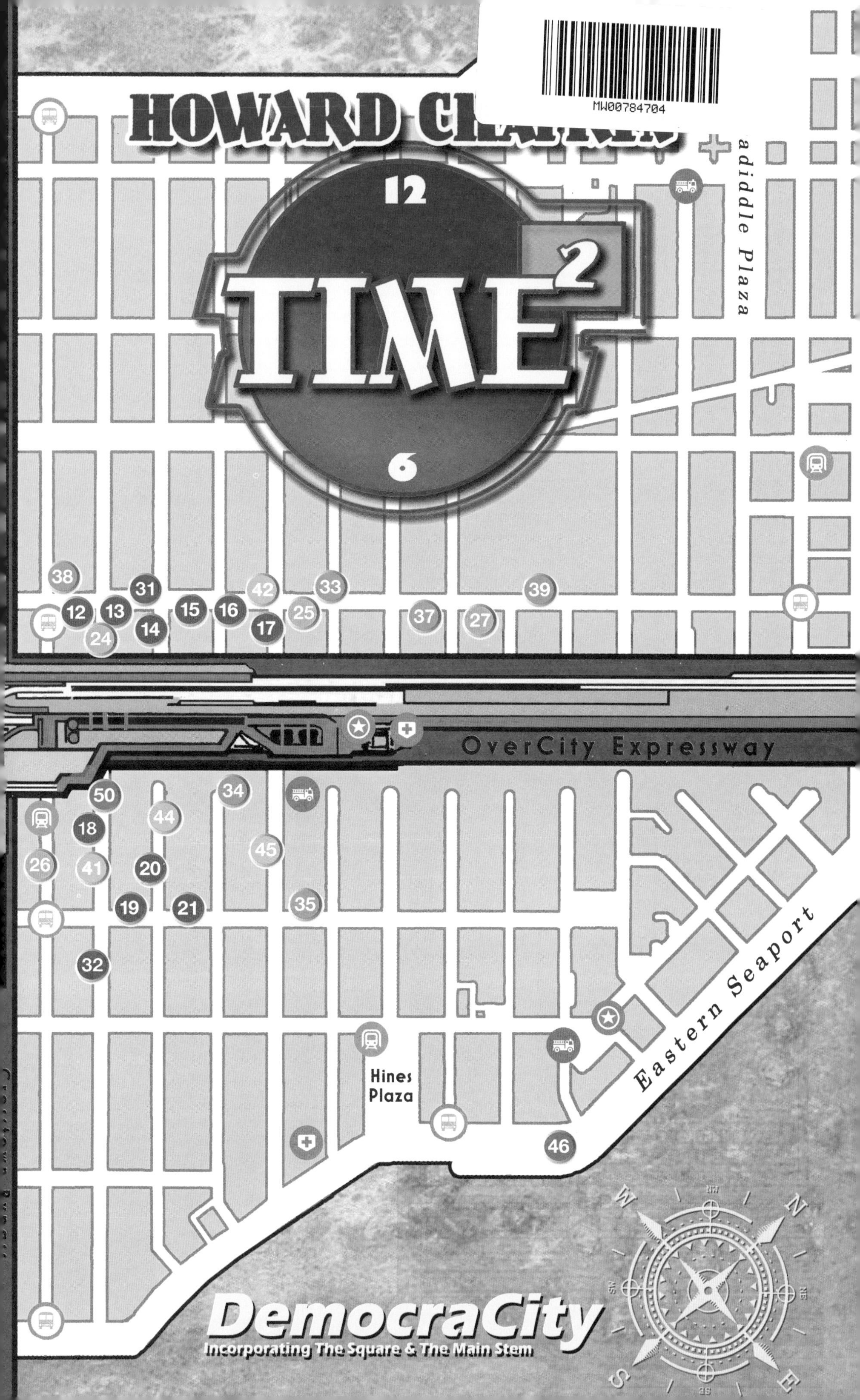

HOWARD CH
12
TIME²
6
adiddle Plaza
OverCity Expressway
Eastern Seaport
Hines Plaza
DemocraCity
Incorporating The Square & The Main Stem

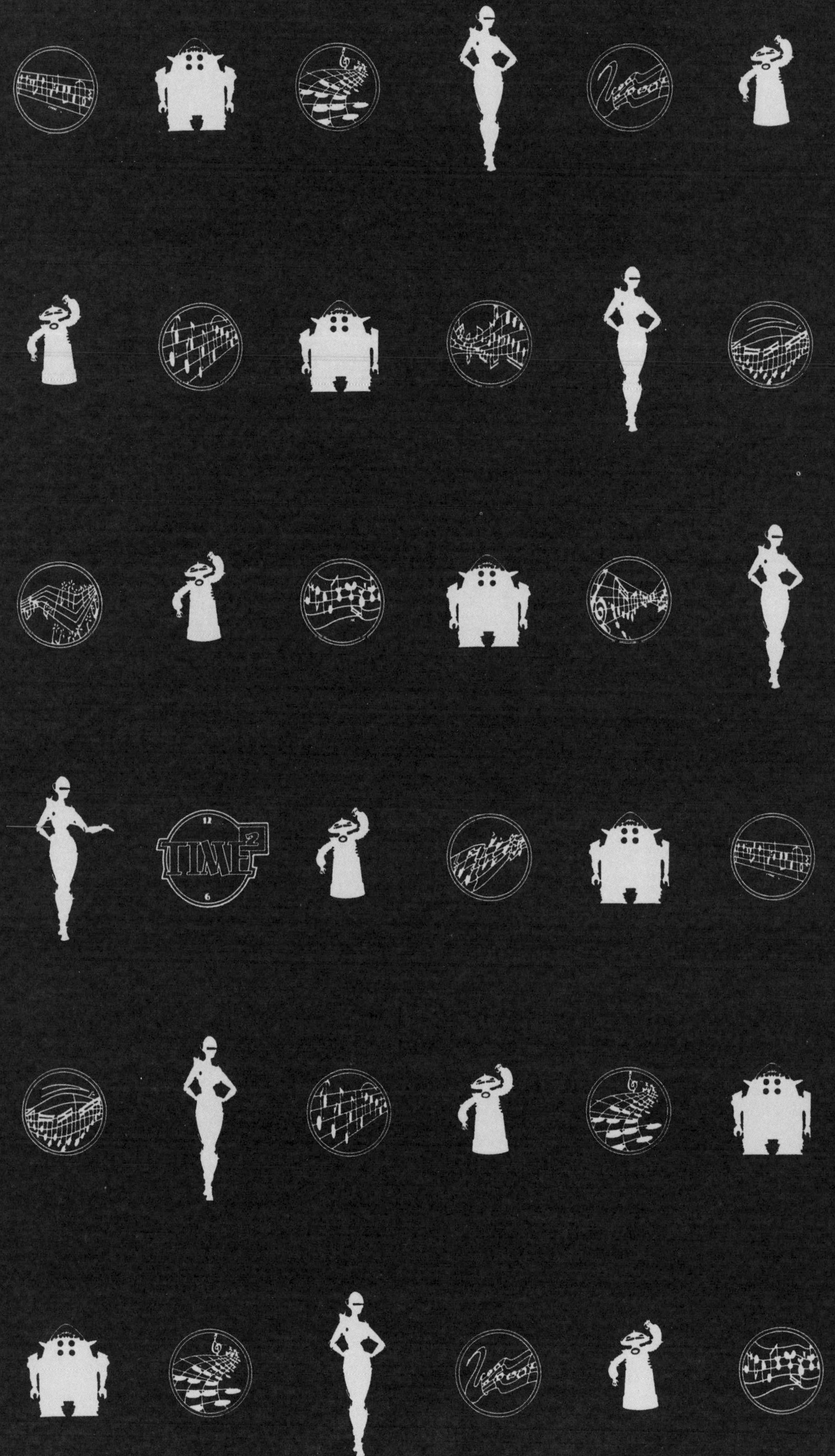
12
TIME 2
6

TIME²

OMNIBUS

A love letter to the Naked City

Story & Art by HOWARD CHAYKIN

LETTERS DESIGN & DIGITAL RECOVERY by KEN BRUZENAK

COVER DIGITAL PAINTING by DON CAMERON

COLORS by LINDA LESSMANN
STEVE OLIFF
RICHARD ORY
YEN NITRO

EDITED by RICK OLIVER
THOMAS K.

HOWARD CHAYKIN

12

TIME²

6

OMNIBUS

TIME² OMNIBUS. First printing. March 2022. Copyright ©
2022 Howard Chaykin, Inc. All rights reserved. Published by
Image Comics, Inc. Office of publication: PO BOX 14457,
Portland, OR 97293. "Time²," the Time² logos, and the
likenesses of all characters herein are trademarks of Howard
Chaykin, Inc., unless otherwise expressly noted. "Image" and
the Image Comics logos are registered trademarks of Image
Comics, Inc. Chapters 1 and 2 originally published by First
Comics. No part of this publication may be reproduced or
transmitted, in any form or by any means (except for short
excerpts for journalistic or review purposes), without the
express written permission of Howard Chaykin, Inc or Image
Comics, Inc. All names, characters, events, institutions, and
places herein are entirely fictional. Any resemblance to
actual persons (living or dead), events, institutions, or places,
without satirical intent, is coincidental.
Printed in China.
ISBN: 978-1-5343-2110-6
Representation: Law Offices of
Harris M. Miller II, P.C.
(rights.inquiries@gmail.com).

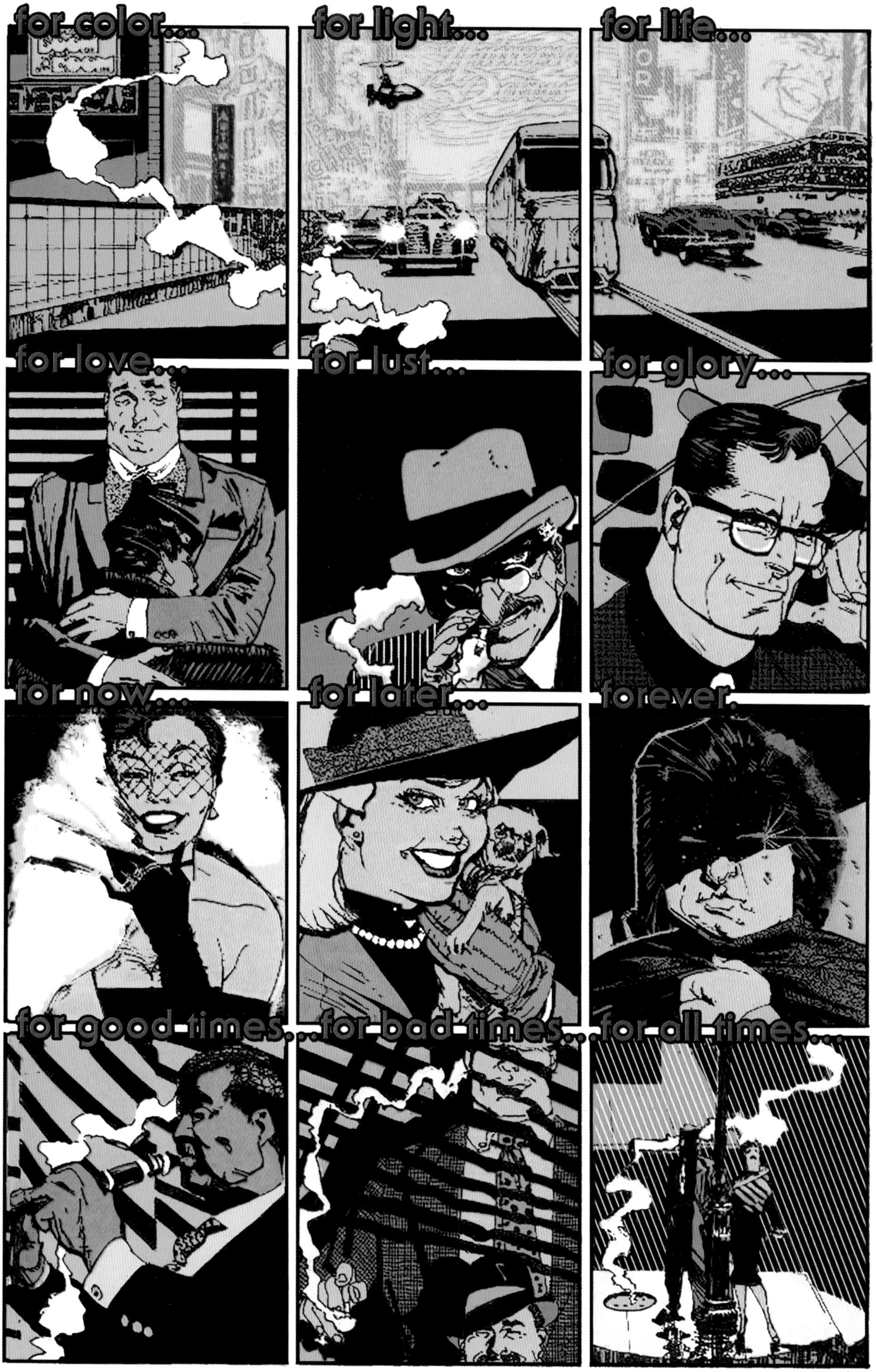
for color...
for light...
for life...
for love...
for lust...
for glory...
for now...
for later...
forever.
for good times...
for bad times...
for all times...

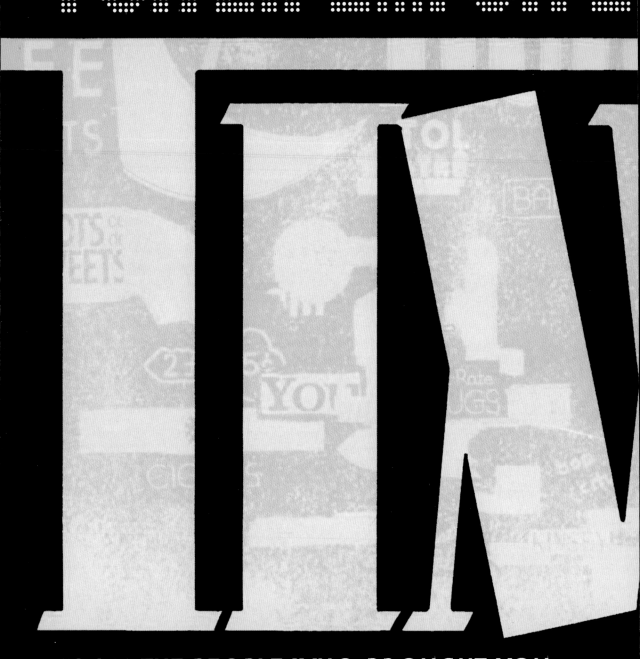

FOR LIFE...FOR L

FROM THE PEOPLE WHO BROUGHT YOU
THE FIRST GREAT COMIC BOOK OF THE '80's--
AMERICAN FLAGG!

A GRAPHIC ALBUM
FOR MATURE READERS
BY HOWARD CHAYKIN

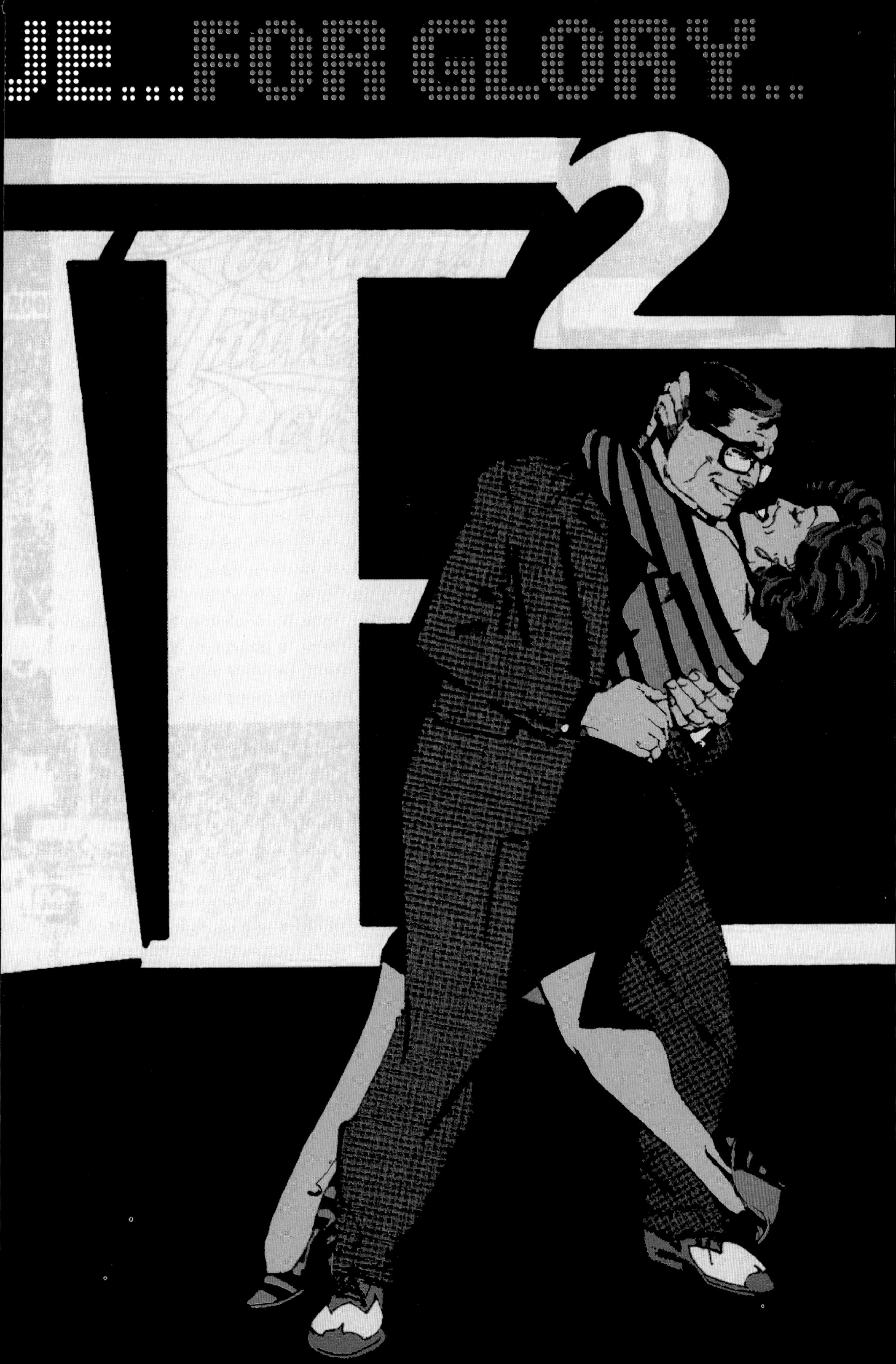
JE...FOR GLORY...

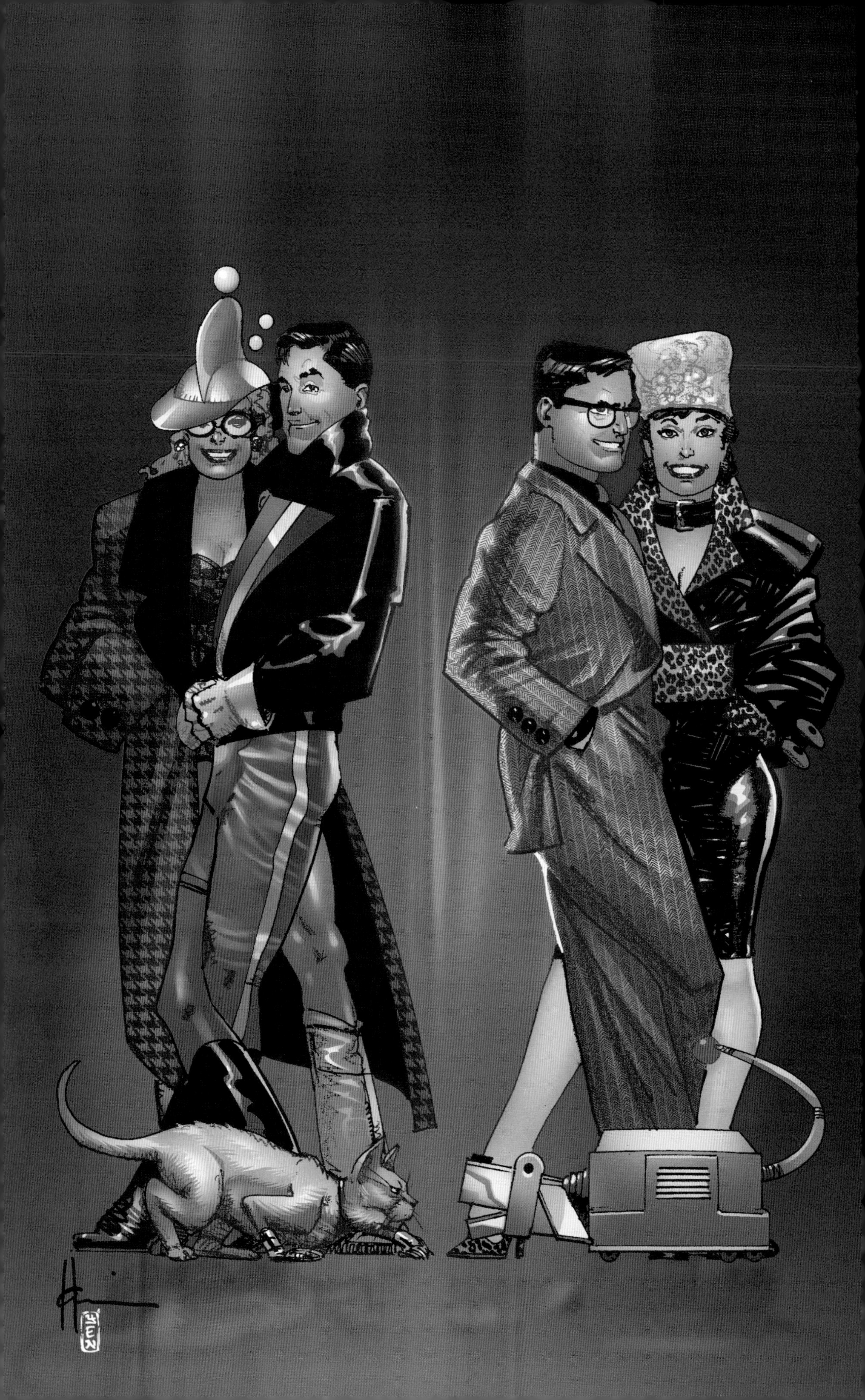

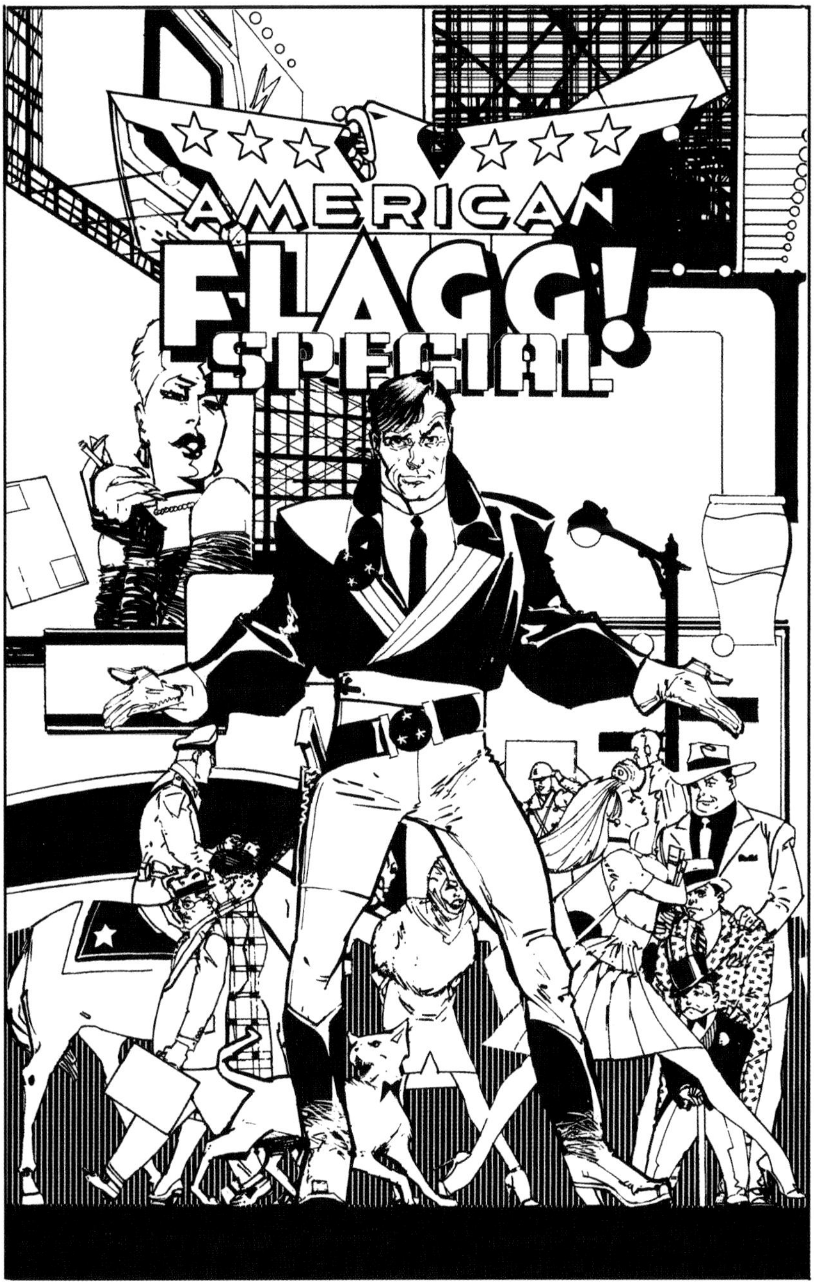
AMERICAN
FLAGG!
SPECIAL
Unlettered cover art for the *American Flagg! Special*

AMERICAN FLAGG! SPECIAL

originally published
JULY, 1986
story and art
HOWARD CHAYKIN
letters
KEN BRUZENAK
color
LINDA LESSMANN
editor
RICK OLIVER

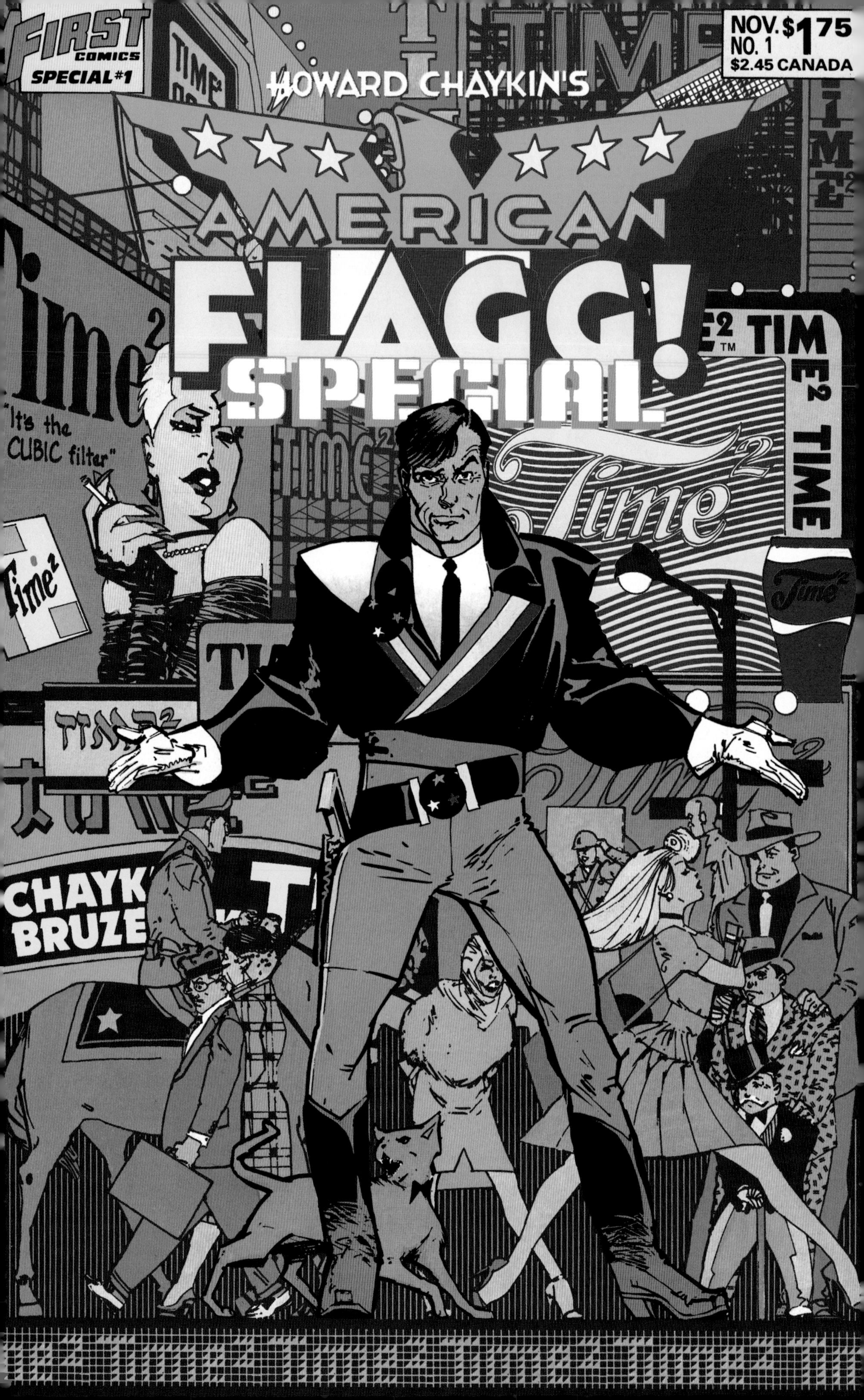
FIRST COMICS
SPECIAL #1
NOV. $1.75
NO. 1
$2.45 CANADA
HOWARD CHAYKIN'S
AMERICAN
FLAGG!
SPECIAL
"It's the CUBIC filter"
CHAYK
BRUZE

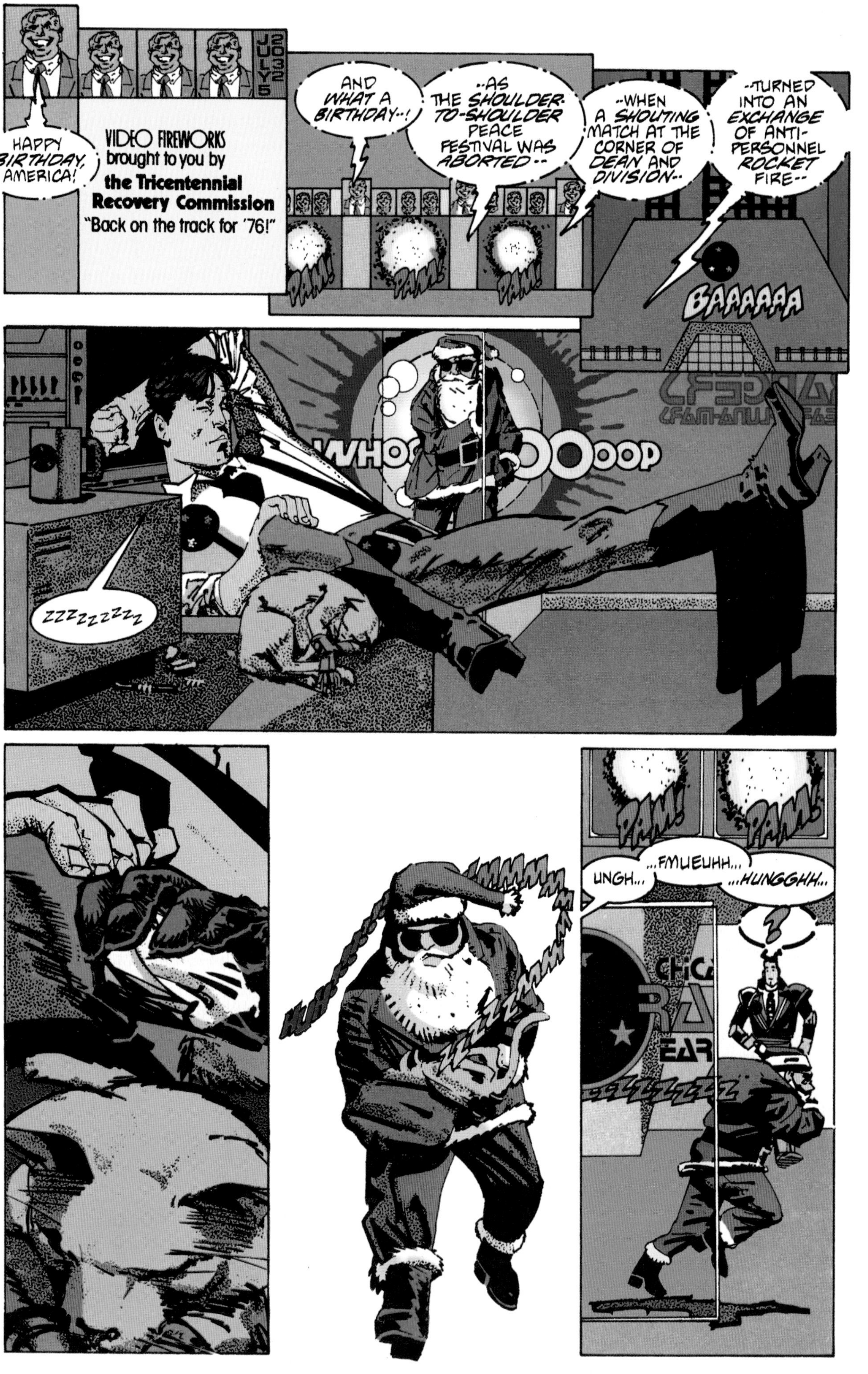
JULY 5 2032
HAPPY BIRTHDAY, AMERICA!
VIDEO FIREWORKS brought to you by the Tricentennial Recovery Commission "Back on the track for '76!"
AND WHAT A BIRTHDAY--!
--AS THE SHOULDER-TO-SHOULDER PEACE FESTIVAL WAS ABORTED--
--WHEN A SHOUTING MATCH AT THE CORNER OF DEAN AND DIVISION--
--TURNED INTO AN EXCHANGE OF ANTI-PERSONNEL ROCKET FIRE--
PAM!
PAM!
PAM!
BAAAAAA
WHOO OOOoop
ZZZzzzzzz
PAM!
PAM!
UNGH...
...FMUEUHH...
...HUNGGHH...
?

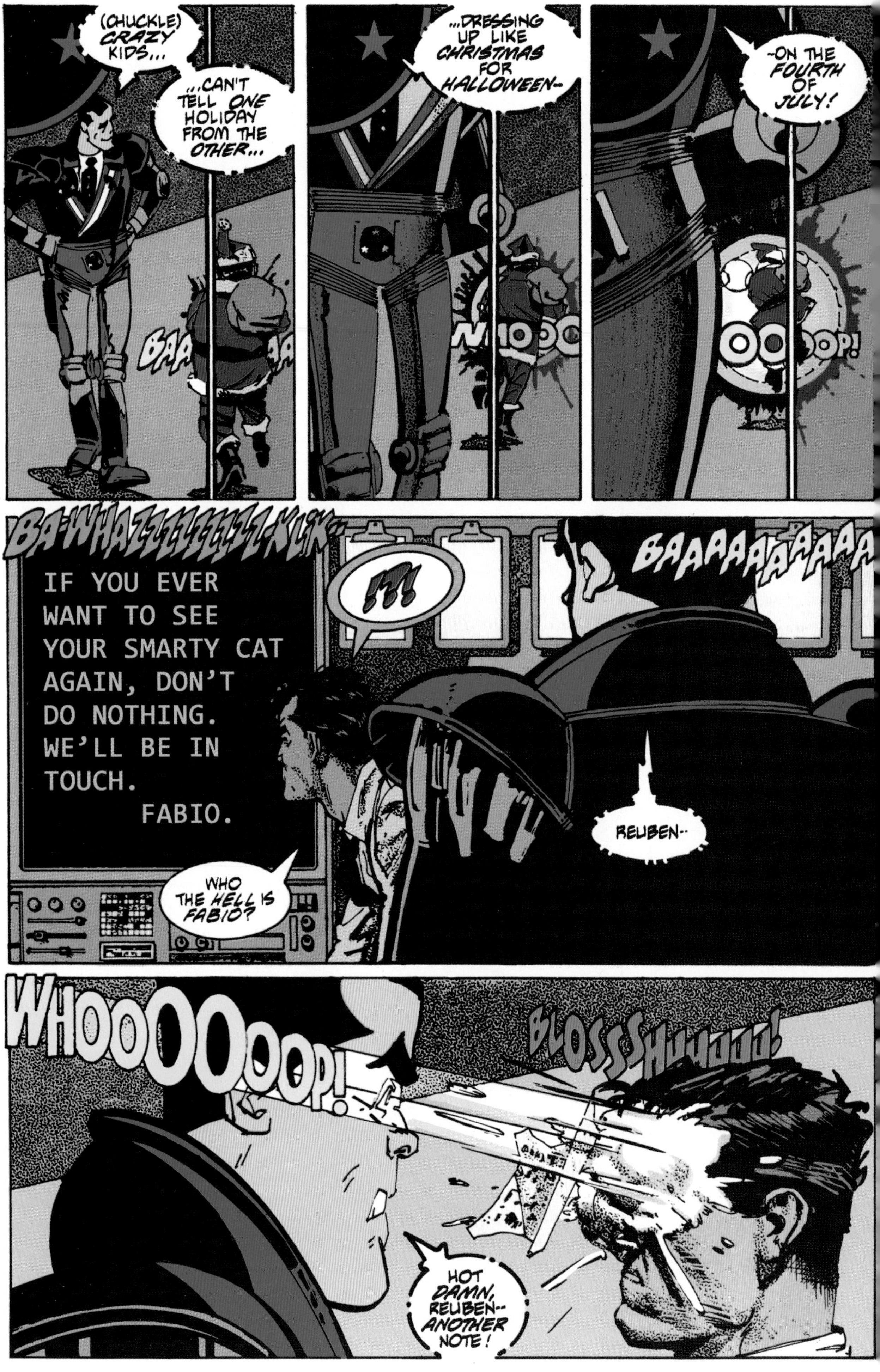

(CHUCKLE) CRAZY KIDS...
...CAN'T TELL ONE HOLIDAY FROM THE OTHER...
...DRESSING UP LIKE CHRISTMAS FOR HALLOWEEN--
-ON THE FOURTH OF JULY!
BA-WHAZZZZZZZZ-KLIK
IF YOU EVER WANT TO SEE YOUR SMARTY CAT AGAIN, DON'T DO NOTHING. WE'LL BE IN TOUCH. FABIO.
!?!
BAAAAAAAAAA
REUBEN--
WHO THE HELL IS FABIO?
WHOOOOOoop!
BLOSSSHuuuuu!
HOT DAMN, REUBEN-- ANOTHER NOTE!

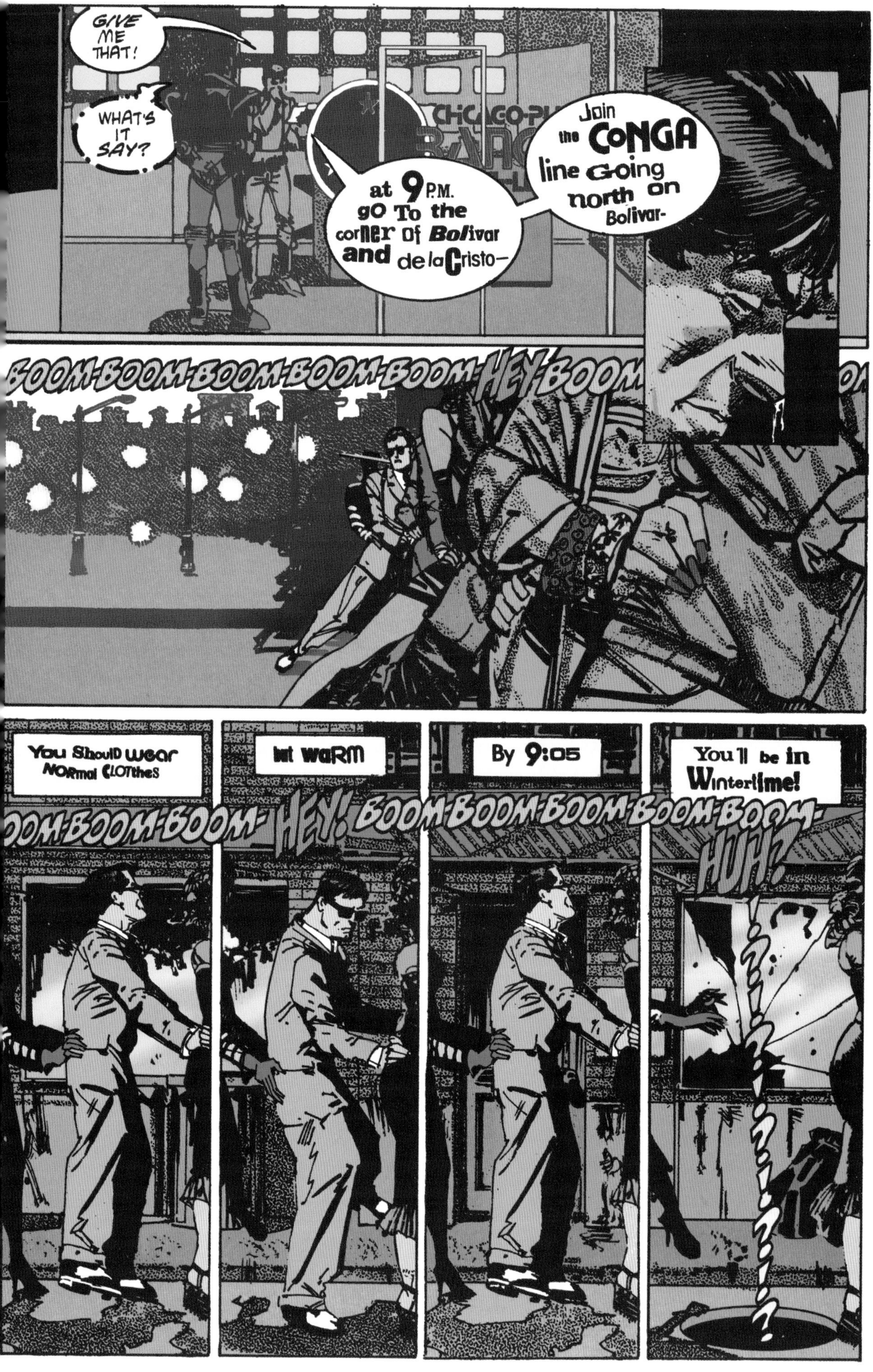
GIVE ME THAT!
WHAT'S IT SAY?
at 9 P.M. gO To the corNer Of Bolivar and de la Cristo—
Join the CONGA line Going north on Bolivar-
BOOM-BOOM-BOOM-BOOM-BOOM-HEY-BOOM
You Should wear NORmal CLOThes
but waRM
By 9:05
You'll be in Wintertime!
OOM-BOOM-BOOM-HEY! BOOM-BOOM-BOOM-BOOM-BOOM-
HUH?

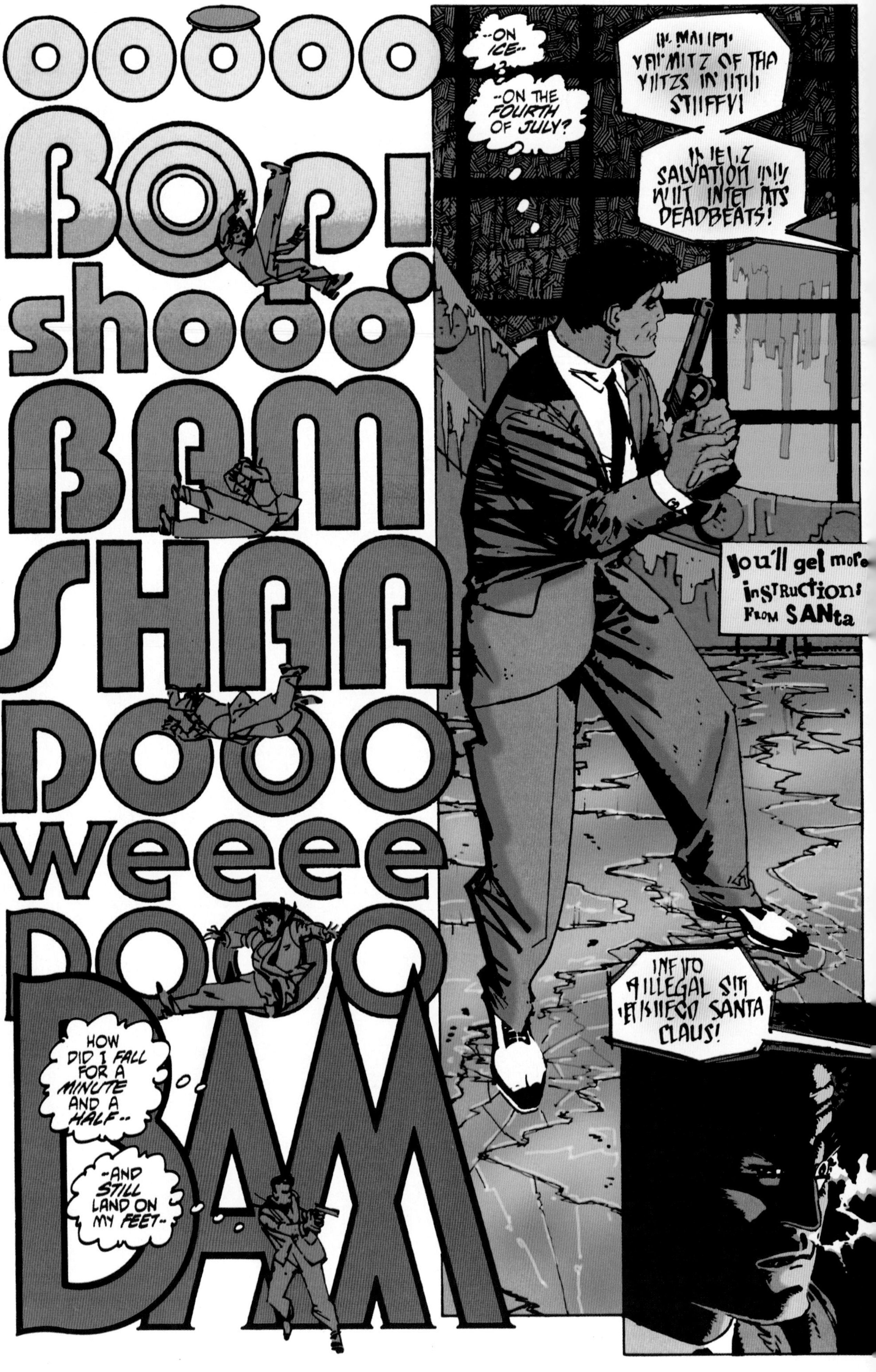

OOOOO
shooo
BAM
SHAA
DOOO
weeee
DOOO
BAM
--ON ICE--
--ON THE FOURTH OF JULY?
OF THA
STIFF
SALVATION
DEADBEATS!
you'll get more instructions FROM SANta
ILLEGAL
SANTA CLAUS!
HOW DID I FALL FOR A MINUTE AND A HALF--
--AND STILL LAND ON MY FEET--

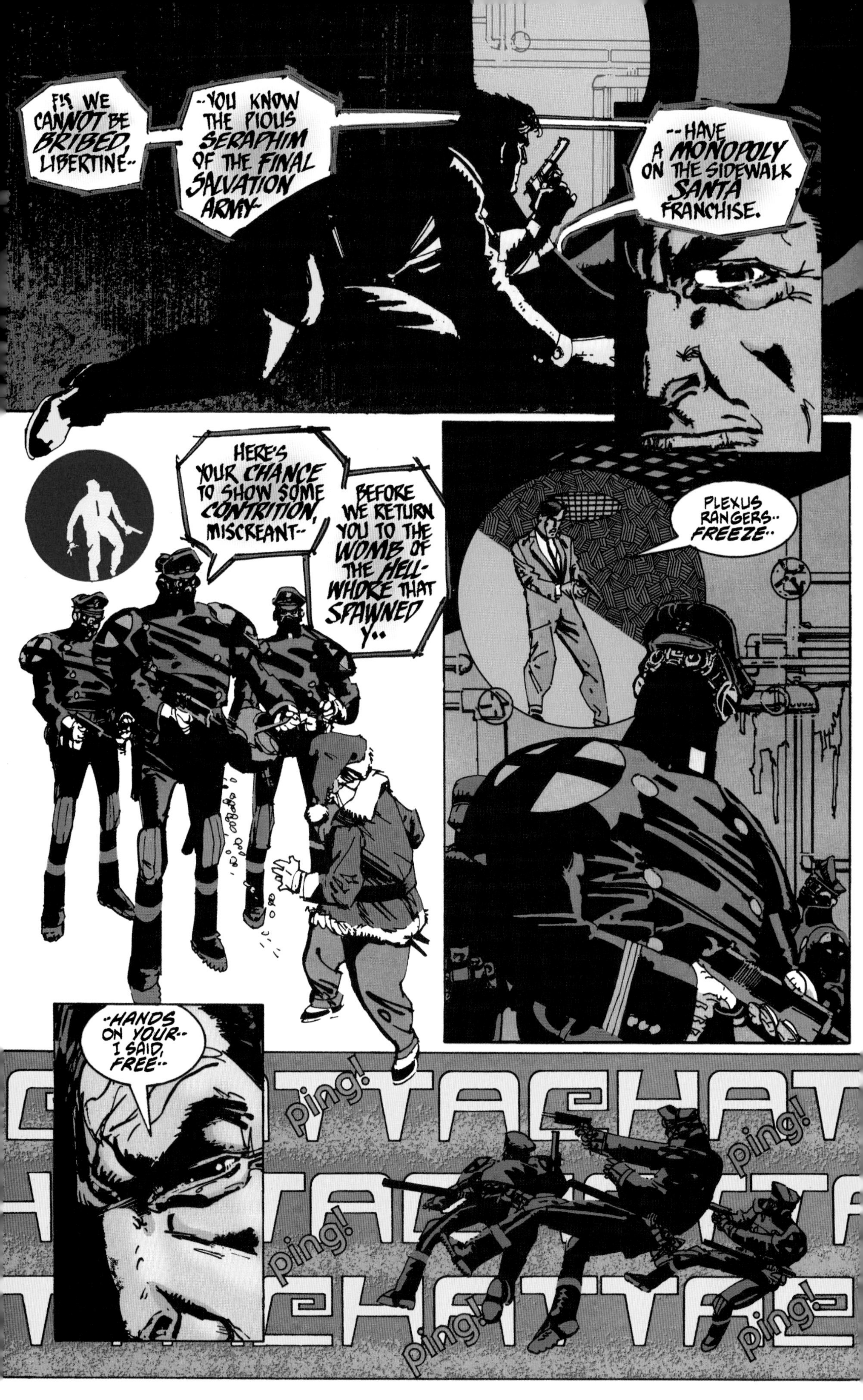
F!S WE CANNOT BE BRIBED, LIBERTINE--
--YOU KNOW THE PIOUS SERAPHIM OF THE FINAL SALVATION ARMY--
--HAVE A MONOPOLY ON THE SIDEWALK SANTA FRANCHISE.
HERE'S YOUR CHANCE TO SHOW SOME CONTRITION, MISCREANT--
BEFORE WE RETURN YOU TO THE WOMB OF THE HELL-WHORE THAT SPAWNED Y--
PLEXUS RANGERS.. FREEZE..
--HANDS ON YOUR-- I SAID, FREE--
ping!
ping!
ping!
ping!
ping!

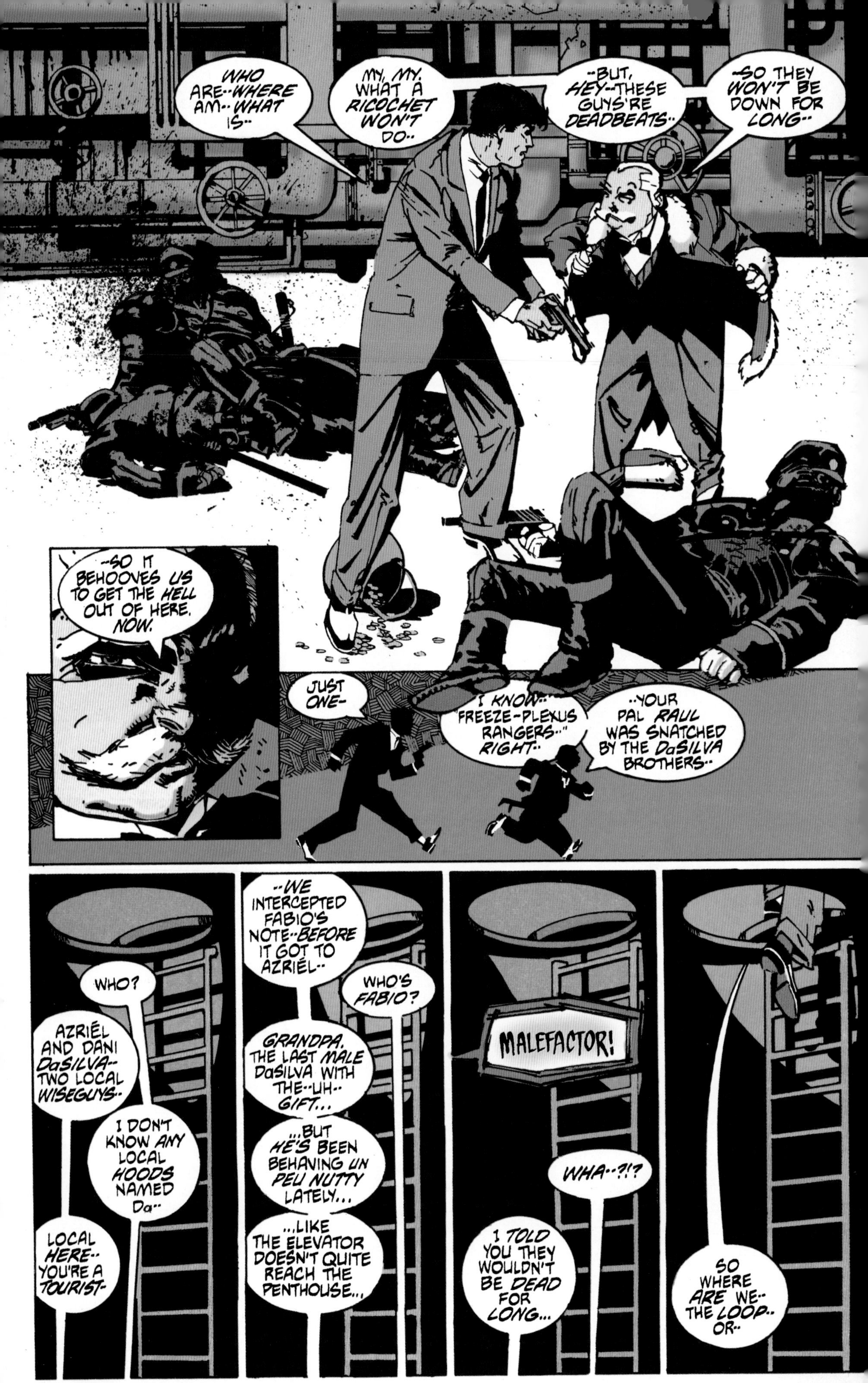
WHO ARE--WHERE AM--WHAT IS--
MY, MY. WHAT A RICOCHET WON'T DO--
--BUT, HEY--THESE GUYS'RE DEADBEATS--
--SO THEY WON'T BE DOWN FOR LONG--
--SO IT BEHOOVES US TO GET THE HELL OUT OF HERE. NOW.
JUST ONE-
I KNOW-- "FREEZE-PLEXUS RANGERS--" RIGHT--
--YOUR PAL RAUL WAS SNATCHED BY THE DaSILVA BROTHERS--
WHO?
AZRIÉL AND DANI DaSILVA-- TWO LOCAL WISEGUYS--
I DON'T KNOW ANY LOCAL HOODS NAMED Da--
LOCAL HERE-- YOU'RE A TOURIST-
--WE INTERCEPTED FABIO'S NOTE--BEFORE IT GOT TO AZRIÉL--
WHO'S FABIO?
GRANDPA. THE LAST MALE DaSILVA WITH THE--UH-- GIFT...
...BUT HE'S BEEN BEHAVING UN PEU NUTTY LATELY...
...LIKE THE ELEVATOR DOESN'T QUITE REACH THE PENTHOUSE...
MALEFACTOR!
WHA--?!?
I TOLD YOU THEY WOULDN'T BE DEAD FOR LONG...
SO WHERE ARE WE-- THE LOOP-- OR--

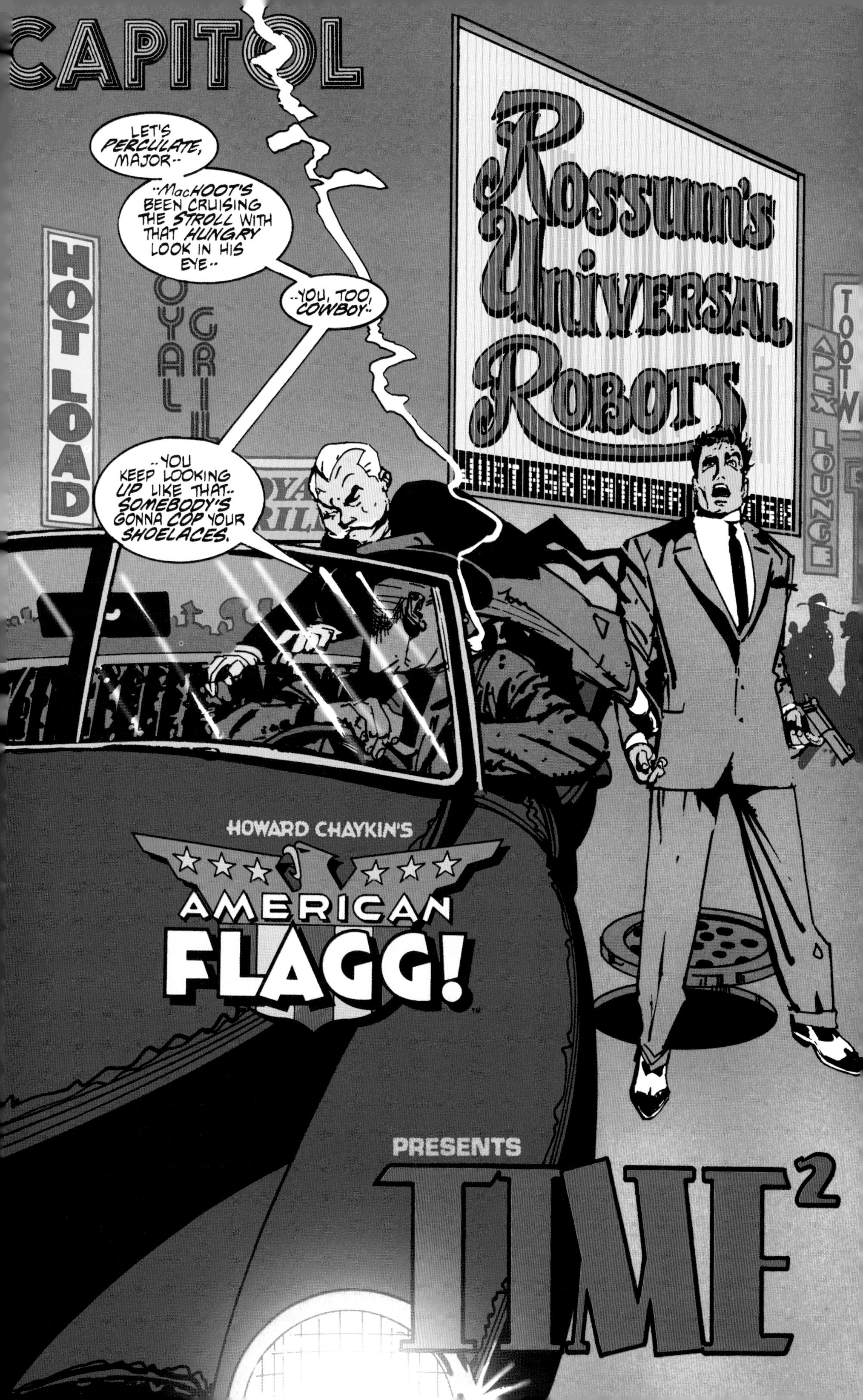
CAPITOL
LET'S PERCULATE, MAJOR--
--MacHOOT'S BEEN CRUISING THE STROLL WITH THAT HUNGRY LOOK IN HIS EYE--
--YOU, TOO, COWBOY--
--YOU KEEP LOOKING UP LIKE THAT-- SOMEBODY'S GONNA COP YOUR SHOELACES.
HOT LOAD
ROYAL GRILL
Rossum's Universal Robots
TOOTWEE
APEX LOUNGE
HOWARD CHAYKIN'S
AMERICAN FLAGG!
PRESENTS
TIME²

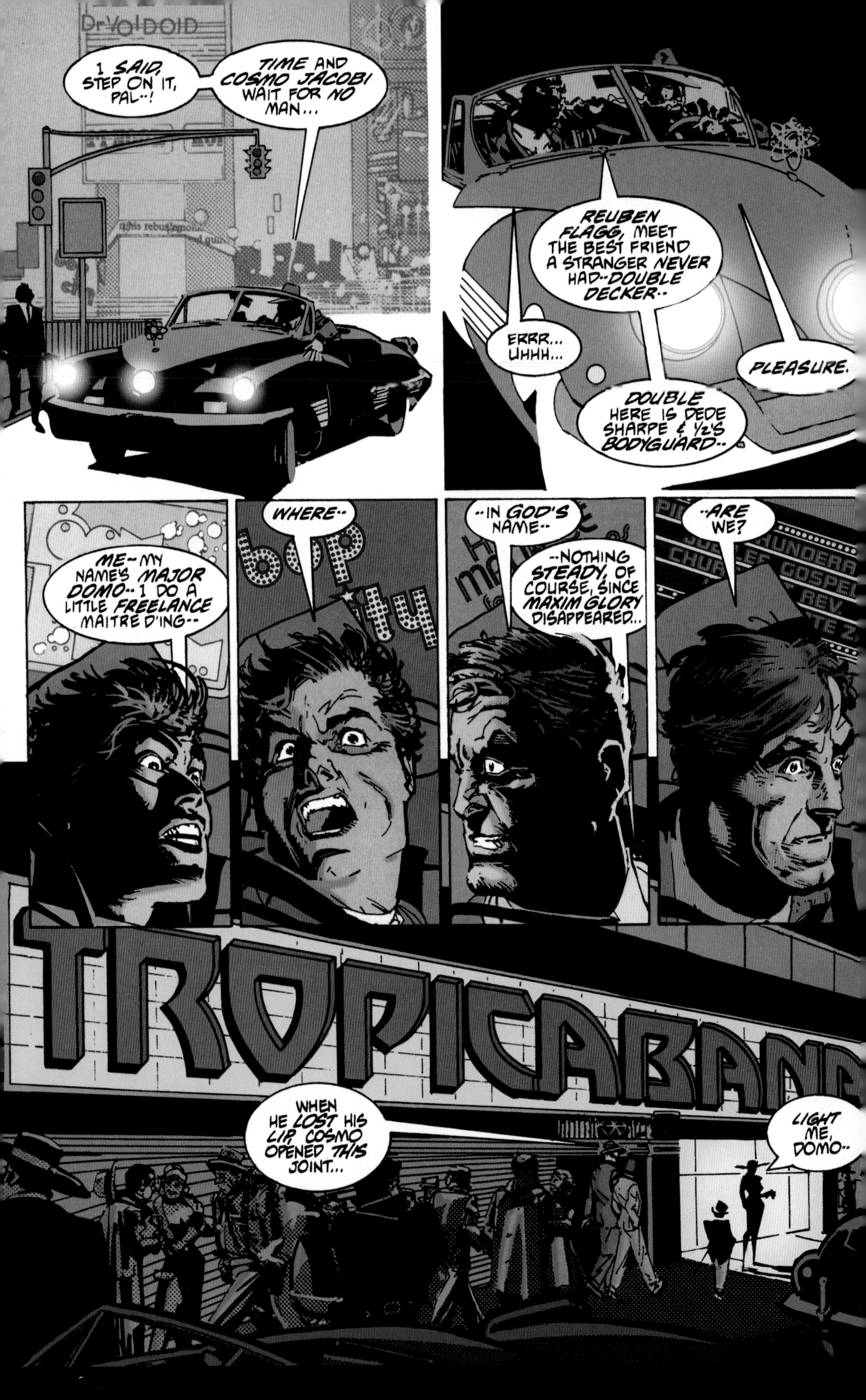
Dr VOLDOID
I SAID, STEP ON IT, PAL--!
TIME AND COSMO JACOBI WAIT FOR NO MAN...
REUBEN FLAGG, MEET THE BEST FRIEND A STRANGER NEVER HAD--DOUBLE DECKER--
ERRR... UHHH...
PLEASURE.
DOUBLE HERE IS DEDE SHARPE & ½'S BODYGUARD--
ME--MY NAME'S MAJOR DOMO-- I DO A LITTLE FREELANCE MAITRE D'ING--
WHERE--
--IN GOD'S NAME--
--NOTHING STEADY, OF COURSE, SINCE MAXIM GLORY DISAPPEARED...
--ARE WE?
TROPICABANA
WHEN HE LOST HIS LIP, COSMO OPENED THIS JOINT...
LIGHT ME, DOMO--

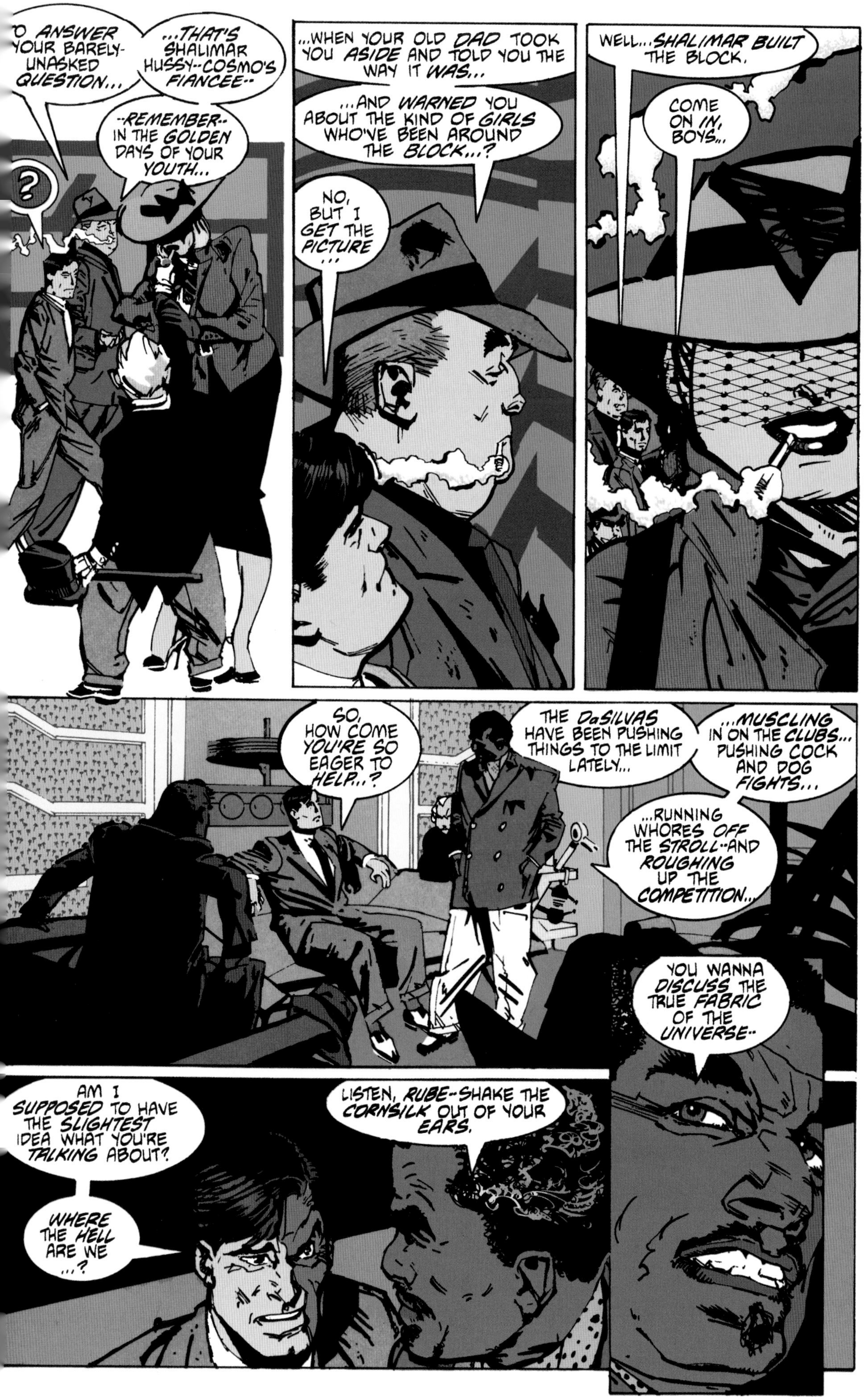
O ANSWER YOUR BARELY-UNASKED QUESTION...
...THAT'S SHALIMAR HUSSY--COSMO'S FIANCEE--
--REMEMBER-- IN THE GOLDEN DAYS OF YOUR YOUTH...
?
...WHEN YOUR OLD DAD TOOK YOU ASIDE AND TOLD YOU THE WAY IT WAS...
...AND WARNED YOU ABOUT THE KIND OF GIRLS WHO'VE BEEN AROUND THE BLOCK...?
NO, BUT I GET THE PICTURE ...
WELL... SHALIMAR BUILT THE BLOCK.
COME ON IN, BOYS...
SO, HOW COME YOU'RE SO EAGER TO HELP...?
THE DaSILVAS HAVE BEEN PUSHING THINGS TO THE LIMIT LATELY...
...MUSCLING IN ON THE CLUBS... PUSHING COCK AND DOG FIGHTS...
...RUNNING WHORES OFF THE STROLL--AND ROUGHING UP THE COMPETITION...
YOU WANNA DISCUSS THE TRUE FABRIC OF THE UNIVERSE--
AM I SUPPOSED TO HAVE THE SLIGHTEST IDEA WHAT YOU'RE TALKING ABOUT?
WHERE THE HELL ARE WE ...?
LISTEN, RUBE--SHAKE THE CORNSILK OUT OF YOUR EARS.

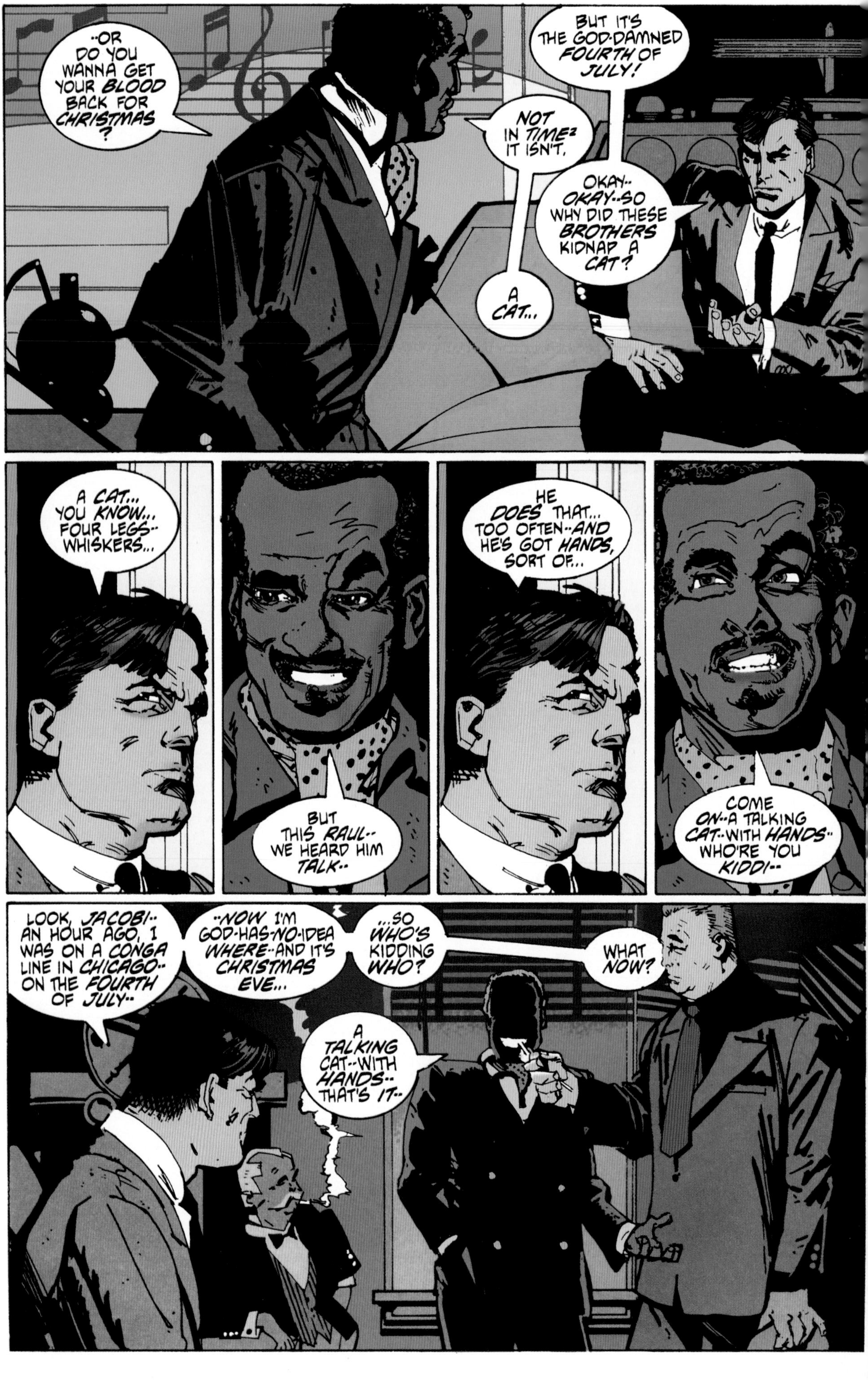

..OR DO YOU WANNA GET YOUR BLOOD BACK FOR CHRISTMAS?
BUT IT'S THE GOD-DAMNED FOURTH OF JULY!
NOT IN TIME² IT ISN'T.
A CAT...
OKAY.. OKAY..SO WHY DID THESE BROTHERS KIDNAP A CAT?
A CAT... YOU KNOW.. FOUR LEGS.. WHISKERS...
BUT THIS RAUL.. WE HEARD HIM TALK..
HE DOES THAT... TOO OFTEN..AND HE'S GOT HANDS, SORT OF...
COME ON..A TALKING CAT..WITH HANDS.. WHO'RE YOU KIDDI--
LOOK, JACOBI.. AN HOUR AGO, I WAS ON A CONGA LINE IN CHICAGO.. ON THE FOURTH OF JULY..
..NOW I'M GOD-HAS-NO-IDEA WHERE..AND IT'S CHRISTMAS EVE...
...SO WHO'S KIDDING WHO?
WHAT NOW?
A TALKING CAT..WITH HANDS.. THAT'S IT..

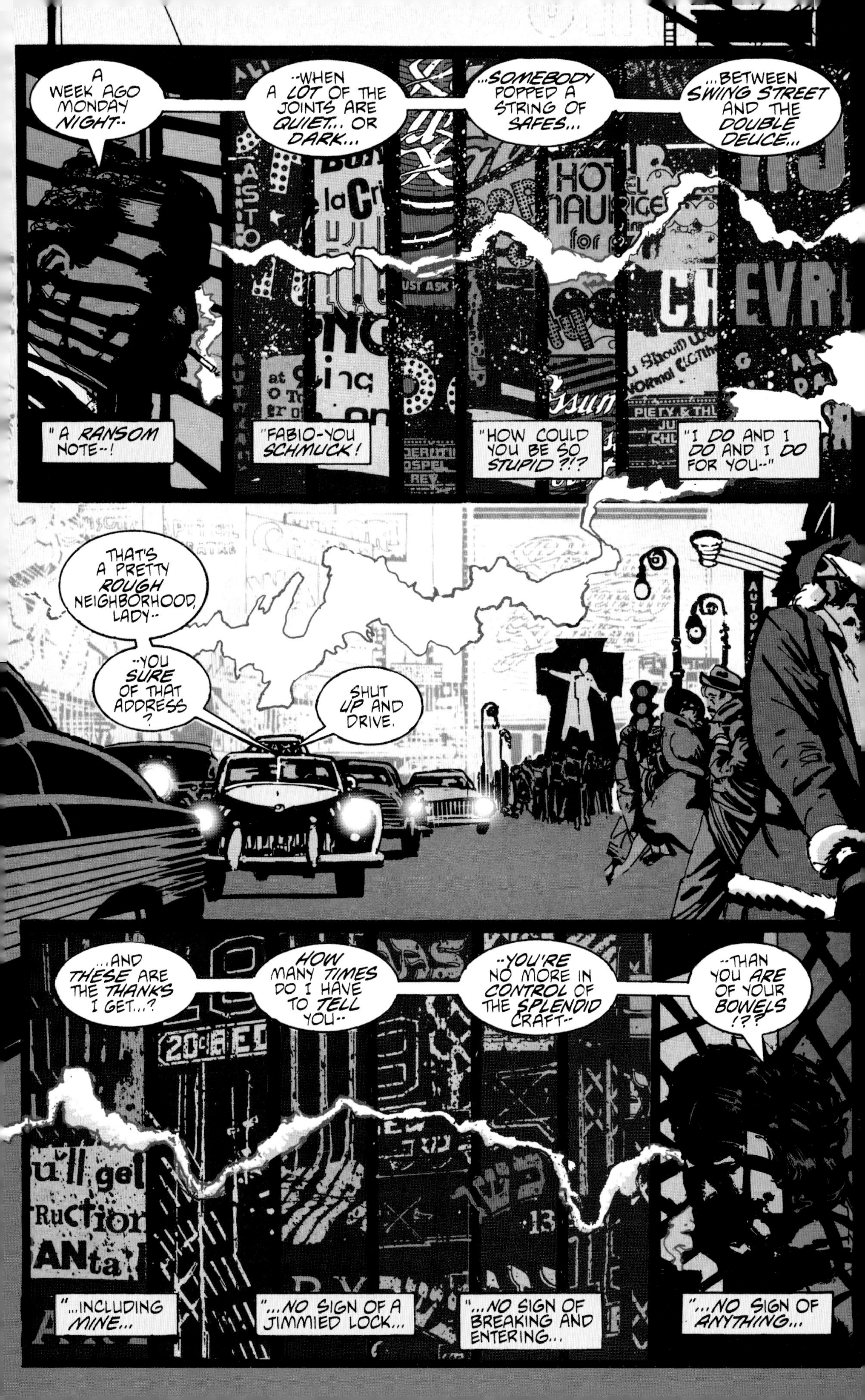
A WEEK AGO MONDAY NIGHT--
--WHEN A LOT OF THE JOINTS ARE QUIET... OR DARK...
...SOMEBODY POPPED A STRING OF SAFES...
...BETWEEN SWING STREET AND THE DOUBLE DEUCE...
"A RANSOM NOTE--!
"FABIO-YOU SCHMUCK!
"HOW COULD YOU BE SO STUPID?!?
"I DO AND I DO AND I DO FOR YOU--"
THAT'S A PRETTY ROUGH NEIGHBORHOOD, LADY--
--YOU SURE OF THAT ADDRESS?
SHUT UP AND DRIVE.
...AND THESE ARE THE THANKS I GET...?
HOW MANY TIMES DO I HAVE TO TELL YOU--
--YOU'RE NO MORE IN CONTROL OF THE SPLENDID CRAFT--
--THAN YOU ARE OF YOUR BOWELS!?
"...INCLUDING MINE...
"...NO SIGN OF A JIMMIED LOCK...
"...NO SIGN OF BREAKING AND ENTERING...
"...NO SIGN OF ANYTHING...

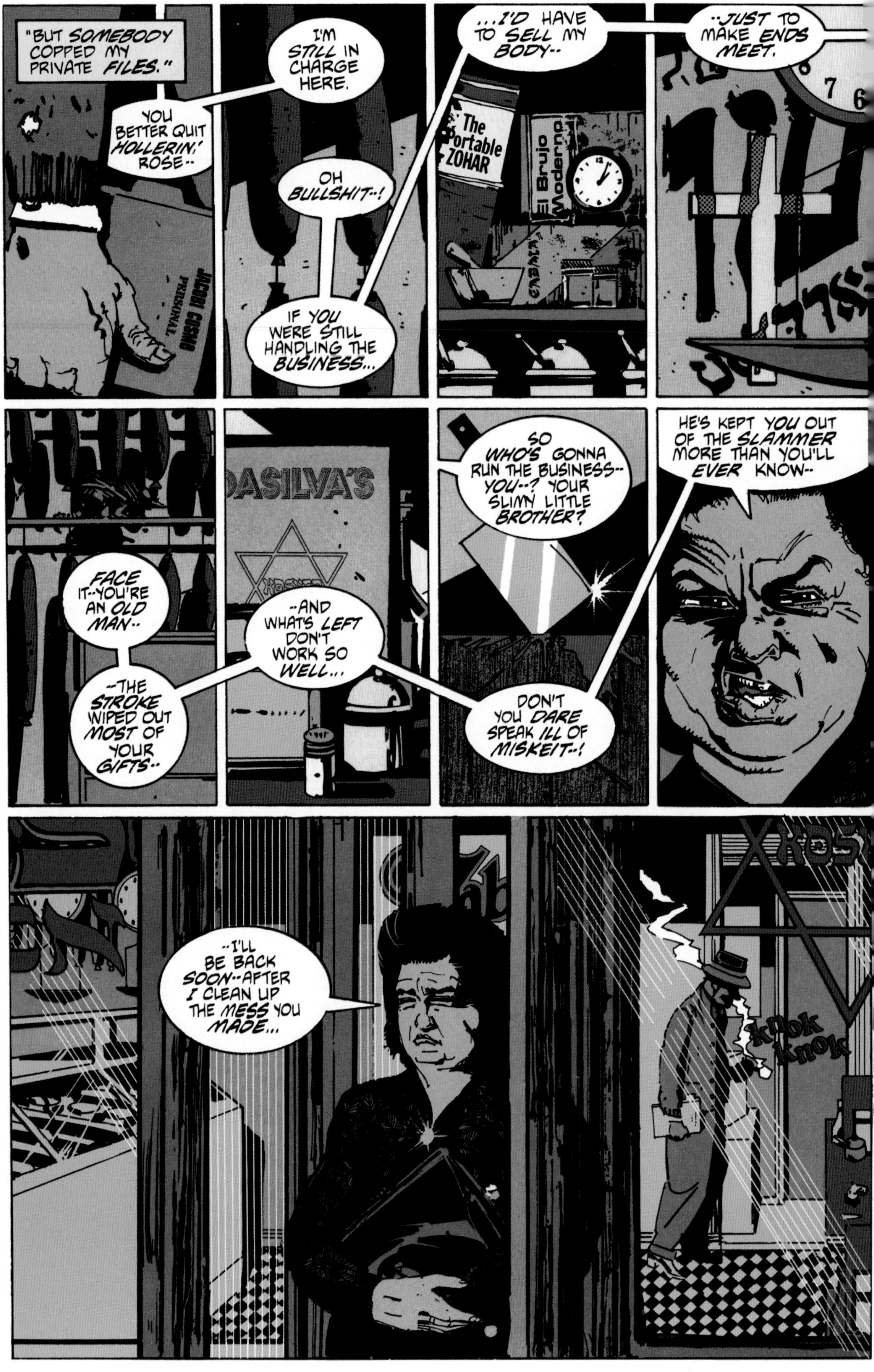
"BUT SOMEBODY COPPED MY PRIVATE FILES."
YOU BETTER QUIT HOLLERIN,' ROSE--
JACOBI COSMO PERSONAL
I'M STILL IN CHARGE HERE.
OH BULLSHIT--!
IF YOU WERE STILL HANDLING THE BUSINESS...
...I'D HAVE TO SELL MY BODY--
The Portable ZOHAR
El Brujo Moderno
--JUST TO MAKE ENDS MEET.
FACE IT--YOU'RE AN OLD MAN--
--THE STROKE WIPED OUT MOST OF YOUR GIFTS--
DASILVA'S
--AND WHAT'S LEFT DON'T WORK SO WELL...
SO WHO'S GONNA RUN THE BUSINESS-- YOU--? YOUR SLIMY LITTLE BROTHER?
DON'T YOU DARE SPEAK ILL OF MISKEIT--!
HE'S KEPT YOU OUT OF THE SLAMMER MORE THAN YOU'LL EVER KNOW--
--I'LL BE BACK SOON--AFTER I CLEAN UP THE MESS YOU MADE...
knok knok

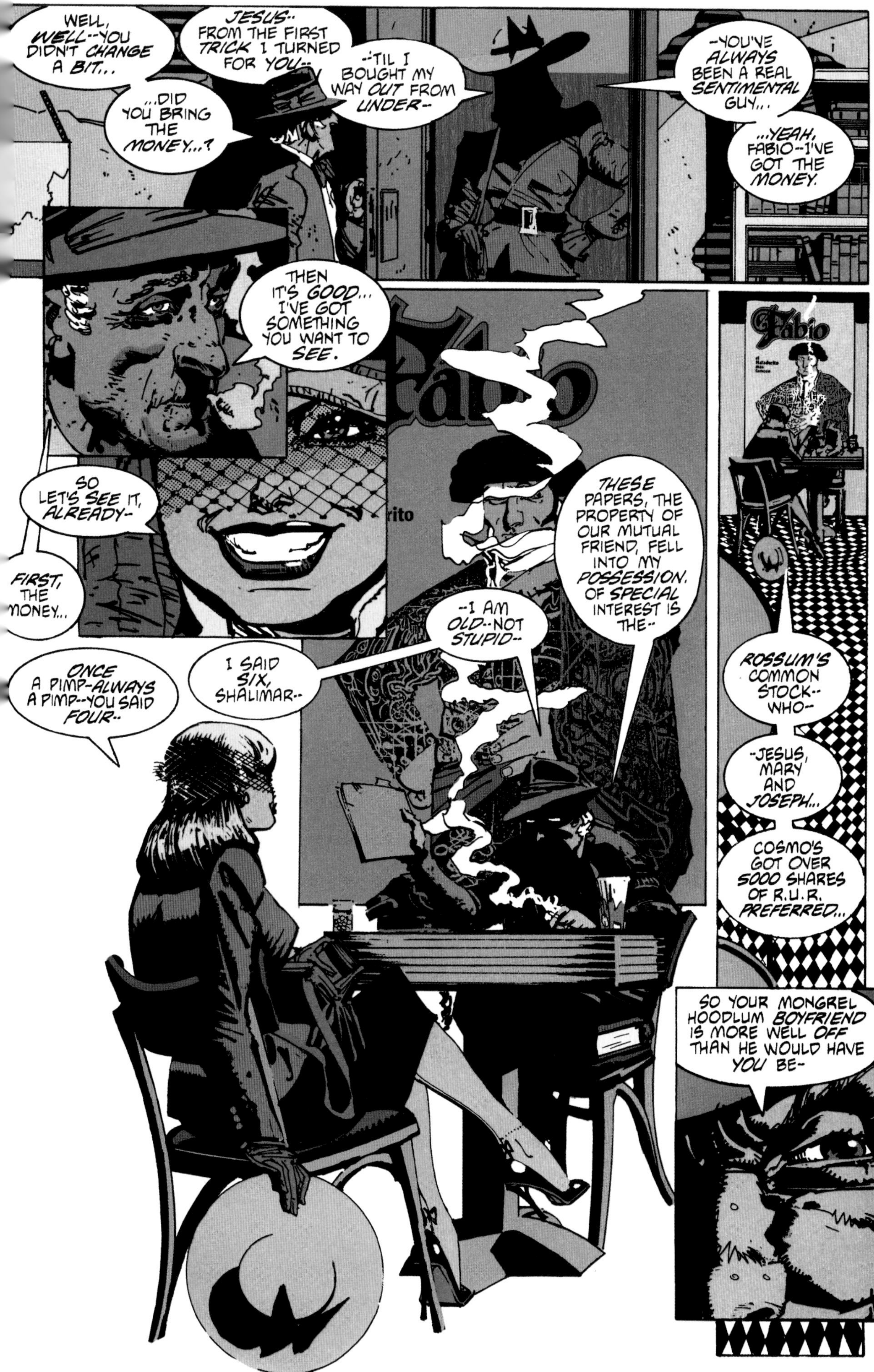
WELL, WELL--YOU DIDN'T CHANGE A BIT...
...DID YOU BRING THE MONEY...?
JESUS.. FROM THE FIRST TRICK I TURNED FOR YOU..
--'TIL I BOUGHT MY WAY OUT FROM UNDER--
--YOU'VE ALWAYS BEEN A REAL SENTIMENTAL GUY...
...YEAH, FABIO--I'VE GOT THE MONEY.
THEN IT'S GOOD... I'VE GOT SOMETHING YOU WANT TO SEE.
SO LET'S SEE IT, ALREADY-
FIRST, THE MONEY...
ONCE A PIMP-ALWAYS A PIMP--YOU SAID FOUR--
I SAID SIX, SHALIMAR--
--I AM OLD--NOT STUPID--
THESE PAPERS, THE PROPERTY OF OUR MUTUAL FRIEND, FELL INTO MY POSSESSION. OF SPECIAL INTEREST IS THE--
ROSSUM'S COMMON STOCK--WHO--
-JESUS, MARY AND JOSEPH...
COSMO'S GOT OVER 5000 SHARES OF R.U.R. PREFERRED...
SO YOUR MONGREL HOODLUM BOYFRIEND IS MORE WELL OFF THAN HE WOULD HAVE YOU BE-

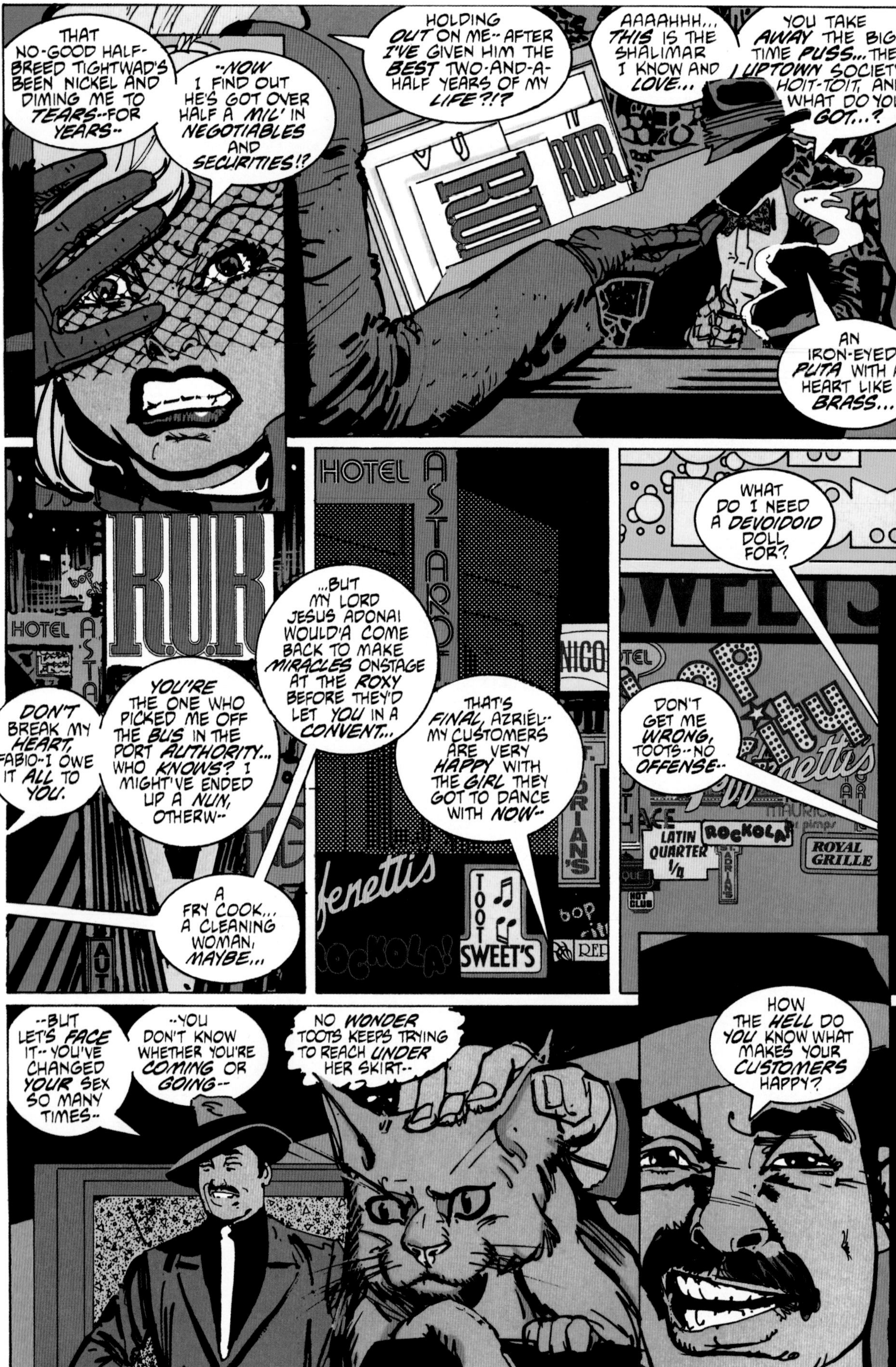
THAT NO-GOOD HALF-BREED TIGHTWAD'S BEEN NICKEL AND DIMING ME TO TEARS--FOR YEARS--
--NOW I FIND OUT HE'S GOT OVER HALF A MIL' IN NEGOTIABLES AND SECURITIES!?
HOLDING OUT ON ME-- AFTER I'VE GIVEN HIM THE BEST TWO-AND-A-HALF YEARS OF MY LIFE?!?
R.U.R.
AAAAHHH... THIS IS THE SHALIMAR I KNOW AND LOVE...
YOU TAKE AWAY THE BIG TIME PUSS... THE UPTOWN SOCIETY HOIT-TOIT, AND WHAT DO YOU GOT...?
AN IRON-EYED PUTA WITH A HEART LIKE BRASS...
DON'T BREAK MY HEART, FABIO--I OWE IT ALL TO YOU.
YOU'RE THE ONE WHO PICKED ME OFF THE BUS IN THE PORT AUTHORITY... WHO KNOWS? I MIGHT'VE ENDED UP A NUN, OTHERW--
...BUT MY LORD JESUS ADONAI WOULD'A COME BACK TO MAKE MIRACLES ONSTAGE AT THE ROXY BEFORE THEY'D LET YOU IN A CONVENT...
A FRY COOK... A CLEANING WOMAN, MAYBE...
THAT'S FINAL, AZRIÉL-- MY CUSTOMERS ARE VERY HAPPY WITH THE GIRL THEY GOT TO DANCE WITH NOW--
TOOT SWEET'S
WHAT DO I NEED A DEVOIDOID DOLL FOR?
DON'T GET ME WRONG, TOOTS--NO OFFENSE--
LATIN QUARTER 1/4
ROCKOLA
ROYAL GRILLE
--BUT LET'S FACE IT--YOU'VE CHANGED YOUR SEX SO MANY TIMES--
--YOU DON'T KNOW WHETHER YOU'RE COMING OR GOING--
NO WONDER TOOTS KEEPS TRYING TO REACH UNDER HER SKIRT--
HOW THE HELL DO YOU KNOW WHAT MAKES YOUR CUSTOMERS HAPPY?

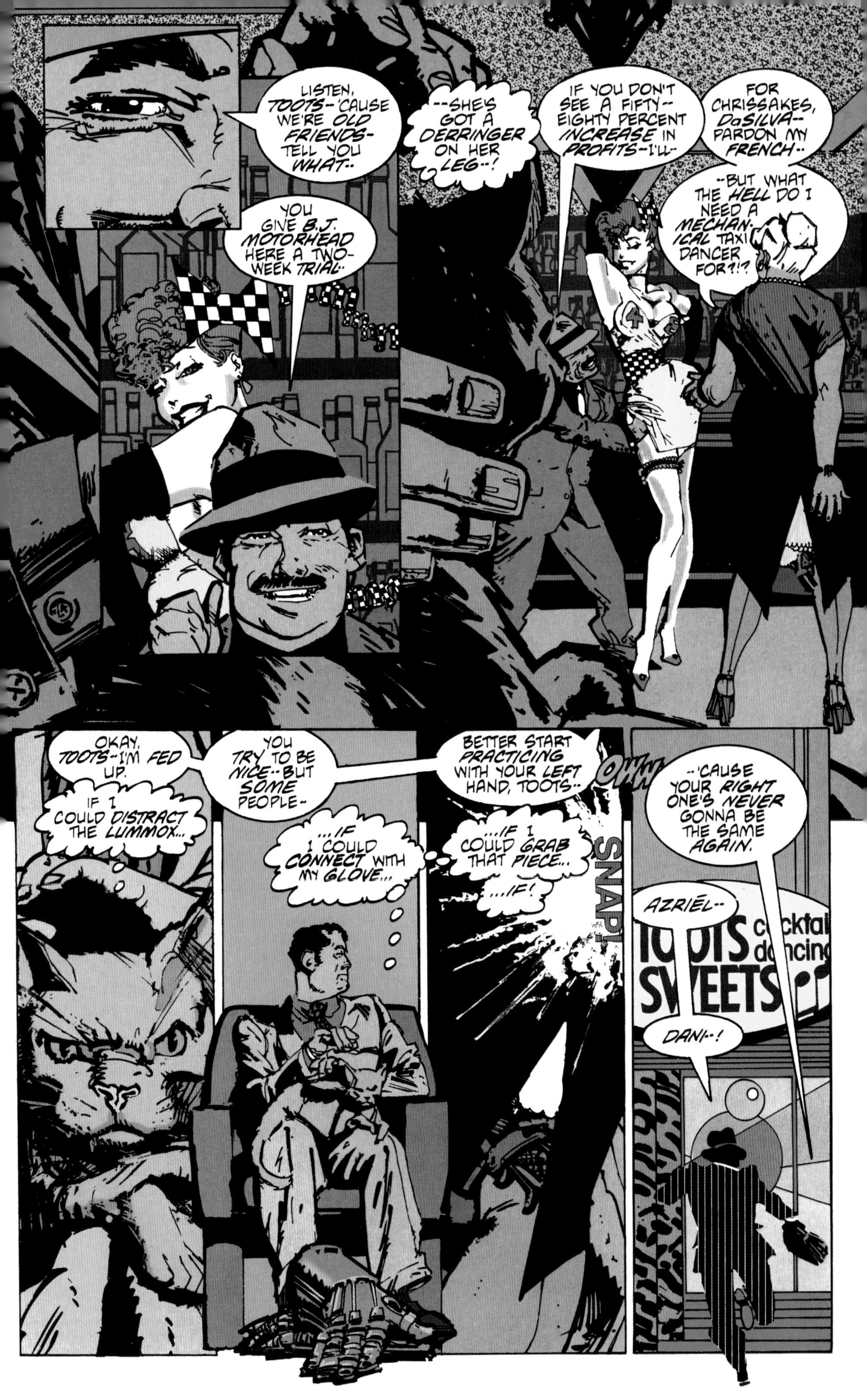
LISTEN, TOOTS--'CAUSE WE'RE OLD FRIENDS-TELL YOU WHAT--
YOU GIVE B.J. MOTORHEAD HERE A TWO-WEEK TRIAL--
--SHE'S GOT A DERRINGER ON HER LEG--!
IF YOU DON'T SEE A FIFTY--EIGHTY PERCENT INCREASE IN PROFITS--I'LL--
FOR CHRISSAKES, DaSILVA--PARDON MY FRENCH--
--BUT WHAT THE HELL DO I NEED A MECHANICAL TAXI DANCER FOR?!?
OKAY, TOOTS--I'M FED UP.
IF I COULD DISTRACT THE LUMMOX...
YOU TRY TO BE NICE--BUT SOME PEOPLE--
...IF I COULD CONNECT WITH MY GLOVE...
BETTER START PRACTICING WITH YOUR LEFT HAND, TOOTS--
...IF I COULD GRAB THAT PIECE...
...IF!
OWW
SNAP!
--'CAUSE YOUR RIGHT ONE'S NEVER GONNA BE THE SAME AGAIN.
AZRIEL--
TOOTS SWEETS cocktails dancing
DANI--!

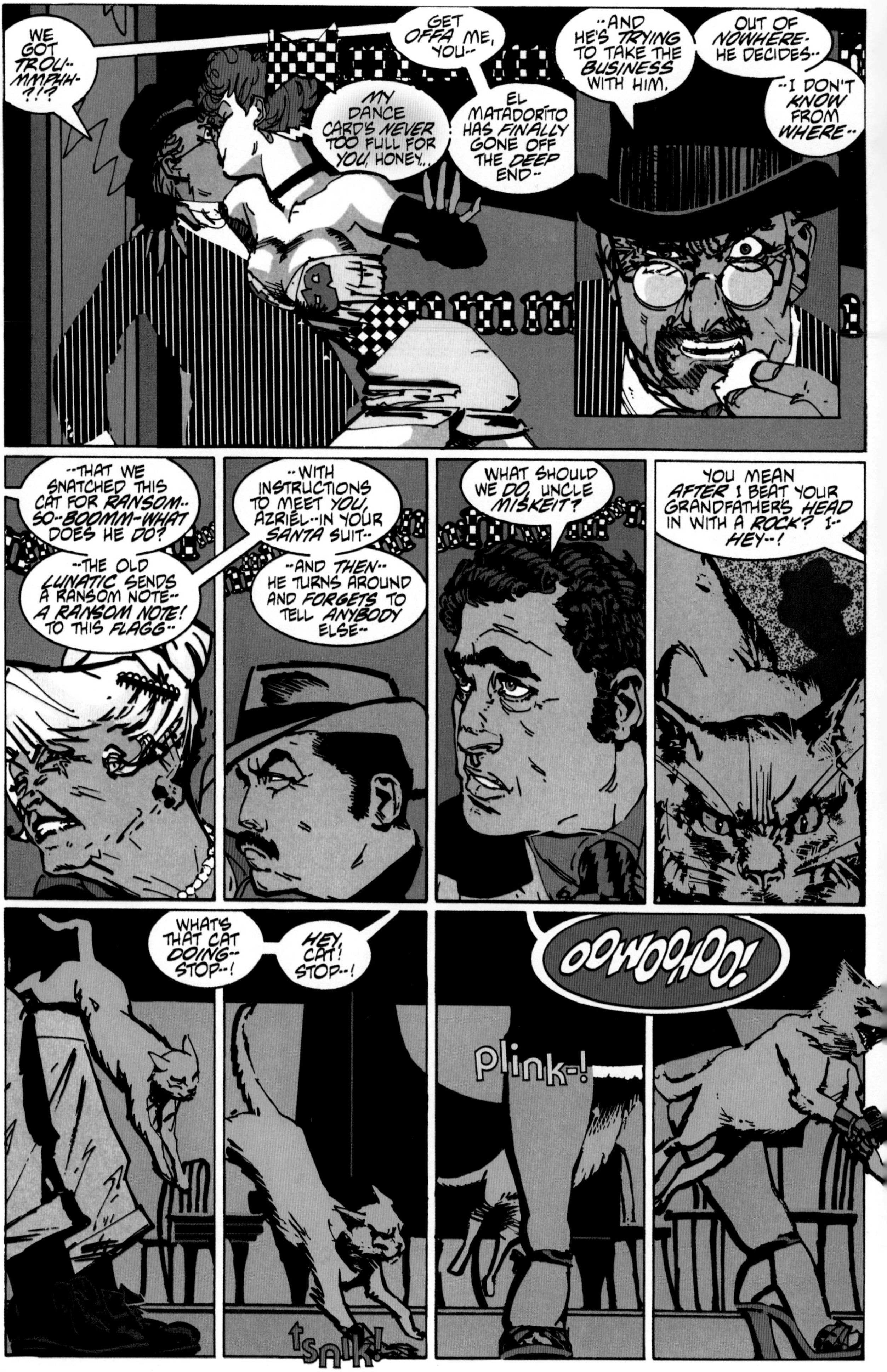
WE GOT TROU-- MMPHH-?!?
GET OFFA ME, YOU--
MY DANCE CARD'S NEVER TOO FULL FOR YOU, HONEY...
EL MATADORITO HAS FINALLY GONE OFF THE DEEP END--
--AND HE'S TRYING TO TAKE THE BUSINESS WITH HIM.
OUT OF NOWHERE-- HE DECIDES--
--I DON'T KNOW FROM WHERE--
--THAT WE SNATCHED THIS CAT FOR RANSOM-- SO--BOOMM--WHAT DOES HE DO?
--THE OLD LUNATIC SENDS A RANSOM NOTE-- A RANSOM NOTE! TO THIS FLAGG--
--WITH INSTRUCTIONS TO MEET YOU, AZRIEL--IN YOUR SANTA SUIT--
--AND THEN-- HE TURNS AROUND AND FORGETS TO TELL ANYBODY ELSE--
WHAT SHOULD WE DO, UNCLE MISKEIT?
YOU MEAN AFTER I BEAT YOUR GRANDFATHER'S HEAD IN WITH A ROCK? I-- HEY--!
WHAT'S THAT CAT DOING-- STOP--!
HEY, CAT! STOP--!
tsnik!
OOWOOHOO!
plink-!

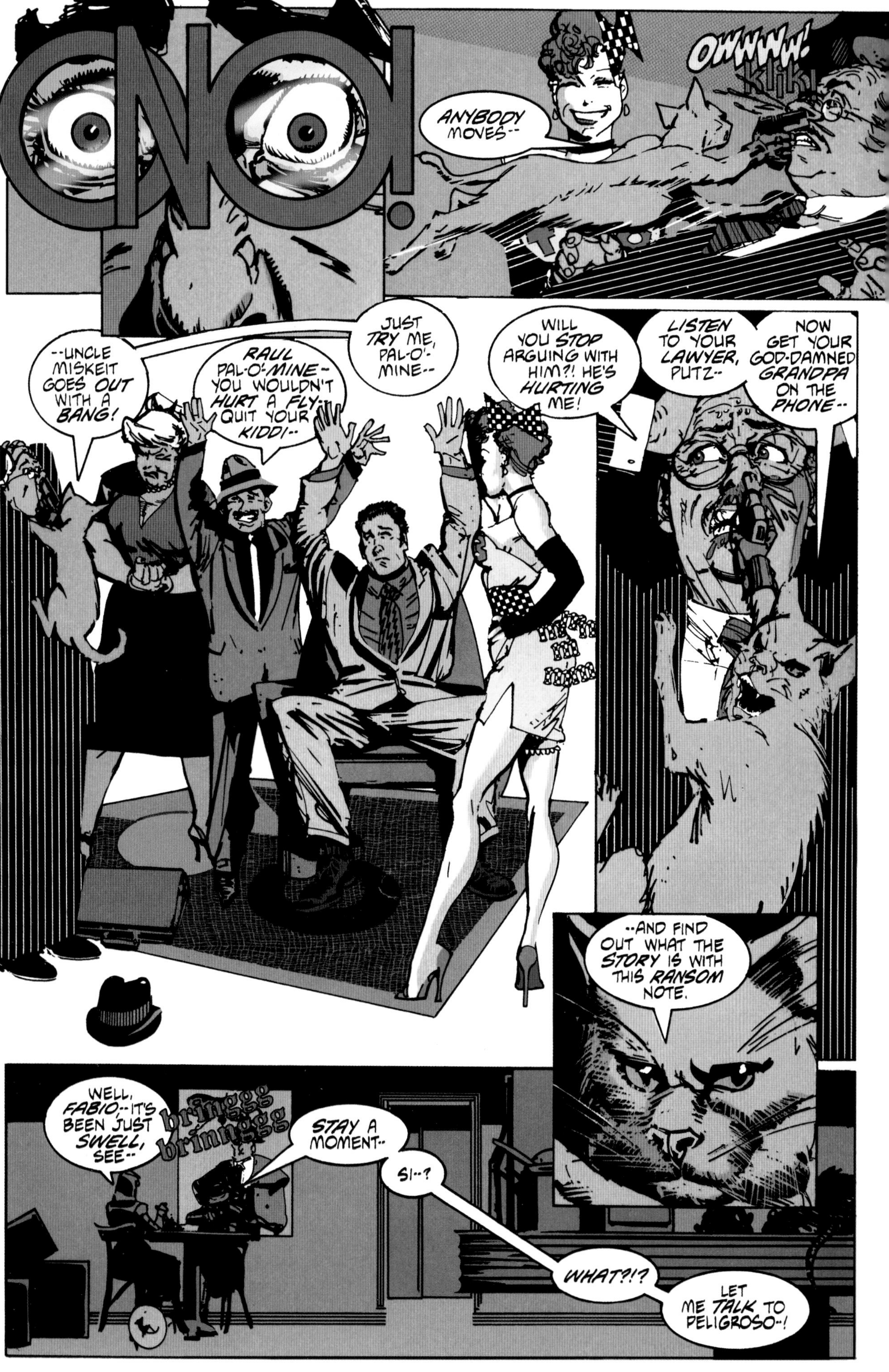
NO!
ANYBODY MOVES--
OWWWW!
klik!
--UNCLE MISKEIT GOES OUT WITH A BANG!
RAUL PAL-O'-MINE-- YOU WOULDN'T HURT A FLY-QUIT YOUR KIDDI--
JUST TRY ME, PAL-O'-MINE--
WILL YOU STOP ARGUING WITH HIM?! HE'S HURTING ME!
LISTEN TO YOUR LAWYER, PUTZ--
NOW GET YOUR GOD-DAMNED GRANDPA ON THE PHONE--
--AND FIND OUT WHAT THE STORY IS WITH THIS RANSOM NOTE.
WELL, FABIO,--IT'S BEEN JUST SWELL, SEE--
bringgg bringggg
STAY A MOMENT--
SI--?
WHAT?!?
LET ME TALK TO PELIGROSO--!

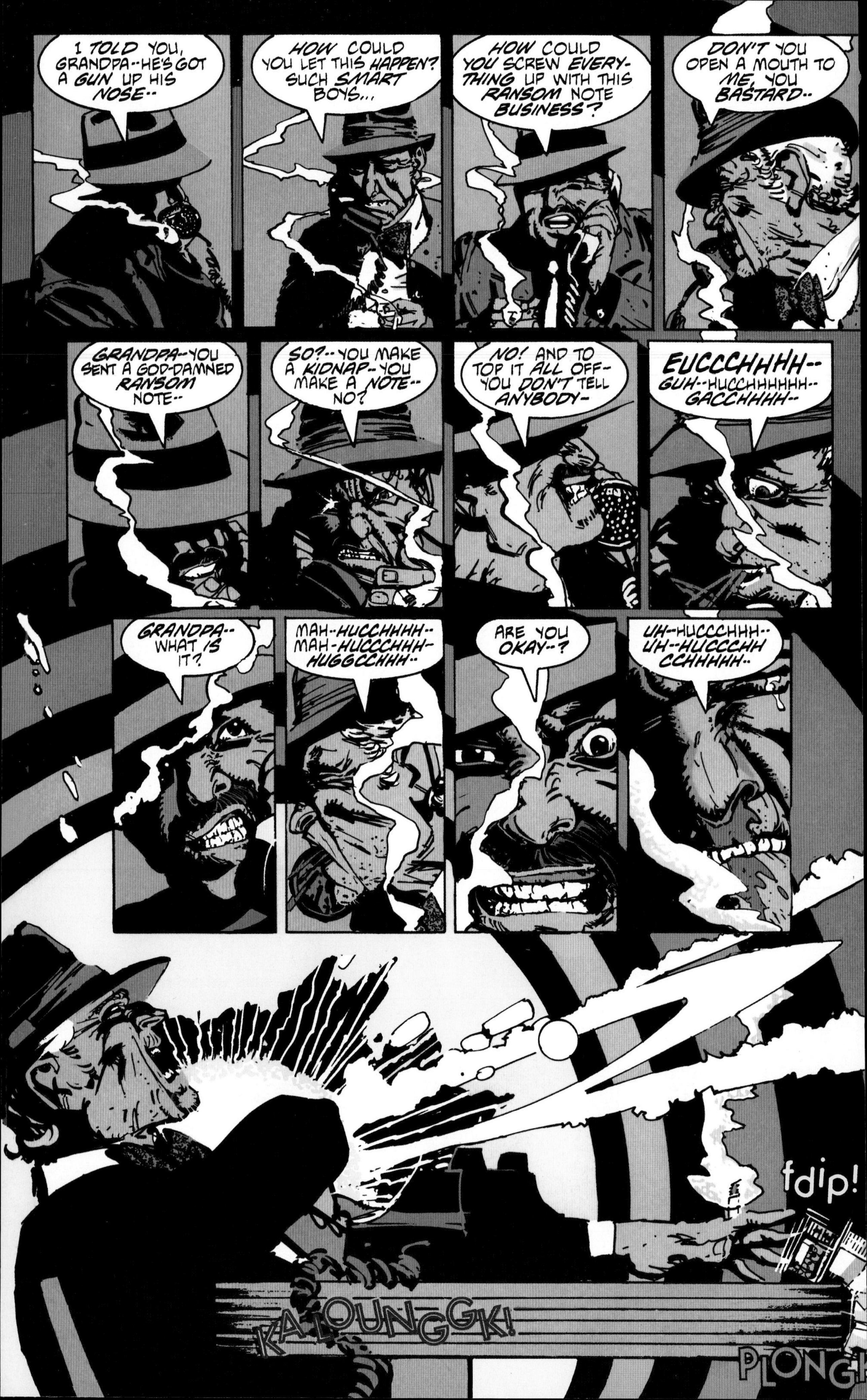
I TOLD YOU, GRANDPA--HE'S GOT A GUN UP HIS NOSE--
HOW COULD YOU LET THIS HAPPEN? SUCH SMART BOYS...
HOW COULD YOU SCREW EVERY-THING UP WITH THIS RANSOM NOTE BUSINESS?
DON'T YOU OPEN A MOUTH TO ME, YOU BASTARD--
GRANDPA--YOU SENT A GOD-DAMNED RANSOM NOTE--
SO?--YOU MAKE A KIDNAP--YOU MAKE A NOTE--NO?
NO! AND TO TOP IT ALL OFF--YOU DON'T TELL ANYBODY--
EUCCCHHHH--GUH--HUCCHHHHHHH--GACCHHHH--
GRANDPA--WHAT IS IT?
MAH--HUCCHHHH--MAH--HUCCCHHH-HUGGCCHHH--
ARE YOU OKAY--?
UH--HUCCCHHH--UH--HUCCCHH CCHHHHH--
fdip!
KALOUNGGK!
PLONG!

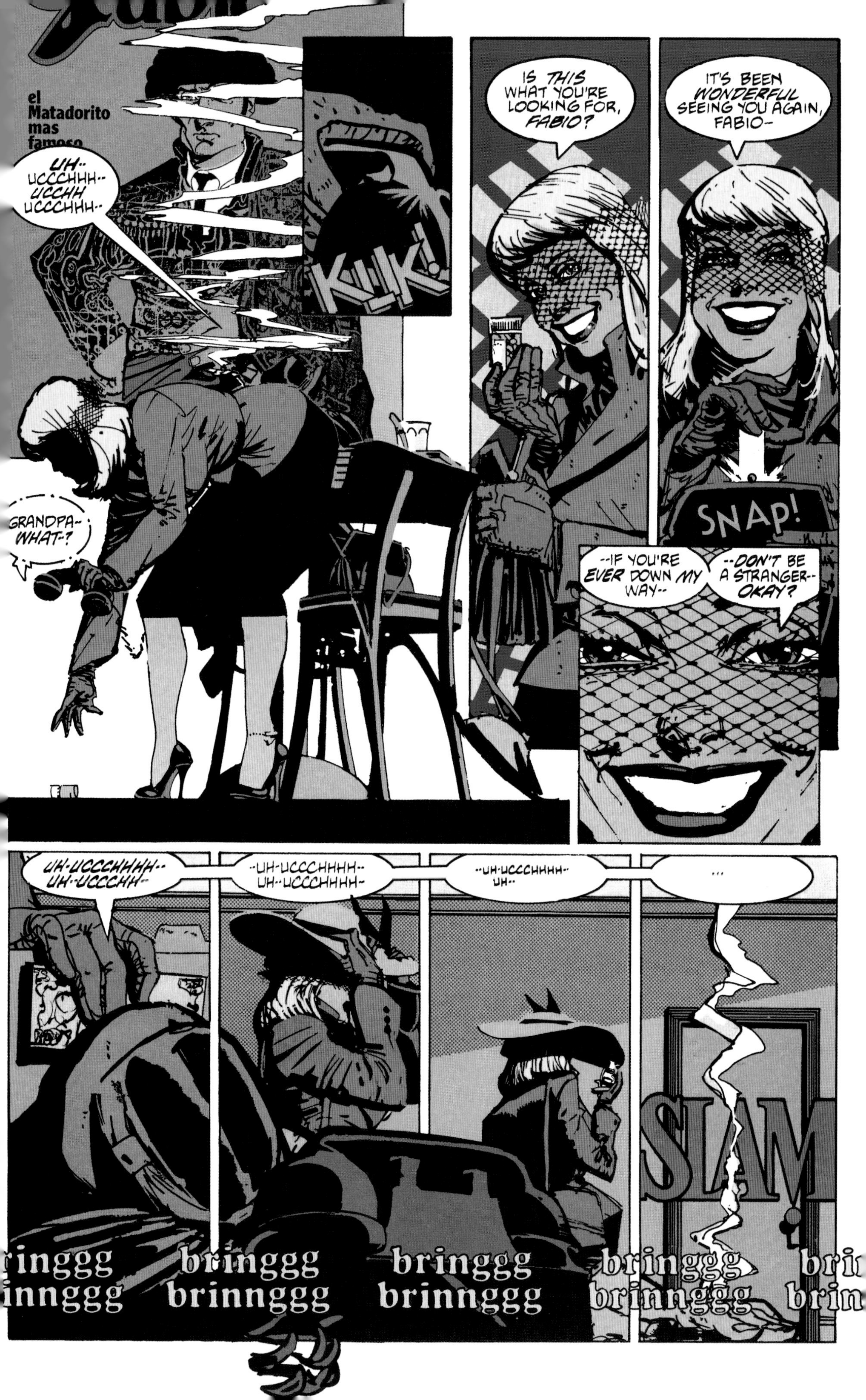
el Matadorito mas famoso
UH-- UCCCHHH-- UCCHH UCCCHHH--
KLIK!
GRANDPA-- WHAT--?
IS THIS WHAT YOU'RE LOOKING FOR, FABIO?
IT'S BEEN WONDERFUL SEEING YOU AGAIN, FABIO--
SNAP!
--IF YOU'RE EVER DOWN MY WAY--
--DON'T BE A STRANGER-- OKAY?
UH-UCCCHHHH-- UH--UCCCHH--
--UH-UCCCHHHH-- UH--UCCCHHHH--
--UH-UCCCHHHH-- UH--
...
SLAM
ringgg bringgg bringgg bringgg bri
innggg brinnggg brinnggg brinnggg brin

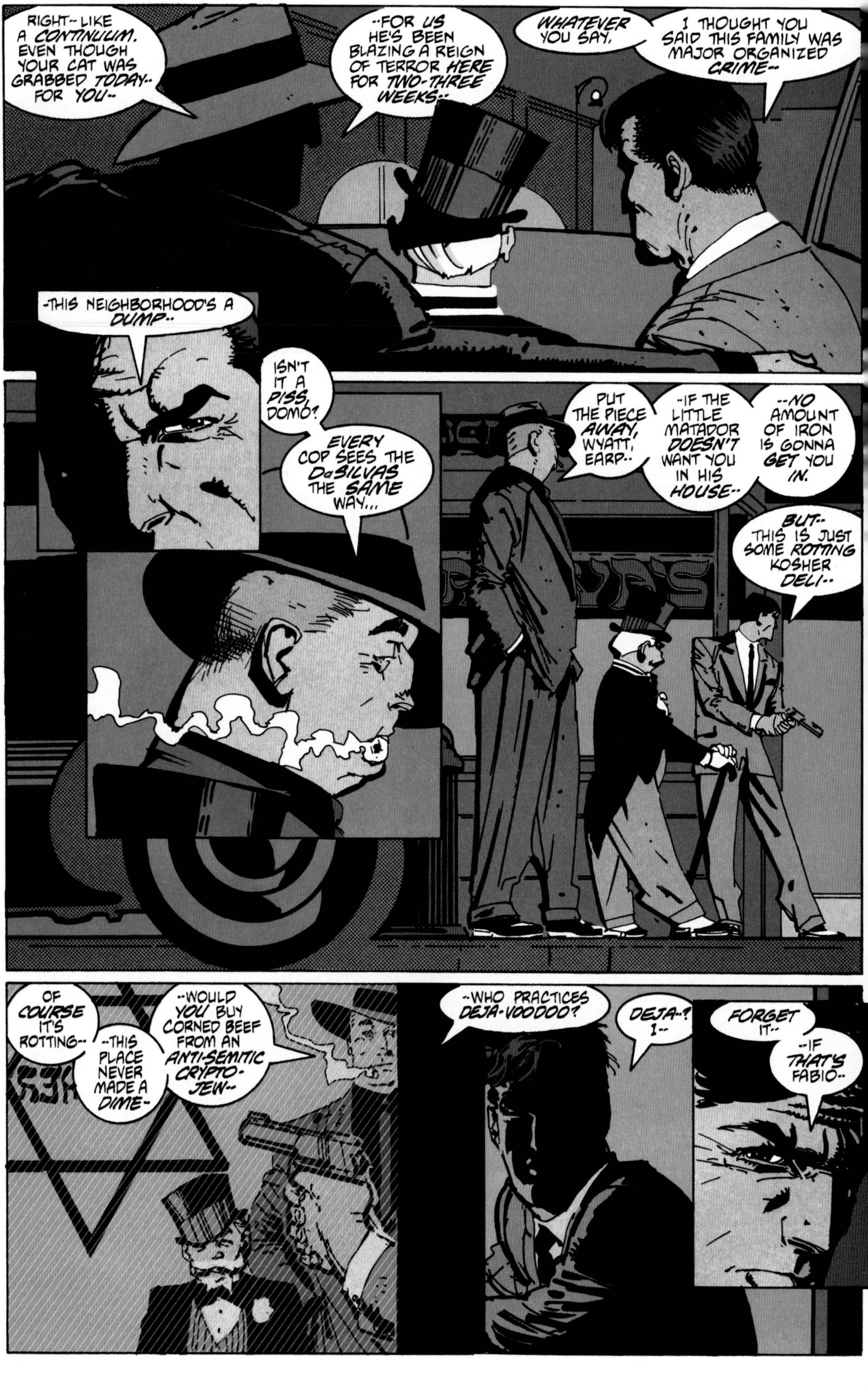
RIGHT--LIKE A CONTINUUM. EVEN THOUGH YOUR CAT WAS GRABBED TODAY-- FOR YOU--
--FOR US HE'S BEEN BLAZING A REIGN OF TERROR HERE FOR TWO-THREE WEEKS--
WHATEVER YOU SAY.
I THOUGHT YOU SAID THIS FAMILY WAS MAJOR ORGANIZED CRIME--
-THIS NEIGHBORHOOD'S A DUMP--
ISN'T IT A PISS, DOMO?
EVERY COP SEES THE DaSILVAS THE SAME WAY...
PUT THE PIECE AWAY, WYATT, EARP--
--IF THE LITTLE MATADOR DOESN'T WANT YOU IN HIS HOUSE--
--NO AMOUNT OF IRON IS GONNA GET YOU IN.
BUT-- THIS IS JUST SOME ROTTING KOSHER DELI--
OF COURSE IT'S ROTTING--
--THIS PLACE NEVER MADE A DIME--
--WOULD YOU BUY CORNED BEEF FROM AN ANTI-SEMITIC CRYPTO-JEW--
--WHO PRACTICES DEJA-VOODOO?
DEJA--? I--
FORGET IT--
--IF THAT'S FABIO--

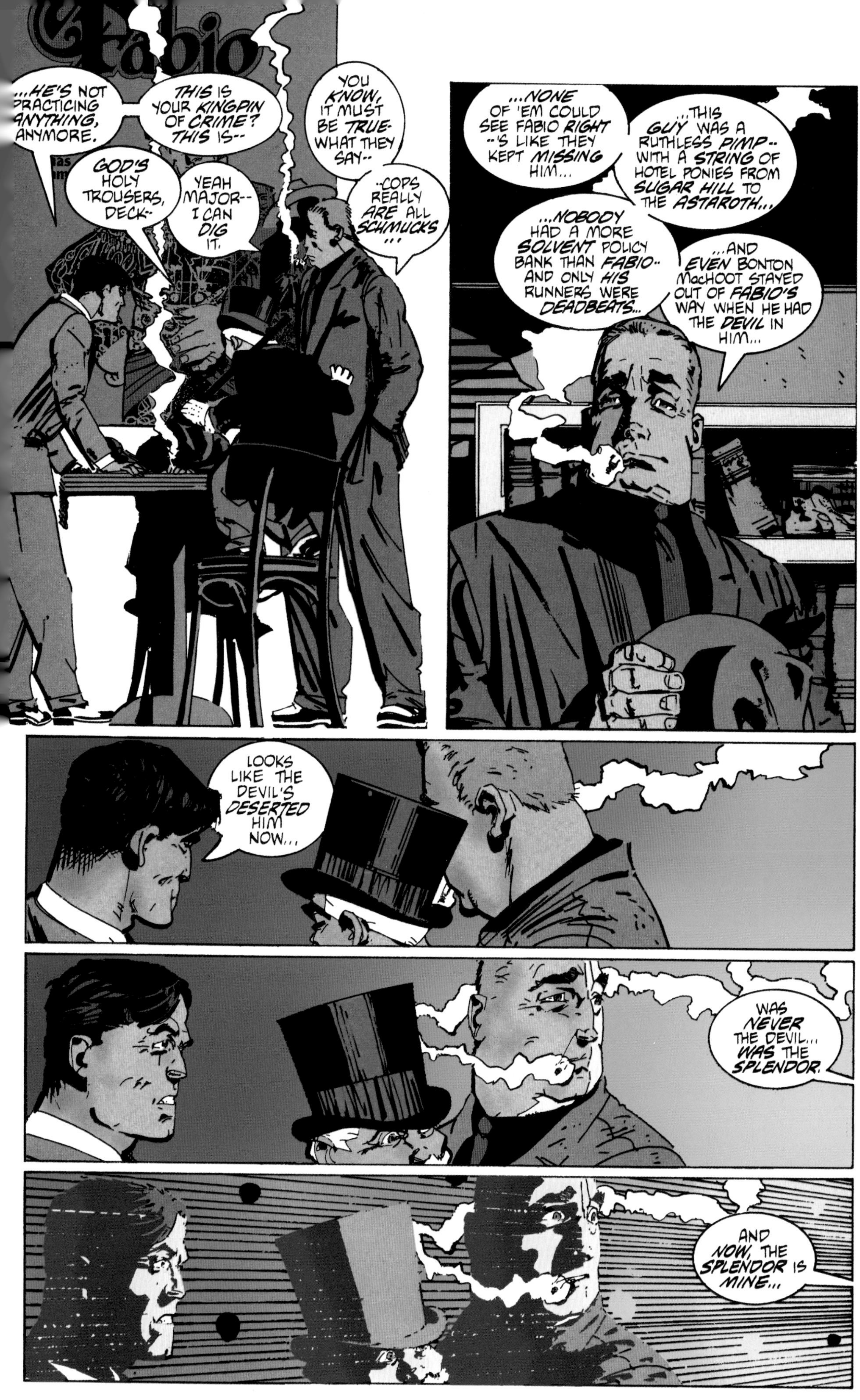
Fabio
...HE'S NOT PRACTICING ANYTHING, ANYMORE.
THIS IS YOUR KINGPIN OF CRIME? THIS IS--
GOD'S HOLY TROUSERS, DECK-
YEAH MAJOR-- I CAN DIG IT.
YOU KNOW, IT MUST BE TRUE- WHAT THEY SAY--
--COPS REALLY ARE ALL SCHMUCKS ...
...NONE OF 'EM COULD SEE FABIO RIGHT --'S LIKE THEY KEPT MISSING HIM...
...THIS GUY WAS A RUTHLESS PIMP-- WITH A STRING OF HOTEL PONIES FROM SUGAR HILL TO THE ASTAROTH...
...NOBODY HAD A MORE SOLVENT POLICY BANK THAN FABIO-- AND ONLY HIS RUNNERS WERE DEADBEATS...
...AND EVEN BONTON MacHOOT STAYED OUT OF FABIO'S WAY WHEN HE HAD THE DEVIL IN HIM...
LOOKS LIKE THE DEVIL'S DESERTED HIM NOW...
WAS NEVER THE DEVIL... WAS THE SPLENDOR.
AND NOW, THE SPLENDOR IS MINE...

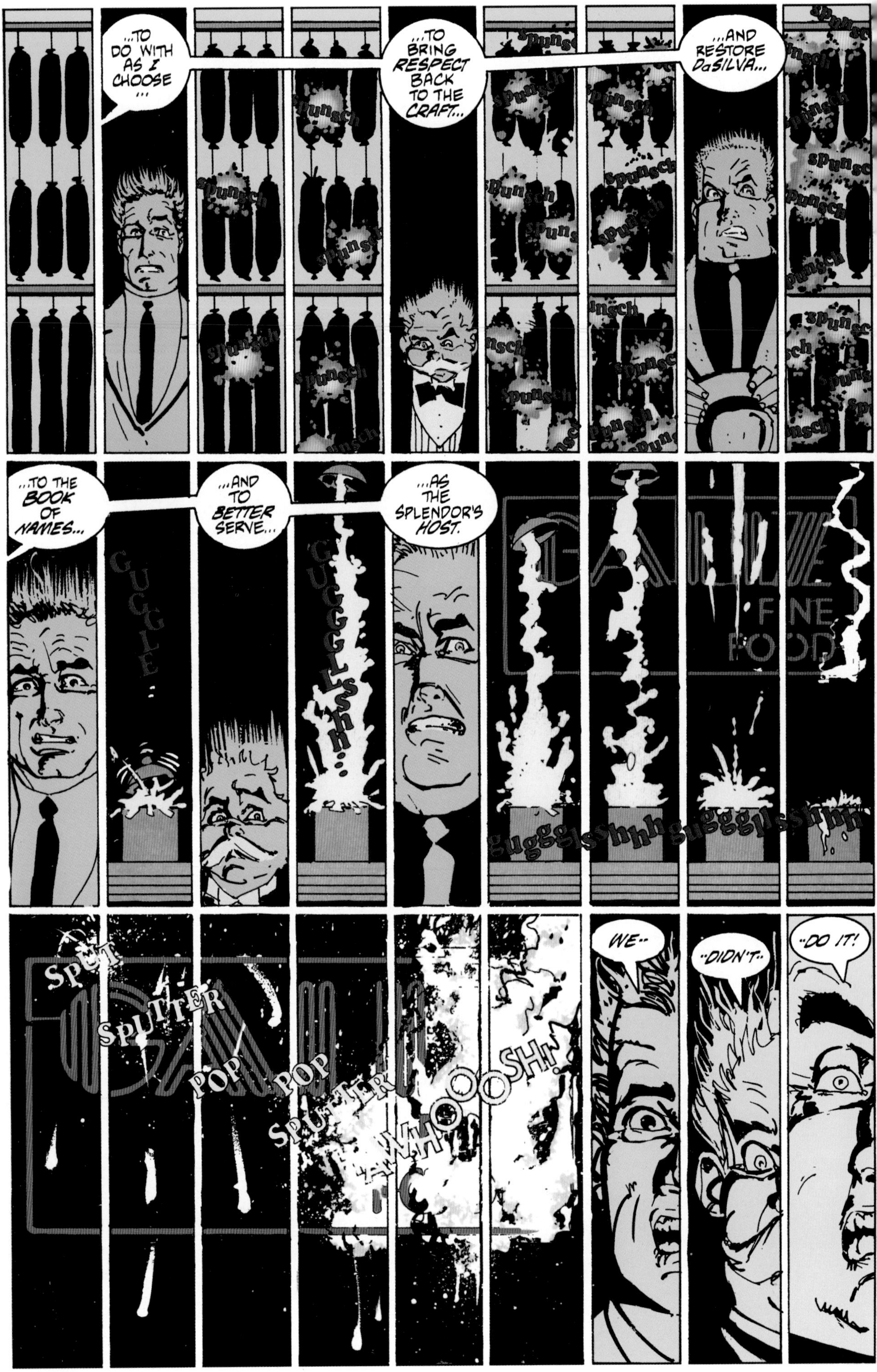
...TO DO WITH AS I CHOOSE ...
spunsch
...TO BRING RESPECT BACK TO THE CRAFT...
...AND RESTORE DaSILVA...
...TO THE BOOK OF NAMES...
GUGGLE
...AND TO BETTER SERVE...
GUGGGLISHH
...AS THE SPLENDOR'S HOST.
FINE FOOD
guggglisshhh
guggglisshhh
SPUT
SPUTTER
POP
POP
SPUTTER
WHOOOSH!
WE--
--DIDN'T--
--DO IT!

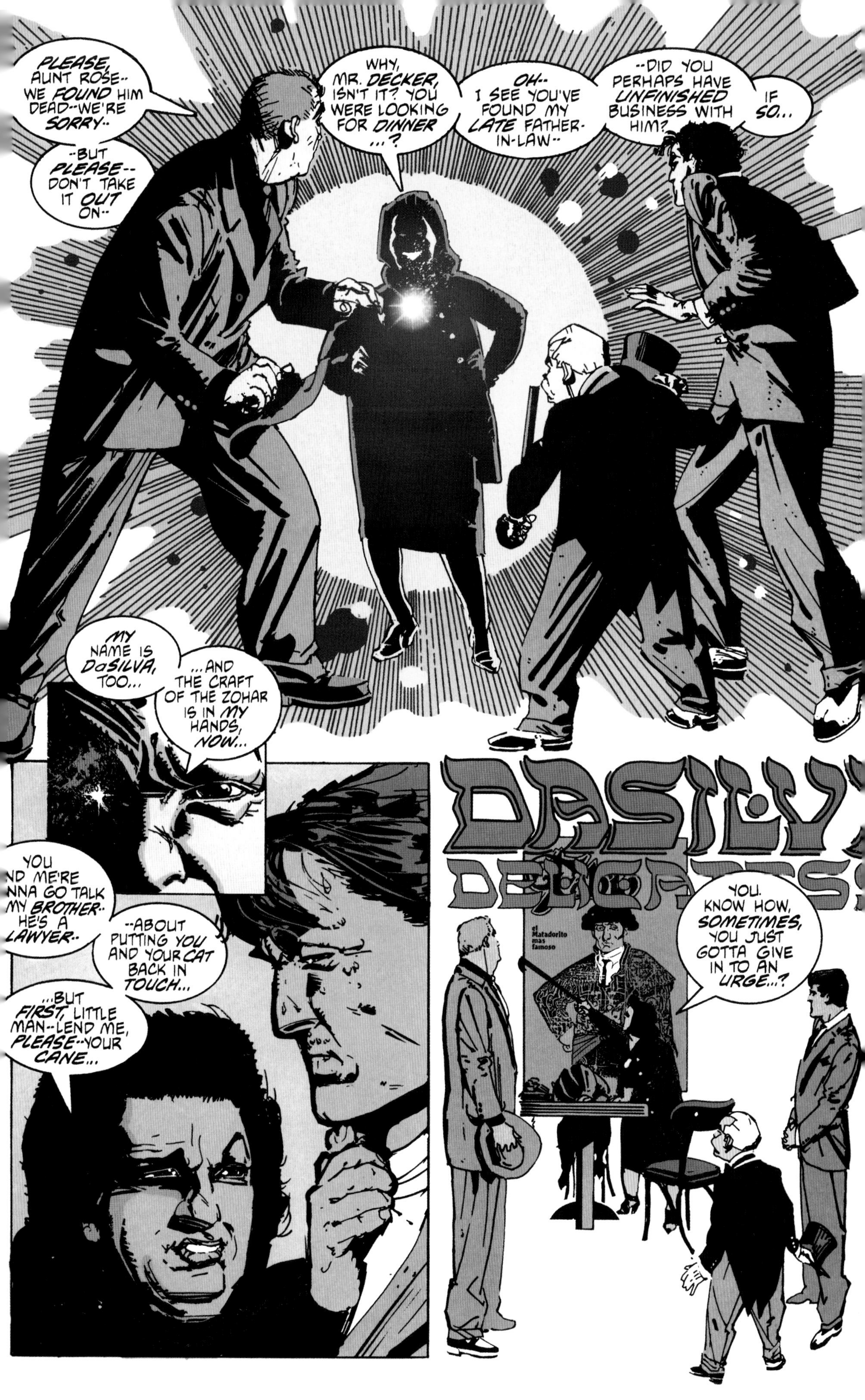
PLEASE, AUNT ROSE.. WE FOUND HIM DEAD--WE'RE SORRY..
--BUT PLEASE--DON'T TAKE IT OUT ON--
WHY, MR. DECKER, ISN'T IT? YOU WERE LOOKING FOR DINNER ...?
OH-- I SEE YOU'VE FOUND MY LATE FATHER-IN-LAW--
--DID YOU PERHAPS HAVE UNFINISHED BUSINESS WITH HIM?
IF SO...
MY NAME IS DaSILVA, TOO...
...AND THE CRAFT OF THE ZOHAR IS IN MY HANDS, NOW...
YOU
ND ME'RE
NNA GO TALK
MY BROTHER..
HE'S A
LAWYER..
--ABOUT PUTTING YOU AND YOUR CAT BACK IN TOUCH...
...BUT FIRST, LITTLE MAN--LEND ME, PLEASE--YOUR CANE...
el Matadorito mas famoso
YOU. KNOW HOW, SOMETIMES, YOU JUST GOTTA GIVE IN TO AN URGE...?

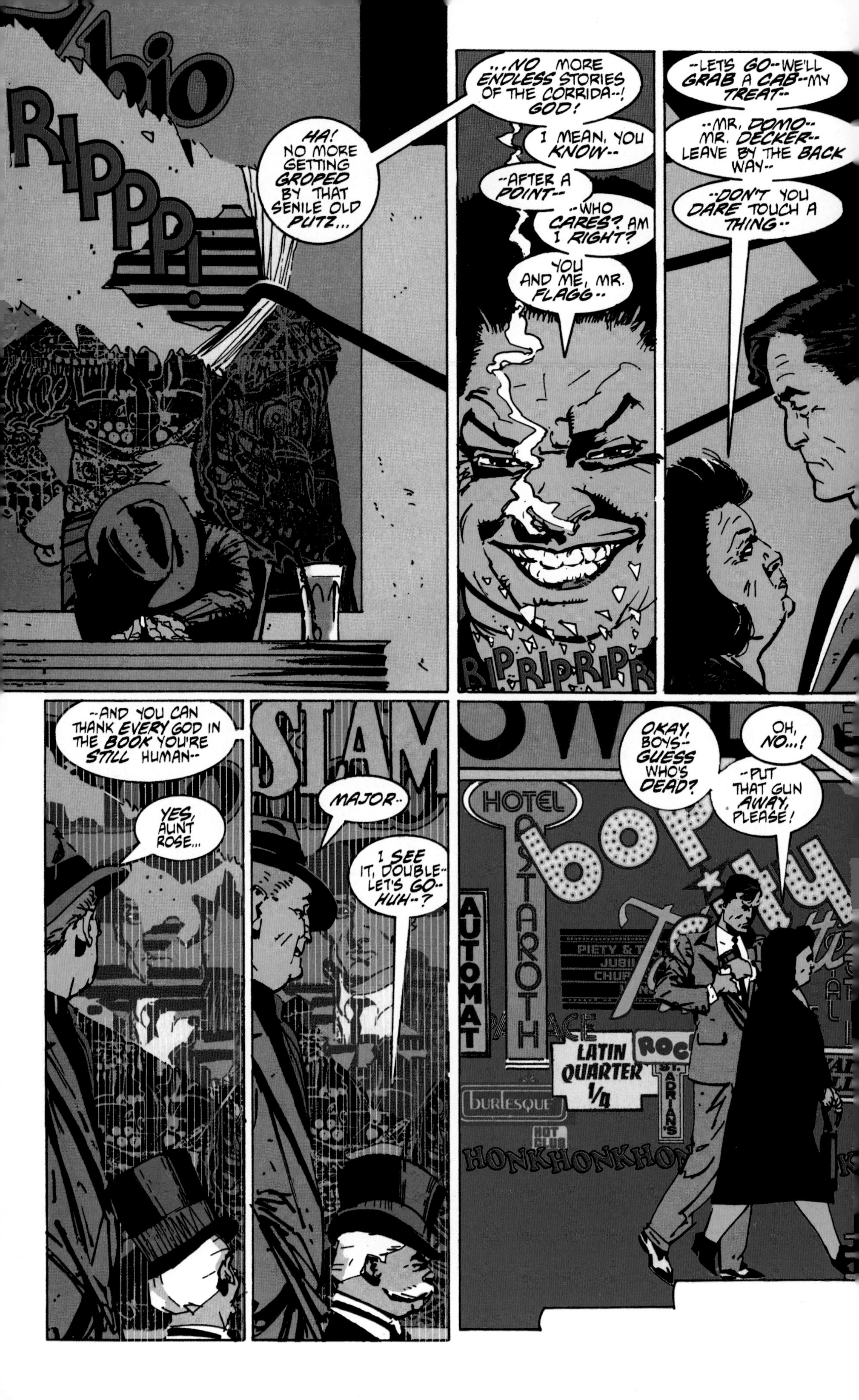
RIPPPP!
HA! NO MORE GETTING GROPED BY THAT SENILE OLD PUTZ...
...NO MORE ENDLESS STORIES OF THE CORRIDA--! GOD!
I MEAN, YOU KNOW--
--AFTER A POINT--
--WHO CARES? AM I RIGHT?
YOU AND ME, MR. FLAGG--
RIPRIPRIPRIPR
--LET'S GO--WE'LL GRAB A CAB--MY TREAT--
--MR. DOMO-- MR. DECKER-- LEAVE BY THE BACK WAY--
--DON'T YOU DARE TOUCH A THING--
--AND YOU CAN THANK EVERY GOD IN THE BOOK YOU'RE STILL HUMAN--
YES, AUNT ROSE...
MAJOR--
I SEE IT, DOUBLE-- LET'S GO-- HUH--?
OKAY, BOYS-- GUESS WHO'S DEAD?
OH, NO...!
--PUT THAT GUN AWAY, PLEASE!
HOTEL
AUTOMAT
ASTAROTH
PALACE
LATIN QUARTER 1/4
burlesque
HOT CLUB
ST. ADRIAN'S
HONKHONKHON

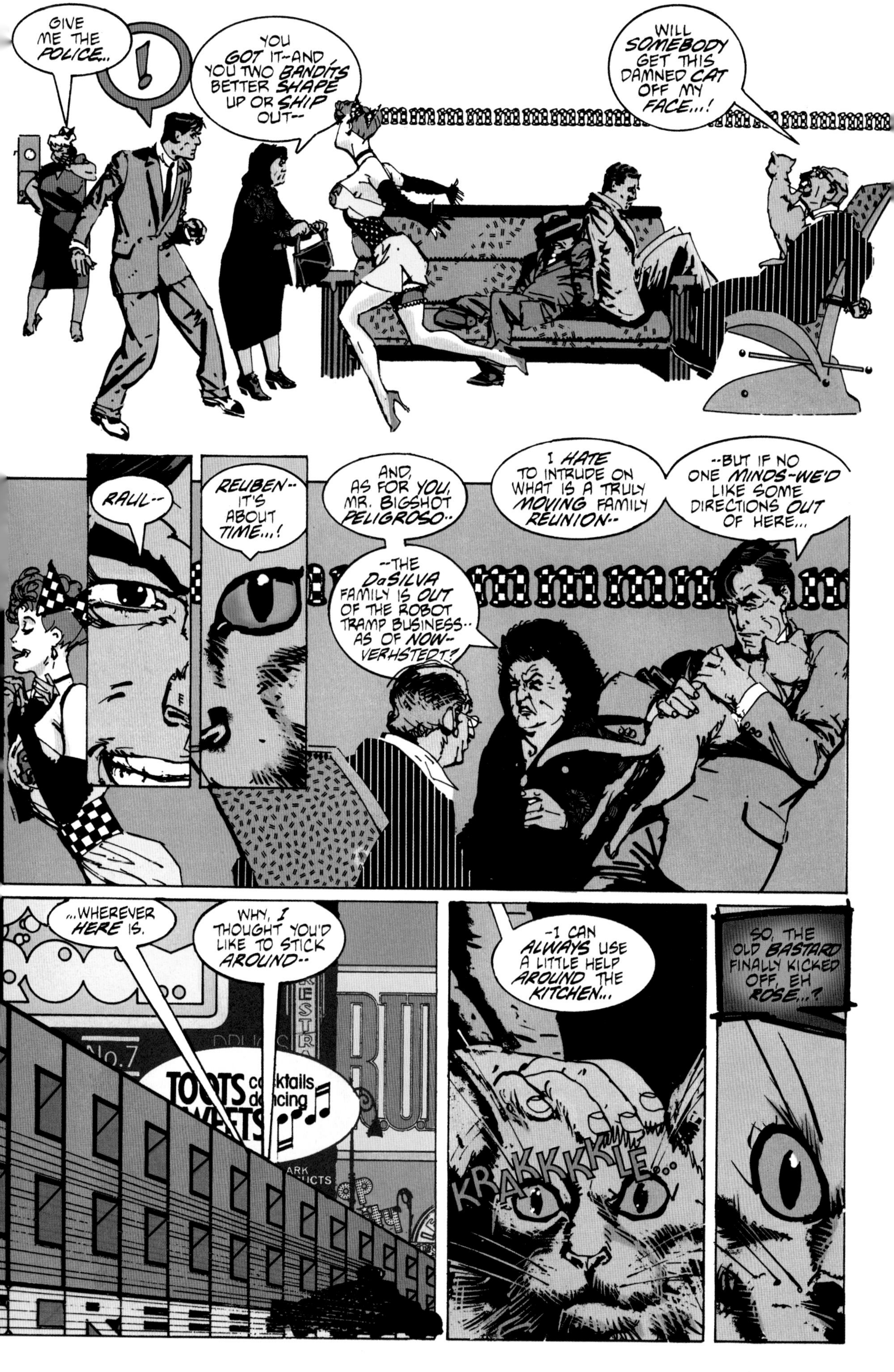
GIVE ME THE POLICE..
!
YOU GOT IT--AND YOU TWO BANDITS BETTER SHAPE UP OR SHIP OUT--
WILL SOMEBODY GET THIS DAMNED CAT OFF MY FACE...!
RAUL--
REUBEN-- IT'S ABOUT TIME...!
AND, AS FOR YOU, MR. BIGSHOT PELIGROSO--
--THE DaSILVA FAMILY IS OUT OF THE ROBOT TRAMP BUSINESS-- AS OF NOW-- VERHSTEDT?
I HATE TO INTRUDE ON WHAT IS A TRULY MOVING FAMILY REUNION--
--BUT IF NO ONE MINDS--WE'D LIKE SOME DIRECTIONS OUT OF HERE...
...WHEREVER HERE IS.
WHY, I THOUGHT YOU'D LIKE TO STICK AROUND--
No.7
TOOTS SWEETS cocktails dancing
-I CAN ALWAYS USE A LITTLE HELP AROUND THE KITCHEN...
KRAKKKKLE...
SO, THE OLD BASTARD FINALLY KICKED OFF, EH ROSE...?

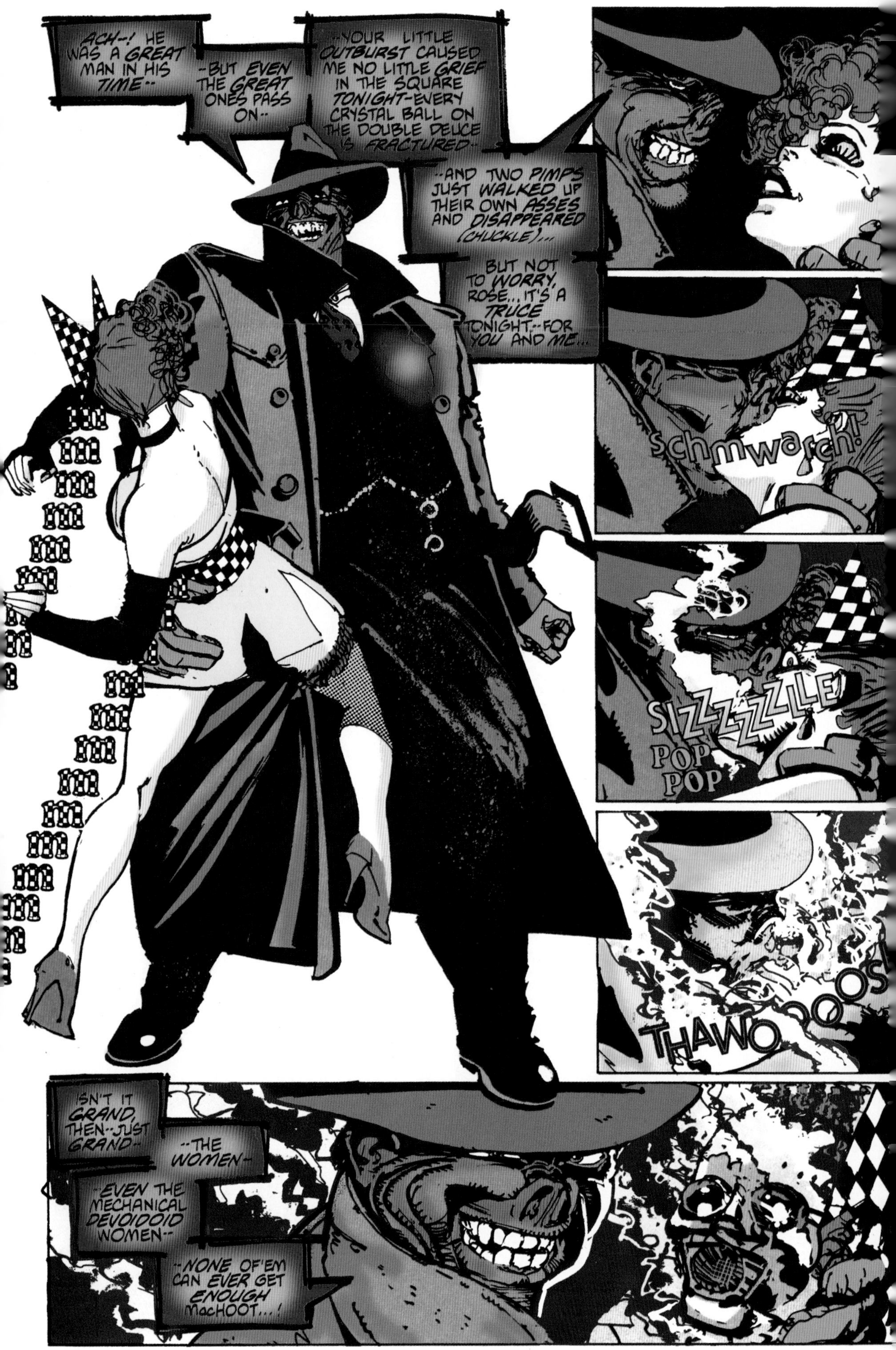
ACH--! HE WAS A GREAT MAN IN HIS TIME--
--BUT EVEN THE GREAT ONES PASS ON--
--YOUR LITTLE OUTBURST CAUSED ME NO LITTLE GRIEF IN THE SQUARE TONIGHT--EVERY CRYSTAL BALL ON THE DOUBLE DEUCE IS FRACTURED--
--AND TWO PIMPS JUST WALKED UP THEIR OWN ASSES AND DISAPPEARED (CHUCKLE)...
BUT NOT TO WORRY, ROSE... IT'S A TRUCE TONIGHT--FOR YOU AND ME...
schmwarch!
SIZZZZZZLE!
POP
POP
THAWOOOOOS
ISN'T IT GRAND, THEN--JUST GRAND--
--THE WOMEN--
--EVEN THE MECHANICAL DEVOIDOID WOMEN--
--NONE OF'EM CAN EVER GET ENOUGH MacHOOT...!

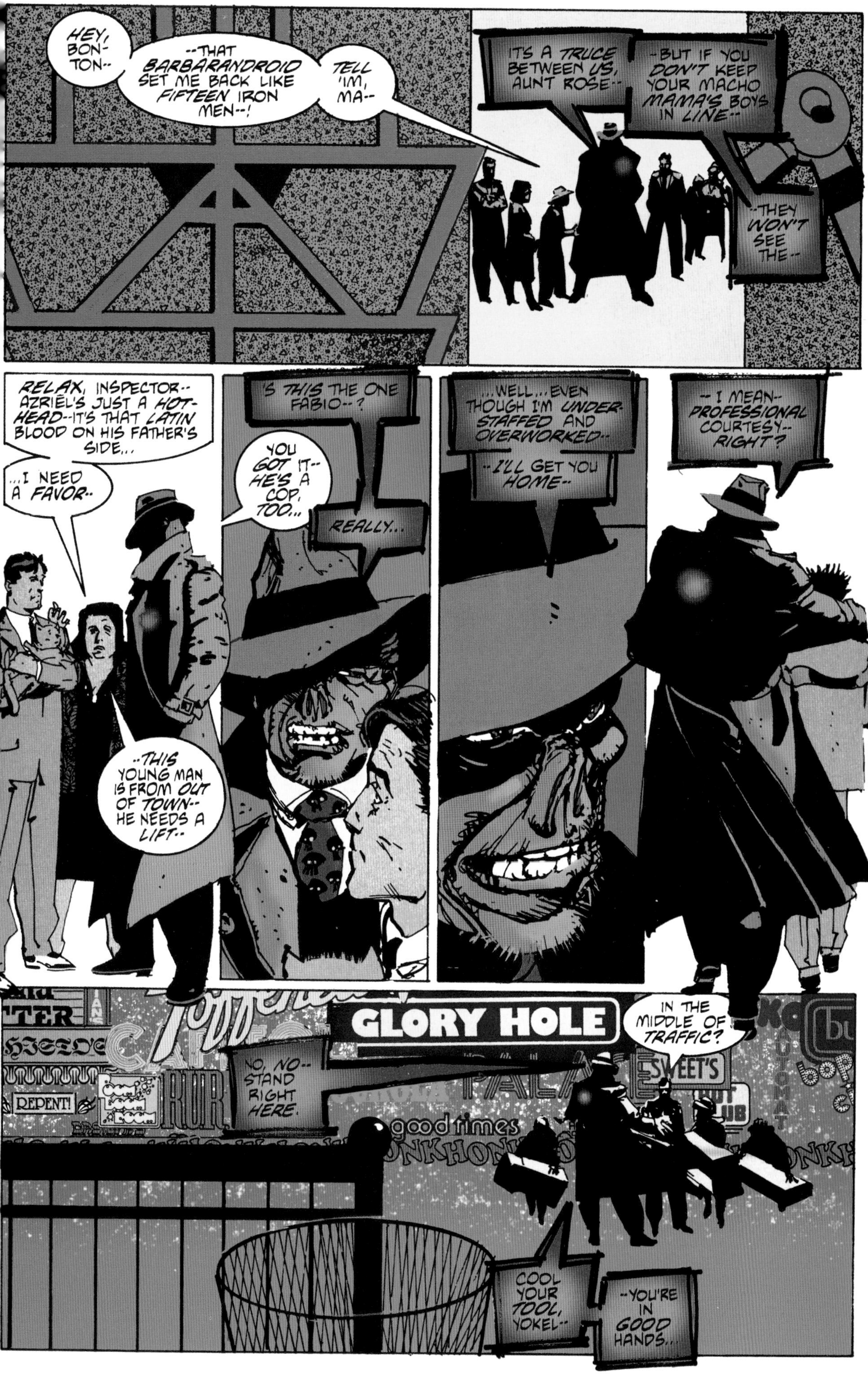
HEY, BON-TON--
--THAT BARBARANDROID SET ME BACK LIKE FIFTEEN IRON MEN--!
TELL 'IM, MA--
IT'S A TRUCE BETWEEN US, AUNT ROSE--
--BUT IF YOU DON'T KEEP YOUR MACHO MAMA'S BOYS IN LINE--
--THEY WON'T SEE THE--
RELAX, INSPECTOR--AZRIEL'S JUST A HOT-HEAD--IT'S THAT LATIN BLOOD ON HIS FATHER'S SIDE...
...I NEED A FAVOR--
--THIS YOUNG MAN IS FROM OUT OF TOWN--HE NEEDS A LIFT--
'S THIS THE ONE FABIO--?
YOU GOT IT--HE'S A COP, TOO...
REALLY...
...WELL...EVEN THOUGH I'M UNDER-STAFFED AND OVERWORKED--
--I'LL GET YOU HOME--
-- I MEAN--PROFESSIONAL COURTESY--RIGHT?
GLORY HOLE
IN THE MIDDLE OF TRAFFIC?
NO, NO--STAND RIGHT HERE.
REPENT!
SWEET'S
good times
COOL YOUR TOOL, YOKEL--
--YOU'RE IN GOOD HANDS...

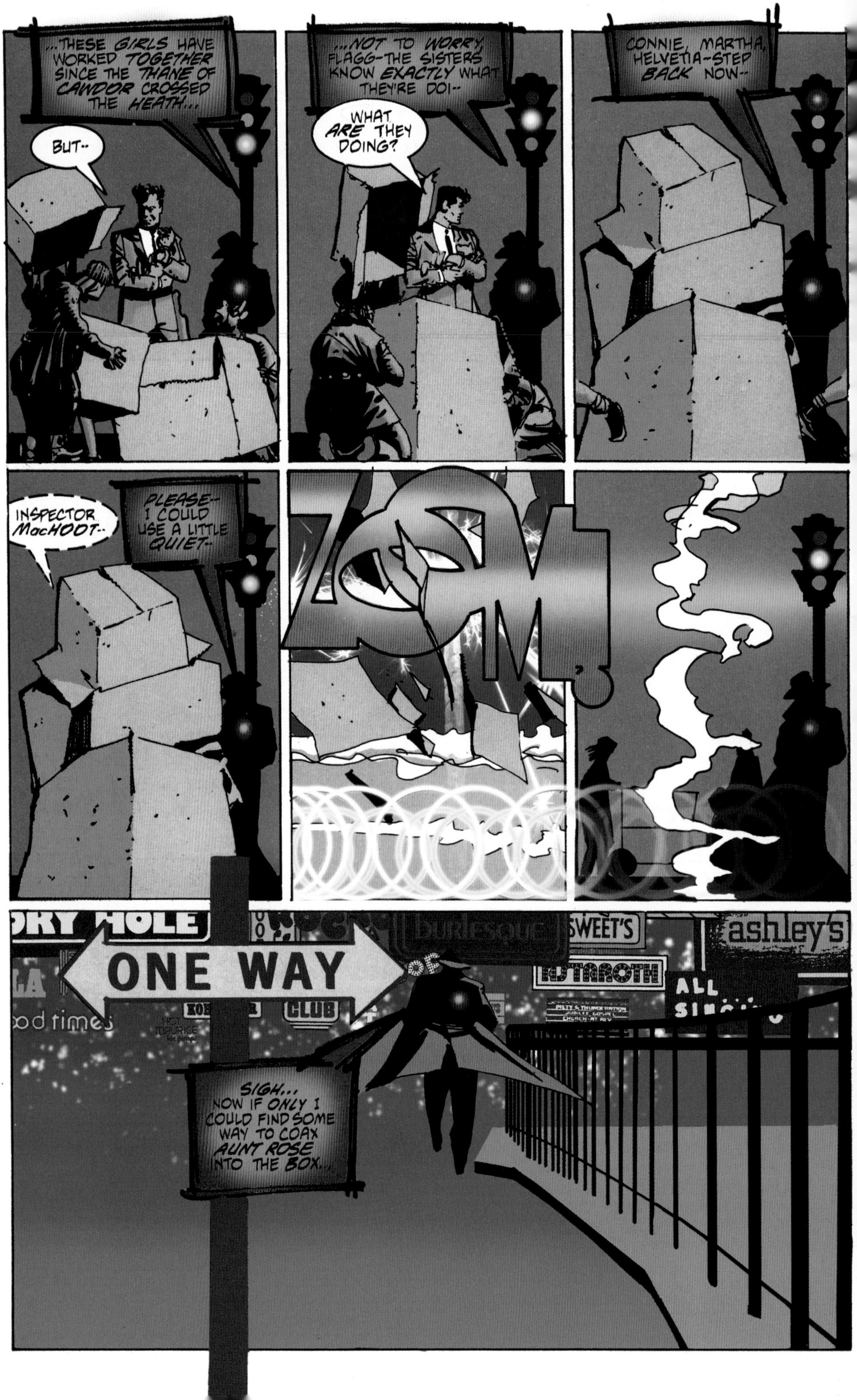
...THESE GIRLS HAVE WORKED TOGETHER SINCE THE THANE OF CAWDOR CROSSED THE HEATH...
BUT..
...NOT TO WORRY, FLAGG--THE SISTERS KNOW EXACTLY WHAT THEY'RE DOI--
WHAT ARE THEY DOING?
CONNIE, MARTHA, HELVETIA--STEP BACK NOW--
INSPECTOR MacHOOT--
PLEASE-- I COULD USE A LITTLE QUIET--
ZOOM
burlesque
SWEET'S
ashley's
ONE WAY
CLUB
ALL
SIGH... NOW IF ONLY I COULD FIND SOME WAY TO COAX AUNT ROSE INTO THE BOX...

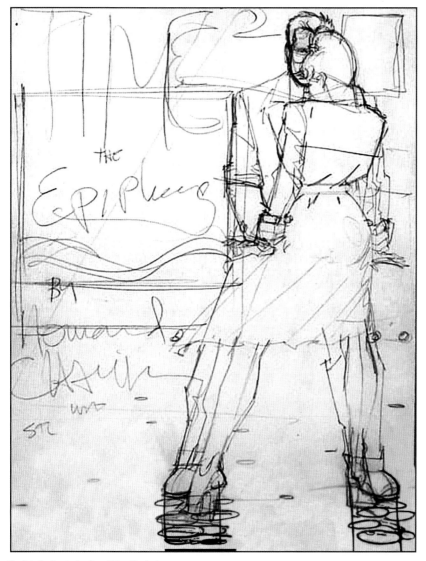

Initial sketch for *The Epiphany* cover.

An intersection of the infinite, where eternity meets forever.

Pulsating with the antic, earthy energy of the heartbeat of the living...and with the sullen, staccato silence of the heartbeat of the undead.

Where Deja-Voodoo and Reincarnimation collide — and zombies and robots bring new meaning to a new lease on life.

Bop Street, the Main Stem, the Stroll, the Double Deuce... these are mean streets, awash with smears of color and light, but nervous, jittery and menacing...

And no matter who you are, or where you are, or when you are —it's always 'round about midnight... $Time^2$.

THE EPIPHANY
originally published
NOVEMBER 1986
story and art
HOWARD CHAYKIN
color
STEVE OLIFF
letters
KEN BRUZENAK
editor
RICK OLIVER

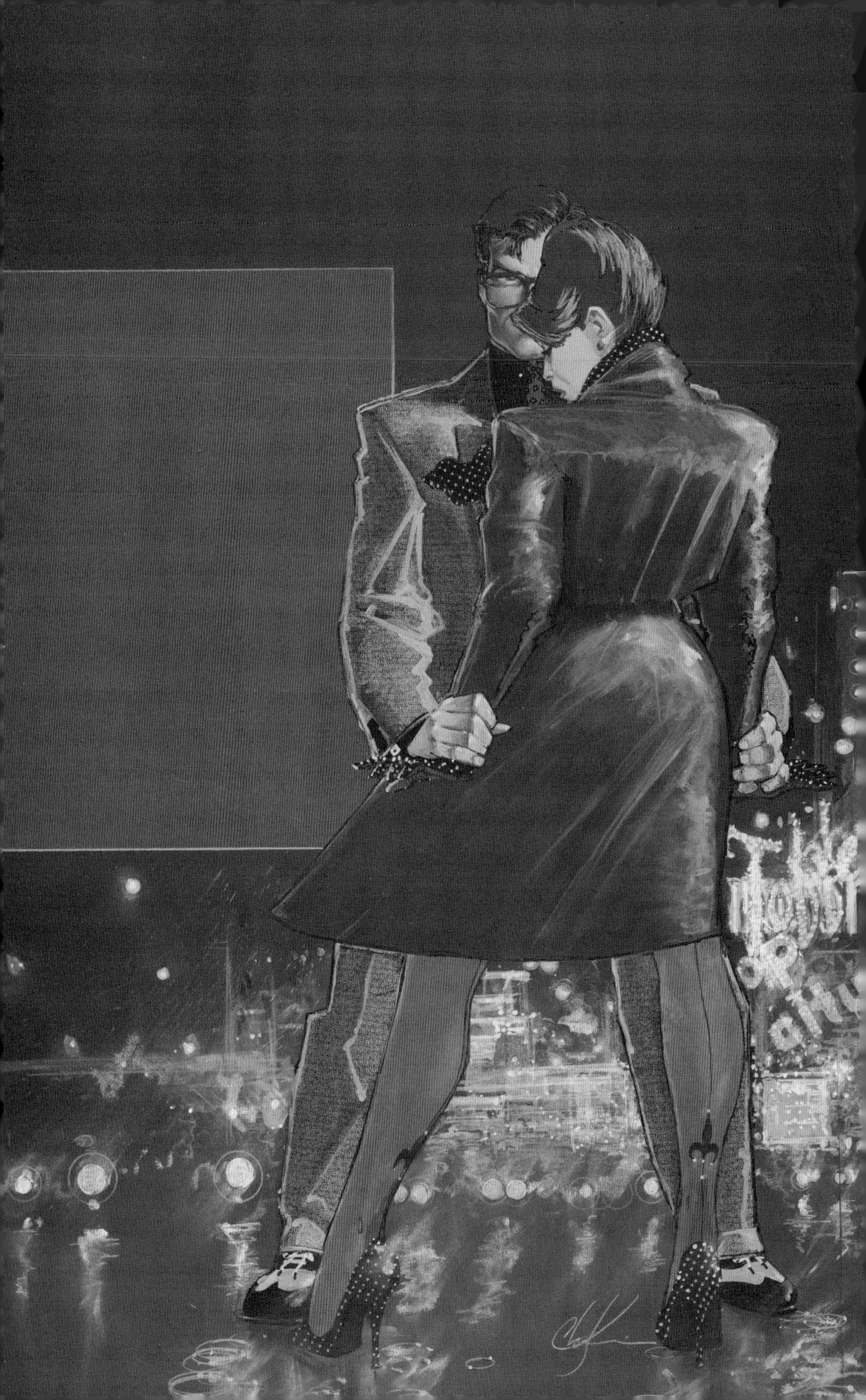

TIME²

The EPIPHANY

A fairy tale of the under city

The EPIPHANY

-NYONE in his right mind thinks these ZOMBIES are a

-ake NO for an ANSWER-with screaming MEEM-*

-early the issue MUST be resolved- SOONER or LATE-*

ere comes that Oh-so-happy vagabond, Mazda lantern held on high-- still searching for an honest man -- Diogenes Pilgrim -- with ²Talk!

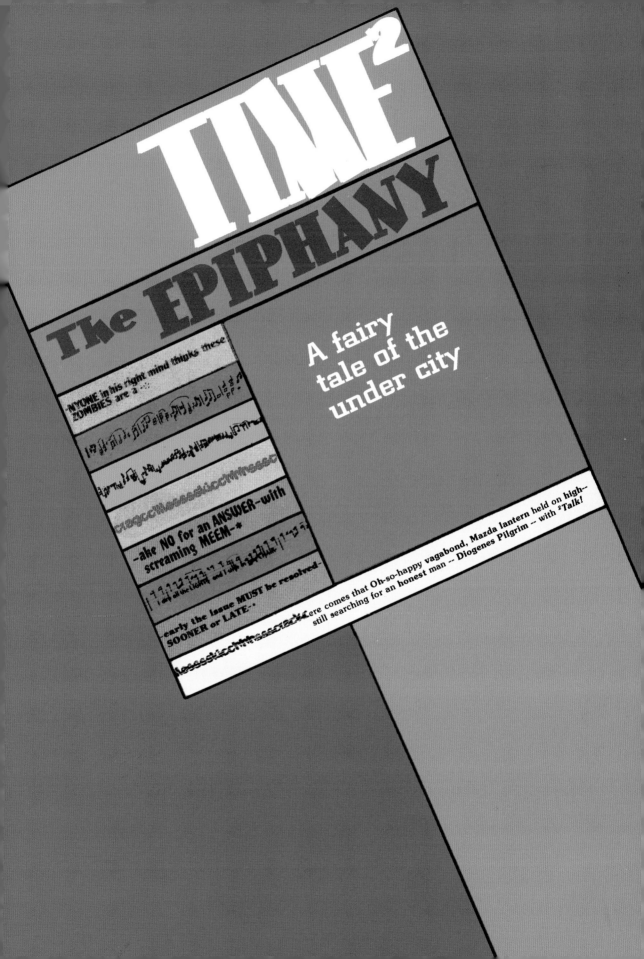

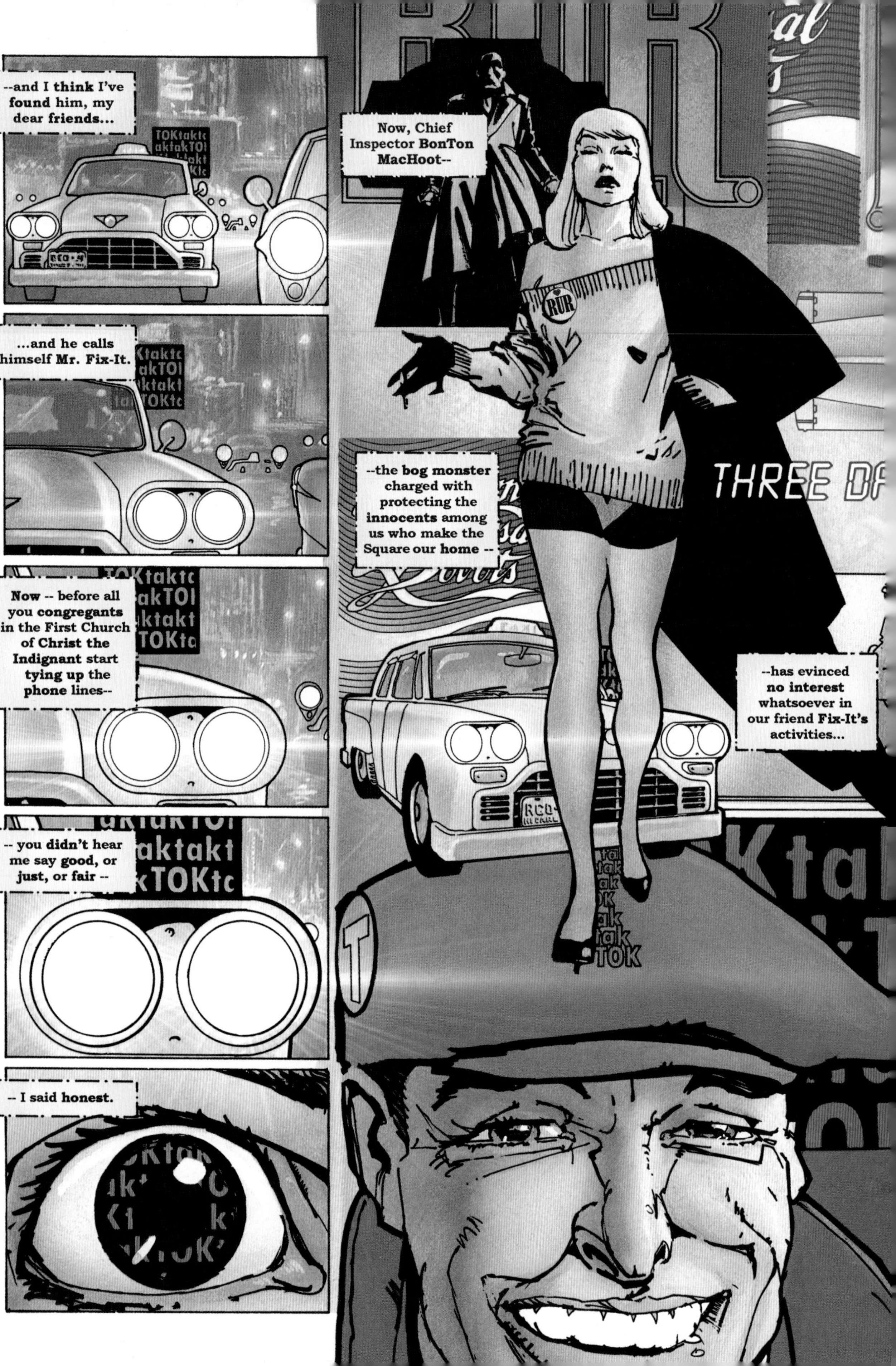
--and I think I've found him, my dear friends...
TOKtaktc aktakTOK
...and he calls himself Mr. Fix-It.
Now, Chief Inspector BonTon MacHoot--
RUR
--the bog monster charged with protecting the innocents among us who make the Square our home --
THREE DA
Now -- before all you congregants in the First Church of Christ the Indignant start tying up the phone lines--
--has evinced no interest whatsoever in our friend Fix-It's activities...
-- you didn't hear me say good, or just, or fair --
-- I said honest.

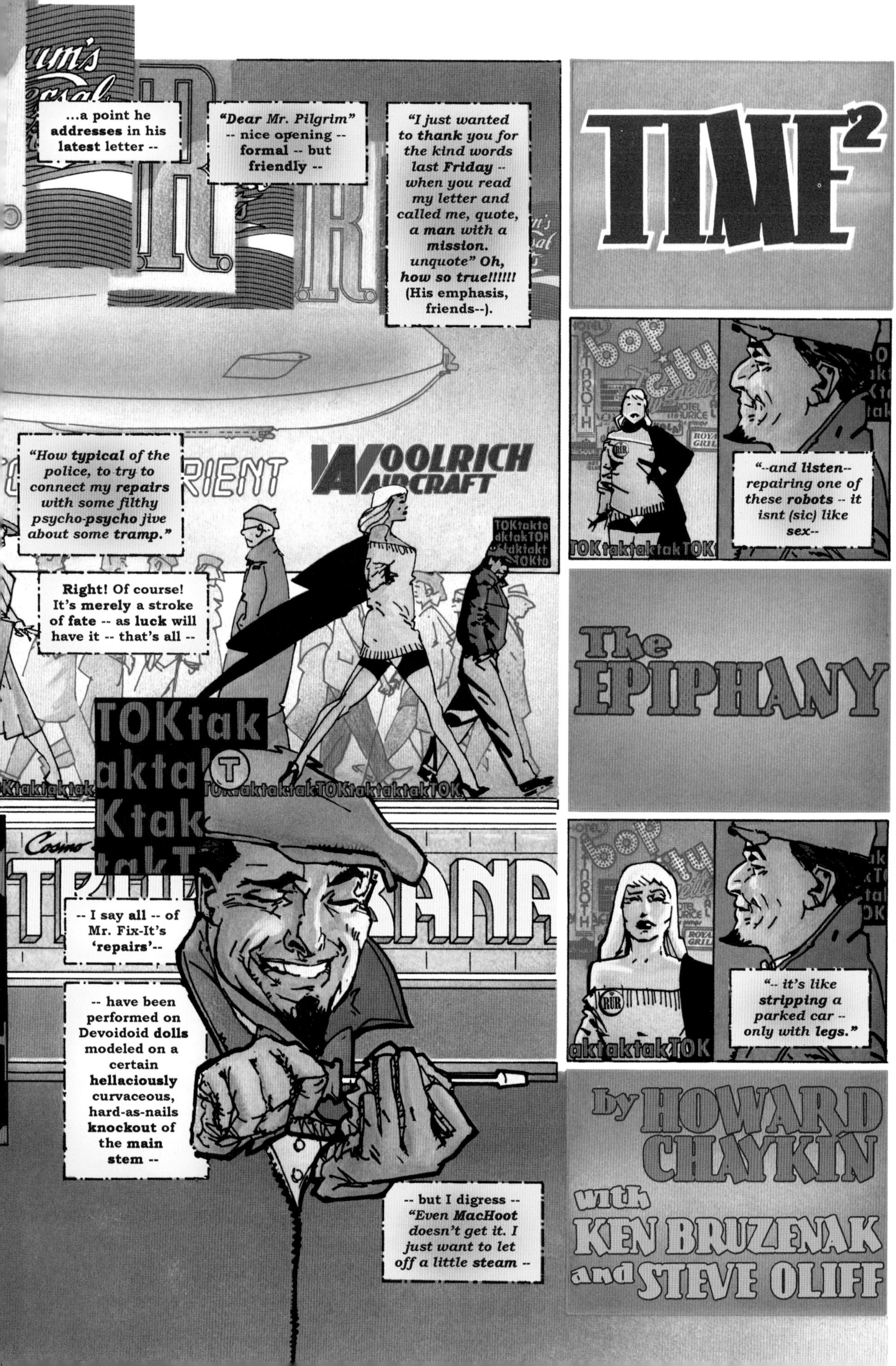
...a point he addresses in his latest letter --
"Dear Mr. Pilgrim" -- nice opening -- formal -- but friendly --
"I just wanted to thank you for the kind words last Friday -- when you read my letter and called me, quote, a man with a mission. unquote" Oh, how so true!!!!!! (His emphasis, friends--).
"How typical of the police, to try to connect my repairs with some filthy psycho-psycho jive about some tramp."
Right! Of course! It's merely a stroke of fate -- as luck will have it -- that's all --
WOOLRICH AIRCRAFT
TOKtak aktak Ktak takT
-- I say all -- of Mr. Fix-It's 'repairs'--
-- have been performed on Devoidoid dolls modeled on a certain hellaciously curvaceous, hard-as-nails knockout of the main stem --
-- but I digress -- "Even MacHoot doesn't get it. I just want to let off a little steam --
TIME²
"--and listen-- repairing one of these robots -- it isnt (sic) like sex--
The EPIPHANY
"-- it's like stripping a parked car -- only with legs."
by HOWARD CHAYKIN with KEN BRUZENAK and STEVE OLIFF

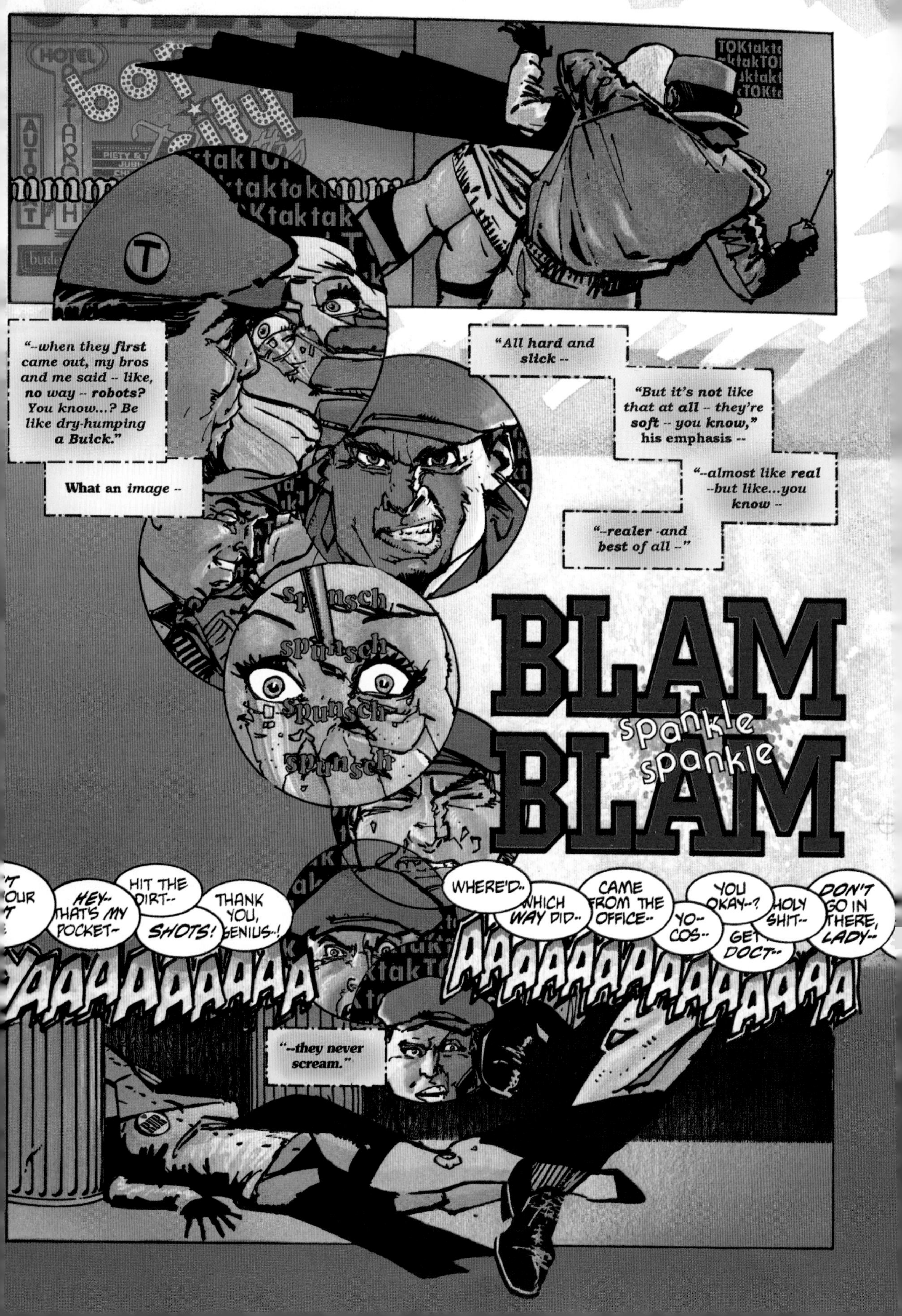

HOTEL
AUTO
PIETY & T
TOKtaktak
"--when they first came out, my bros and me said -- like, no way -- robots? You know...? Be like dry-humping a Buick."
What an image --
"All hard and slick --
"But it's not like that at all -- they're soft -- you know," his emphasis --
"--almost like real --but like...you know --
"--realer -and best of all --"
spunsch
spunsch
spunsch
spunsch
BLAM
spankle
BLAM
spankle
HEY-- THAT'S MY POCKET--
HIT THE DIRT--
SHOTS!
THANK YOU, GENIUS--!
WHERE'D--
WHICH WAY DID--
CAME FROM THE OFFICE--
YO-COS--
YOU OKAY--?
HOLY SHIT--
DON'T GO IN THERE, LADY--
AAAAAAAAA
AAAAAAAAAAAAAA
"--they never scream."

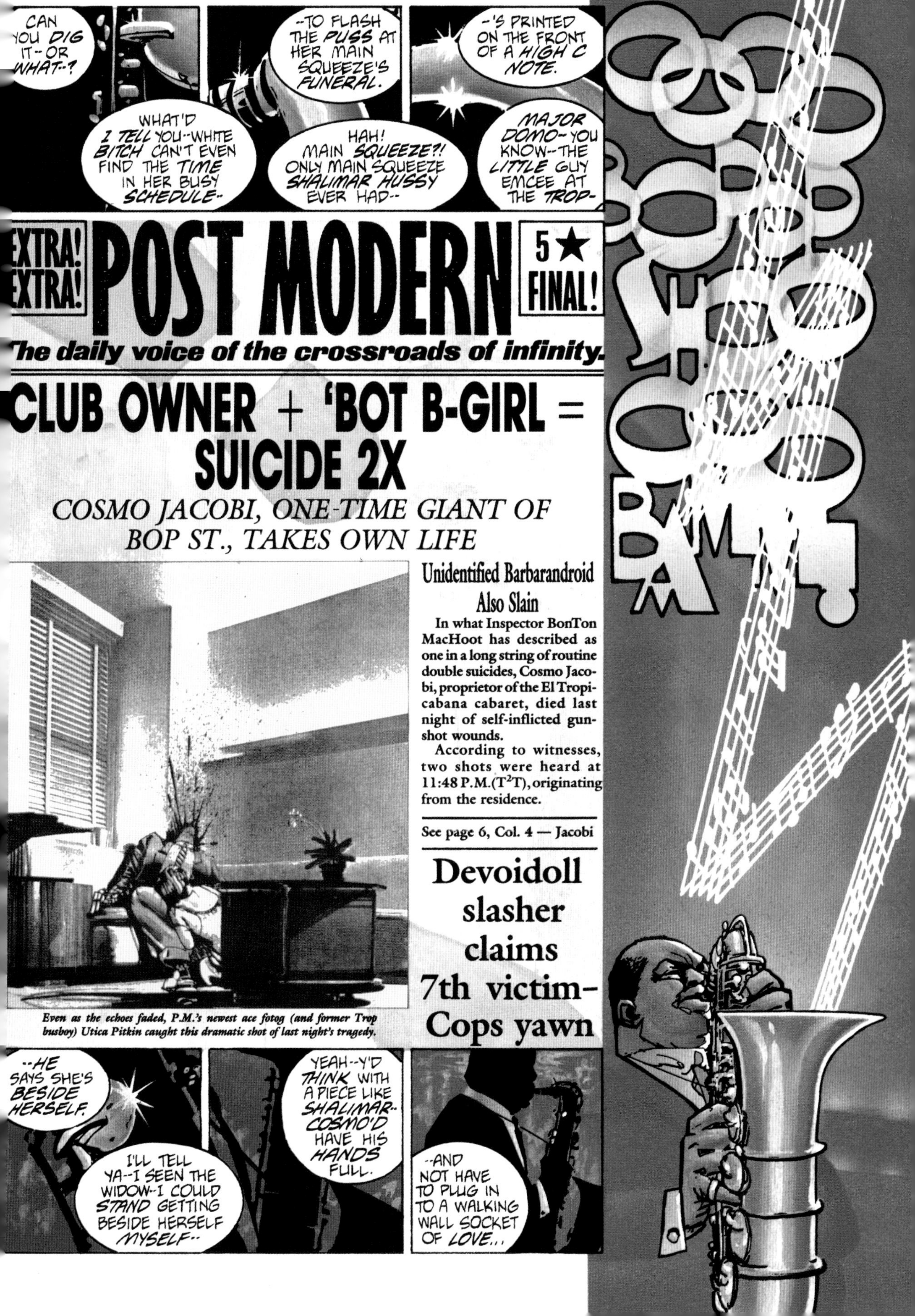

CAN YOU DIG IT--OR WHAT--?
WHAT'D I TELL YOU--WHITE BITCH CAN'T EVEN FIND THE TIME IN HER BUSY SCHEDULE--
--TO FLASH THE PUSS AT HER MAIN SQUEEZE'S FUNERAL.
HAH! MAIN SQUEEZE?! ONLY MAIN SQUEEZE SHALIMAR HUSSY EVER HAD--
--'S PRINTED ON THE FRONT OF A HIGH C NOTE.
MAJOR DOMO--YOU KNOW--THE LITTLE GUY EMCEE AT THE TROP-
EXTRA! EXTRA!
POST MODERN
5 ★ FINAL!
The daily voice of the crossroads of infinity.
CLUB OWNER + 'BOT B-GIRL = SUICIDE 2X
COSMO JACOBI, ONE-TIME GIANT OF BOP ST., TAKES OWN LIFE
Unidentified Barbarandroid Also Slain
In what Inspector BonTon MacHoot has described as one in a long string of routine double suicides, Cosmo Jacobi, proprietor of the El Tropicabana cabaret, died last night of self-inflicted gunshot wounds.
According to witnesses, two shots were heard at 11:48 P.M.(T^2T), originating from the residence.
See page 6, Col. 4 — Jacobi
Even as the echoes faded, P.M.'s newest ace fotog (and former Trop busboy) Utica Pitkin caught this dramatic shot of last night's tragedy.
Devoidoll slasher claims 7th victim-Cops yawn
--HE SAYS SHE'S BESIDE HERSELF.
I'LL TELL YA--I SEEN THE WIDOW--I COULD STAND GETTING BESIDE HERSELF MYSELF--
YEAH--Y'D THINK WITH A PIECE LIKE SHALIMAR--COSMO'D HAVE HIS HANDS FULL.
--AND NOT HAVE TO PLUG IN TO A WALKING WALL SOCKET OF LOVE...

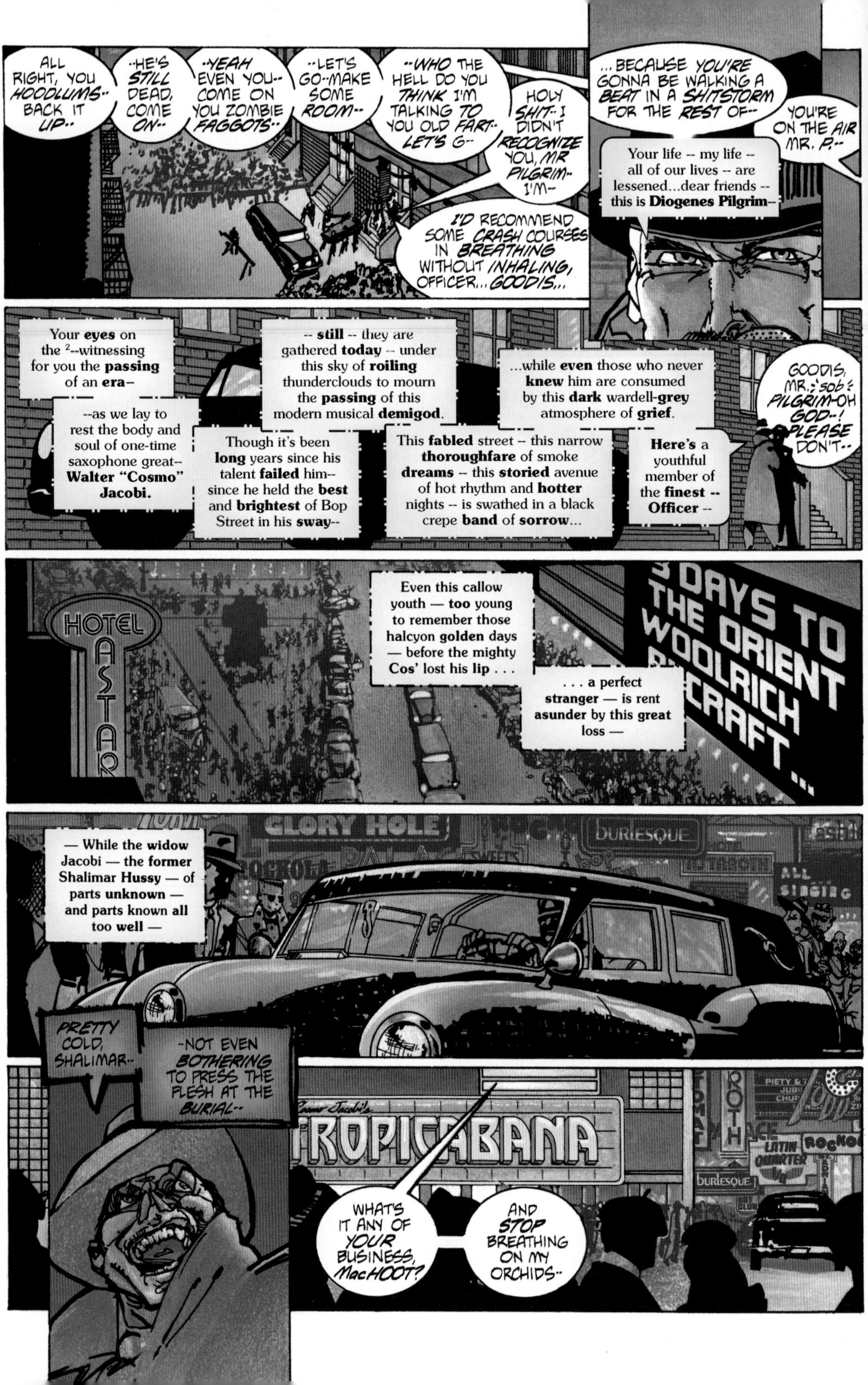
ALL RIGHT, YOU HOODLUMS-- BACK IT UP--
--HE'S STILL DEAD, COME ON--
--YEAH EVEN YOU-- COME ON YOU ZOMBIE FAGGOTS--
--LET'S GO--MAKE SOME ROOM--
--WHO THE HELL DO YOU THINK I'M TALKING TO YOU OLD FART-- LET'S G--
HOLY SHIT-- I DIDN'T RECOGNIZE YOU, MR PILGRIM-- I'M--
I'D RECOMMEND SOME CRASH COURSES IN BREATHING WITHOUT INHALING, OFFICER... GOODIS...
...BECAUSE YOU'RE GONNA BE WALKING A BEAT IN A SHITSTORM FOR THE REST OF--
YOU'RE ON THE AIR MR. P.--
Your life -- my life -- all of our lives -- are lessened...dear friends -- this is Diogenes Pilgrim--
Your eyes on the 2--witnessing for you the passing of an era--
--as we lay to rest the body and soul of one-time saxophone great-- Walter "Cosmo" Jacobi.
-- still -- they are gathered today -- under this sky of roiling thunderclouds to mourn the passing of this modern musical demigod.
Though it's been long years since his talent failed him-- since he held the best and brightest of Bop Street in his sway--
...while even those who never knew him are consumed by this dark wardell-grey atmosphere of grief.
This fabled street -- this narrow thoroughfare of smoke dreams -- this storied avenue of hot rhythm and hotter nights -- is swathed in a black crepe band of sorrow...
Here's a youthful member of the finest -- Officer --
GOODIS, MR.--sob-- PILGRIM--OH GOD--! PLEASE DON'T--
HOTEL ASTAR
DAYS TO THE ORIENT WOOLRICH CRAFT...
Even this callow youth — too young to remember those halcyon golden days — before the mighty Cos' lost his lip . . .
. . . a perfect stranger — is rent asunder by this great loss —
GLORY HOLE
BURLESQUE
— While the widow Jacobi — the former Shalimar Hussy — of parts unknown — and parts known all too well —
PRETTY COLD, SHALIMAR--
--NOT EVEN BOTHERING TO PRESS THE FLESH AT THE BURIAL--
TROPICABANA
LATIN QUARTER
burlesque
WHAT'S IT ANY OF YOUR BUSINESS, MacHOOT?
AND STOP BREATHING ON MY ORCHIDS--

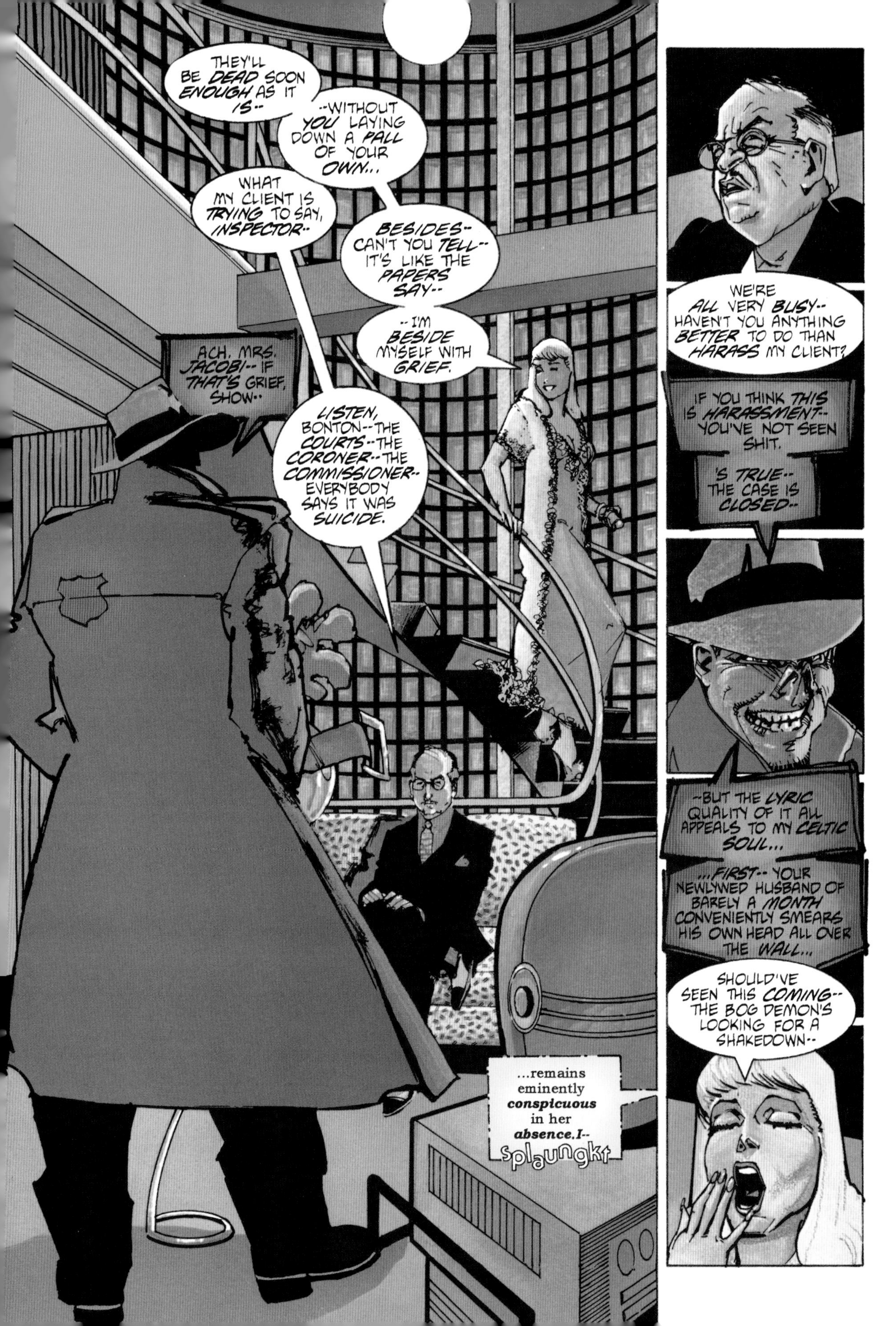
THEY'LL BE DEAD SOON ENOUGH AS IT IS--
--WITHOUT YOU LAYING DOWN A PALL OF YOUR OWN...
WHAT MY CLIENT IS TRYING TO SAY, INSPECTOR--
BESIDES-- CAN'T YOU TELL-- IT'S LIKE THE PAPERS SAY--
--I'M BESIDE MYSELF WITH GRIEF.
ACH. MRS. JACOBI-- IF THAT'S GRIEF, SHOW--
LISTEN, BONTON--THE COURTS--THE CORONER--THE COMMISSIONER-- EVERYBODY SAYS IT WAS SUICIDE.
...remains eminently conspicuous in her absence. I--
splaungkt
WE'RE ALL VERY BUSY-- HAVEN'T YOU ANYTHING BETTER TO DO THAN HARASS MY CLIENT?
IF YOU THINK THIS IS HARASSMENT-- YOU'VE NOT SEEN SHIT.
'S TRUE-- THE CASE IS CLOSED--
--BUT THE LYRIC QUALITY OF IT ALL APPEALS TO MY CELTIC SOUL...
...FIRST-- YOUR NEWLYWED HUSBAND OF BARELY A MONTH CONVENIENTLY SMEARS HIS OWN HEAD ALL OVER THE WALL...
SHOULD'VE SEEN THIS COMING-- THE BOG DEMON'S LOOKING FOR A SHAKEDOWN--

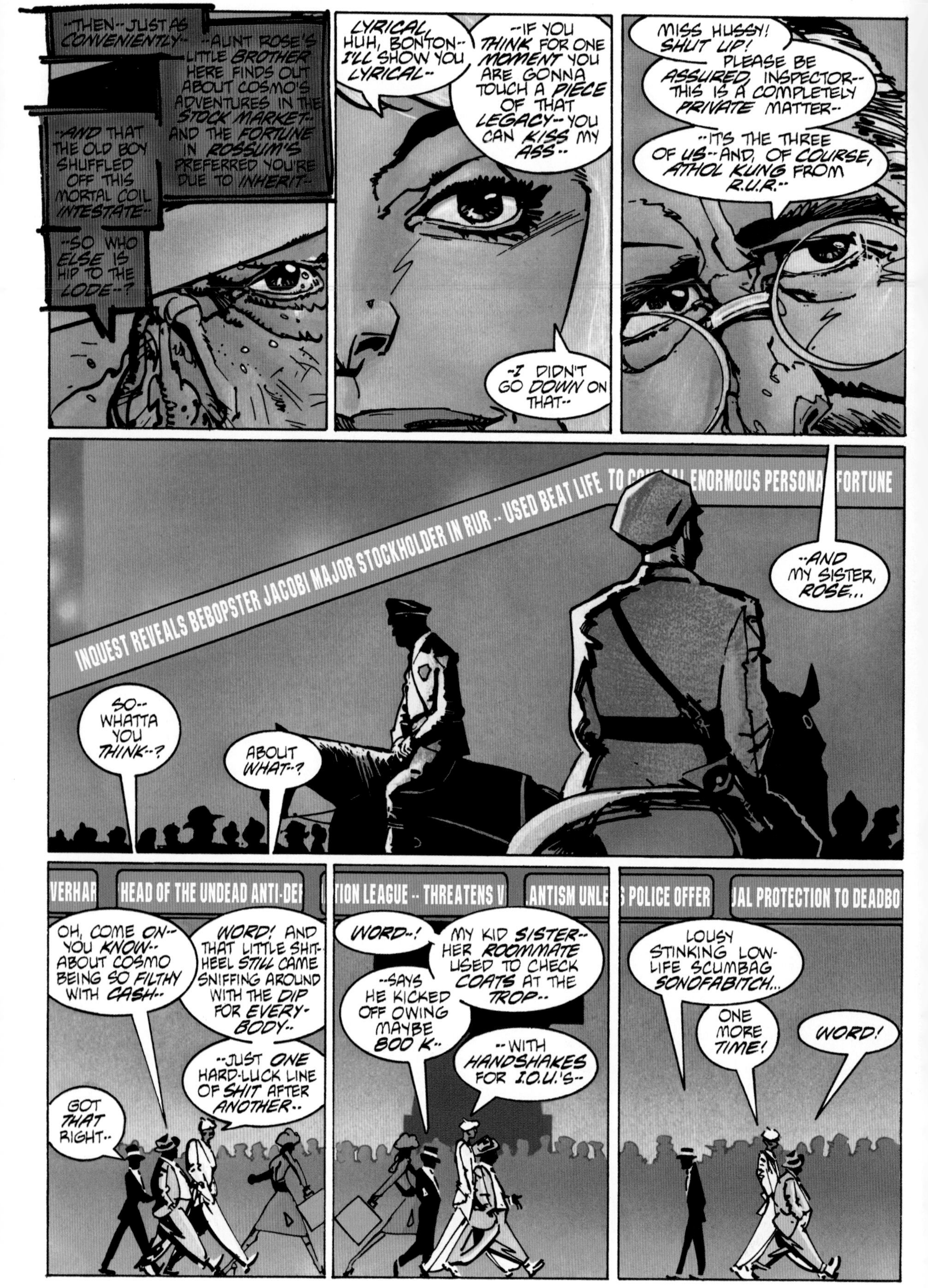
--THEN--JUST AS CONVENIENTLY--
--AUNT ROSE'S LITTLE BROTHER HERE FINDS OUT ABOUT COSMO'S ADVENTURES IN THE STOCK MARKET--
AND THE FORTUNE IN ROSSUM'S PREFERRED YOU'RE DUE TO INHERIT--
--AND THAT THE OLD BOY SHUFFLED OFF THIS MORTAL COIL INTESTATE--
--SO WHO ELSE IS HIP TO THE LODE--?
LYRICAL, HUH, BONTON-- I'LL SHOW YOU LYRICAL--
--IF YOU THINK FOR ONE MOMENT YOU ARE GONNA TOUCH A PIECE OF THAT LEGACY--YOU CAN KISS MY ASS--
--I DIDN'T GO DOWN ON THAT--
MISS HUSSY! SHUT UP!
PLEASE BE ASSURED, INSPECTOR-- THIS IS A COMPLETELY PRIVATE MATTER--
--IT'S THE THREE OF US--AND, OF COURSE, ATHOL KUNG FROM R.U.R.--
INQUEST REVEALS BEBOPSTER JACOBI MAJOR STOCKHOLDER IN RUR -- USED BEAT LIFE TO CO ENORMOUS PERSONA FORTUNE
--AND MY SISTER, ROSE...
SO-- WHATTA YOU THINK--?
ABOUT WHAT--?
VERHAR HEAD OF THE UNDEAD ANTI-DEF TION LEAGUE -- THREATENS V ANTISM UNLE POLICE OFFER JAL PROTECTION TO DEADBO
OH, COME ON-- YOU KNOW-- ABOUT COSMO BEING SO FILTHY WITH CASH--
WORD! AND THAT LITTLE SHIT-HEEL STILL CAME SNIFFING AROUND WITH THE DIP FOR EVERY-BODY--
--JUST ONE HARD-LUCK LINE OF SHIT AFTER ANOTHER--
GOT THAT RIGHT--
WORD--!
MY KID SISTER-- HER ROOMMATE USED TO CHECK COATS AT THE TROP--
--SAYS HE KICKED OFF OWING MAYBE 800 K--
--WITH HANDSHAKES FOR I.O.U.'s--
LOUSY STINKING LOW-LIFE SCUMBAG SONOFABITCH...
ONE MORE TIME!
WORD!

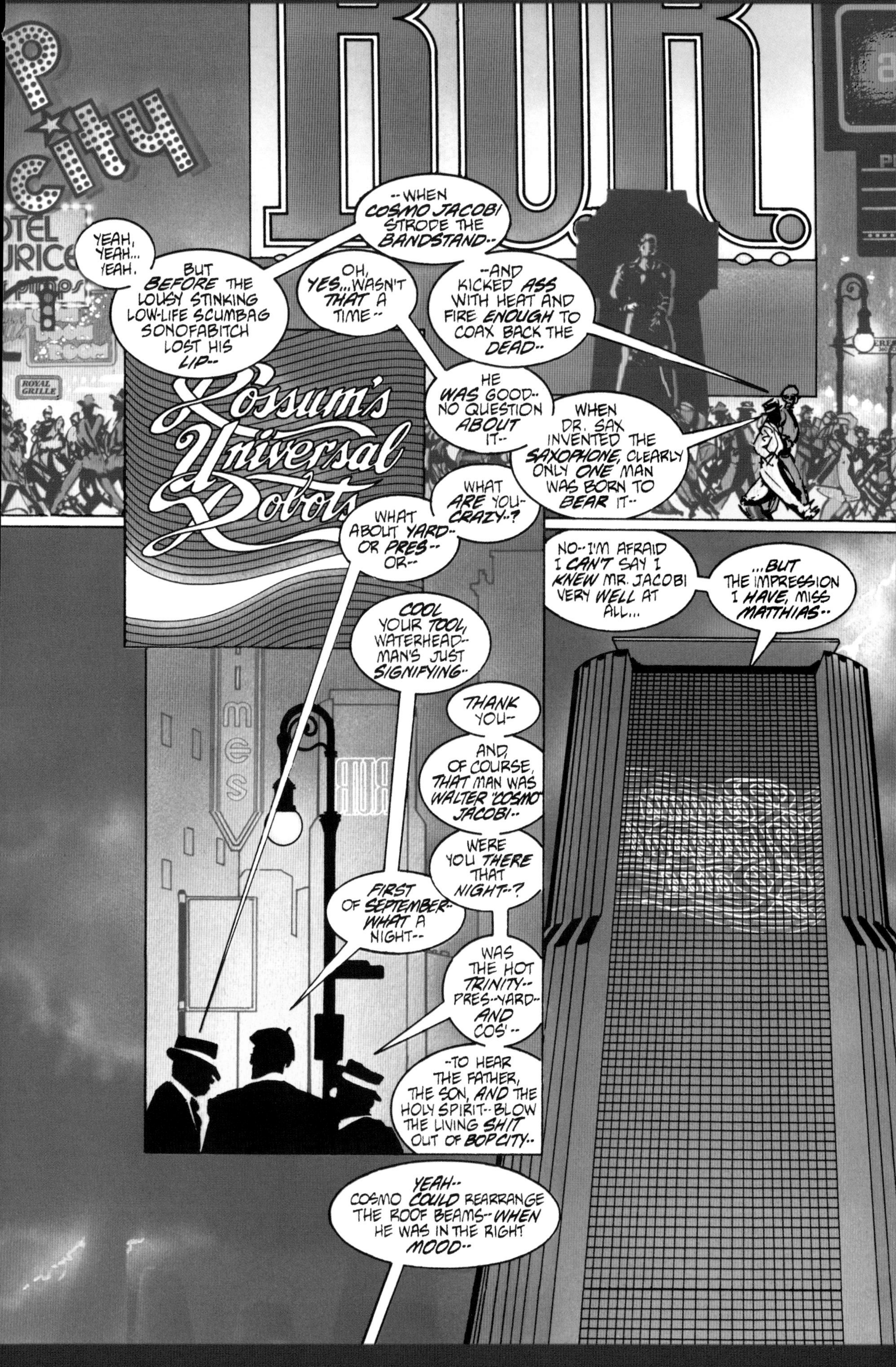
--WHEN COSMO JACOBI STRODE THE BANDSTAND--
--AND KICKED ASS WITH HEAT AND FIRE ENOUGH TO COAX BACK THE DEAD--
YEAH, YEAH... YEAH.
BUT BEFORE THE LOUSY STINKING LOW-LIFE SCUMBAG SONOFABITCH LOST HIS LIP--
OH, YES...WASN'T THAT A TIME--
HE WAS GOOD-- NO QUESTION ABOUT IT--
WHEN DR. SAX INVENTED THE SAXOPHONE, CLEARLY ONLY ONE MAN WAS BORN TO BEAR IT--
WHAT ARE YOU-- CRAZY--?
WHAT ABOUT YARD-- OR PRES-- OR--
COOL YOUR TOOL, WATERHEAD-- MAN'S JUST SIGNIFYING--
ROYAL GRILLE
Rossum's Universal Robots
NO--I'M AFRAID I CAN'T SAY I KNEW MR. JACOBI VERY WELL AT ALL...
...BUT THE IMPRESSION I HAVE, MISS MATTHIAS--
THANK YOU-
AND, OF COURSE, THAT MAN WAS WALTER "COSMO" JACOBI--
WERE YOU THERE THAT NIGHT--?
FIRST OF SEPTEMBER-- WHAT A NIGHT--
WAS THE HOT TRINITY-- PRES--YARD-- AND COS'--
--TO HEAR THE FATHER, THE SON, AND THE HOLY SPIRIT-- BLOW THE LIVING SHIT OUT OF BOP CITY--
YEAH-- COSMO COULD REARRANGE THE ROOF BEAMS--WHEN HE WAS IN THE RIGHT MOOD--

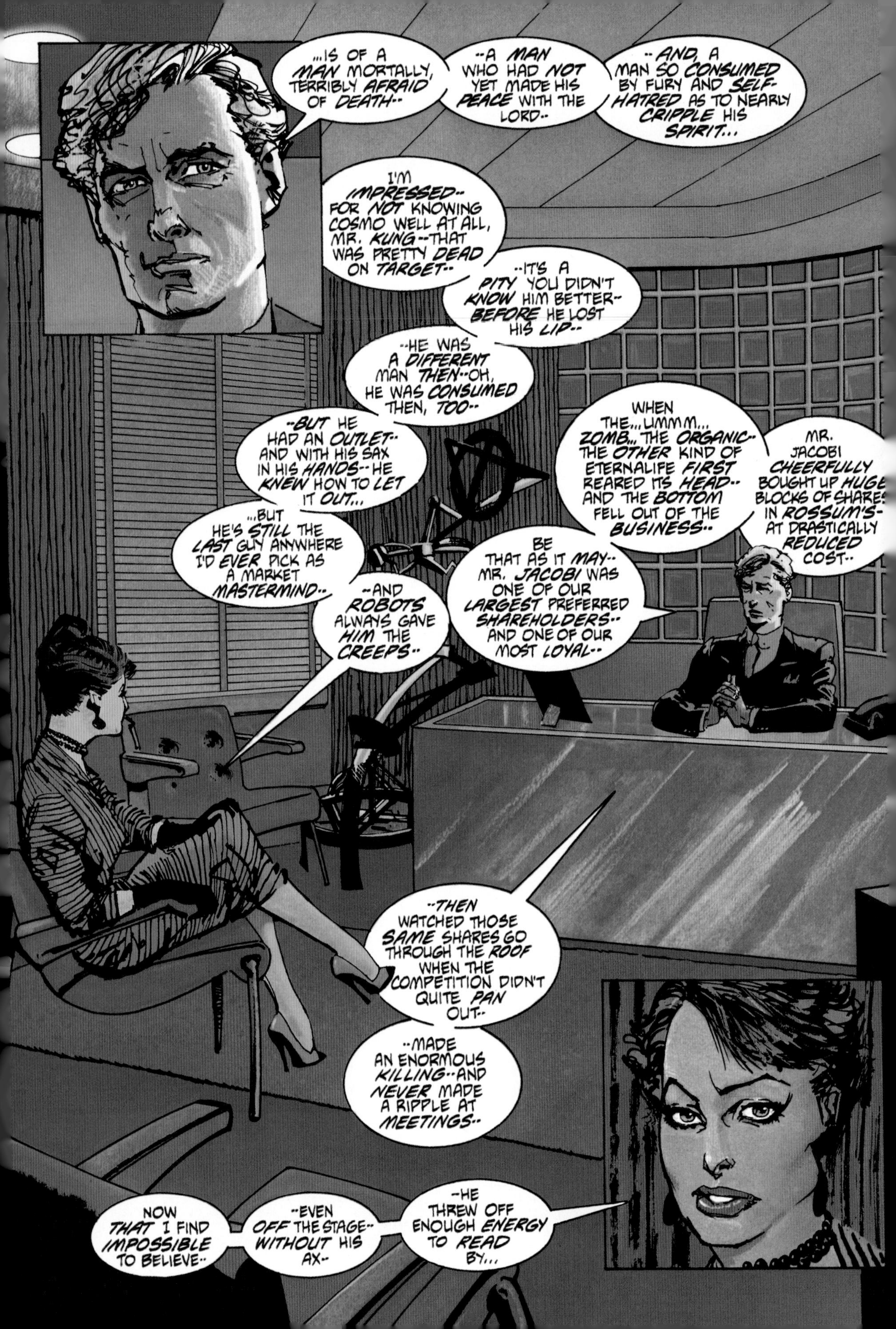
...IS OF A MAN MORTALLY, TERRIBLY AFRAID OF DEATH--
--A MAN WHO HAD NOT YET MADE HIS PEACE WITH THE LORD--
--AND, A MAN SO CONSUMED BY FURY AND SELF-HATRED AS TO NEARLY CRIPPLE HIS SPIRIT...
I'M IMPRESSED-- FOR NOT KNOWING COSMO WELL AT ALL, MR. KUNG--THAT WAS PRETTY DEAD ON TARGET--
--IT'S A PITY YOU DIDN'T KNOW HIM BETTER-- BEFORE HE LOST HIS LIP--
--HE WAS A DIFFERENT MAN THEN--OH, HE WAS CONSUMED THEN, TOO--
--BUT HE HAD AN OUTLET-- AND WITH HIS SAX IN HIS HANDS--HE KNEW HOW TO LET IT OUT...
...BUT HE'S STILL THE LAST GUY ANYWHERE I'D EVER PICK AS A MARKET MASTERMIND--
--AND ROBOTS ALWAYS GAVE HIM THE CREEPS--
WHEN THE... UMMM... ZOMB... THE ORGANIC-- THE OTHER KIND OF ETERNALIFE FIRST REARED ITS HEAD-- AND THE BOTTOM FELL OUT OF THE BUSINESS--
MR. JACOBI CHEERFULLY BOUGHT UP HUGE BLOCKS OF SHARES IN ROSSUM'S-- AT DRASTICALLY REDUCED COST--
BE THAT AS IT MAY-- MR. JACOBI WAS ONE OF OUR LARGEST PREFERRED SHAREHOLDERS-- AND ONE OF OUR MOST LOYAL--
--THEN WATCHED THOSE SAME SHARES GO THROUGH THE ROOF WHEN THE COMPETITION DIDN'T QUITE PAN OUT--
--MADE AN ENORMOUS KILLING--AND NEVER MADE A RIPPLE AT MEETINGS--
NOW THAT I FIND IMPOSSIBLE TO BELIEVE--
--EVEN OFF THE STAGE-- WITHOUT HIS AX--
--HE THREW OFF ENOUGH ENERGY TO READ BY...

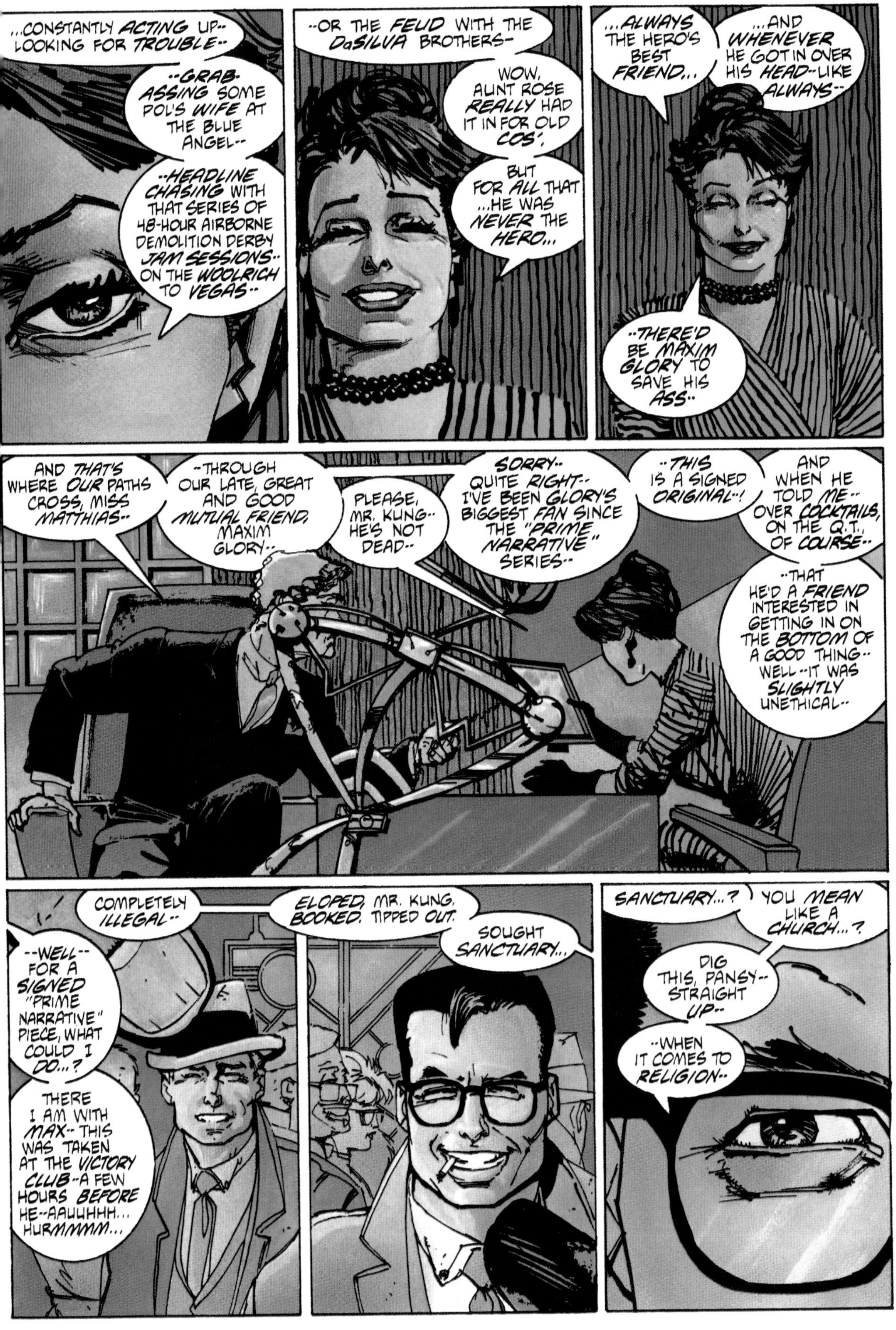
...CONSTANTLY ACTING UP-- LOOKING FOR TROUBLE--
--GRAB-ASSING SOME POL'S WIFE AT THE BLUE ANGEL--
--HEADLINE CHASING WITH THAT SERIES OF 48-HOUR AIRBORNE DEMOLITION DERBY JAM SESSIONS-- ON THE WOOLRICH TO VEGAS--
--OR THE FEUD WITH THE DaSILVA BROTHERS--
WOW, AUNT ROSE REALLY HAD IT IN FOR OLD COS'.
BUT FOR ALL THAT ...HE WAS NEVER THE HERO...
...ALWAYS THE HERO'S BEST FRIEND...
...AND WHENEVER HE GOT IN OVER HIS HEAD--LIKE ALWAYS--
--THERE'D BE MAXIM GLORY TO SAVE HIS ASS--
AND THAT'S WHERE OUR PATHS CROSS, MISS MATTHIAS--
--THROUGH OUR LATE, GREAT AND GOOD MUTUAL FRIEND, MAXIM GLORY--
PLEASE, MR. KUNG-- HE'S NOT DEAD--
SORRY-- QUITE RIGHT-- I'VE BEEN GLORY'S BIGGEST FAN SINCE THE "PRIME NARRATIVE" SERIES--
--THIS IS A SIGNED ORIGINAL--!
AND WHEN HE TOLD ME-- OVER COCKTAILS, ON THE Q.T., OF COURSE--
--THAT HE'D A FRIEND INTERESTED IN GETTING IN ON THE BOTTOM OF A GOOD THING-- WELL--IT WAS SLIGHTLY UNETHICAL--
COMPLETELY ILLEGAL--
--WELL-- FOR A SIGNED "PRIME NARRATIVE" PIECE, WHAT COULD I DO...?
THERE I AM WITH MAX-- THIS WAS TAKEN AT THE VICTORY CLUB--A FEW HOURS BEFORE HE--AAUUHHH... HURMMMM...
ELOPED, MR. KUNG. BOOKED. TIPPED OUT.
SOUGHT SANCTUARY...
SANCTUARY...?
YOU MEAN LIKE A CHURCH...?
DIG THIS, PANSY-- STRAIGHT UP--
--WHEN IT COMES TO RELIGION--

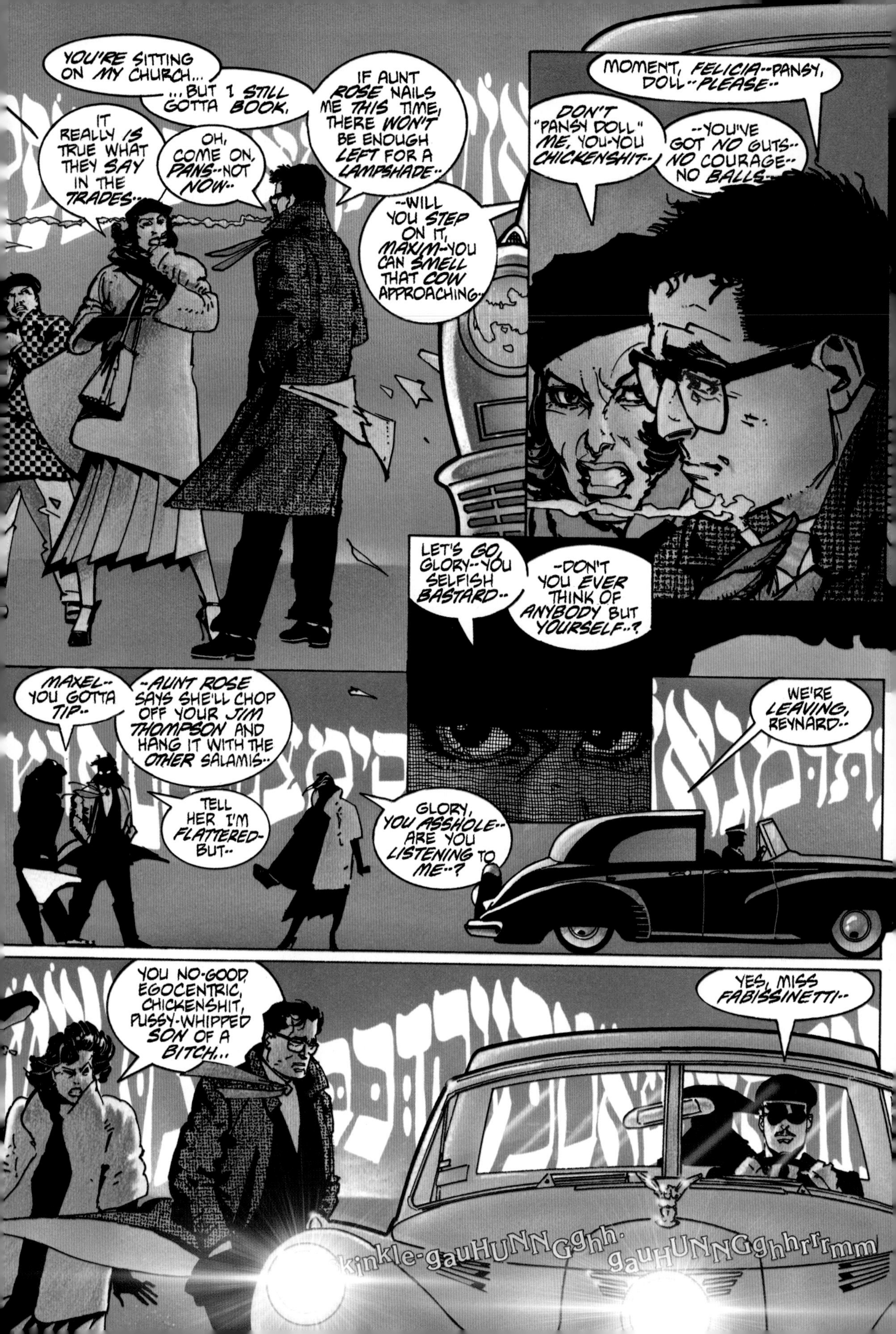
YOU'RE SITTING ON MY CHURCH...
...BUT I STILL GOTTA BOOK.
IT REALLY IS TRUE WHAT THEY SAY IN THE TRADES..
OH, COME ON, PANS--NOT NOW--
IF AUNT ROSE NAILS ME THIS TIME, THERE WON'T BE ENOUGH LEFT FOR A LAMPSHADE--
--WILL YOU STEP ON IT, MAXIM--YOU CAN SMELL THAT COW APPROACHING..
MOMENT, FELICIA--PANSY, DOLL--PLEASE--
DON'T "PANSY DOLL" ME, YOU-YOU CHICKENSHIT--
--YOU'VE GOT NO GUTS-- NO COURAGE-- NO BALLS--
LET'S GO, GLORY--YOU SELFISH BASTARD--
--DON'T YOU EVER THINK OF ANYBODY BUT YOURSELF--?
MAXEL-- YOU GOTTA TIP--
--AUNT ROSE SAYS SHE'LL CHOP OFF YOUR JIM THOMPSON AND HANG IT WITH THE OTHER SALAMIS--
TELL HER I'M FLATTERED-BUT--
GLORY, YOU ASSHOLE-- ARE YOU LISTENING TO ME--?
WE'RE LEAVING, REYNARD--
YOU NO-GOOD, EGOCENTRIC, CHICKENSHIT, PUSSY-WHIPPED SON OF A BITCH...
YES, MISS FABISSINETTI--
kinkle-gauHUNNGghh. gauHUNNGghhrrrmm

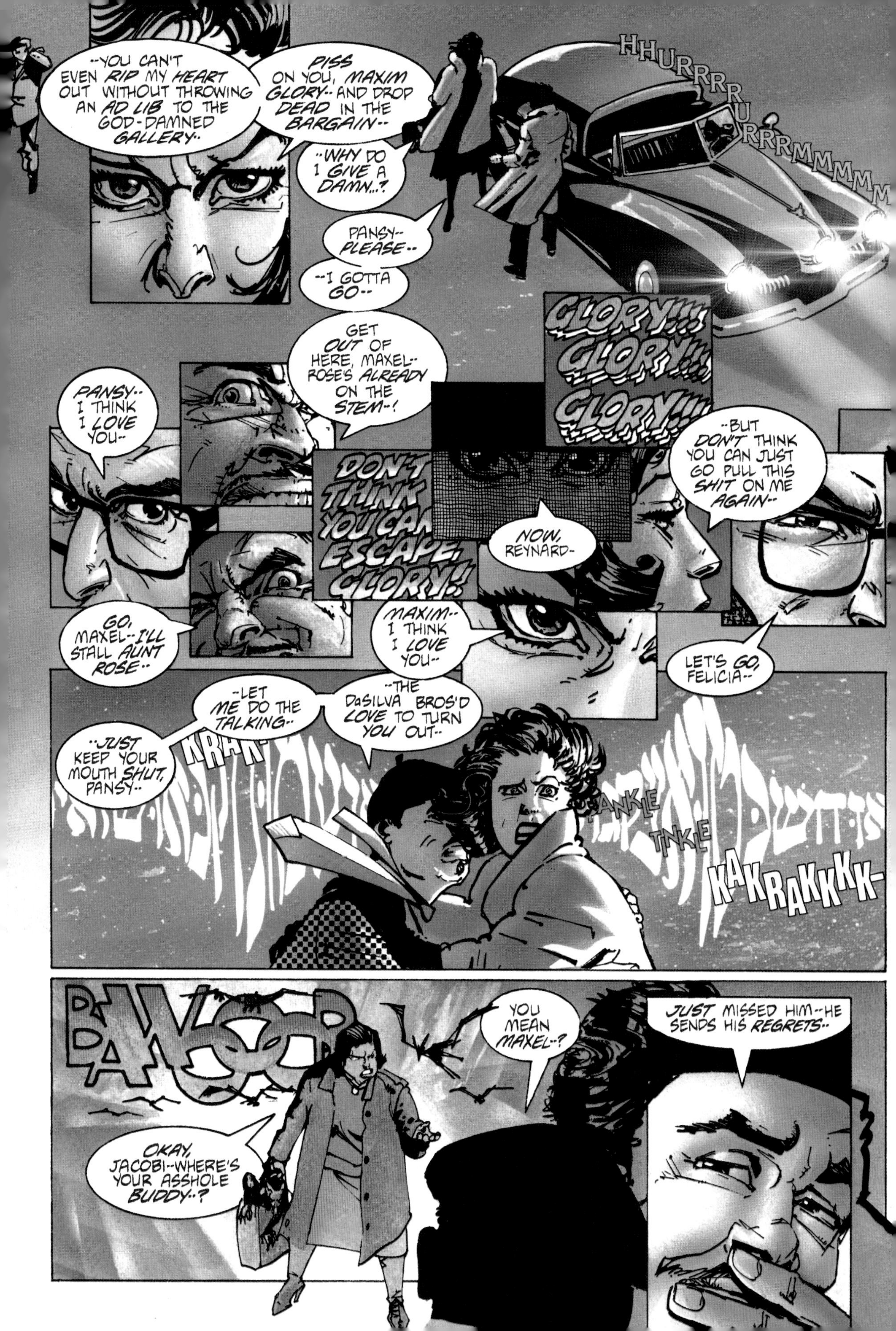
--YOU CAN'T EVEN RIP MY HEART OUT WITHOUT THROWING AN AD LIB TO THE GOD-DAMNED GALLERY--
PISS ON YOU, MAXIM GLORY-- AND DROP DEAD IN THE BARGAIN--
--WHY DO I GIVE A DAMN...?
HHURRRRRURRRRMMMMMMM
PANSY-- PLEASE--
--I GOTTA GO--
GET OUT OF HERE, MAXEL-- ROSE'S ALREADY ON THE STEM--!
GLORY!!! GLORY!!! GLORY!!!
PANSY-- I THINK I LOVE YOU--
DON'T THINK YOU CAN ESCAPE, GLORY!!
NOW, REYNARD--
--BUT DON'T THINK YOU CAN JUST GO PULL THIS SHIT ON ME AGAIN--
GO, MAXEL--I'LL STALL AUNT ROSE--
MAXIM-- I THINK I LOVE YOU--
LET'S GO, FELICIA--
--JUST KEEP YOUR MOUTH SHUT, PANSY--
--LET ME DO THE TALKING--
--THE DaSILVA BROS'D LOVE TO TURN YOU OUT--
KRAK
TINKLE
KAKRAKKKK-
YOU MEAN MAXEL--?
JUST MISSED HIM--HE SENDS HIS REGRETS--
OKAY, JACOBI--WHERE'S YOUR ASSHOLE BUDDY--?

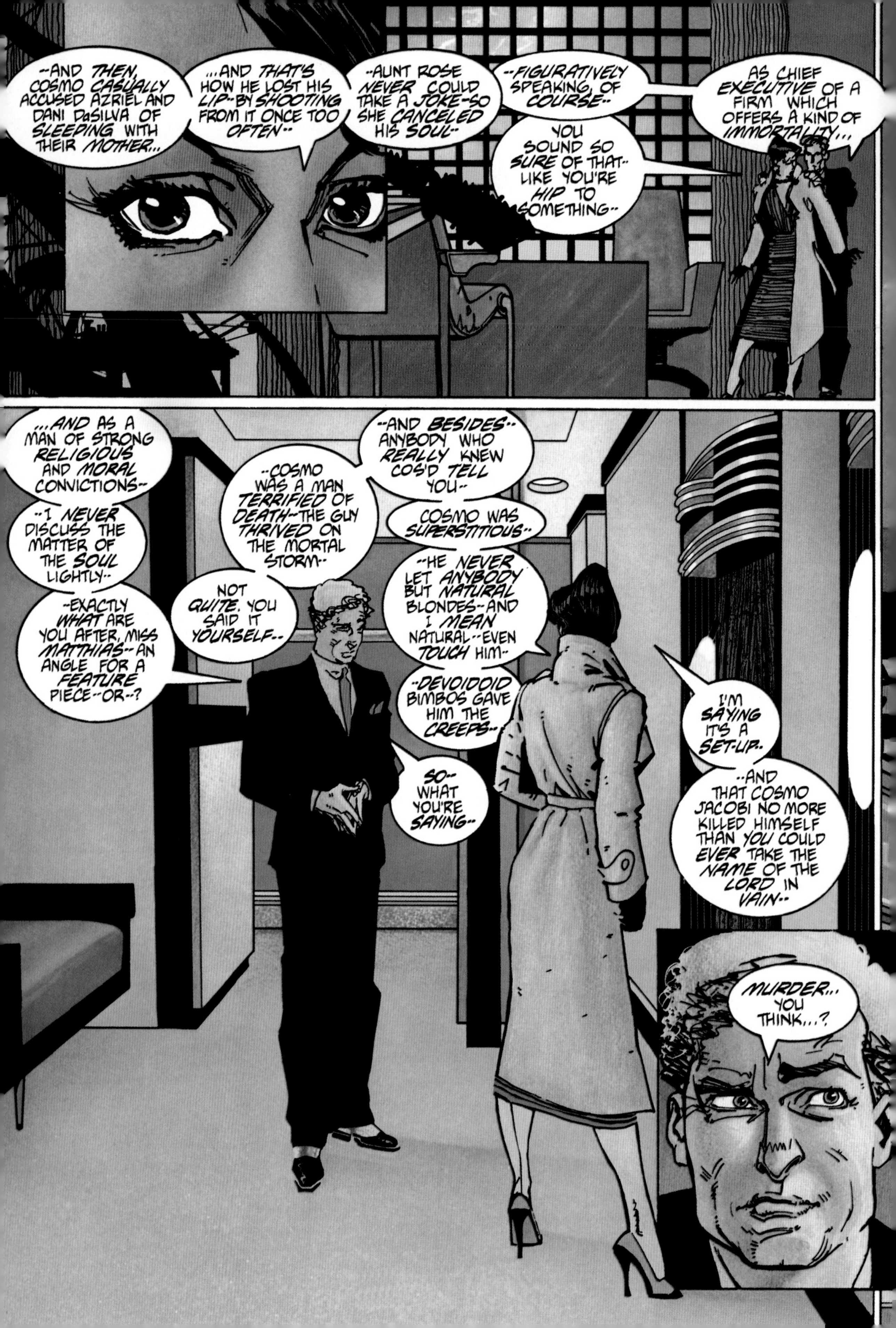
--AND THEN, COSMO CASUALLY ACCUSED AZRIEL AND DANI DaSILVA OF SLEEPING WITH THEIR MOTHER...
...AND THAT'S HOW HE LOST HIS LIP--BY SHOOTING FROM IT ONCE TOO OFTEN--
--AUNT ROSE NEVER COULD TAKE A JOKE--SO SHE CANCELED HIS SOUL--
--FIGURATIVELY SPEAKING, OF COURSE--
YOU SOUND SO SURE OF THAT-- LIKE YOU'RE HIP TO SOMETHING--
AS CHIEF EXECUTIVE OF A FIRM WHICH OFFERS A KIND OF IMMORTALITY...
...AND AS A MAN OF STRONG RELIGIOUS AND MORAL CONVICTIONS--
--I NEVER DISCUSS THE MATTER OF THE SOUL LIGHTLY--
--EXACTLY WHAT ARE YOU AFTER, MISS MATTHIAS--AN ANGLE FOR A FEATURE PIECE--OR--?
--COSMO WAS A MAN TERRIFIED OF DEATH--THE GUY THRIVED ON THE MORTAL STORM--
NOT QUITE. YOU SAID IT YOURSELF--
--AND BESIDES-- ANYBODY WHO REALLY KNEW COS'D TELL YOU--
COSMO WAS SUPERSTITIOUS--
--HE NEVER LET ANYBODY BUT NATURAL BLONDES--AND I MEAN NATURAL--EVEN TOUCH HIM--
--DEVOIDOID BIMBOS GAVE HIM THE CREEPS--
SO-- WHAT YOU'RE SAYING--
I'M SAYING IT'S A SET-UP..
--AND THAT COSMO JACOBI NO MORE KILLED HIMSELF THAN YOU COULD EVER TAKE THE NAME OF THE LORD IN VAIN--
MURDER... YOU THINK...?

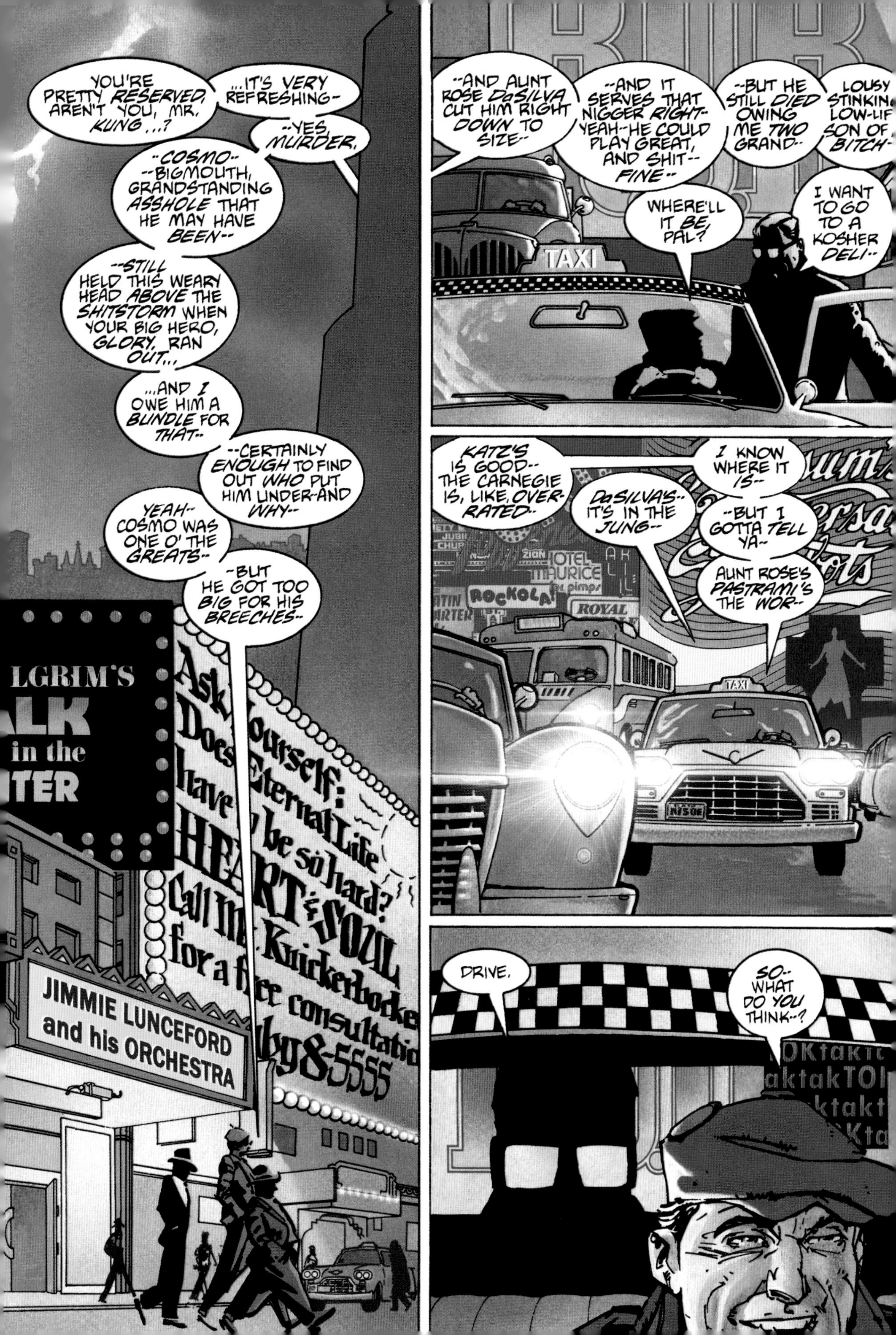
YOU'RE PRETTY RESERVED, AREN'T YOU, MR. KUNG...?
...IT'S VERY REFRESHING--
--YES, MURDER.
--COSMO-- --BIGMOUTH, GRANDSTANDING ASSHOLE THAT HE MAY HAVE BEEN--
--STILL HELD THIS WEARY HEAD ABOVE THE SHITSTORM WHEN YOUR BIG HERO, GLORY, RAN OUT...
...AND I OWE HIM A BUNDLE FOR THAT--
--CERTAINLY ENOUGH TO FIND OUT WHO PUT HIM UNDER--AND WHY--
YEAH-- COSMO WAS ONE O' THE GREATS--
--BUT HE GOT TOO BIG FOR HIS BREECHES--
LGRIM'S
ALK
in the
TER
JIMMIE LUNCEFORD and his ORCHESTRA
--AND AUNT ROSE DaSILVA CUT HIM RIGHT DOWN TO SIZE--
--AND IT SERVES THAT NIGGER RIGHT-- YEAH--HE COULD PLAY GREAT, AND SHIT--FINE--
--BUT HE STILL DIED OWING ME TWO GRAND--
LOUSY STINKIN LOW-LIF SON OF BITCH--
TAXI
WHERE'LL IT BE, PAL?
I WANT TO GO TO A KOSHER DELI--
KATZ'S IS GOOD-- THE CARNEGIE IS, LIKE, OVER-RATED--
I KNOW WHERE IT IS--
DaSILVA'S-- IT'S IN THE JUNG--
--BUT I GOTTA TELL YA--
AUNT ROSE'S PASTRAMI'S THE WOR--
HOTEL MAURICE
ROCKOLA!
ROYAL
TAXI
DRIVE.
SO-- WHAT DO YOU THINK--?

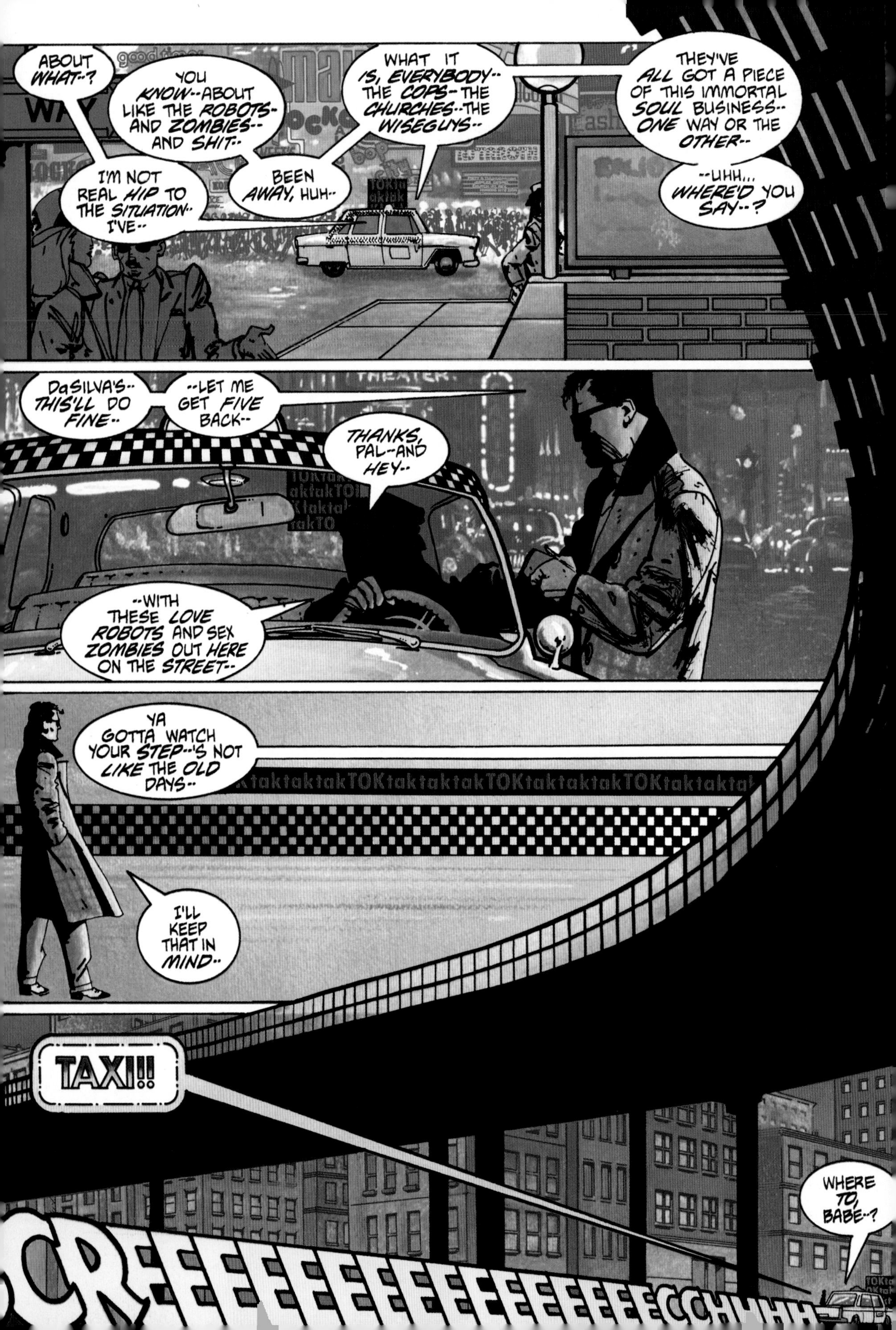
ABOUT WHAT--?
YOU KNOW--ABOUT LIKE THE ROBOTS- AND ZOMBIES-- AND SHIT--
I'M NOT REAL HIP TO THE SITUATION-- I'VE--
BEEN AWAY, HUH--
WHAT IT IS, EVERYBODY-- THE COPS-- THE CHURCHES--THE WISEGUYS--
THEY'VE ALL GOT A PIECE OF THIS IMMORTAL SOUL BUSINESS-- ONE WAY OR THE OTHER--
--UHH... WHERE'D YOU SAY--?
DaSILVA'S-- THIS'LL DO FINE--
--LET ME GET FIVE BACK--
THANKS, PAL--AND HEY--
--WITH THESE LOVE ROBOTS AND SEX ZOMBIES OUT HERE ON THE STREET--
YA GOTTA WATCH YOUR STEP--'S NOT LIKE THE OLD DAYS--
taktaktakTOKtaktaktakTOKtaktaktakTOKtaktak
I'LL KEEP THAT IN MIND--
TAXI!!
SCREEEEEEEEEEEEEEEEEEECCHHHH
WHERE TO, BABE--?

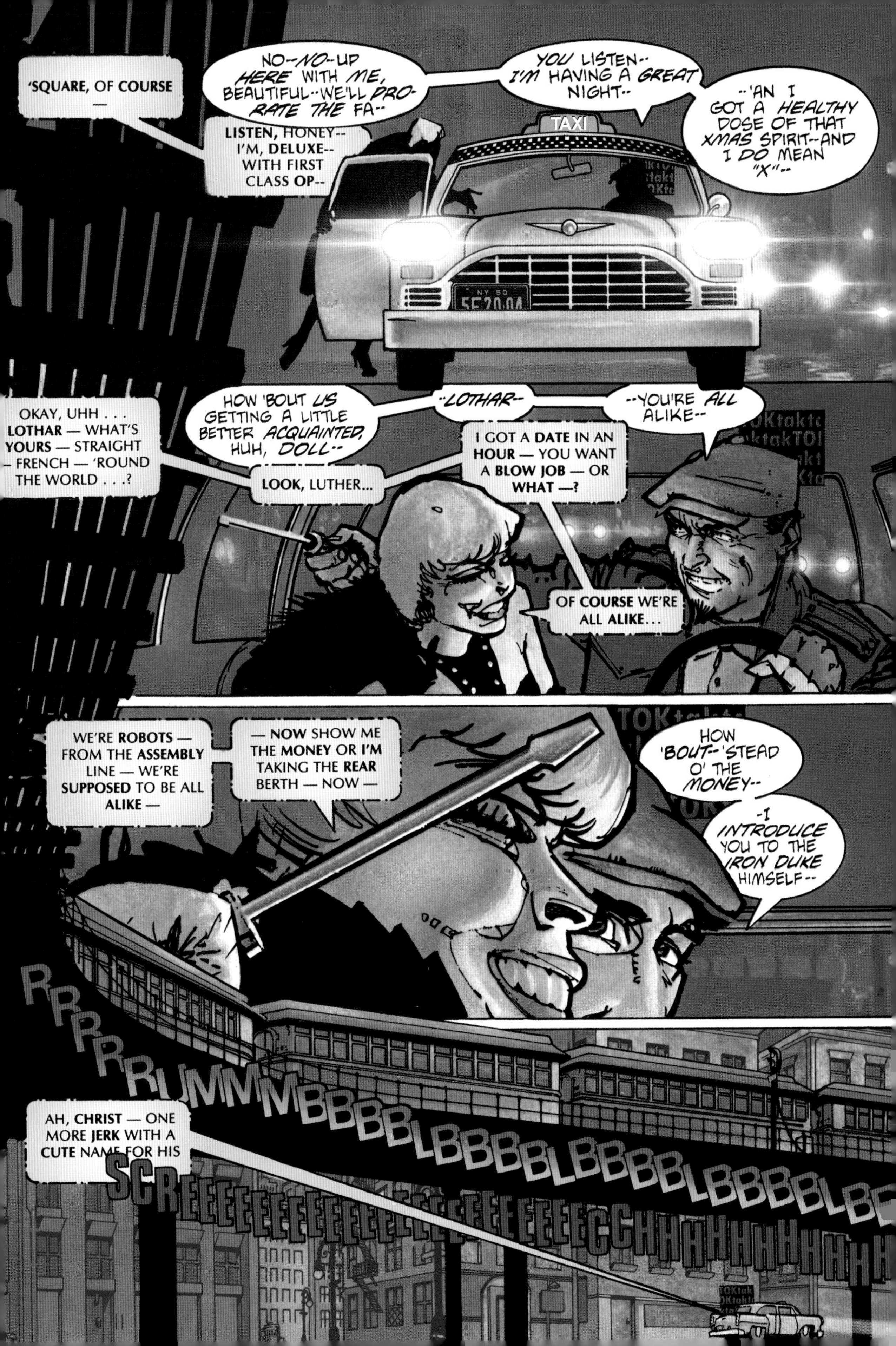
'SQUARE, OF COURSE —
NO--NO--UP HERE WITH ME, BEAUTIFUL--WE'LL PRO-RATE THE FA--
LISTEN, HONEY-- I'M, DELUXE-- WITH FIRST CLASS OP--
YOU LISTEN-- I'M HAVING A GREAT NIGHT--
TAXI
--'AN I GOT A HEALTHY DOSE OF THAT XMAS SPIRIT--AND I DO MEAN "X"--
NY 50
5E 20 04
OKAY, UHH . . . LOTHAR — WHAT'S YOURS — STRAIGHT — FRENCH — 'ROUND THE WORLD . . .?
HOW 'BOUT US GETTING A LITTLE BETTER ACQUAINTED, HUH, DOLL--
LOOK, LUTHER...
--LOTHAR--
I GOT A DATE IN AN HOUR — YOU WANT A BLOW JOB — OR WHAT —?
--YOU'RE ALL ALIKE--
OF COURSE WE'RE ALL ALIKE...
WE'RE ROBOTS — FROM THE ASSEMBLY LINE — WE'RE SUPPOSED TO BE ALL ALIKE —
— NOW SHOW ME THE MONEY OR I'M TAKING THE REAR BERTH — NOW —
HOW 'BOUT--'STEAD O' THE MONEY--
-I INTRODUCE YOU TO THE IRON DUKE HIMSELF--
RRRRRUMMMMBBBBLBBBBBLBBBBBLBBBBBLB
AH, CHRIST — ONE MORE JERK WITH A CUTE NAME FOR HIS
SCREEEEEEEEEEEEEEEEEEEEEEEEECCHHHHHHHHHHH

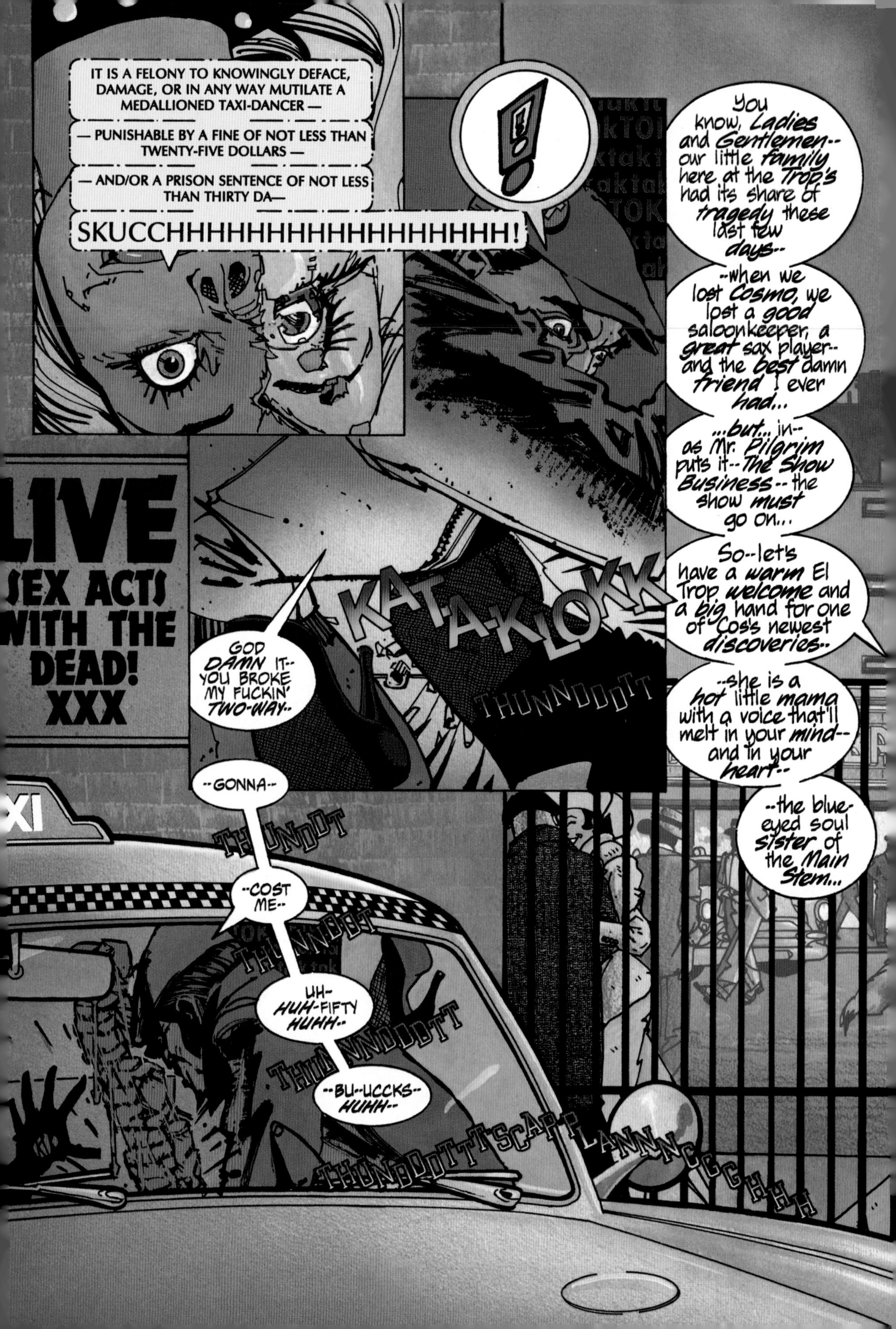
IT IS A FELONY TO KNOWINGLY DEFACE, DAMAGE, OR IN ANY WAY MUTILATE A MEDALLIONED TAXI-DANCER —
— PUNISHABLE BY A FINE OF NOT LESS THAN TWENTY-FIVE DOLLARS —
— AND/OR A PRISON SENTENCE OF NOT LESS THAN THIRTY DA—
SKUCCHHHHHHHHHHHHHHHHHH!
!
You know, Ladies and Gentlemen-- our little family here at the Trop's had its share of tragedy these last few days--
--when we lost Cosmo, we lost a good saloonkeeper, a great sax player-- and the best damn friend I ever had...
...but... in-- as Mr. Pilgrim puts it--The Show Business-- the show must go on...
So--let's have a warm El Trop welcome and a big hand for one of Cos's newest discoveries--
--she is a hot little mama with a voice that'll melt in your mind-- and in your heart--
--the blue-eyed soul sister of the Main Stem...
LIVE SEX ACTS WITH THE DEAD! XXX
KAT-A-KLOKK
GOD DAMN IT-- YOU BROKE MY FUCKIN' TWO-WAY--
--GONNA--
--COST ME--
UH-HUH-FIFTY HUHH--
--BU--UCCKS-- HUHH--

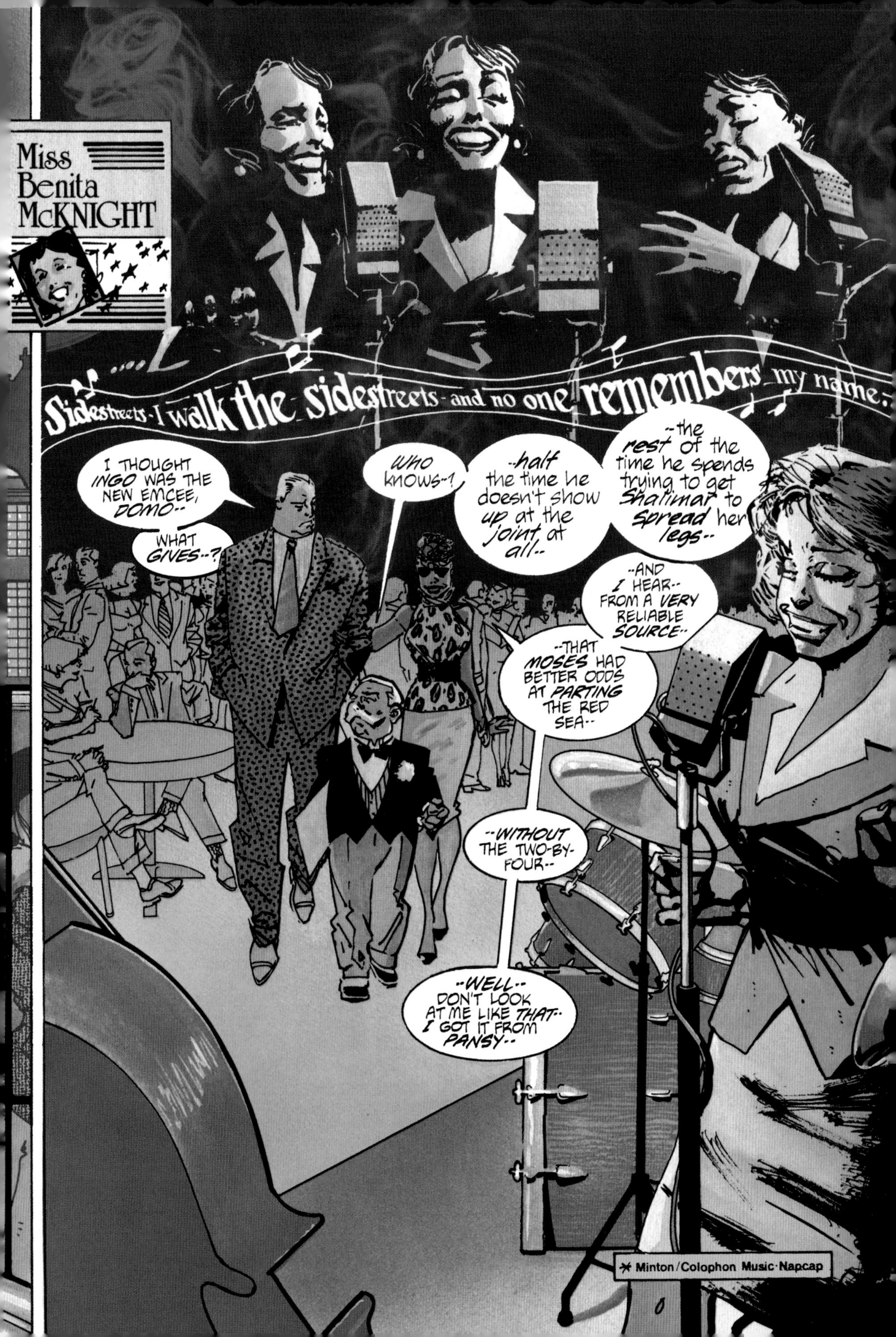

Miss Benita McKNIGHT
...Sidestreets - I walk the sidestreets - and no one remembers my name...
I THOUGHT INGO WAS THE NEW EMCEE, DOMO--
WHAT GIVES--?
Who knows--!
--half the time he doesn't show up at the joint at all--
--the rest of the time he spends trying to get Shalimar to spread her legs--
--AND I HEAR-- FROM A VERY RELIABLE SOURCE--
--THAT MOSES HAD BETTER ODDS AT PARTING THE RED SEA--
--WITHOUT THE TWO-BY-FOUR--
--WELL-- DON'T LOOK AT ME LIKE THAT-- I GOT IT FROM PANSY--
* Minton/Colophon Music·Napcap

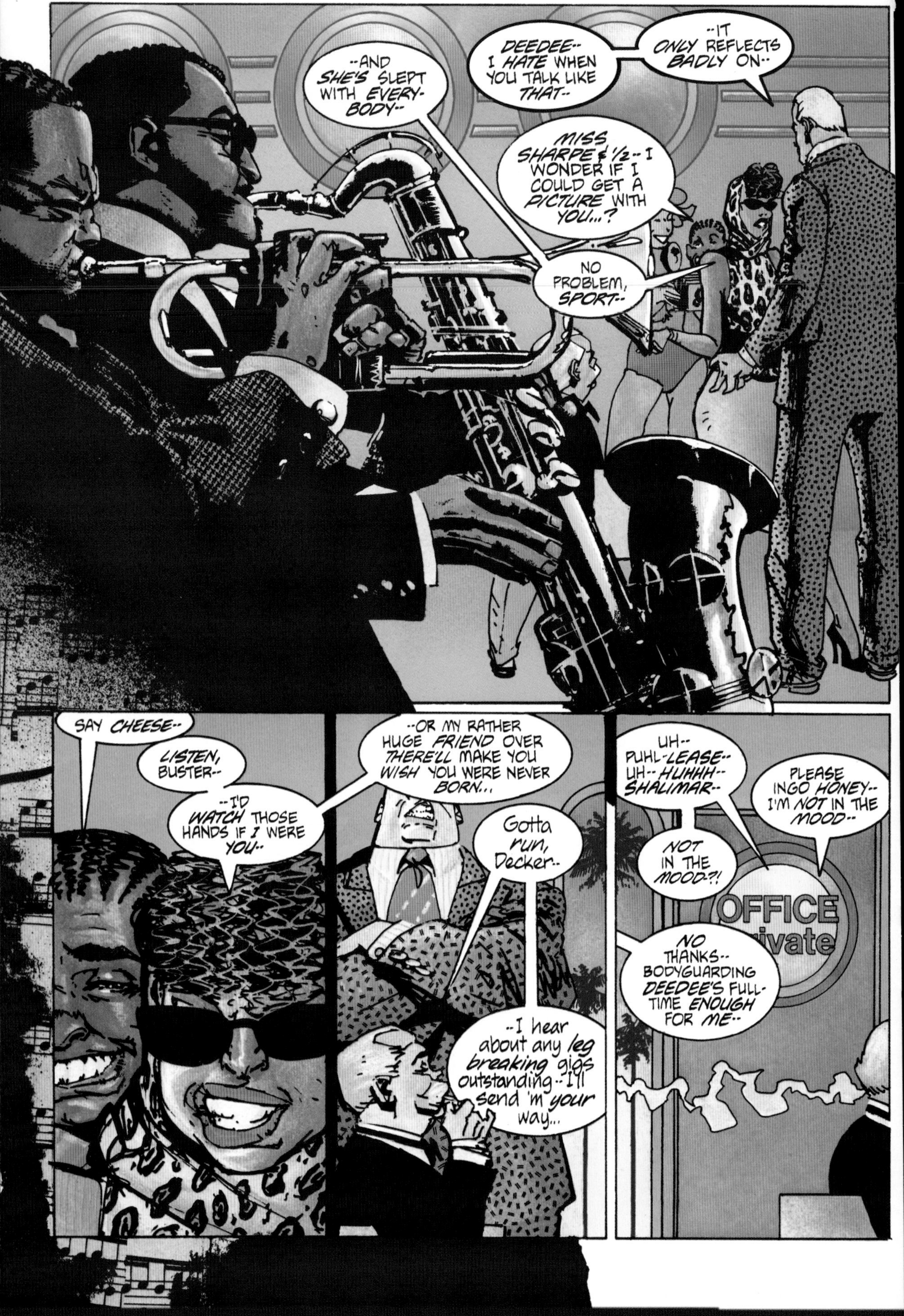
--AND SHE'S SLEPT WITH EVERY-BODY--
DEEDEE-- I HATE WHEN YOU TALK LIKE THAT--
--IT ONLY REFLECTS BADLY ON--
MISS SHARPE & 1/2-- I WONDER IF I COULD GET A PICTURE WITH YOU...?
NO PROBLEM, SPORT--
SAY CHEESE--
LISTEN, BUSTER--
--I'D WATCH THOSE HANDS IF I WERE YOU--
--OR MY RATHER HUGE FRIEND OVER THERE'LL MAKE YOU WISH YOU WERE NEVER BORN...
Gotta run, Decker--
--I hear about any leg breaking gigs outstanding--I'll send 'm your way...
UH-- PUHL-LEASE-- UH-- HUHHH-- SHALIMAR--
PLEASE INGO HONEY-- I'M NOT IN THE MOOD--
NOT IN THE MOOD?!
OFFICE
...rivate
NO THANKS-- BODYGUARDING DEEDEE'S FULL-TIME ENOUGH FOR ME--

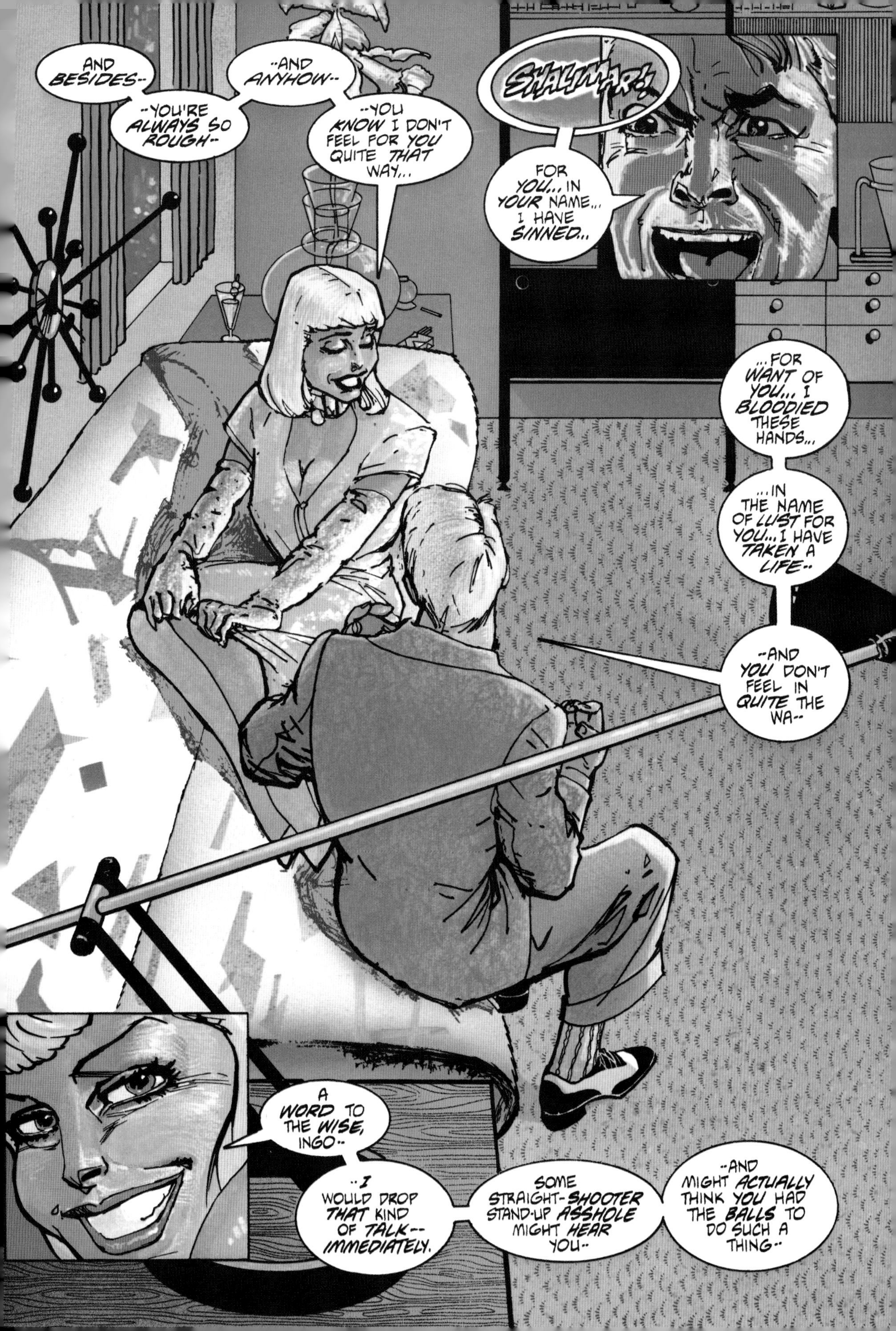
AND BESIDES--
--YOU'RE ALWAYS SO ROUGH--
--AND ANYHOW--
--YOU KNOW I DON'T FEEL FOR YOU QUITE THAT WAY...
SHALYMAR!
FOR YOU... IN YOUR NAME... I HAVE SINNED...
...FOR WANT OF YOU... I BLOODIED THESE HANDS...
...IN THE NAME OF LUST FOR YOU... I HAVE TAKEN A LIFE--
--AND YOU DON'T FEEL IN QUITE THE WA--
A WORD TO THE WISE, INGO--
--I WOULD DROP THAT KIND OF TALK-- IMMEDIATELY.
SOME STRAIGHT-SHOOTER STAND-UP ASSHOLE MIGHT HEAR YOU--
--AND MIGHT ACTUALLY THINK YOU HAD THE BALLS TO DO SUCH A THING--

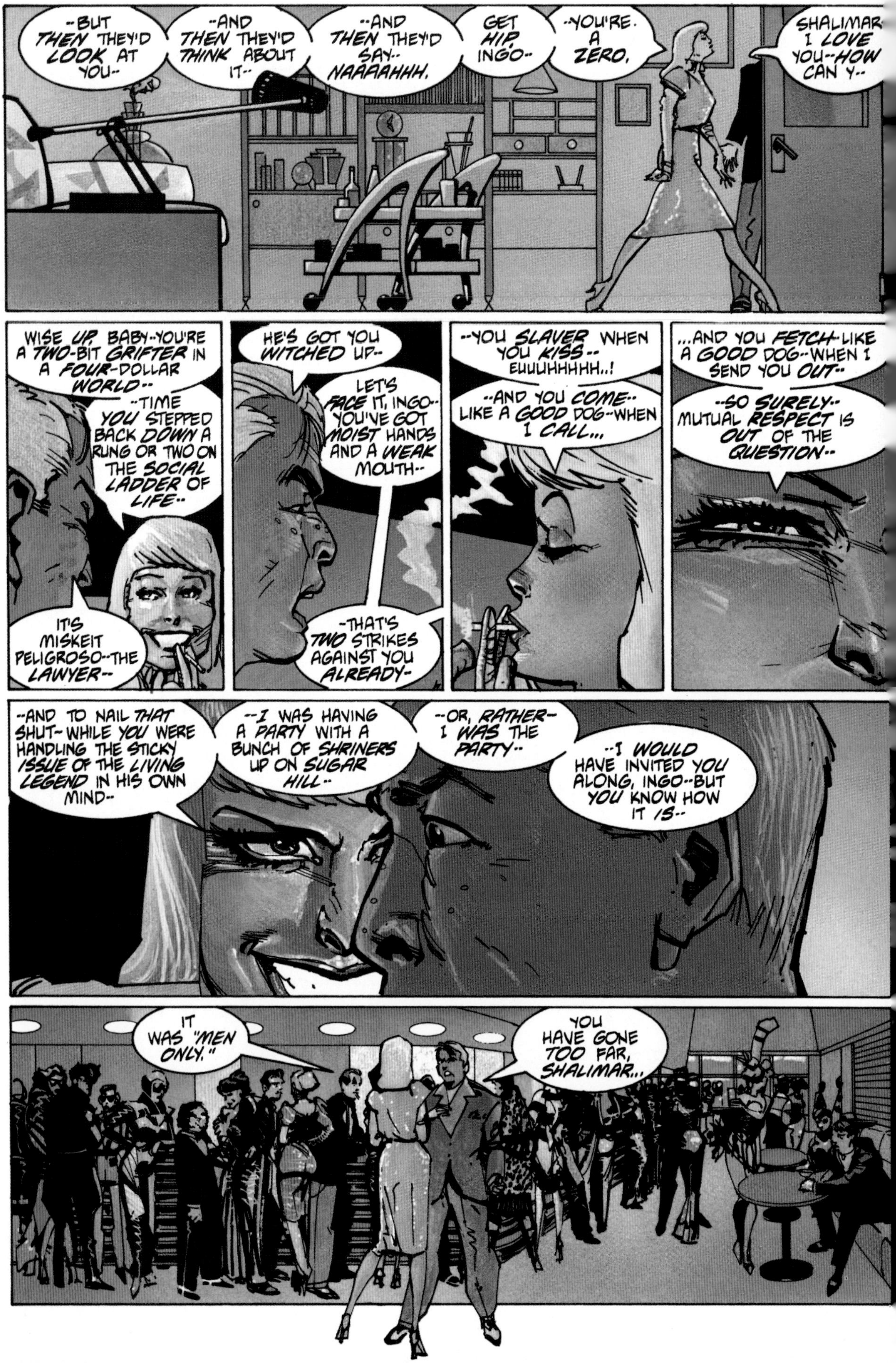
--BUT THEN THEY'D LOOK AT YOU--
--AND THEN THEY'D THINK ABOUT IT--
--AND THEN THEY'D SAY-- NAAAAAHHH.
GET HIP, INGO--
--YOU'RE. A ZERO.
SHALIMAR I LOVE YOU--HOW CAN Y--
WISE UP, BABY--YOU'RE A TWO-BIT GRIFTER IN A FOUR-DOLLAR WORLD--
--TIME YOU STEPPED BACK DOWN A RUNG OR TWO ON THE SOCIAL LADDER OF LIFE--
IT'S MISKEIT PELIGROSO--THE LAWYER--
HE'S GOT YOU WITCHED UP--
LET'S FACE IT, INGO--YOU'VE GOT MOIST HANDS AND A WEAK MOUTH--
--THAT'S TWO STRIKES AGAINST YOU ALREADY--
--YOU SLAVER WHEN YOU KISS-- EUUUHHHHH..!
--AND YOU COME-- LIKE A GOOD DOG--WHEN I CALL...
...AND YOU FETCH--LIKE A GOOD DOG--WHEN I SEND YOU OUT--
--SO SURELY-- MUTUAL RESPECT IS OUT OF THE QUESTION--
--AND TO NAIL THAT SHUT--WHILE YOU WERE HANDLING THE STICKY ISSUE OF THE LIVING LEGEND IN HIS OWN MIND--
--I WAS HAVING A PARTY WITH A BUNCH OF SHRINERS UP ON SUGAR HILL--
--OR, RATHER-- I WAS THE PARTY--
--I WOULD HAVE INVITED YOU ALONG, INGO--BUT YOU KNOW HOW IT IS--
IT WAS "MEN ONLY."
YOU HAVE GONE TOO FAR, SHALIMAR...

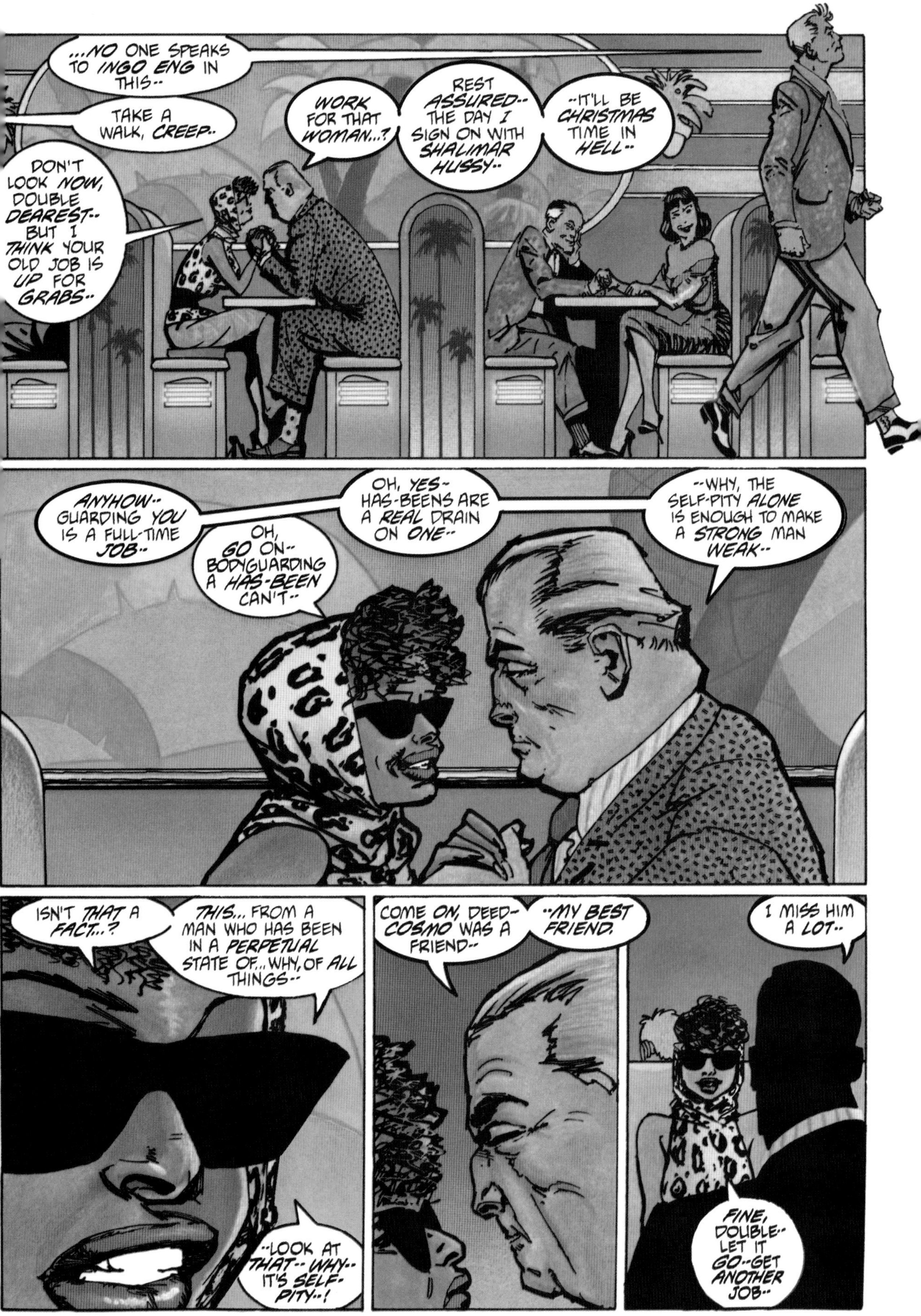
...NO ONE SPEAKS TO INGO ENG IN THIS--
TAKE A WALK, CREEP--
DON'T LOOK NOW, DOUBLE DEAREST-- BUT I THINK YOUR OLD JOB IS UP FOR GRABS--
WORK FOR THAT WOMAN...?
REST ASSURED-- THE DAY I SIGN ON WITH SHALIMAR HUSSY--
--IT'LL BE CHRISTMAS TIME IN HELL--
ANYHOW-- GUARDING YOU IS A FULL-TIME JOB--
OH, GO ON-- BODYGUARDING A HAS-BEEN CAN'T--
OH, YES-- HAS-BEENS ARE A REAL DRAIN ON ONE--
--WHY, THE SELF-PITY ALONE IS ENOUGH TO MAKE A STRONG MAN WEAK--
ISN'T THAT A FACT...?
THIS... FROM A MAN WHO HAS BEEN IN A PERPETUAL STATE OF... WHY, OF ALL THINGS--
--LOOK AT THAT-- WHY-- IT'S SELF-PITY--!
COME ON, DEED-- COSMO WAS A FRIEND--
--MY BEST FRIEND.
I MISS HIM A LOT--
FINE, DOUBLE-- LET IT GO--GET ANOTHER JOB--

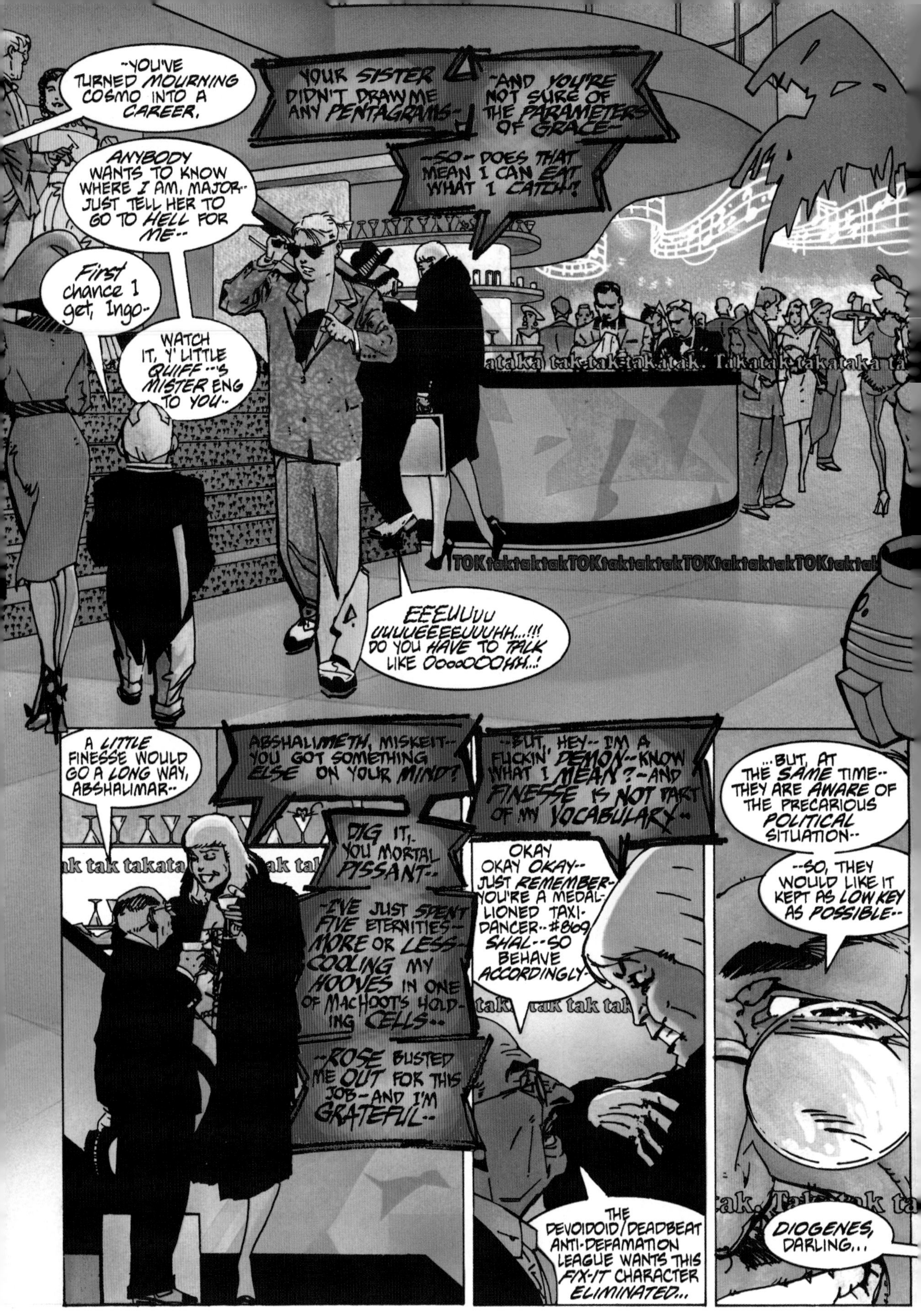
--YOU'VE TURNED MOURNING COSMO INTO A CAREER.
YOUR SISTER DIDN'T DRAW ME ANY PENTAGRAMS--
-AND YOU'RE NOT SURE OF THE PARAMETERS OF GRACE--
--SO--DOES THAT MEAN I CAN EAT WHAT I CATCH?
ANYBODY WANTS TO KNOW WHERE I AM, MAJOR-- JUST TELL HER TO GO TO HELL FOR ME--
First chance I get, Ingo--
WATCH IT, Y' LITTLE QUIFF--'S MISTER ENG TO YOU--
ataka tak-tak-takatak. Takatak takataka ta
TOKtaktaktakTOKtaktaktakTOKtaktaktakTOKtaktak
EEEUUUU UUUUEEEEUUUHH...!!! DO YOU HAVE TO TALK LIKE OOOOOOOHH...!
A LITTLE FINESSE WOULD GO A LONG WAY, ABSHALIMAR--
ABSHALIMETH, MISKEIT-- YOU GOT SOMETHING ELSE ON YOUR MIND?
DIG IT, YOU MORTAL PISSANT--
-I'VE JUST SPENT FIVE ETERNITIES--MORE OR LESS--COOLING MY HOOVES IN ONE OF MACHOOT'S HOLDING CELLS--
--ROSE BUSTED ME OUT FOR THIS JOB--AND I'M GRATEFUL--
--BUT, HEY--I'M A FUCKIN' DEMON--KNOW WHAT I MEAN?--AND FINESSE IS NOT PART OF MY VOCABULARY--
OKAY OKAY OKAY-- JUST REMEMBER-- YOU'RE A MEDALLIONED TAXI-DANCER--#869 SHAL--SO BEHAVE ACCORDINGLY-
THE DEVOIDOID/DEADBEAT ANTI-DEFAMATION LEAGUE WANTS THIS FIX-IT CHARACTER ELIMINATED...
...BUT, AT THE SAME TIME-- THEY ARE AWARE OF THE PRECARIOUS POLITICAL SITUATION--
--SO, THEY WOULD LIKE IT KEPT AS LOW KEY AS POSSIBLE--
DIOGENES, DARLING...

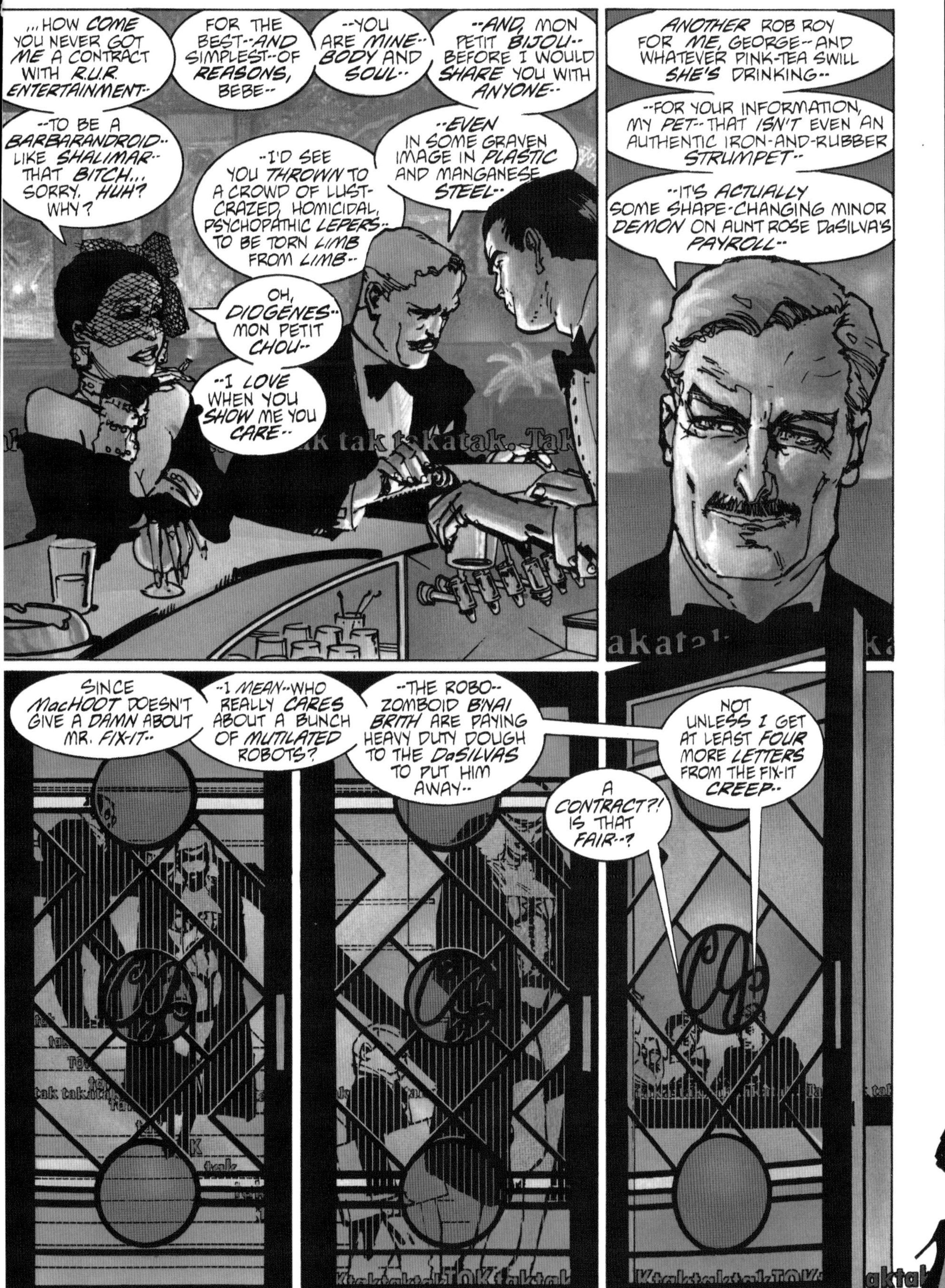
...HOW COME YOU NEVER GOT ME A CONTRACT WITH R.U.R. ENTERTAINMENT--
--TO BE A BARBARANDROID-- LIKE SHALIMAR-- THAT BITCH... SORRY. HUH? WHY?
FOR THE BEST--AND SIMPLEST--OF REASONS, BEBE--
--YOU ARE MINE-- BODY AND SOUL--
--AND, MON PETIT BIJOU-- BEFORE I WOULD SHARE YOU WITH ANYONE--
--EVEN IN SOME GRAVEN IMAGE IN PLASTIC AND MANGANESE STEEL--
--I'D SEE YOU THROWN TO A CROWD OF LUST-CRAZED, HOMICIDAL, PSYCHOPATHIC LEPERS-- TO BE TORN LIMB FROM LIMB--
OH, DIOGENES-- MON PETIT CHOU--
--I LOVE WHEN YOU SHOW ME YOU CARE--
tak tak takatak. Tak
ANOTHER ROB ROY FOR ME, GEORGE--AND WHATEVER PINK-TEA SWILL SHE'S DRINKING--
--FOR YOUR INFORMATION, MY PET--THAT ISN'T EVEN AN AUTHENTIC IRON-AND-RUBBER STRUMPET--
--IT'S ACTUALLY SOME SHAPE-CHANGING MINOR DEMON ON AUNT ROSE DaSILVA'S PAYROLL--
akatak
SINCE MacHOOT DOESN'T GIVE A DAMN ABOUT MR. FIX-IT--
--I MEAN--WHO REALLY CARES ABOUT A BUNCH OF MUTILATED ROBOTS?
--THE ROBO-ZOMBOID B'NAI BRITH ARE PAYING HEAVY DUTY DOUGH TO THE DaSILVAS TO PUT HIM AWAY--
A CONTRACT?! IS THAT FAIR--?
NOT UNLESS I GET AT LEAST FOUR MORE LETTERS FROM THE FIX-IT CREEP--
Ktaktaktak TOK taktak
Ktaktaktak TOK taktak
aktak

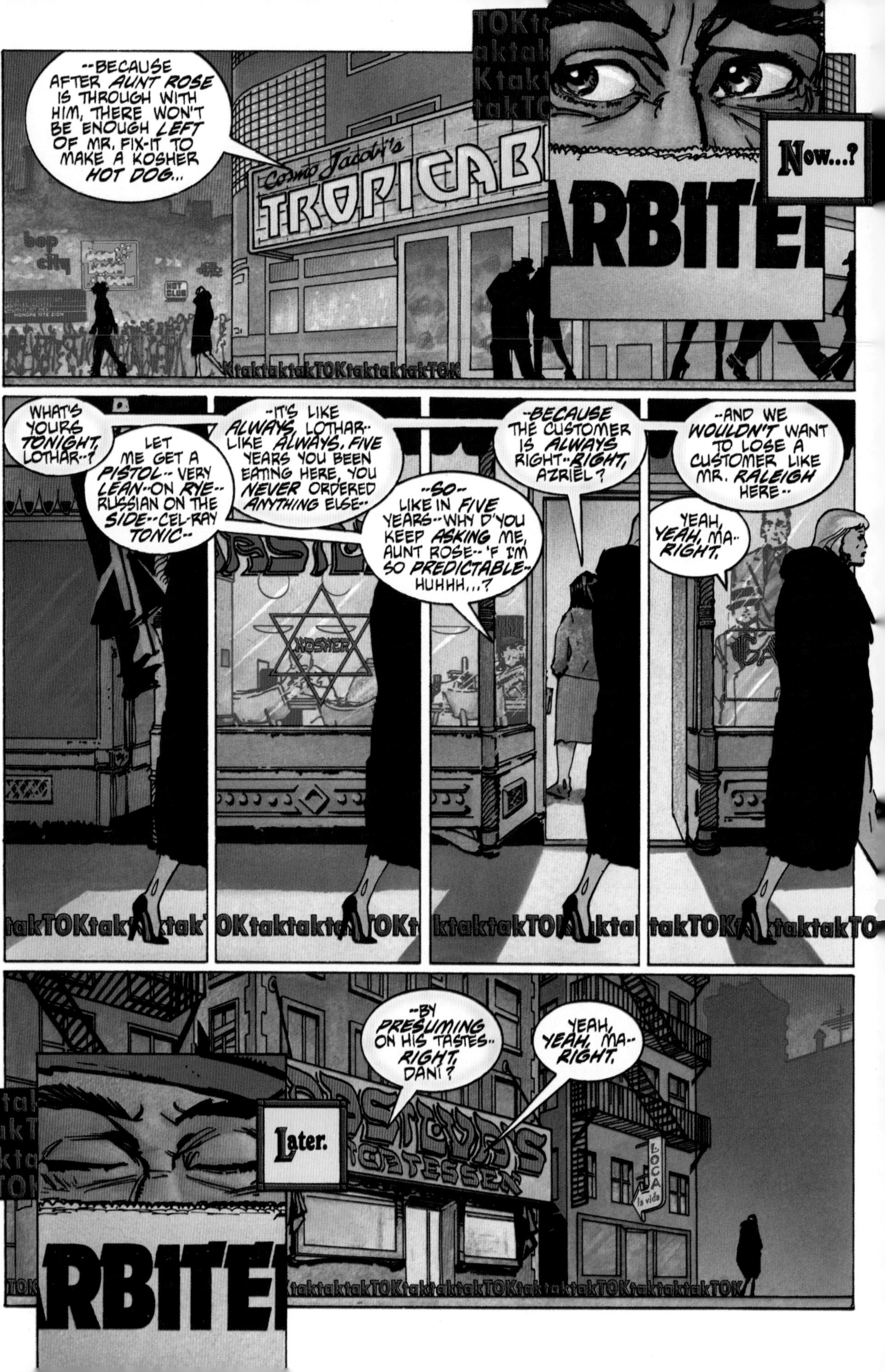
--BECAUSE AFTER AUNT ROSE IS THROUGH WITH HIM, THERE WON'T BE ENOUGH LEFT OF MR. FIX-IT TO MAKE A KOSHER HOT DOG...
Now...?
KtaktaktakTOKtaktaktakTOK
WHAT'S YOURS TONIGHT, LOTHAR--?
LET ME GET A PISTOL-- VERY LEAN--ON RYE-- RUSSIAN ON THE SIDE--CEL-RAY TONIC--
--IT'S LIKE ALWAYS, LOTHAR-- LIKE ALWAYS. FIVE YEARS YOU BEEN EATING HERE, YOU NEVER ORDERED ANYTHING ELSE--
--SO-- LIKE IN FIVE YEARS--WHY D'YOU KEEP ASKING ME, AUNT ROSE-- 'F I'M SO PREDICTABLE-- HUHHH...?
--BECAUSE THE CUSTOMER IS ALWAYS RIGHT--RIGHT, AZRIEL?
--AND WE WOULDN'T WANT TO LOSE A CUSTOMER LIKE MR. RALEIGH HERE--
YEAH, YEAH, MA-- RIGHT.
KOSHER
Later.
--BY PRESUMING ON HIS TASTES-- RIGHT, DANI?
YEAH, YEAH, MA-- RIGHT.
LOCA
la vida
ktaktaktakTOKtaktaktakTOKtaktaktakTOK

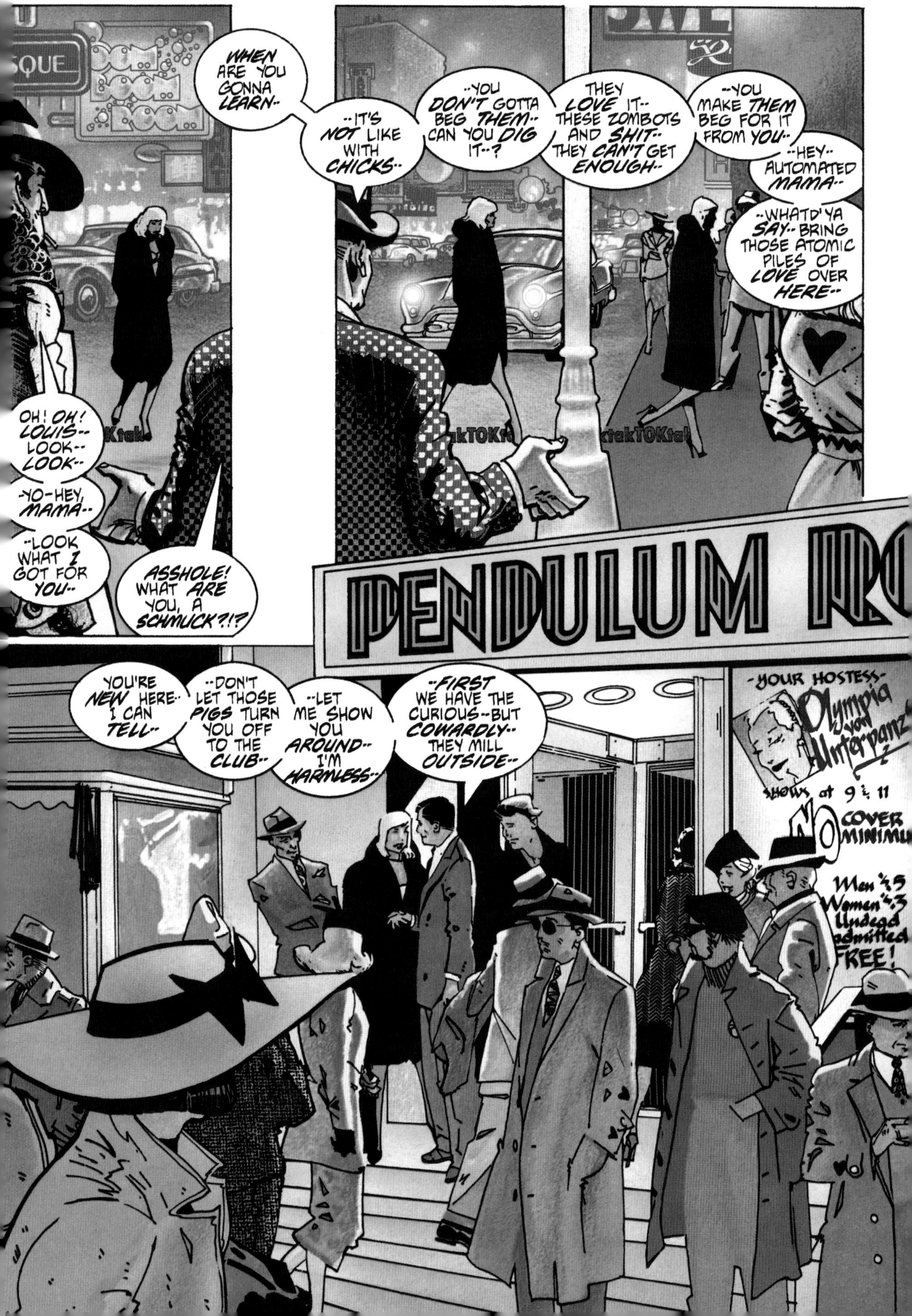
SQUE
WHEN ARE YOU GONNA LEARN--
--IT'S NOT LIKE WITH CHICKS--
--YOU DON'T GOTTA BEG THEM-- CAN YOU DIG IT--?
THEY LOVE IT-- THESE ZOMBOTS AND SHIT-- THEY CAN'T GET ENOUGH--
--YOU MAKE THEM BEG FOR IT FROM YOU--
--HEY-- AUTOMATED MAMA--
--WHATD'YA SAY-- BRING THOSE ATOMIC PILES OF LOVE OVER HERE--
OH! OH! LOUIS-- LOOK-- LOOK--
-YO-HEY, MAMA--
--LOOK WHAT I GOT FOR YOU--
ASSHOLE! WHAT ARE YOU, A SCHMUCK?!?
PENDULUM RO
YOU'RE NEW HERE-- I CAN TELL--
--DON'T LET THOSE PIGS TURN YOU OFF TO THE CLUB--
--LET ME SHOW YOU AROUND-- I'M HARMLESS--
--FIRST WE HAVE THE CURIOUS--BUT COWARDLY-- THEY MILL OUTSIDE--
-YOUR HOSTESS-
Olympia von Unterpanz
shows at 9 & 11
NO COVER MINIMU
Men $5
Women $3
Undead admitted FREE!

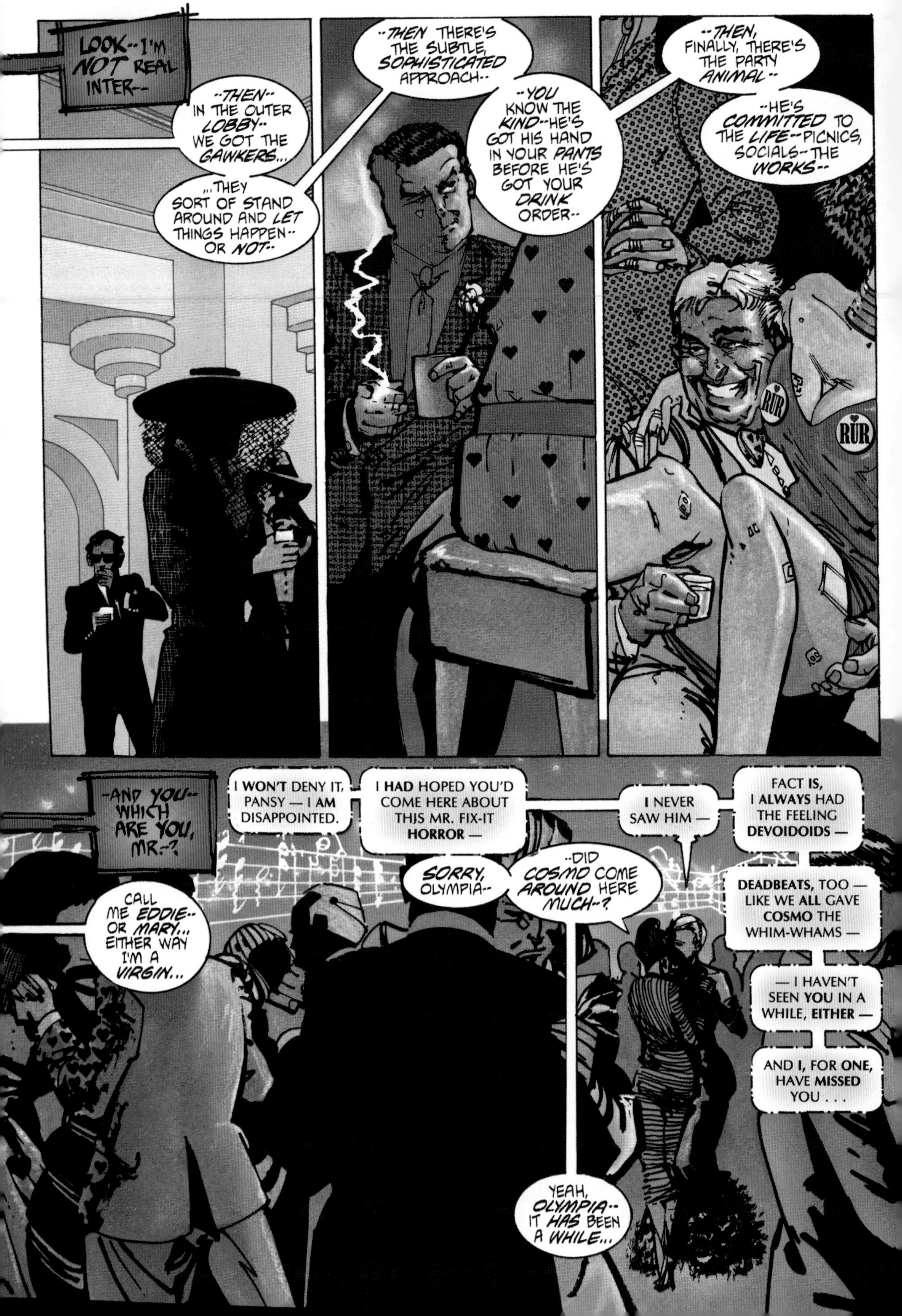
LOOK--I'M NOT REAL INTER--
--THEN-- IN THE OUTER LOBBY-- WE GOT THE GAWKERS...
...THEY SORT OF STAND AROUND AND LET THINGS HAPPEN-- OR NOT--
--THEN THERE'S THE SUBTLE, SOPHISTICATED APPROACH--
--YOU KNOW THE KIND--HE'S GOT HIS HAND IN YOUR PANTS BEFORE HE'S GOT YOUR DRINK ORDER--
--THEN, FINALLY, THERE'S THE PARTY ANIMAL--
--HE'S COMMITTED TO THE LIFE--PICNICS, SOCIALS--THE WORKS--
RUR
RUR
-AND YOU-- WHICH ARE YOU, MR.--?
CALL ME EDDIE-- OR MARY... EITHER WAY I'M A VIRGIN...
I WON'T DENY IT, PANSY — I AM DISAPPOINTED.
I HAD HOPED YOU'D COME HERE ABOUT THIS MR. FIX-IT HORROR —
SORRY, OLYMPIA--
--DID COSMO COME AROUND HERE MUCH--?
I NEVER SAW HIM —
FACT IS, I ALWAYS HAD THE FEELING DEVOIDOIDS —
DEADBEATS, TOO — LIKE WE ALL GAVE COSMO THE WHIM-WHAMS —
— I HAVEN'T SEEN YOU IN A WHILE, EITHER —
AND I, FOR ONE, HAVE MISSED YOU . . .
YEAH, OLYMPIA-- IT HAS BEEN A WHILE...

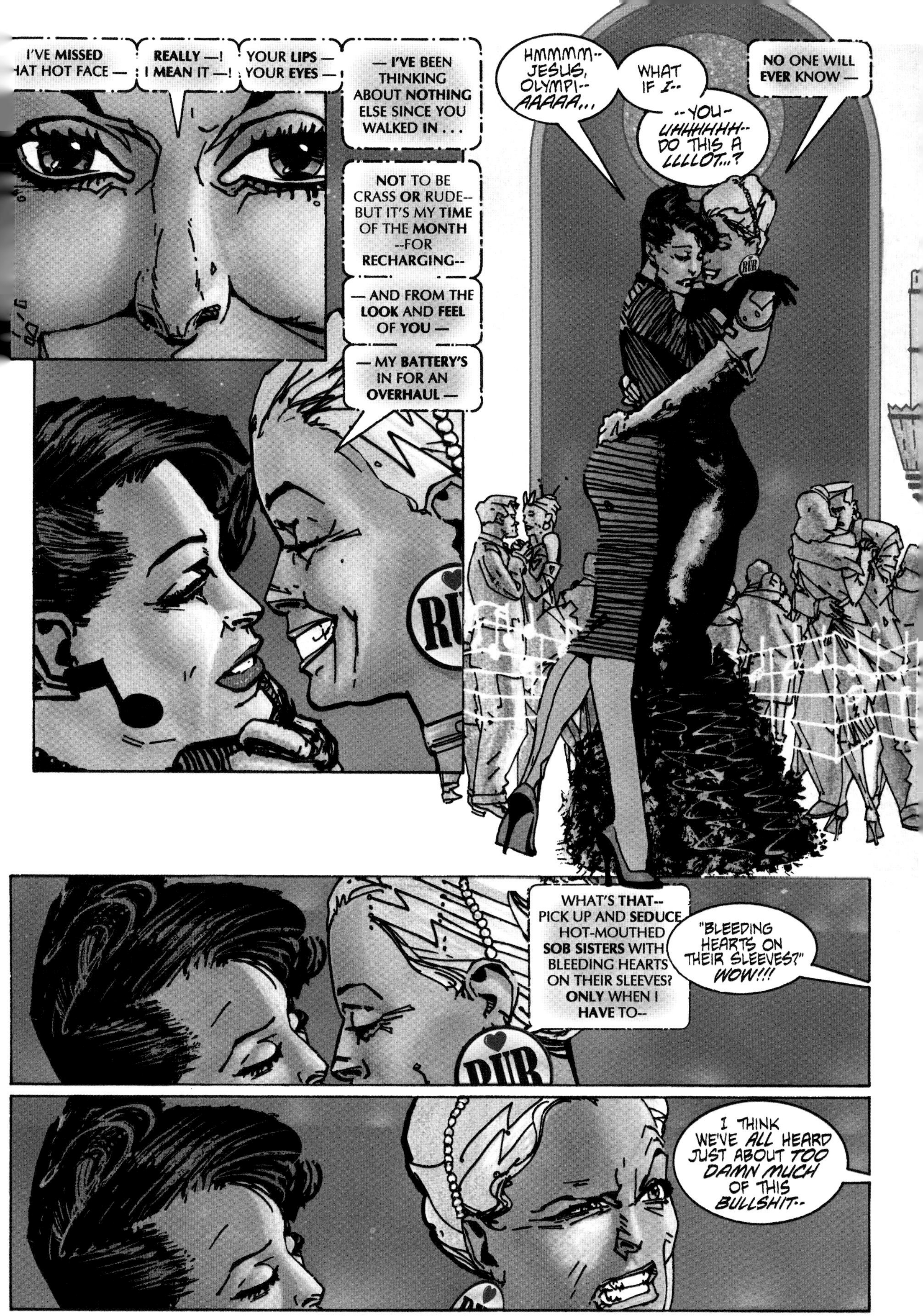

I'VE MISSED THAT HOT FACE —
REALLY —! I MEAN IT —!
YOUR LIPS — YOUR EYES —
— I'VE BEEN THINKING ABOUT NOTHING ELSE SINCE YOU WALKED IN . . .
NOT TO BE CRASS OR RUDE-- BUT IT'S MY TIME OF THE MONTH --FOR RECHARGING--
— AND FROM THE LOOK AND FEEL OF YOU —
— MY BATTERY'S IN FOR AN OVERHAUL —
HMMMM-- JESUS, OLYMPI-- AAAAA...
WHAT IF I--
--YOU-- UHHHHHH-- DO THIS A LLLLOT...?
NO ONE WILL EVER KNOW —
RUR
WHAT'S THAT-- PICK UP AND SEDUCE HOT-MOUTHED SOB SISTERS WITH BLEEDING HEARTS ON THEIR SLEEVES? ONLY WHEN I HAVE TO--
"BLEEDING HEARTS ON THEIR SLEEVES?" WOW!!!
I THINK WE'VE ALL HEARD JUST ABOUT TOO DAMN MUCH OF THIS BULLSHIT--

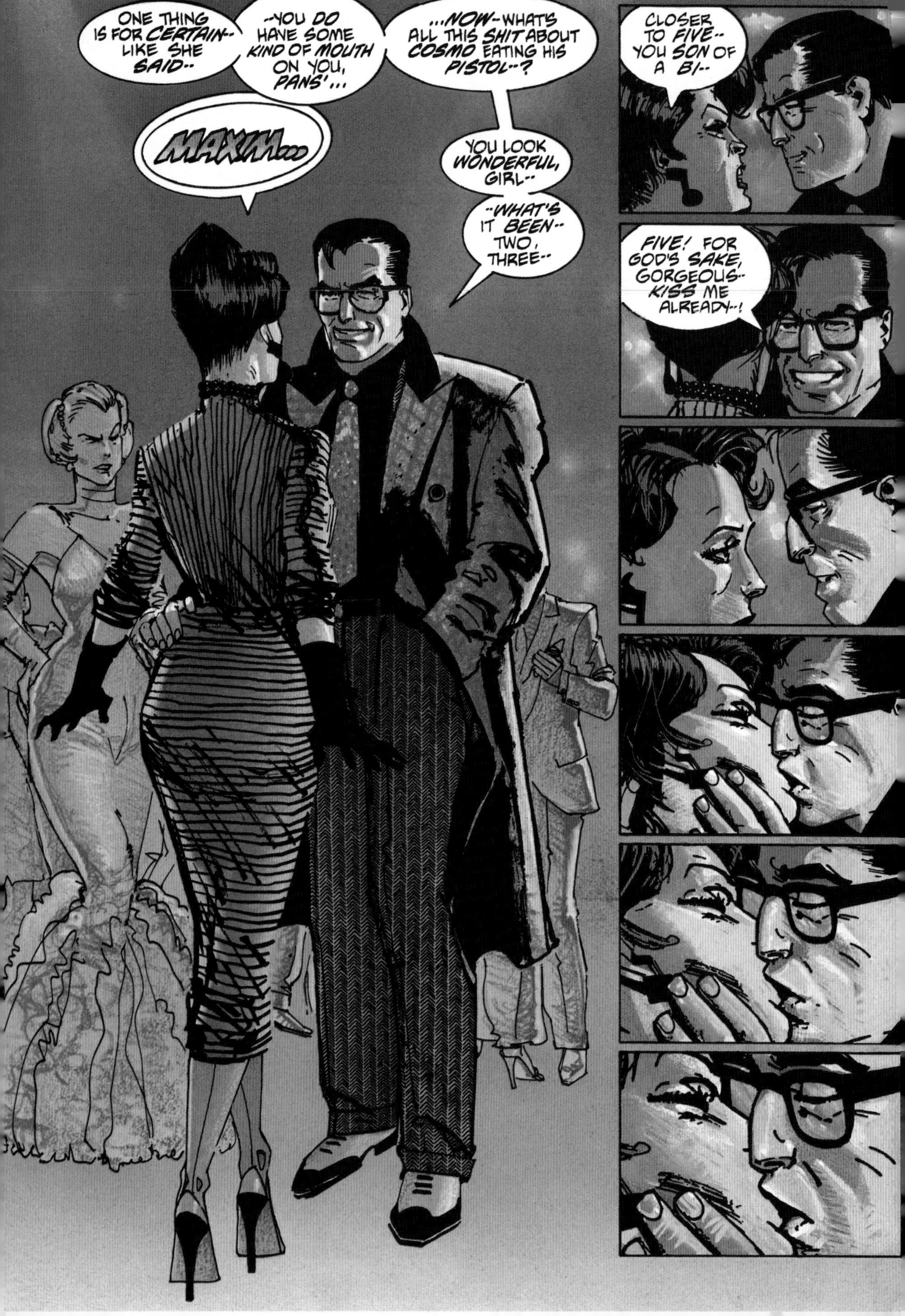

ONE THING IS FOR CERTAIN-- LIKE SHE SAID--
--YOU DO HAVE SOME KIND OF MOUTH ON YOU, PANS'...
...NOW--WHAT'S ALL THIS SHIT ABOUT COSMO EATING HIS PISTOL--?
MAXIM...
YOU LOOK WONDERFUL, GIRL--
--WHAT'S IT BEEN-- TWO, THREE--
CLOSER TO FIVE-- YOU SON OF A BI--
FIVE! FOR GOD'S SAKE, GORGEOUS-- KISS ME ALREADY--!

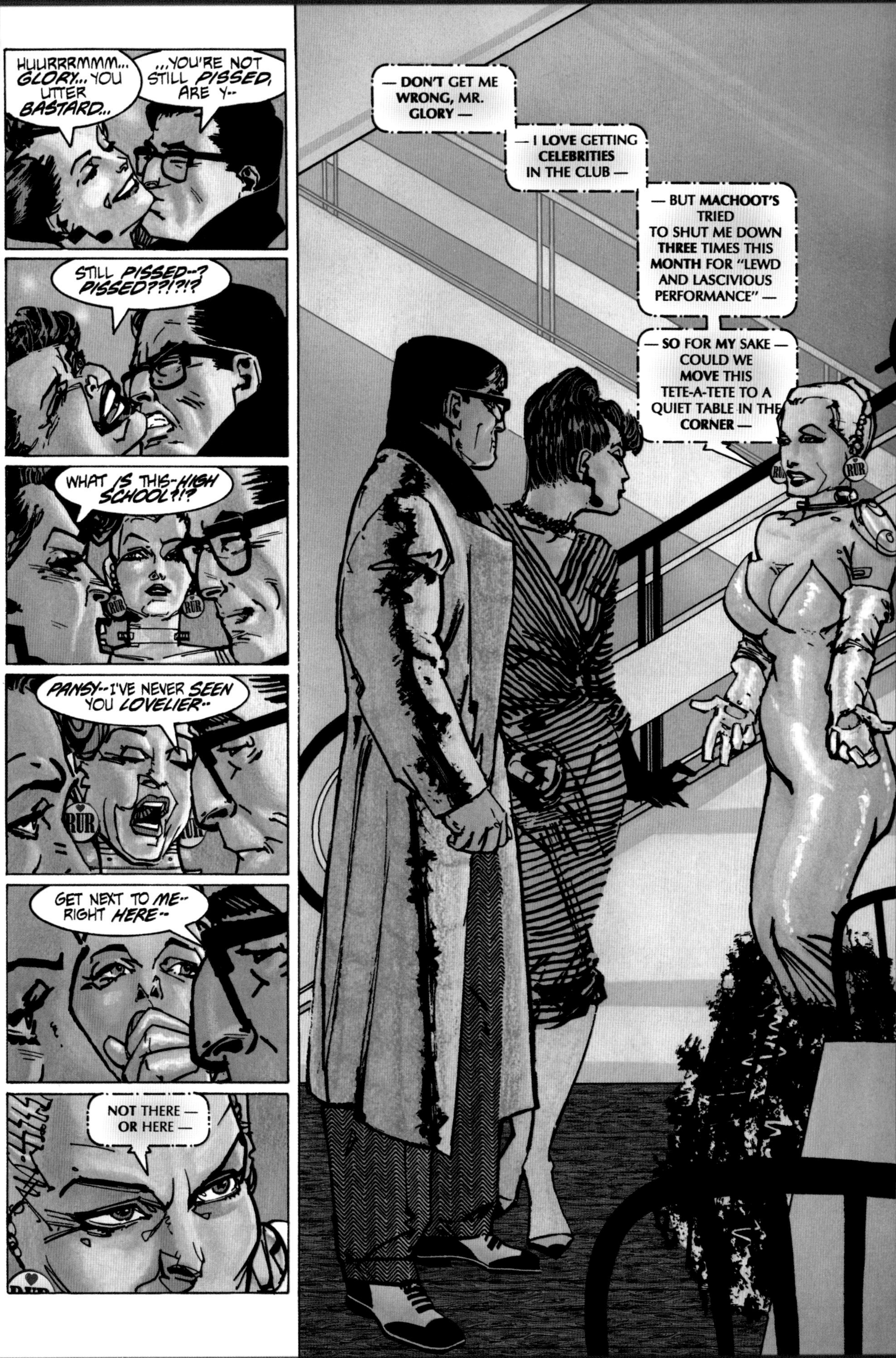
HUURRRMMM... GLORY... YOU UTTER BASTARD...
...YOU'RE NOT STILL PISSED, ARE Y--
STILL PISSED--? PISSED??!?!?
WHAT IS THIS--HIGH SCHOOL?!?
PANSY--I'VE NEVER SEEN YOU LOVELIER--
GET NEXT TO ME-- RIGHT HERE--
NOT THERE — OR HERE —
— DON'T GET ME WRONG, MR. GLORY —
— I LOVE GETTING CELEBRITIES IN THE CLUB —
— BUT MACHOOT'S TRIED TO SHUT ME DOWN THREE TIMES THIS MONTH FOR "LEWD AND LASCIVIOUS PERFORMANCE" —
— SO FOR MY SAKE — COULD WE MOVE THIS TETE-A-TETE TO A QUIET TABLE IN THE CORNER —

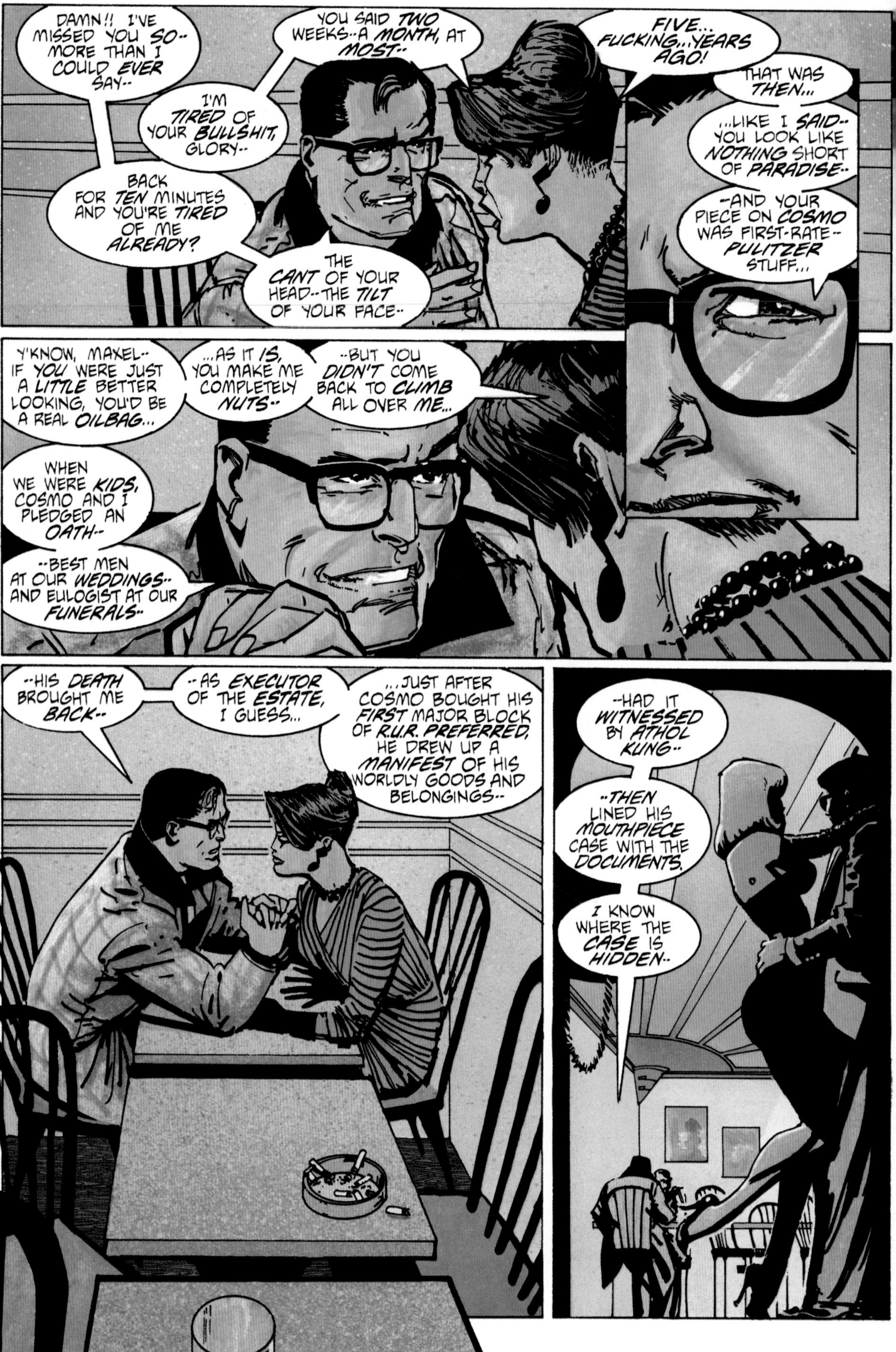
DAMN!! I'VE MISSED YOU SO-- MORE THAN I COULD EVER SAY--
YOU SAID TWO WEEKS--A MONTH, AT MOST--
FIVE... FUCKING... YEARS AGO!
I'M TIRED OF YOUR BULLSHIT, GLORY--
THAT WAS THEN...
...LIKE I SAID-- YOU LOOK LIKE NOTHING SHORT OF PARADISE--
BACK FOR TEN MINUTES AND YOU'RE TIRED OF ME ALREADY?
--AND YOUR PIECE ON COSMO WAS FIRST-RATE-- PULITZER STUFF...
THE CANT OF YOUR HEAD--THE TILT OF YOUR FACE--
Y'KNOW, MAXEL-- IF YOU WERE JUST A LITTLE BETTER LOOKING, YOU'D BE A REAL OILBAG...
...AS IT IS, YOU MAKE ME COMPLETELY NUTS--
--BUT YOU DIDN'T COME BACK TO CLIMB ALL OVER ME...
WHEN WE WERE KIDS, COSMO AND I PLEDGED AN OATH--
--BEST MEN AT OUR WEDDINGS-- AND EULOGIST AT OUR FUNERALS--
--HIS DEATH BROUGHT ME BACK--
--AS EXECUTOR OF THE ESTATE, I GUESS...
...JUST AFTER COSMO BOUGHT HIS FIRST MAJOR BLOCK OF R.U.R. PREFERRED, HE DREW UP A MANIFEST OF HIS WORLDLY GOODS AND BELONGINGS--
--HAD IT WITNESSED BY ATHOL KUNG--
--THEN LINED HIS MOUTHPIECE CASE WITH THE DOCUMENTS.
I KNOW WHERE THE CASE IS HIDDEN--

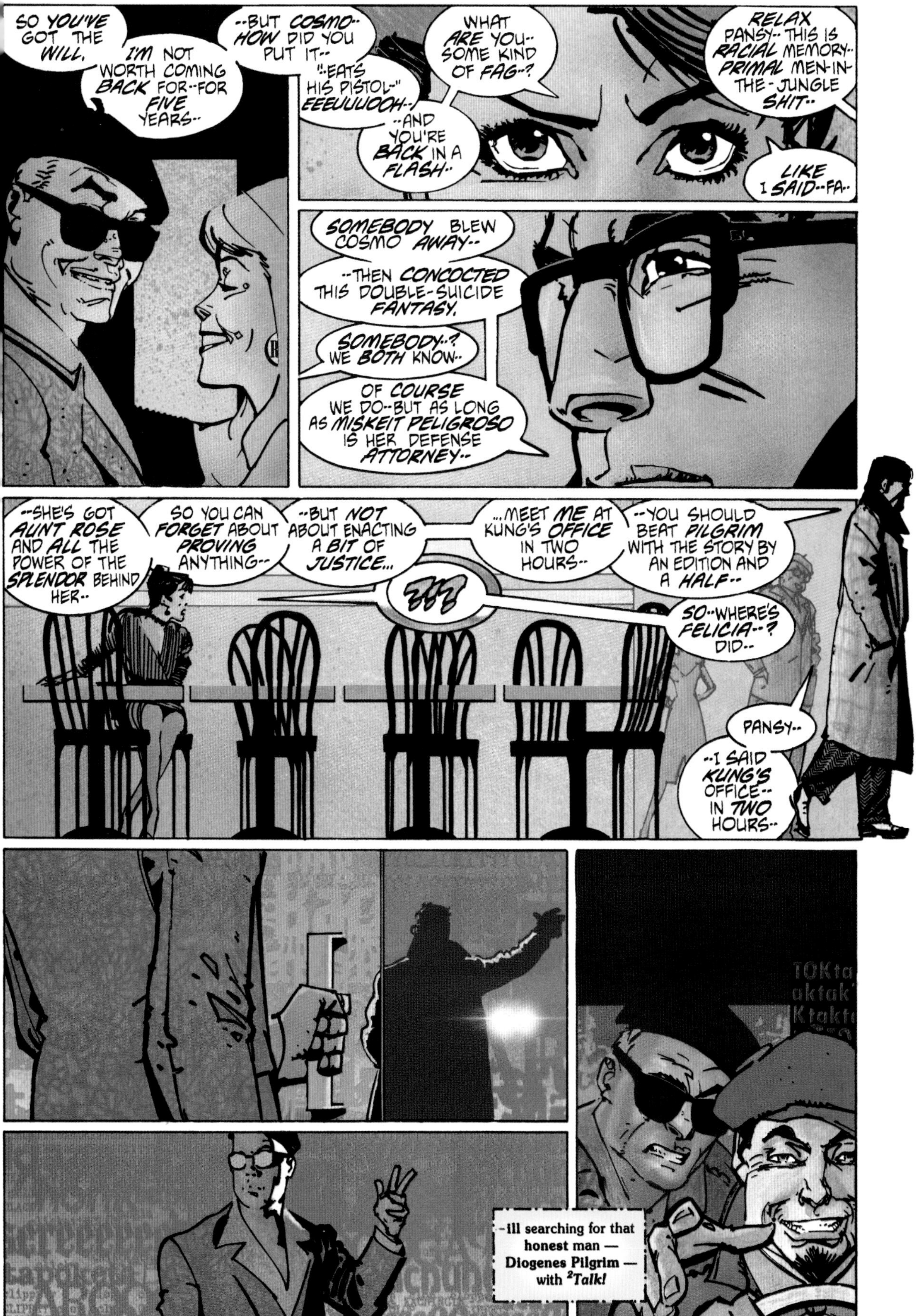
SO YOU'VE GOT THE WILL.
I'M NOT WORTH COMING BACK FOR--FOR FIVE YEARS--
--BUT COSMO-- HOW DID YOU PUT IT--
"--EATS HIS PISTOL--" EEEUUUOOH--!
--AND YOU'RE BACK IN A FLASH--
WHAT ARE YOU-- SOME KIND OF FAG--?
RELAX PANSY-- THIS IS RACIAL MEMORY-- PRIMAL MEN-IN-THE-JUNGLE SHIT--
LIKE I SAID--FA--
SOMEBODY BLEW COSMO AWAY--
--THEN CONCOCTED THIS DOUBLE-SUICIDE FANTASY.
SOMEBODY--? WE BOTH KNOW--
OF COURSE WE DO--BUT AS LONG AS MISKEIT PELIGROSO IS HER DEFENSE ATTORNEY--
--SHE'S GOT AUNT ROSE AND ALL THE POWER OF THE SPLENDOR BEHIND HER--
SO YOU CAN FORGET ABOUT PROVING ANYTHING--
--BUT NOT ABOUT ENACTING A BIT OF JUSTICE...
...MEET ME AT KUNG'S OFFICE IN TWO HOURS--
--YOU SHOULD BEAT PILGRIM WITH THE STORY BY AN EDITION AND A HALF--
SO--WHERE'S FELICIA--? DID--
PANSY--
--I SAID KUNG'S OFFICE-- IN TWO HOURS--
-ill searching for that honest man — Diogenes Pilgrim — with ²Talk!

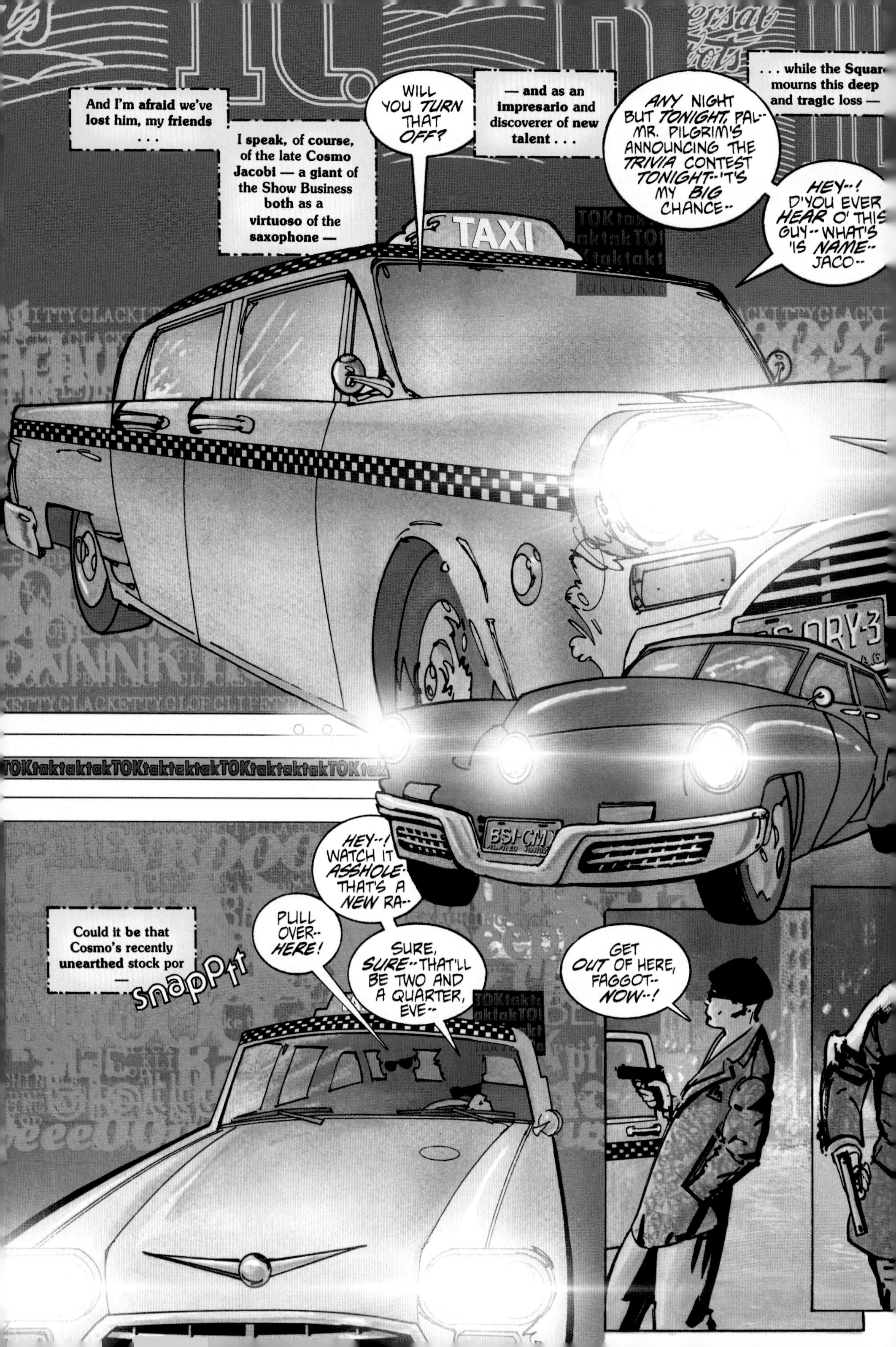

And I'm afraid we've lost him, my friends . . .
I speak, of course, of the late Cosmo Jacobi — a giant of the Show Business both as a virtuoso of the saxophone —
WILL YOU TURN THAT OFF?
— and as an impresario and discoverer of new talent . . .
ANY NIGHT BUT TONIGHT, PAL-- MR. PILGRIM'S ANNOUNCING THE TRIVIA CONTEST TONIGHT--'T'S MY BIG CHANCE--
. . . while the Square mourns this deep and tragic loss —
HEY--! D'YOU EVER HEAR O' THIS GUY--WHAT'S 'IS NAME-- JACO--
TAXI
TOKtaktaktakTOKtaktaktakTOKtaktaktakTOKtak
HEY--! WATCH IT ASSHOLE-- THAT'S A NEW RA--
Could it be that Cosmo's recently unearthed stock por —
snapPft
PULL OVER-- HERE!
SURE, SURE--THAT'LL BE TWO AND A QUARTER, EVE--
GET OUT OF HERE, FAGGOT-- NOW--!

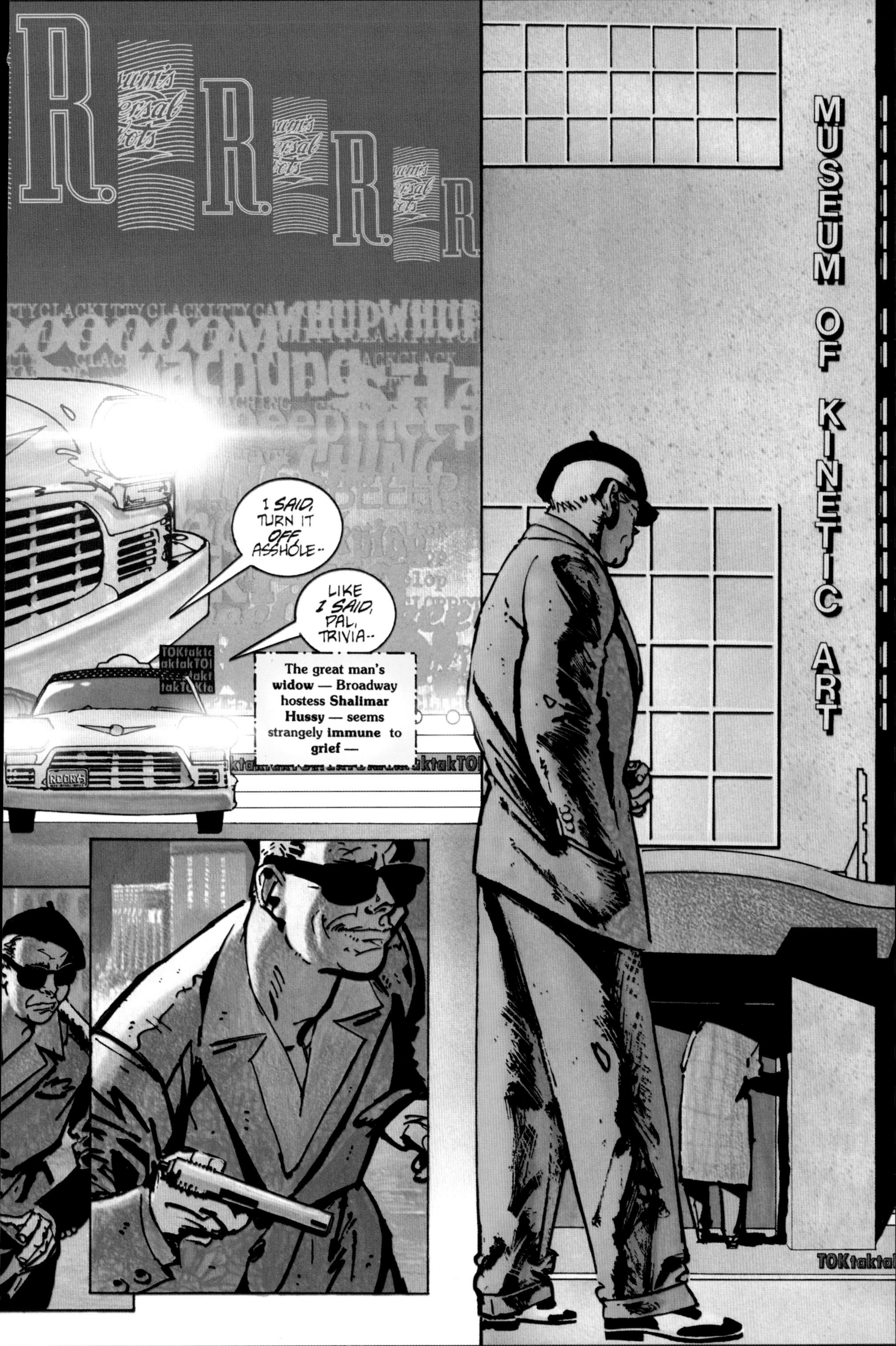
I SAID, TURN IT OFF ASSHOLE--
LIKE I SAID, PAL, TRIVIA--
The great man's widow — Broadway hostess Shalimar Hussy — seems strangely immune to grief —
MUSEUM OF KINETIC ART

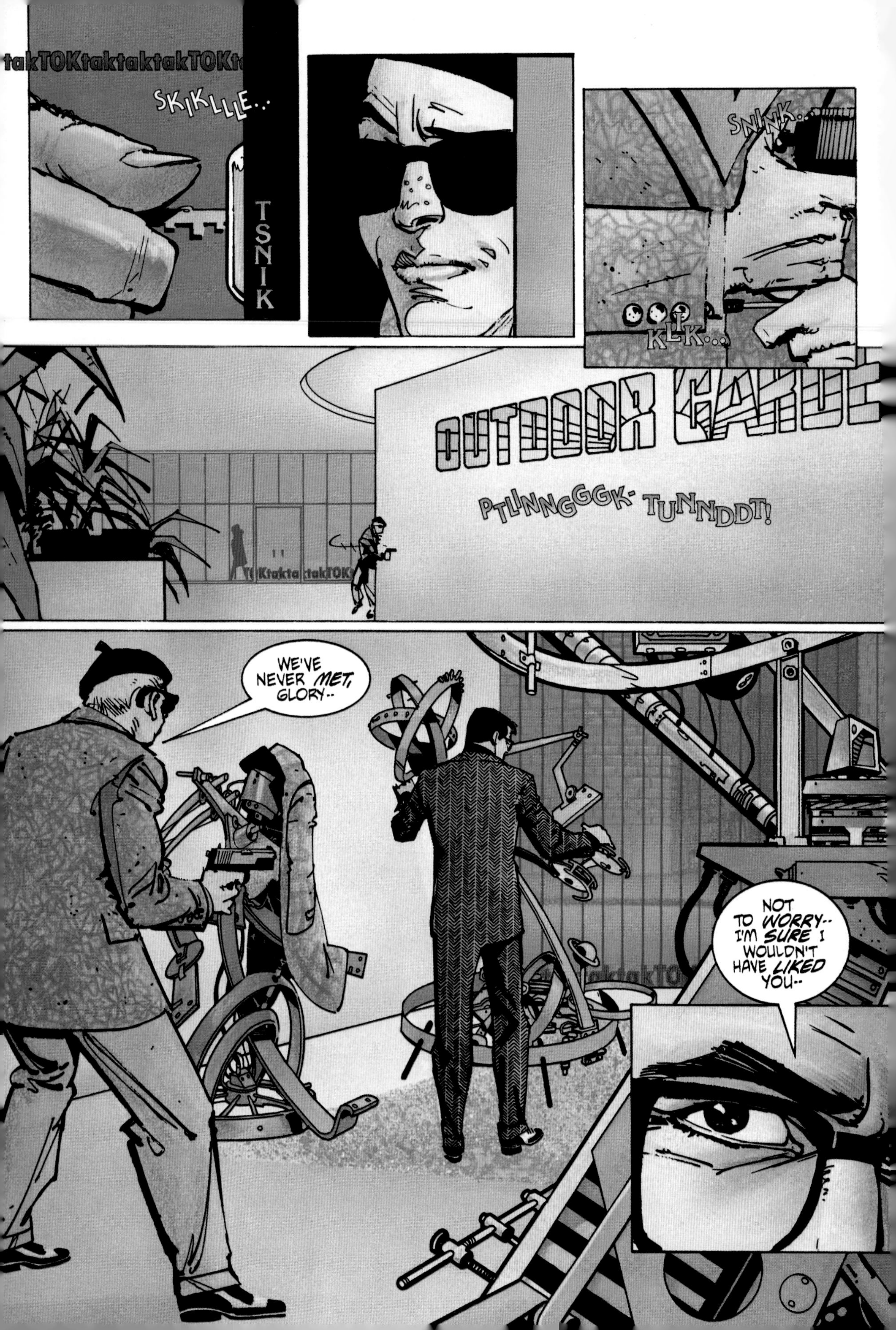
takTOKtaktaktakTOKta
SKIKLLLE..
TSNIK
SNINK..
KLIK..
OUTDOOR
PTLINNGGGK- TUNNDDT!
TOKtakta takTOK
WE'VE NEVER MET, GLORY..
NOT TO WORRY.. I'M SURE I WOULDN'T HAVE LIKED YOU..
taktakTOK

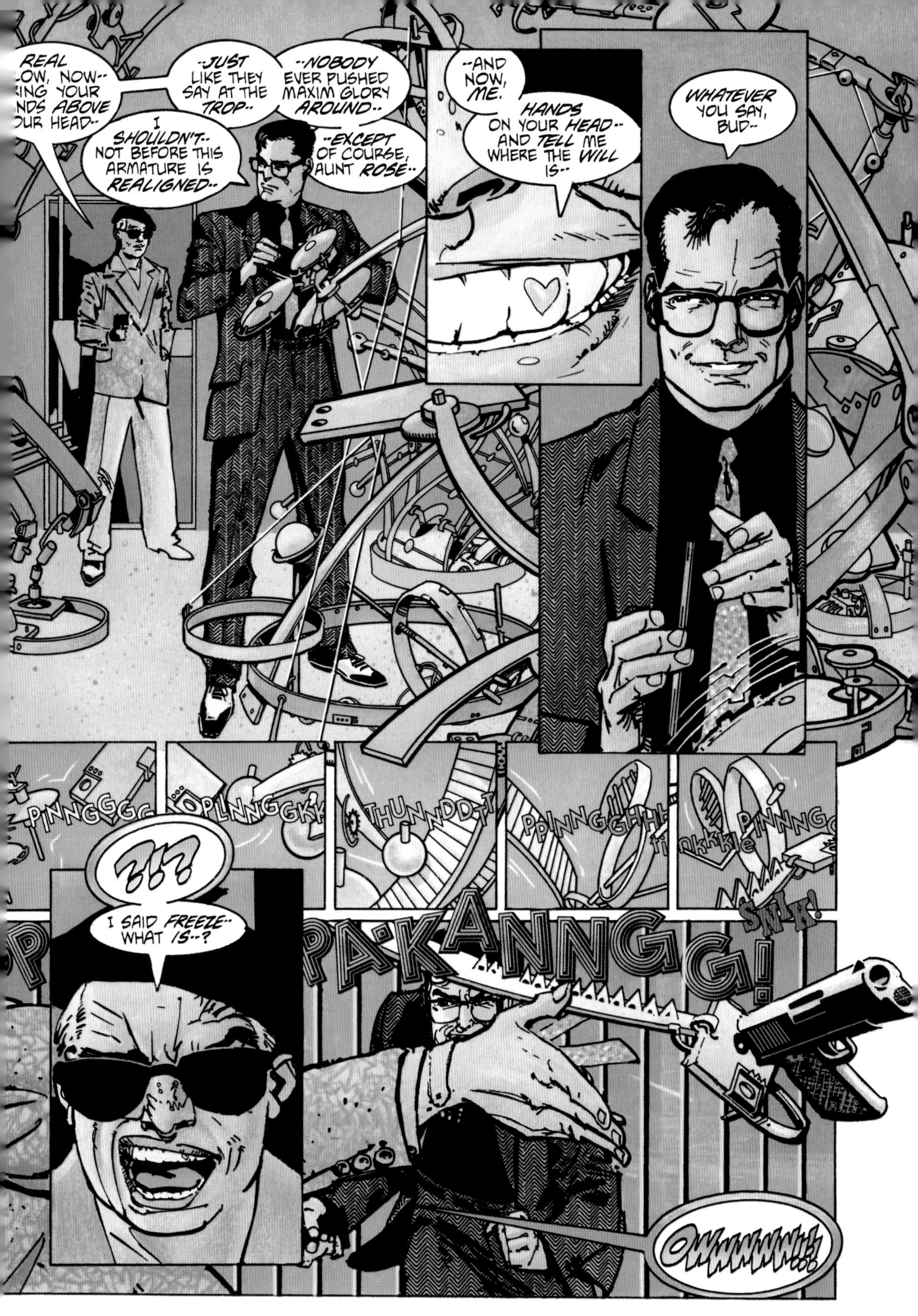
REAL ...LOW, NOW-- ...ING YOUR ...NDS ABOVE ...UR HEAD--
--JUST LIKE THEY SAY AT THE TROP--
--NOBODY EVER PUSHED MAXIM GLORY AROUND--
I SHOULDN'T-- NOT BEFORE THIS ARMATURE IS REALIGNED--
--EXCEPT OF COURSE, AUNT ROSE--
--AND NOW, ME.
HANDS ON YOUR HEAD-- AND TELL ME WHERE THE WILL IS--
WHATEVER YOU SAY, BUD--
PINNGGGG
PLINNGGKK
THUNNDD-T
PPINNGGHHH
tinkkkle
PINNNGG
??!
I SAID FREEZE-- WHAT IS--?
PA-KANNGG!
SNIK!
OWWWWWW!!

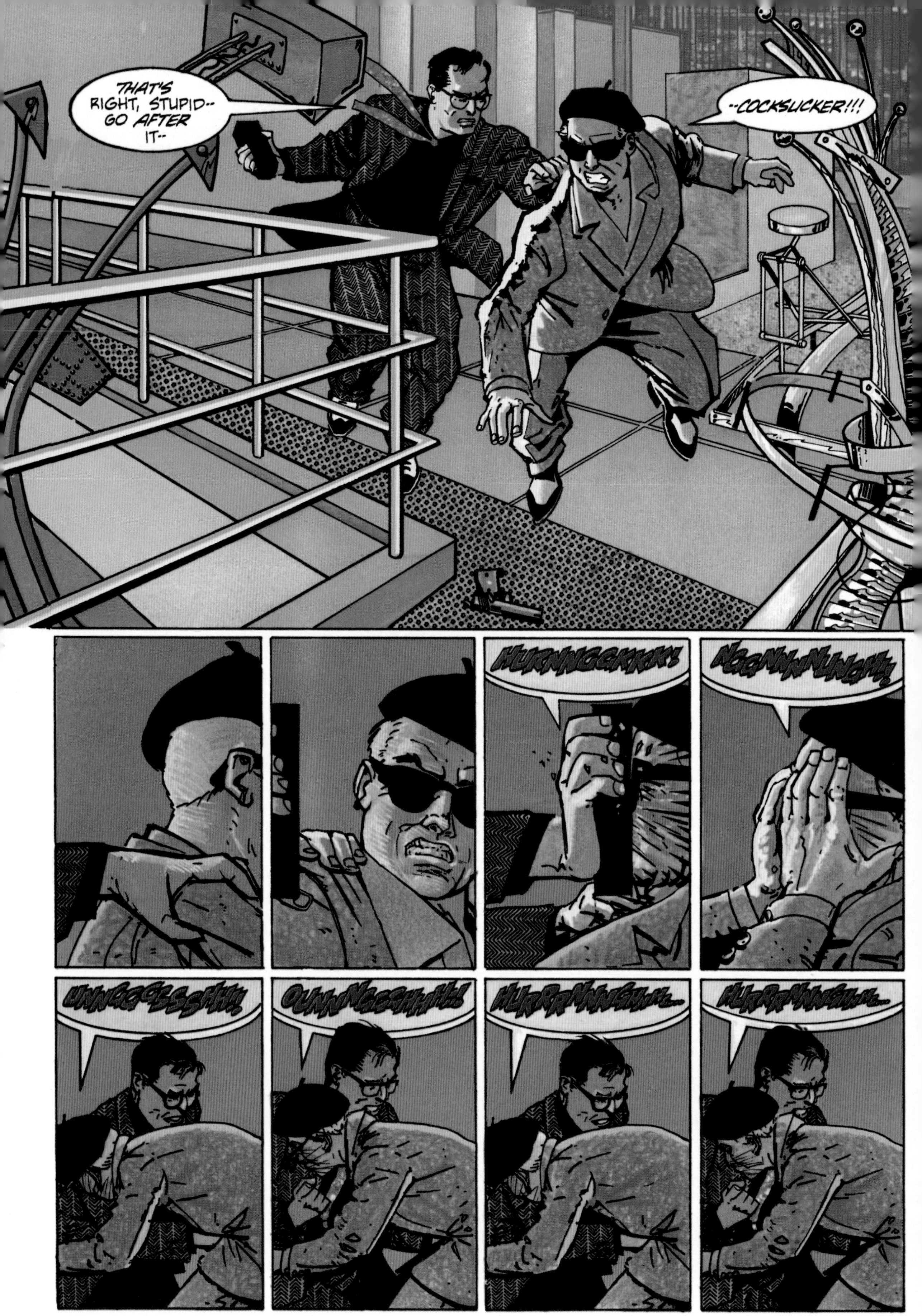
THAT'S RIGHT, STUPID-- GO AFTER IT--
--COCKSUCKER!!!

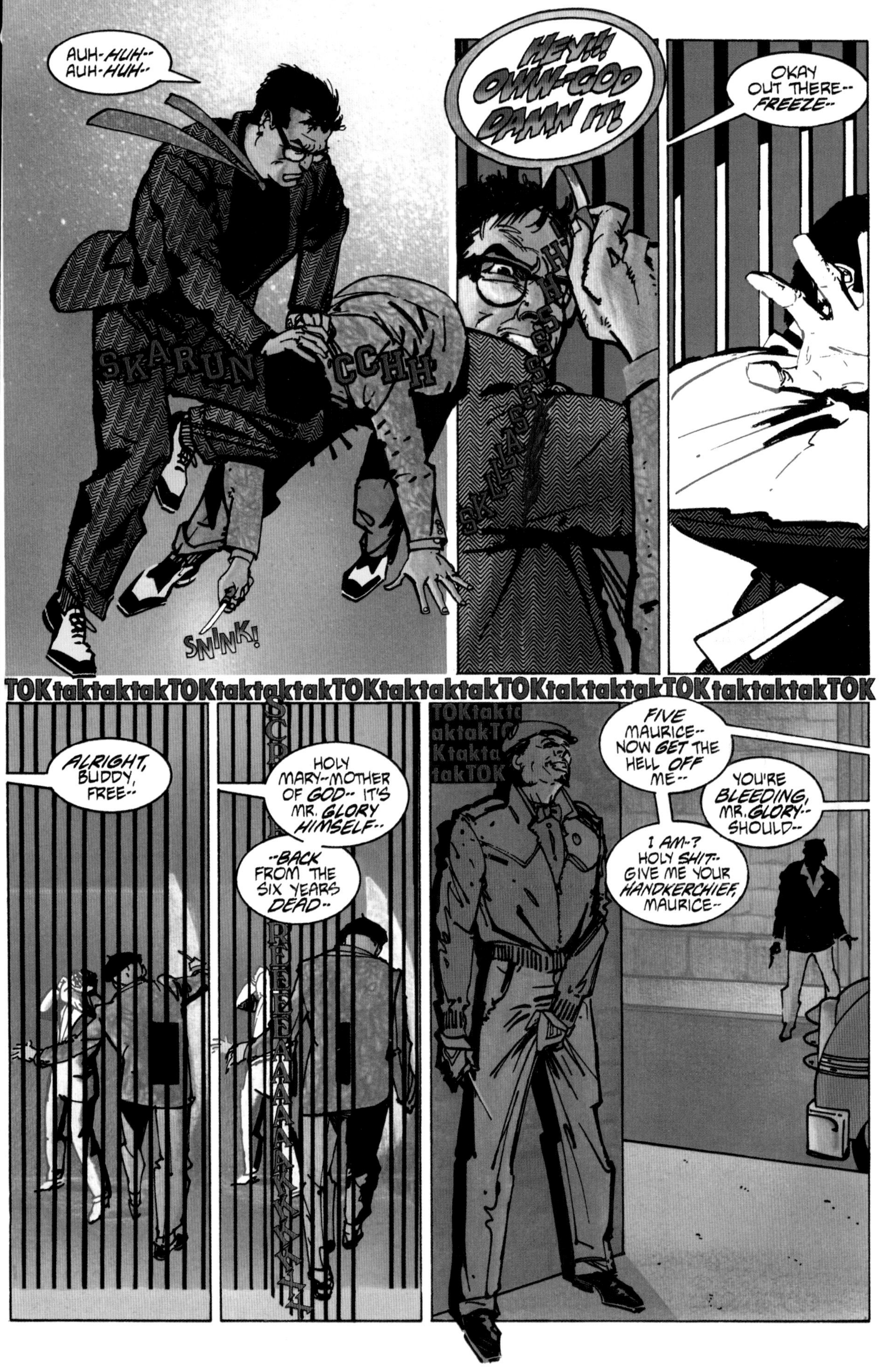
AUH-HUH-- AUH-HUH--
SKARUN
CCHH
SNINK!
HEY!! OWW-GOD DAMN IT!
SKLLASSSHH
OKAY OUT THERE-- FREEZE--
TOKtaktaktakTOKtaktaktakTOKtaktaktakTOKtaktaktakTOKtaktaktakTOK
ALRIGHT, BUDDY, FREE--
HOLY MARY--MOTHER OF GOD-- IT'S MR. GLORY HIMSELF--
--BACK FROM THE SIX YEARS DEAD--
TOKtaktaktakTOKtaktaktakTOK
FIVE MAURICE-- NOW GET THE HELL OFF ME--
YOU'RE BLEEDING, MR. GLORY-- SHOULD--
I AM--? HOLY SHIT-- GIVE ME YOUR HANDKERCHIEF, MAURICE--

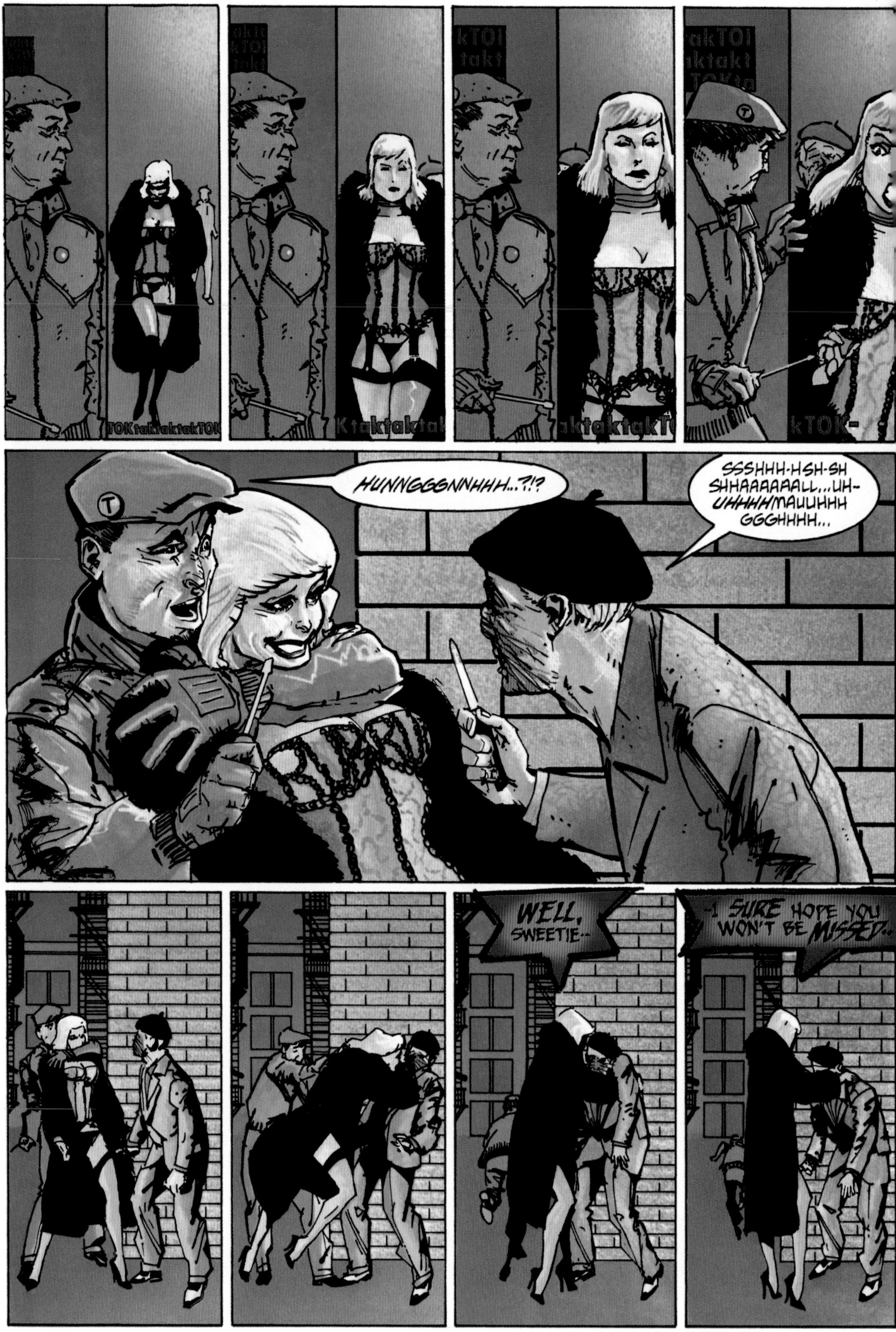
TOKtaktaktakTOK
Ktaktaktak
aktaktakTO
kTOK-
HUNNGGGNNHHH...?!?
SSSHHH-HSH-SH
SHHAAAAAALL...UH-
UHHHHMAUUHHH
GGGHHHH...
WELL,
SWEETIE--
--I SURE HOPE YOU
WON'T BE MISSED...

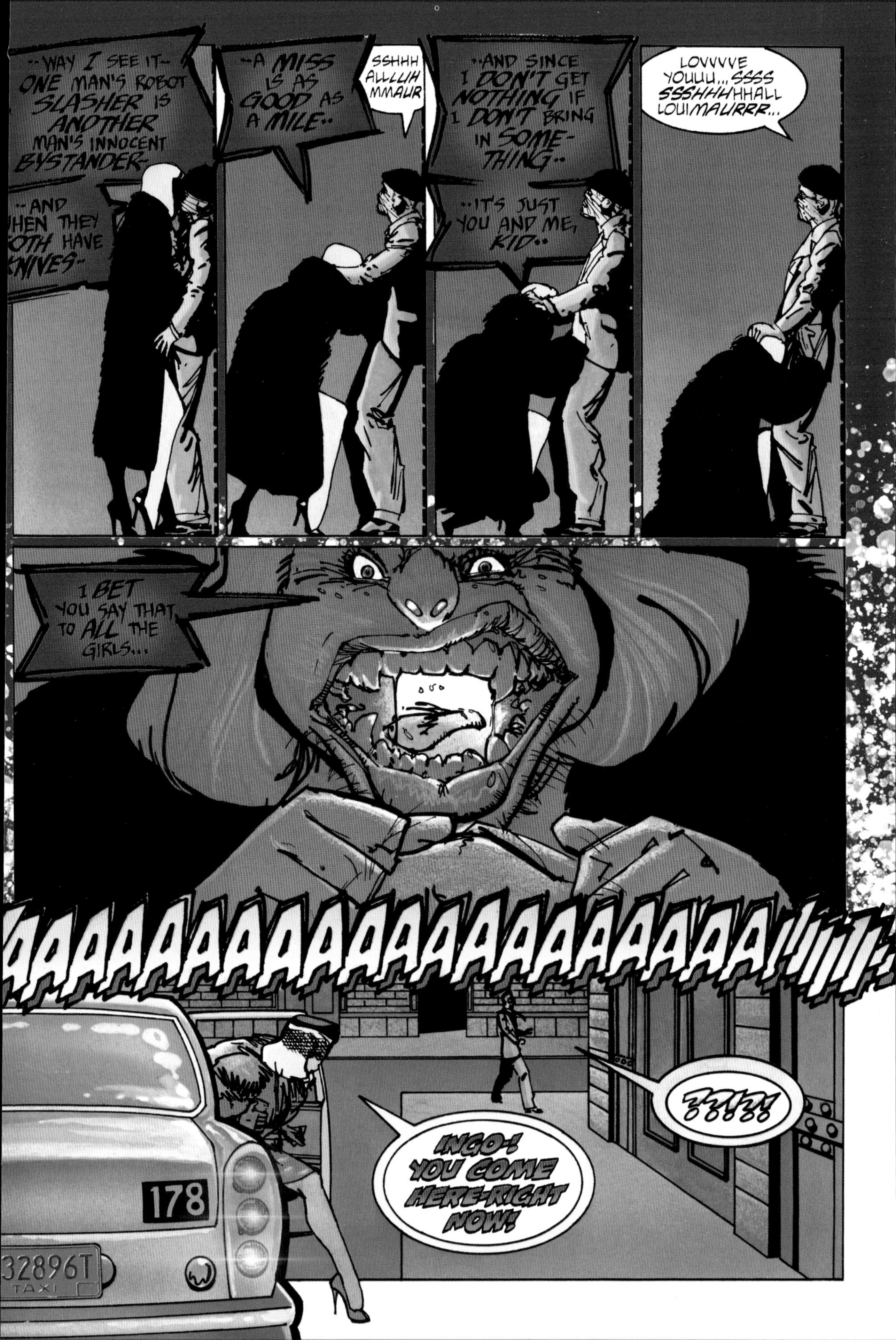

--WAY I SEE IT-- ONE MAN'S ROBOT SLASHER IS ANOTHER MAN'S INNOCENT BYSTANDER--
--AND HEN THEY OTH HAVE KNIVES--
--A MISS IS AS GOOD AS A MILE--
SSHHH ALLLUH MMAUR
--AND SINCE I DON'T GET NOTHING IF I DON'T BRING IN SOME-THING--
--IT'S JUST YOU AND ME, KID--
LOVVVVE YOUUU... SSSS SSSHHHHHALL LOUIMAURRR...
I BET YOU SAY THAT TO ALL THE GIRLS...
AAAAAAAAAAAAAAAAAAAAIIIII!
INGO-! YOU COME HERE-RIGHT NOW!
178
32896T
TAXI

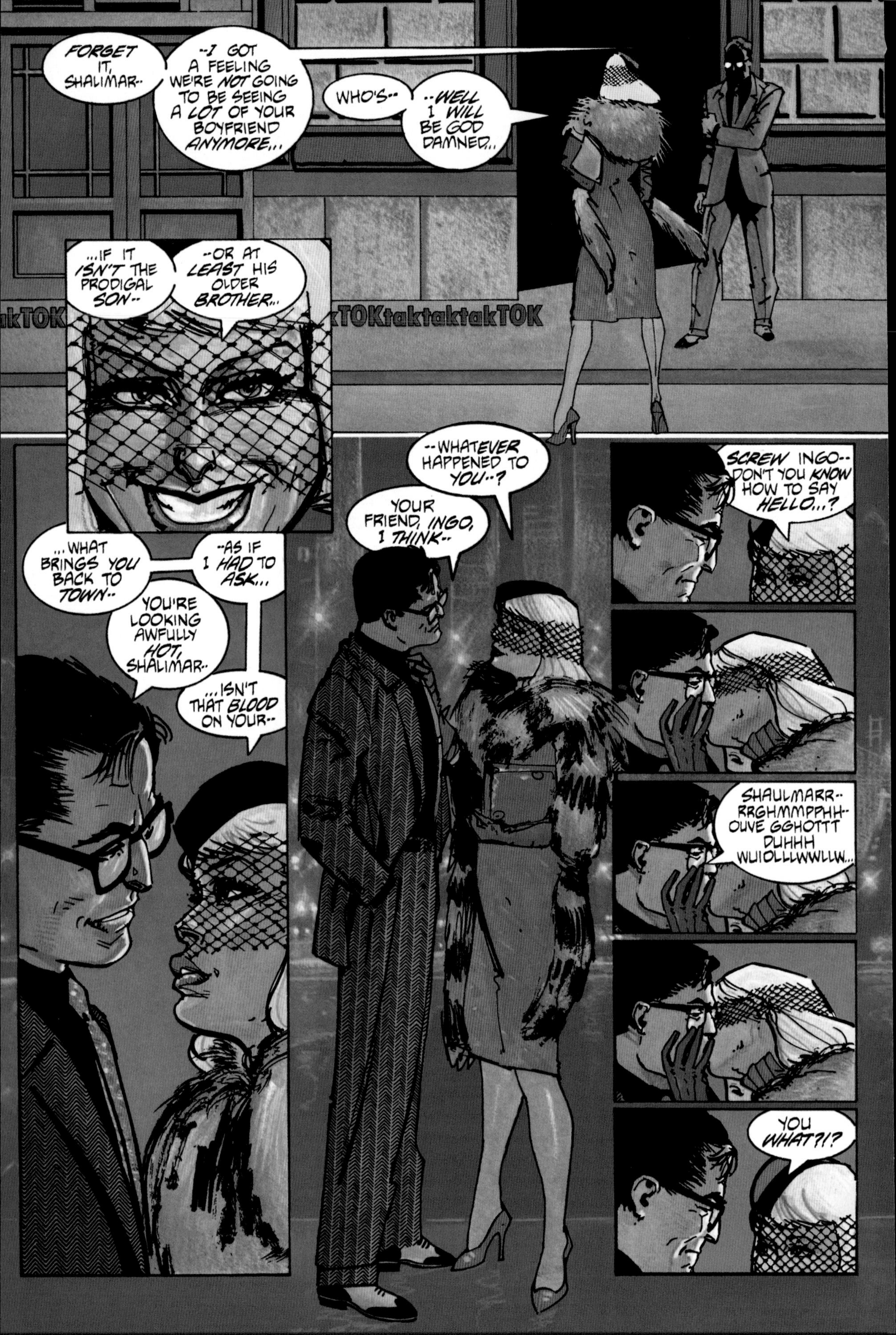
FORGET IT, SHALIMAR--
--I GOT A FEELING WE'RE NOT GOING TO BE SEEING A LOT OF YOUR BOYFRIEND ANYMORE...
WHO'S--
...WELL I WILL BE GOD DAMNED...
...IF IT ISN'T THE PRODIGAL SON--
--OR AT LEAST HIS OLDER BROTHER...
taktakTOKtaktaktakTOK
--WHATEVER HAPPENED TO YOU..?
YOUR FRIEND, INGO, I THINK--
SCREW INGO-- DON'T YOU KNOW HOW TO SAY HELLO...?
...WHAT BRINGS YOU BACK TO TOWN--
--AS IF I HAD TO ASK...
YOU'RE LOOKING AWFULLY HOT, SHALIMAR--
...ISN'T THAT BLOOD ON YOUR--
SHAULMARR-- RRGHMMPPHH-- OUVE GGHOTTT DUHHH WUIOLLLWWLLW...
YOU WHAT?!?

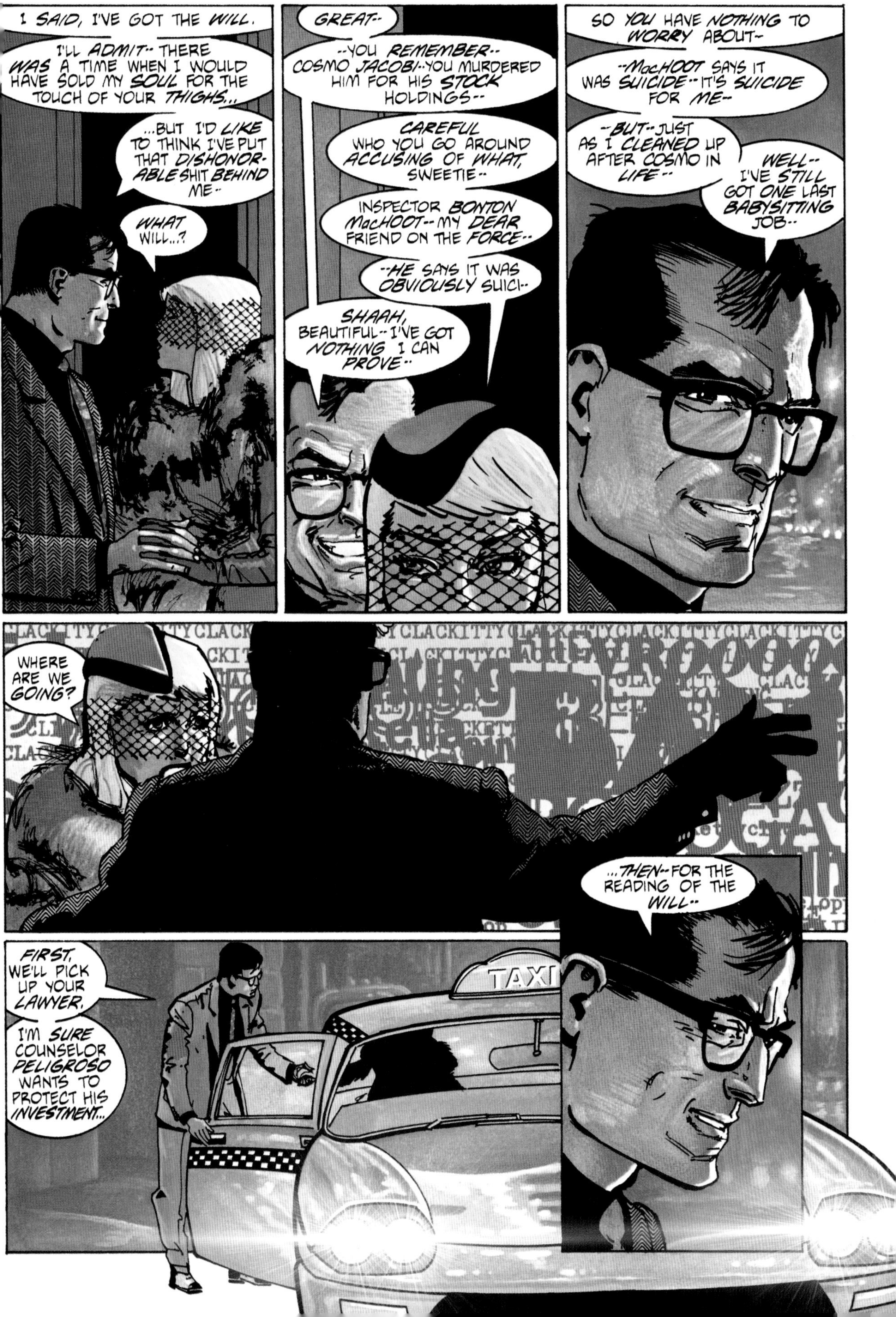

I SAID, I'VE GOT THE WILL.
I'LL ADMIT-- THERE WAS A TIME WHEN I WOULD HAVE SOLD MY SOUL FOR THE TOUCH OF YOUR THIGHS...
...BUT I'D LIKE TO THINK I'VE PUT THAT DISHONOR-ABLE SHIT BEHIND ME--
WHAT WILL...?
GREAT--
--YOU REMEMBER-- COSMO JACOBI--YOU MURDERED HIM FOR HIS STOCK HOLDINGS--
CAREFUL WHO YOU GO AROUND ACCUSING OF WHAT, SWEETIE--
INSPECTOR BONTON MacHOOT-- MY DEAR FRIEND ON THE FORCE--
--HE SAYS IT WAS OBVIOUSLY SUICI--
SHAAH, BEAUTIFUL-- I'VE GOT NOTHING I CAN PROVE--
SO YOU HAVE NOTHING TO WORRY ABOUT--
--MacHOOT SAYS IT WAS SUICIDE-- IT'S SUICIDE FOR ME--
--BUT-- JUST AS I CLEANED UP AFTER COSMO IN LIFE--
WELL-- I'VE STILL GOT ONE LAST BABYSITTING JOB--
WHERE ARE WE GOING?
...THEN-- FOR THE READING OF THE WILL--
FIRST, WE'LL PICK UP YOUR LAWYER.
I'M SURE COUNSELOR PELIGROSO WANTS TO PROTECT HIS INVESTMENT...
TAXI

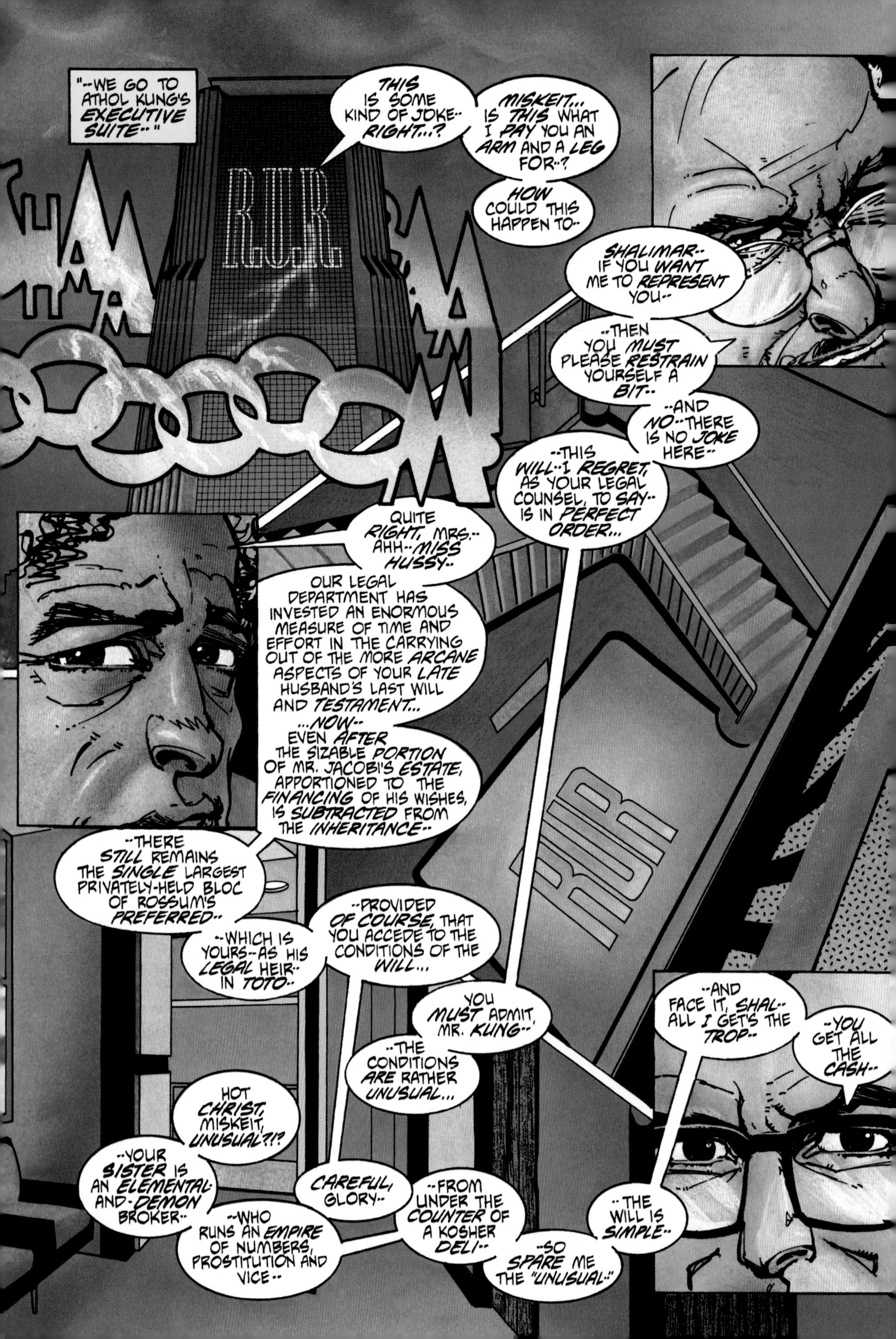

"--WE GO TO ATHOL KUNG'S EXECUTIVE SUITE--"
R.U.R.
THIS IS SOME KIND OF JOKE-- RIGHT...?
MISKEIT... IS THIS WHAT I PAY YOU AN ARM AND A LEG FOR--?
HOW COULD THIS HAPPEN TO--
SHALIMAR-- IF YOU WANT ME TO REPRESENT YOU--
--THEN YOU MUST PLEASE RESTRAIN YOURSELF A BIT--
--AND NO--THERE IS NO JOKE HERE--
--THIS WILL--I REGRET, AS YOUR LEGAL COUNSEL, TO SAY-- IS IN PERFECT ORDER...
QUITE RIGHT, MRS.-- AHH--MISS HUSSY--
OUR LEGAL DEPARTMENT HAS INVESTED AN ENORMOUS MEASURE OF TIME AND EFFORT IN THE CARRYING OUT OF THE MORE ARCANE ASPECTS OF YOUR LATE HUSBAND'S LAST WILL AND TESTAMENT... ...NOW-- EVEN AFTER THE SIZABLE PORTION OF MR. JACOBI'S ESTATE, APPORTIONED TO THE FINANCING OF HIS WISHES, IS SUBTRACTED FROM THE INHERITANCE--
--THERE STILL REMAINS THE SINGLE LARGEST PRIVATELY-HELD BLOC OF ROSSUM'S PREFERRED--
--WHICH IS YOURS--AS HIS LEGAL HEIR-- IN TOTO--
--PROVIDED OF COURSE, THAT YOU ACCEDE TO THE CONDITIONS OF THE WILL...
RUR
YOU MUST ADMIT, MR. KUNG--
--THE CONDITIONS ARE RATHER UNUSUAL...
--AND FACE IT, SHAL-- ALL I GET'S THE TROP--
--YOU GET ALL THE CASH--
HOT CHRIST, MISKEIT, UNUSUAL?!?
--YOUR SISTER IS AN ELEMENTAL-AND-DEMON BROKER--
--WHO RUNS AN EMPIRE OF NUMBERS, PROSTITUTION AND VICE--
CAREFUL, GLORY--
--FROM UNDER THE COUNTER OF A KOSHER DELI--
--THE WILL IS SIMPLE--
--SO SPARE ME THE "UNUSUAL."

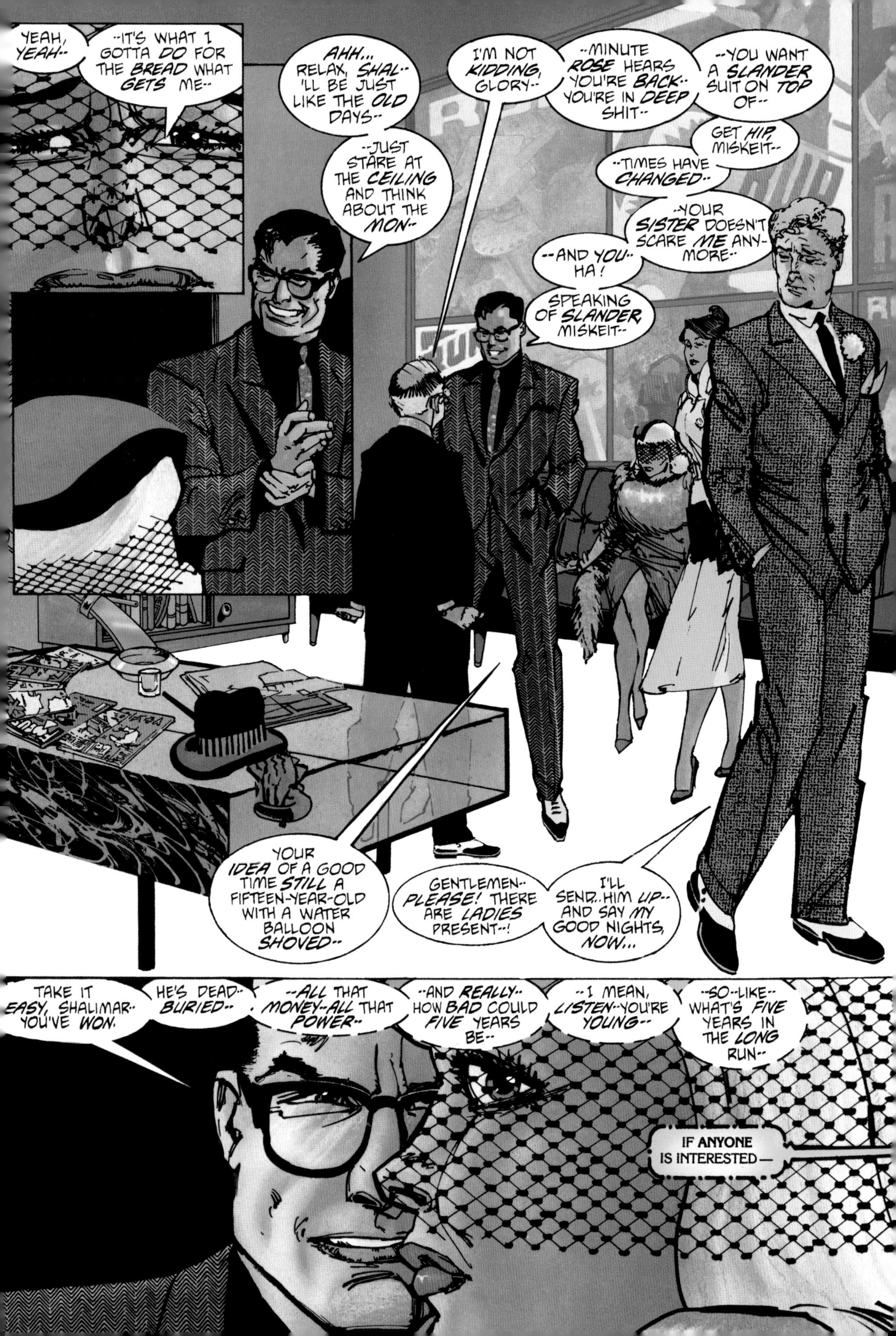
YEAH, YEAH--
--IT'S WHAT I GOTTA DO FOR THE BREAD WHAT GETS ME--
AHH... RELAX, SHAL-- 'LL BE JUST LIKE THE OLD DAYS--
--JUST STARE AT THE CEILING AND THINK ABOUT THE MON--
I'M NOT KIDDING, GLORY--
--MINUTE ROSE HEARS YOU'RE BACK-- YOU'RE IN DEEP SHIT--
--YOU WANT A SLANDER SUIT ON TOP OF--
GET HIP, MISKEIT--
--TIMES HAVE CHANGED--
--YOUR SISTER DOESN'T SCARE ME ANY-MORE--
--AND YOU-- HA!
SPEAKING OF SLANDER, MISKEIT--
YOUR IDEA OF A GOOD TIME STILL A FIFTEEN-YEAR-OLD WITH A WATER BALLOON SHOVED--
GENTLEMEN-- PLEASE! THERE ARE LADIES PRESENT--!
I'LL SEND.. HIM UP-- AND SAY MY GOOD NIGHTS, NOW...
TAKE IT EASY, SHALIMAR-- YOU'VE WON.
HE'S DEAD-- BURIED--
--ALL THAT MONEY--ALL THAT POWER--
--AND REALLY-- HOW BAD COULD FIVE YEARS BE--
--I MEAN, LISTEN--YOU'RE YOUNG--
--SO--LIKE-- WHAT'S FIVE YEARS IN THE LONG RUN--
IF ANYONE IS INTERESTED—

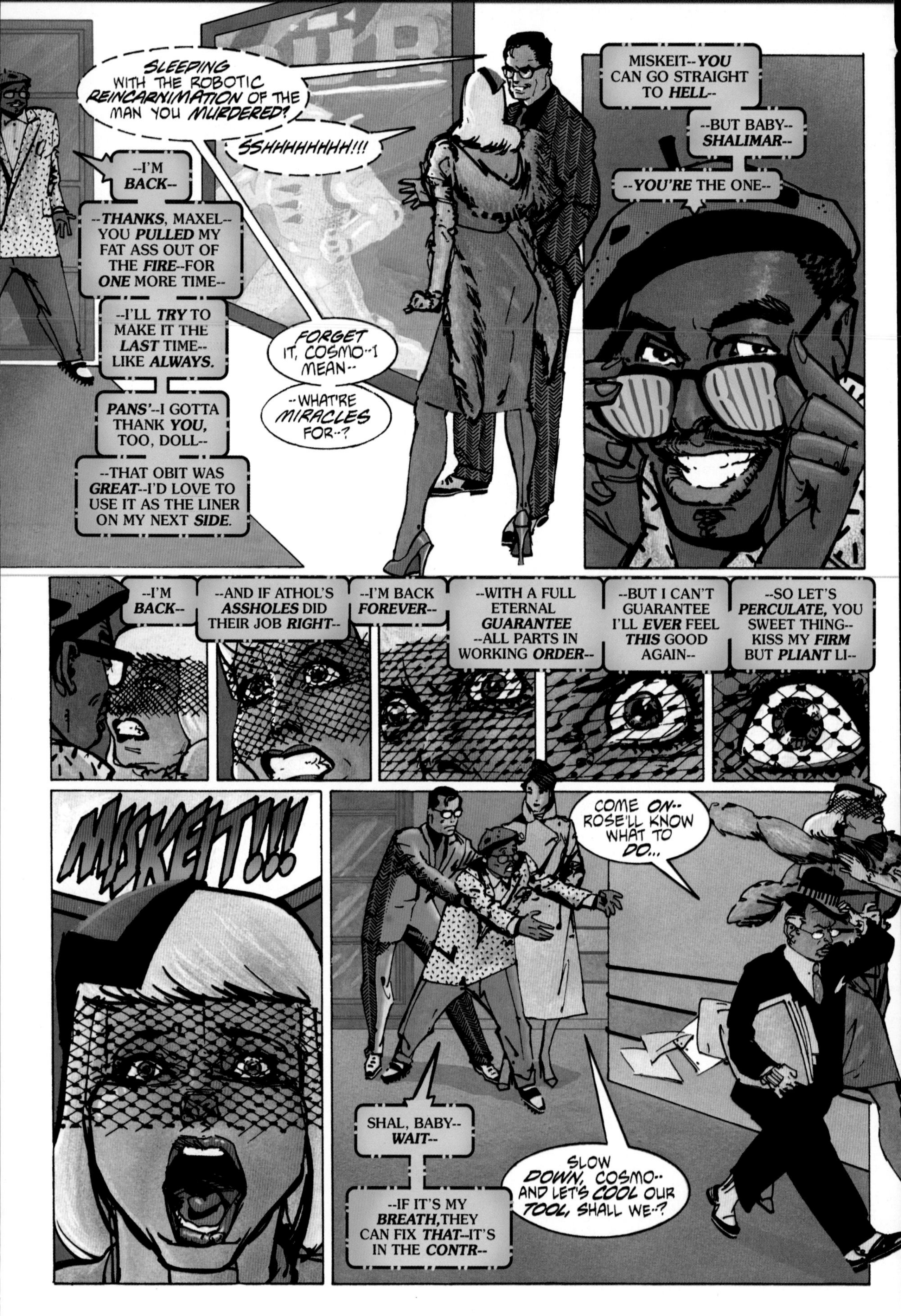

SLEEPING WITH THE ROBOTIC REINCARNIMATION OF THE MAN YOU MURDERED?
SSHHHHHHHH!!!
--I'M BACK--
--THANKS, MAXEL--YOU PULLED MY FAT ASS OUT OF THE FIRE--FOR ONE MORE TIME--
--I'LL TRY TO MAKE IT THE LAST TIME--LIKE ALWAYS.
PANS'--I GOTTA THANK YOU, TOO, DOLL--
--THAT OBIT WAS GREAT--I'D LOVE TO USE IT AS THE LINER ON MY NEXT SIDE.
FORGET IT, COSMO--I MEAN--
--WHAT'RE MIRACLES FOR--?
MISKEIT--YOU CAN GO STRAIGHT TO HELL--
--BUT BABY--SHALIMAR--
--YOU'RE THE ONE--
--I'M BACK--
--AND IF ATHOL'S ASSHOLES DID THEIR JOB RIGHT--
--I'M BACK FOREVER--
--WITH A FULL ETERNAL GUARANTEE --ALL PARTS IN WORKING ORDER--
--BUT I CAN'T GUARANTEE I'LL EVER FEEL THIS GOOD AGAIN--
--SO LET'S PERCULATE, YOU SWEET THING--KISS MY FIRM BUT PLIANT LI--
MISKEIT!!!
COME ON--ROSE'LL KNOW WHAT TO DO...
SHAL, BABY--WAIT--
--IF IT'S MY BREATH, THEY CAN FIX THAT--IT'S IN THE CONTR--
SLOW DOWN, COSMO--AND LET'S COOL OUR TOOL, SHALL WE--?

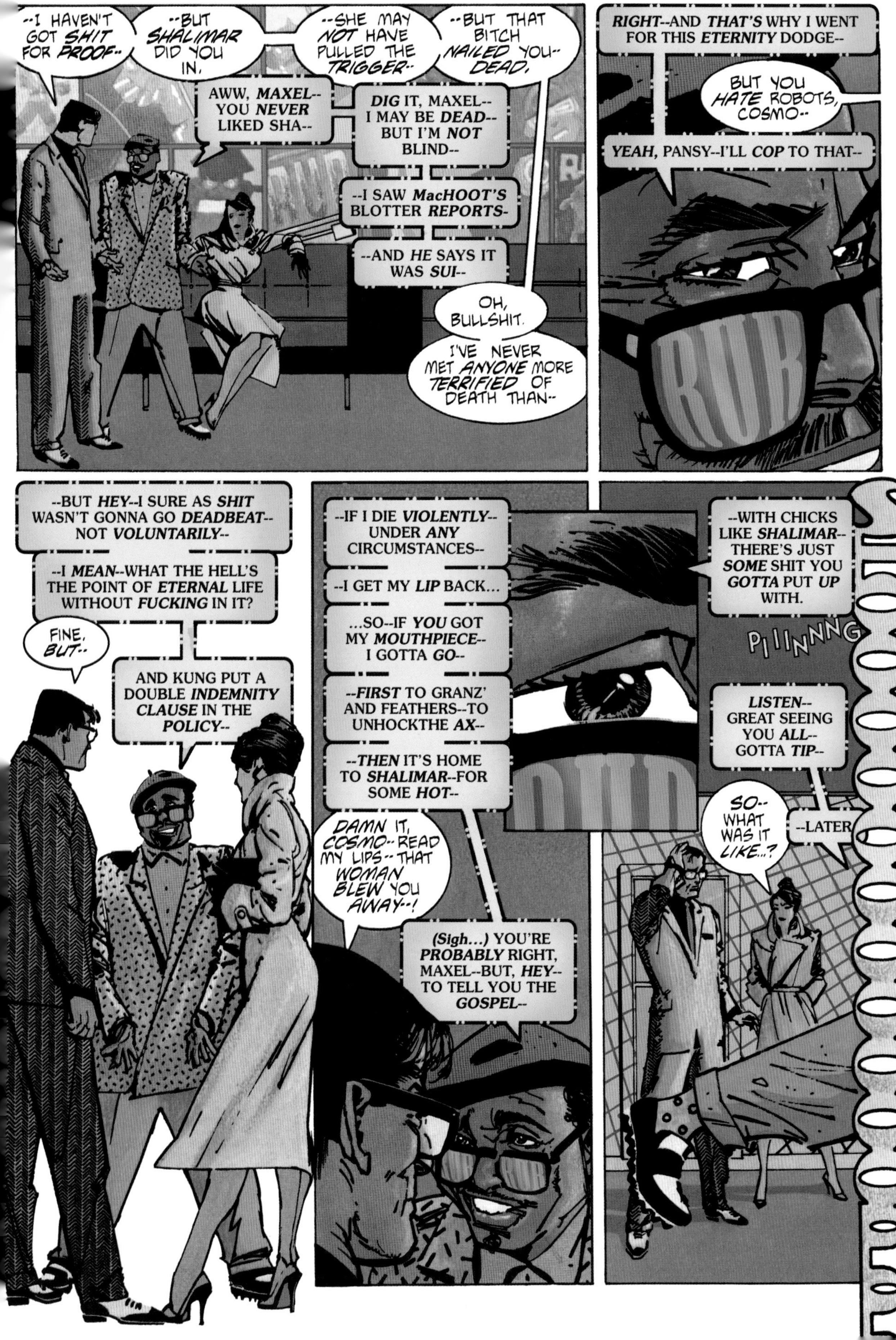
--I HAVEN'T GOT SHIT FOR PROOF--
--BUT SHALIMAR DID YOU IN,
--SHE MAY NOT HAVE PULLED THE TRIGGER--
--BUT THAT BITCH NAILED YOU--DEAD,
AWW, MAXEL--YOU NEVER LIKED SHA--
DIG IT, MAXEL--I MAY BE DEAD--BUT I'M NOT BLIND--
--I SAW MacHOOT'S BLOTTER REPORTS-
--AND HE SAYS IT WAS SUI--
OH, BULLSHIT.
I'VE NEVER MET ANYONE MORE TERRIFIED OF DEATH THAN--
RIGHT--AND THAT'S WHY I WENT FOR THIS ETERNITY DODGE--
BUT YOU HATE ROBOTS, COSMO--
YEAH, PANSY--I'LL COP TO THAT--
--BUT HEY--I SURE AS SHIT WASN'T GONNA GO DEADBEAT--NOT VOLUNTARILY--
--I MEAN--WHAT THE HELL'S THE POINT OF ETERNAL LIFE WITHOUT FUCKING IN IT?
FINE, BUT--
AND KUNG PUT A DOUBLE INDEMNITY CLAUSE IN THE POLICY--
--IF I DIE VIOLENTLY--UNDER ANY CIRCUMSTANCES--
--I GET MY LIP BACK...
...SO--IF YOU GOT MY MOUTHPIECE--I GOTTA GO--
--FIRST TO GRANZ' AND FEATHERS--TO UNHOCKTHE AX--
--THEN IT'S HOME TO SHALIMAR--FOR SOME HOT--
DAMN IT, COSMO--READ MY LIPS--THAT WOMAN BLEW YOU AWAY--!
(Sigh...) YOU'RE PROBABLY RIGHT, MAXEL--BUT, HEY--TO TELL YOU THE GOSPEL--
--WITH CHICKS LIKE SHALIMAR--THERE'S JUST SOME SHIT YOU GOTTA PUT UP WITH.
PIIINNNG
LISTEN--GREAT SEEING YOU ALL--GOTTA TIP--
SO--WHAT WAS IT LIKE...?
--LATER

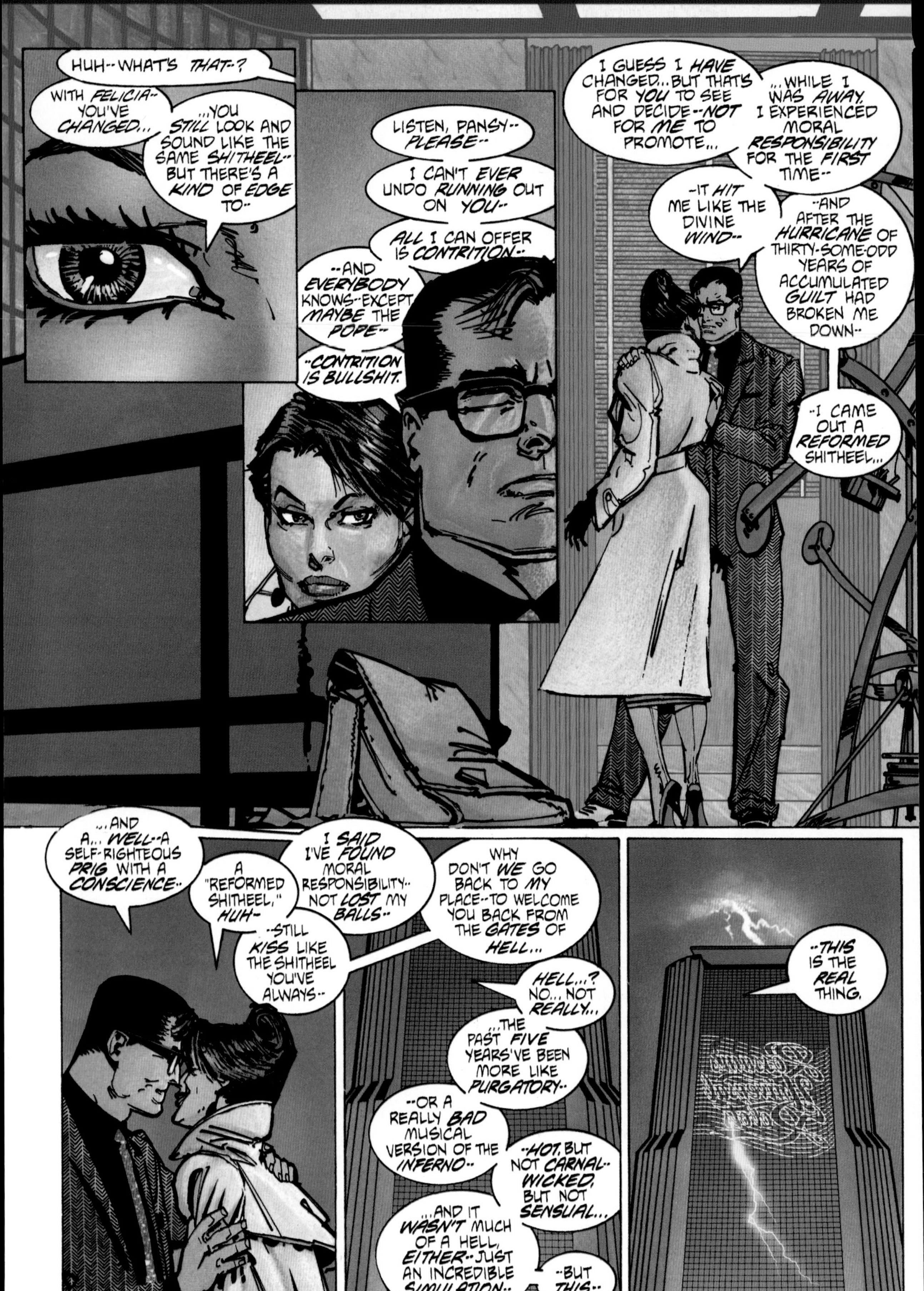
HUH-- WHAT'S THAT--?
WITH FELICIA-- YOU'VE CHANGED...
...YOU STILL LOOK AND SOUND LIKE THE SAME SHITHEEL-- BUT THERE'S A KIND OF EDGE TO--
LISTEN, PANSY-- PLEASE--
I CAN'T EVER UNDO RUNNING OUT ON YOU--
ALL I CAN OFFER IS CONTRITION--
--AND EVERYBODY KNOWS-- EXCEPT MAYBE THE POPE--
--CONTRITION IS BULLSHIT.
I GUESS I HAVE CHANGED... BUT THAT'S FOR YOU TO SEE AND DECIDE--NOT FOR ME TO PROMOTE...
...WHILE I WAS AWAY, I EXPERIENCED MORAL RESPONSIBILITY FOR THE FIRST TIME--
--IT HIT ME LIKE THE DIVINE WIND--
--AND AFTER THE HURRICANE OF THIRTY-SOME-ODD YEARS OF ACCUMULATED GUILT HAD BROKEN ME DOWN--
--I CAME OUT A REFORMED SHITHEEL...
...AND A... WELL--A SELF-RIGHTEOUS PRIG WITH A CONSCIENCE--
A "REFORMED SHITHEEL," HUH--
I SAID I'VE FOUND MORAL RESPONSIBILITY-- NOT LOST MY BALLS--
--STILL KISS LIKE THE SHITHEEL YOU'VE ALWAYS--
WHY DON'T WE GO BACK TO MY PLACE--TO WELCOME YOU BACK FROM THE GATES OF HELL...
HELL...? NO... NOT REALLY...
...THE PAST FIVE YEARS'VE BEEN MORE LIKE PURGATORY--
--OR A REALLY BAD MUSICAL VERSION OF THE INFERNO--
--HOT, BUT NOT CARNAL-- WICKED, BUT NOT SENSUAL...
...AND IT WASN'T MUCH OF A HELL, EITHER-- JUST AN INCREDIBLE SIMULATION--
--BUT THIS--
--THIS IS THE REAL THING.

A tuned-out guy...
a turned-on doll...
and a psychosexual police
car on the prowl...

First it is an undertone,
subtle and tentative,
honking and choking behind
the blunt clamor of the
klaxon fugue...

Then it is a harmony,
gliding erotically against
the subdued roar of the wet
midnight street...

Now it is a counterpoint,
seductively retracing the
melody, reclaiming its
elegance from the urban
ensemble...

And finally a voice,
growling and caressing
a language beyond human
comprehension —yet rife
with meaning, both
universal and transcendent...

...there'll be hell to pay.

This version of the *Black Mariah* cover was completed, but ultimately rejected.

The SATISFACTION of BLACK MARIAH

originally published
SEPTEMBER, 1987
story and art
HOWARD CHAYKIN
color
**STEVE OLIFF
& RICHARD ORY**
letters
KEN BRUZENAK
special thanks
JOHN MOORE
editor
RICK OLIVER

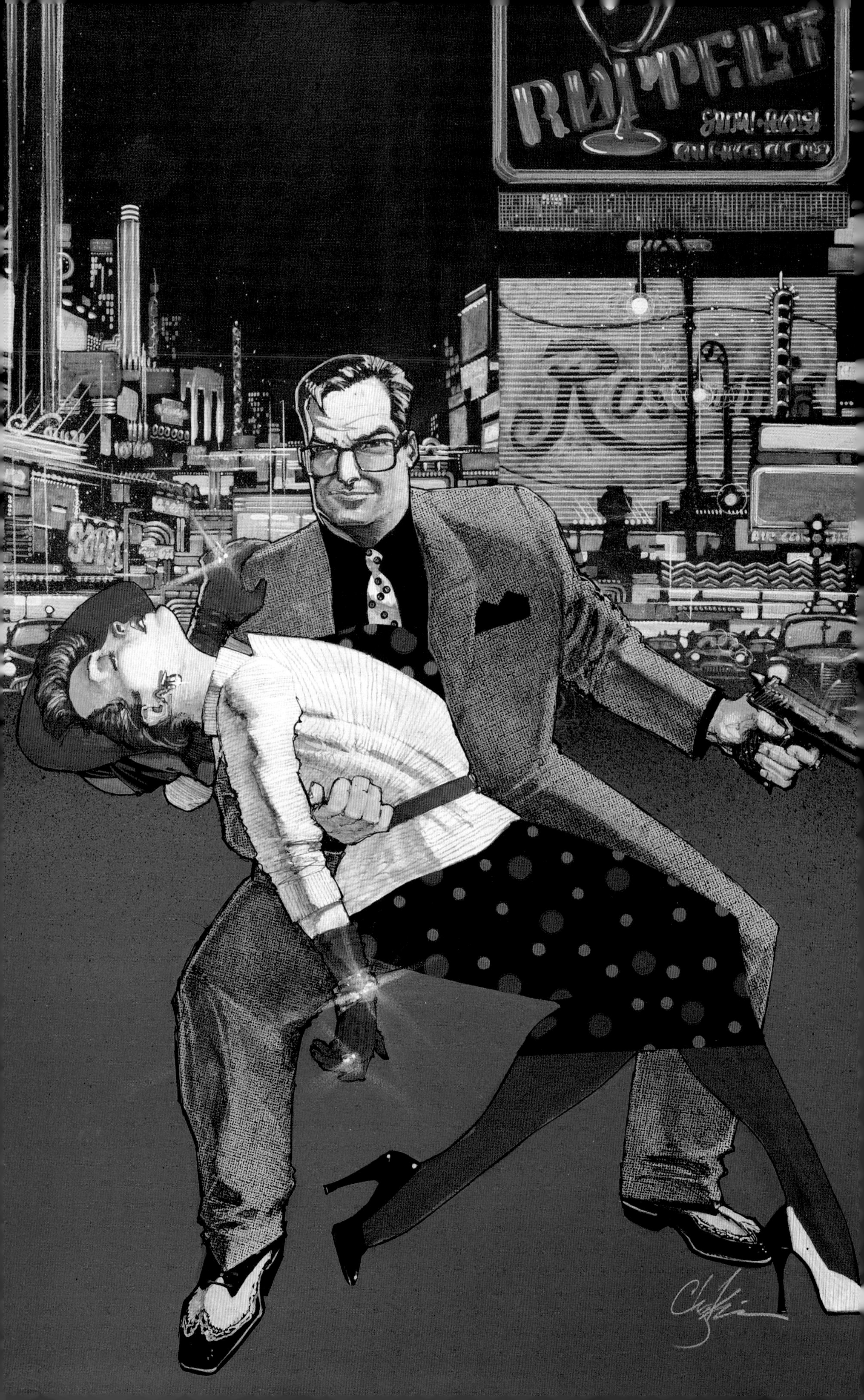

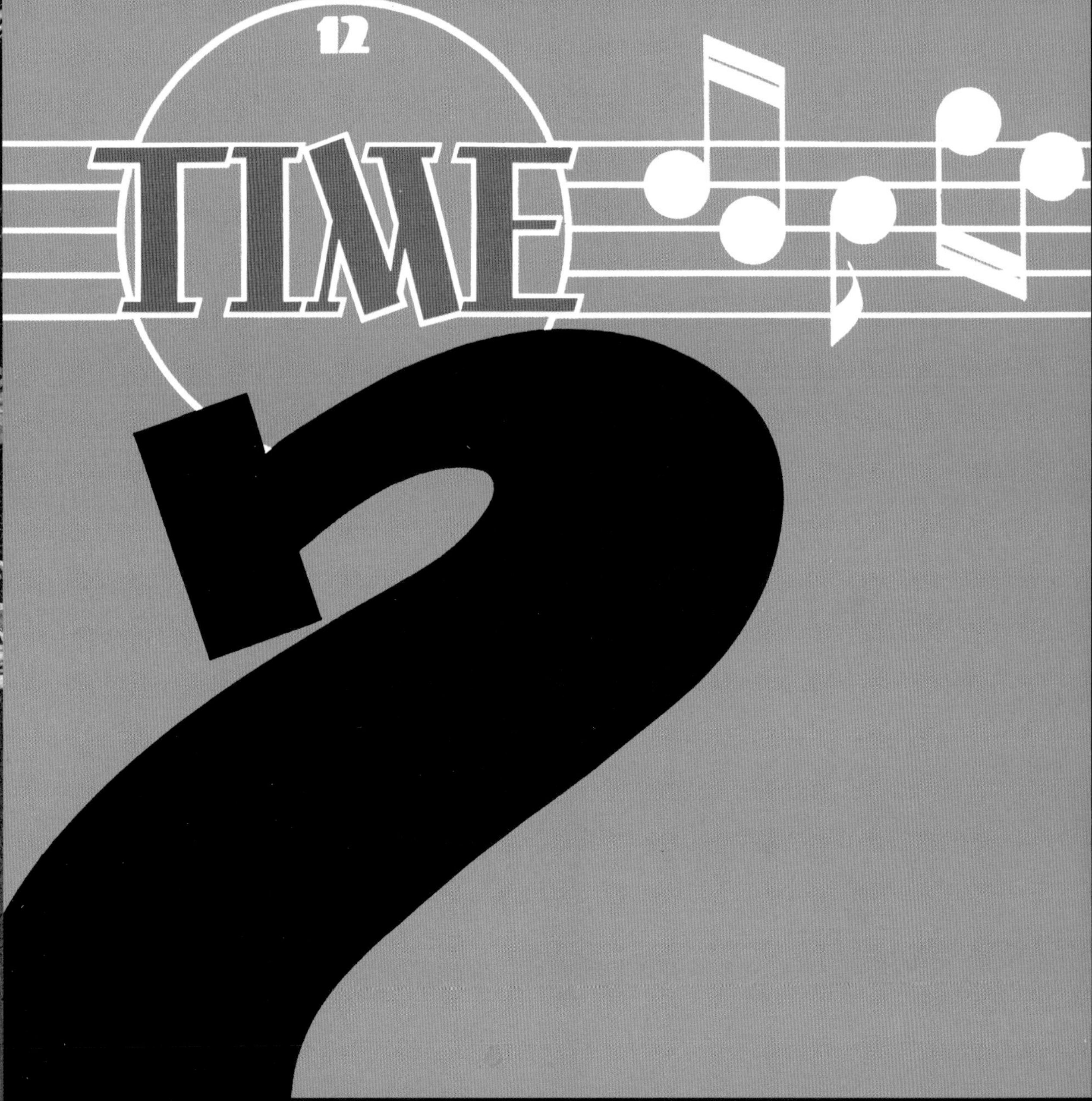
12
TIME
2

The SATISFACTION of BLACK MARIAH

A charm to soothe the savage breast

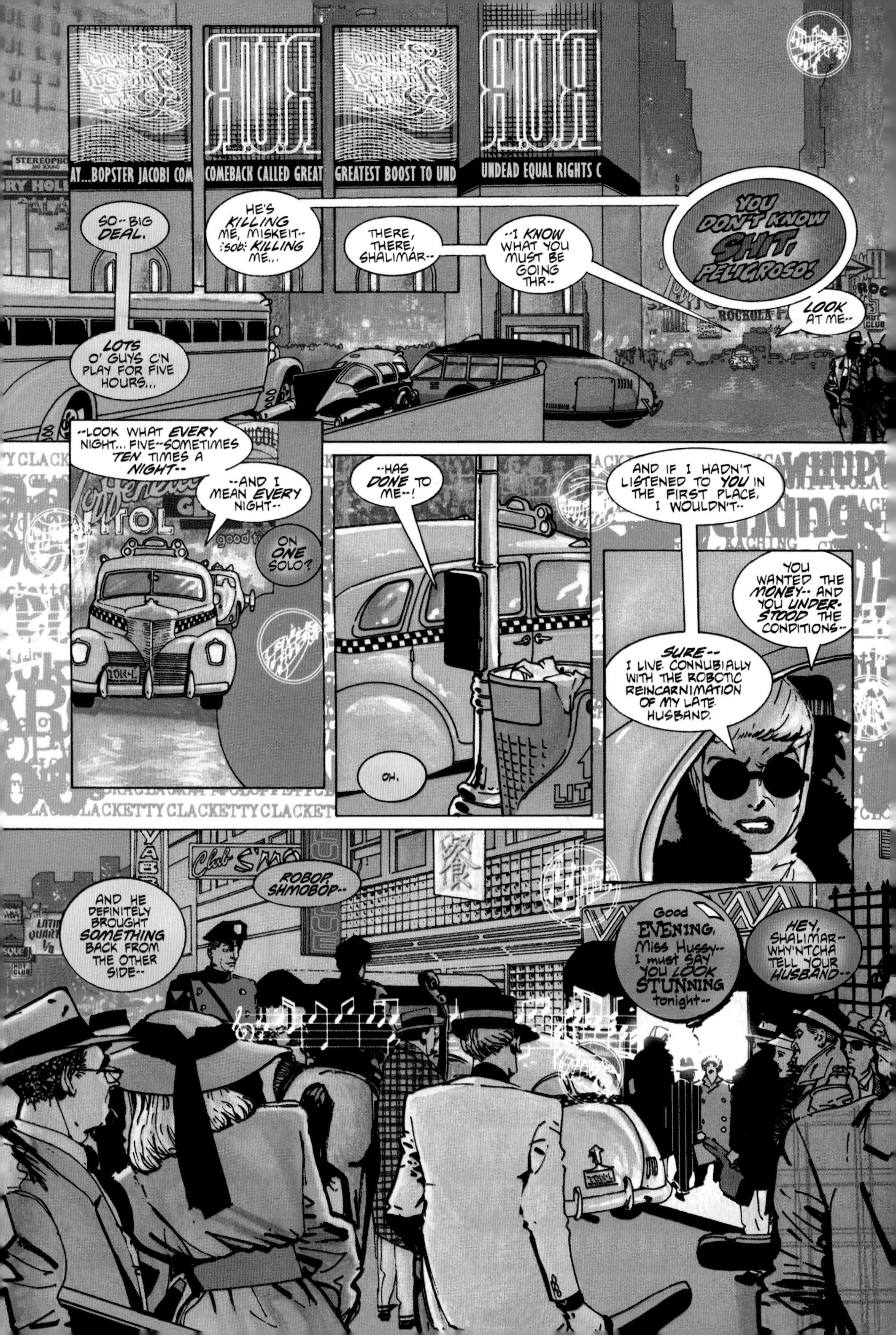
AY...BOPSTER JACOBI COM
COMEBACK CALLED GREAT
GREATEST BOOST TO UND
UNDEAD EQUAL RIGHTS C
SO--BIG DEAL.
HE'S KILLING ME, MISKEIT-- :SOB: KILLING ME...
THERE, THERE, SHALIMAR--
--I KNOW WHAT YOU MUST BE GOING THR--
YOU DON'T KNOW SHIT, PELIGROSO!
LOOK AT ME--
LOTS O' GUYS C'N PLAY FOR FIVE HOURS...
--LOOK WHAT EVERY NIGHT... FIVE--SOMETIMES TEN TIMES A NIGHT--
--AND I MEAN EVERY NIGHT--
ON ONE SOLO?
--HAS DONE TO ME--!
OH.
AND IF I HADN'T LISTENED TO YOU IN THE FIRST PLACE, I WOULDN'T--
YOU WANTED THE MONEY-- AND YOU UNDER-STOOD THE CONDITIONS--
SURE-- I LIVE CONNUBIALLY WITH THE ROBOTIC REINCARNIMATION OF MY LATE HUSBAND.
CLACKETTY CLACKETTY CLACKET
ROBOP, SHMOBOP--
AND HE DEFINITELY BROUGHT SOMETHING BACK FROM THE OTHER SIDE--
Good EVENING, Miss Hussy-- I must SAY you LOOK STUNNING tonight--
HEY, SHALIMAR-- WHY'NTCHA TELL YOUR HUSBAND--

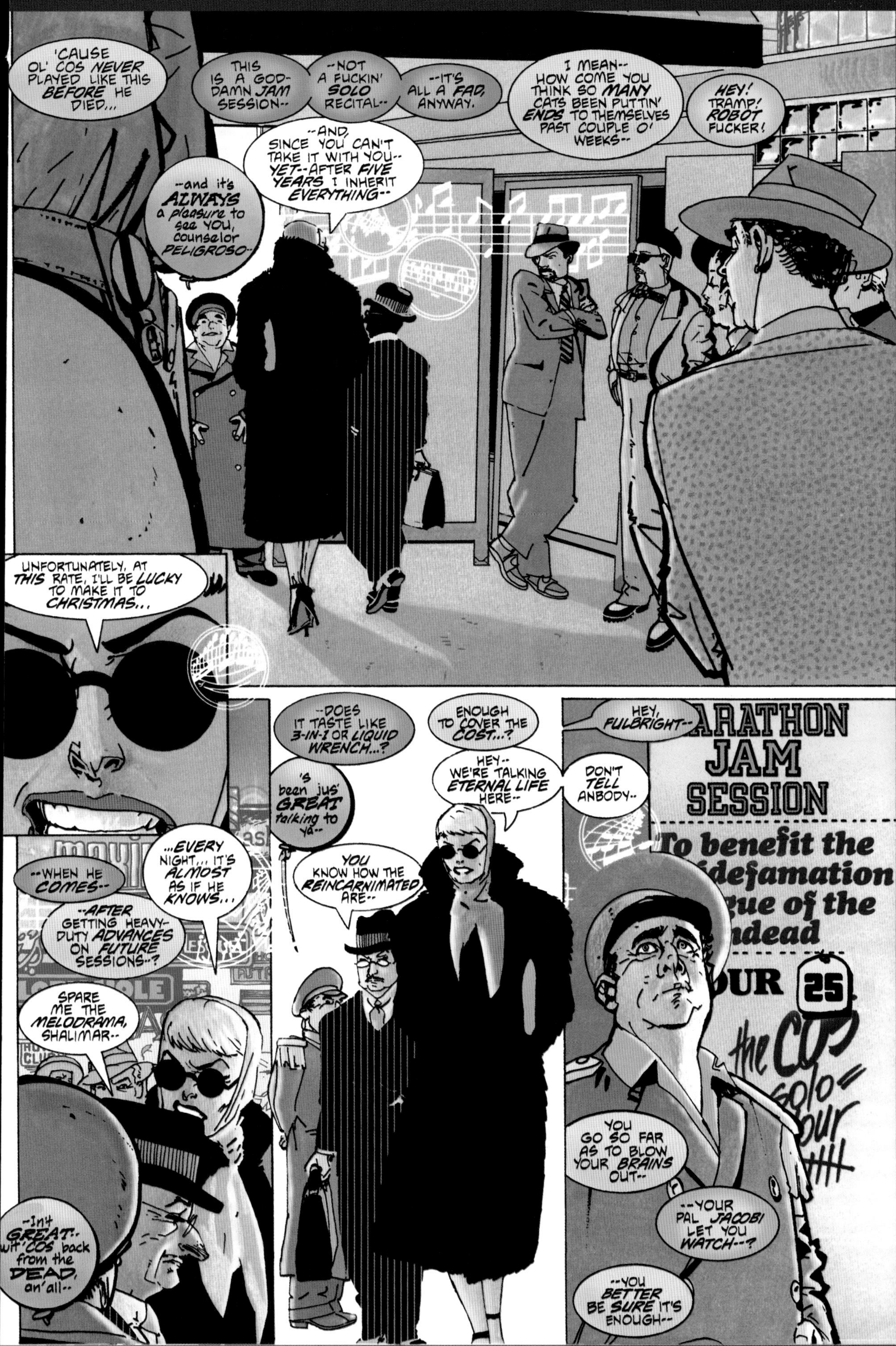
'CAUSE OL' COS NEVER PLAYED LIKE THIS BEFORE HE DIED...
THIS IS A GOD-DAMN JAM SESSION--
--NOT A FUCKIN' SOLO RECITAL--
--IT'S ALL A FAD, ANYWAY.
I MEAN-- HOW COME YOU THINK SO MANY CATS BEEN PUTTIN' ENDS TO THEMSELVES PAST COUPLE O' WEEKS--
HEY! TRAMP! ROBOT FUCKER!
--and it's ALWAYS a pleasure to see YOU, counselor PELIGROSO--
--AND, SINCE YOU CAN'T TAKE IT WITH YOU--YET--AFTER FIVE YEARS I INHERIT EVERYTHING--
UNFORTUNATELY, AT THIS RATE, I'LL BE LUCKY TO MAKE IT TO CHRISTMAS...
--DOES IT TASTE LIKE 3-IN-1 OR LIQUID WRENCH...?
ENOUGH TO COVER THE COST...?
HEY, FULBRIGHT--
ARATHON
JAM
SESSION
To benefit the
defamation
gue of the
ndead
OUR 25
HEY-- WE'RE TALKING ETERNAL LIFE HERE--
DON'T TELL ANBODY--
's been jus' GREAT talking to ya--
--WHEN HE COMES--
...EVERY NIGHT... IT'S ALMOST AS IF HE KNOWS...
--AFTER GETTING HEAVY-DUTY ADVANCES ON FUTURE SESSIONS--?
YOU KNOW HOW THE REINCARNIMATED ARE--
SPARE ME THE MELODRAMA, SHALIMAR--
YOU GO SO FAR AS TO BLOW YOUR BRAINS OUT--
--YOUR PAL JACOBI LET YOU WATCH--?
-Int GREAT.. wit' COS back from the DEAD, an'all--
--YOU BETTER BE SURE IT'S ENOUGH--

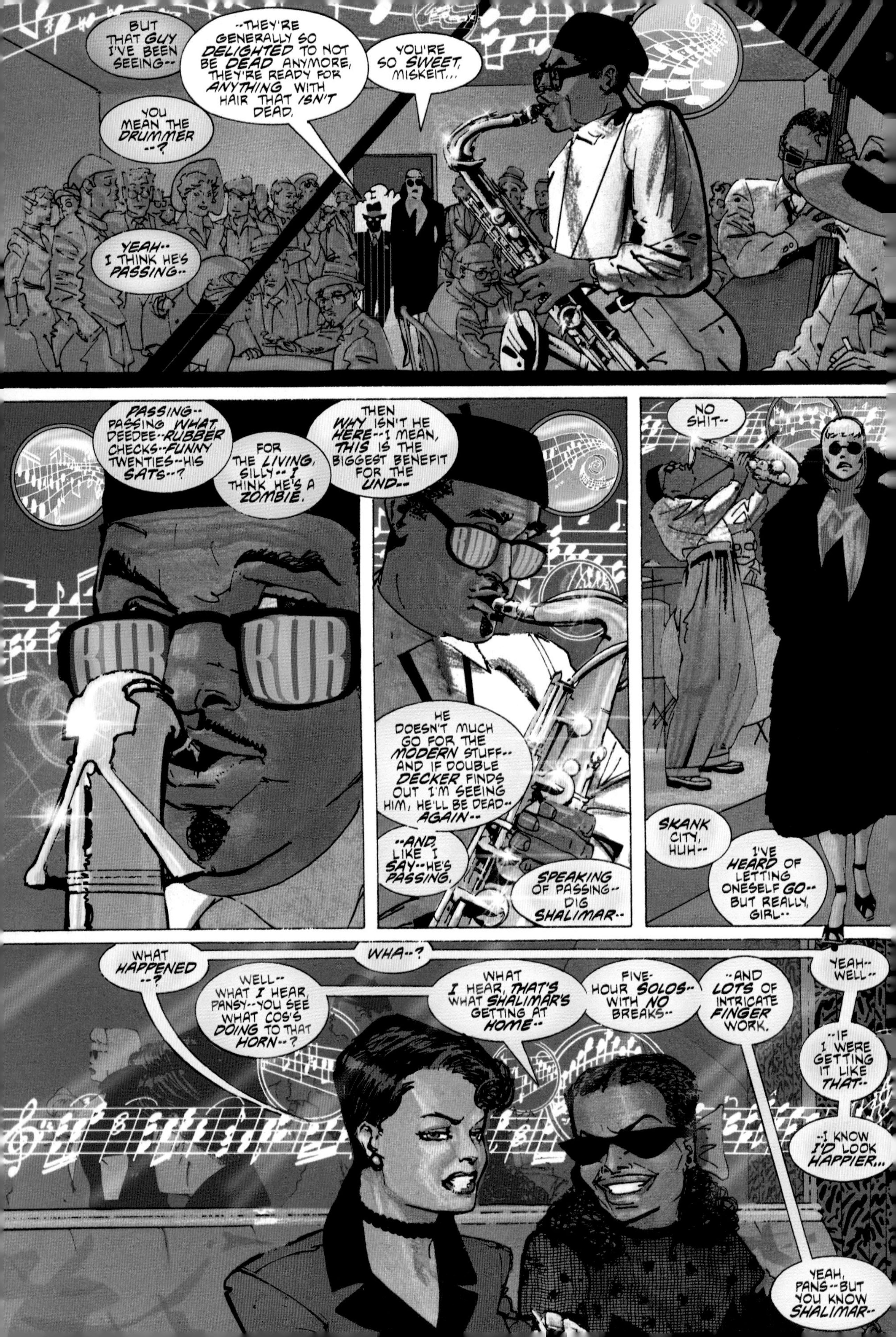
BUT THAT GUY I'VE BEEN SEEING--
--THEY'RE GENERALLY SO DELIGHTED TO NOT BE DEAD ANYMORE, THEY'RE READY FOR ANYTHING WITH HAIR THAT ISN'T DEAD.
YOU'RE SO SWEET, MISKEIT...
YOU MEAN THE DRUMMER --?
YEAH-- I THINK HE'S PASSING--
PASSING-- PASSING WHAT, DEEDEE--RUBBER CHECKS--FUNNY TWENTIES--HIS SATS--?
FOR THE LIVING, SILLY-- I THINK HE'S A ZOMBIE.
THEN WHY ISN'T HE HERE--I MEAN, THIS IS THE BIGGEST BENEFIT FOR THE UND--
RUB RUB
RUB RUB
HE DOESN'T MUCH GO FOR THE MODERN STUFF-- AND IF DOUBLE DECKER FINDS OUT I'M SEEING HIM, HE'LL BE DEAD-- AGAIN--
--AND, LIKE I SAY--HE'S PASSING.
SPEAKING OF PASSING-- DIG SHALIMAR--
NO SHIT--
SKANK CITY, HUH--
I'VE HEARD OF LETTING ONESELF GO-- BUT REALLY, GIRL--
WHAT HAPPENED --?
WHA--?
WELL-- WHAT I HEAR, PANSY--YOU SEE WHAT COS'S DOING TO THAT HORN--?
WHAT I HEAR, THAT'S WHAT SHALIMAR'S GETTING AT HOME--
FIVE-HOUR SOLOS-- WITH NO BREAKS--
--AND LOTS OF INTRICATE FINGER WORK.
YEAH-- WELL--
--IF I WERE GETTING IT LIKE THAT--
--I KNOW I'D LOOK HAPPIER...
YEAH, PANS--BUT YOU KNOW SHALIMAR--

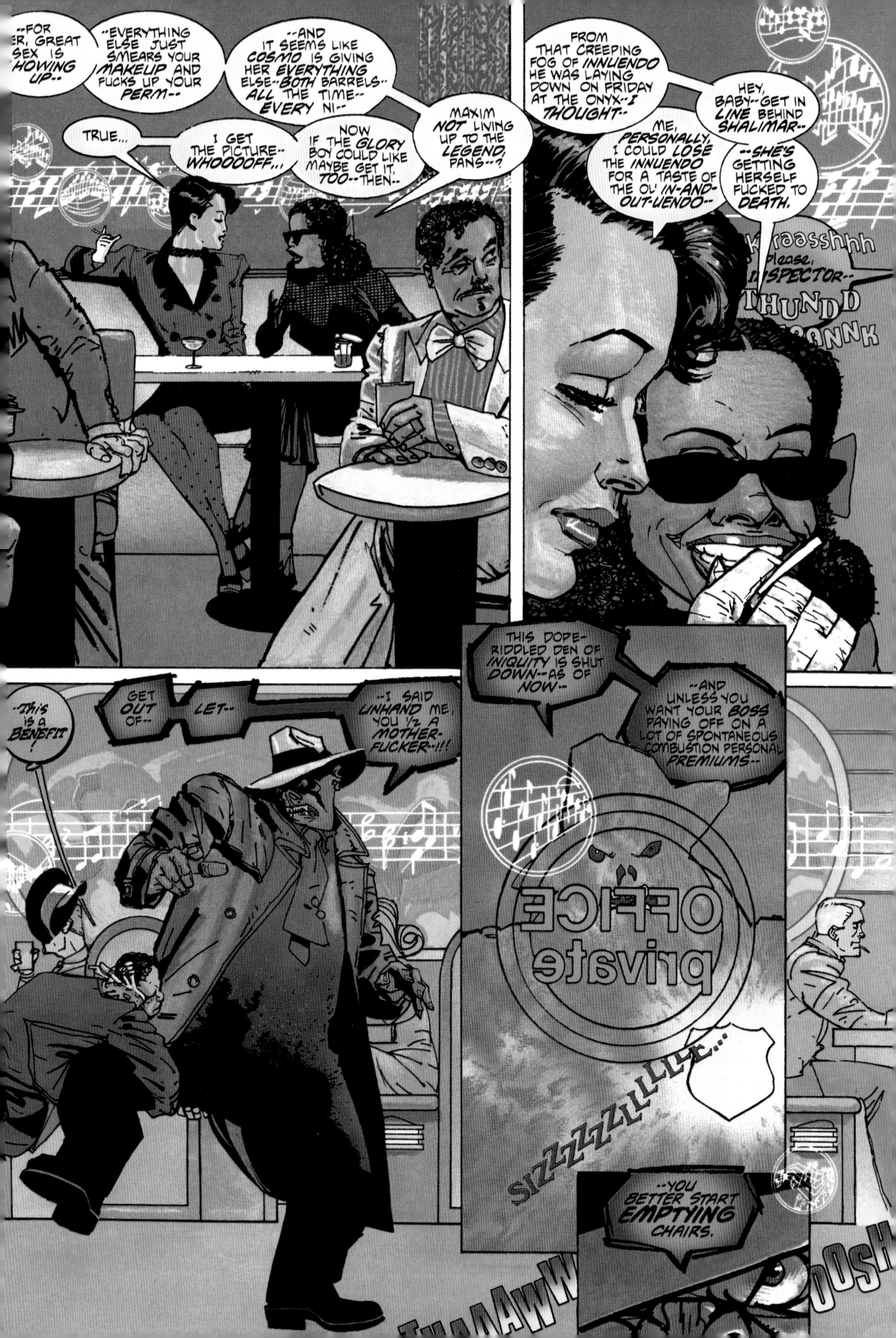
--FOR
ER, GREAT SEX IS HOWING UP--
"EVERYTHING ELSE JUST SMEARS YOUR MAKEUP AND FUCKS UP YOUR PERM--
--AND IT SEEMS LIKE COSMO IS GIVING HER EVERYTHING ELSE--BOTH BARRELS--ALL THE TIME--EVERY NI--
TRUE...
I GET THE PICTURE--WHOOOOFF...
NOW IF THE GLORY BOY COULD LIKE MAYBE GET IT, TOO--THEN--
MAXIM NOT LIVING UP TO THE LEGEND, PANS--?
FROM THAT CREEPING FOG OF INNUENDO HE WAS LAYING DOWN ON FRIDAY AT THE ONYX--I THOUGHT--
ME, PERSONALLY, I COULD LOSE THE INNUENDO FOR A TASTE OF THE OL' IN-AND-OUT-UENDO--
HEY, BABY--GET IN LINE BEHIND SHALIMAR--
--SHE'S GETTING HERSELF FUCKED TO DEATH.
raasshhh
please,
SPECTOR--
THUNDD
ANNK
THIS DOPE-RIDDLED DEN OF INIQUITY IS SHUT DOWN--AS OF NOW--
--AND UNLESS YOU WANT YOUR BOSS PAYING OFF ON A LOT OF SPONTANEOUS COMBUSTION PERSONAL PREMIUMS--
--This is a BENEFIT!
GET OUT OF--
LET--
--I SAID UNHAND ME, YOU ½ A MOTHER-FUCKER--!!!
OFFICE
private
SIZZZZZZLLLLLE...
--YOU BETTER START EMPTYING CHAIRS.
THAAAWW
OOSH

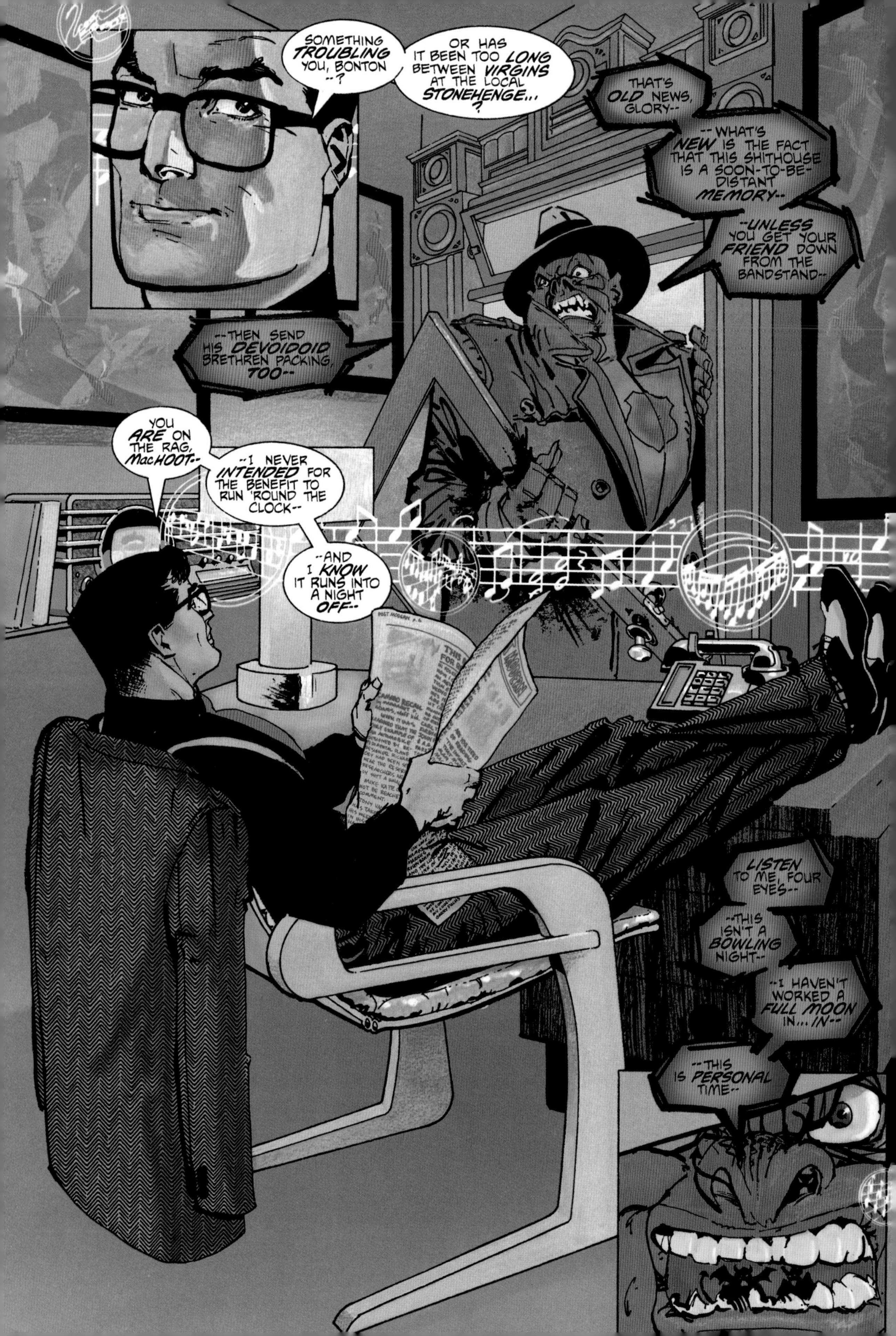
SOMETHING TROUBLING YOU, BONTON --?
OR HAS IT BEEN TOO LONG BETWEEN VIRGINS AT THE LOCAL STONEHENGE...?
THAT'S OLD NEWS, GLORY--
--WHAT'S NEW IS THE FACT THAT THIS SHITHOUSE IS A SOON-TO-BE-DISTANT MEMORY--
--UNLESS YOU GET YOUR FRIEND DOWN FROM THE BANDSTAND--
--THEN SEND HIS DEVOIDOID BRETHREN PACKING, TOO--
YOU ARE ON THE RAG, MacHOOT--
--I NEVER INTENDED FOR THE BENEFIT TO RUN 'ROUND THE CLOCK--
--AND I KNOW IT RUNS INTO A NIGHT OFF--
LISTEN TO ME, FOUR EYES--
--THIS ISN'T A BOWLING NIGHT--
--I HAVEN'T WORKED A FULL MOON IN... IN--
--THIS IS PERSONAL TIME--

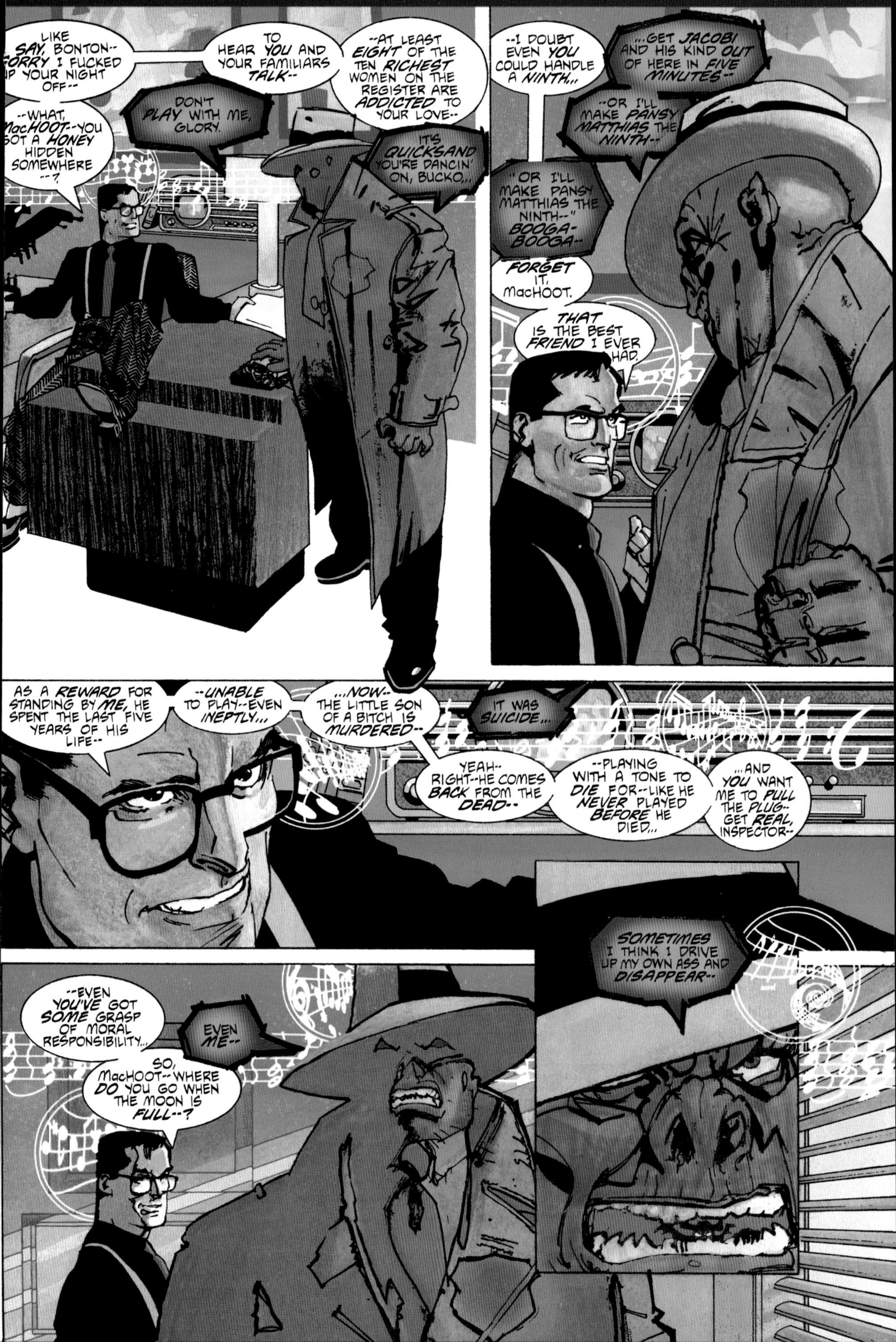

LIKE SAY, BONTON--
SORRY I FUCKED UP YOUR NIGHT OFF--
--WHAT, MacHOOT--YOU GOT A HONEY HIDDEN SOMEWHERE--?
TO HEAR YOU AND YOUR FAMILIARS TALK--
DON'T PLAY WITH ME, GLORY.
--AT LEAST EIGHT OF THE TEN RICHEST WOMEN ON THE REGISTER ARE ADDICTED TO YOUR LOVE--
IT'S QUICKSAND YOU'RE DANCIN' ON, BUCKO...
--I DOUBT EVEN YOU COULD HANDLE A NINTH...
...GET JACOBI AND HIS KIND OUT OF HERE IN FIVE MINUTES--
--OR I'LL MAKE PANSY MATTHIAS THE NINTH--
"OR I'LL MAKE PANSY MATTHIAS THE NINTH--" BOOGA-BOOGA--
FORGET IT, MacHOOT.
THAT IS THE BEST FRIEND I EVER HAD.
AS A REWARD FOR STANDING BY ME, HE SPENT THE LAST FIVE YEARS OF HIS LIFE--
--UNABLE TO PLAY--EVEN INEPTLY...
...NOW--THE LITTLE SON OF A BITCH IS MURDERED--
IT WAS SUICIDE...
YEAH--RIGHT--HE COMES BACK FROM THE DEAD--
--PLAYING WITH A TONE TO DIE FOR--LIKE HE NEVER PLAYED BEFORE HE DIED...
...AND YOU WANT ME TO PULL THE PLUG--GET REAL, INSPECTOR--
--EVEN YOU'VE GOT SOME GRASP OF MORAL RESPONSIBILITY...
EVEN ME--
SO, MacHOOT--WHERE DO YOU GO WHEN THE MOON IS FULL--?
SOMETIMES I THINK I DRIVE UP MY OWN ASS AND DISAPPEAR--

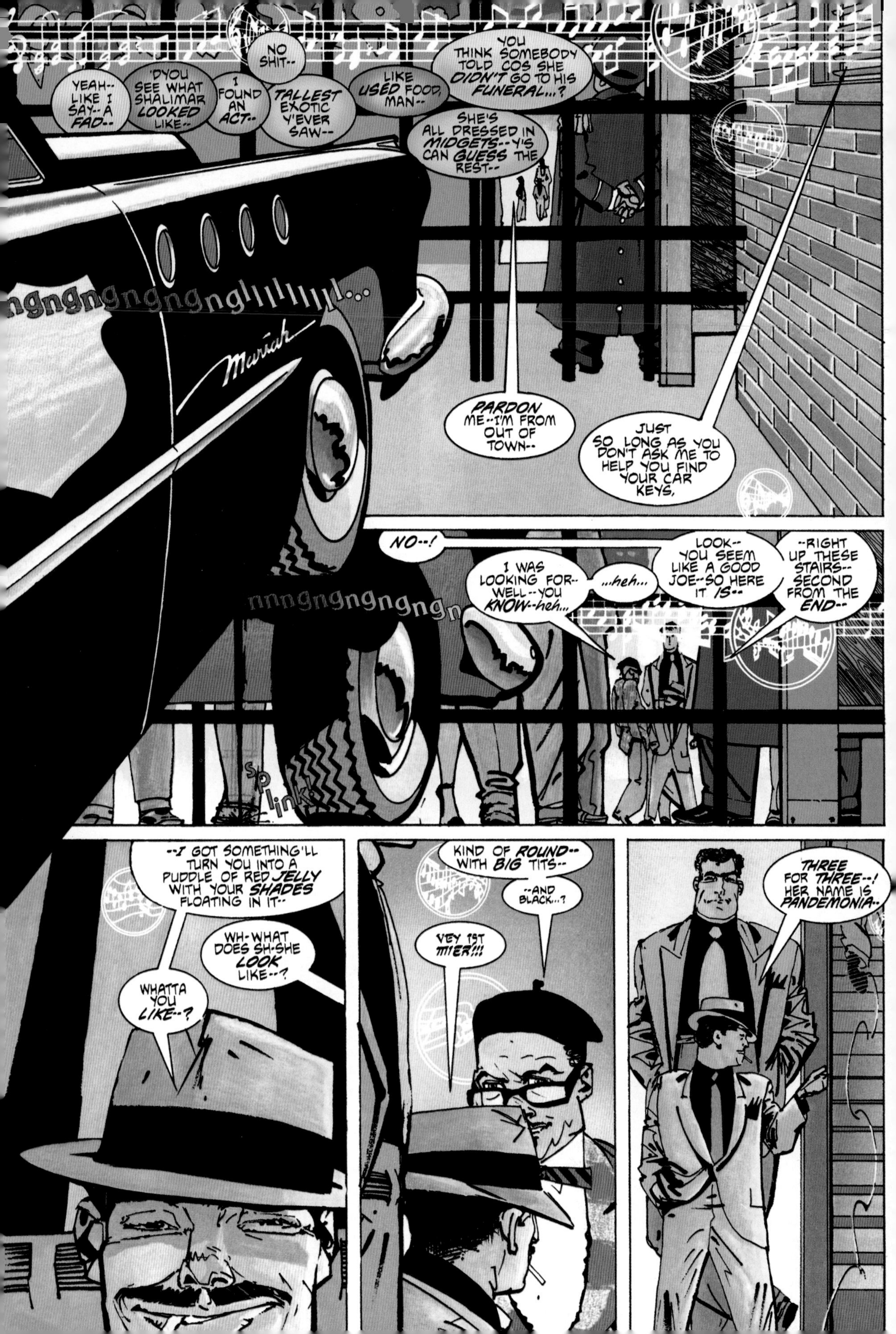

YEAH-- LIKE I SAY-- A FAD--
'DYOU SEE WHAT SHALIMAR LOOKED LIKE--
I FOUND AN ACT--
NO SHIT--
TALLEST EXOTIC Y'EVER SAW--
LIKE USED FOOD, MAN--
YOU THINK SOMEBODY TOLD COS SHE DIDN'T GO TO HIS FUNERAL...?
SHE'S ALL DRESSED IN MIDGETS--Y'S CAN GUESS THE REST--
nngngngngngngngngl l l l l l l l l...
Mariah
PARDON ME--I'M FROM OUT OF TOWN--
JUST SO LONG AS YOU DON'T ASK ME TO HELP YOU FIND YOUR CAR KEYS,
NO--!
I WAS LOOKING FOR-- WELL--YOU KNOW--heh...
...heh...
LOOK-- YOU SEEM LIKE A GOOD JOE--SO HERE IT IS--
--RIGHT UP THESE STAIRS-- SECOND FROM THE END--
nnngngngngngngn
splink!
--I GOT SOMETHING'LL TURN YOU INTO A PUDDLE OF RED JELLY WITH YOUR SHADES FLOATING IN IT--
WH-WHAT DOES SH-SHE LOOK LIKE--?
WHATTA YOU LIKE--?
KIND OF ROUND-- WITH BIG TITS--
--AND BLACK...?
VEY IST MIER!!!
THREE FOR THREE--! HER NAME IS PANDEMONIA--

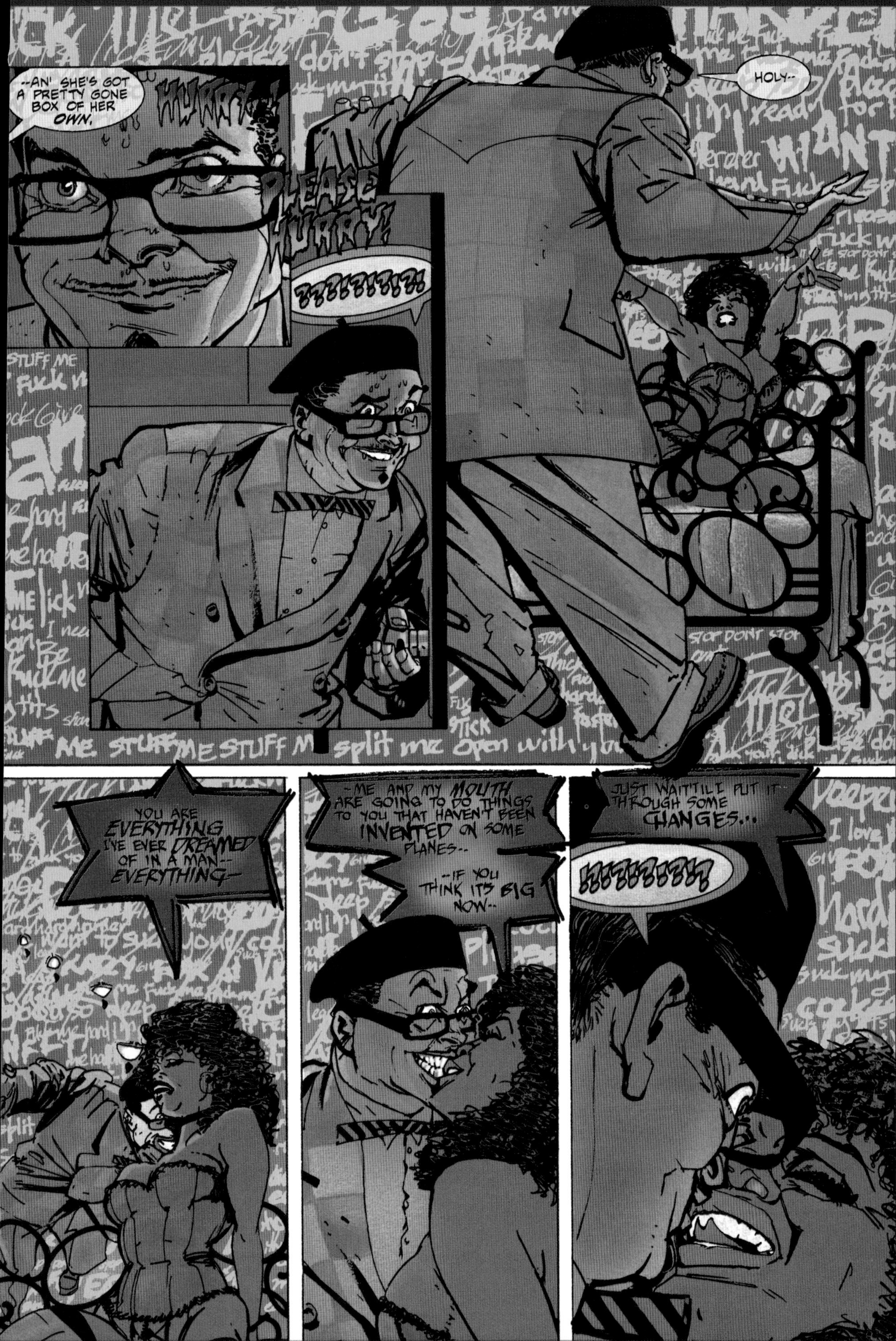
--AN' SHE'S GOT A PRETTY GONE BOX OF HER OWN.
PLEASE HURRY!
HOLY--
YOU ARE EVERYTHING I'VE EVER DREAMED OF IN A MAN-- EVERYTHING--
--ME AND MY MOUTH ARE GOING TO DO THINGS TO YOU THAT HAVEN'T BEEN INVENTED ON SOME PLANES--
--IF YOU THINK IT'S BIG NOW--
JUST WAIT 'TIL I PUT IT THROUGH SOME CHANGES...

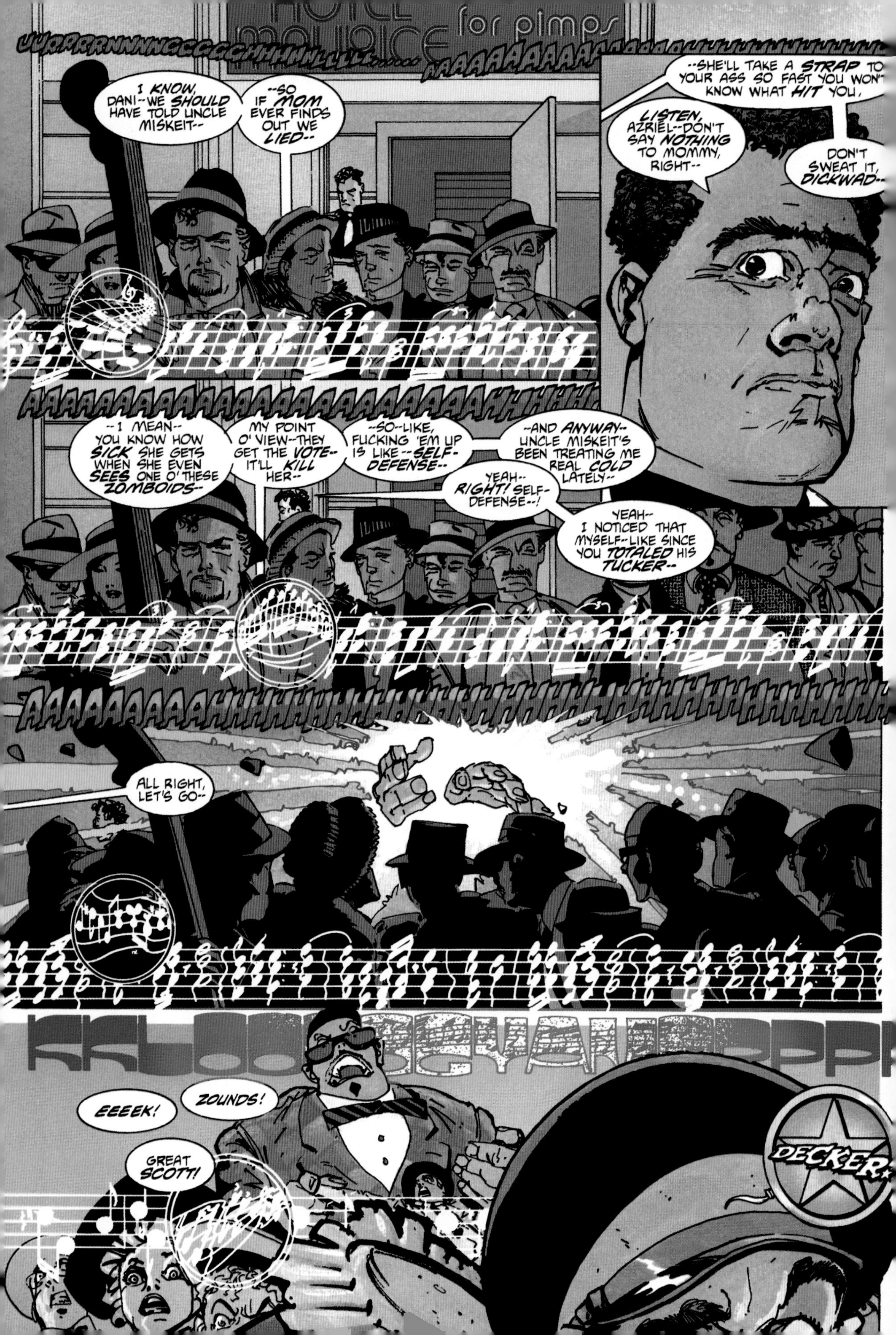

HOTEL MAURICE for pimps
UURRRRNNNNGGGGGCHHHNLLLL.... AAAAAAAAAAAAaaaaa
I KNOW, DANI--WE SHOULD HAVE TOLD UNCLE MISKEIT--
--SO IF MOM EVER FINDS OUT WE LIED--
--SHE'LL TAKE A STRAP TO YOUR ASS SO FAST YOU WON'T KNOW WHAT HIT YOU.
LISTEN, AZRIEL--DON'T SAY NOTHING TO MOMMY, RIGHT--
DON'T SWEAT IT, DICKWAD--
AAAAAAAAAAAAAAAAAAAAAAAAAHHHHH
--I MEAN--YOU KNOW HOW SICK SHE GETS WHEN SHE EVEN SEES ONE O' THESE ZOMBOIDS--
MY POINT O' VIEW--THEY GET THE VOTE--IT'LL KILL HER--
--SO--LIKE, FUCKING 'EM UP IS LIKE--SELF-DEFENSE--
--AND ANYWAY--UNCLE MISKEIT'S BEEN TREATING ME REAL COLD LATELY--
YEAH--RIGHT! SELF-DEFENSE--!
YEAH--I NOTICED THAT MYSELF--LIKE SINCE YOU TOTALED HIS TUCKER--
AAAAAAAAAHHHHHHHHHHHHHHHHHHHHHHHHHHHHHHH
ALL RIGHT, LET'S GO--
EEEEK!
ZOUNDS!
GREAT SCOTT!
DECKER

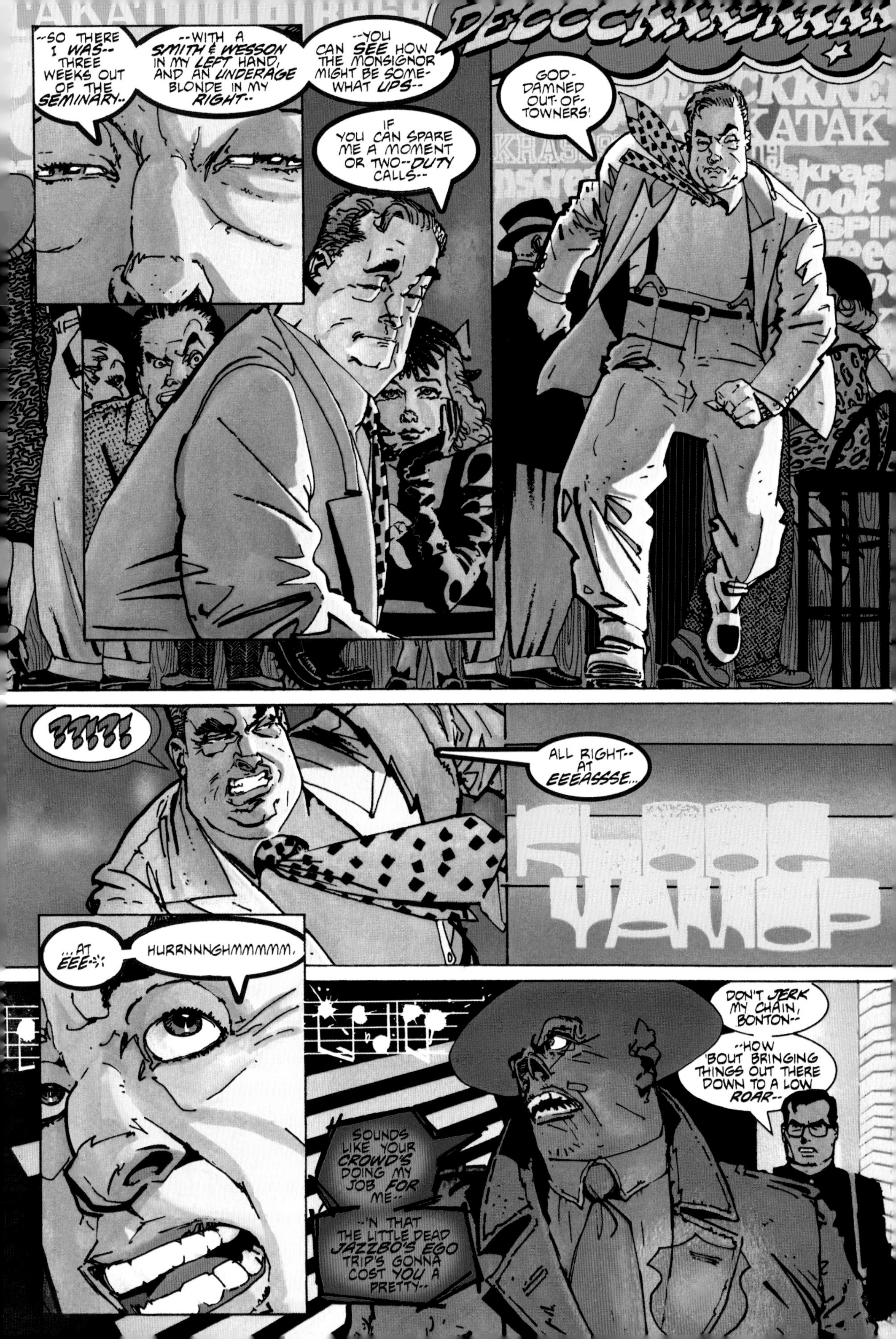
--SO THERE I WAS--THREE WEEKS OUT OF THE SEMINARY..
--WITH A SMITH & WESSON IN MY LEFT HAND, AND AN UNDERAGE BLONDE IN MY RIGHT--
--YOU CAN SEE HOW THE MONSIGNOR MIGHT BE SOMEWHAT UPS--
IF YOU CAN SPARE ME A MOMENT OR TWO--DUTY CALLS--
GOD-DAMNED OUT-OF-TOWNERS!
????!
ALL RIGHT--AT EEEASSSE...
...AT EEE--!
HURRNNNGHMMMMM.
DON'T JERK MY CHAIN, BONTON--
--HOW 'BOUT BRINGING THINGS OUT THERE DOWN TO A LOW ROAR--
SOUNDS LIKE YOUR CROWD'S DOING MY JOB FOR ME--
--'N THAT THE LITTLE DEAD JAZZBO'S EGO TRIP'S GONNA COST YOU A PRETTY--

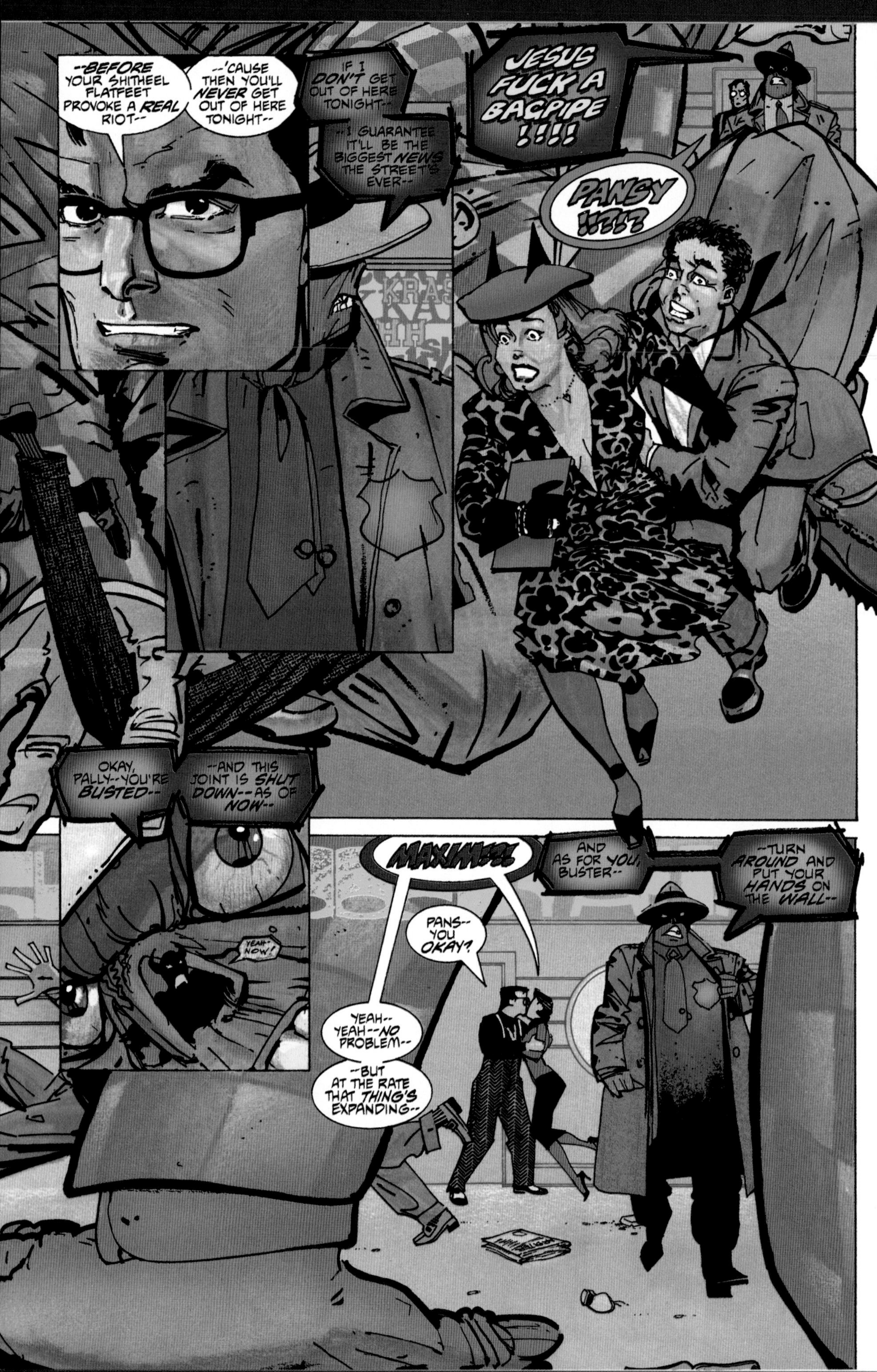
--BEFORE YOUR SHITHEEL FLATFEET PROVOKE A REAL RIOT--
--'CAUSE THEN YOU'LL NEVER GET OUT OF HERE TONIGHT--
IF I DON'T GET OUT OF HERE TONIGHT--
--I GUARANTEE IT'LL BE THE BIGGEST NEWS THE STREET'S EVER--
JESUS FUCK A BAGPIPE !!!!
PANSY !!??
OKAY, PALLY--YOU'RE BUSTED--
--AND THIS JOINT IS SHUT DOWN--AS OF NOW--
YEAH NOW!
MAXIMS!!
AND AS FOR YOU, BUSTER--
--TURN AROUND AND PUT YOUR HANDS ON THE WALL--
PANS-- YOU OKAY?
YEAH-- YEAH--NO PROBLEM--
--BUT AT THE RATE THAT THING'S EXPANDING--

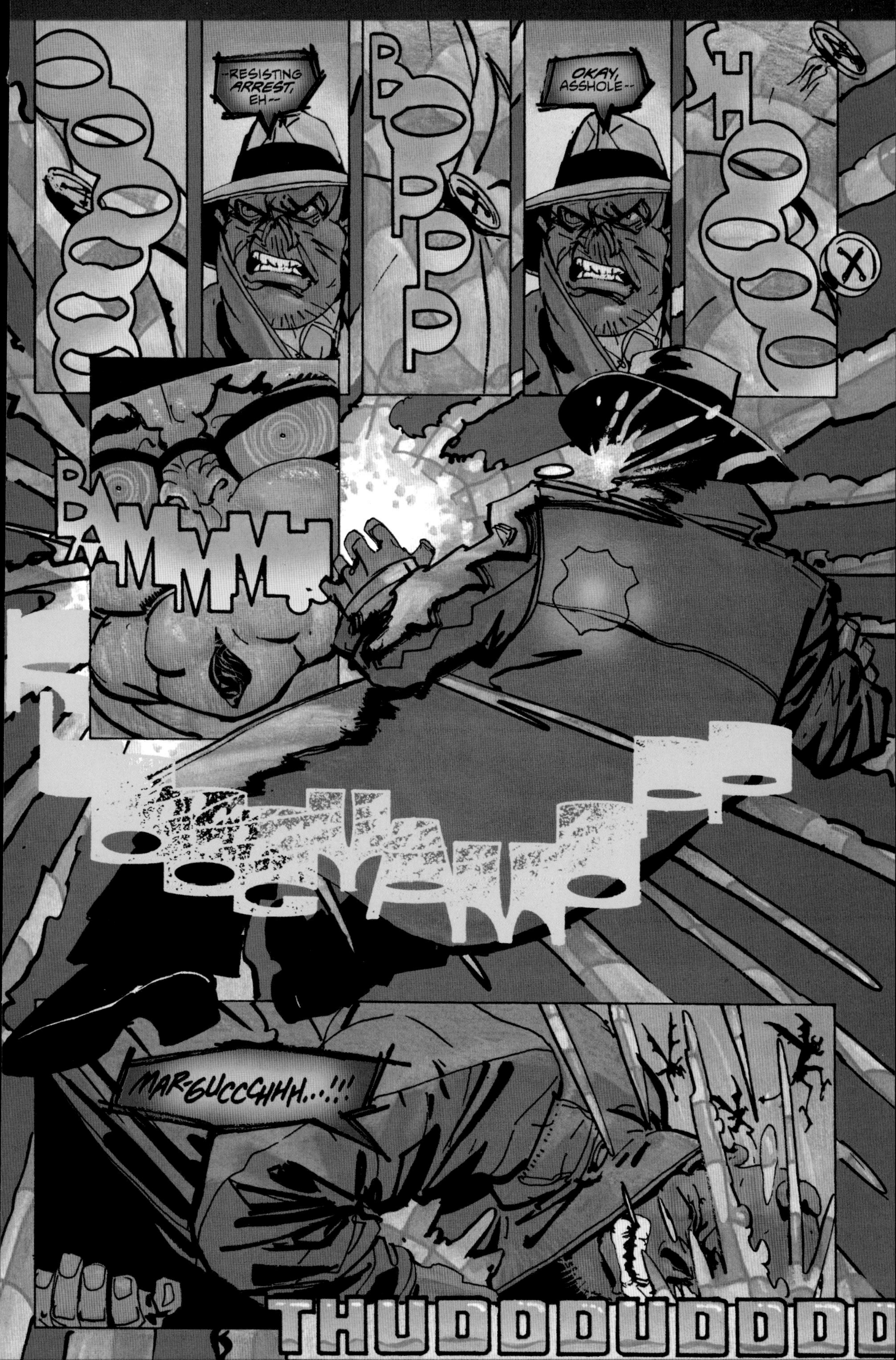
--RESISTING ARREST, EH--
OKAY, ASSHOLE--
MAR-GUCCCHHH...!!!

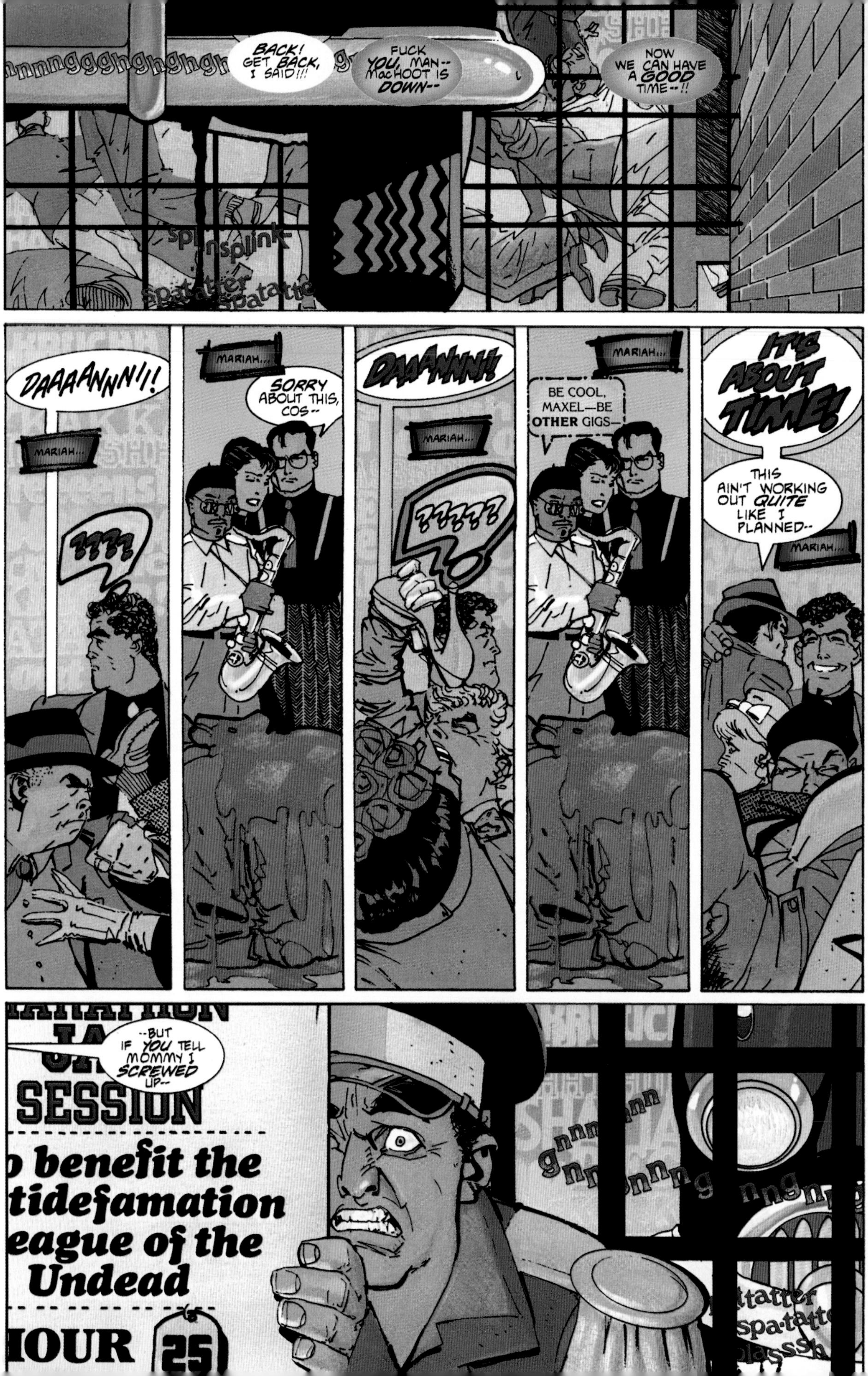
nnnngggghghghghg
BACK! GET BACK, I SAID!!!
FUCK YOU, MAN-- MacHOOT IS DOWN--
NOW WE CAN HAVE A GOOD TIME--!!
splinsplink
spatatter spatatte
DAAAANNN!!!
MARIAH...
????
MARIAH...
SORRY ABOUT THIS, COS--
DAAANNN!
MARIAH...
?????
MARIAH...
BE COOL, MAXEL--BE OTHER GIGS--
IT'S ABOUT TIME!
THIS AIN'T WORKING OUT QUITE LIKE I PLANNED--
MARIAH...
--BUT IF YOU TELL MOMMY I SCREWED UP--
SESSION
benefit the
tidefamation
eague of the
Undead
HOUR 25
gnnnnannn
gnnnnnnngnng
tatter spa·tatte
lassh

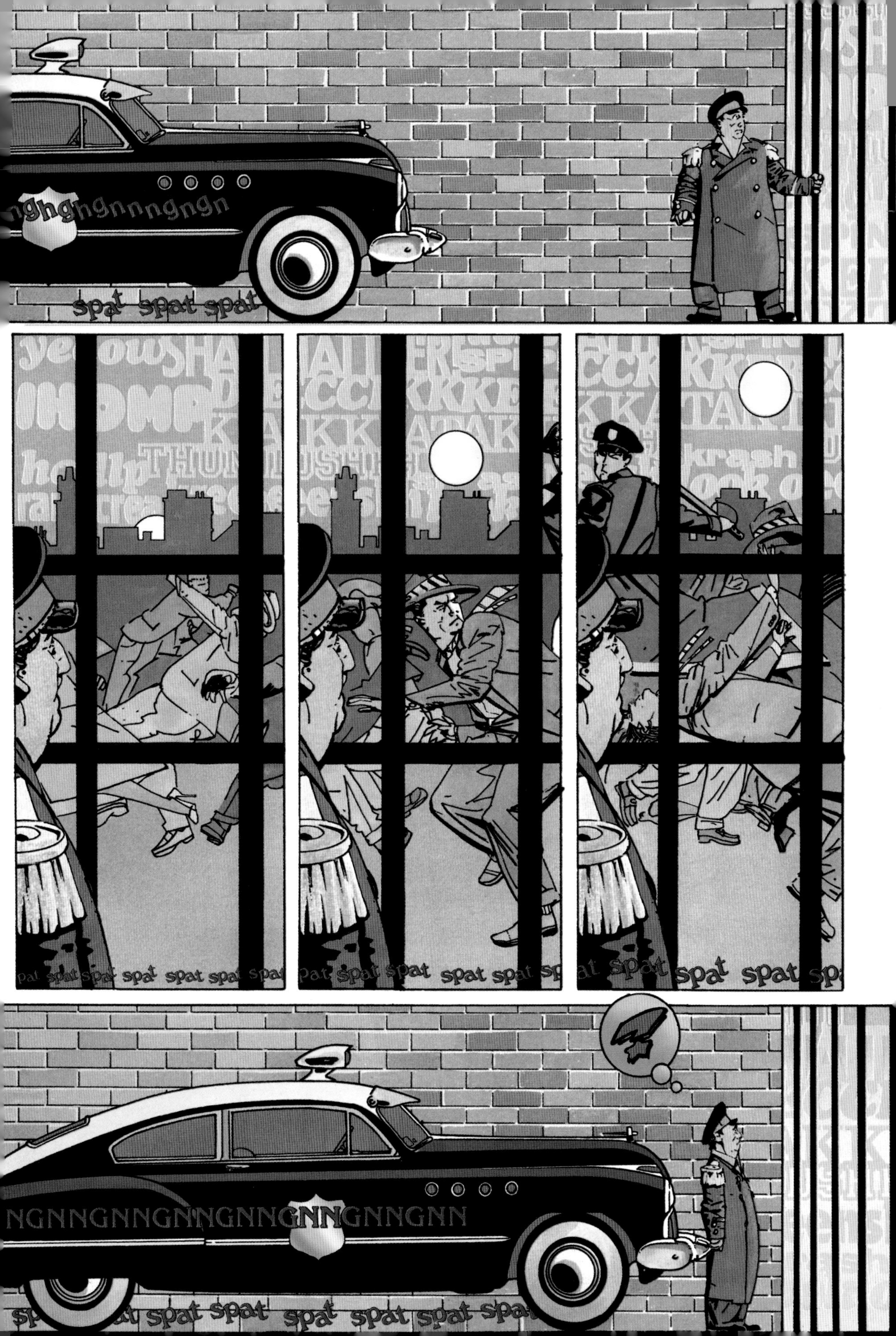
nghghghgnnngngn
spat spat spat
spat spat spat spat spat spat
spat spat spat spat spat
spat spat spat
spat spat spat spat spat spat

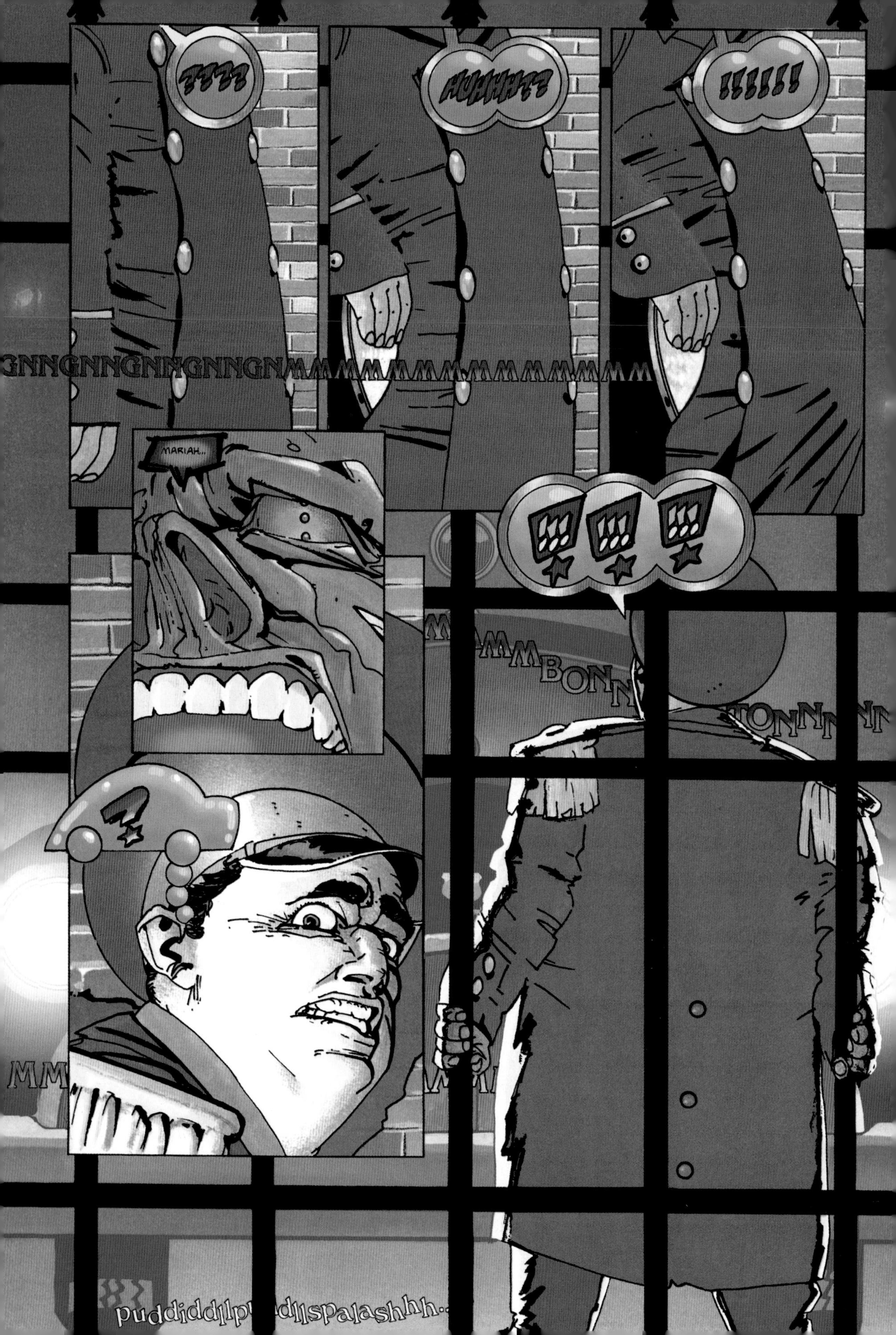
????
HUHHH??
!!!!!!
GNNNGNNNGNNNGNMMMMMMMMMMMMMMMMMM
MARIAH...
MMMMMBONN
TONNNNN
MMM
puddiddllpu dllspalashhh...

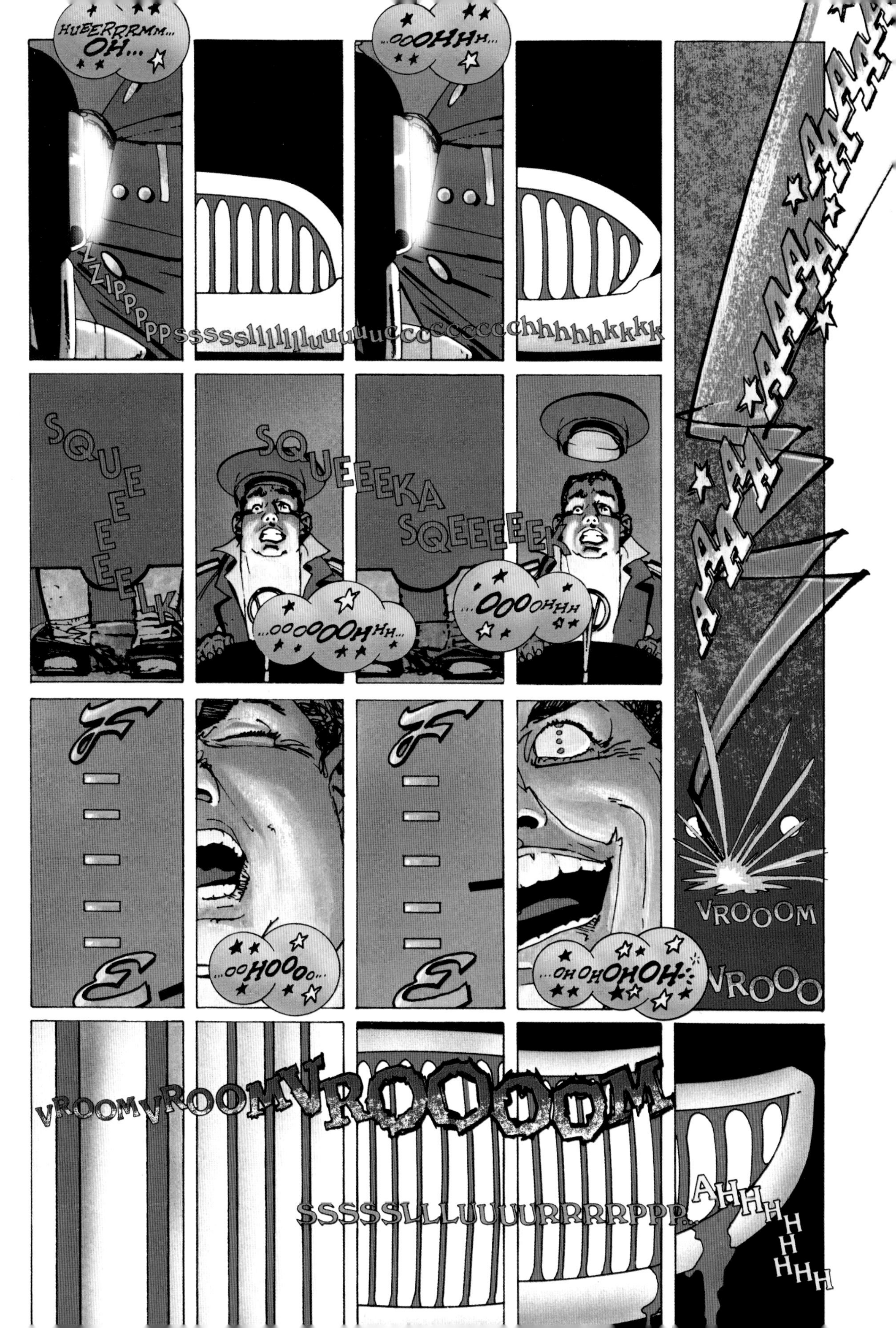

HUEERRRMM... OH...
...OOOHHH...
ZZIPPPPPPSSSSSSLLLLLLLUUUUUCCCCCCCCCCCHHHHHKKKK
AAAAAAAAAAAAAAAHHHHH
SQUEEEEEELK
SQUEEEEKA
SQEEEEEEEK
...OOOOOOHHH...
...OOOOHHH
...OOHOOOO...
...OHOHOHOH
VROOOM
VROOO
VROOMVROOMVROOOOOM
SSSSSSLLLUUUURRRRPPPP...
AHHHHHHHH

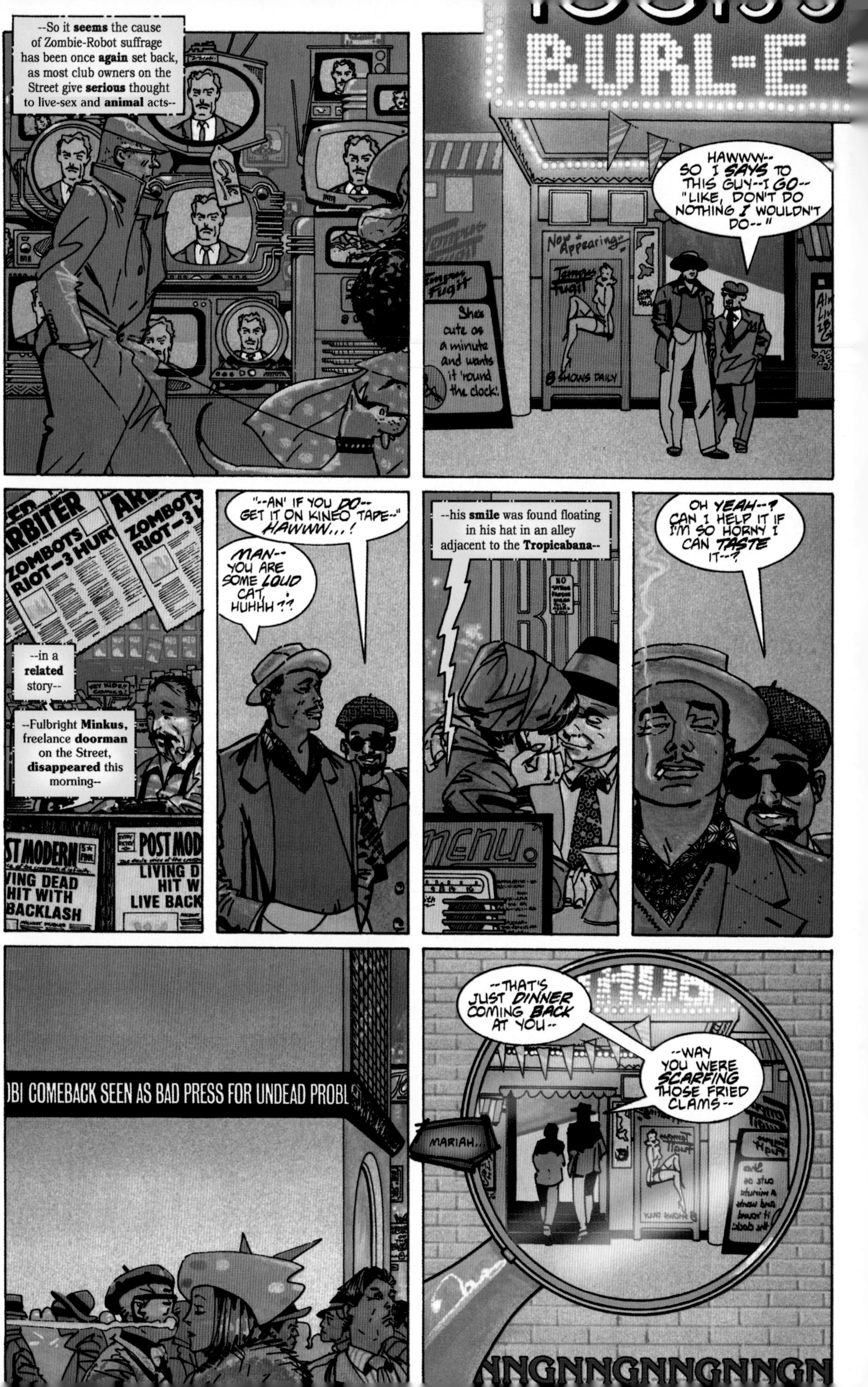

--So it seems the cause of Zombie-Robot suffrage has been once again set back, as most club owners on the Street give serious thought to live-sex and animal acts--
BURL-E-
HAWWW-- SO I SAYS TO THIS GUY--I GO-- "LIKE, DON'T DO NOTHING I WOULDN'T DO--"
Now Appearing
Tempus Fugit
She's cute as a minute and wants it 'round the clock!
8 SHOWS DAILY
ARBITER
ZOMBOTS RIOT--3 HURT
--in a related story--
--Fulbright Minkus, freelance doorman on the Street, disappeared this morning--
POST MODERN
LIVING DEAD HIT WITH BACKLASH
"--AN' IF YOU DO-- GET IT ON KINEO TAPE--" HAWWW...!
MAN-- YOU ARE SOME LOUD CAT, HUHHH??
--his smile was found floating in his hat in an alley adjacent to the Tropicabana--
menu.
OH YEAH--? CAN I HELP IT IF I'M SO HORNY I CAN TASTE IT--?
OBI COMEBACK SEEN AS BAD PRESS FOR UNDEAD PROBL
MARIAH..
--THAT'S JUST DINNER COMING BACK AT YOU--
--WAY YOU WERE SCARFING THOSE FRIED CLAMS--
NNGNNGNGNNGNGNNGN

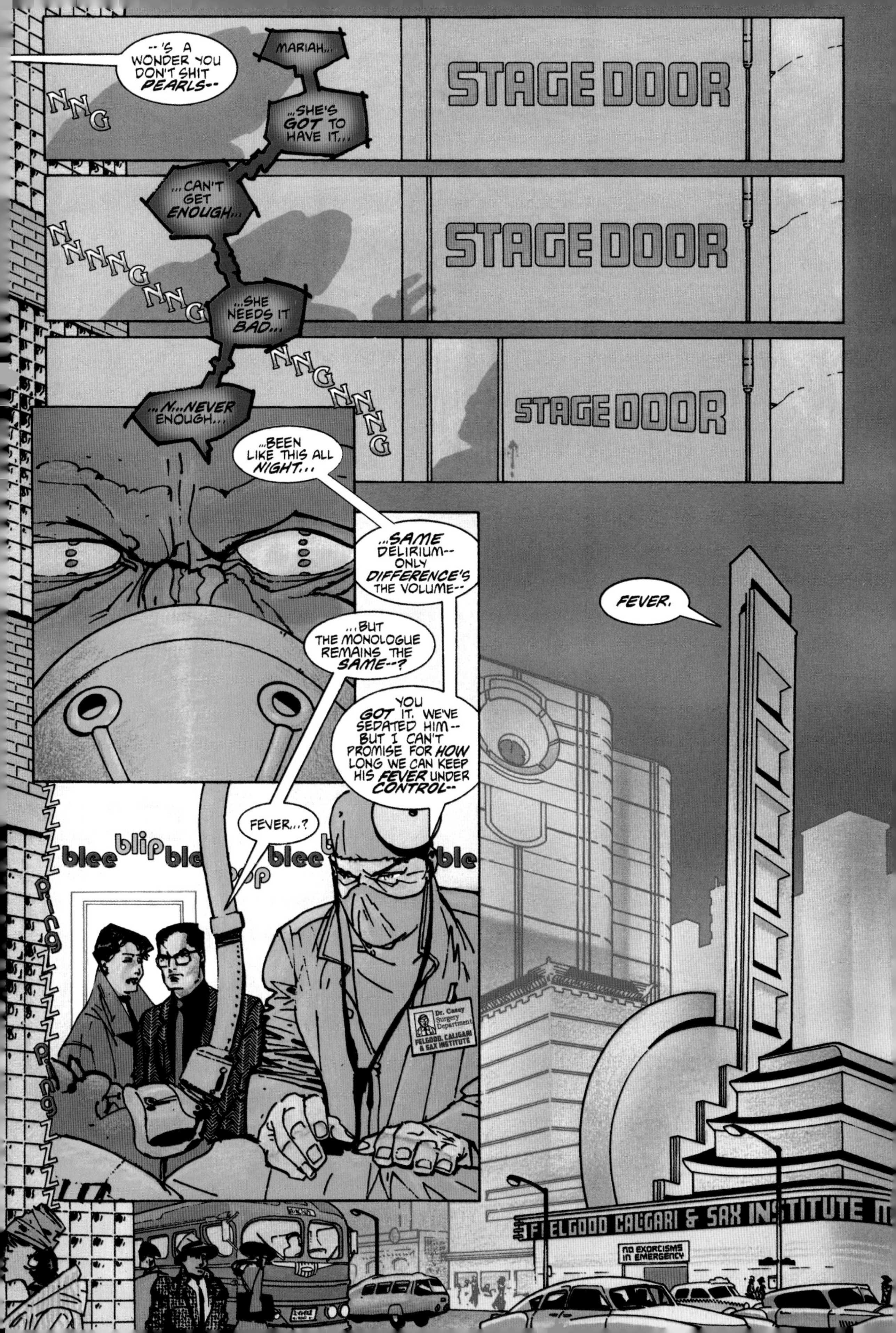

--'S A WONDER YOU DON'T SHIT PEARLS--
MARIAH...
...SHE'S GOT TO HAVE IT...
NNG
STAGE DOOR
...CAN'T GET ENOUGH...
NNNNGNNG
...SHE NEEDS IT BAD...
STAGE DOOR
...N...NEVER ENOUGH...
NNGNNNG
STAGE DOOR
...BEEN LIKE THIS ALL NIGHT...
...SAME DELIRIUM--ONLY DIFFERENCE'S THE VOLUME--
...BUT THE MONOLOGUE REMAINS THE SAME--?
YOU GOT IT. WE'VE SEDATED HIM--BUT I CAN'T PROMISE FOR HOW LONG WE CAN KEEP HIS FEVER UNDER CONTROL--
FEVER...?
FEVER.
bleeblipbleebopbleeblible
ping
ping
Dr. Casey Surgery Department FELGOOD, CALIGARI & SAX INSTITUTE
FEELGOOD CALIGARI & SAX INSTITUTE
NO EXORCISMS IN EMERGENCY

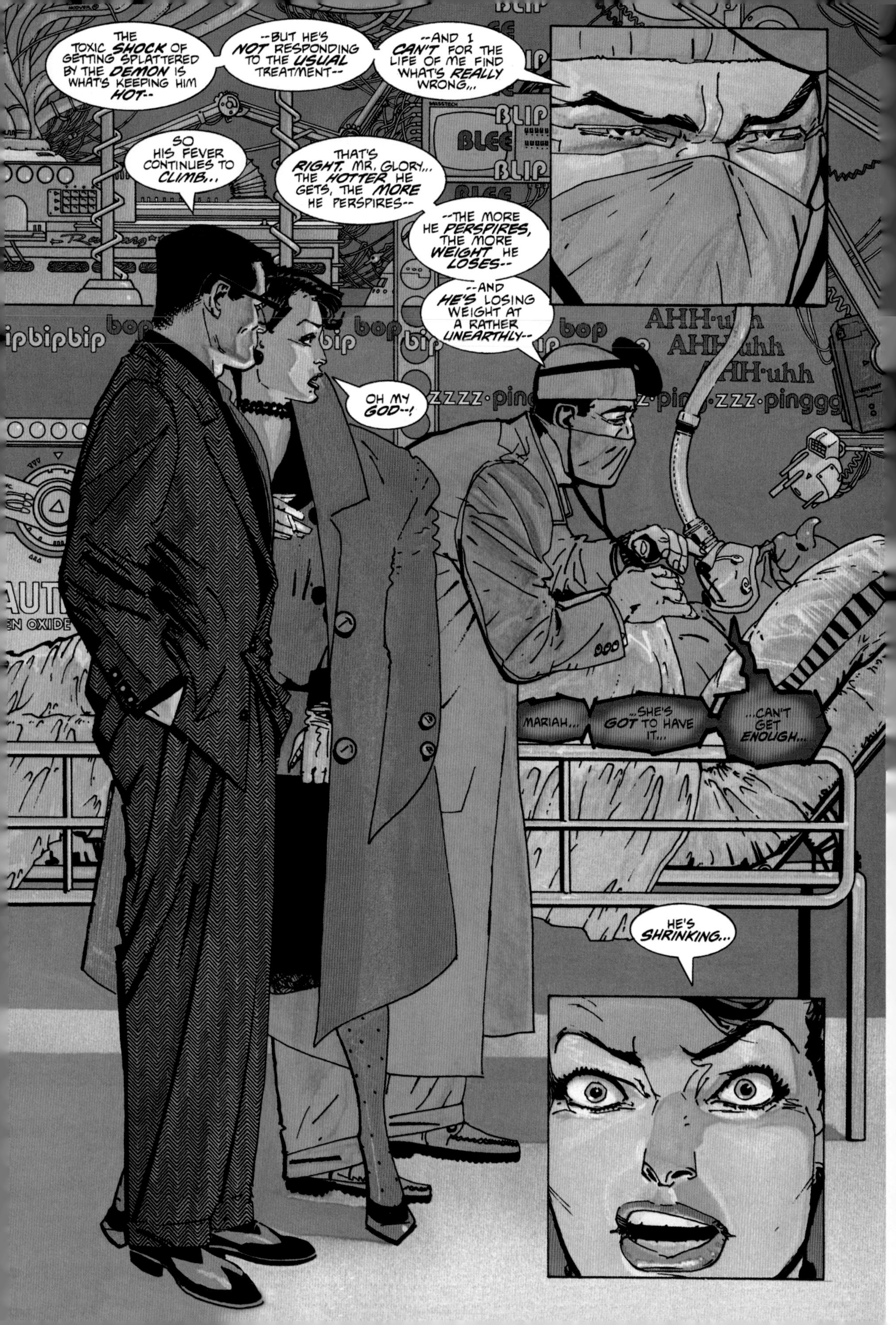

THE TOXIC SHOCK OF GETTING SPLATTERED BY THE DEMON IS WHAT'S KEEPING HIM HOT--
--BUT HE'S NOT RESPONDING TO THE USUAL TREATMENT--
--AND I CAN'T FOR THE LIFE OF ME FIND WHAT'S REALLY WRONG...
SO HIS FEVER CONTINUES TO CLIMB...
THAT'S RIGHT, MR. GLORY... THE HOTTER HE GETS, THE MORE HE PERSPIRES--
--THE MORE HE PERSPIRES, THE MORE WEIGHT HE LOSES--
--AND HE'S LOSING WEIGHT AT A RATHER UNEARTHLY--
OH MY GOD--!
MARIAH...
...SHE'S GOT TO HAVE IT...
...CAN'T GET ENOUGH...
HE'S SHRINKING...
BLIP
BLEE
bipbipbip
bop
AHH·uhh AHH·uhh AHH·uhh
zzzz·pingg·zzz·pinggg

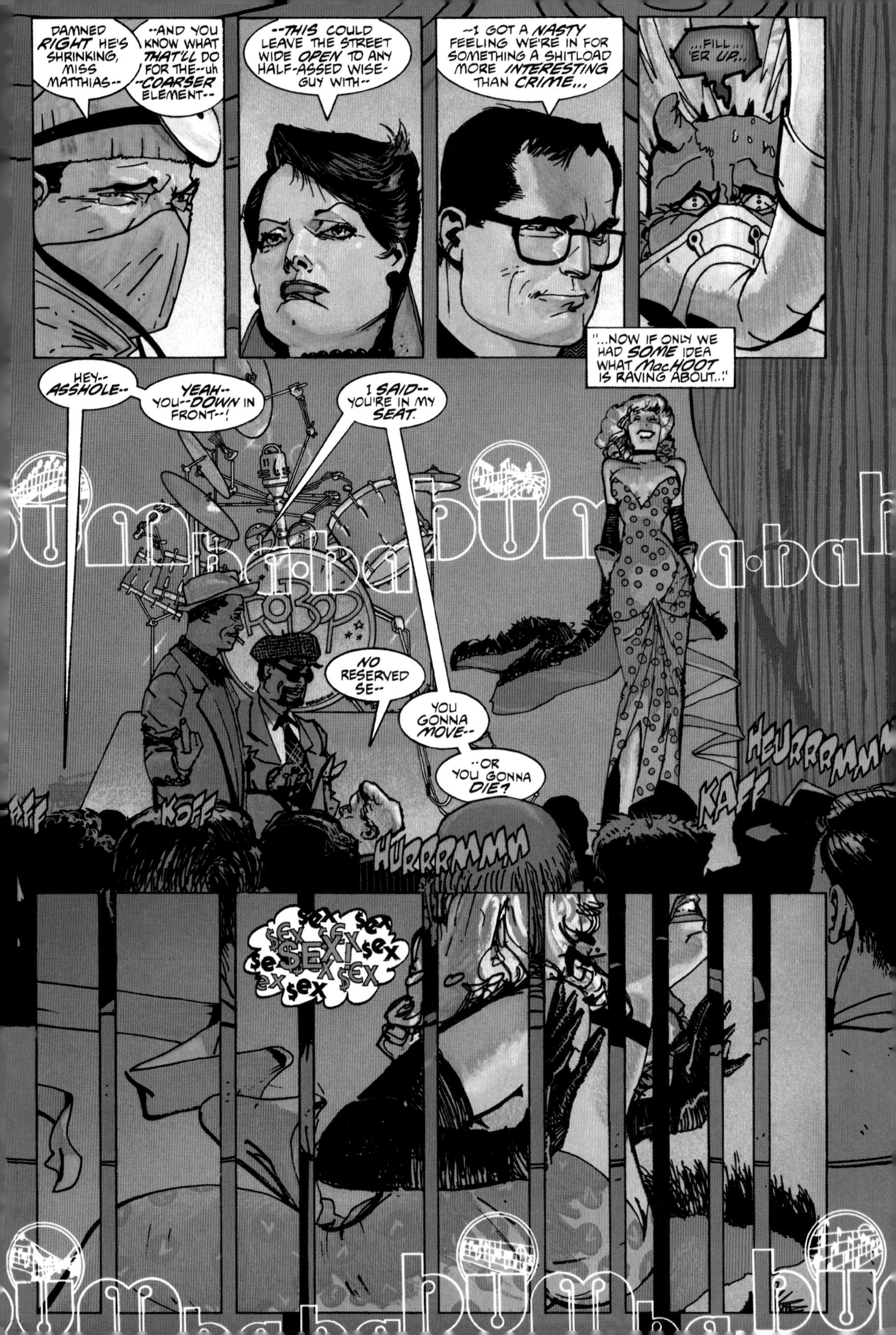

DAMNED RIGHT HE'S SHRINKING, MISS MATTHIAS--
--AND YOU KNOW WHAT THAT'LL DO FOR THE--uh --COARSER ELEMENT--
--THIS COULD LEAVE THE STREET WIDE OPEN TO ANY HALF-ASSED WISE-GUY WITH--
--I GOT A NASTY FEELING WE'RE IN FOR SOMETHING A SHITLOAD MORE INTERESTING THAN CRIME...
...FILL... 'ER UP...
"...NOW IF ONLY WE HAD SOME IDEA WHAT MacHOOT IS RAVING ABOUT..."
HEY-- ASSHOLE--
YEAH-- YOU--DOWN IN FRONT--!
I SAID-- YOU'RE IN MY SEAT.
bum-ba-bum-ba-ba
NO RESERVED SE--
YOU GONNA MOVE--
--OR YOU GONNA DIE?
KOFF
HEURRRMMM
KAFF
HURRRMMMN
$EX SEX $EX! SEX $EX sex
bum-ba-bum-ba-bum

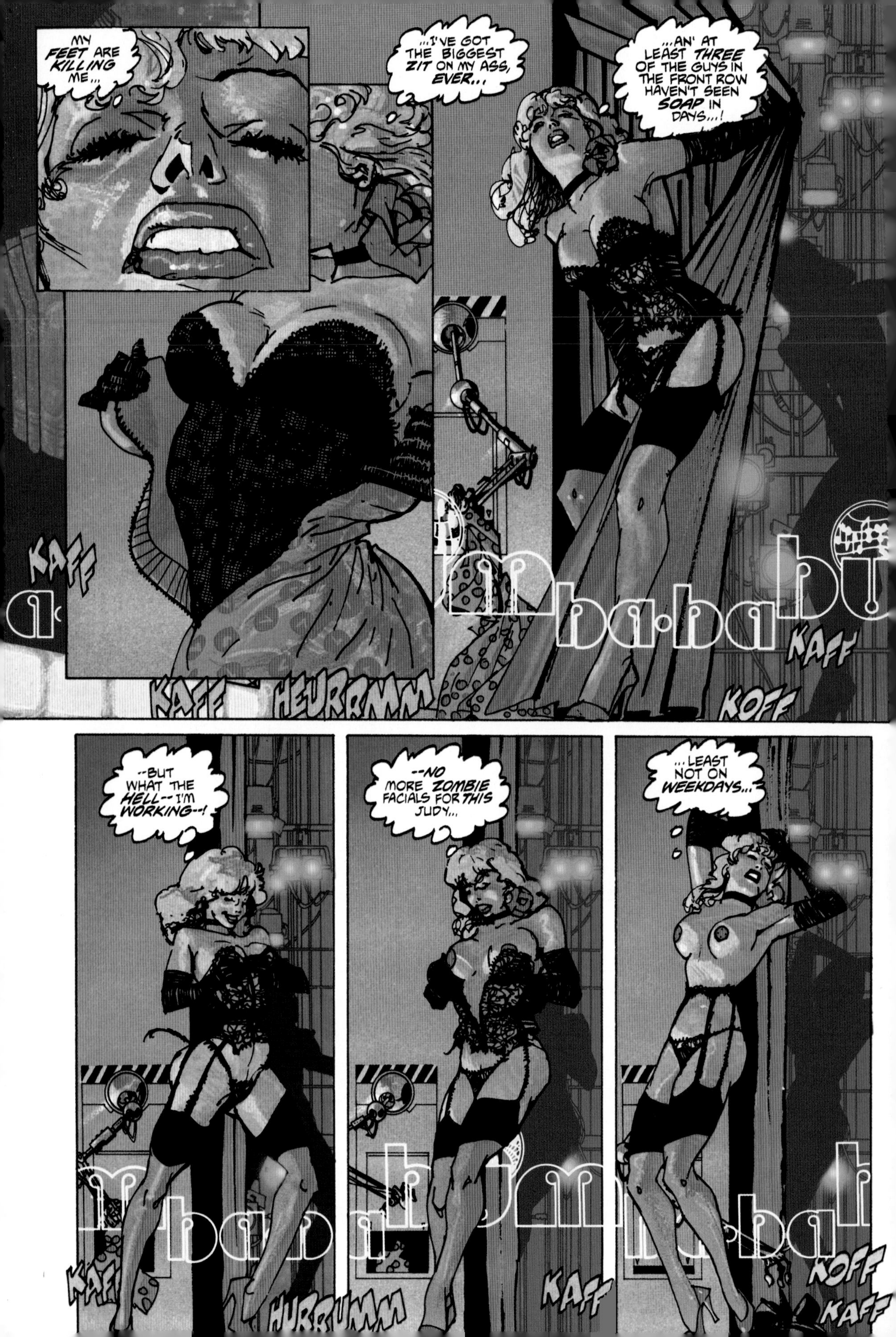
MY FEET ARE KILLING ME...
...I'VE GOT THE BIGGEST ZIT ON MY ASS, EVER...
...AN' AT LEAST THREE OF THE GUYS IN THE FRONT ROW HAVEN'T SEEN SOAP IN DAYS...!
KAFF
ba·ba
KAFF
KAFF
HEURRMM
KOFF
--BUT WHAT THE HELL--I'M WORKING--!
--NO MORE ZOMBIE FACIALS FOR THIS JUDY...
...LEAST NOT ON WEEKDAYS...
KAFF
HURRUMM
KAFF
KOFF
KAFF

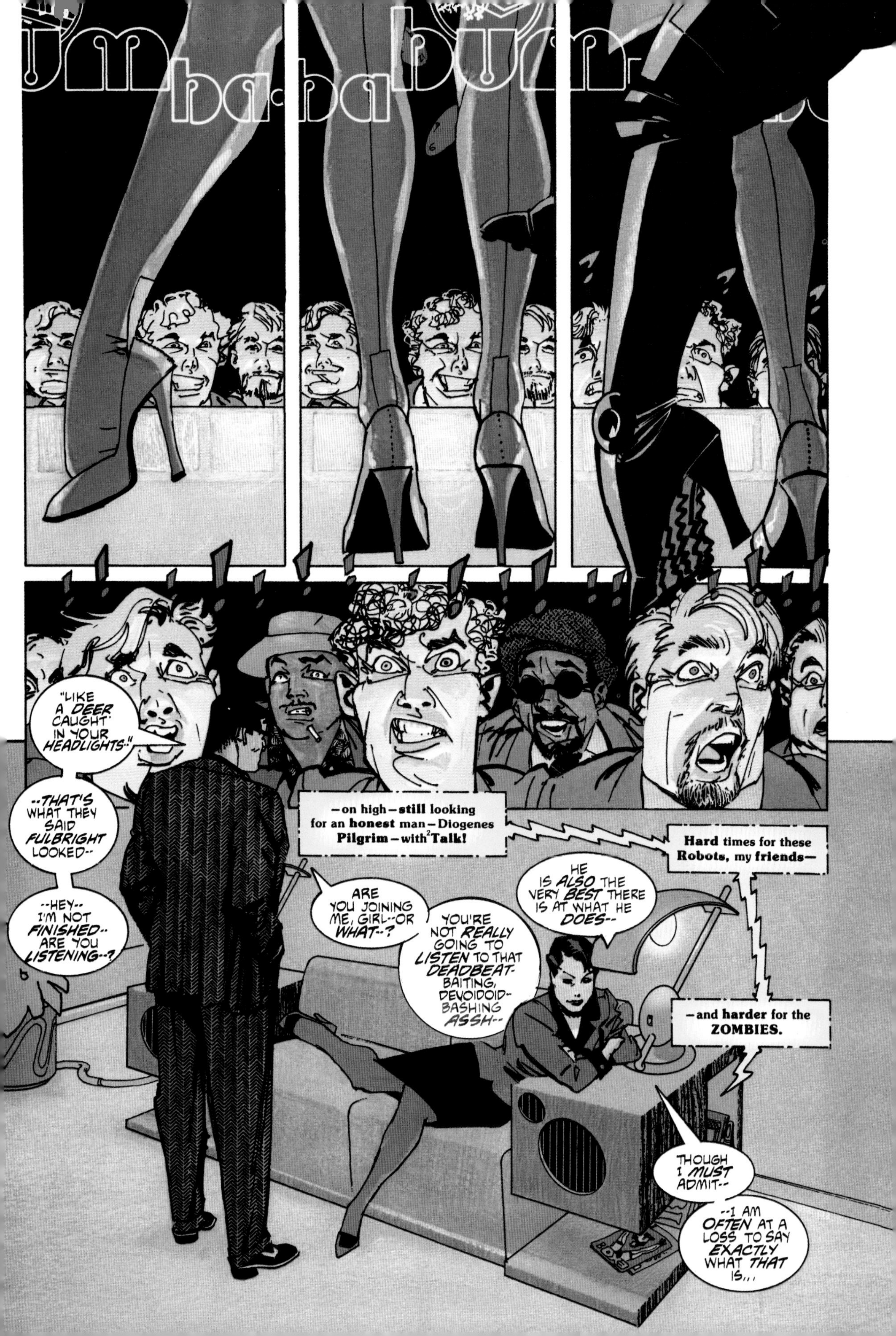
bum ba-ba bum
"LIKE A DEER CAUGHT IN YOUR HEADLIGHTS."
--THAT'S WHAT THEY SAID FULBRIGHT LOOKED--
--HEY-- I'M NOT FINISHED-- ARE YOU LISTENING--?
—on high—still looking for an honest man—Diogenes Pilgrim—with² Talk!
Hard times for these Robots, my friends—
ARE YOU JOINING ME, GIRL--OR WHAT--?
YOU'RE NOT REALLY GOING TO LISTEN TO THAT DEADBEAT-BAITING, DEVOIDOID-BASHING ASSH--
HE IS ALSO THE VERY BEST THERE IS AT WHAT HE DOES--
—and harder for the ZOMBIES.
THOUGH I MUST ADMIT--
--I AM OFTEN AT A LOSS TO SAY EXACTLY WHAT THAT IS...

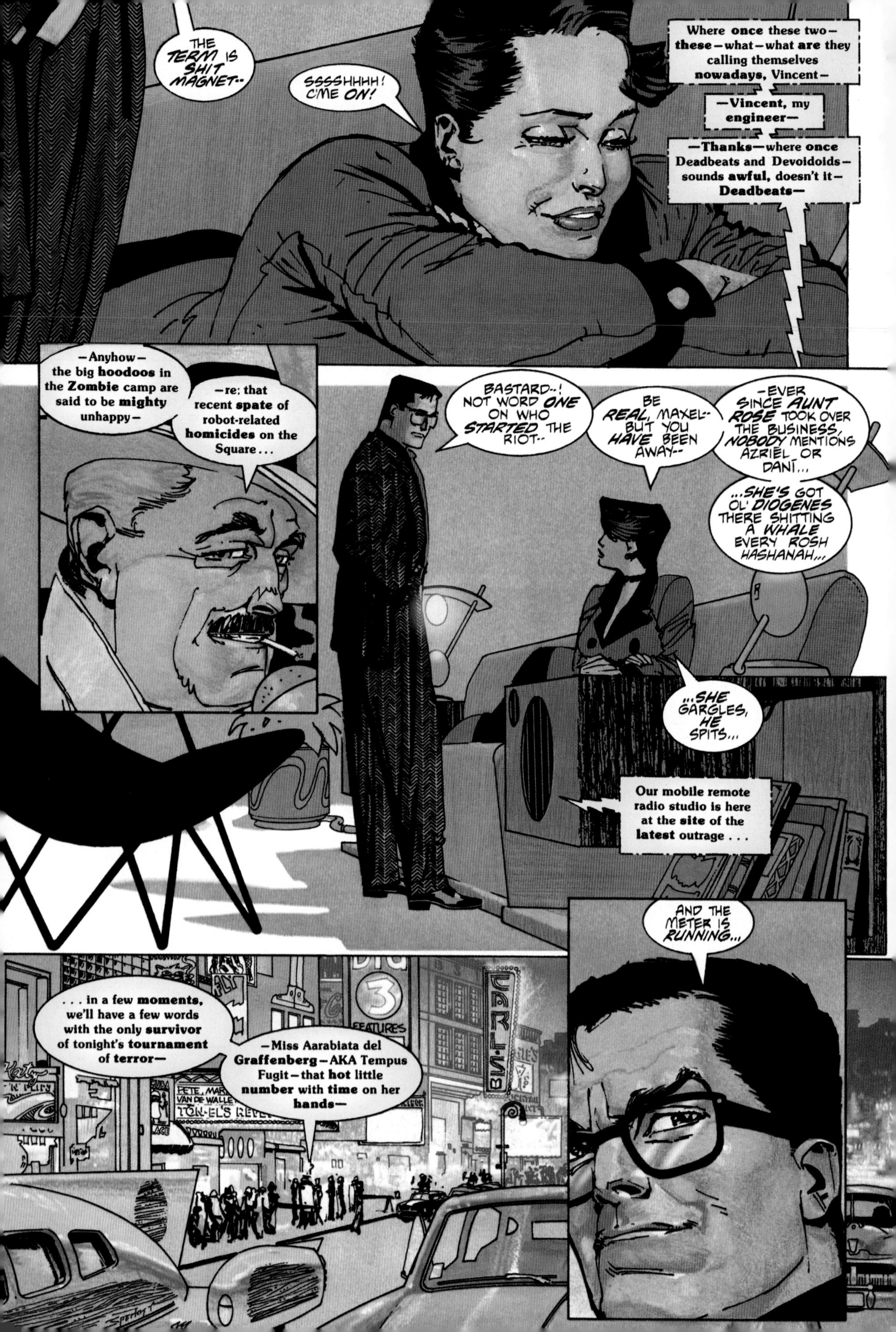
THE TERM IS SHIT MAGNET..
SSSSHHHH! C'ME ON!
Where once these two—these—what—what are they calling themselves nowadays, Vincent—
—Vincent, my engineer—
—Thanks—where once Deadbeats and Devoidoids—sounds awful, doesn't it—Deadbeats—
—Anyhow—the big hoodoos in the Zombie camp are said to be mighty unhappy—
—re: that recent spate of robot-related homicides on the Square . . .
BASTARD..! NOT WORD ONE ON WHO STARTED THE RIOT..
BE REAL, MAXEL.. BUT YOU HAVE BEEN AWAY..
—EVER SINCE AUNT ROSE TOOK OVER THE BUSINESS, NOBODY MENTIONS AZRIEL OR DANI...
...SHE'S GOT OL' DIOGENES THERE SHITTING A WHALE EVERY ROSH HASHANAH...
...SHE GARGLES, HE SPITS...
Our mobile remote radio studio is here at the site of the latest outrage . . .
AND THE METER IS RUNNING...
. . . in a few moments, we'll have a few words with the only survivor of tonight's tournament of terror—
—Miss Aarabiata del Graffenberg—AKA Tempus Fugit—that hot little number with time on her hands—
3
FEATURES
CARL'S
PETE, MAR
VAN DE WALLE
TON-EL'S REVE

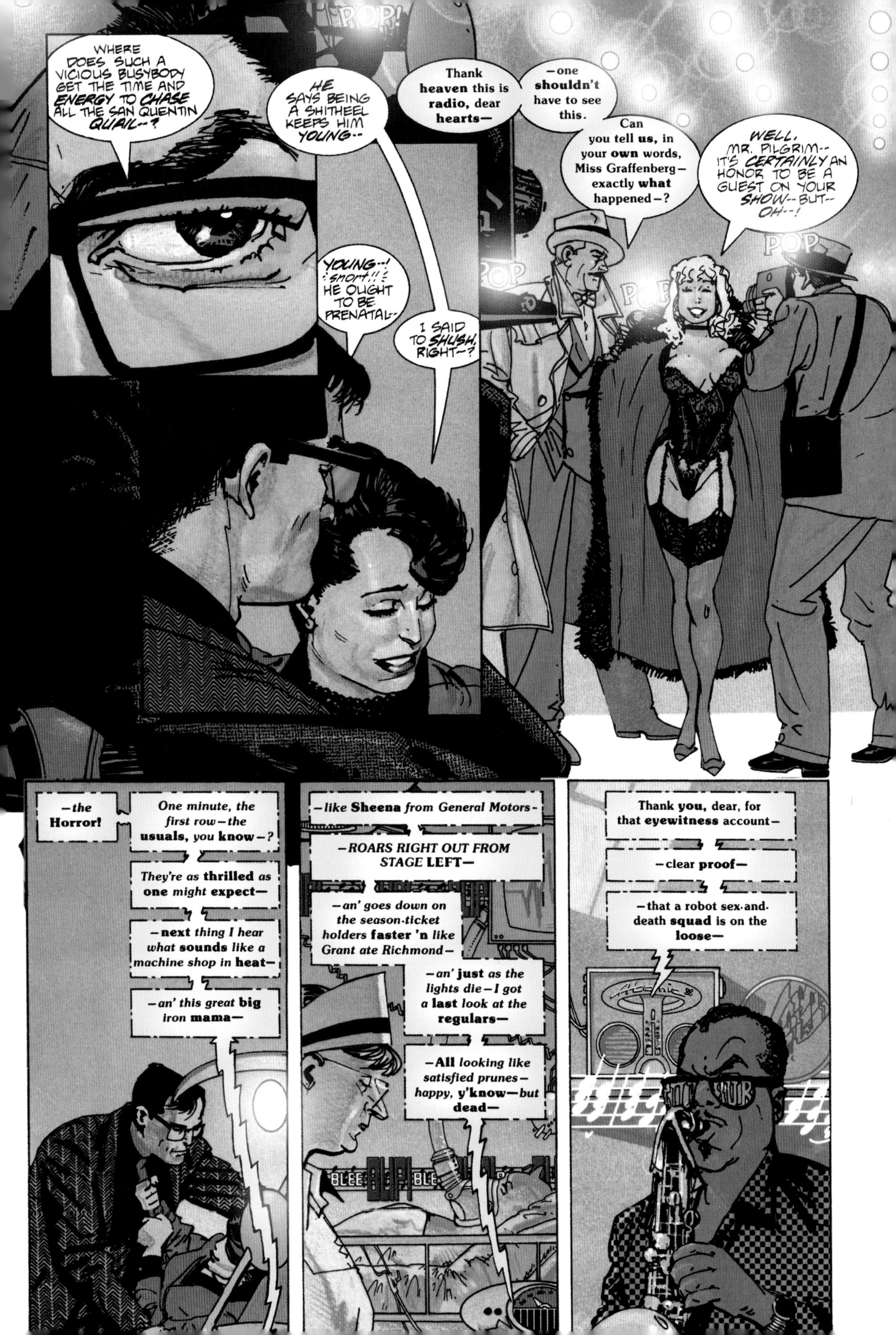
POP!
WHERE DOES SUCH A VICIOUS BUSYBODY GET THE TIME AND ENERGY TO CHASE ALL THE SAN QUENTIN QUAIL--?
HE SAYS BEING A SHITHEEL KEEPS HIM YOUNG--
YOUNG--! snort!! HE OUGHT TO BE PRENATAL--
I SAID TO SHUSH, RIGHT--?
Thank heaven this is radio, dear hearts—
—one shouldn't have to see this.
Can you tell us, in your own words, Miss Graffenberg—exactly what happened—?
WELL, MR. PILGRIM-- IT'S CERTAINLY AN HONOR TO BE A GUEST ON YOUR SHOW--BUT-- OH--!
POP
POP
POP
—the Horror!
One minute, the first row—the usuals, you know—?
They're as thrilled as one might expect—
—next thing I hear what sounds like a machine shop in heat—
—an' this great big iron mama—
—like Sheena from General Motors—
—ROARS RIGHT OUT FROM STAGE LEFT—
—an' goes down on the season-ticket holders faster 'n like Grant ate Richmond—
—an' just as the lights die—I got a last look at the regulars—
—All looking like satisfied prunes—happy, y'know—but dead—
BLEE BLEE
Thank you, dear, for that eyewitness account—
—clear proof—
—that a robot sex-and-death squad is on the loose—

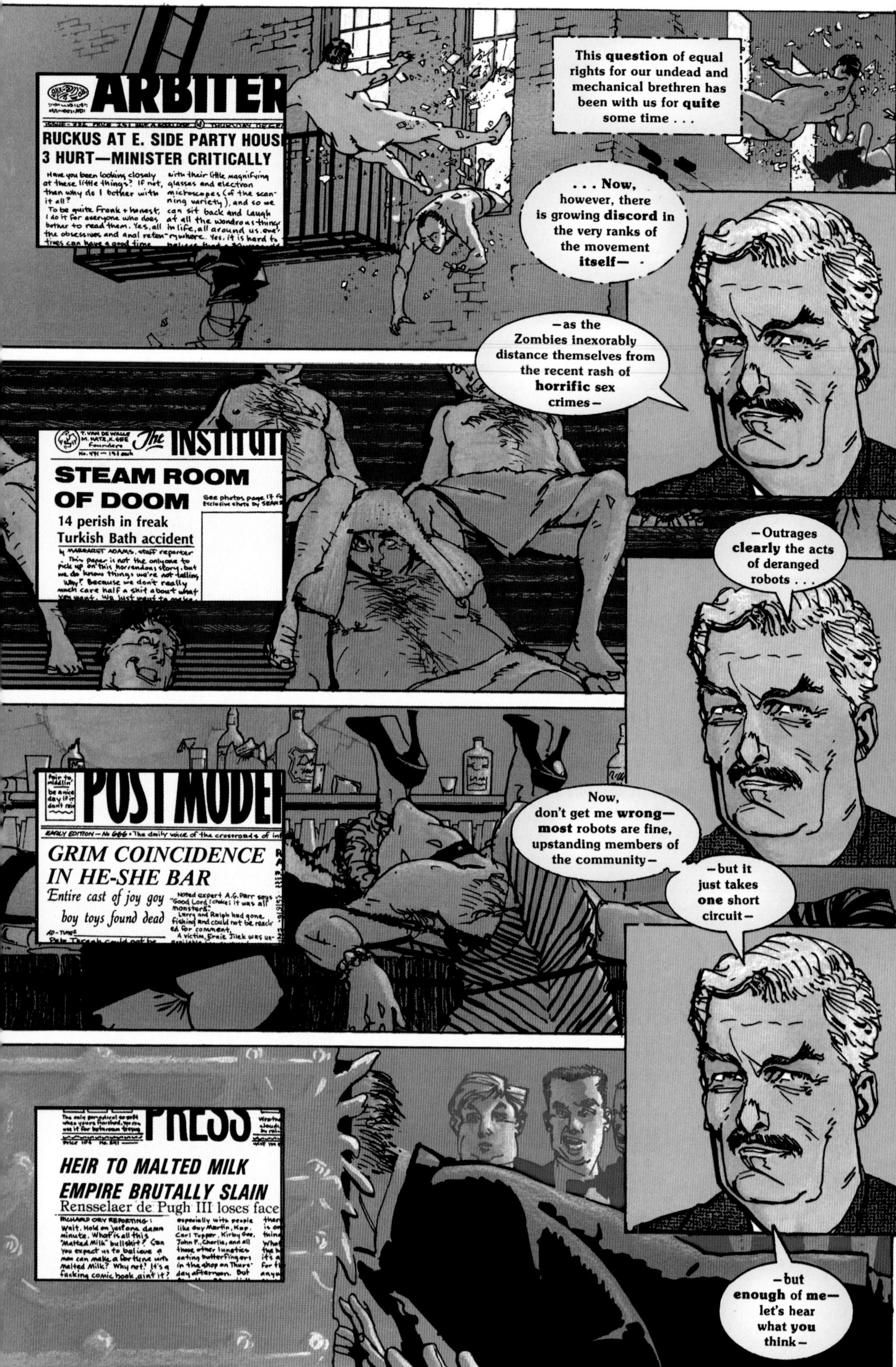

ARBITER
RUCKUS AT E. SIDE PARTY HOUS
3 HURT—MINISTER CRITICALLY
This question of equal rights for our undead and mechanical brethren has been with us for quite some time . . .
. . . Now, however, there is growing discord in the very ranks of the movement itself—
—as the Zombies inexorably distance themselves from the recent rash of horrific sex crimes—
The INSTITUT
STEAM ROOM OF DOOM
14 perish in freak Turkish Bath accident
—Outrages clearly the acts of deranged robots . . .
POST MODER
GRIM COINCIDENCE IN HE-SHE BAR
Entire cast of joy goy boy toys found dead
Now, don't get me wrong—most robots are fine, upstanding members of the community—
—but it just takes one short circuit—
PRESS
HEIR TO MALTED MILK EMPIRE BRUTALLY SLAIN
Rensselaer de Pugh III loses face
—but enough of me—let's hear what you think—

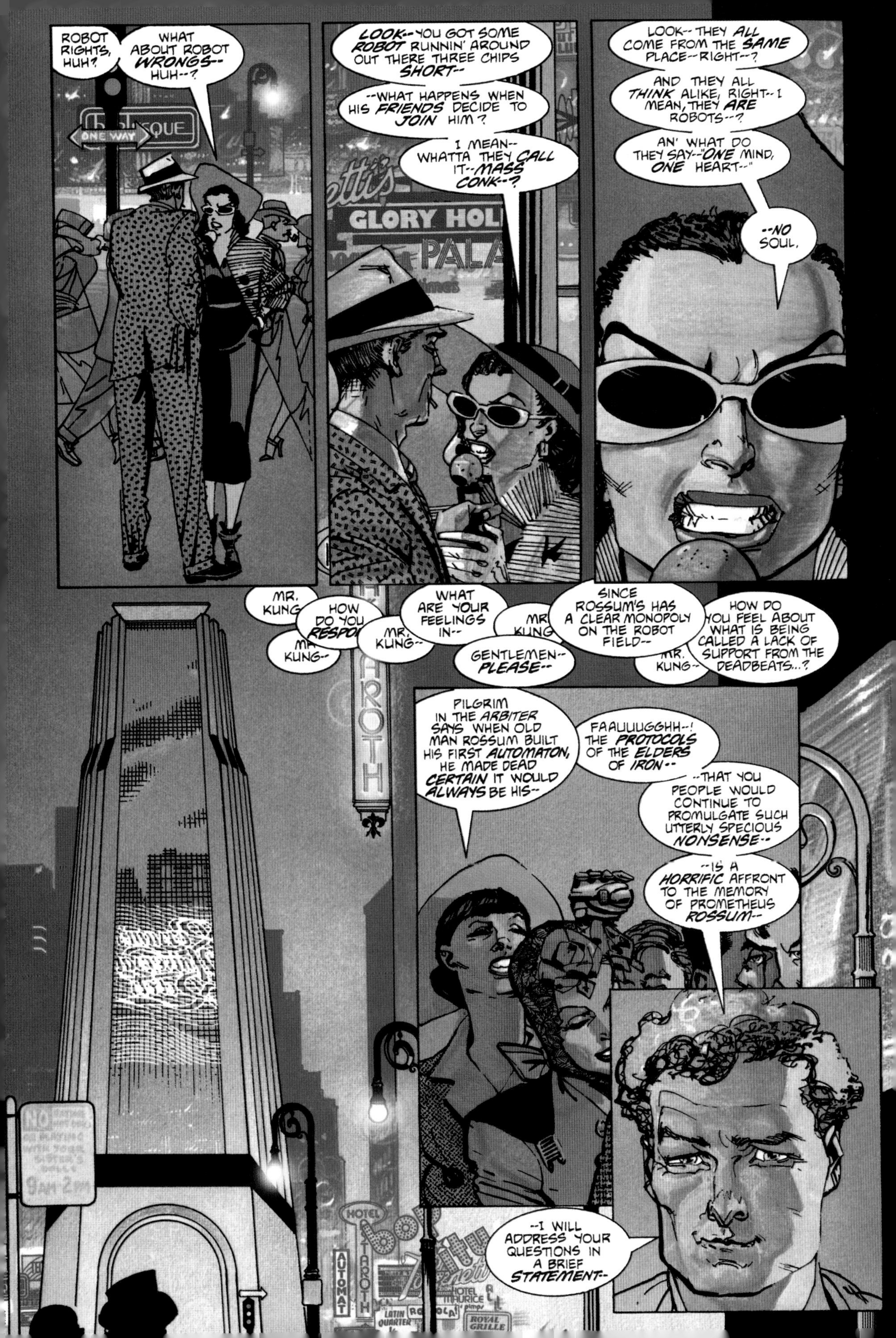
ROBOT RIGHTS, HUH?
WHAT ABOUT ROBOT WRONGS--HUH--?
LOOK--YOU GOT SOME ROBOT RUNNIN' AROUND OUT THERE THREE CHIPS SHORT--
--WHAT HAPPENS WHEN HIS FRIENDS DECIDE TO JOIN HIM?
I MEAN--WHATTA THEY CALL IT--MASS CONK--?
LOOK--THEY ALL COME FROM THE SAME PLACE--RIGHT--?
AND THEY ALL THINK ALIKE, RIGHT--I MEAN, THEY ARE ROBOTS--?
AN' WHAT DO THEY SAY--"ONE MIND, ONE HEART--"
--NO SOUL.
ONE WAY
GLORY HOL
MR. KUNG--
HOW DO YOU RESPO
MR. KUNG--
MR. KUNG--
WHAT ARE YOUR FEELINGS IN--
MR. KUNG
GENTLEMEN--PLEASE--
SINCE ROSSUM'S HAS A CLEAR MONOPOLY ON THE ROBOT FIELD--
MR. KUNG--
HOW DO YOU FEEL ABOUT WHAT IS BEING CALLED A LACK OF SUPPORT FROM THE DEADBEATS...?
PILGRIM IN THE ARBITER SAYS WHEN OLD MAN ROSSUM BUILT HIS FIRST AUTOMATON, HE MADE DEAD CERTAIN IT WOULD ALWAYS BE HIS--
FAAUUUGGHH--! THE PROTOCOLS OF THE ELDERS OF IRON--
--THAT YOU PEOPLE WOULD CONTINUE TO PROMULGATE SUCH UTTERLY SPECIOUS NONSENSE--
--IS A HORRIFIC AFFRONT TO THE MEMORY OF PROMETHEUS ROSSUM--
--I WILL ADDRESS YOUR QUESTIONS IN A BRIEF STATEMENT--
STAROTH
HOTEL
AUTOMAT
HOTEL MAURICE
LATIN QUARTER
ROYAL GRILLE

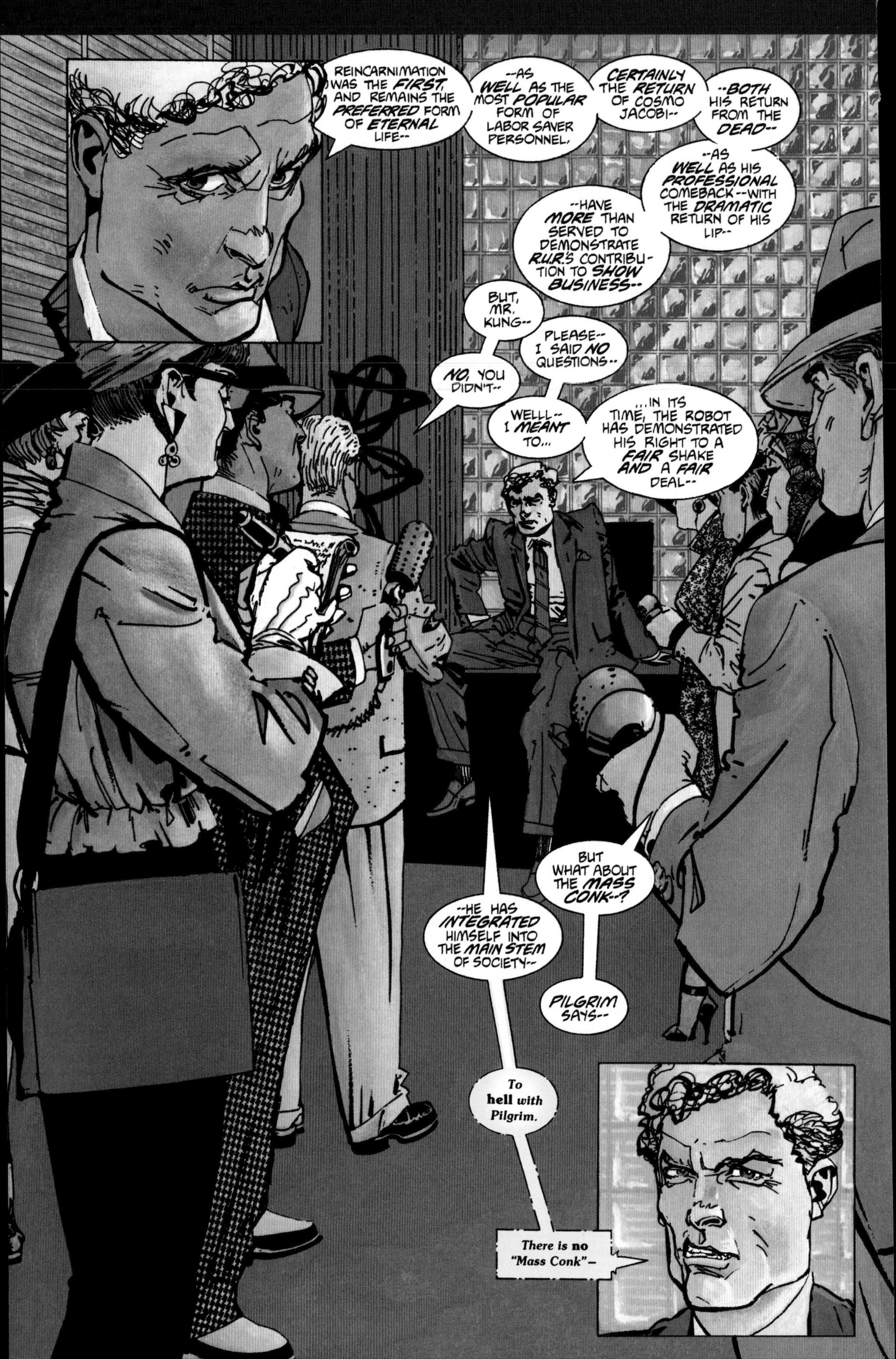
REINCARNIMATION WAS THE FIRST, AND REMAINS THE PREFERRED FORM OF ETERNAL LIFE--
--AS WELL AS THE MOST POPULAR FORM OF LABOR SAVER PERSONNEL,
CERTAINLY THE RETURN OF COSMO JACOBI--
--BOTH HIS RETURN FROM THE DEAD--
--AS WELL AS HIS PROFESSIONAL COMEBACK--WITH THE DRAMATIC RETURN OF HIS LIP--
--HAVE MORE THAN SERVED TO DEMONSTRATE R.U.R.'S CONTRIBUTION TO SHOW BUSINESS--
BUT, MR. KUNG--
PLEASE-- I SAID NO QUESTIONS--
NO, YOU DIDN'T--
WELLL-- I MEANT TO...
...IN ITS TIME, THE ROBOT HAS DEMONSTRATED HIS RIGHT TO A FAIR SHAKE AND A FAIR DEAL--
BUT WHAT ABOUT THE MASS CONK--?
--HE HAS INTEGRATED HIMSELF INTO THE MAIN STEM OF SOCIETY--
PILGRIM SAYS--
To hell with Pilgrim.
There is no "Mass Conk"–

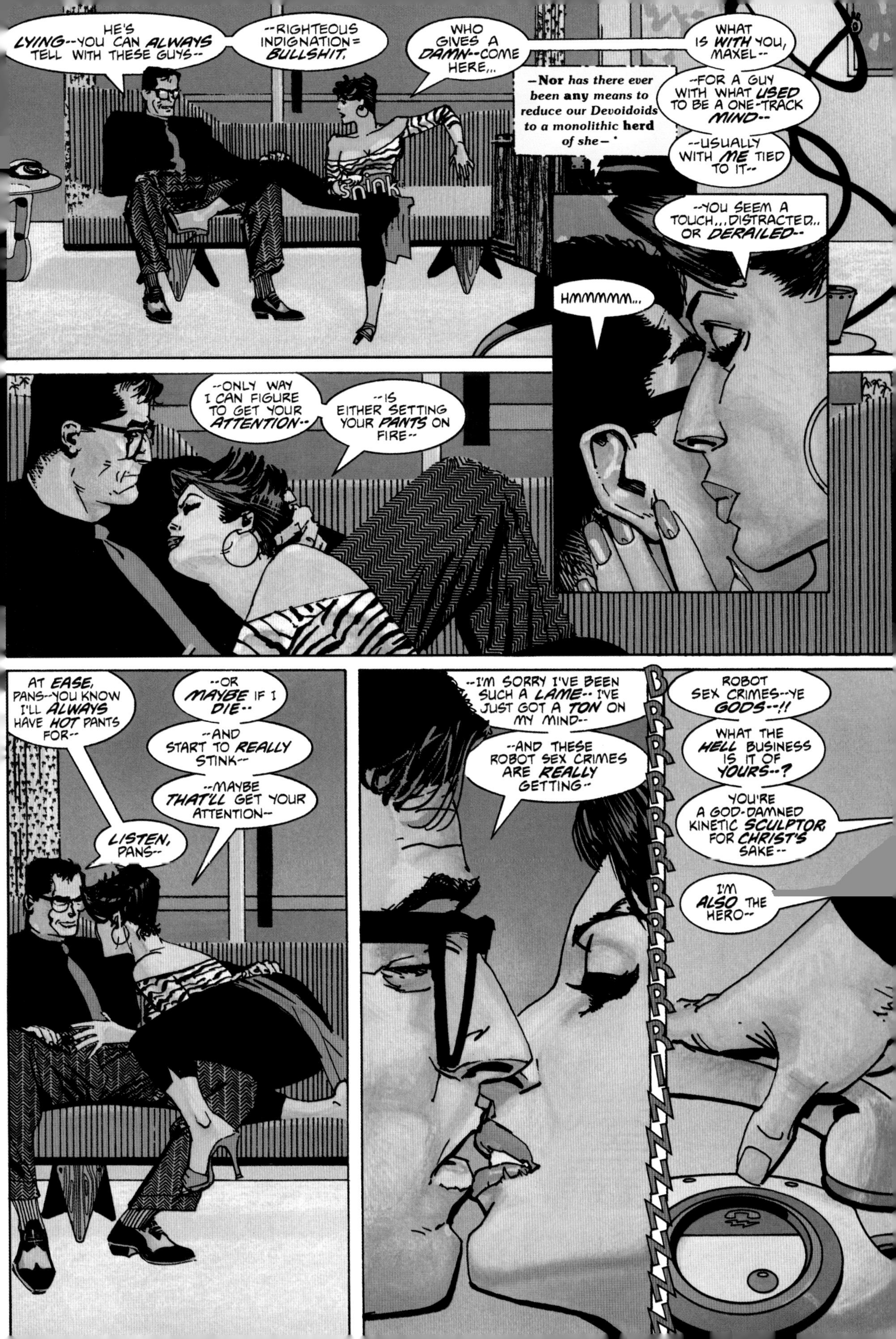
HE'S LYING--YOU CAN ALWAYS TELL WITH THESE GUYS--
--RIGHTEOUS INDIGNATION= BULLSHIT.
WHO GIVES A DAMN--COME HERE,..
—Nor has there ever been any means to reduce our Devoidoids to a monolithic herd of she—'
WHAT IS WITH YOU, MAXEL--
--FOR A GUY WITH WHAT USED TO BE A ONE-TRACK MIND--
--USUALLY WITH ME TIED TO IT--
--YOU SEEM A TOUCH,,,DISTRACTED,.. OR DERAILED--
HMMMMM,..
--ONLY WAY I CAN FIGURE TO GET YOUR ATTENTION--
--IS EITHER SETTING YOUR PANTS ON FIRE--
AT EASE, PANS--YOU KNOW I'LL ALWAYS HAVE HOT PANTS FOR--
--OR MAYBE IF I DIE--
--AND START TO REALLY STINK--
--MAYBE THAT'LL GET YOUR ATTENTION--
LISTEN, PANS--
--I'M SORRY I'VE BEEN SUCH A LAME-- I'VE JUST GOT A TON ON MY MIND--
--AND THESE ROBOT SEX CRIMES ARE REALLY GETTING--
BRRRRRRRRRRRRRRRRRRING
ROBOT SEX CRIMES--YE GODS--!!
WHAT THE HELL BUSINESS IS IT OF YOURS--?
YOU'RE A GOD-DAMNED KINETIC SCULPTOR, FOR CHRIST'S SAKE--
I'M ALSO THE HERO--

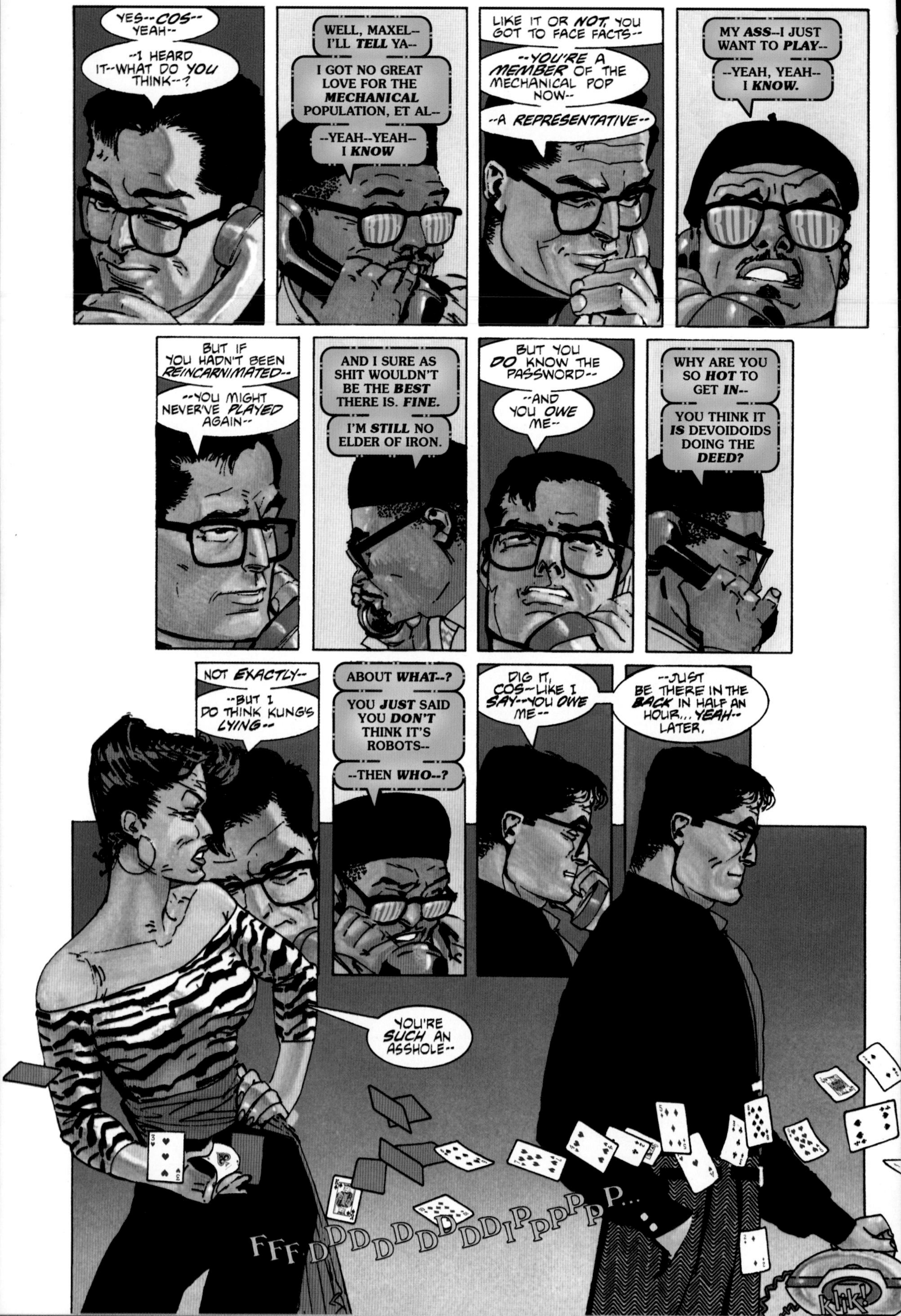

YES--COS--
YEAH--
--I HEARD IT--WHAT DO YOU THINK--?
WELL, MAXEL-- I'LL TELL YA--
I GOT NO GREAT LOVE FOR THE MECHANICAL POPULATION, ET AL--
--YEAH--YEAH-- I KNOW
LIKE IT OR NOT, YOU GOT TO FACE FACTS--
--YOU'RE A MEMBER OF THE MECHANICAL POP NOW--
--A REPRESENTATIVE--
MY ASS--I JUST WANT TO PLAY--
--YEAH, YEAH-- I KNOW.
BUT IF YOU HADN'T BEEN REINCARNIMATED--
--YOU MIGHT NEVER'VE PLAYED AGAIN--
AND I SURE AS SHIT WOULDN'T BE THE BEST THERE IS. FINE.
I'M STILL NO ELDER OF IRON.
BUT YOU DO KNOW THE PASSWORD--
--AND YOU OWE ME--
WHY ARE YOU SO HOT TO GET IN--
YOU THINK IT IS DEVOIDOIDS DOING THE DEED?
NOT EXACTLY--
--BUT I DO THINK KUNG'S LYING--
ABOUT WHAT--?
YOU JUST SAID YOU DON'T THINK IT'S ROBOTS--
--THEN WHO--?
DIG IT, COS--LIKE I SAY--YOU OWE ME--
--JUST BE THERE IN THE BACK IN HALF AN HOUR... YEAH-- LATER.
YOU'RE SUCH AN ASSHOLE--
FFFDDDDDDDDDIPPPPPP...
klik!

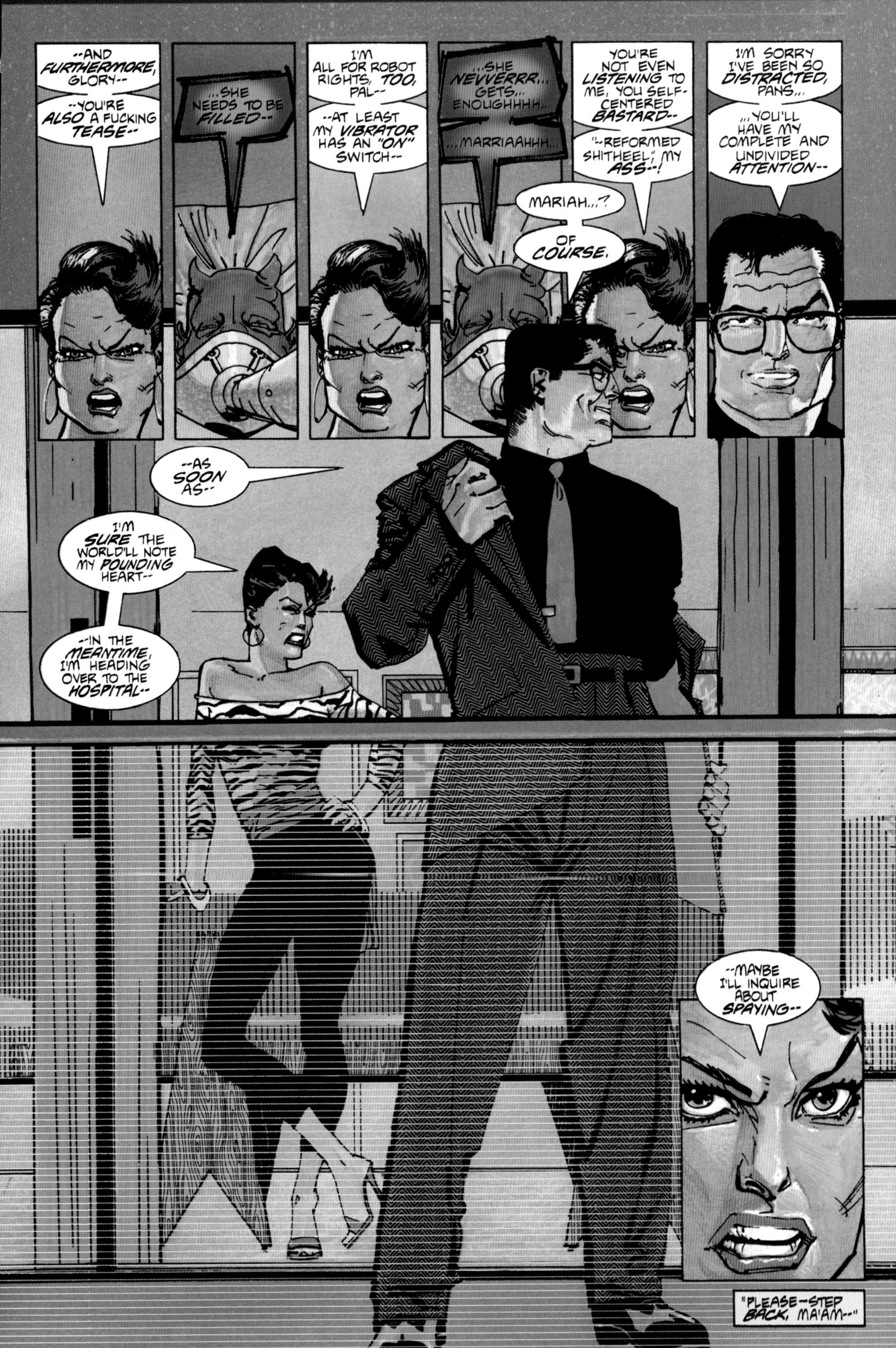
--AND FURTHERMORE, GLORY--
--YOU'RE ALSO A FUCKING TEASE--
...SHE NEEDS TO BE FILLED--
I'M ALL FOR ROBOT RIGHTS, TOO, PAL--
--AT LEAST MY VIBRATOR HAS AN "ON" SWITCH--
...SHE NEVVERRR... GETS... ENOUGHHHHH...
...MARRIAAHHH...
YOU'RE NOT EVEN LISTENING TO ME, YOU SELF-CENTERED BASTARD--
"--REFORMED SHITHEEL," MY ASS--!
MARIAH...?
OF COURSE.
I'M SORRY I'VE BEEN SO DISTRACTED, PANS...
...YOU'LL HAVE MY COMPLETE AND UNDIVIDED ATTENTION--
--AS SOON AS--
I'M SURE THE WORLD'LL NOTE MY POUNDING HEART--
--IN THE MEANTIME, I'M HEADING OVER TO THE HOSPITAL--
--MAYBE I'LL INQUIRE ABOUT SPAYING--
"PLEASE--STEP BACK, MA'AM--"

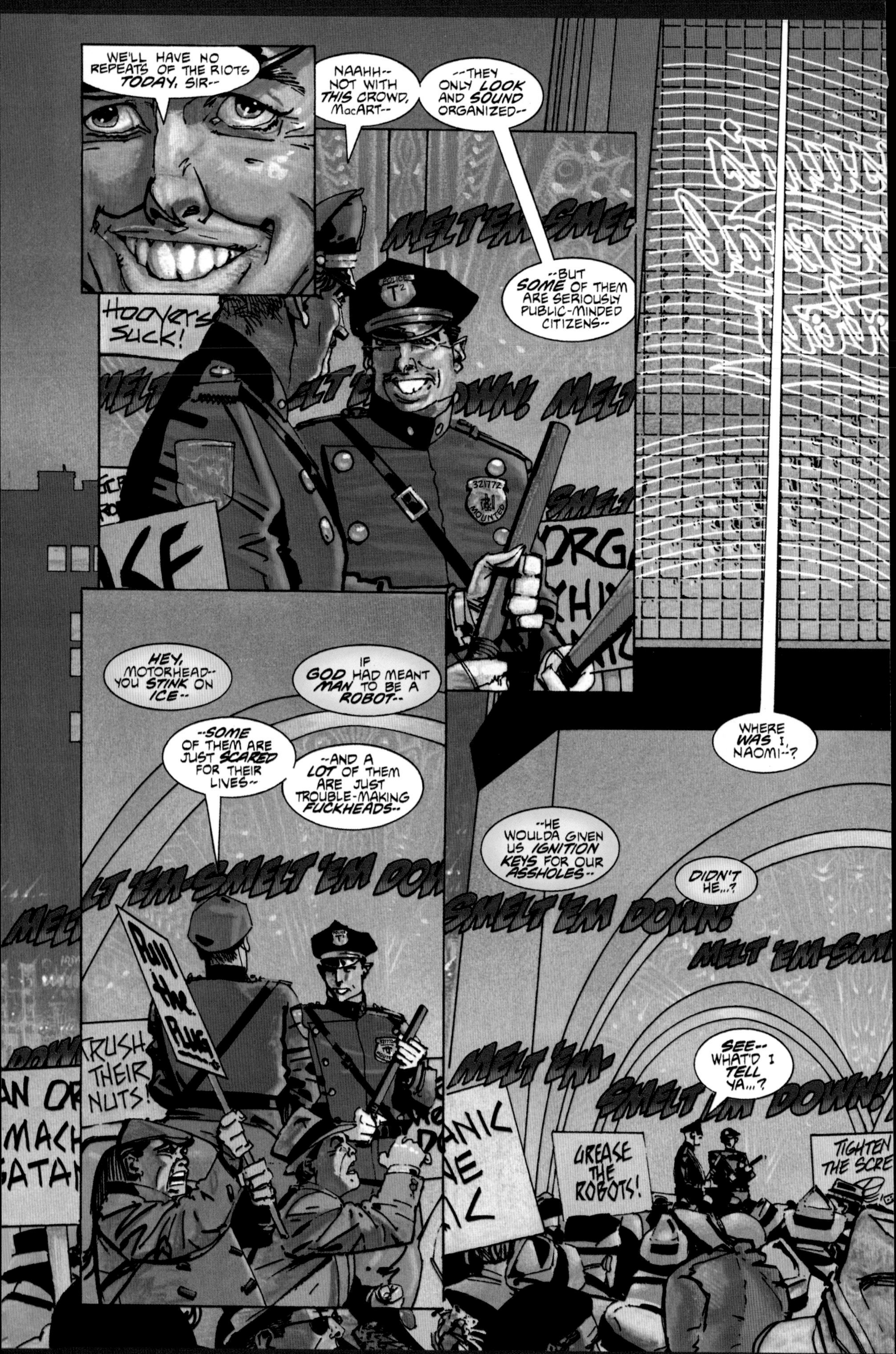

WE'LL HAVE NO REPEATS OF THE RIOTS TODAY, SIR--
NAAHH-- NOT WITH THIS CROWD, MacART--
--THEY ONLY LOOK AND SOUND ORGANIZED--
MELT 'EM-SMEL
--BUT SOME OF THEM ARE SERIOUSLY PUBLIC-MINDED CITIZENS--
Hoovers Suck!
SMELT 'EM DOWN! MELT
HEY, MOTORHEAD-- YOU STINK ON ICE--
IF GOD HAD MEANT MAN TO BE A ROBOT--
--SOME OF THEM ARE JUST SCARED FOR THEIR LIVES--
--AND A LOT OF THEM ARE JUST TROUBLE-MAKING FUCKHEADS--
WHERE WAS I, NAOMI--?
--HE WOULDA GIVEN US IGNITION KEYS FOR OUR ASSHOLES--
DIDN'T HE...?
MELT 'EM-SMELT 'EM DOWN
SMELT 'EM DOWN!
MELT 'EM-SM
Pull the Plug
CRUSH THEIR NUTS!
SEE-- WHAT'D I TELL YA...?
MELT 'EM-
SMELT 'EM DOWN!
GREASE THE ROBOTS!
TIGHTEN THE SCRE

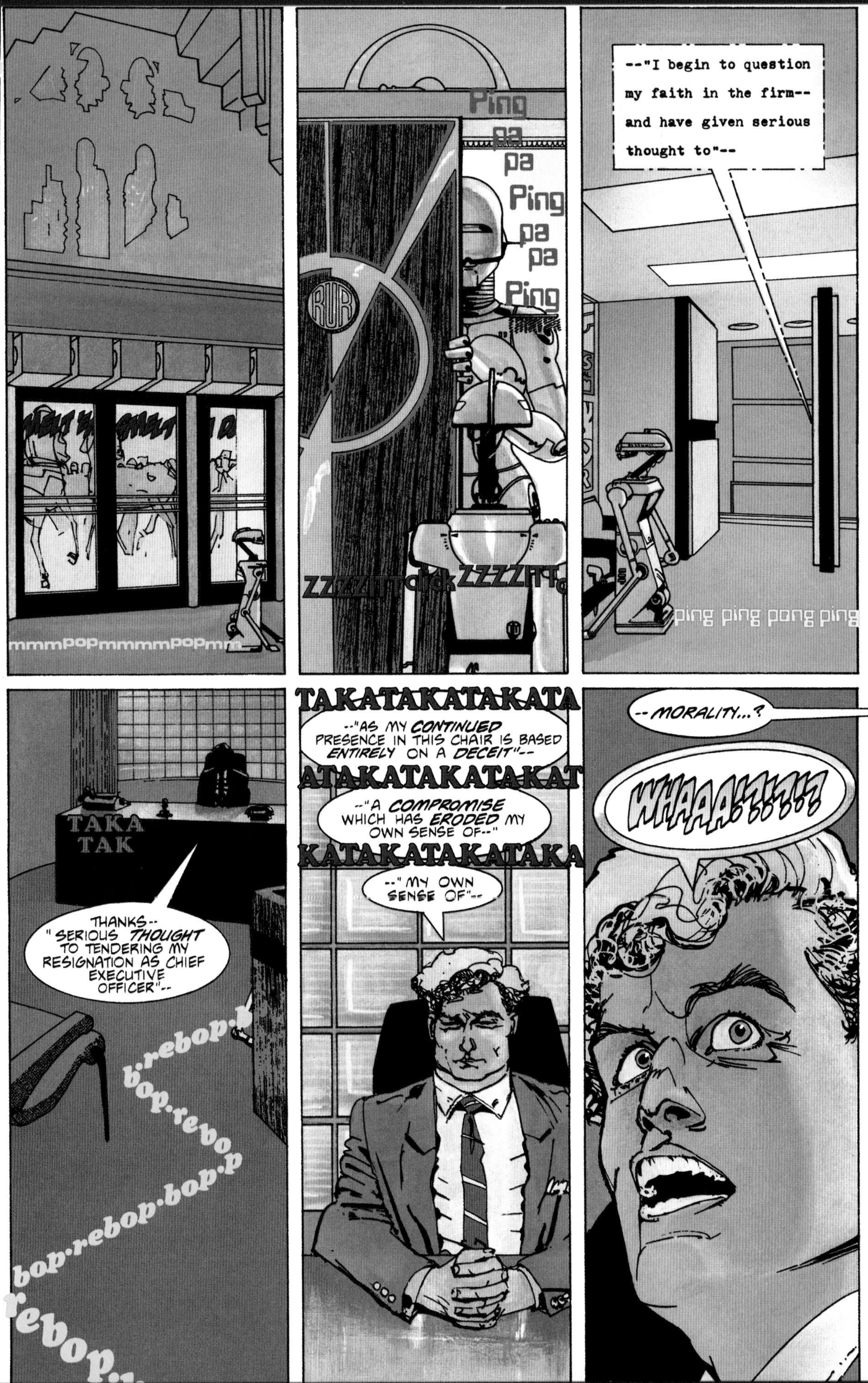
mmmPOPmmmmPOPmm
Ping
pa
pa
Ping
pa
pa
Ping
RUR
ZZZZIT click ZZZZIT
--"I begin to question my faith in the firm--and have given serious thought to"--
ping ping pong ping
TAKA
TAK
THANKS-- "SERIOUS THOUGHT TO TENDERING MY RESIGNATION AS CHIEF EXECUTIVE OFFICER"--
b·rebop·b
bop·rebop
bop·rebop·bop·p
bop·rebop
TAKATAKATAKATA
--"AS MY CONTINUED PRESENCE IN THIS CHAIR IS BASED ENTIRELY ON A DECEIT"--
ATAKATAKATAKAT
--"A COMPROMISE WHICH HAS ERODED MY OWN SENSE OF--"
KATAKATAKATAKA
--"MY OWN SENSE OF"--
--MORALITY...?
WHAAA!?!?!?

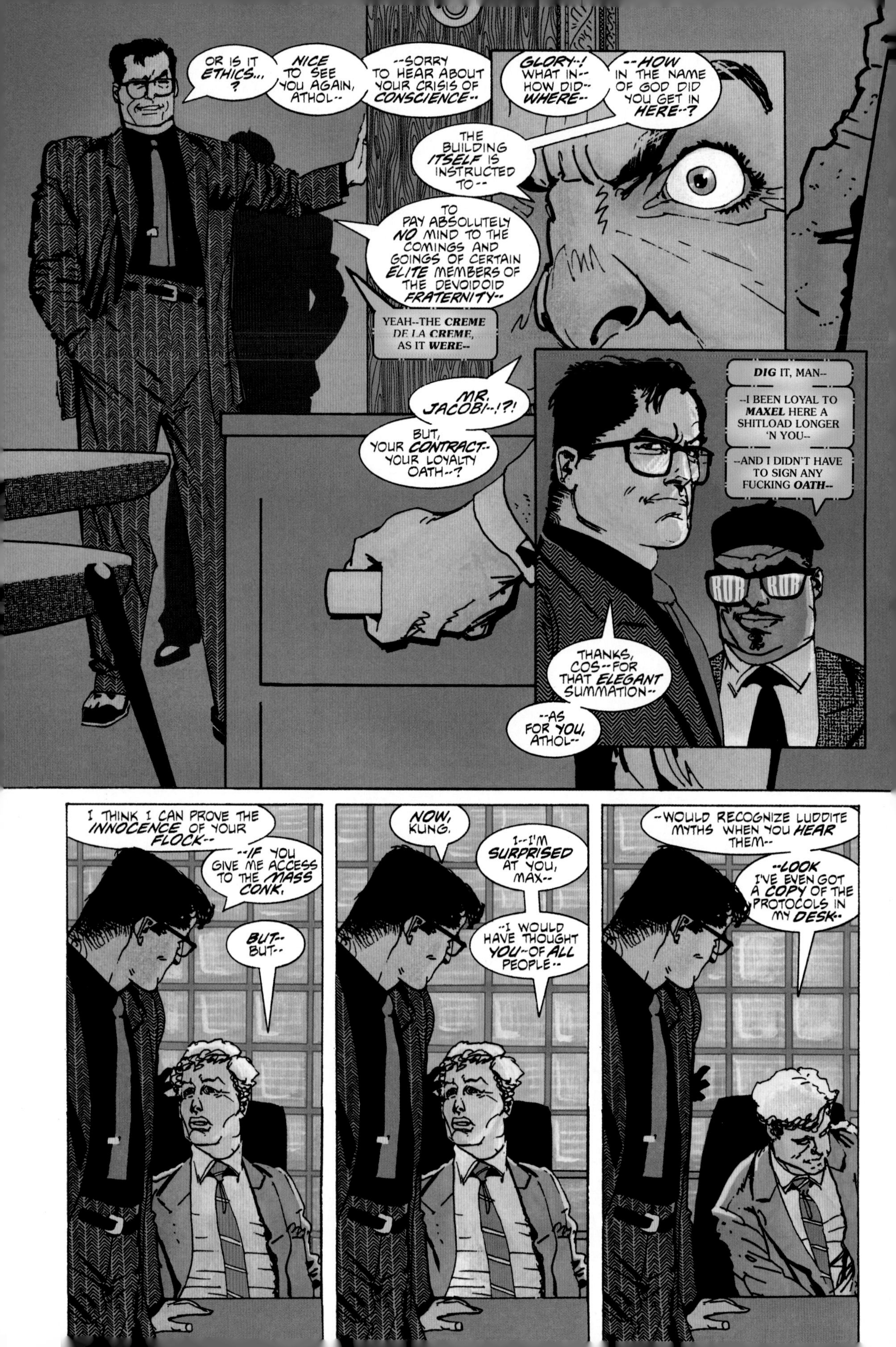
OR IS IT ETHICS... ?
NICE TO SEE YOU AGAIN, ATHOL--
--SORRY TO HEAR ABOUT YOUR CRISIS OF CONSCIENCE--
GLORY--! WHAT IN-- HOW DID-- WHERE--
--HOW IN THE NAME OF GOD DID YOU GET IN HERE--?
THE BUILDING ITSELF IS INSTRUCTED TO--
TO PAY ABSOLUTELY NO MIND TO THE COMINGS AND GOINGS OF CERTAIN ELITE MEMBERS OF THE DEVOIDOID FRATERNITY--
YEAH--THE CREME DE LA CREME, AS IT WERE--
MR. JACOBI--!?!
BUT, YOUR CONTRACT-- YOUR LOYALTY OATH--?
DIG IT, MAN--
--I BEEN LOYAL TO MAXEL HERE A SHITLOAD LONGER 'N YOU--
--AND I DIDN'T HAVE TO SIGN ANY FUCKING OATH--
THANKS, COS--FOR THAT ELEGANT SUMMATION--
--AS FOR YOU, ATHOL--
I THINK I CAN PROVE THE INNOCENCE OF YOUR FLOCK--
--IF YOU GIVE ME ACCESS TO THE MASS CONK.
BUT-- BUT--
NOW, KUNG.
I--I'M SURPRISED AT YOU, MAX--
--I WOULD HAVE THOUGHT YOU--OF ALL PEOPLE--
--WOULD RECOGNIZE LUDDITE MYTHS WHEN YOU HEAR THEM--
--LOOK I'VE EVEN GOT A COPY OF THE PROTOCOLS IN MY DESK--

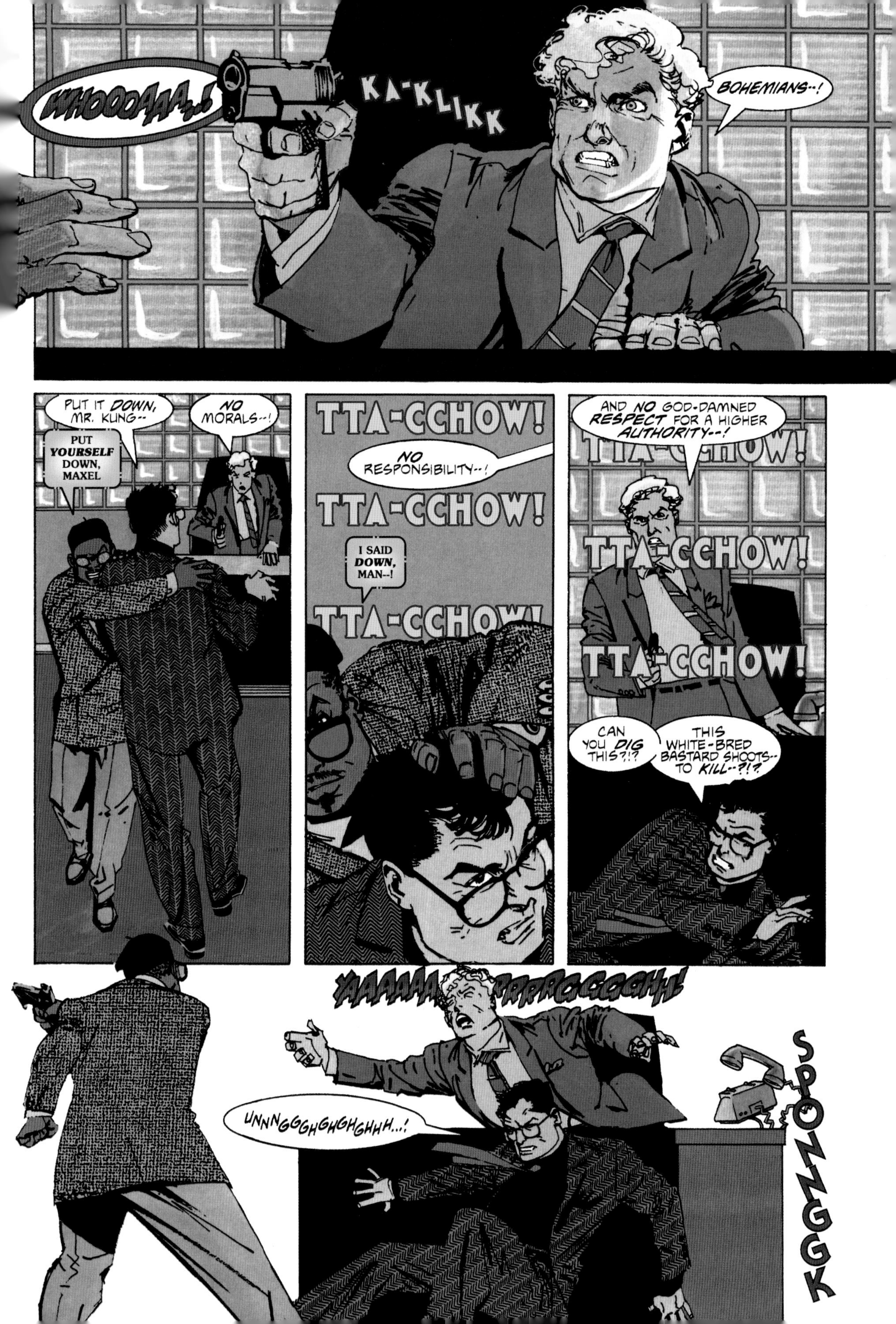
WHOOOAAA..!
KA-KLIKK
BOHEMIANS--!
PUT IT DOWN, MR. KUNG--
PUT YOURSELF DOWN, MAXEL
NO MORALS--!
TTA-CCHOW!
NO RESPONSIBILITY--!
TTA-CCHOW!
I SAID DOWN, MAN--!
TTA-CCHOW!
AND NO GOD-DAMNED RESPECT FOR A HIGHER AUTHORITY--!
TTA-CCHOW!
TTA-CCHOW!
TTA-CCHOW!
CAN YOU DIG THIS?!?
THIS WHITE-BRED BASTARD SHOOTS-- TO KILL--?!?
YAAAAAARRRRGGGGHH!
UNNNGGGHGHGHGHHH...!
SPONGGK

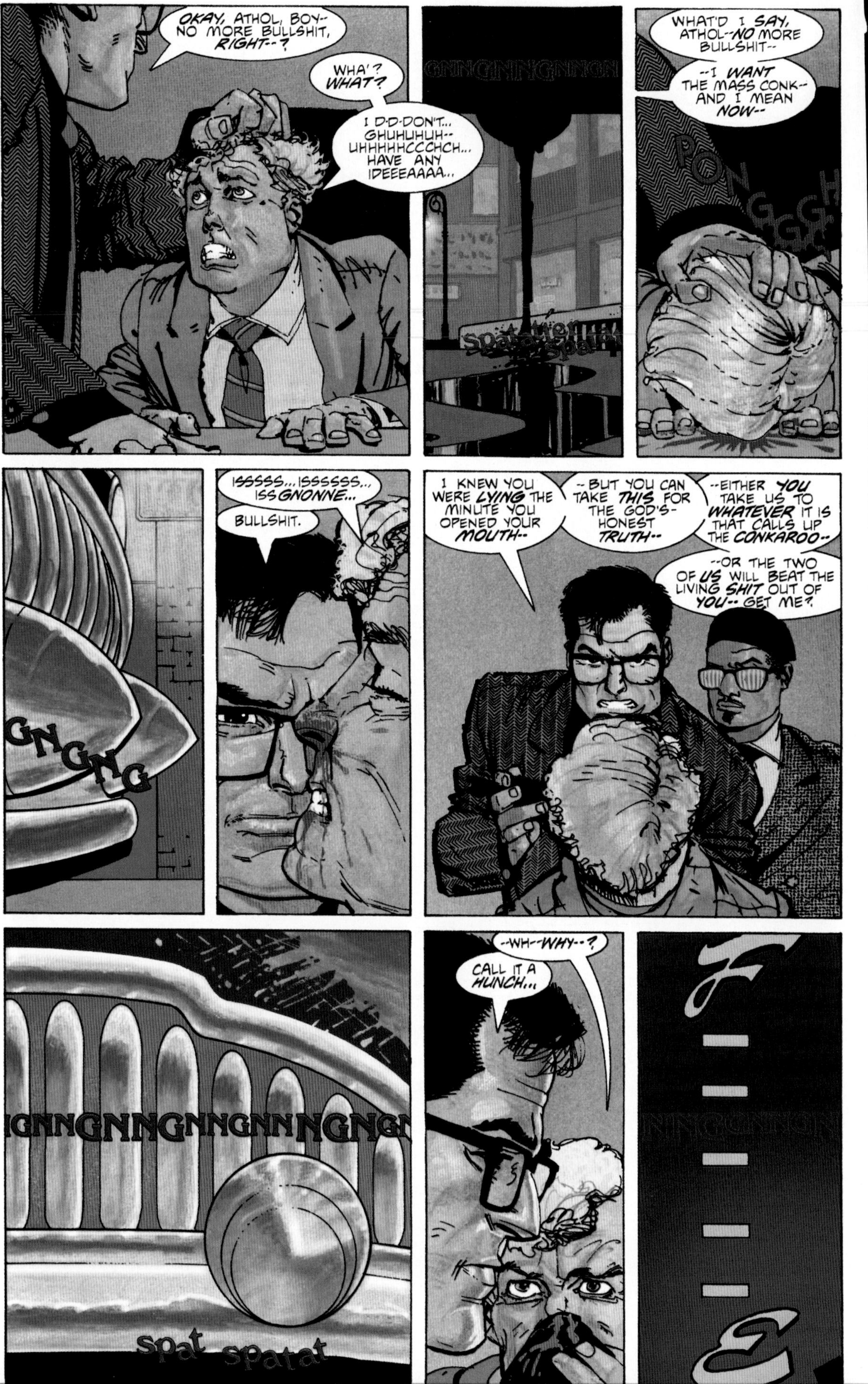
OKAY, ATHOL, BOY-- NO MORE BULLSHIT, RIGHT--?
WHA'? WHAT?
I D-D-DON'T... GHUHUHUH-- UHHHHHCCCHCH... HAVE ANY IDEEEAAAA...
GNNNGNNNGNNNGN
spatatter spatat
WHAT'D I SAY, ATHOL--NO MORE BULLSHIT--
--I WANT THE MASS CONK-- AND I MEAN NOW--
PONGGGH
GNGNG
ISSSSS...ISSSSSS... ISSGNONNE...
BULLSHIT.
I KNEW YOU WERE LYING THE MINUTE YOU OPENED YOUR MOUTH--
--BUT YOU CAN TAKE THIS FOR THE GOD'S-HONEST TRUTH--
--EITHER YOU TAKE US TO WHATEVER IT IS THAT CALLS UP THE CONKAROO--
--OR THE TWO OF US WILL BEAT THE LIVING SHIT OUT OF YOU-- GET ME?
NGNNGNNGNNGNNNGNGN
spat spatatat
--WH--WHY--?
CALL IT A HUNCH...

OLD MR. ROSSUM *NEVER* INTENDED--

SPARE ME, ATHOL--

--OLD MR. *ROSSUM* WAS A *MEAN-*SPIRITED, UNION-BUSTING *BASTARD*--

spat spat spat spat

YOUR *CALLOUS* DISREGARD FOR YOUR OATH IN BOND SHOULD *FRIGHTEN* YOU, MR. JACOBI--

--IT DEMONSTRATES AN *UTTER* LACK OF CHARACTER--

GNNNGNNGNNG

I'LL SAY THIS FOR THE *LAST* TIME--

--I AM A ROBOT BY *CONVENIENCE*--

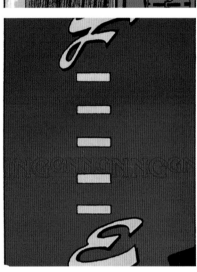

CONVENIENCE OR *NOT,* YOU SILLY LITTLE MAN--YOU'RE *STUCK* WITH IT--

--AND-- IF *THIS* HAPPENS--

YES--!

ROBOTIC *SUFFRAGE* WILL BE SET BACK--MAYBE *FOREVER*--

JUST *WATCH* THAT "LITTLE MAN" *SHIT*--

THIS--YOU MEAN THE MASS *CONK*--?

HEY--! ALL'S I WANNA DO IS *PLAY*--

WHICH, I LEAP TO *REMIND* YOU, YOU WERE UTTERLY *INCAPABLE* OF DOING IN THE LAST FIVE YEARS OF YOUR *LIFE...*

EXCUSE ME--BUT ROBOTS GIVE ME THE *CREEPS,* MAN--

IMPRESSED...?

X. MACHINA president nt relations

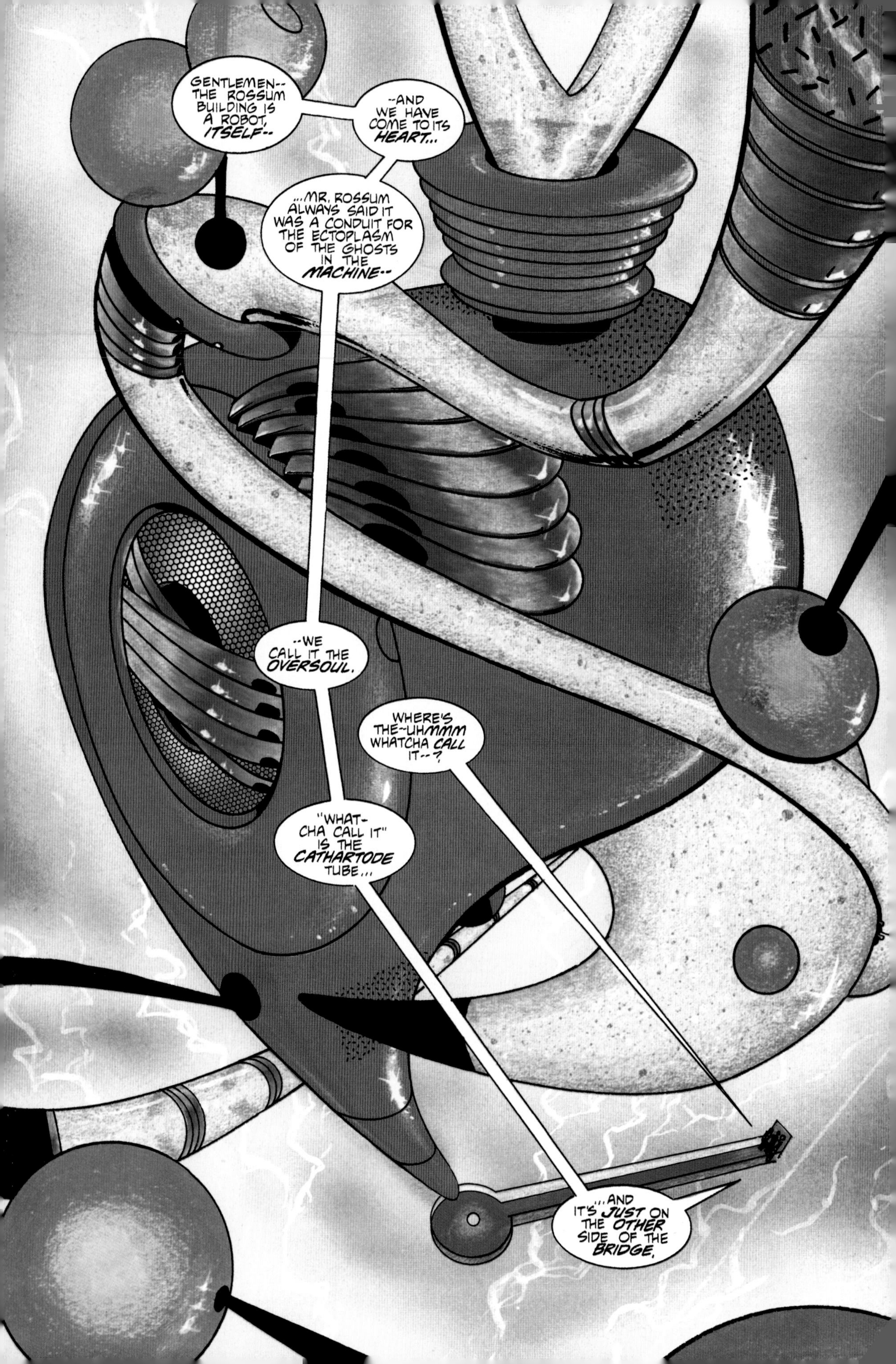
GENTLEMEN-- THE ROSSUM BUILDING IS A ROBOT, ITSELF--
--AND WE HAVE COME TO ITS HEART...
...MR. ROSSUM ALWAYS SAID IT WAS A CONDUIT FOR THE ECTOPLASM OF THE GHOSTS IN THE MACHINE--
--WE CALL IT THE OVERSOUL.
WHERE'S THE--UHMMM WHATCHA CALL IT--?
"WHAT-CHA CALL IT" IS THE CATHARTODE TUBE...
...AND IT'S JUST ON THE OTHER SIDE OF THE BRIDGE.

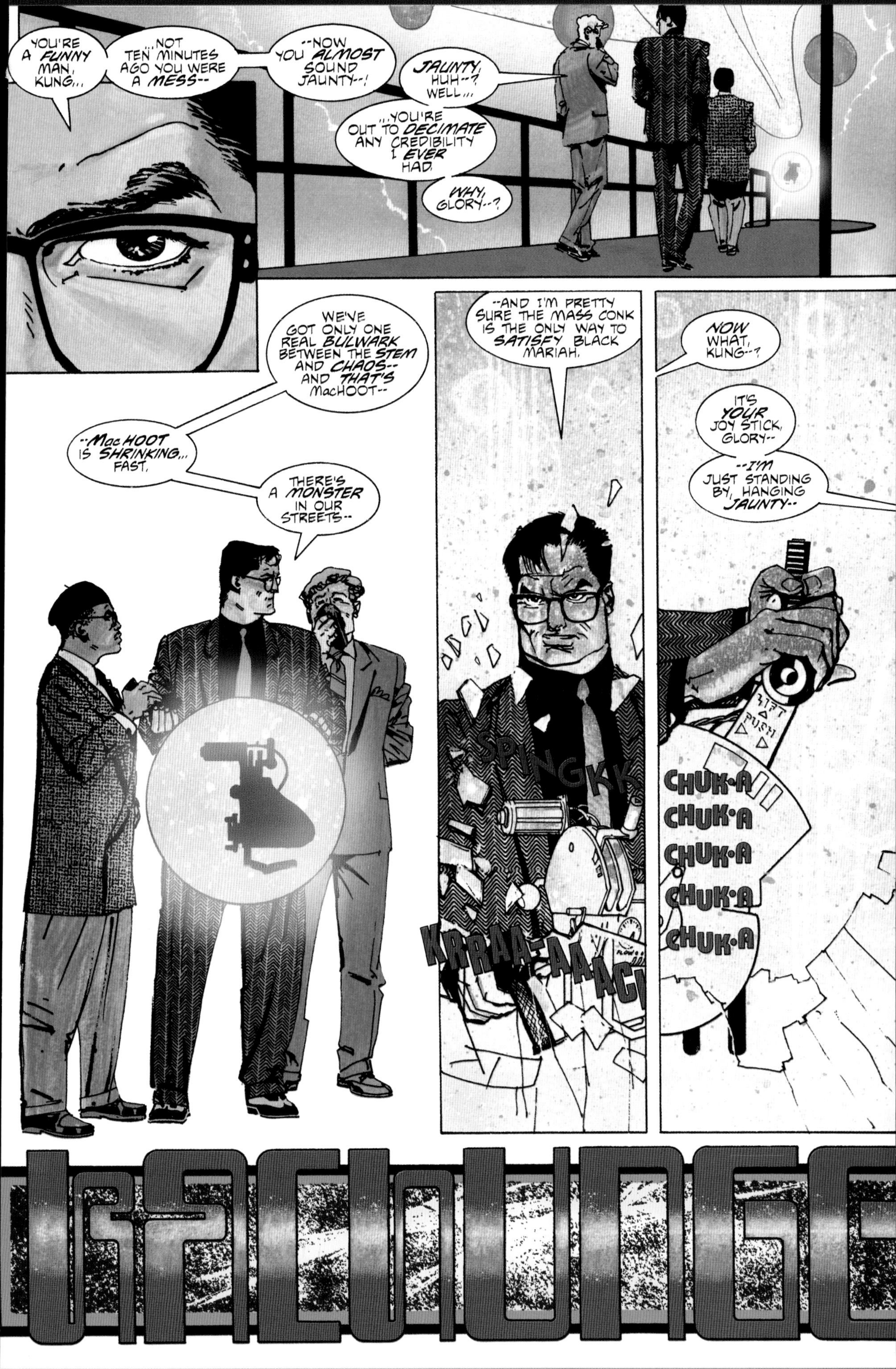
YOU'RE A FUNNY MAN, KUNG...
...NOT TEN MINUTES AGO YOU WERE A MESS--
--NOW YOU ALMOST SOUND JAUNTY--!
JAUNTY, HUH--? WELL...
...YOU'RE OUT TO DECIMATE ANY CREDIBILITY I EVER HAD.
WHY, GLORY--?
WE'VE GOT ONLY ONE REAL BULWARK BETWEEN THE STEM AND CHAOS-- AND THAT'S MacHOOT--
--MacHOOT IS SHRINKING... FAST.
THERE'S A MONSTER IN OUR STREETS--
--AND I'M PRETTY SURE THE MASS CONK IS THE ONLY WAY TO SATISFY BLACK MARIAH.
SPINGKK
KRRAA-AAAC
NOW WHAT, KUNG--?
IT'S YOUR JOY STICK, GLORY--
--I'M JUST STANDING BY, HANGING JAUNTY--
CHUK-A
CHUK-A
CHUK-A
CHUK-A
CHUK-A

KA-CHUNNGGKK
KA-CHUNNGGKKK
NAOMI
ROSSUM'S
KA-CHUNNGGK
ROSSUM
KA-CHUNNGGKK
RUR
KA-CHUNNGGKK
RUR
KA-CHUNNGGKI
RUR
KA-CHUNNGGKI
KA-CHUNNGGHKKK
DOC-TOR DOG
RUR
KA-CHUNNGGKKI
JUKEBOT
KA-CHUNNGGKKI
ROSSUMS
KA-CHUNNGGKKK
RUR
KA-CHUNNGGKK
RUR
WATCH THE
KA-CHUNNGGKI
RUR RUR
KA-CHUNNGGKKK
RUR
KA-CHUNNGGKKKK
ROSSUM
KA-CHUNNGGK
GOTTA BOOK, MAXEL-- DIG YOU LATER.

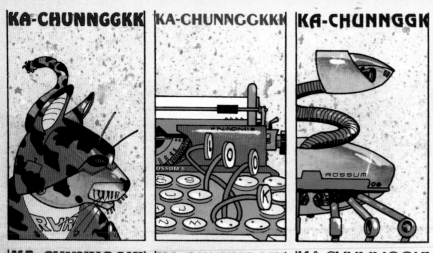

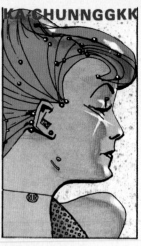

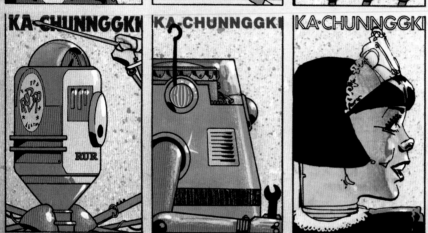

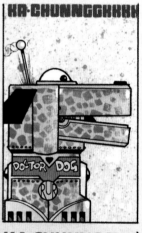

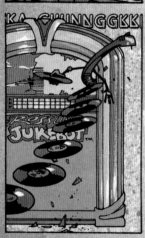

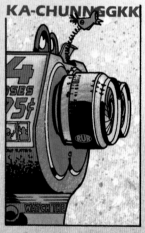

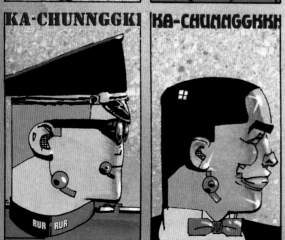

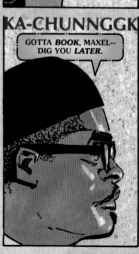

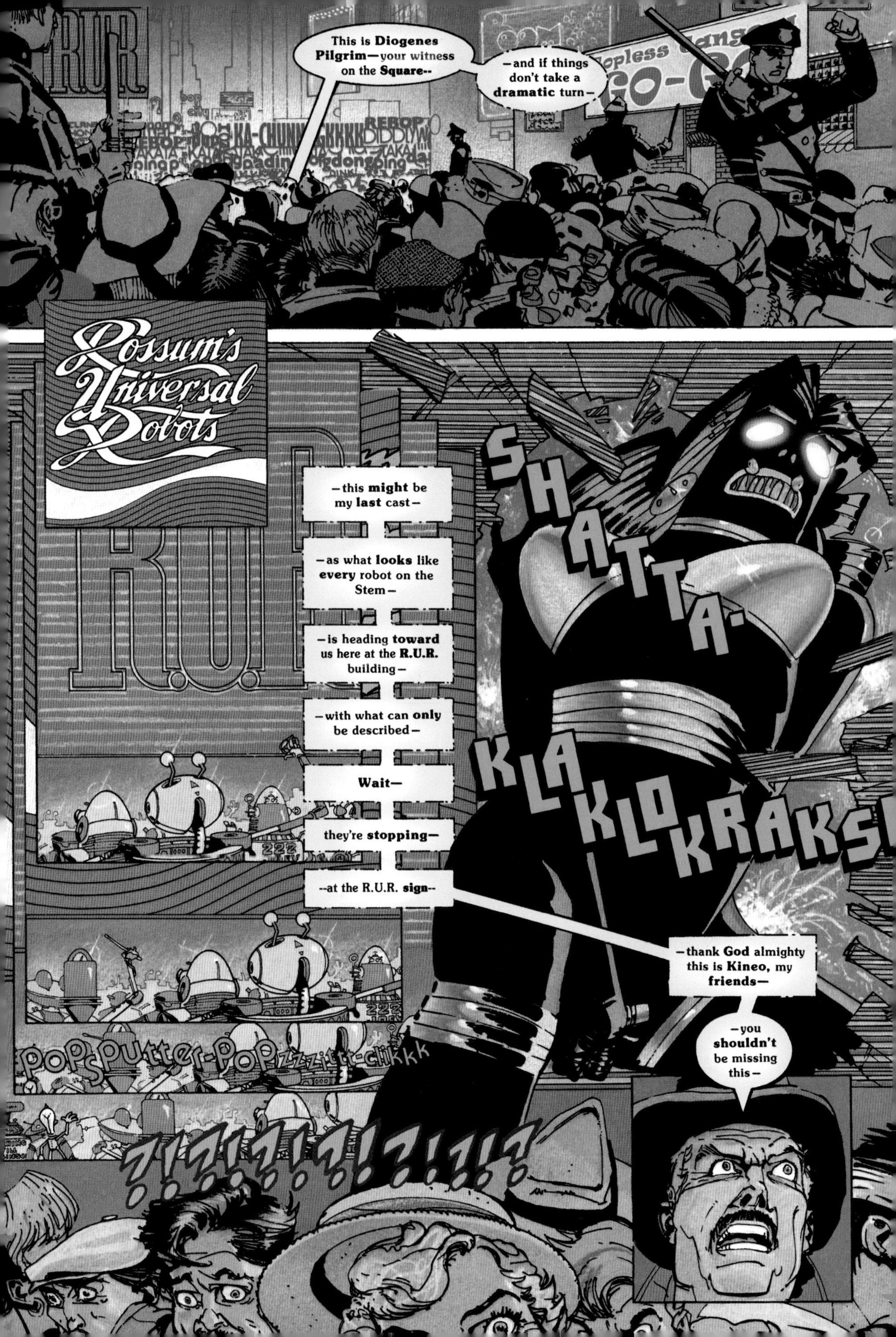

R.U.R.
This is Diogenes Pilgrim—your witness on the Square--
—and if things don't take a dramatic turn—
Topless
GO-GO
KA-CHUNNGKKKK
REBOP
Rossum's Universal Robots
R.U.R.
—this might be my last cast—
—as what looks like every robot on the Stem—
—is heading toward us here at the R.U.R. building—
—with what can only be described—
Wait—
they're stopping—
--at the R.U.R. sign--
SHATTA-
KLAKLOKRAKS
POPSPUTTER-POPZZZITT-CLIKKK
?!?!?!?!?!?!?
—thank God almighty this is Kineo, my friends—
—you shouldn't be missing this—

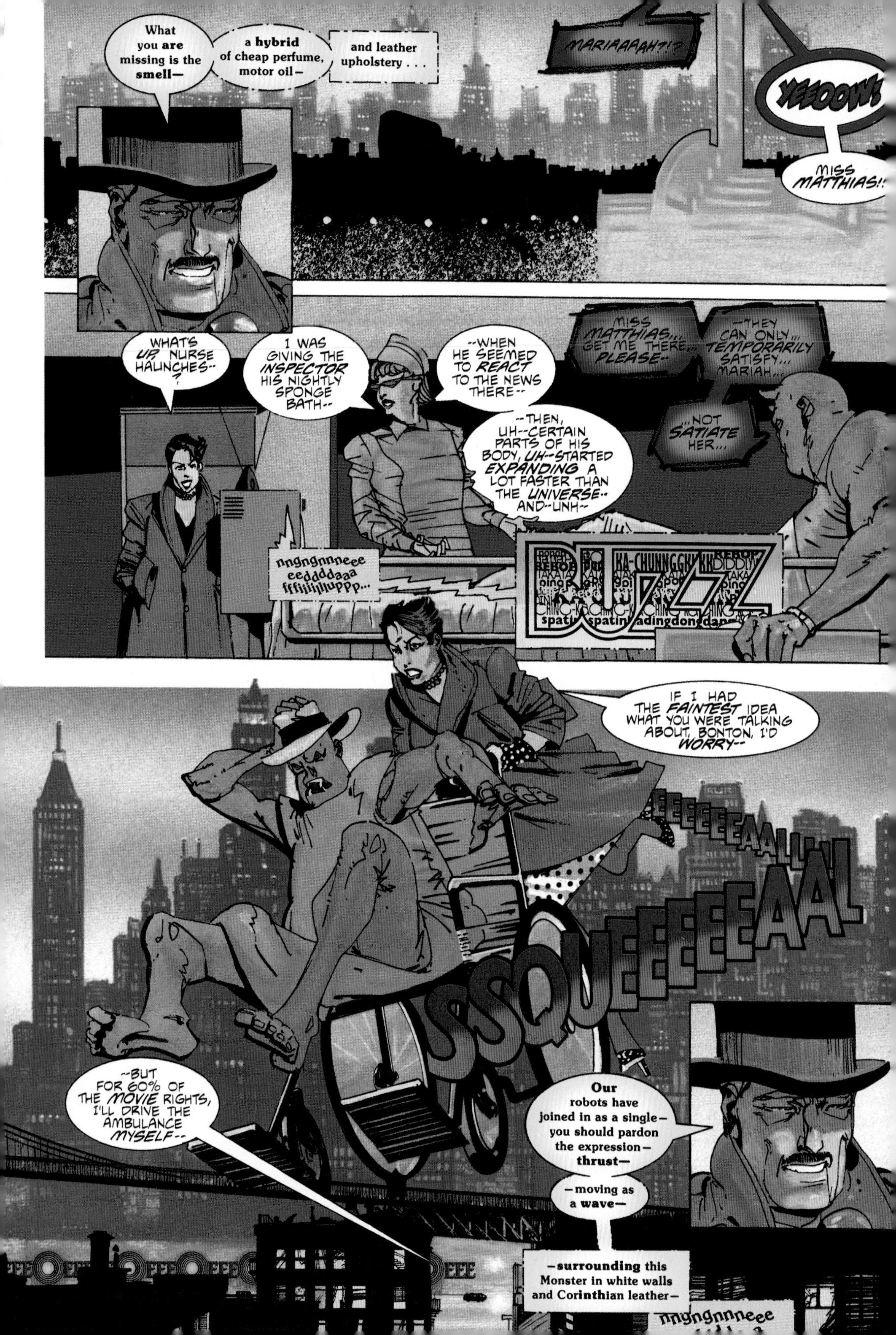
What you are missing is the smell—
a hybrid of cheap perfume, motor oil—
and leather upholstery . . .
MARIAAAAH?!?
YEEOOW!
MISS MATTHIAS!!
WHAT'S UP, NURSE HAUNCHES--?
I WAS GIVING THE INSPECTOR HIS NIGHTLY SPONGE BATH--
--WHEN HE SEEMED TO REACT TO THE NEWS THERE--
--THEN, UH--CERTAIN PARTS OF HIS BODY, UH--STARTED EXPANDING A LOT FASTER THAN THE UNIVERSE--AND--UNH--
MISS MATTHIAS... GET ME THERE... PLEASE--
--THEY CAN ONLY... TEMPORARILY SATISFY... MARIAH...
...NOT SATIATE HER...
nngngnnneee eeddddaaa ffiiiiiilllupppp...
KA-CHUNNGGHKKK
IF I HAD THE FAINTEST IDEA WHAT YOU WERE TALKING ABOUT, BONTON, I'D WORRY--
SSQUEEEEEEAAL
--BUT FOR 60% OF THE MOVIE RIGHTS, I'LL DRIVE THE AMBULANCE MYSELF--
Our robots have joined in as a single—you should pardon the expression—thrust—
—moving as a wave—
—surrounding this Monster in white walls and Corinthian leather—
nngngnnneee

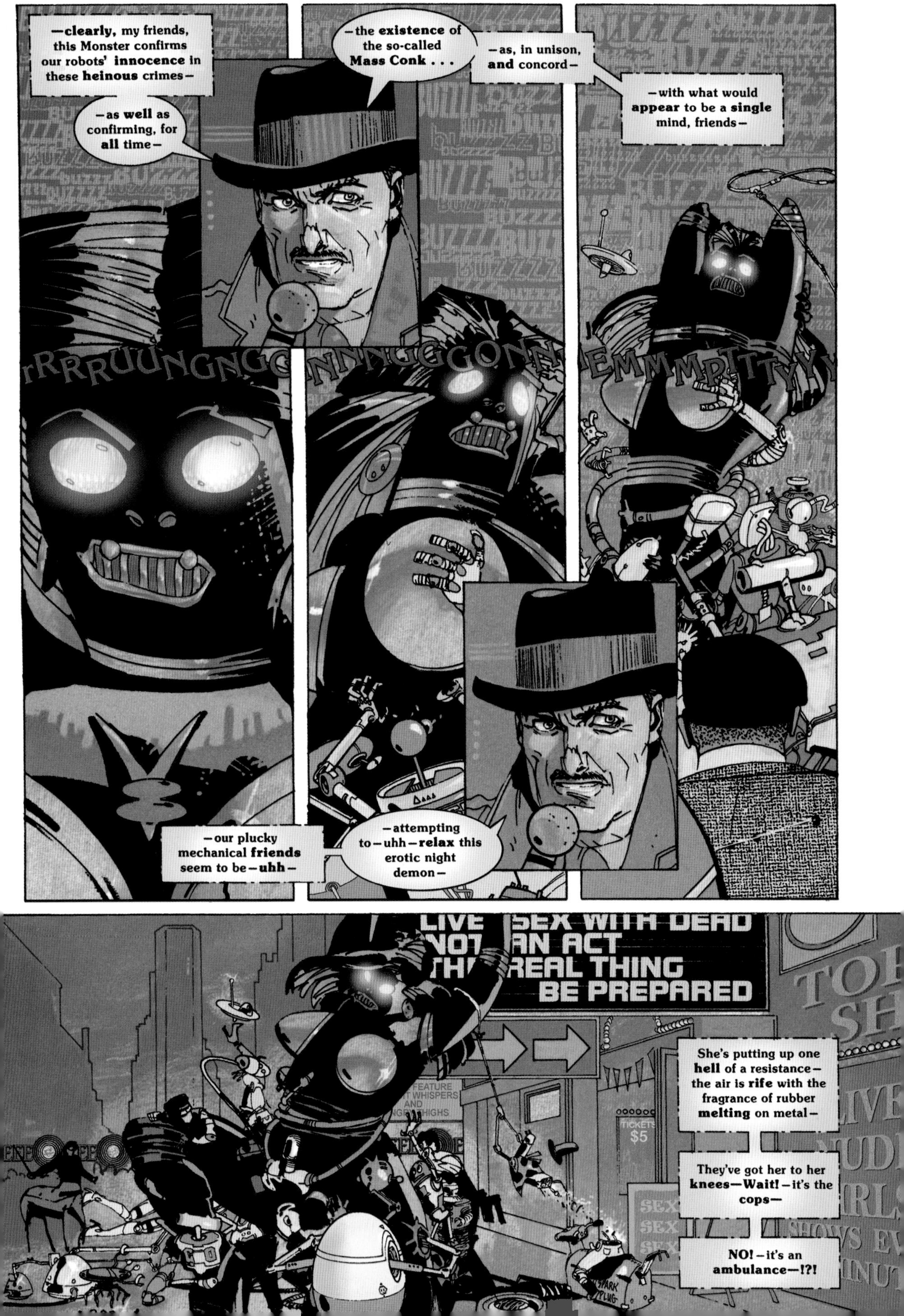
—clearly, my friends, this Monster confirms our robots' innocence in these heinous crimes—
—as well as confirming, for all time—
—the existence of the so-called Mass Conk . . .
—as, in unison, and concord—
—with what would appear to be a single mind, friends—
—our plucky mechanical friends seem to be—uhh—
—attempting to—uhh—relax this erotic night demon—
LIVE SEX WITH DEAD
REAL THING
BE PREPARED
TICKETS $5
She's putting up one hell of a resistance—the air is rife with the fragrance of rubber melting on metal—
They've got her to her knees—Wait!—it's the cops—
NO!—it's an ambulance—!?!

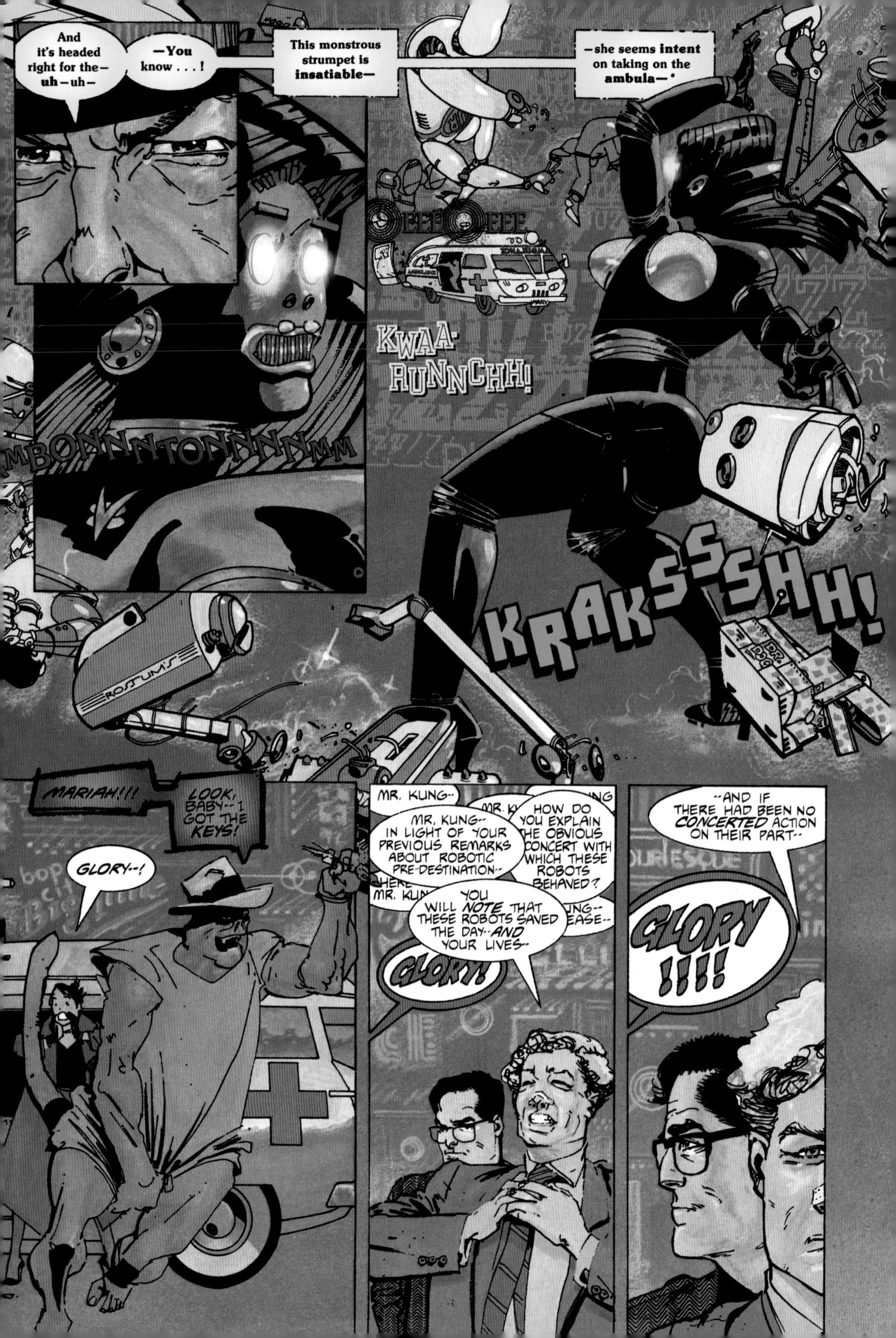
And it's headed right for the—uh—uh—
—You know . . . !
This monstrous strumpet is insatiable—
—she seems intent on taking on the ambula—*
KWAA-RUNNCHH!
KRAKSSSHH!
MARIAH!!!
LOOK, BABY-- I GOT THE KEYS!
GLORY--!
MR. KUNG--
MR. KUNG-- IN LIGHT OF YOUR PREVIOUS REMARKS ABOUT ROBOTIC PRE-DESTINATION--
HOW DO YOU EXPLAIN THE OBVIOUS CONCERT WITH WHICH THESE ROBOTS BEHAVED?
YOU WILL NOTE THAT THESE ROBOTS SAVED THE DAY--AND YOUR LIVES--
GLORY!
--AND IF THERE HAD BEEN NO CONCERTED ACTION ON THEIR PART--
GLORY !!!!

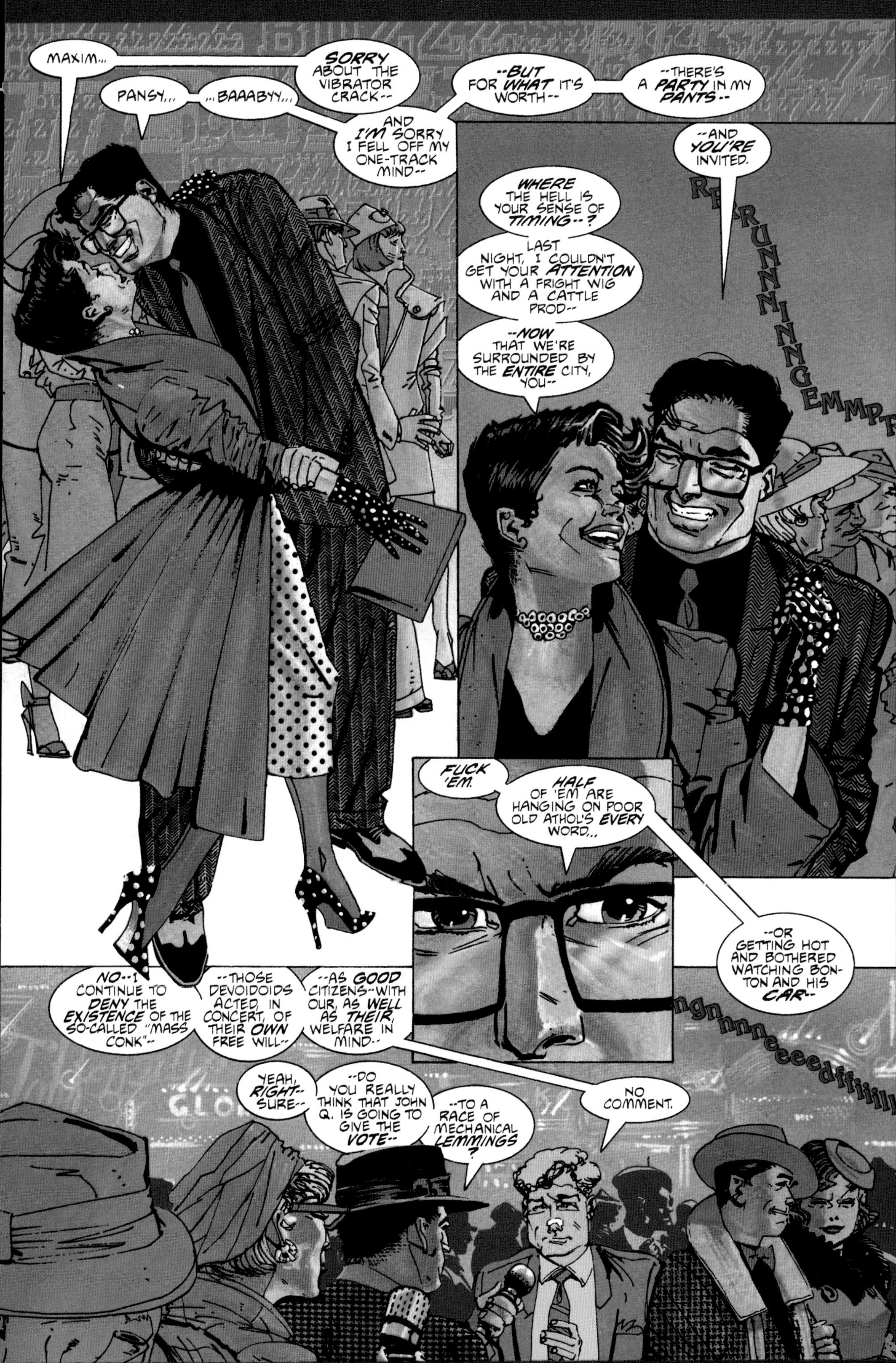

MAXIM...
PANSY...
...BAAAABYY...
SORRY ABOUT THE VIBRATOR CRACK--
AND I'M SORRY I FELL OFF MY ONE-TRACK MIND--
--BUT FOR WHAT IT'S WORTH--
--THERE'S A PARTY IN MY PANTS--
--AND YOU'RE INVITED.
WHERE THE HELL IS YOUR SENSE OF TIMING--?
LAST NIGHT, I COULDN'T GET YOUR ATTENTION WITH A FRIGHT WIG AND A CATTLE PROD--
--NOW THAT WE'RE SURROUNDED BY THE ENTIRE CITY, YOU--
FUCK 'EM.
HALF OF 'EM ARE HANGING ON POOR OLD ATHOL'S EVERY WORD...
--OR GETTING HOT AND BOTHERED WATCHING BON-TON AND HIS CAR--
NO--I CONTINUE TO DENY THE EXISTENCE OF THE SO-CALLED "MASS CONK"--
--THOSE DEVOIDOIDS ACTED, IN CONCERT, OF THEIR OWN FREE WILL--
--AS GOOD CITIZENS--WITH OUR, AS WELL AS THEIR, WELFARE IN MIND--
YEAH, RIGHT--SURE--
--DO YOU REALLY THINK THAT JOHN Q. IS GOING TO GIVE THE VOTE--
--TO A RACE OF MECHANICAL LEMMINGS?
NO COMMENT.

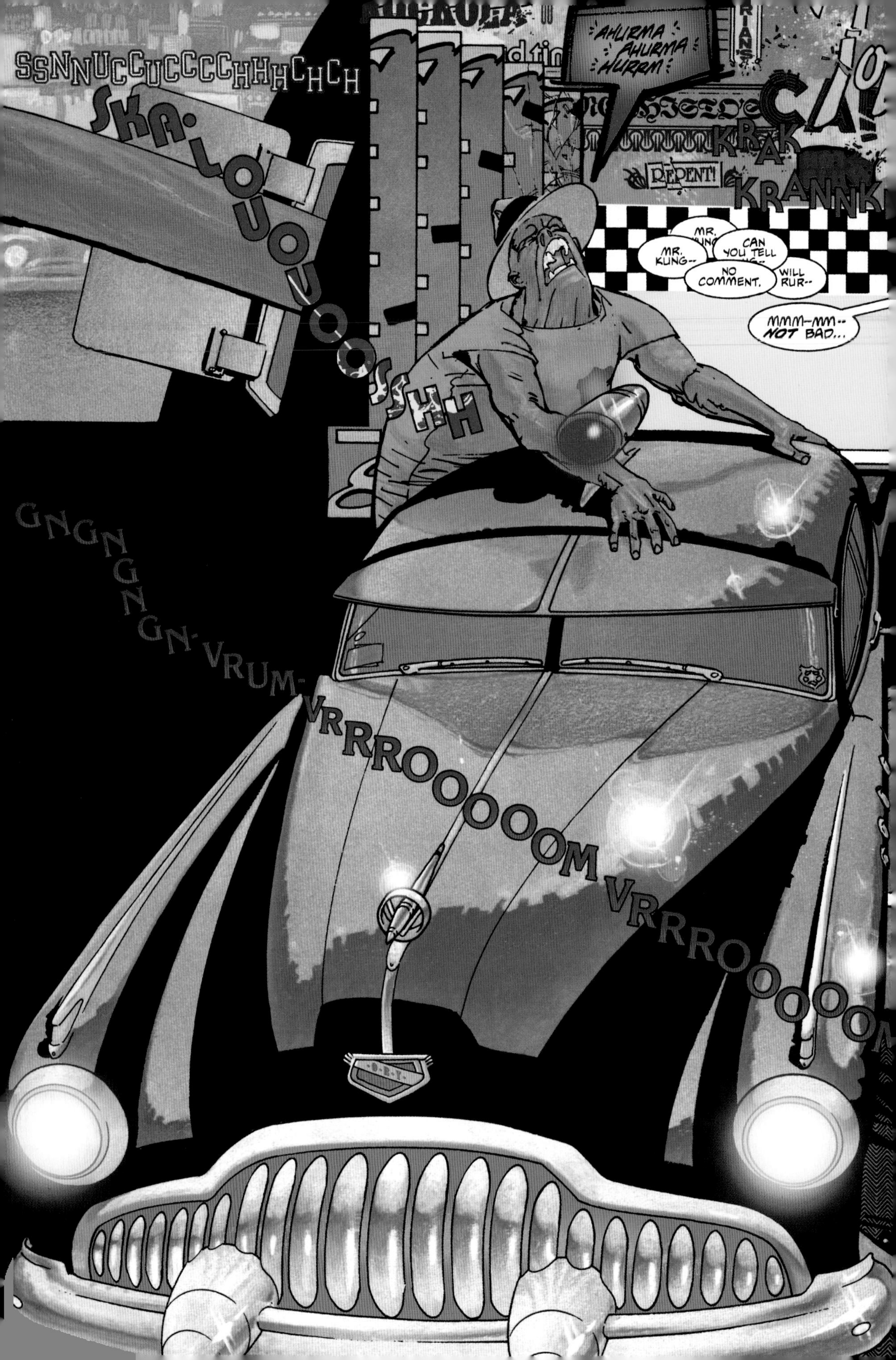
SSNNUCCUCCCCHHHCHCH
SKA-LOUOUOUOOSHH
AHURMA AHURMA HURRM
KRAK
KRANNK
REPENT!
MR. KUNG--
CAN YOU TELL
NO COMMENT.
WILL RUR--
MMM-MM-- ***NOT*** BAD...
GNGNGNGN-VRUM-VRRROOOOOOM VRRROOOOOM

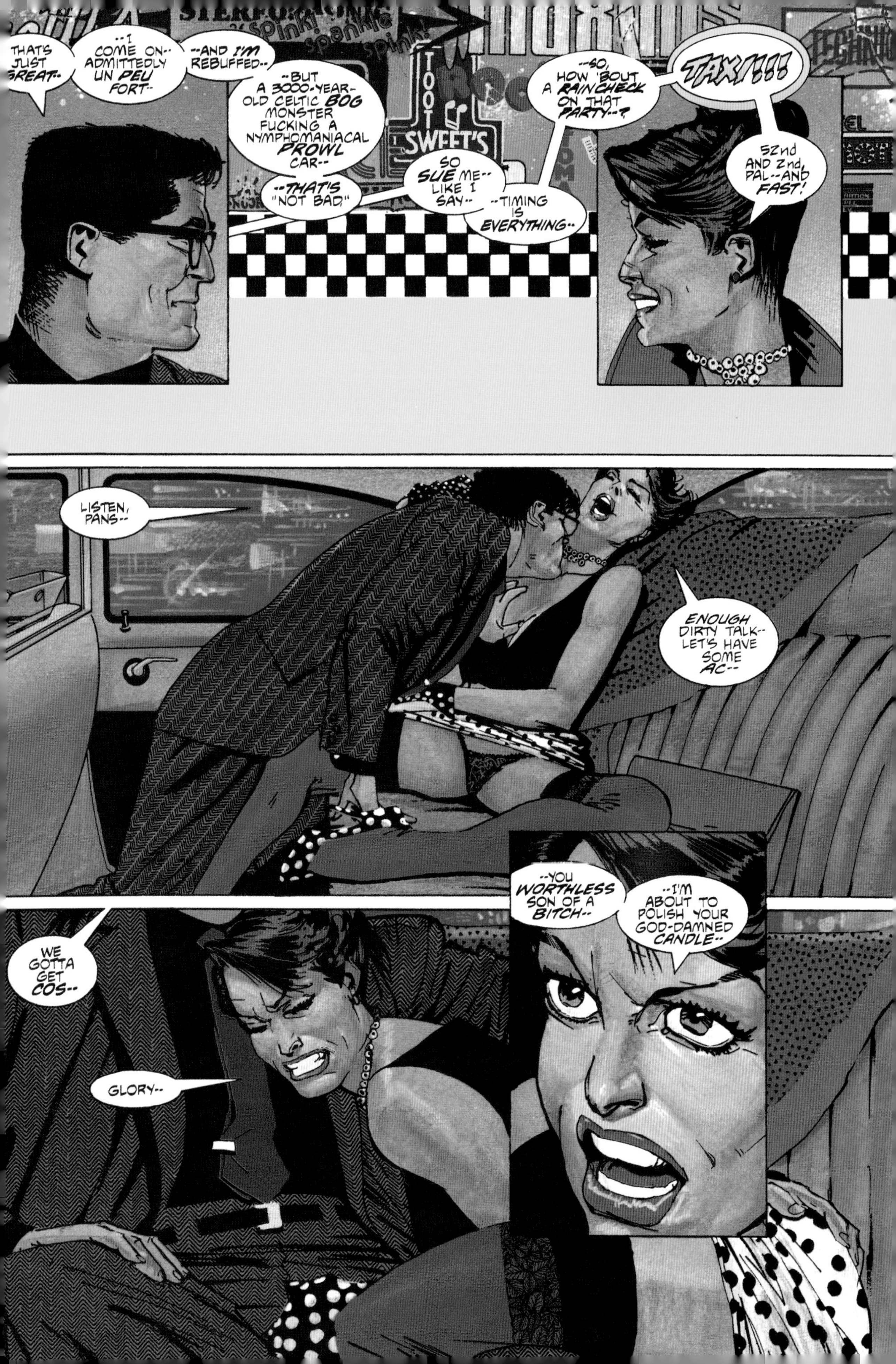
THAT'S JUST GREAT--
--I COME ON-- ADMITTEDLY UN PEU FORT--
--AND I'M REBUFFED--
--BUT A 3000-YEAR-OLD CELTIC BOG MONSTER FUCKING A NYMPHOMANIACAL PROWL CAR--
--THAT'S "NOT BAD."
SO SUE ME-- LIKE I SAY--
--TIMING IS EVERYTHING--
--SO, HOW 'BOUT A RAINCHECK ON THAT PARTY--?
TAXI!!!!
52nd AND 2nd, PAL--AND FAST!
TOOT
SWEET'S
LISTEN, PANS--
ENOUGH DIRTY TALK-- LET'S HAVE SOME AC--
WE GOTTA GET COS--
GLORY--
--YOU WORTHLESS SON OF A BITCH--
--I'M ABOUT TO POLISH YOUR GOD-DAMNED CANDLE--

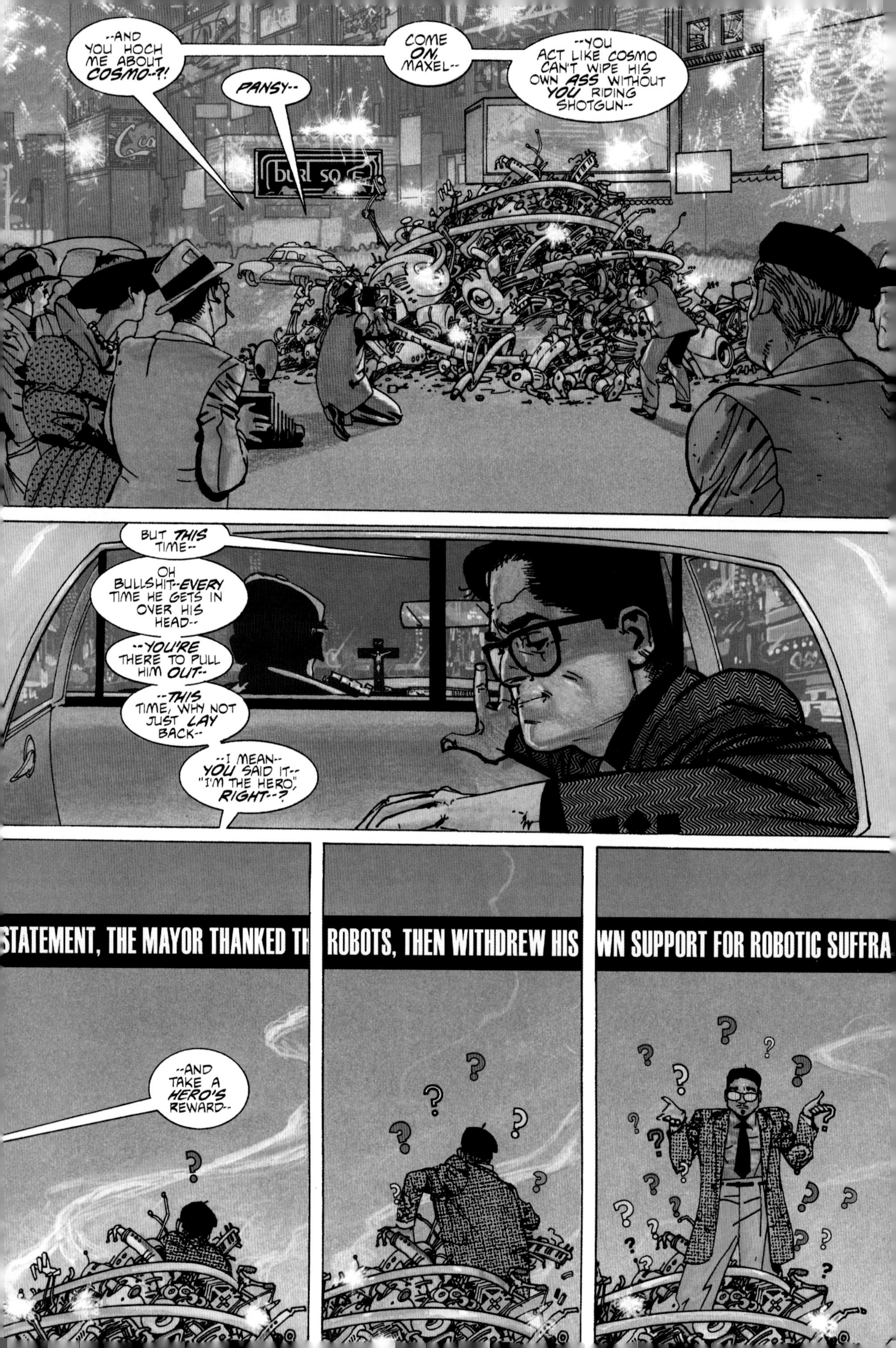
--AND YOU HOCH ME ABOUT COSMO--?!
PANSY--
COME ON, MAXEL--
--YOU ACT LIKE COSMO CAN'T WIPE HIS OWN ASS WITHOUT YOU RIDING SHOTGUN--
BUT THIS TIME--
OH BULLSHIT--EVERY TIME HE GETS IN OVER HIS HEAD--
--YOU'RE THERE TO PULL HIM OUT--
--THIS TIME, WHY NOT JUST LAY BACK--
--I MEAN--YOU SAID IT--"I'M THE HERO," RIGHT--?
STATEMENT, THE MAYOR THANKED TH
ROBOTS, THEN WITHDREW HIS
WN SUPPORT FOR ROBOTIC SUFFRA
--AND TAKE A HERO'S REWARD--

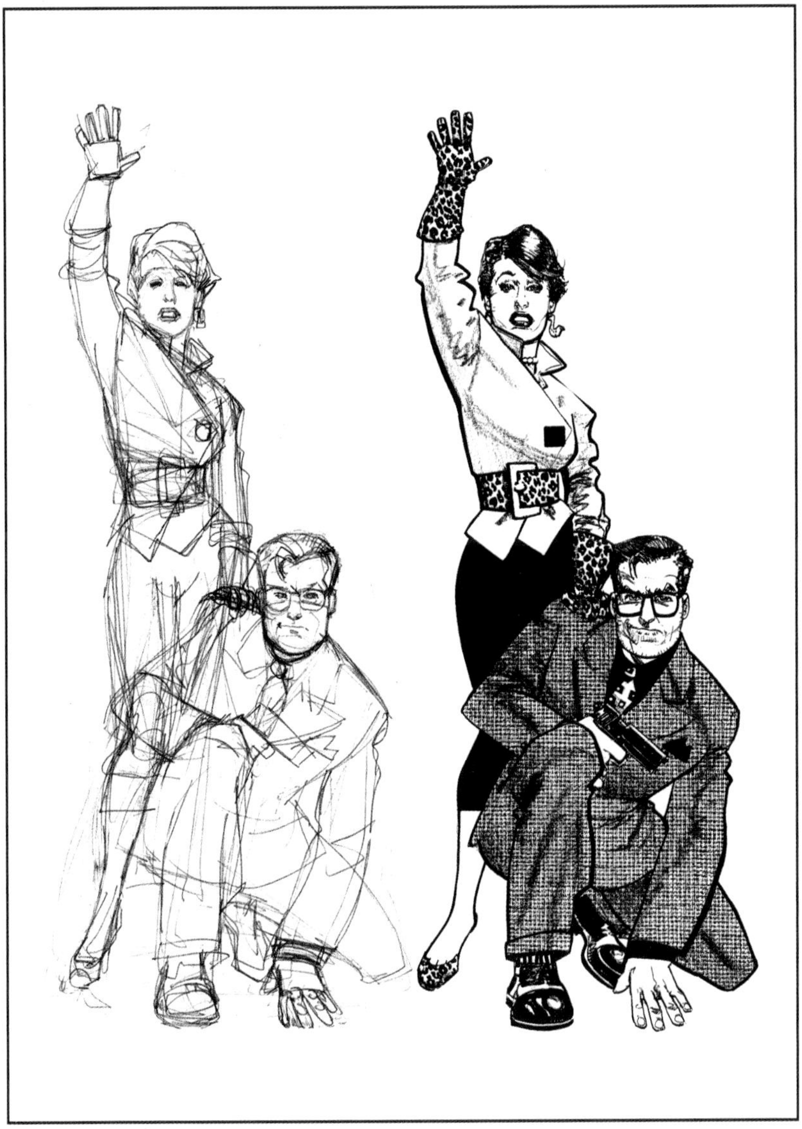

Initial sketch and inked versions of the *Hallowed Ground*[0] cover.

At the intersection of infinity,
where eternity meets forever...

...When forgotten ghosts
ring changes in an orchestra
lost to time.

When tomorrow is haunted
by that rhapsody of memory,
recollections of things to come.

When a lost soul gone forever
returns to find it's still on the
hit parade.

When yesterday sings that
old siren song, and still finds
it sweet and lowdown.

When a longtime love
disappears at dawn, and a
solo scarcely heard floats
out an open door to forever
haunt your days.

WHAT WAS.
WHAT IS.
WHAT WILL...
AND NEVER WILL...
BE.

Every dream, every prayer,
every fear, found forever
at the crossroads of memory
and imagination.

As ever...Always.

Welcome home.

Time².

HALLOWED GROUND⁰

story and art
HOWARD CHAYKIN
color
YEN NITRO
letters
KEN BRUZENAK
special thanks
CALVIN NYE
RAMON TORREZ
editor
THOMAS K.

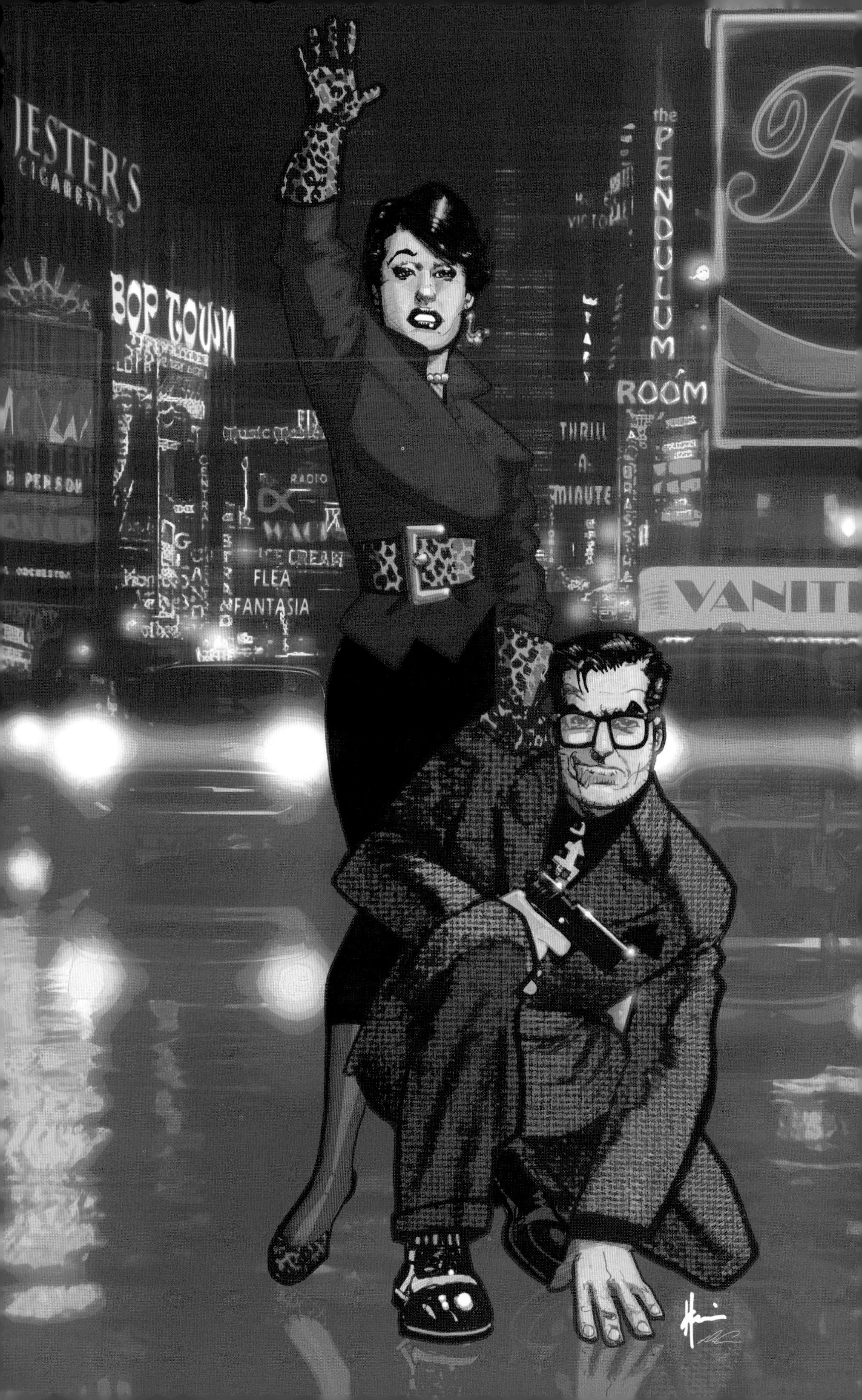
JESTER'S
CIGARETTES
BOP TOWN
the PENDULUM ROOM
THRILL A MINUTE
RADIO
ICE CREAM
FLEA
FANTASIA

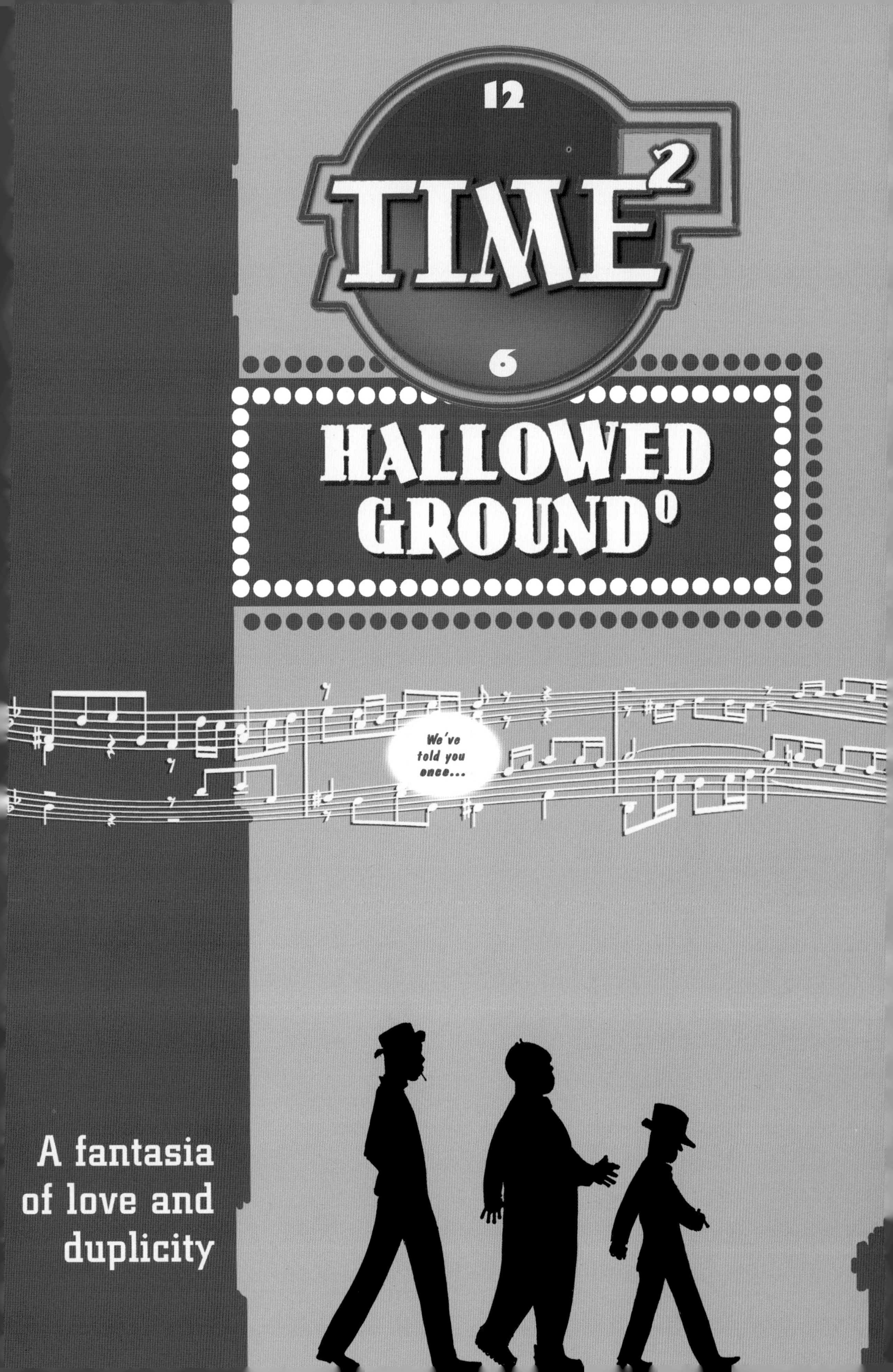
12
TIME²
6
HALLOWED
GROUND⁰
We've told you once...
A fantasia of love and duplicity

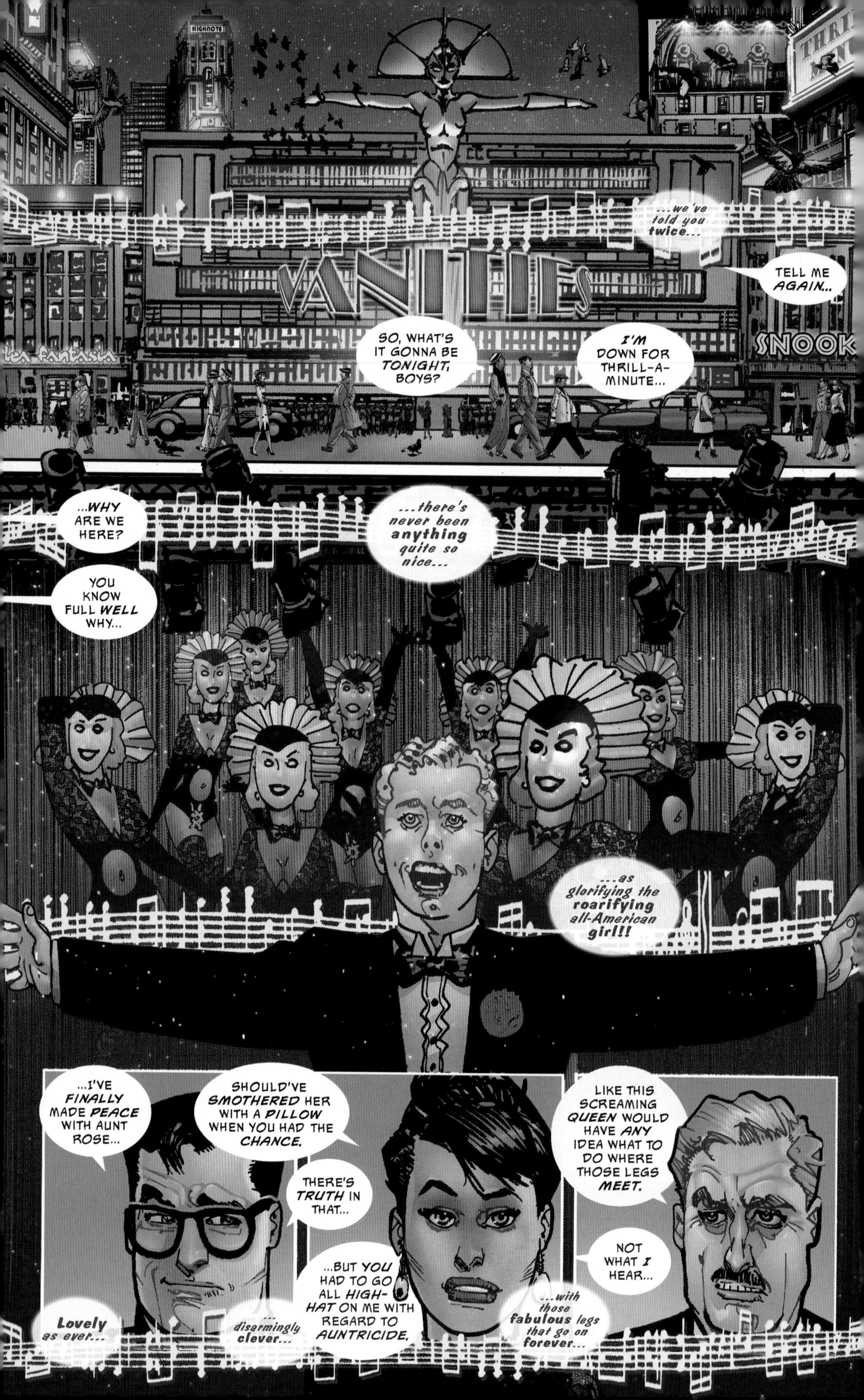

HIGHNOTE
...we've told you twice...
TELL ME AGAIN...
VANITIES
la fantasia
SNOOK
SO, WHAT'S IT GONNA BE TONIGHT, BOYS?
I'M DOWN FOR THRILL-A-MINUTE...
...WHY ARE WE HERE?
...there's never been anything quite so nice...
YOU KNOW FULL WELL WHY...
...as glorifying the roarifying all-American girl!!!
...I'VE FINALLY MADE PEACE WITH AUNT ROSE...
SHOULD'VE SMOTHERED HER WITH A PILLOW WHEN YOU HAD THE CHANCE.
THERE'S TRUTH IN THAT...
...BUT YOU HAD TO GO ALL HIGH-HAT ON ME WITH REGARD TO AUNTRICIDE.
LIKE THIS SCREAMING QUEEN WOULD HAVE ANY IDEA WHAT TO DO WHERE THOSE LEGS MEET.
NOT WHAT I HEAR...
Lovely as ever...
...disarmingly clever...
...with those fabulous legs that go on forever...

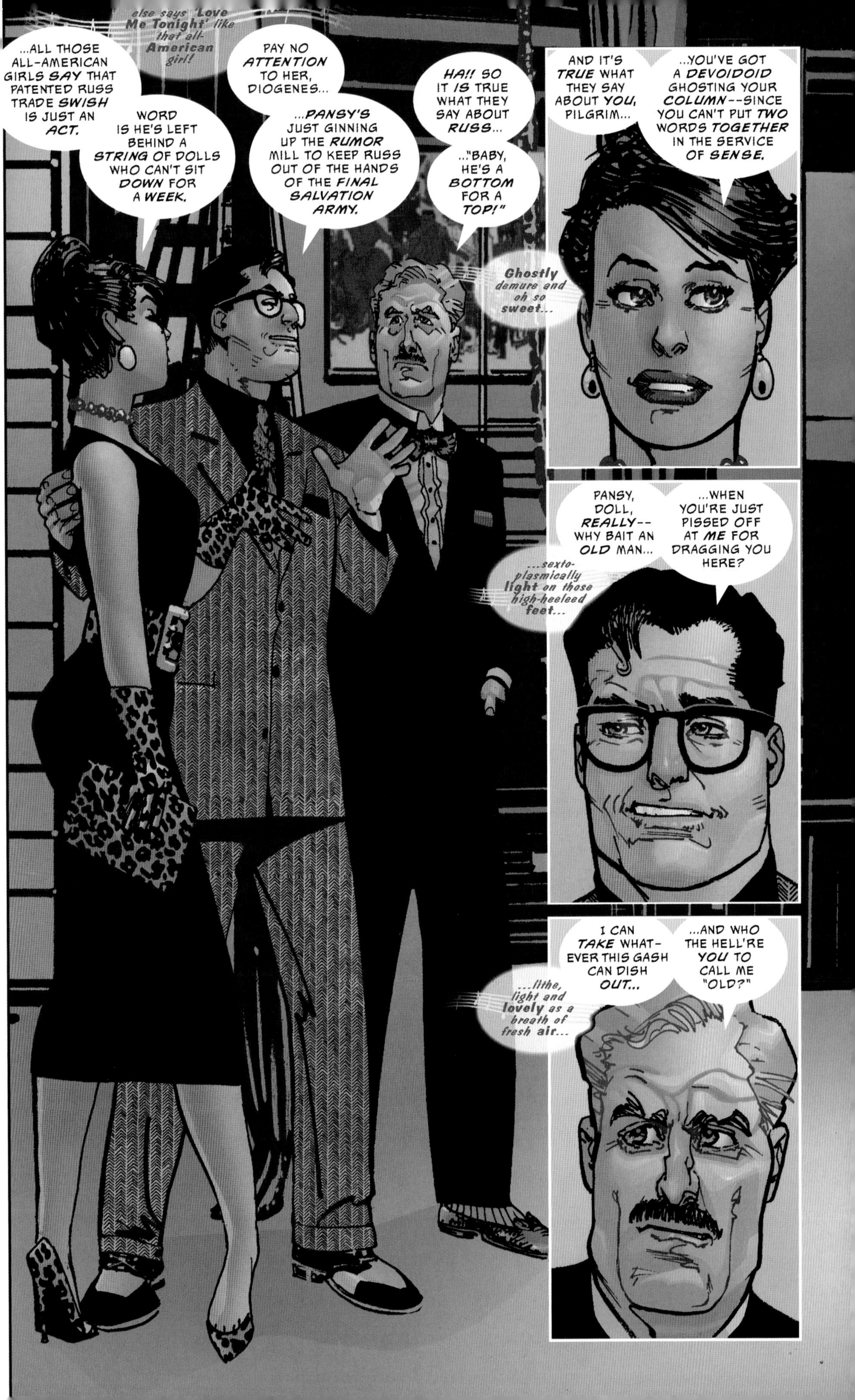

else says 'Love Me Tonight' like that all-American girl!
...ALL THOSE ALL-AMERICAN GIRLS SAY THAT PATENTED RUSS TRADE SWISH IS JUST AN ACT.
WORD IS HE'S LEFT BEHIND A STRING OF DOLLS WHO CAN'T SIT DOWN FOR A WEEK.
PAY NO ATTENTION TO HER, DIOGENES...
...PANSY'S JUST GINNING UP THE RUMOR MILL TO KEEP RUSS OUT OF THE HANDS OF THE FINAL SALVATION ARMY.
HA!! SO IT IS TRUE WHAT THEY SAY ABOUT RUSS...
..."BABY, HE'S A BOTTOM FOR A TOP!"
Ghostly demure and oh so sweet...
AND IT'S TRUE WHAT THEY SAY ABOUT YOU, PILGRIM...
...YOU'VE GOT A DEVOIDOID GHOSTING YOUR COLUMN--SINCE YOU CAN'T PUT TWO WORDS TOGETHER IN THE SERVICE OF SENSE.
PANSY, DOLL, REALLY-- WHY BAIT AN OLD MAN...
...WHEN YOU'RE JUST PISSED OFF AT ME FOR DRAGGING YOU HERE?
...sexto-plasmically light on those high-heeleed feet...
I CAN TAKE WHAT-EVER THIS GASH CAN DISH OUT...
...AND WHO THE HELL'RE YOU TO CALL ME "OLD?"
...lithe, light and lovely as a breath of fresh air...

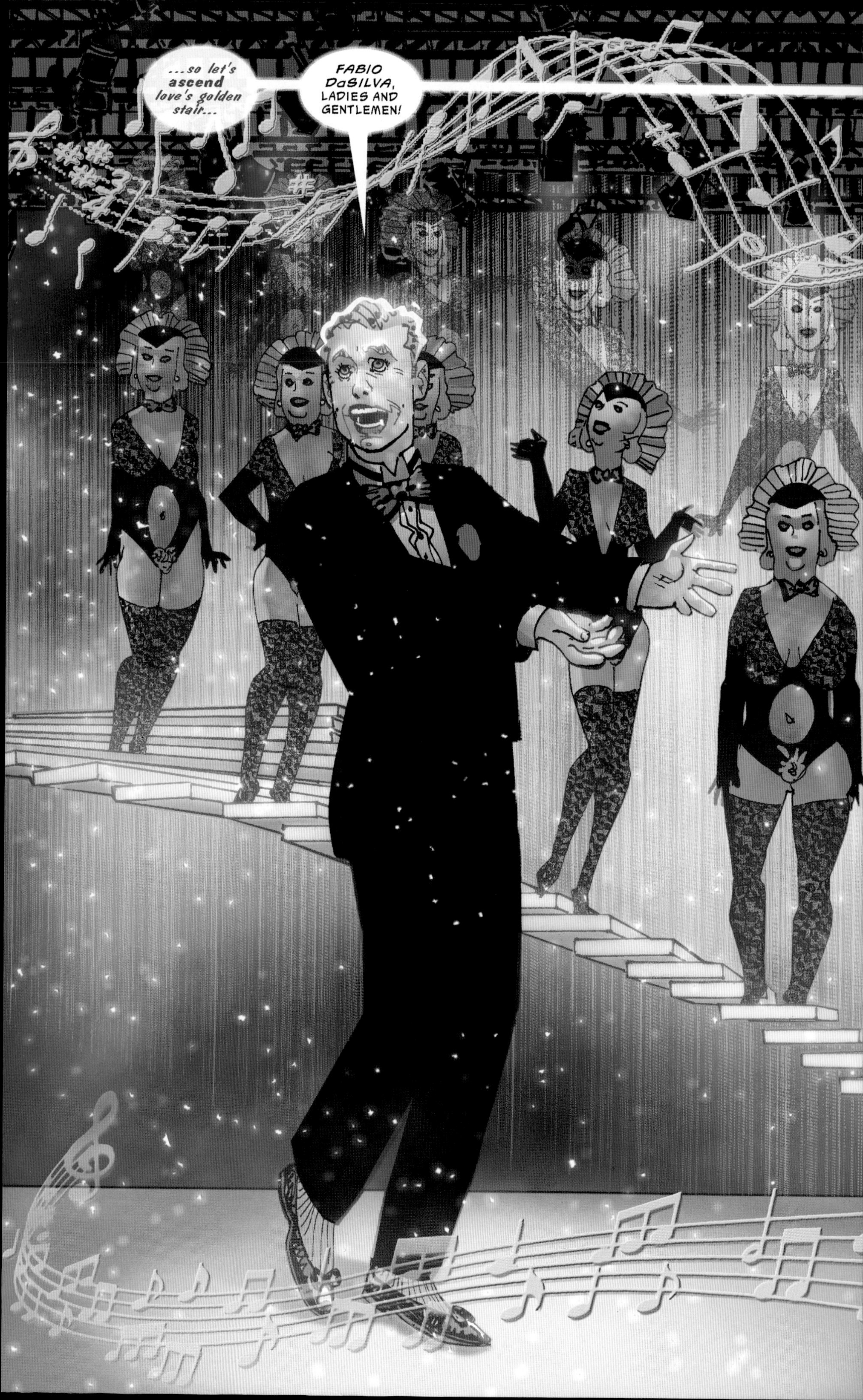
...so let's **ascend** love's golden stair...
FABIO DaSILVA, LADIES AND GENTLEMEN!

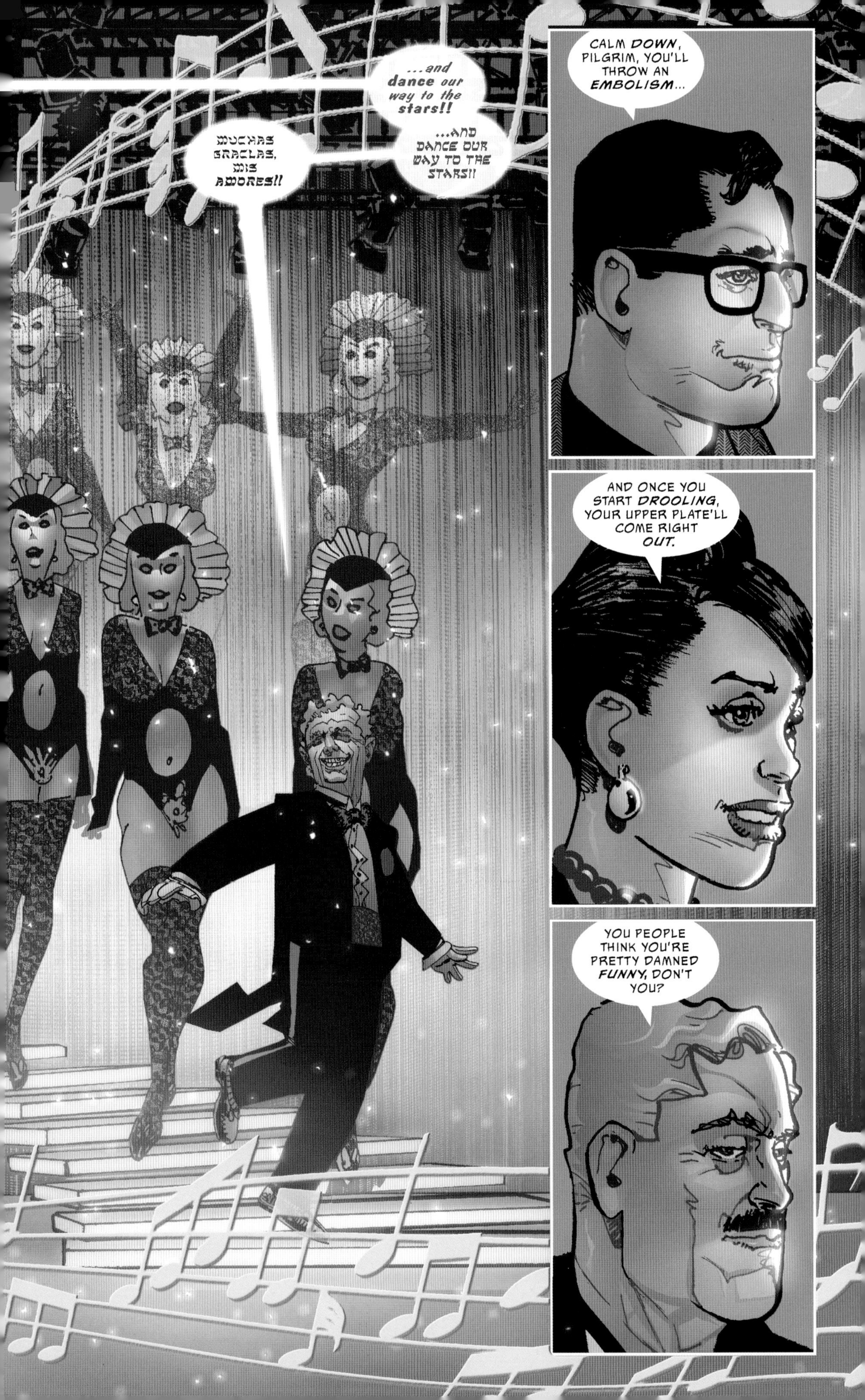
...and dance our way to the stars!!
MUCHAS GRACIAS, MIS AMORES!!
...AND DANCE OUR WAY TO THE STARS!!
CALM DOWN, PILGRIM, YOU'LL THROW AN EMBOLISM...
AND ONCE YOU START DROOLING, YOUR UPPER PLATE'LL COME RIGHT OUT.
YOU PEOPLE THINK YOU'RE PRETTY DAMNED FUNNY, DON'T YOU?

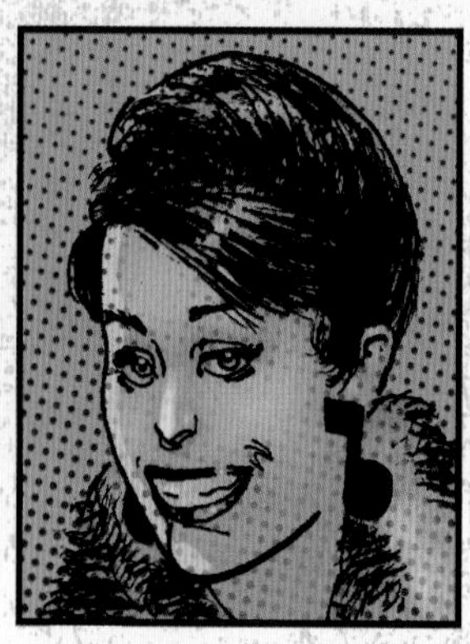

PANSY'S PASSIONS

by PANSY MATTHIAS

Yours truly and the main squeeze on the Main Stem sneaked ourselves into a rehearsal of Toots Sweet's revue, ALL IS VANITY, last night, and the girls were, you should pardon the expression, gloriously gorgeous.

Not our organical girls, natch, but their shades, reincarnimated by R.U.R. in its latest bid to take the Time out of Time².

One of the evening's delights was the surprise appearance of Fabio DaSilva, the world's premier midget bullfighter--who brought the butch to the otherwise all-too-girly proceedings.

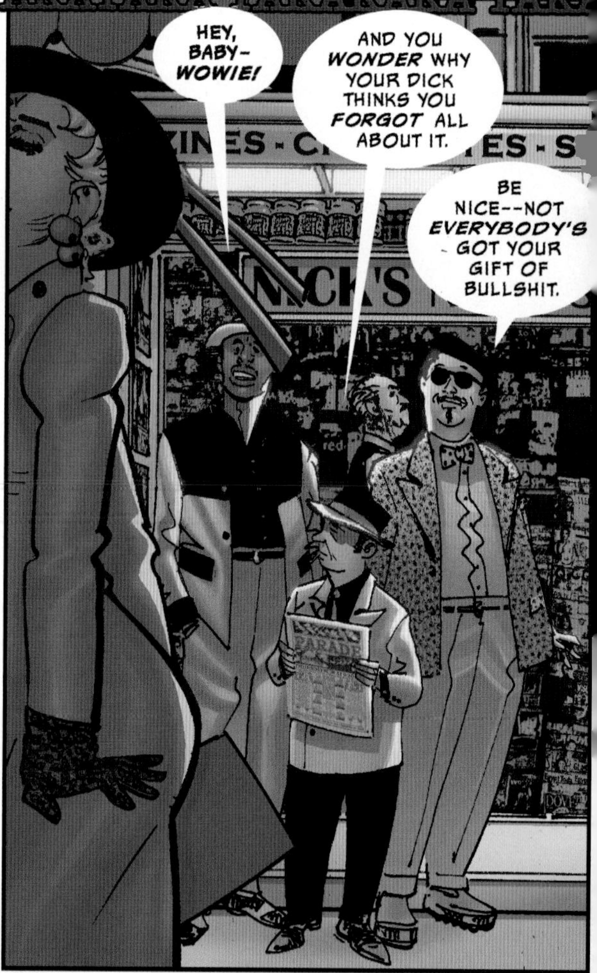
KATAKA TAKA TAK TAK TAKATAKATAKA TAKAKAKA TAKA
HEY, BABY-*WOWIE!*
AND YOU *WONDER* WHY YOUR DICK THINKS YOU *FORGOT* ALL ABOUT IT.
BE NICE--NOT *EVERYBODY'S* GOT YOUR GIFT OF BULLSHIT.
NICK'S

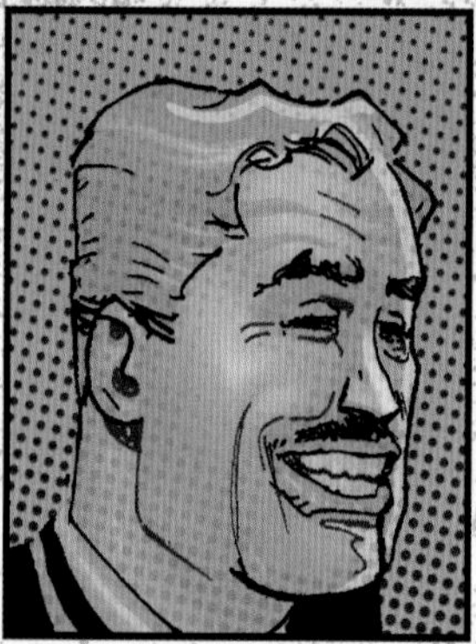

THE LAMP IS LIT

by DIOGENES PILGRIM

Looking for an honest man...your eyes on the main stem spent last evening at a critics' preview of the usually incomparable Toots Sweet's latest footlight treat, ALL IS VANITY...

...Sad to say, this edition just lacks that certain *joi de whoopie* we've come to expect from Toots and her ensemble...

...Instead, we got an unhealthy dose of *je ne sais queerbait* in the person of Russ Trade, a regular Lispering Smith, y'ask me.

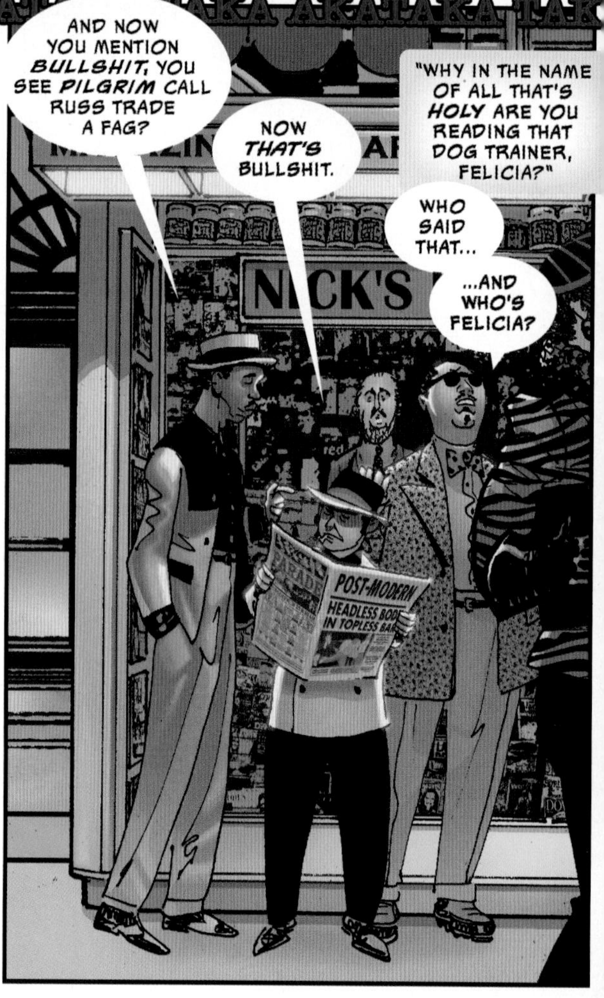
AND NOW YOU MENTION *BULLSHIT,* YOU SEE *PILGRIM* CALL RUSS TRADE A FAG?
NOW *THAT'S* BULLSHIT.
"WHY IN THE NAME OF ALL THAT'S *HOLY* ARE YOU READING THAT DOG TRAINER, FELICIA?"
WHO SAID THAT...
...AND WHO'S FELICIA?
NICK'S
POST-MODERN
HEADLESS BODY IN TOPLESS BAR

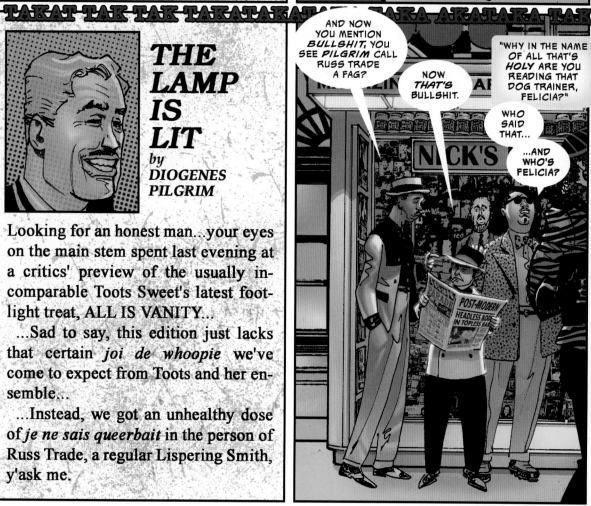

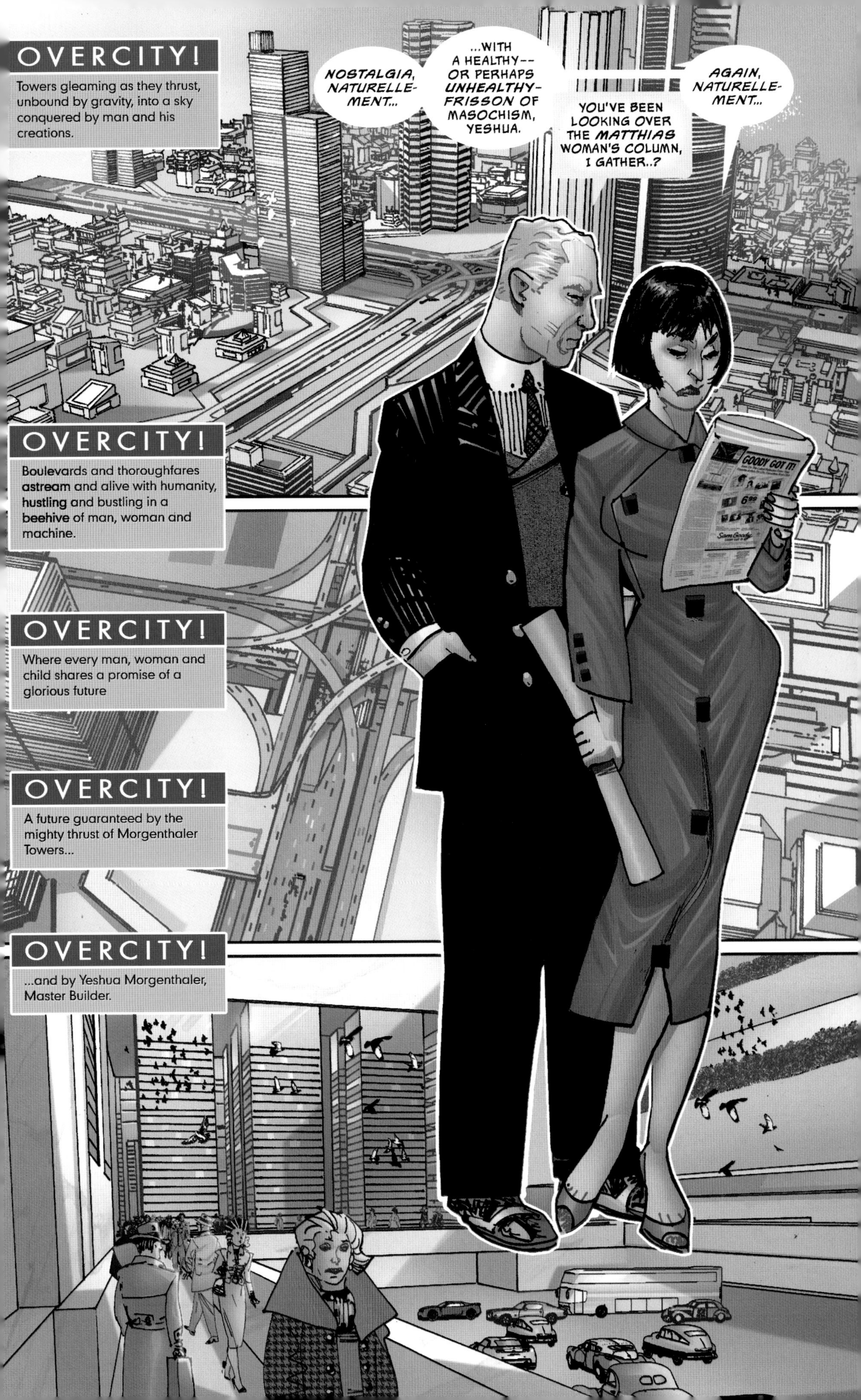
OVERCITY!
Towers gleaming as they thrust, unbound by gravity, into a sky conquered by man and his creations.
NOSTALGIA, NATURELLE-MENT...
...WITH A HEALTHY--OR PERHAPS UNHEALTHY-FRISSON OF MASOCHISM, YESHUA.
YOU'VE BEEN LOOKING OVER THE MATTHIAS WOMAN'S COLUMN, I GATHER..?
AGAIN, NATURELLE-MENT...
OVERCITY!
Boulevards and thoroughfares astream and alive with humanity, hustling and bustling in a beehive of man, woman and machine.
GOODY GOT IT!
6.99
Sam Goody
OVERCITY!
Where every man, woman and child shares a promise of a glorious future
OVERCITY!
A future guaranteed by the mighty thrust of Morgenthaler Towers...
OVERCITY!
...and by Yeshua Morgenthaler, Master Builder.

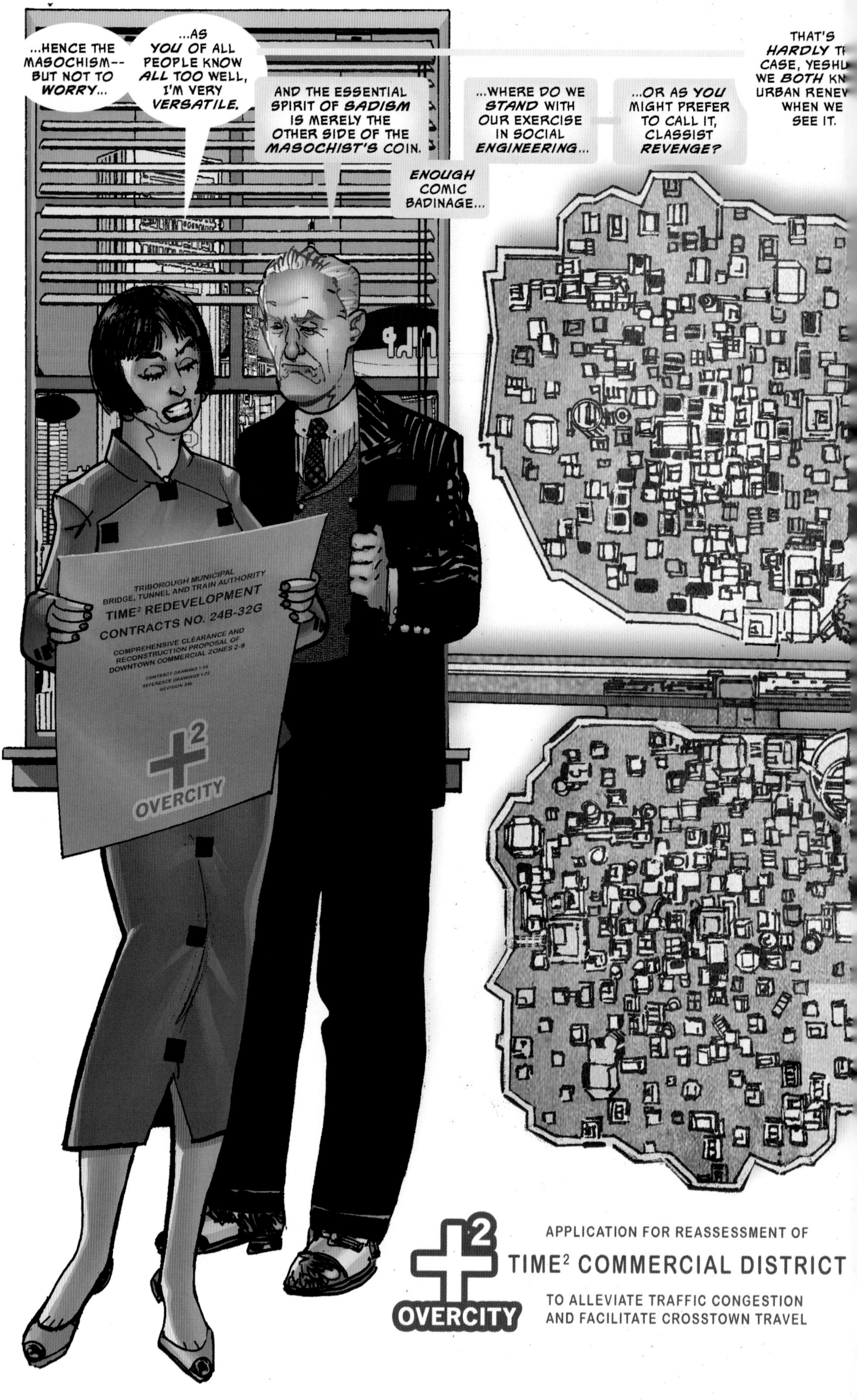
...HENCE THE MASOCHISM-- BUT NOT TO WORRY...
...AS YOU OF ALL PEOPLE KNOW ALL TOO WELL, I'M VERY VERSATILE.
AND THE ESSENTIAL SPIRIT OF SADISM IS MERELY THE OTHER SIDE OF THE MASOCHIST'S COIN.
ENOUGH COMIC BADINAGE...
...WHERE DO WE STAND WITH OUR EXERCISE IN SOCIAL ENGINEERING...
...OR AS YOU MIGHT PREFER TO CALL IT, CLASSIST REVENGE?
THAT'S HARDLY T
CASE, YESH
WE BOTH KN
URBAN RENEV
WHEN WE
SEE IT.
TRIBOROUGH MUNICIPAL
BRIDGE, TUNNEL AND TRAIN AUTHORITY
TIME² REDEVELOPMENT
CONTRACTS NO. 24B-32G
COMPREHENSIVE CLEARANCE AND RECONSTRUCTION PROPOSAL OF DOWNTOWN COMMERCIAL ZONES 2-9
OVERCITY
OVERCITY
APPLICATION FOR REASSESSMENT OF
TIME² COMMERCIAL DISTRICT
TO ALLEVIATE TRAFFIC CONGESTION AND FACILITATE CROSSTOWN TRAVEL

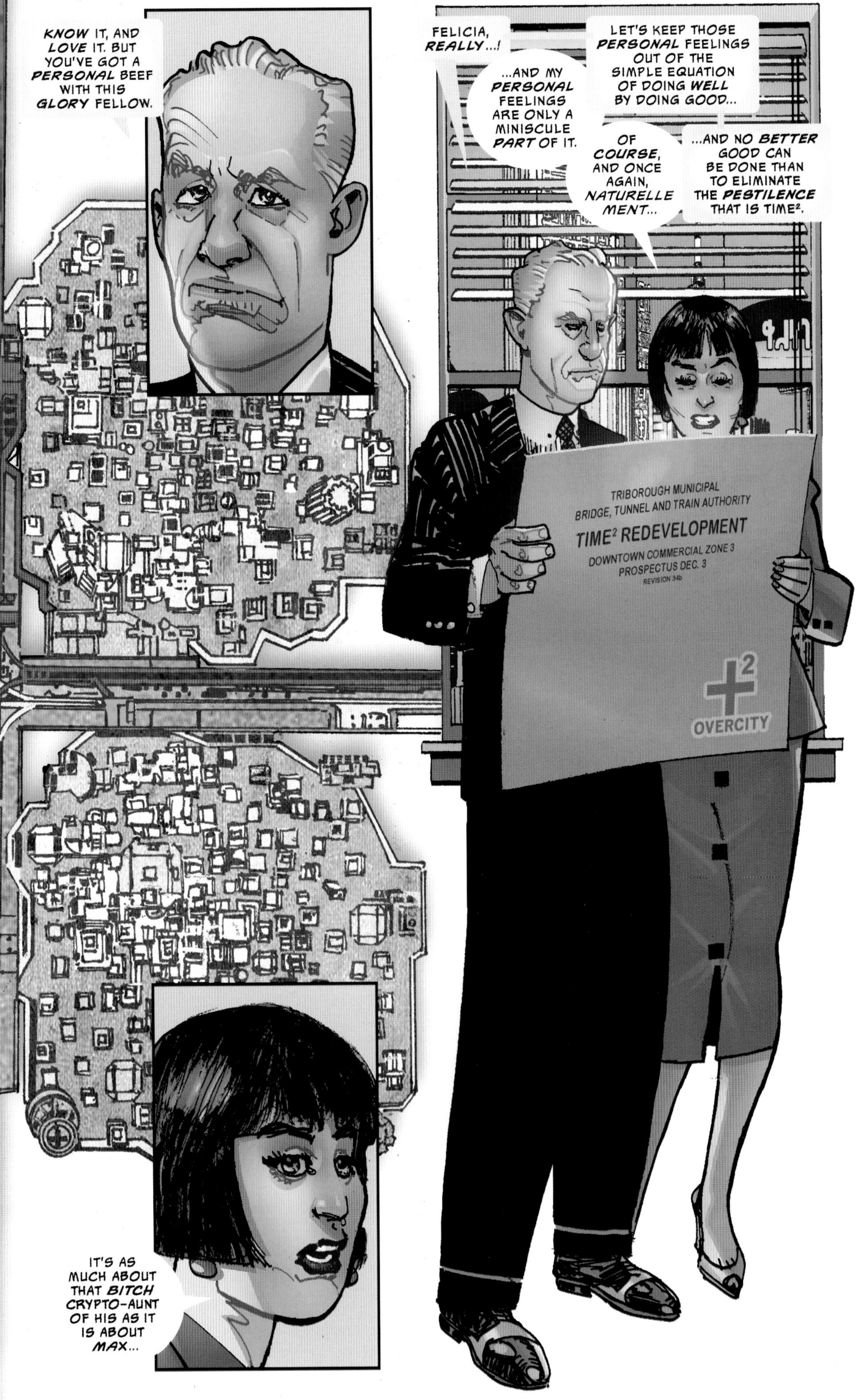
KNOW IT, AND LOVE IT. BUT YOU'VE GOT A PERSONAL BEEF WITH THIS GLORY FELLOW.
IT'S AS MUCH ABOUT THAT BITCH CRYPTO-AUNT OF HIS AS IT IS ABOUT MAX...
FELICIA, REALLY...!
...AND MY PERSONAL FEELINGS ARE ONLY A MINISCULE PART OF IT.
LET'S KEEP THOSE PERSONAL FEELINGS OUT OF THE SIMPLE EQUATION OF DOING WELL BY DOING GOOD...
OF COURSE, AND ONCE AGAIN, NATURELLE MENT...
...AND NO BETTER GOOD CAN BE DONE THAN TO ELIMINATE THE PESTILENCE THAT IS TIME².
TRIBOROUGH MUNICIPAL
BRIDGE, TUNNEL AND TRAIN AUTHORITY
TIME² REDEVELOPMENT
DOWNTOWN COMMERCIAL ZONE 3
PROSPECTUS DEC. 3
REVISION 34b
T²
OVERCITY

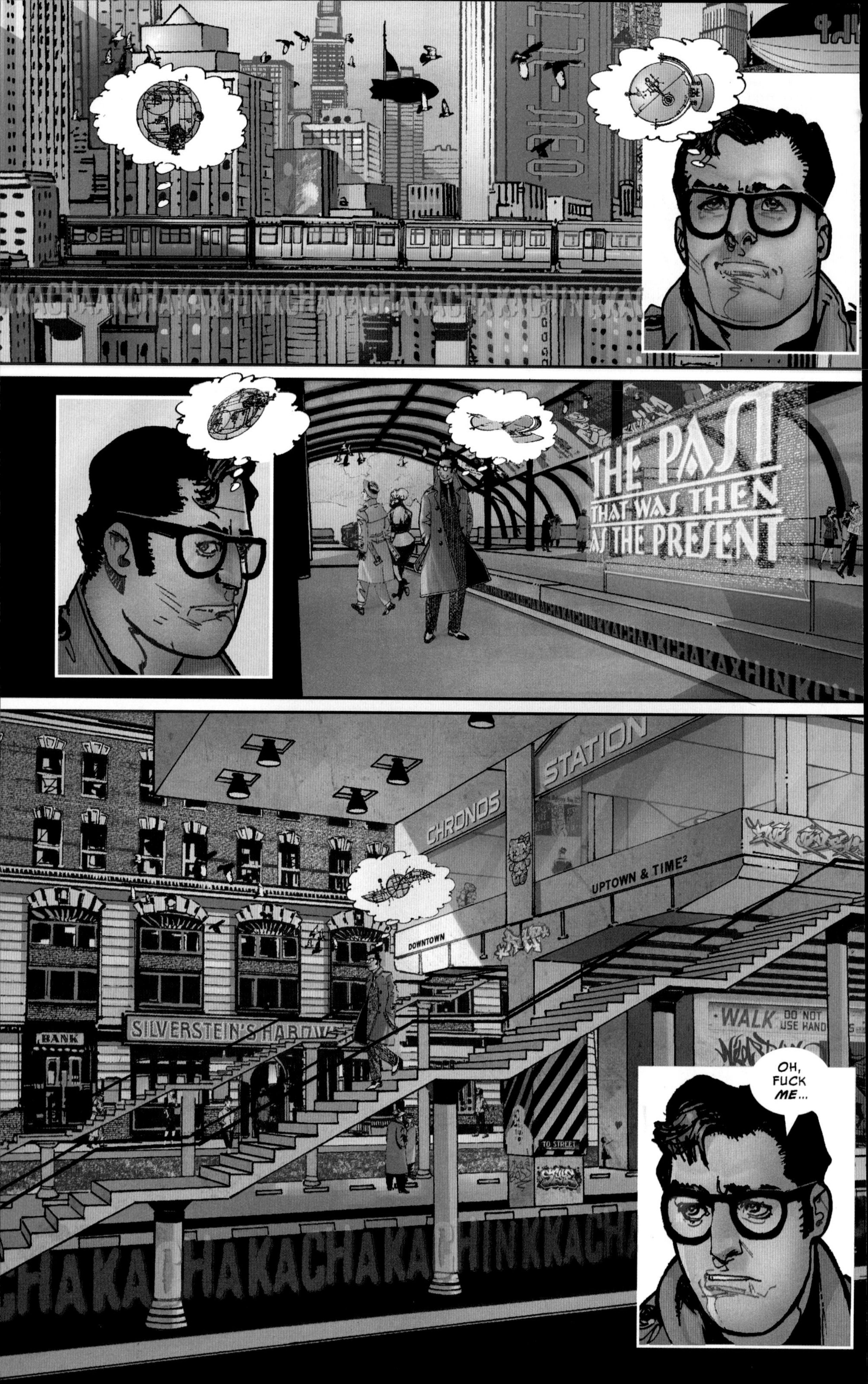
THE PAST
THAT WAS THEN
AS THE PRESENT
CHRONOS
STATION
UPTOWN & TIME²
DOWNTOWN
SILVERSTEIN'S HARDW
BANK
WALK DO NOT USE HAND
TO STREET
OH, FUCK *ME*...

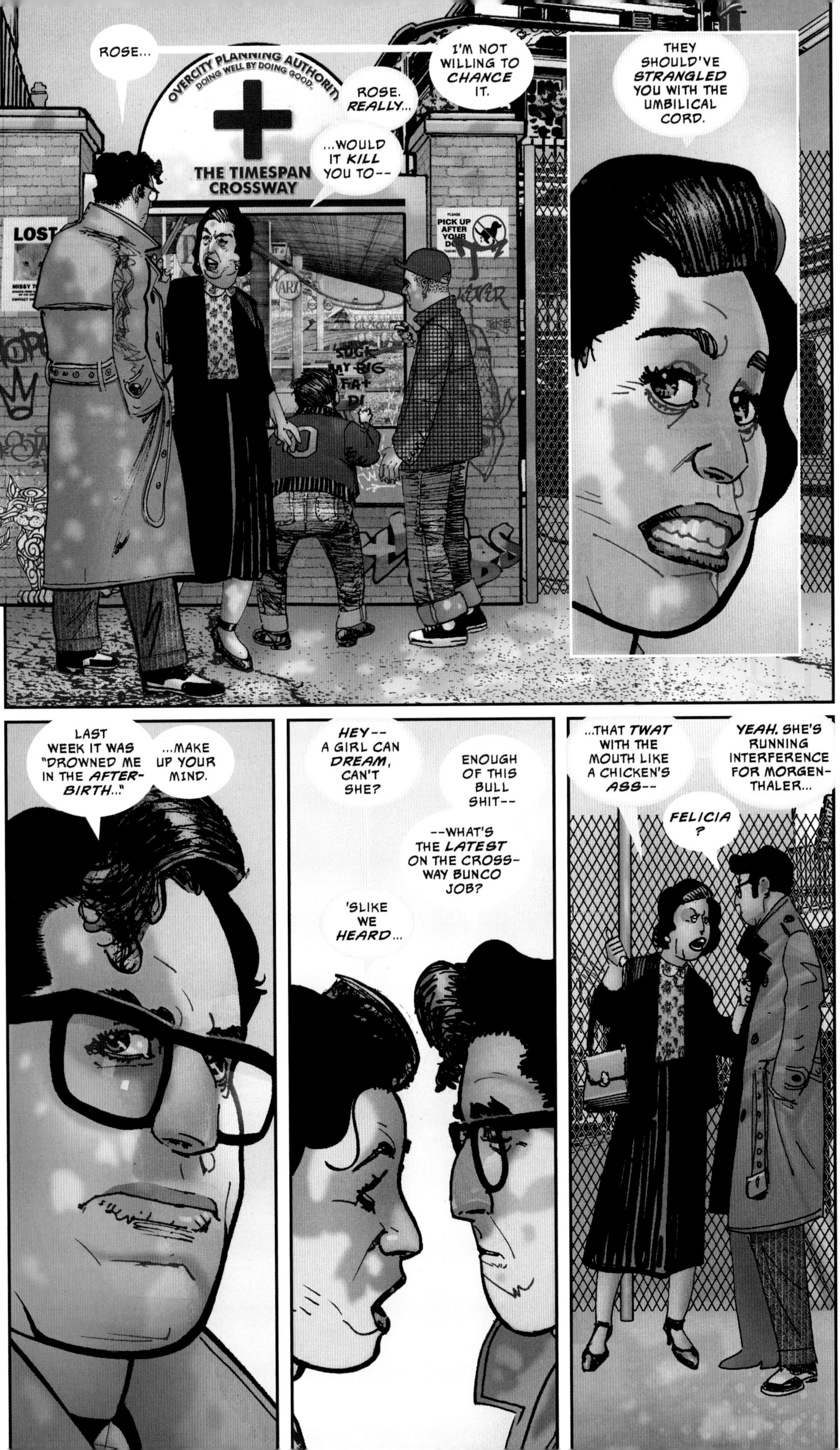
ROSE...
OVERCITY PLANNING AUTHORITY
DOING WELL BY DOING GOOD.
THE TIMESPAN CROSSWAY
ROSE. REALLY...
...WOULD IT KILL YOU TO--
I'M NOT WILLING TO CHANCE IT.
LOST
PICK UP AFTER YOUR DOG
THEY SHOULD'VE STRANGLED YOU WITH THE UMBILICAL CORD.
LAST WEEK IT WAS "DROWNED ME IN THE AFTER-BIRTH..."
...MAKE UP YOUR MIND.
HEY-- A GIRL CAN DREAM, CAN'T SHE?
ENOUGH OF THIS BULL SHIT--
--WHAT'S THE LATEST ON THE CROSS-WAY BUNCO JOB?
'SLIKE WE HEARD...
...THAT TWAT WITH THE MOUTH LIKE A CHICKEN'S ASS--
FELICIA?
YEAH. SHE'S RUNNING INTERFERENCE FOR MORGEN-THALER...

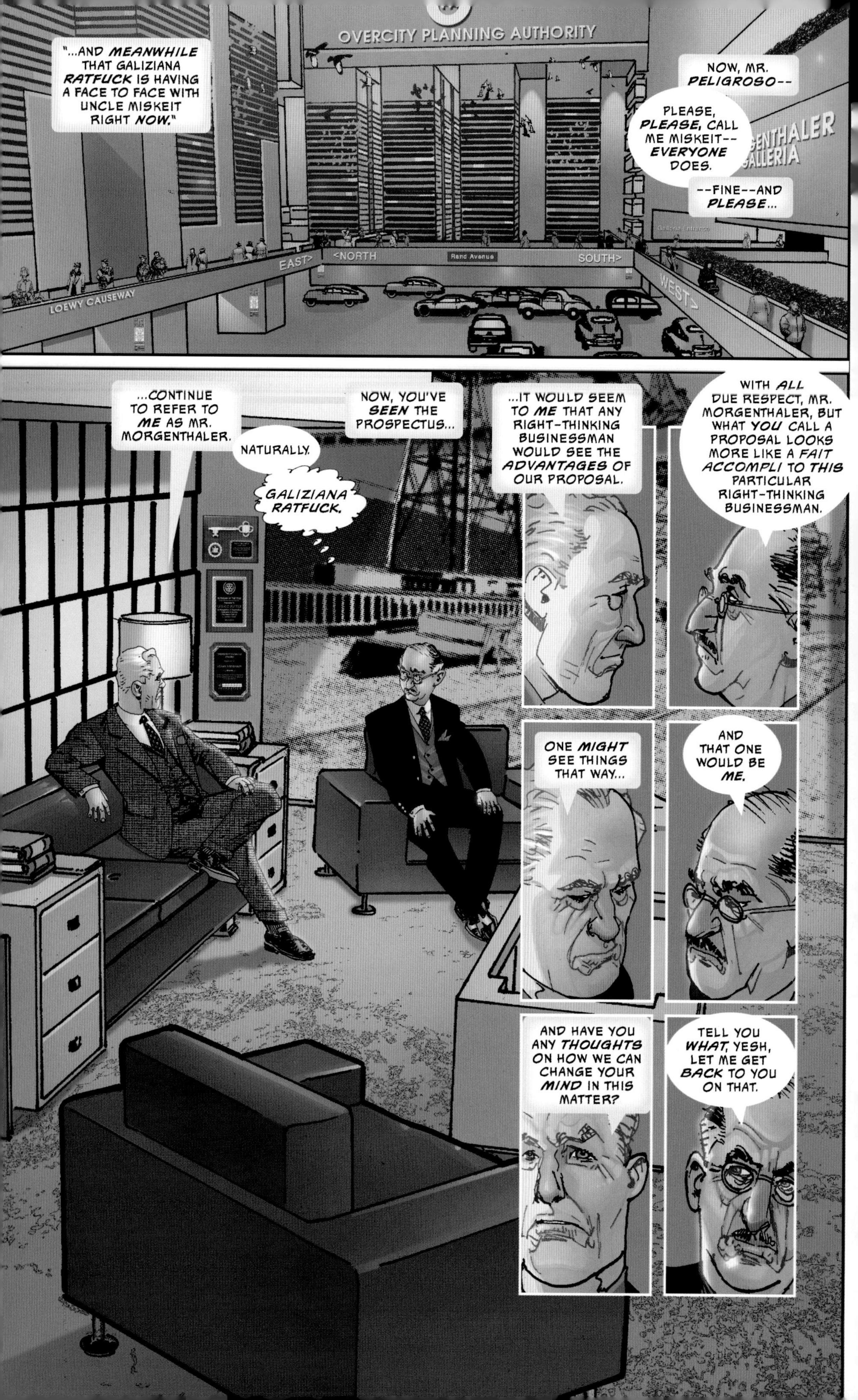
OVERCITY PLANNING AUTHORITY
"...AND MEANWHILE THAT GALIZIANA RATFUCK IS HAVING A FACE TO FACE WITH UNCLE MISKEIT RIGHT NOW."
NOW, MR. PELIGROSO--
PLEASE, PLEASE, CALL ME MISKEIT-- EVERYONE DOES.
GENTHALER
--FINE--AND PLEASE...
EAST>
<NORTH
Rand Avenue
SOUTH>
WEST>
LOEWY CAUSEWAY
...CONTINUE TO REFER TO ME AS MR. MORGENTHALER.
NATURALLY.
GALIZIANA RATFUCK.
NOW, YOU'VE SEEN THE PROSPECTUS...
...IT WOULD SEEM TO ME THAT ANY RIGHT-THINKING BUSINESSMAN WOULD SEE THE ADVANTAGES OF OUR PROPOSAL.
WITH ALL DUE RESPECT, MR. MORGENTHALER, BUT WHAT YOU CALL A PROPOSAL LOOKS MORE LIKE A FAIT ACCOMPLI TO THIS PARTICULAR RIGHT-THINKING BUSINESSMAN.
ONE MIGHT SEE THINGS THAT WAY...
AND THAT ONE WOULD BE ME.
AND HAVE YOU ANY THOUGHTS ON HOW WE CAN CHANGE YOUR MIND IN THIS MATTER?
TELL YOU WHAT, YESH, LET ME GET BACK TO YOU ON THAT.

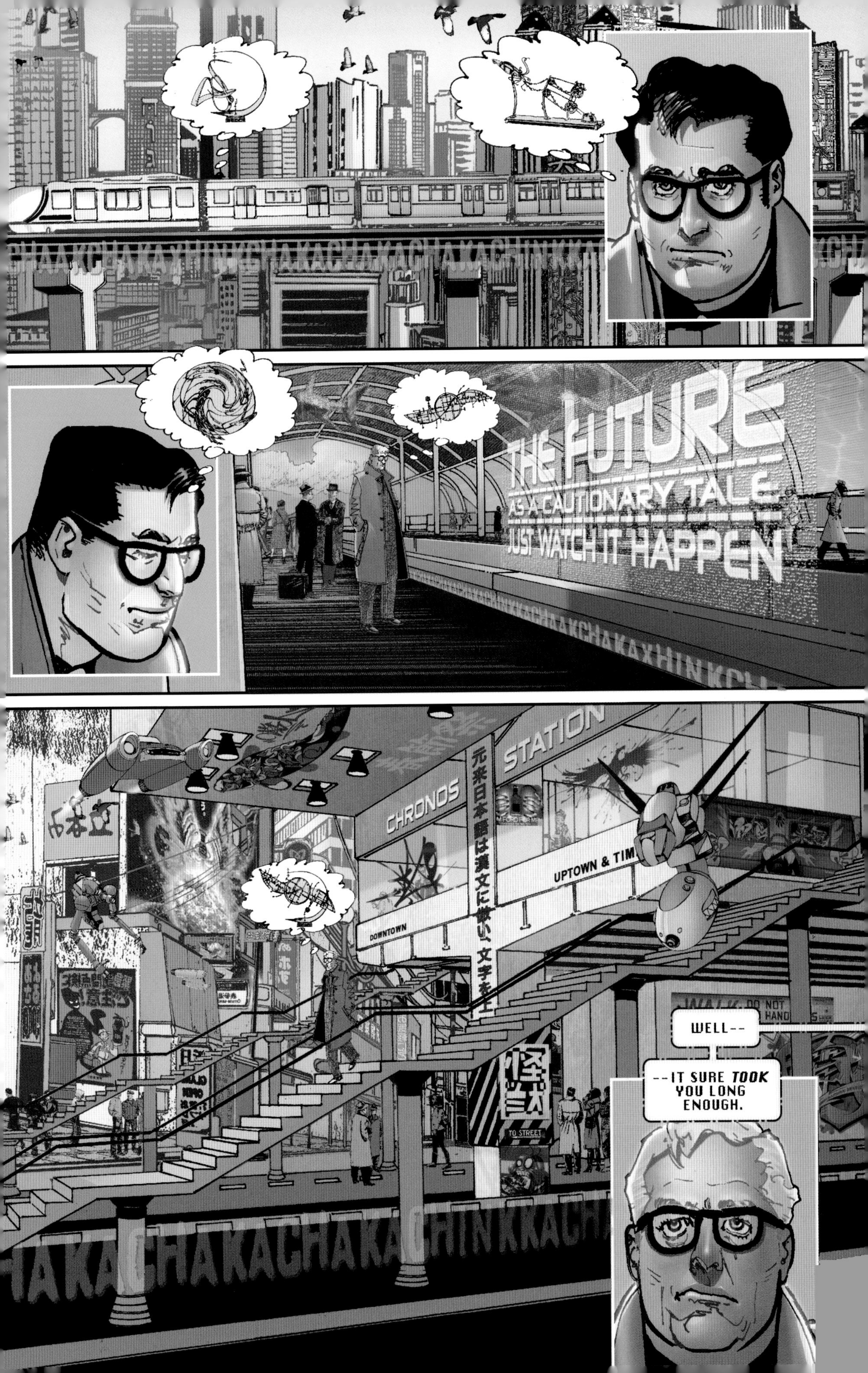
THE FUTURE
AS A CAUTIONARY TALE.
JUST WATCH IT HAPPEN
CHRONOS STATION
元来日本語は漢文に倣い、文字を上
UPTOWN & TIM
DOWNTOWN
TO STREET
WALK DO NOT
WELL--
--IT SURE *TOOK* YOU LONG ENOUGH.

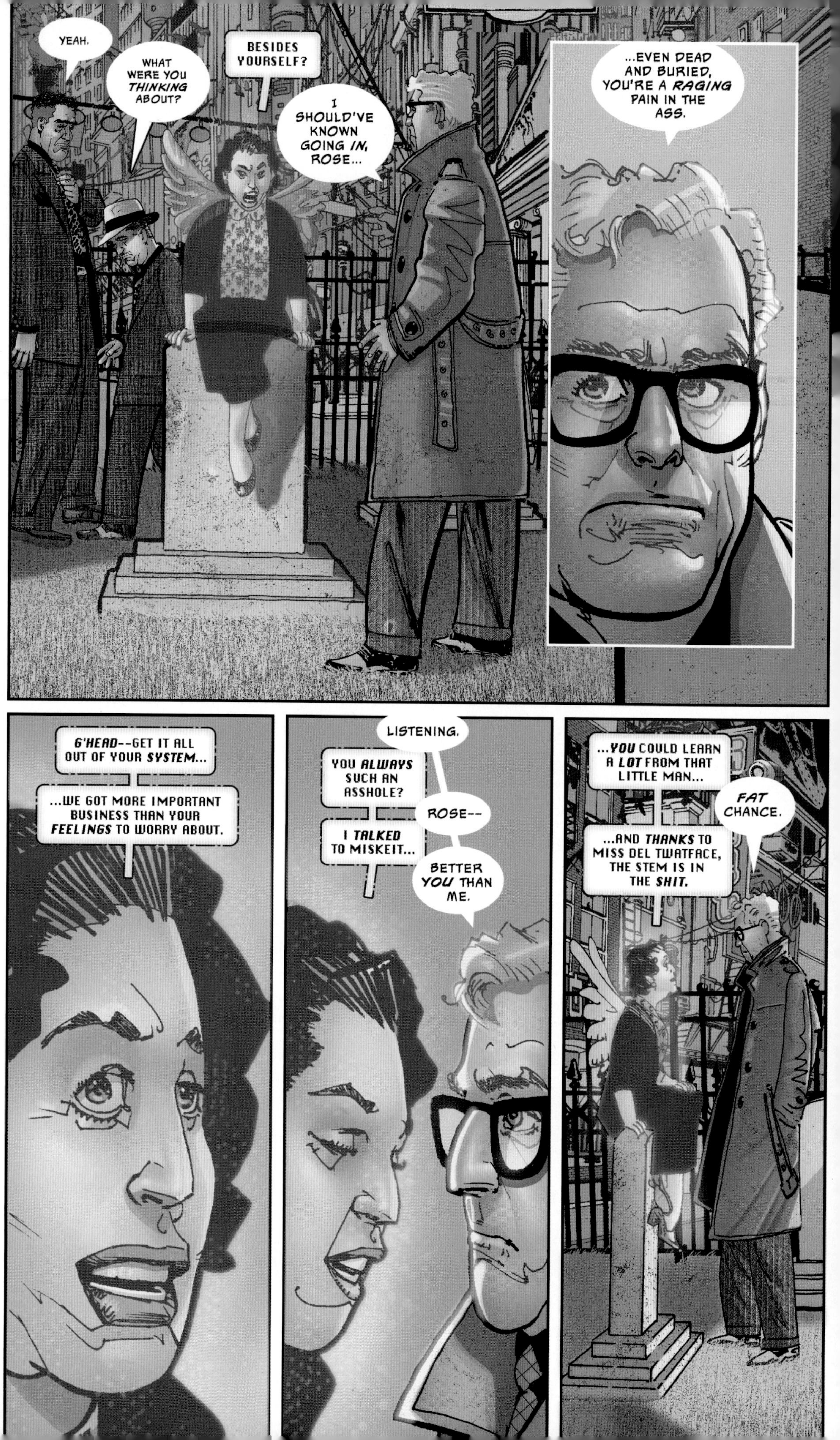
YEAH.
WHAT WERE YOU THINKING ABOUT?
BESIDES YOURSELF?
I SHOULD'VE KNOWN GOING IN, ROSE...
...EVEN DEAD AND BURIED, YOU'RE A RAGING PAIN IN THE ASS.
G'HEAD--GET IT ALL OUT OF YOUR SYSTEM...
...WE GOT MORE IMPORTANT BUSINESS THAN YOUR FEELINGS TO WORRY ABOUT.
LISTENING.
YOU ALWAYS SUCH AN ASSHOLE?
ROSE--
I TALKED TO MISKEIT...
BETTER YOU THAN ME.
...YOU COULD LEARN A LOT FROM THAT LITTLE MAN...
FAT CHANCE.
...AND THANKS TO MISS DEL TWATFACE, THE STEM IS IN THE SHIT.

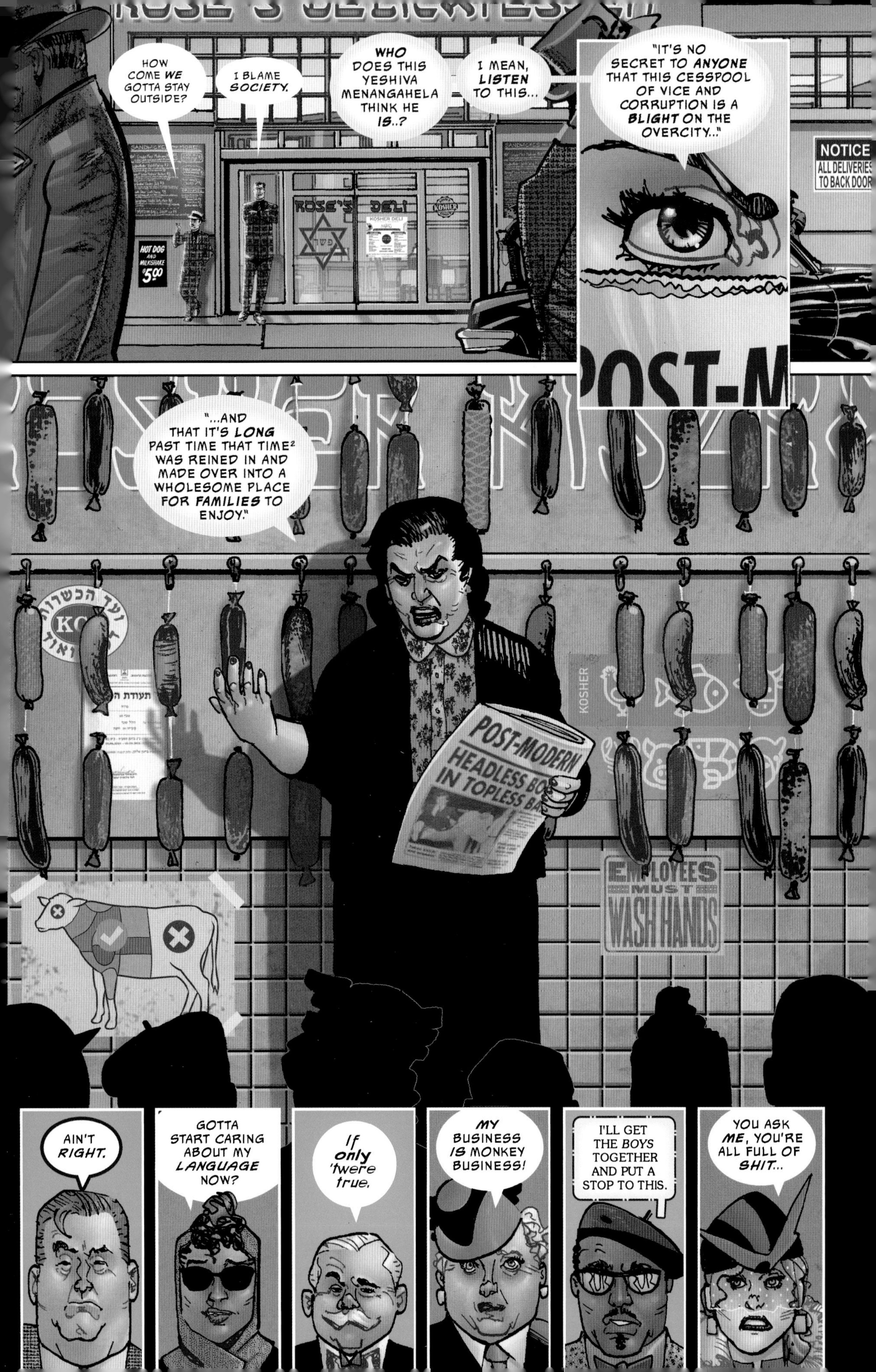
ROSE'S DELICATESSEN
HOW COME WE GOTTA STAY OUTSIDE?
I BLAME SOCIETY.
WHO DOES THIS YESHIVA MENANGAHELA THINK HE IS..?
I MEAN, LISTEN TO THIS...
"IT'S NO SECRET TO ANYONE THAT THIS CESSPOOL OF VICE AND CORRUPTION IS A BLIGHT ON THE OVERCITY..."
NOTICE ALL DELIVERIES TO BACK DOOR
HOT DOG AND MILKSHAKE $5.00
ROSE'S DELI
KOSHER
POST-M
"...AND THAT IT'S LONG PAST TIME THAT TIME² WAS REINED IN AND MADE OVER INTO A WHOLESOME PLACE FOR FAMILIES TO ENJOY."
POST-MODERN
HEADLESS BO IN TOPLESS BA
KOSHER
EMPLOYEES MUST WASH HANDS
AIN'T RIGHT.
GOTTA START CARING ABOUT MY LANGUAGE NOW?
If only 'twere true.
MY BUSINESS IS MONKEY BUSINESS!
I'LL GET THE BOYS TOGETHER AND PUT A STOP TO THIS.
YOU ASK ME, YOU'RE ALL FULL OF SHIT...

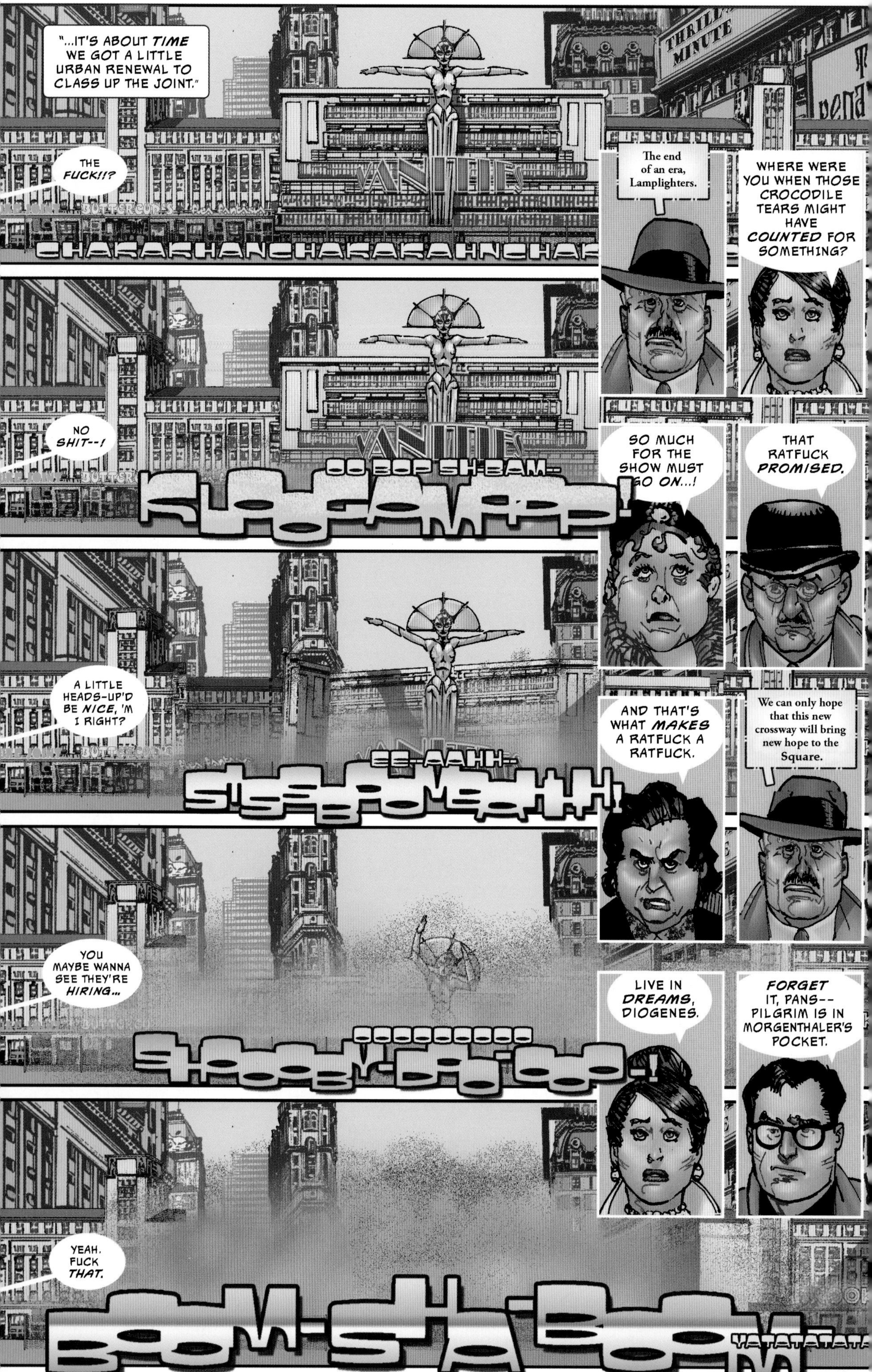
"...IT'S ABOUT *TIME* WE GOT A LITTLE URBAN RENEWAL TO CLASS UP THE JOINT."
THRILL MINUTE
VANITIES
THE *FUCK!!?*
The end of an era, Lamplighters.
WHERE WERE YOU WHEN THOSE CROCODILE TEARS MIGHT HAVE *COUNTED* FOR SOMETHING?
NO *SHIT--!*
OO BOP SH-BAM--
SO MUCH FOR THE SHOW MUST GO *ON*...!
THAT RATFUCK *PROMISED.*
A LITTLE HEADS-UP'D BE *NICE*, 'M I RIGHT?
EE-AAHH--
AND THAT'S WHAT *MAKES* A RATFUCK A RATFUCK.
We can only hope that this new crossway will bring new hope to the Square.
YOU MAYBE WANNA SEE THEY'RE *HIRING*...
LIVE IN *DREAMS*, DIOGENES.
FORGET IT, PANS-- PILGRIM IS IN MORGENTHALER'S POCKET.
YEAH. FUCK *THAT.*
BOOM-SHA-BOOM
YATATATAT

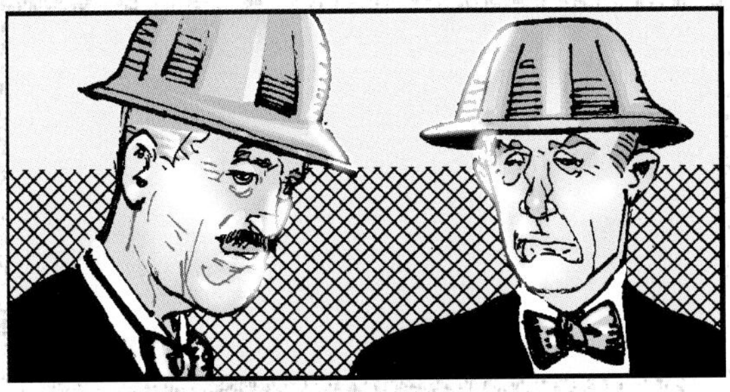

THE LAMP IS LIT

by **DIOGENES PILGRIM**

Looking for an honest man... and we've found him, Lamplighters, in the person of Yeshua Morgenthaler.

This privileged son of the OverCity has done right by our humble Square, and brought to bear a man-sized piece of that privilege to bring a little light and love to the Main Stem....

In his own words, Mr Morgenthaler said: "The TimeSpan Crossway, connecting the OverCity and Time[2] will bring new life, and not incidentally, new business to the so-called Main Stem."

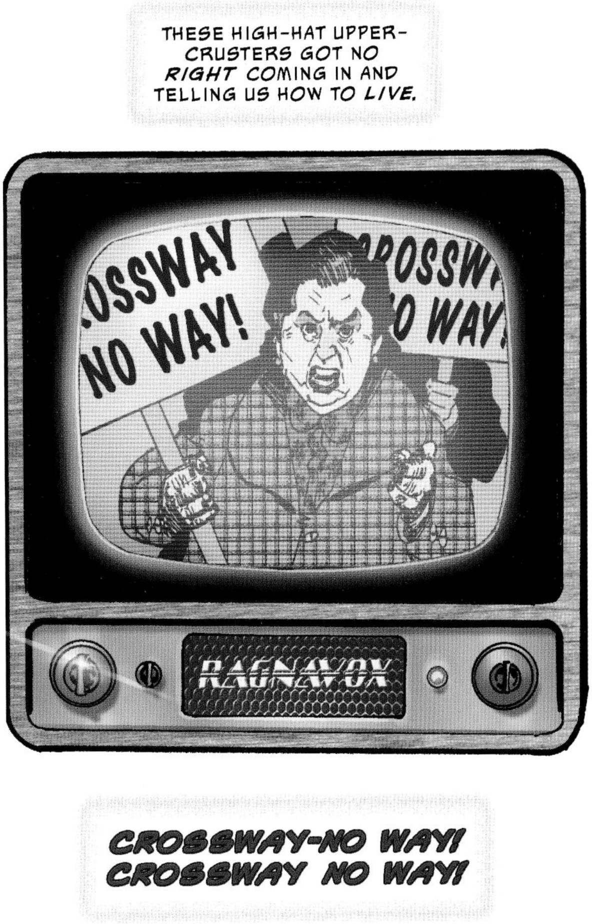
THESE HIGH-HAT UPPER-CRUSTERS GOT NO *RIGHT* COMING IN AND TELLING US HOW TO *LIVE.*
CROSSWAY NO WAY!
CROSSWAY NO WAY!
RAGNAVOX
CROSSWAY-NO WAY! CROSSWAY NO WAY!

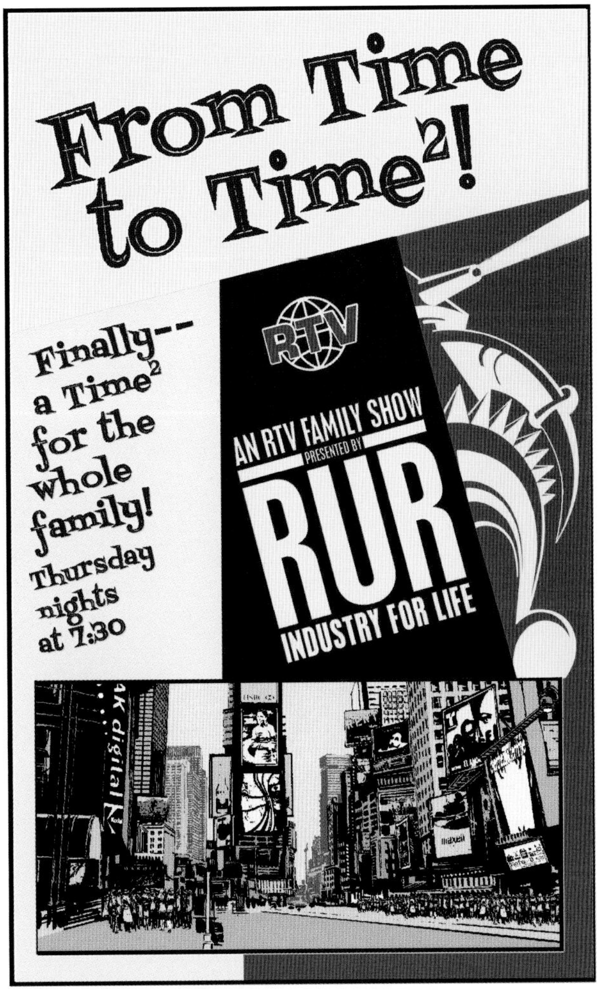
From Time to Time²!
Finally-- a Time² for the whole family! Thursday nights at 7:30
RTV
AN RTV FAMILY SHOW PRESENTED BY
RUR
INDUSTRY FOR LIFE

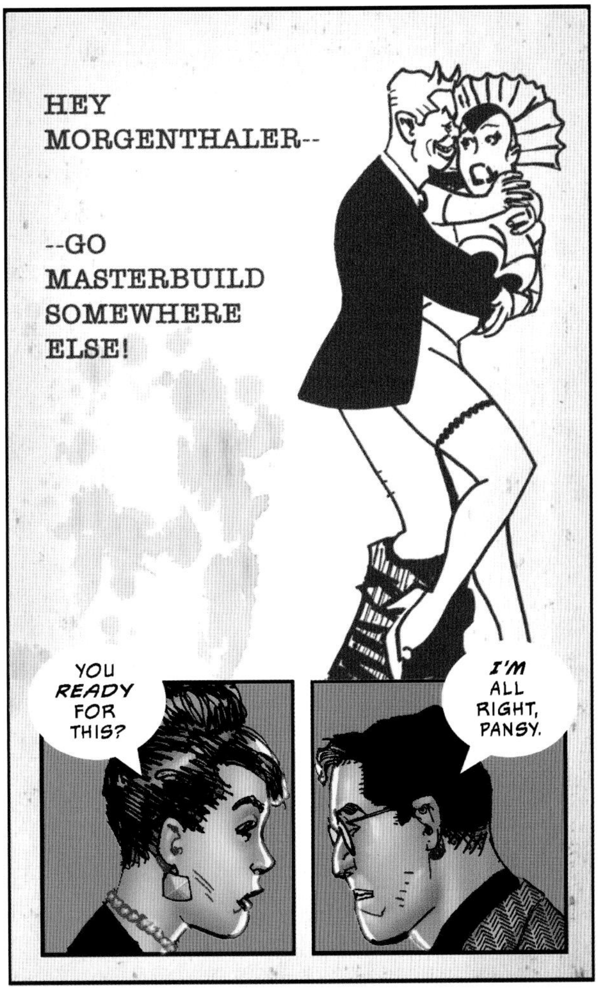
HEY MORGENTHALER--
--GO MASTERBUILD SOMEWHERE ELSE!
YOU *READY* FOR THIS?
I'M ALL RIGHT, PANSY.

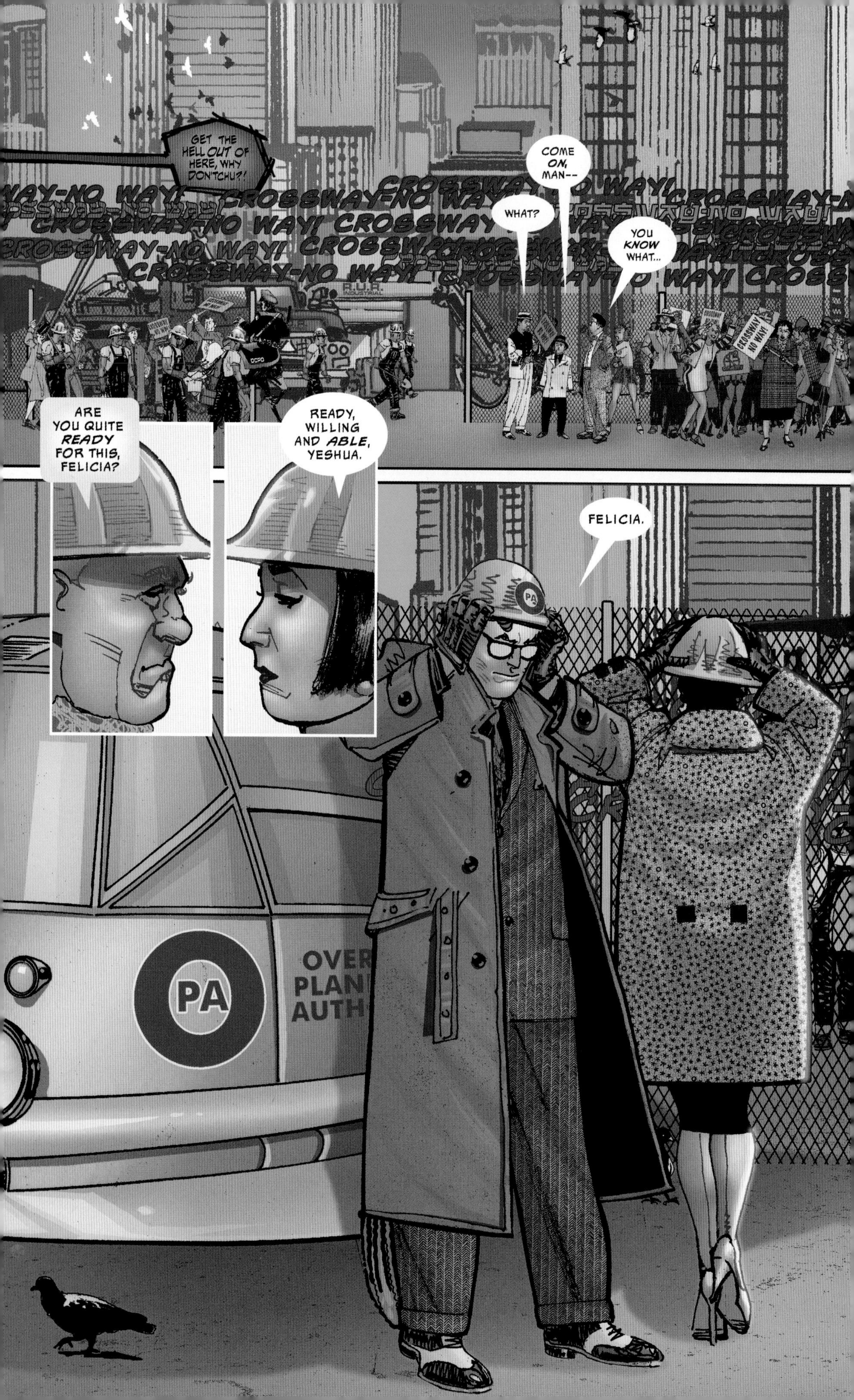
GET THE HELL OUT OF HERE, WHY DON'TCHU?!
CROSSWAY-NO WAY! CROSSWAY-NO WAY! CROSSWAY-NO WAY!
COME ON, MAN--
WHAT?
YOU KNOW WHAT...
ARE YOU QUITE READY FOR THIS, FELICIA?
READY, WILLING AND ABLE, YESHUA.
FELICIA.
PA
OVER PLAN AUTH

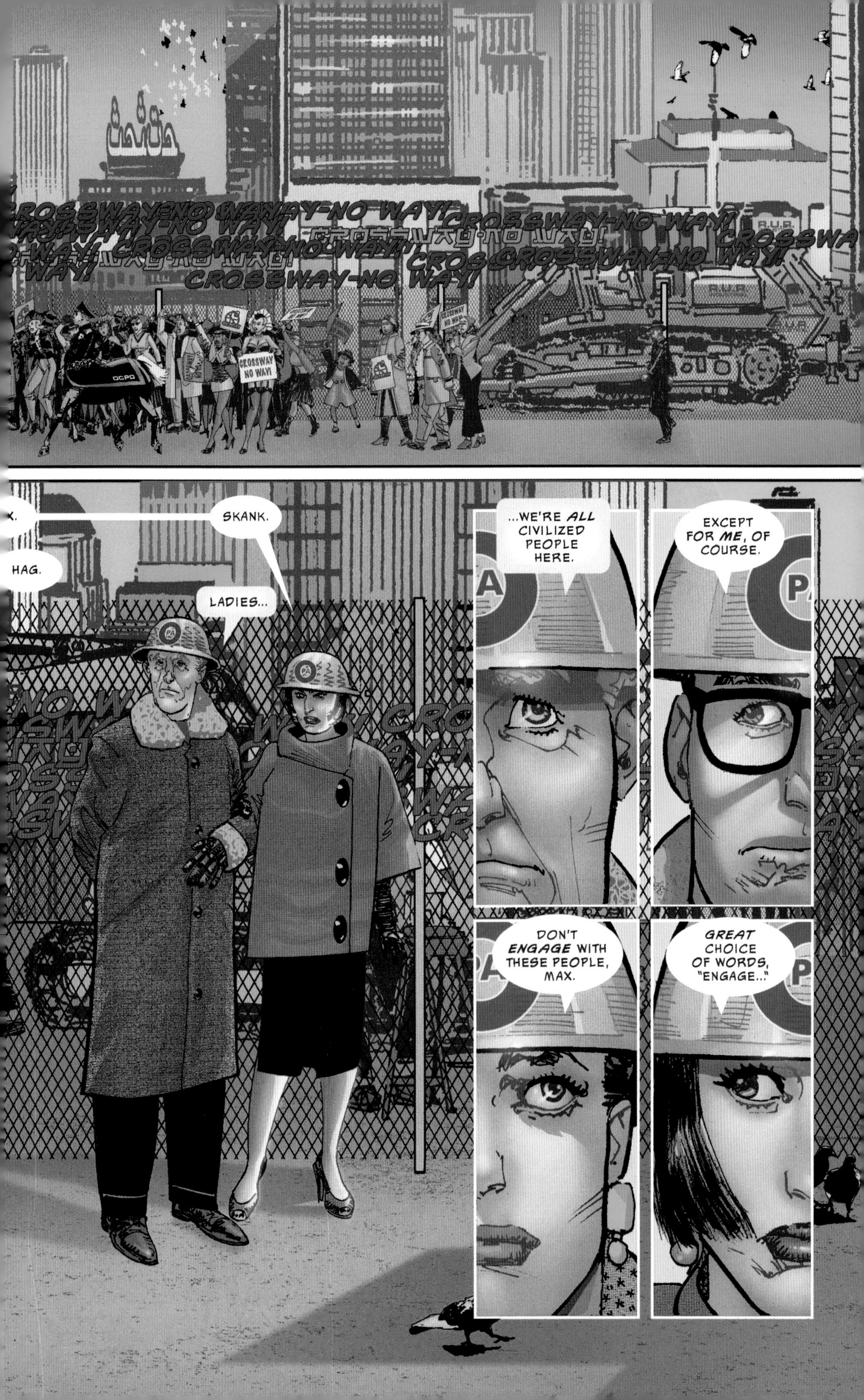
CROSSWAY–NO WAY!
CROSSWAY–NO WAY!
CROSSWAY–NO WAY!
CROSSWAY–NO WAY!
CROSSWAY–NO WAY!
CROSSWAY NO WAY!
X.
SKANK.
HAG.
LADIES...
...WE'RE *ALL* CIVILIZED PEOPLE HERE.
EXCEPT FOR *ME*, OF COURSE.
DON'T *ENGAGE* WITH THESE PEOPLE, MAX.
GREAT CHOICE OF WORDS, "ENGAGE..."

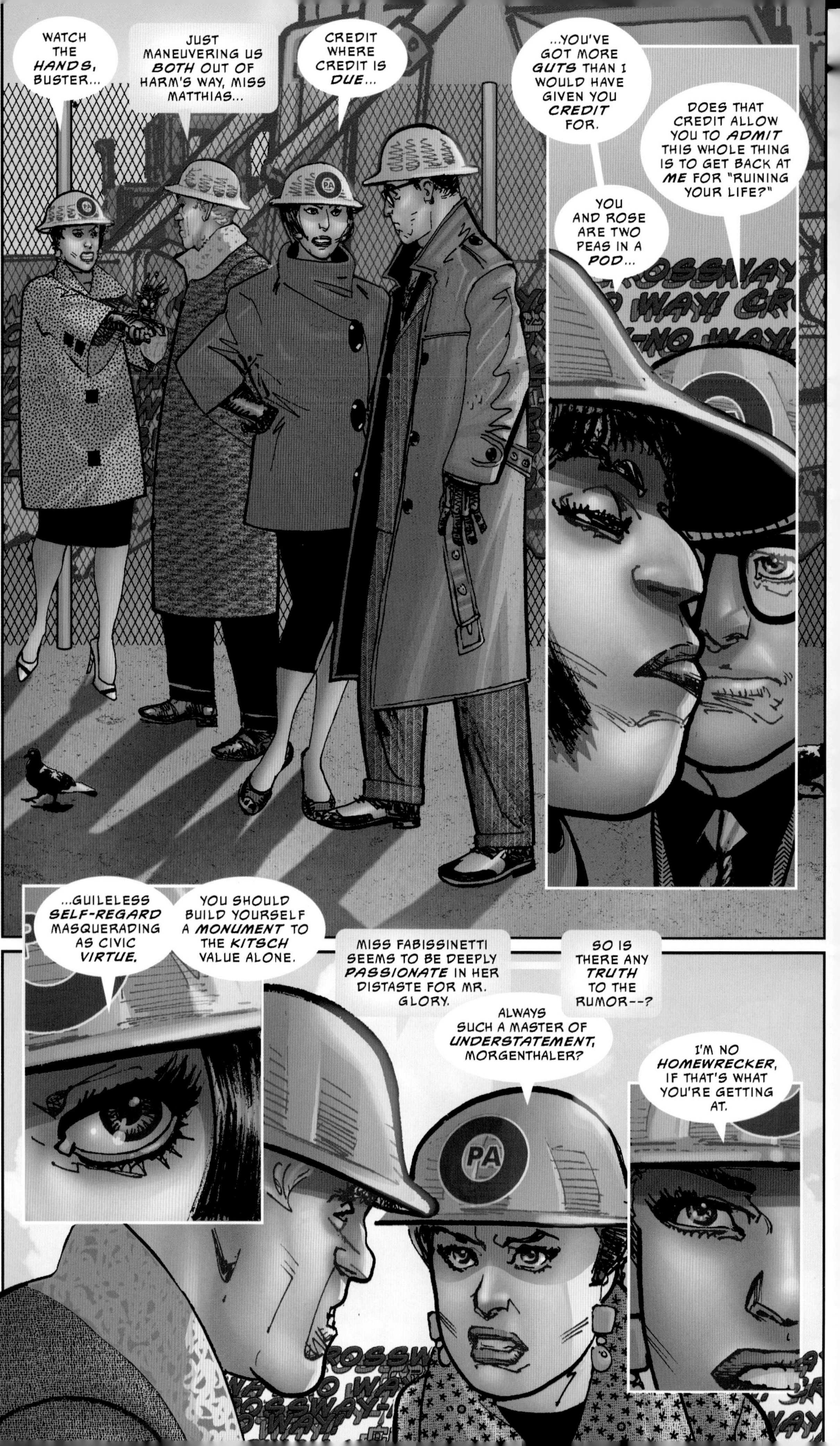

WATCH THE *HANDS*, BUSTER...
JUST MANEUVERING US *BOTH* OUT OF HARM'S WAY, MISS MATTHIAS...
CREDIT WHERE CREDIT IS *DUE*...
...YOU'VE GOT MORE *GUTS* THAN I WOULD HAVE GIVEN YOU *CREDIT* FOR.
YOU AND ROSE ARE TWO PEAS IN A *POD*...
DOES THAT CREDIT ALLOW YOU TO *ADMIT* THIS WHOLE THING IS TO GET BACK AT *ME* FOR "RUINING YOUR LIFE?"
...GUILELESS *SELF-REGARD* MASQUERADING AS CIVIC *VIRTUE.*
YOU SHOULD BUILD YOURSELF A *MONUMENT* TO THE *KITSCH* VALUE ALONE.
MISS FABISSINETTI SEEMS TO BE DEEPLY *PASSIONATE* IN HER DISTASTE FOR MR. GLORY.
SO IS THERE ANY *TRUTH* TO THE RUMOR--?
ALWAYS SUCH A MASTER OF *UNDERSTATEMENT*, MORGENTHALER?
I'M NO *HOMEWRECKER*, IF THAT'S WHAT YOU'RE GETTING AT.

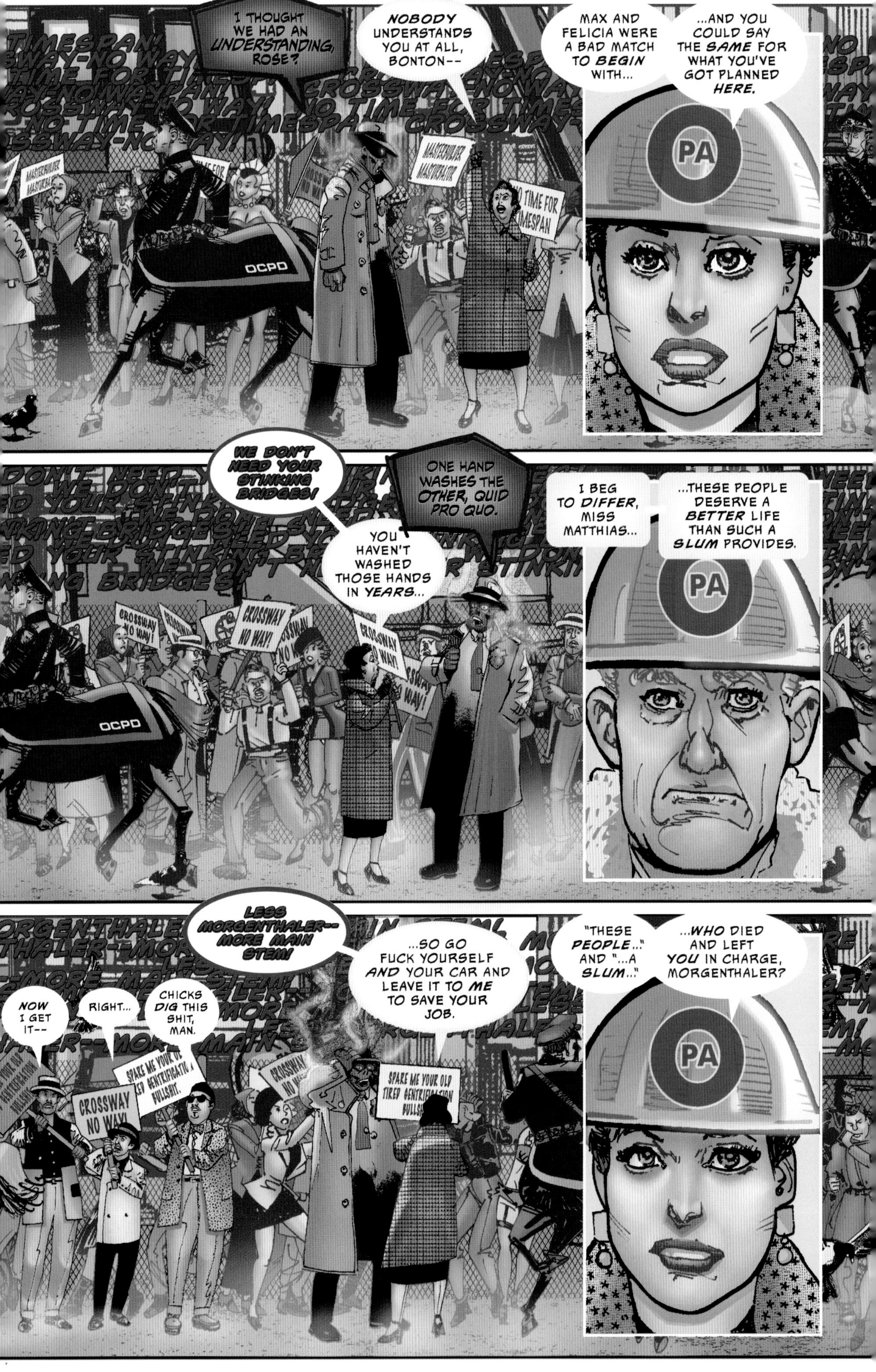
I THOUGHT WE HAD AN UNDERSTANDING, ROSE?
NOBODY UNDERSTANDS YOU AT ALL, BONTON--
MAX AND FELICIA WERE A BAD MATCH TO BEGIN WITH...
...AND YOU COULD SAY THE SAME FOR WHAT YOU'VE GOT PLANNED HERE.
MASTERBUILDER MASTURBATOR
NO TIME FOR TIMESPAN
OCPD
PA
WE DON'T NEED YOUR STINKING BRIDGES!
ONE HAND WASHES THE OTHER, QUID PRO QUO.
YOU HAVEN'T WASHED THOSE HANDS IN YEARS...
I BEG TO DIFFER, MISS MATTHIAS...
...THESE PEOPLE DESERVE A BETTER LIFE THAN SUCH A SLUM PROVIDES.
CROSSWAY NO WAY!
OCPD
PA
LESS MORGENTHALER-- MORE MAIN STEM!
NOW I GET IT--
RIGHT...
CHICKS DIG THIS SHIT, MAN.
...SO GO FUCK YOURSELF AND YOUR CAR AND LEAVE IT TO ME TO SAVE YOUR JOB.
"THESE PEOPLE..." AND "...A SLUM..."
...WHO DIED AND LEFT YOU IN CHARGE, MORGENTHALER?
CROSSWAY NO WAY!
SPARE ME YOUR OLD TIRED GENTRIFICATION BULLSH

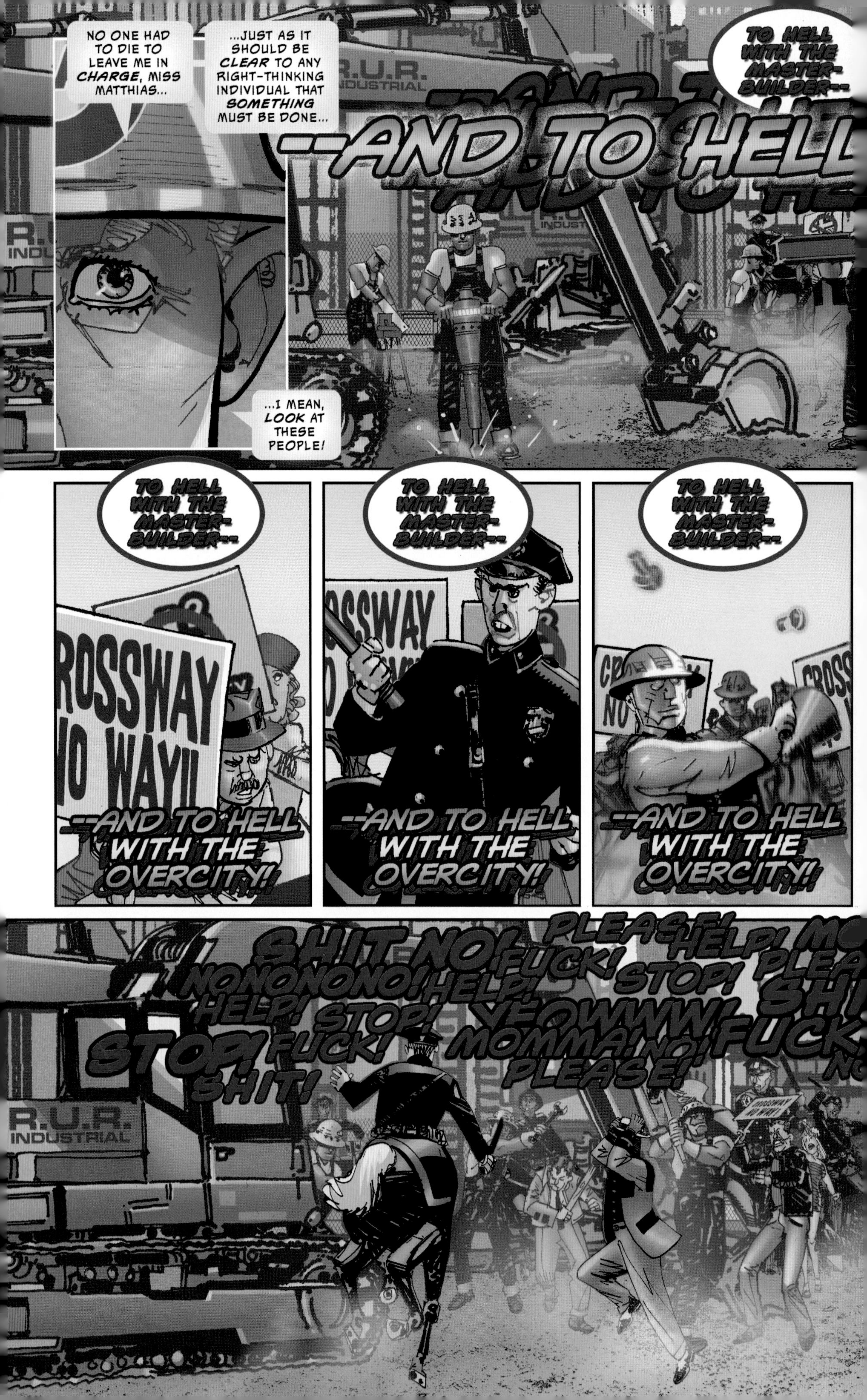

NO ONE HAD TO DIE TO LEAVE ME IN *CHARGE*, MISS MATTHIAS...
...JUST AS IT SHOULD BE *CLEAR* TO ANY RIGHT-THINKING INDIVIDUAL THAT *SOMETHING* MUST BE DONE...
TO HELL WITH THE MASTER-BUILDER--
--AND TO HELL
R.U.R. INDUSTRIAL
...I MEAN, *LOOK* AT THESE PEOPLE!
TO HELL WITH THE MASTER-BUILDER--
ROSSWAY NO WAY!!
--AND TO HELL WITH THE OVERCITY!
TO HELL WITH THE MASTER-BUILDER--
ROSSWAY
--AND TO HELL WITH THE OVERCITY!
TO HELL WITH THE MASTER-BUILDER--
--AND TO HELL WITH THE OVERCITY!
SHIT NO! PLEASE! HELP!
NONONONO! FUCK! STOP!
HELP! STOP! HELP! YEOWWW!
STOP! FUCK! MOMMA! NO! FUCK!
SHIT! PLEASE!
R.U.R. INDUSTRIAL

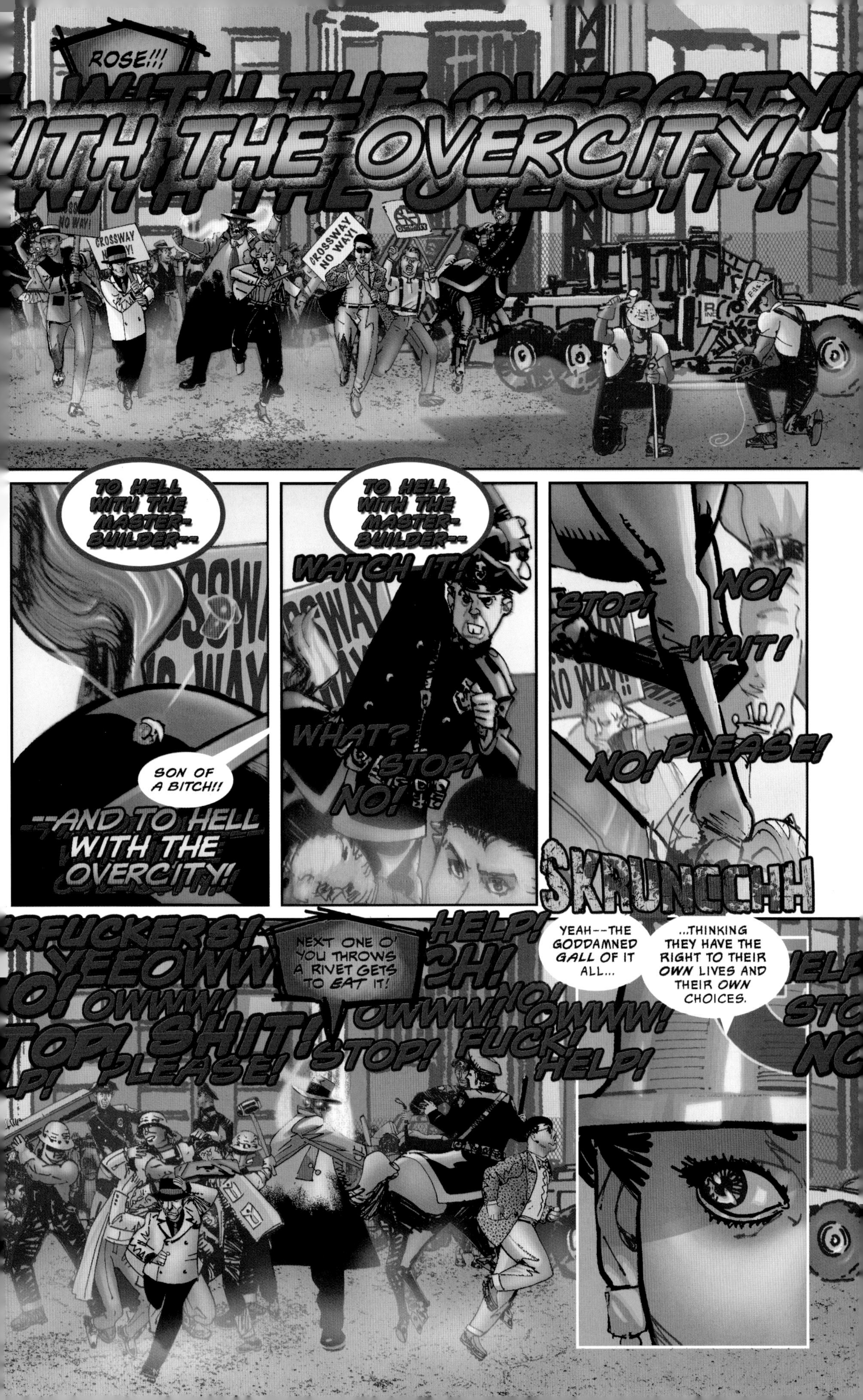

ROSE!!!
WITH THE OVERCITY!
CROSSWAY NO WAY!
TO HELL WITH THE MASTER-BUILDER--
SON OF A BITCH!!
--AND TO HELL WITH THE OVERCITY!!
TO HELL WITH THE MASTER-BUILDER--
WATCH IT!
WHAT? STOP! NO!
STOP! NO! WAIT! NO! PLEASE!
SKRUNCCHH
NEXT ONE O' YOU THROWS A RIVET GETS TO EAT IT!
YEEOWW! OWWW! SHIT! PLEASE! STOP! HELP! OWWW! NO! FUCK! HELP!
YEAH--THE GODDAMNED GALL OF IT ALL...
...THINKING THEY HAVE THE RIGHT TO THEIR OWN LIVES AND THEIR OWN CHOICES.

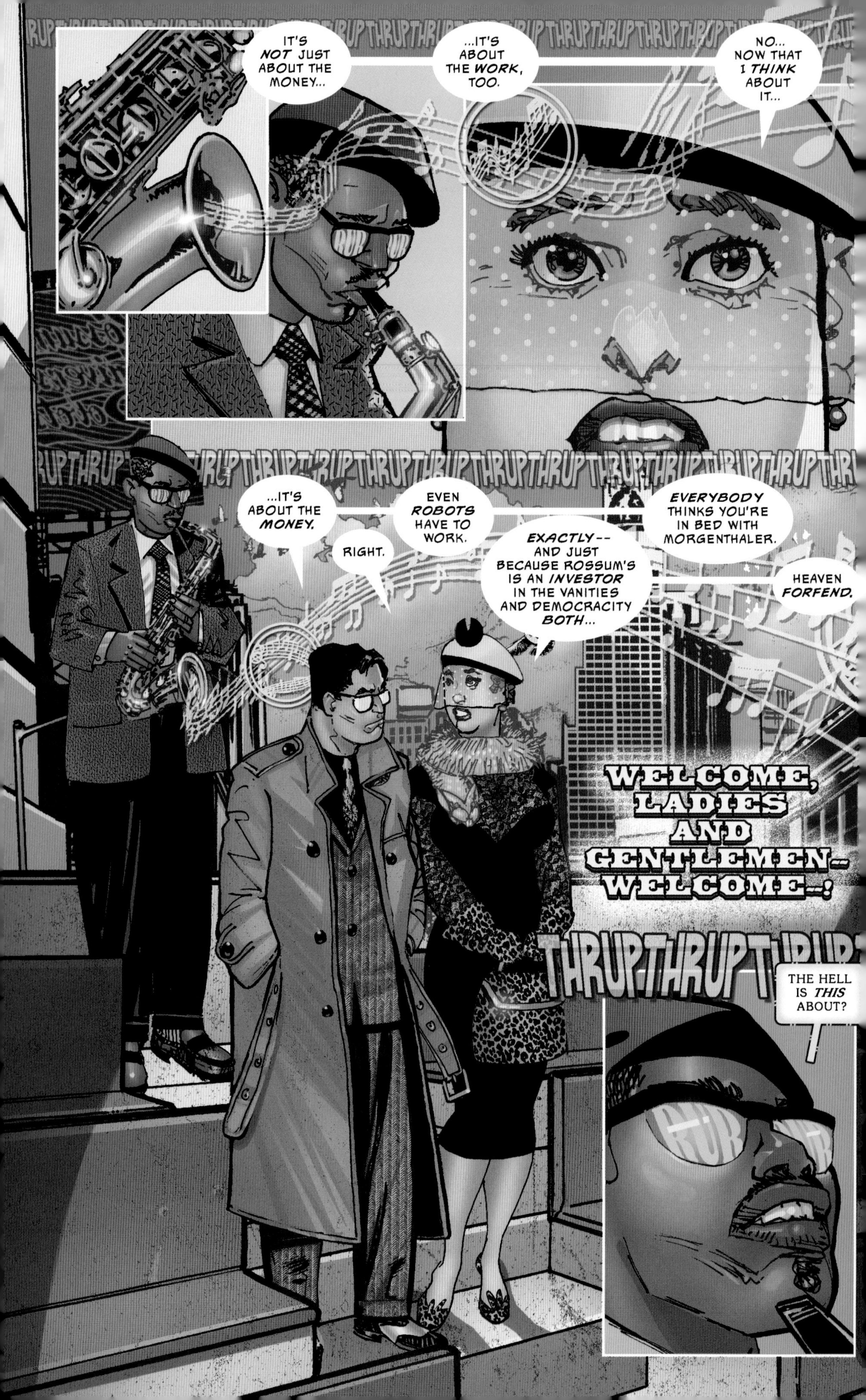
THRUPTHRUPTHRUPTHRUP
IT'S NOT JUST ABOUT THE MONEY...
...IT'S ABOUT THE WORK, TOO.
NO... NOW THAT I THINK ABOUT IT...
THRUPTHRUPTHRUPTHRUP
...IT'S ABOUT THE MONEY.
RIGHT.
EVEN ROBOTS HAVE TO WORK.
EXACTLY-- AND JUST BECAUSE ROSSUM'S IS AN INVESTOR IN THE VANITIES AND DEMOCRACITY BOTH...
EVERYBODY THINKS YOU'RE IN BED WITH MORGENTHALER.
HEAVEN FORFEND.
WELCOME, LADIES AND GENTLEMEN-- WELCOME--!
THRUPTHRUP
THE HELL IS THIS ABOUT?

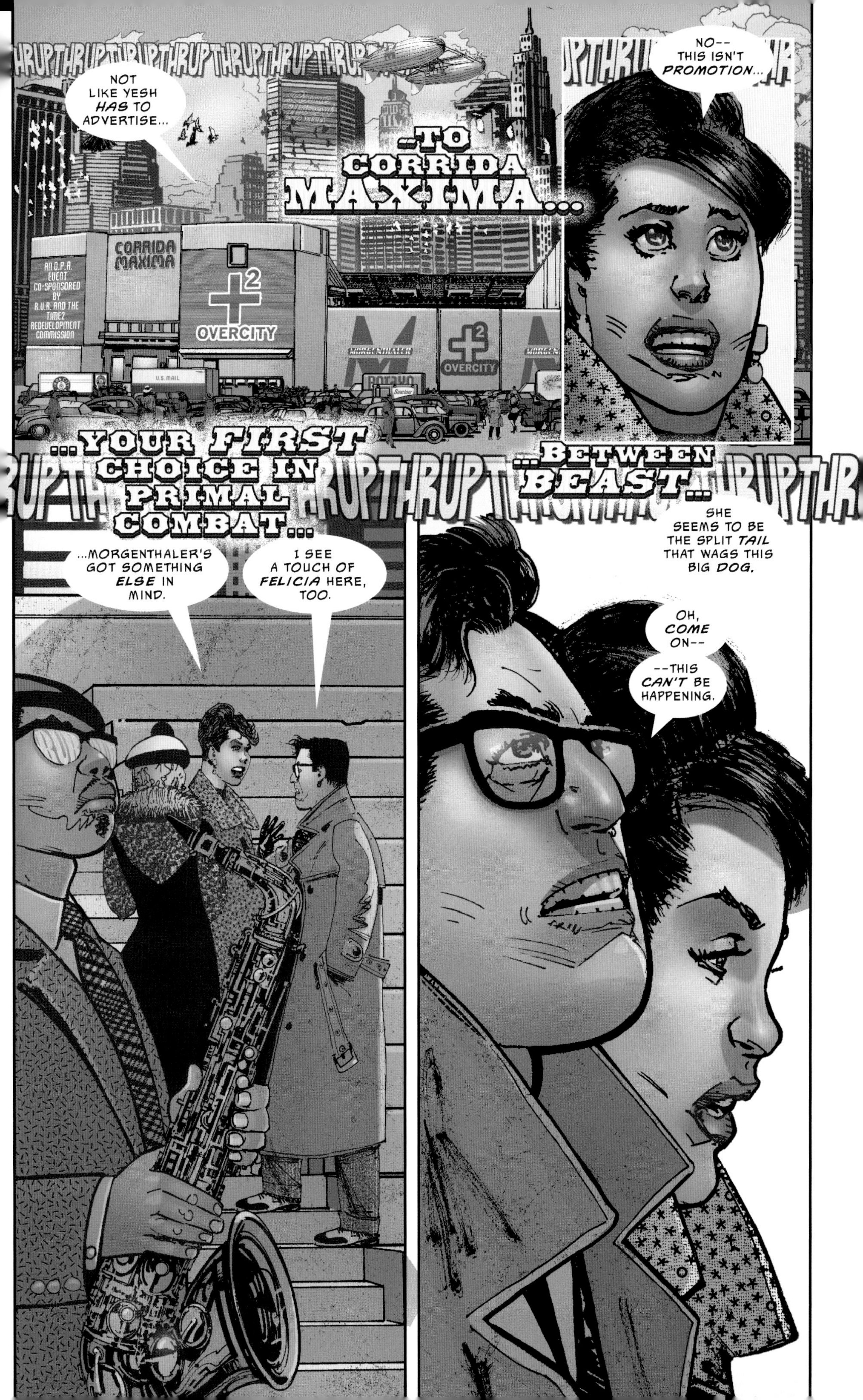
THRUPTHRUPTHRUPTHRUPTHRUPTHRUPTHRUPTHRUPTHRUP
NOT LIKE YESH HAS TO ADVERTISE...
-TO CORRIDA MAXIMA...
CORRIDA MAXIMA
AN O.P.A. EVENT CO-SPONSORED BY R.U.R. AND THE TIME2 REDEVELOPMENT COMMISSION
OVERCITY
MORGENTHALER
U.S. MAIL
NO-- THIS ISN'T PROMOTION...
...YOUR FIRST CHOICE IN PRIMAL COMBAT...
...BETWEEN BEAST...
...MORGENTHALER'S GOT SOMETHING ELSE IN MIND.
I SEE A TOUCH OF FELICIA HERE, TOO.
SHE SEEMS TO BE THE SPLIT TAIL THAT WAGS THIS BIG DOG.
OH, COME ON--
--THIS CAN'T BE HAPPENING.

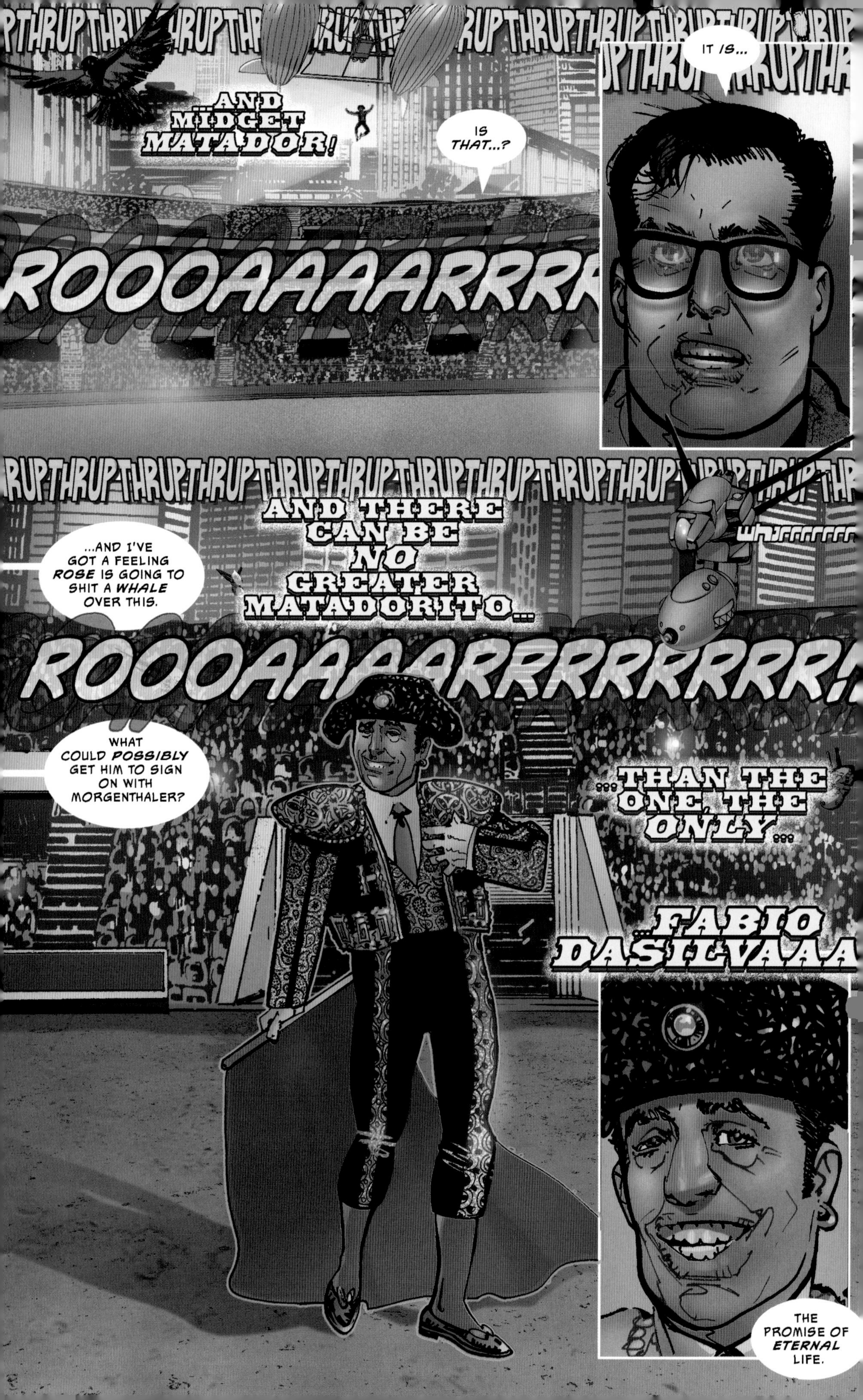
THRUPTHRUPTHRUPTHRUPTHRUP
...AND MIDGET MATADOR!
IS THAT...?
IT IS...
ROOOAAAAARRRR
THRUPTHRUPTHRUPTHRUPTHRUP
AND THERE CAN BE NO GREATER MATADORITO...
...AND I'VE GOT A FEELING ROSE IS GOING TO SHIT A WHALE OVER THIS.
WHIRRRRRRR
ROOOAAAAARRRRRRRR!
WHAT COULD POSSIBLY GET HIM TO SIGN ON WITH MORGENTHALER?
...THAN THE ONE, THE ONLY...
...FABIO DASILVAAA
THE PROMISE OF ETERNAL LIFE.

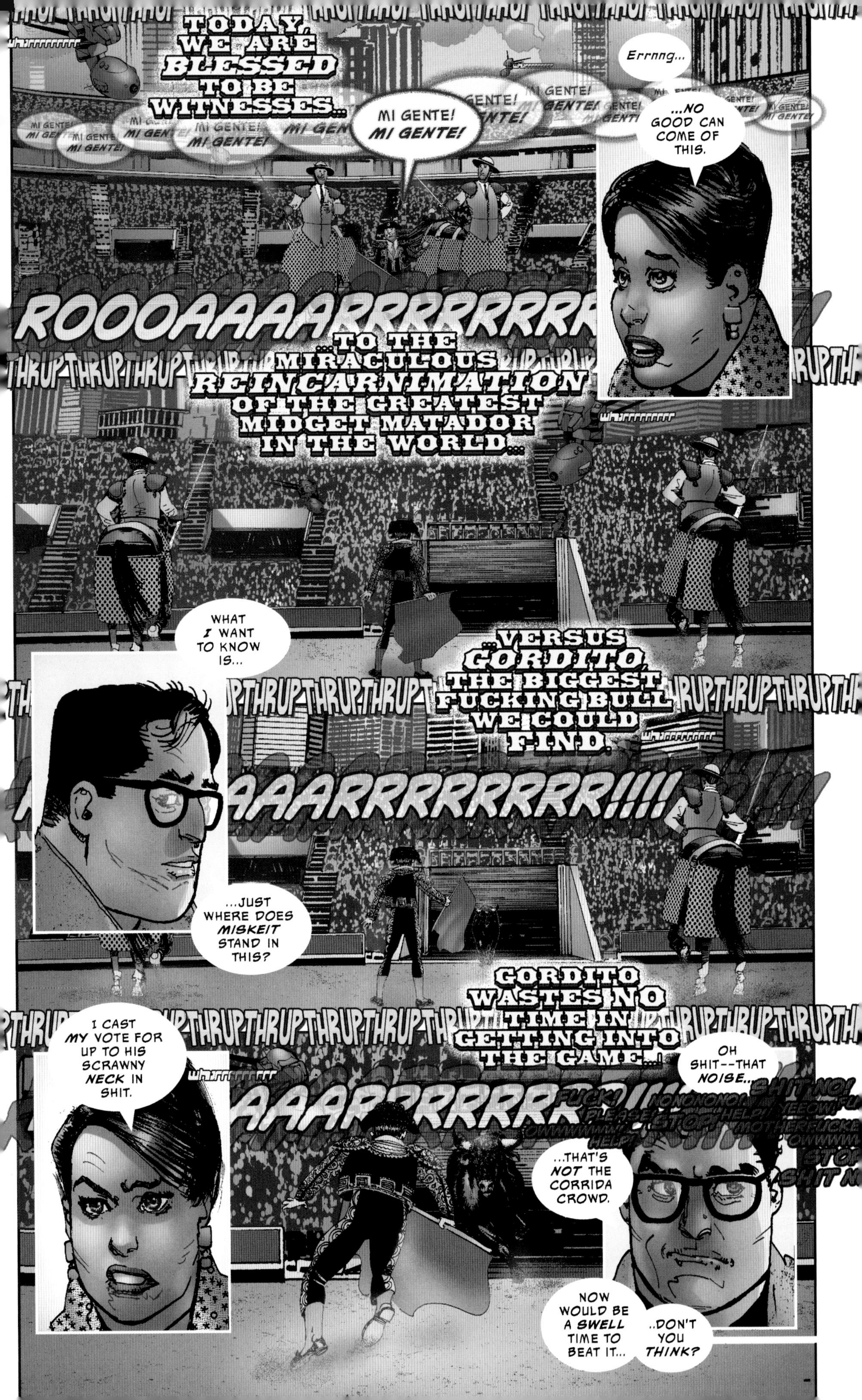
TODAY, WE ARE BLESSED TO BE WITNESSES...
MI GENTE! MI GENTE!
Errrng...
...NO GOOD CAN COME OF THIS.
ROOOAAAAARRRRRRR
...TO THE MIRACULOUS REINCARNIMATION OF THE GREATEST MIDGET MATADOR IN THE WORLD...
THRUP THRUP THRUP
WHAT I WANT TO KNOW IS...
...VERSUS GORDITO, THE BIGGEST FUCKING BULL WE COULD FIND.
AAARRRRRRRR!!!!
...JUST WHERE DOES MISKEIT STAND IN THIS?
GORDITO WASTES NO TIME IN GETTING INTO THE GAME...!
I CAST MY VOTE FOR UP TO HIS SCRAWNY NECK IN SHIT.
OH SHIT--THAT NOISE...
AAARRRRRRR
...THAT'S NOT THE CORRIDA CROWD.
NOW WOULD BE A SWELL TIME TO BEAT IT...
..DON'T YOU THINK?

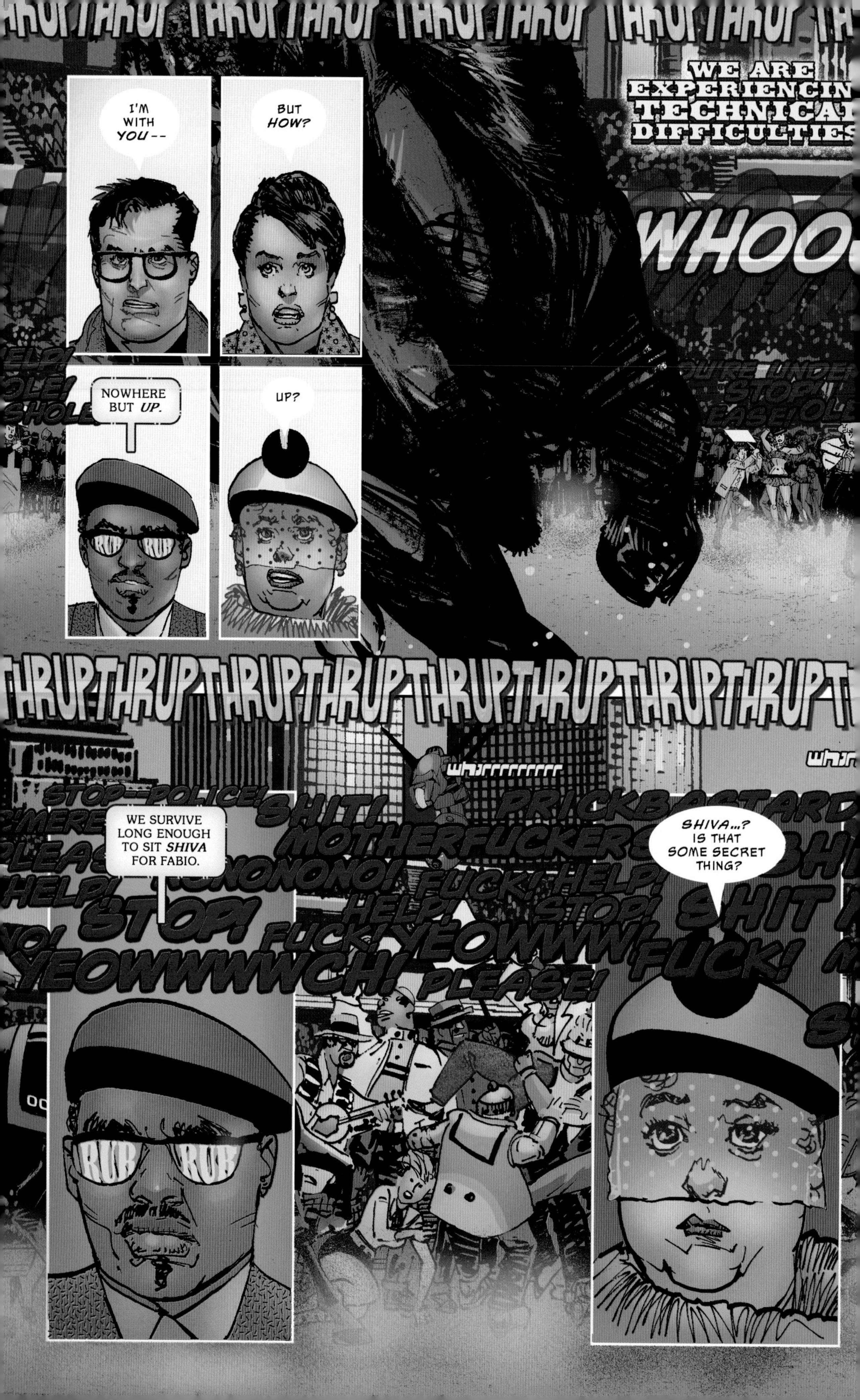

I'M WITH YOU--
BUT HOW?
WE ARE EXPERIENCIN TECHNICAL DIFFICULTIES
WHOO
NOWHERE BUT UP.
UP?
THRUPTHRUPTHRUPTHRUPTHRUPTHRUPTHRUPTHRUP
whirrrrrrrrr
STOP--POLICE!
SHIT!
PRICKBASTARD
MOTHERFUCKERS
WE SURVIVE LONG ENOUGH TO SIT SHIVA FOR FABIO.
SHIVA...? IS THAT SOME SECRET THING?
NONONONO!
FUCK! HELP!
HELP!
STOP!
STOP!
SHIT
FUCK! YEOWWW!
YEOWWWWCH!
PLEASE!
FUCK!

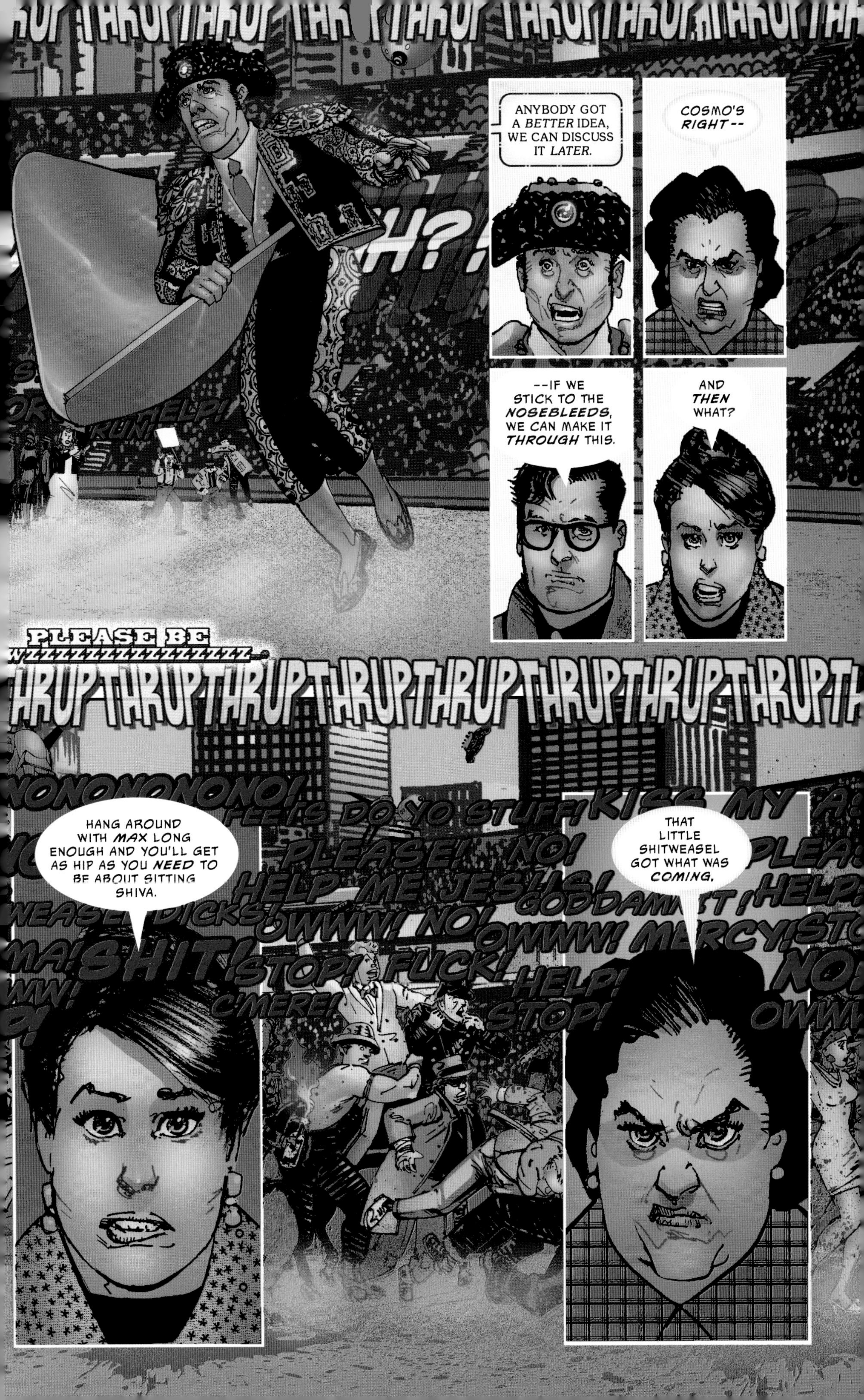
ANYBODY GOT A BETTER IDEA, WE CAN DISCUSS IT LATER.
COSMO'S RIGHT--
--IF WE STICK TO THE NOSEBLEEDS, WE CAN MAKE IT THROUGH THIS.
AND THEN WHAT?
PLEASE BE
THRUP THRUP THRUP THRUP THRUP THRUP THRUP THRUP
NONONONONONO!
HANG AROUND WITH MAX LONG ENOUGH AND YOU'LL GET AS HIP AS YOU NEED TO BE ABOUT SITTING SHIVA.
PLEASE! NO!
HELP ME JESUS!
OWWW! NO!
SHIT!
STOP! FUCK!
C'MERE!
KISS MY
GODDAMMIT!
OWWW! MERCY!
HELP!
STOP!
THAT LITTLE SHITWEASEL GOT WHAT WAS COMING.

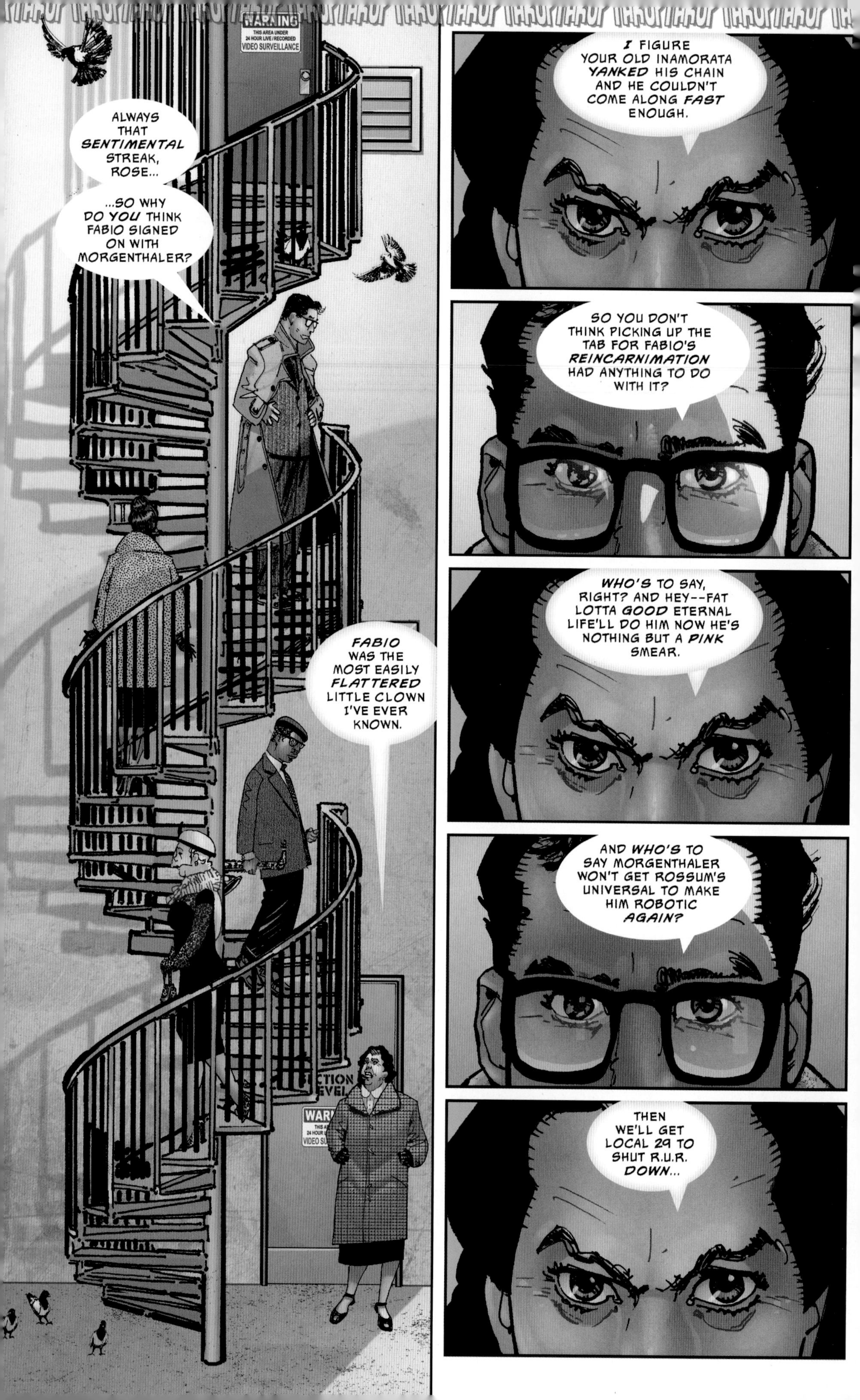
WARNING
THIS AREA UNDER
24 HOUR LIVE/RECORDED
VIDEO SURVEILLANCE
ALWAYS THAT *SENTIMENTAL* STREAK, ROSE...
...SO WHY DO *YOU* THINK FABIO SIGNED ON WITH MORGENTHALER?
FABIO WAS THE MOST EASILY *FLATTERED* LITTLE CLOWN I'VE EVER KNOWN.
I FIGURE YOUR OLD INAMORATA *YANKED* HIS CHAIN AND HE COULDN'T COME ALONG *FAST* ENOUGH.
SO YOU DON'T THINK PICKING UP THE TAB FOR FABIO'S *REINCARNIMATION* HAD ANYTHING TO DO WITH IT?
WHO'S TO SAY, RIGHT? AND HEY--FAT LOTTA *GOOD* ETERNAL LIFE'LL DO HIM NOW HE'S NOTHING BUT A *PINK* SMEAR.
AND *WHO'S* TO SAY MORGENTHALER WON'T GET ROSSUM'S UNIVERSAL TO MAKE HIM ROBOTIC *AGAIN?*
THEN WE'LL GET LOCAL 29 TO SHUT R.U.R. *DOWN*...

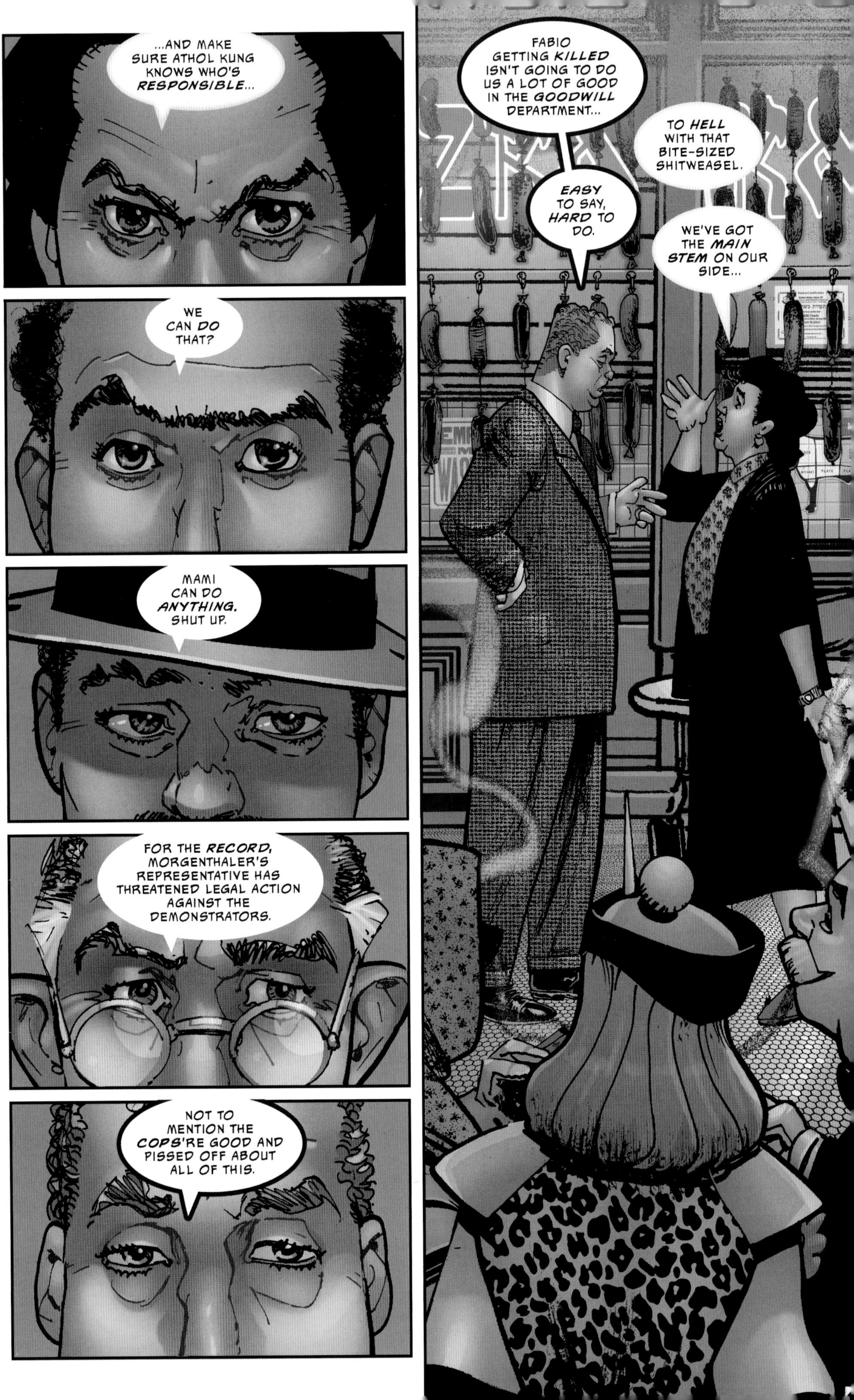
...AND MAKE SURE ATHOL KUNG KNOWS WHO'S RESPONSIBLE...
WE CAN DO THAT?
MAMI CAN DO ANYTHING. SHUT UP.
FOR THE RECORD, MORGENTHALER'S REPRESENTATIVE HAS THREATENED LEGAL ACTION AGAINST THE DEMONSTRATORS.
NOT TO MENTION THE COPS'RE GOOD AND PISSED OFF ABOUT ALL OF THIS.
FABIO GETTING KILLED ISN'T GOING TO DO US A LOT OF GOOD IN THE GOODWILL DEPARTMENT...
TO HELL WITH THAT BITE-SIZED SHITWEASEL.
EASY TO SAY, HARD TO DO.
WE'VE GOT THE MAIN STEM ON OUR SIDE...

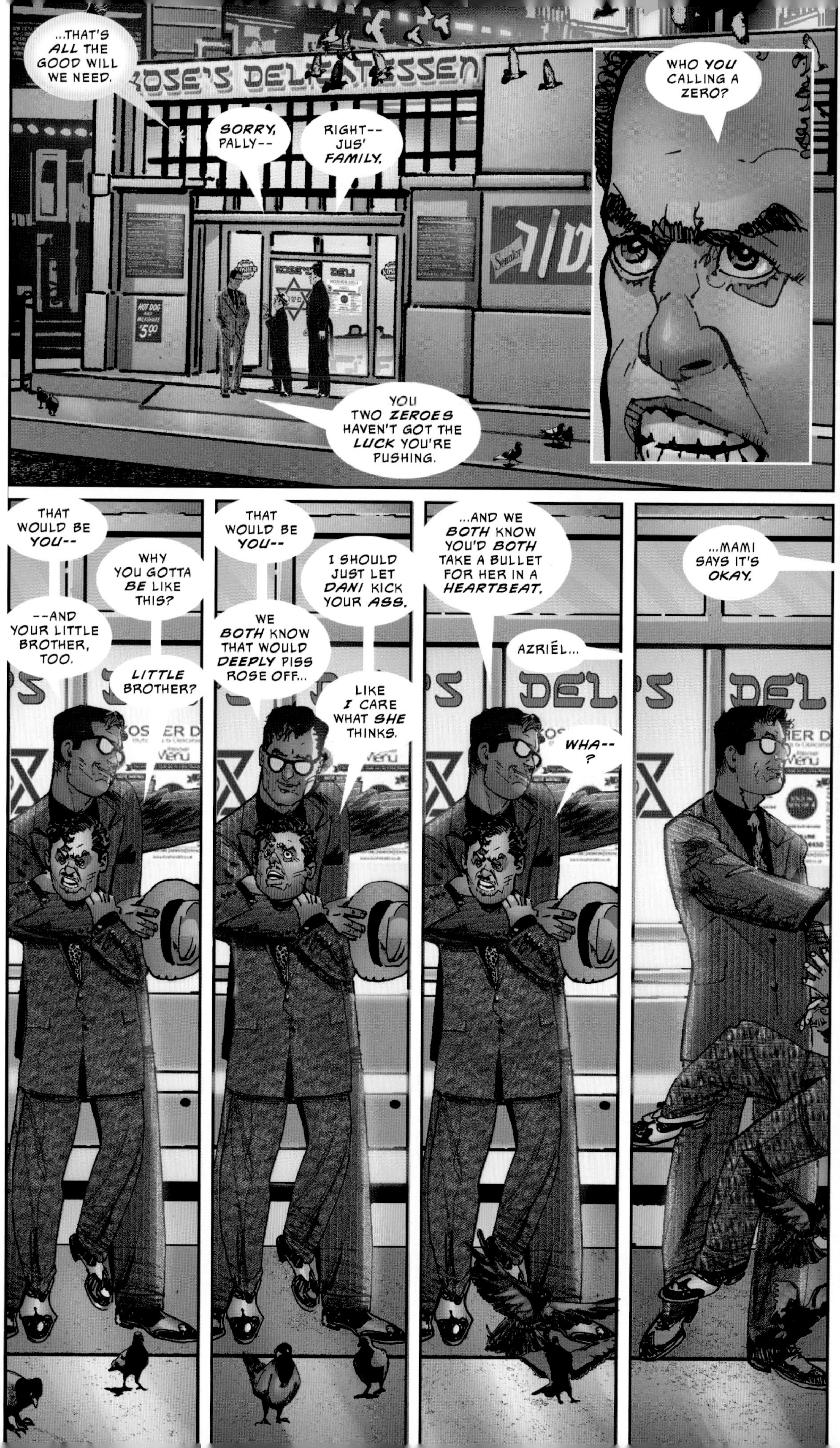

...THAT'S ALL THE GOOD WILL WE NEED.
ROSE'S DELICATESSEN
SORRY, PALLY--
RIGHT-- JUS' FAMILY.
HOT DOG AND MILKSHAKE $5.00
KOSHER
ROSE'S DELI
KOSHER DELI
Senator
YOU TWO ZEROES HAVEN'T GOT THE LUCK YOU'RE PUSHING.
WHO YOU CALLING A ZERO?
THAT WOULD BE YOU--
--AND YOUR LITTLE BROTHER, TOO.
WHY YOU GOTTA BE LIKE THIS?
LITTLE BROTHER?
THAT WOULD BE YOU--
WE BOTH KNOW THAT WOULD DEEPLY PISS ROSE OFF...
I SHOULD JUST LET DANI KICK YOUR ASS.
LIKE I CARE WHAT SHE THINKS.
...AND WE BOTH KNOW YOU'D BOTH TAKE A BULLET FOR HER IN A HEARTBEAT.
AZRIÉL...
WHA-- ?
...MAMI SAYS IT'S OKAY.

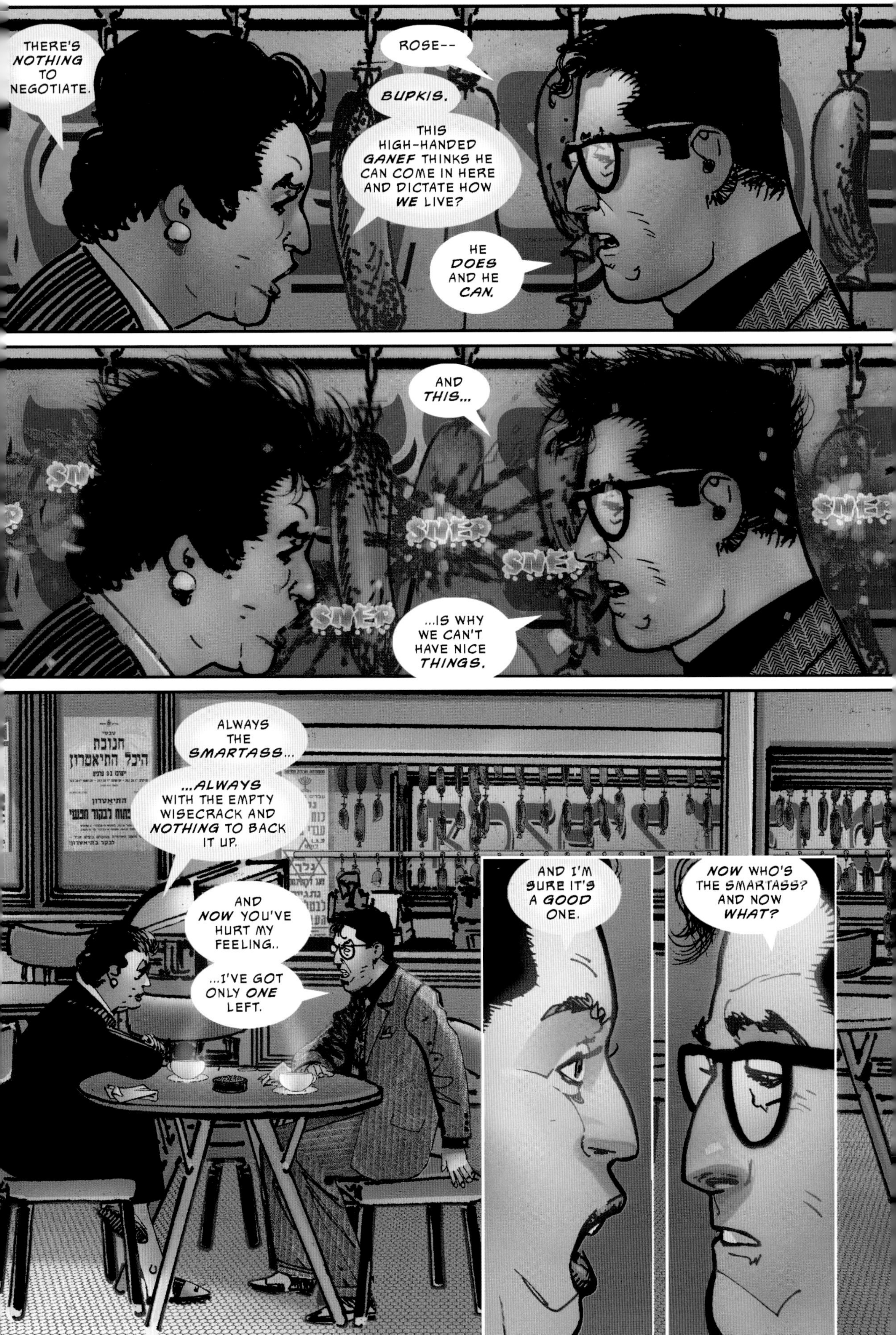
THERE'S NOTHING TO NEGOTIATE.
ROSE--
BUPKIS.
THIS HIGH-HANDED GANEF THINKS HE CAN COME IN HERE AND DICTATE HOW WE LIVE?
HE DOES AND HE CAN.
AND THIS...
SMEP
SMEP
SMEP
SMEP
...IS WHY WE CAN'T HAVE NICE THINGS.
ALWAYS THE SMARTASS...
...ALWAYS WITH THE EMPTY WISECRACK AND NOTHING TO BACK IT UP.
AND NOW YOU'VE HURT MY FEELING..
...I'VE GOT ONLY ONE LEFT.
AND I'M SURE IT'S A GOOD ONE.
NOW WHO'S THE SMARTASS? AND NOW WHAT?

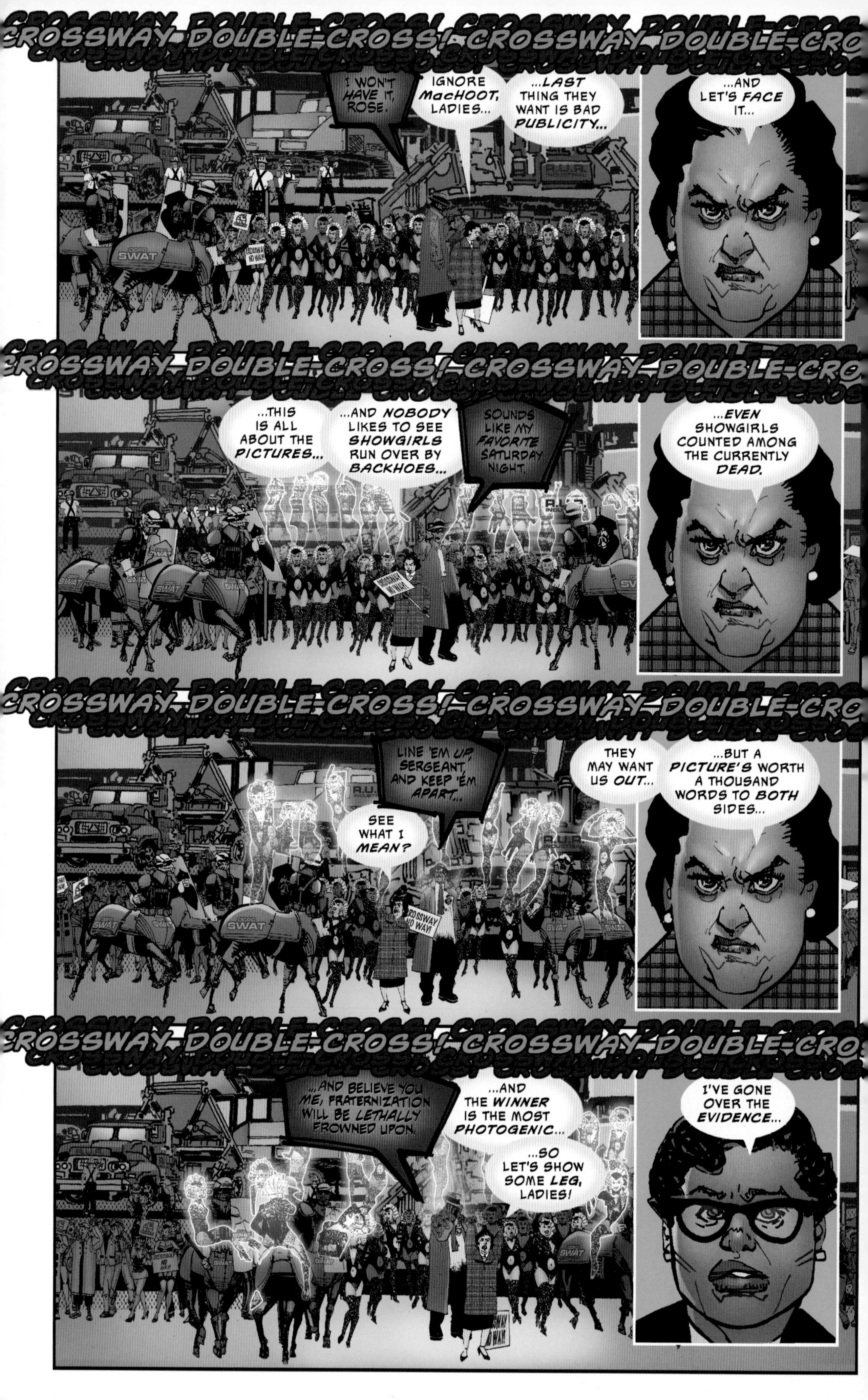
CROSSWAY DOUBLE-CROSS! CROSSWAY DOUBLE-CRO
I WON'T HAVE IT, ROSE.
IGNORE MacHOOT, LADIES...
...LAST THING THEY WANT IS BAD PUBLICITY...
...AND LET'S FACE IT...
SWAT
CROSSWAY NO WAY!
R.U.R. INDUSTRIAL
CROSSWAY DOUBLE-CROSS! CROSSWAY DOUBLE-CRO
...THIS IS ALL ABOUT THE PICTURES...
...AND NOBODY LIKES TO SEE SHOWGIRLS RUN OVER BY BACKHOES...
SOUNDS LIKE MY FAVORITE SATURDAY NIGHT.
...EVEN SHOWGIRLS COUNTED AMONG THE CURRENTLY DEAD.
SWAT
CROSSWAY DOUBLE-CROSS! CROSSWAY DOUBLE-CRO
LINE 'EM UP, SERGEANT, AND KEEP 'EM APART...
SEE WHAT I MEAN?
THEY MAY WANT US OUT...
...BUT A PICTURE'S WORTH A THOUSAND WORDS TO BOTH SIDES...
CROSSWAY NO WAY!
SWAT
CROSSWAY DOUBLE-CROSS! CROSSWAY DOUBLE-CRO
...AND BELIEVE YOU ME, FRATERNIZATION WILL BE LETHALLY FROWNED UPON.
...AND THE WINNER IS THE MOST PHOTOGENIC...
...SO LET'S SHOW SOME LEG, LADIES!
I'VE GONE OVER THE EVIDENCE...
SWAT

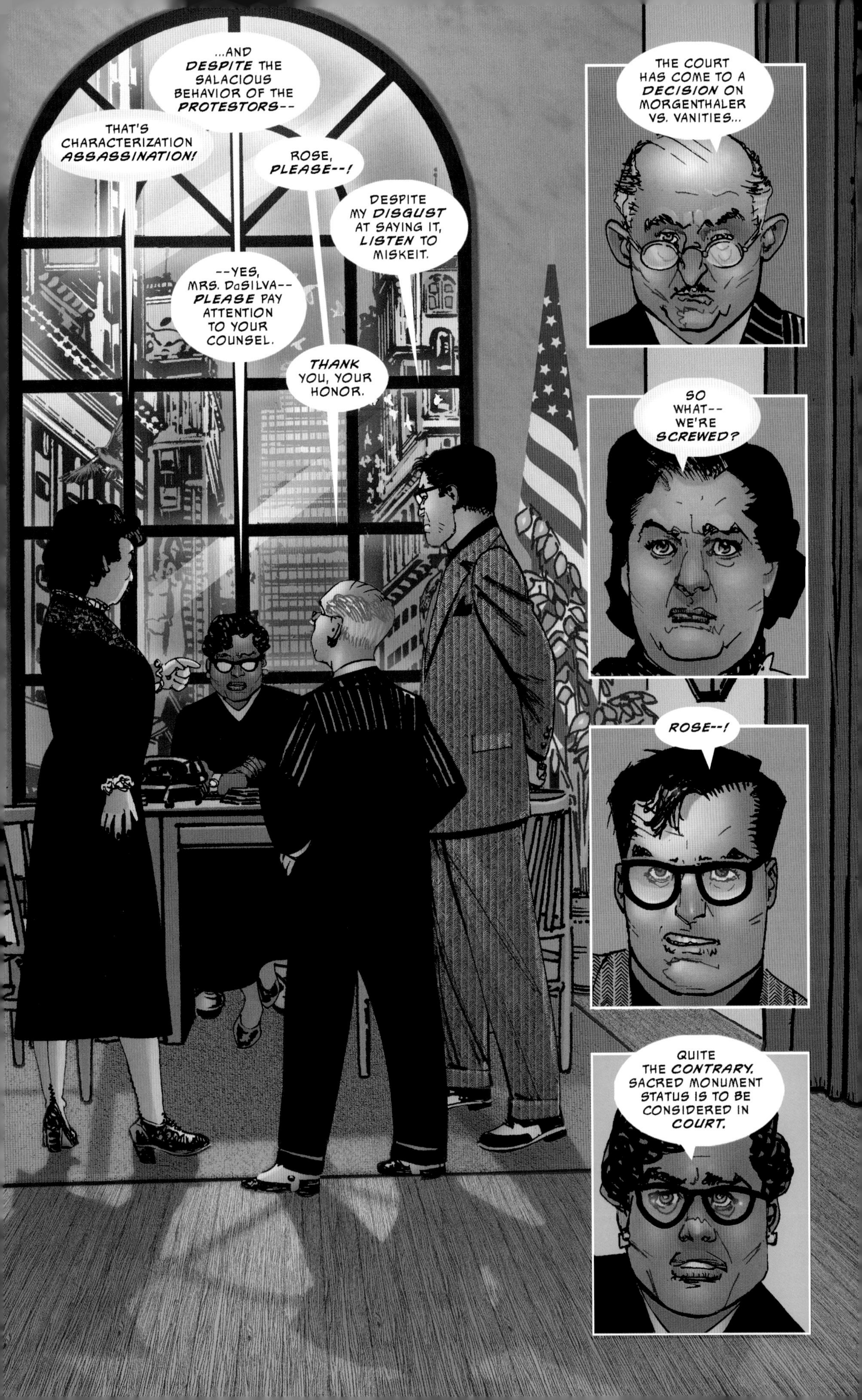
...AND DESPITE THE SALACIOUS BEHAVIOR OF THE PROTESTORS--
THAT'S CHARACTERIZATION ASSASSINATION!
ROSE, PLEASE--!
DESPITE MY DISGUST AT SAYING IT, LISTEN TO MISKEIT.
--YES, MRS. DaSILVA-- PLEASE PAY ATTENTION TO YOUR COUNSEL.
THANK YOU, YOUR HONOR.
THE COURT HAS COME TO A DECISION ON MORGENTHALER VS. VANITIES...
SO WHAT-- WE'RE SCREWED?
ROSE--!
QUITE THE CONTRARY. SACRED MONUMENT STATUS IS TO BE CONSIDERED IN COURT.

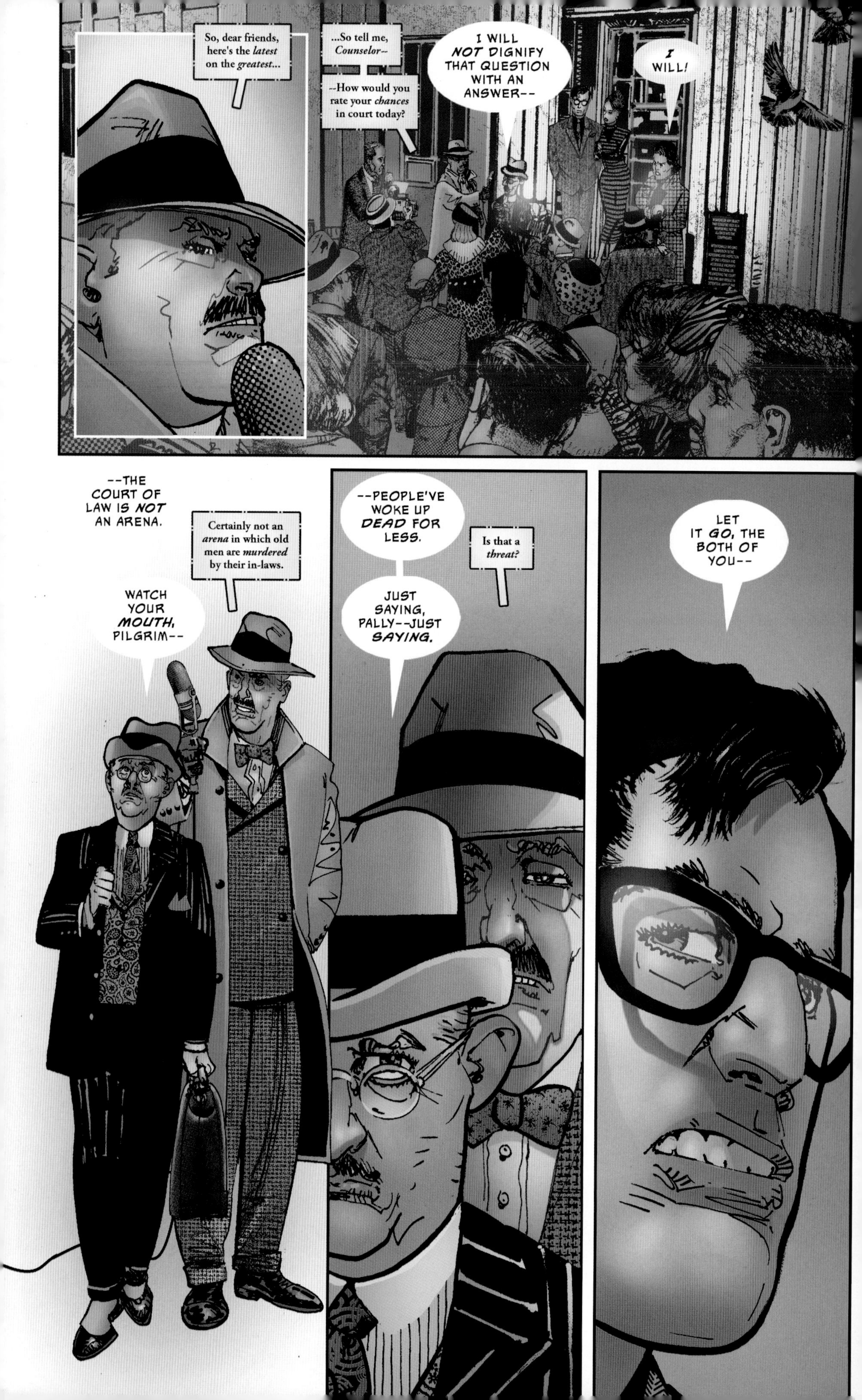
So, dear friends, here's the *latest* on the *greatest*...
...So tell me, *Counselor*--
--How would you rate your *chances* in court today?
I WILL *NOT* DIGNIFY THAT QUESTION WITH AN ANSWER--
I WILL!
--THE COURT OF LAW IS *NOT* AN ARENA.
Certainly not an *arena* in which old men are *murdered* by their in-laws.
WATCH YOUR *MOUTH*, PILGRIM--
--PEOPLE'VE WOKE UP *DEAD* FOR LESS.
Is that a *threat*?
JUST SAYING, PALLY--JUST *SAYING*.
LET IT *GO*, THE BOTH OF YOU--

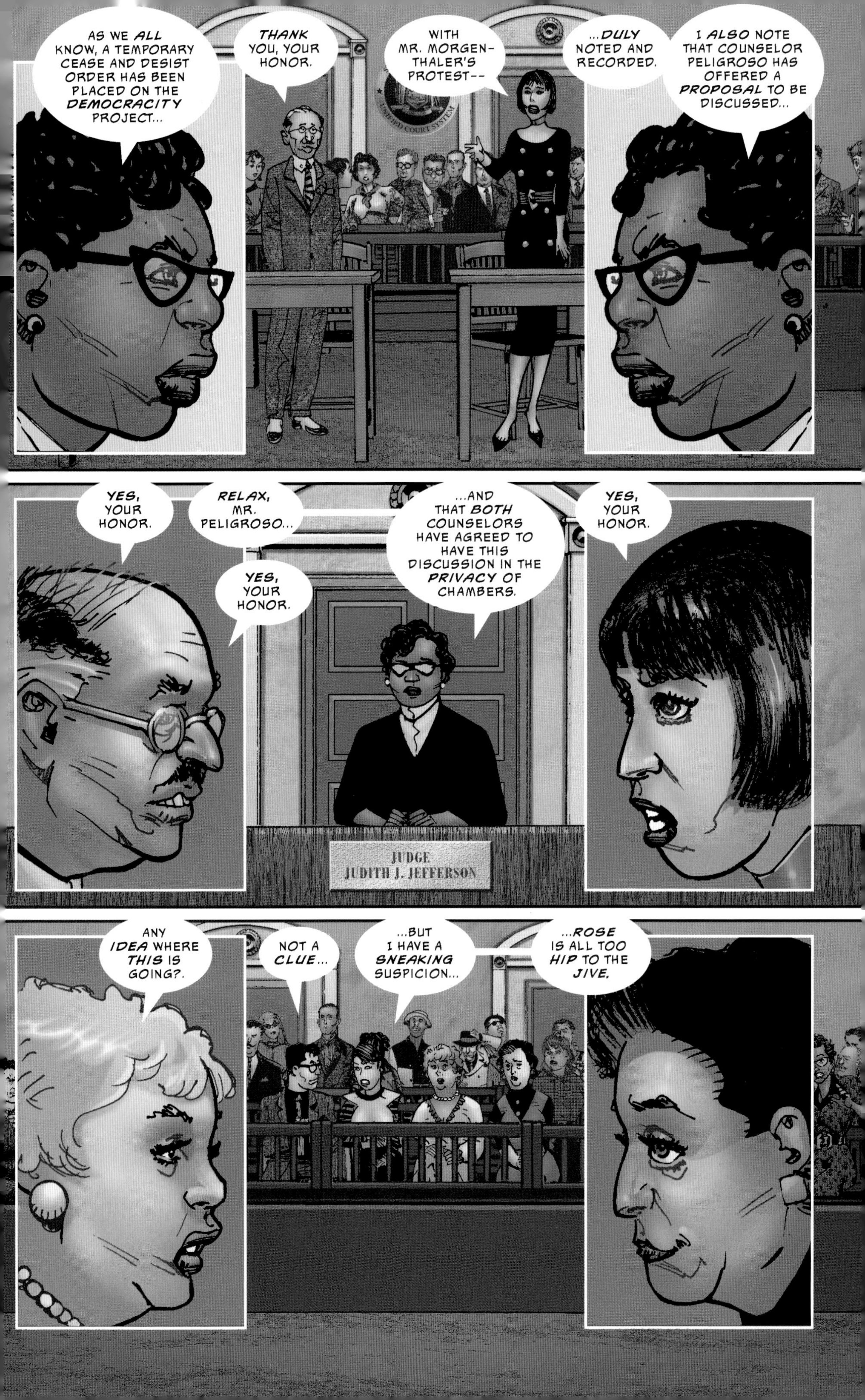
AS WE ALL KNOW, A TEMPORARY CEASE AND DESIST ORDER HAS BEEN PLACED ON THE DEMOCRACITY PROJECT...
THANK YOU, YOUR HONOR.
WITH MR. MORGENTHALER'S PROTEST--
...DULY NOTED AND RECORDED.
I ALSO NOTE THAT COUNSELOR PELIGROSO HAS OFFERED A PROPOSAL TO BE DISCUSSED...
YES, YOUR HONOR.
RELAX, MR. PELIGROSO...
YES, YOUR HONOR.
...AND THAT BOTH COUNSELORS HAVE AGREED TO HAVE THIS DISCUSSION IN THE PRIVACY OF CHAMBERS.
YES, YOUR HONOR.
JUDGE JUDITH J. JEFFERSON
ANY IDEA WHERE THIS IS GOING?.
NOT A CLUE...
...BUT I HAVE A SNEAKING SUSPICION...
...ROSE IS ALL TOO HIP TO THE JIVE.

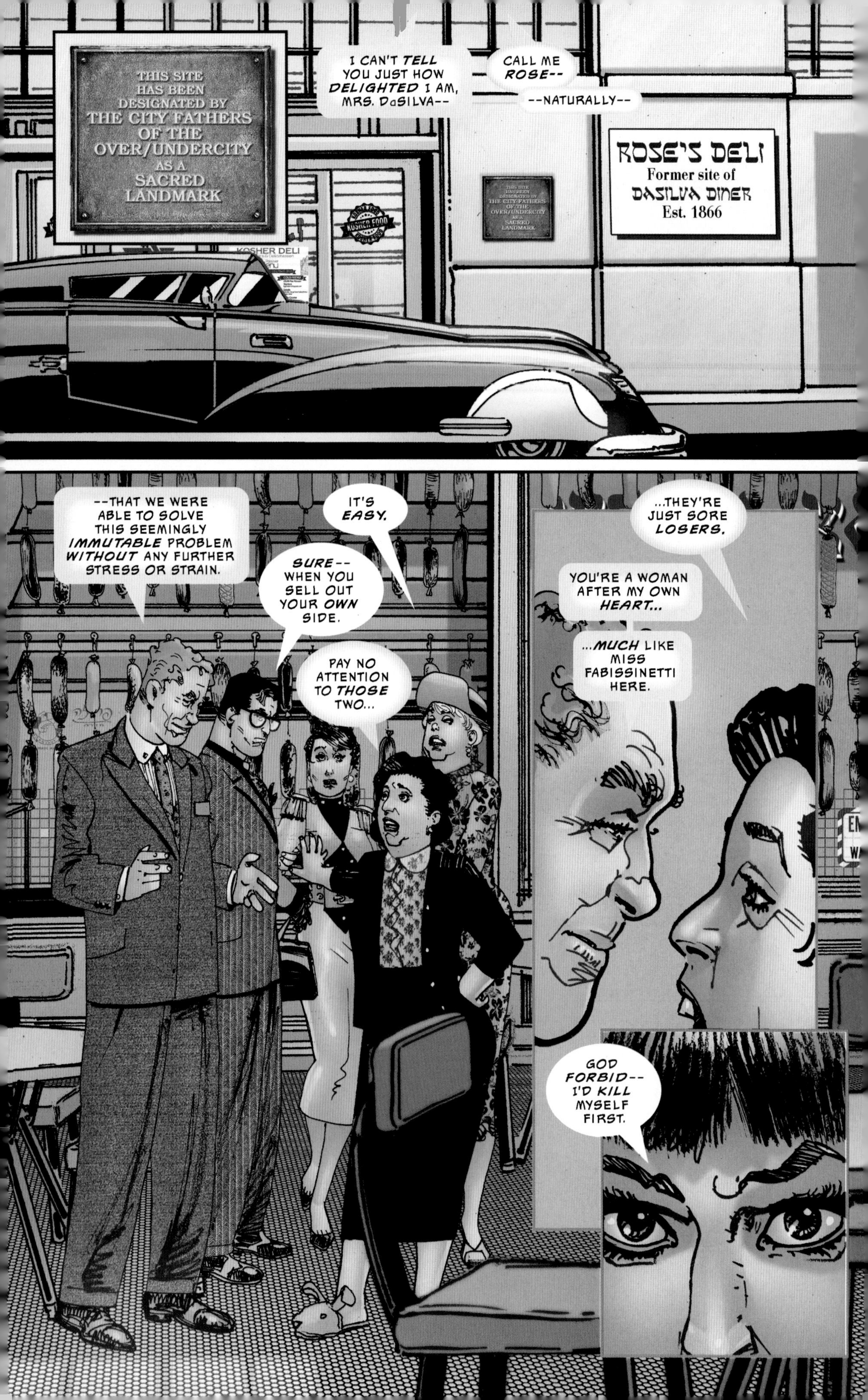
THIS SITE HAS BEEN DESIGNATED BY THE CITY FATHERS OF THE OVER/UNDERCITY AS A SACRED LANDMARK
I CAN'T TELL YOU JUST HOW DELIGHTED I AM, MRS. DaSILVA--
CALL ME ROSE--
--NATURALLY--
ROSE'S DELI
Former site of
DASILVA DINER
Est. 1866
KOSHER FOOD
KOSHER DELI
--THAT WE WERE ABLE TO SOLVE THIS SEEMINGLY IMMUTABLE PROBLEM WITHOUT ANY FURTHER STRESS OR STRAIN.
IT'S EASY.
SURE-- WHEN YOU SELL OUT YOUR OWN SIDE.
PAY NO ATTENTION TO THOSE TWO...
...THEY'RE JUST SORE LOSERS.
YOU'RE A WOMAN AFTER MY OWN HEART...
...MUCH LIKE MISS FABISSINETTI HERE.
GOD FORBID-- I'D KILL MYSELF FIRST.

"--What a *day*, ladies and gentlemen..."
"...*What* a day!"
"To the *delight* of millions--*millions*, I say...!"
DON'T *JUDGE* ME...
"...the Main Stem is no *longer* just a little part of little old Time^2..."
NEVER.
"...but it's now a part of the *unified* whole..."
WE'LL LEAVE *THAT* TO FABIO WHEN HE COMES *BACK*.
"...the whole that is *DemocraCity!*"
NOT GONNA HAPPEN.

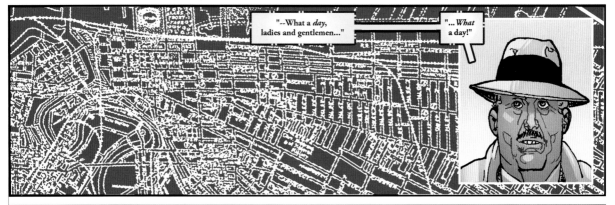

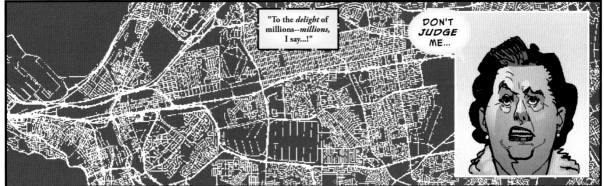

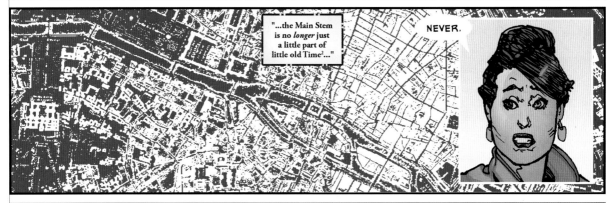

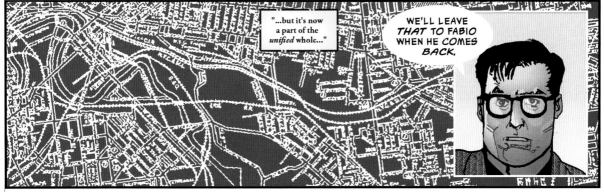

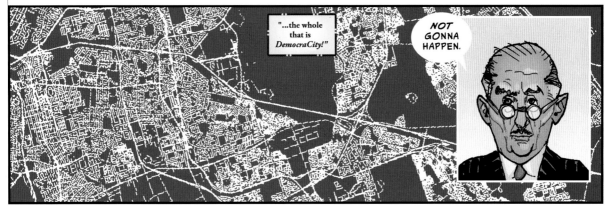

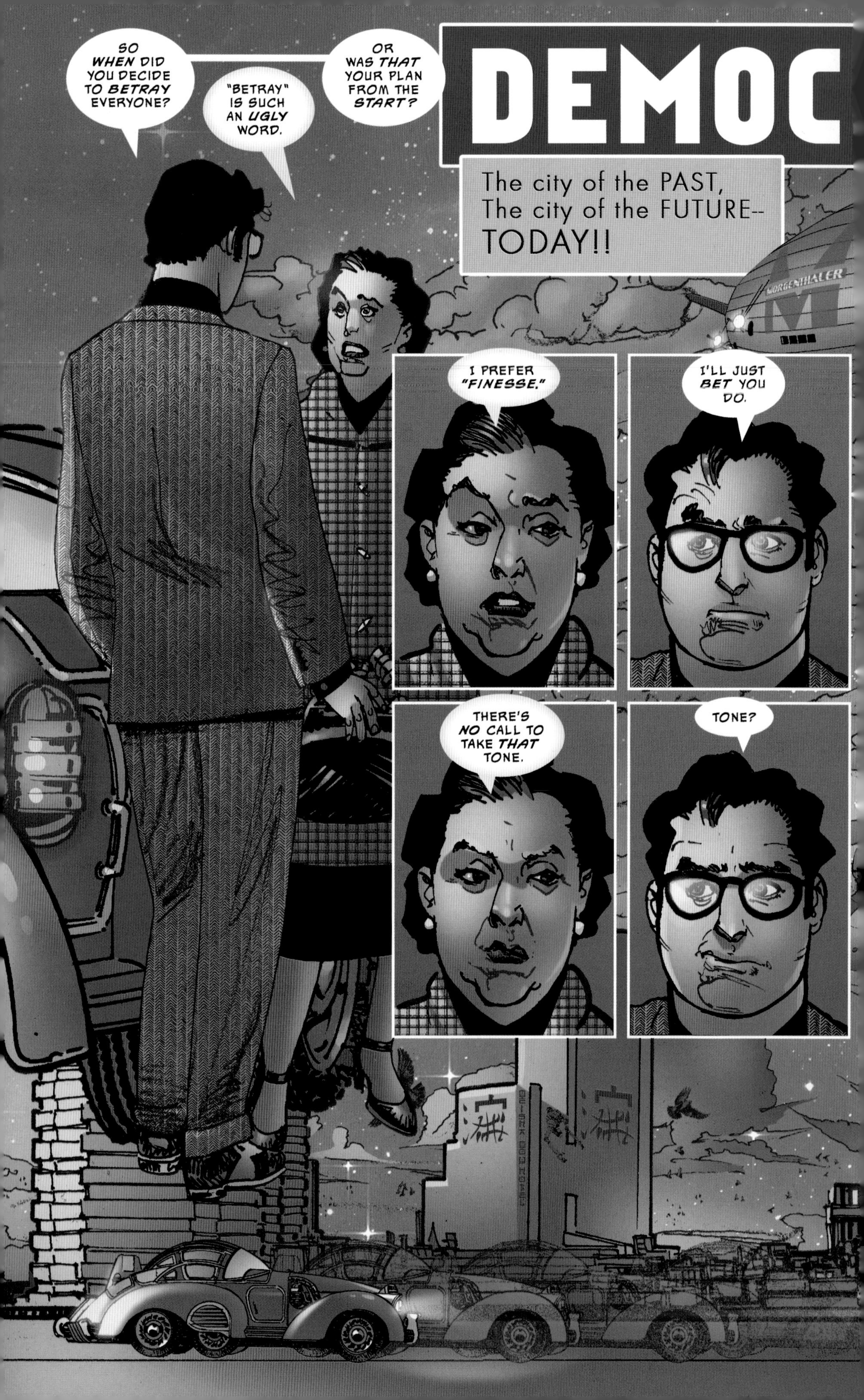
DEMOC
The city of the PAST,
The city of the FUTURE--
TODAY!!
SO WHEN DID YOU DECIDE TO BETRAY EVERYONE?
"BETRAY" IS SUCH AN UGLY WORD.
OR WAS THAT YOUR PLAN FROM THE START?
I PREFER "FINESSE."
I'LL JUST BET YOU DO.
THERE'S NO CALL TO TAKE THAT TONE.
TONE?
MORGENTHALER

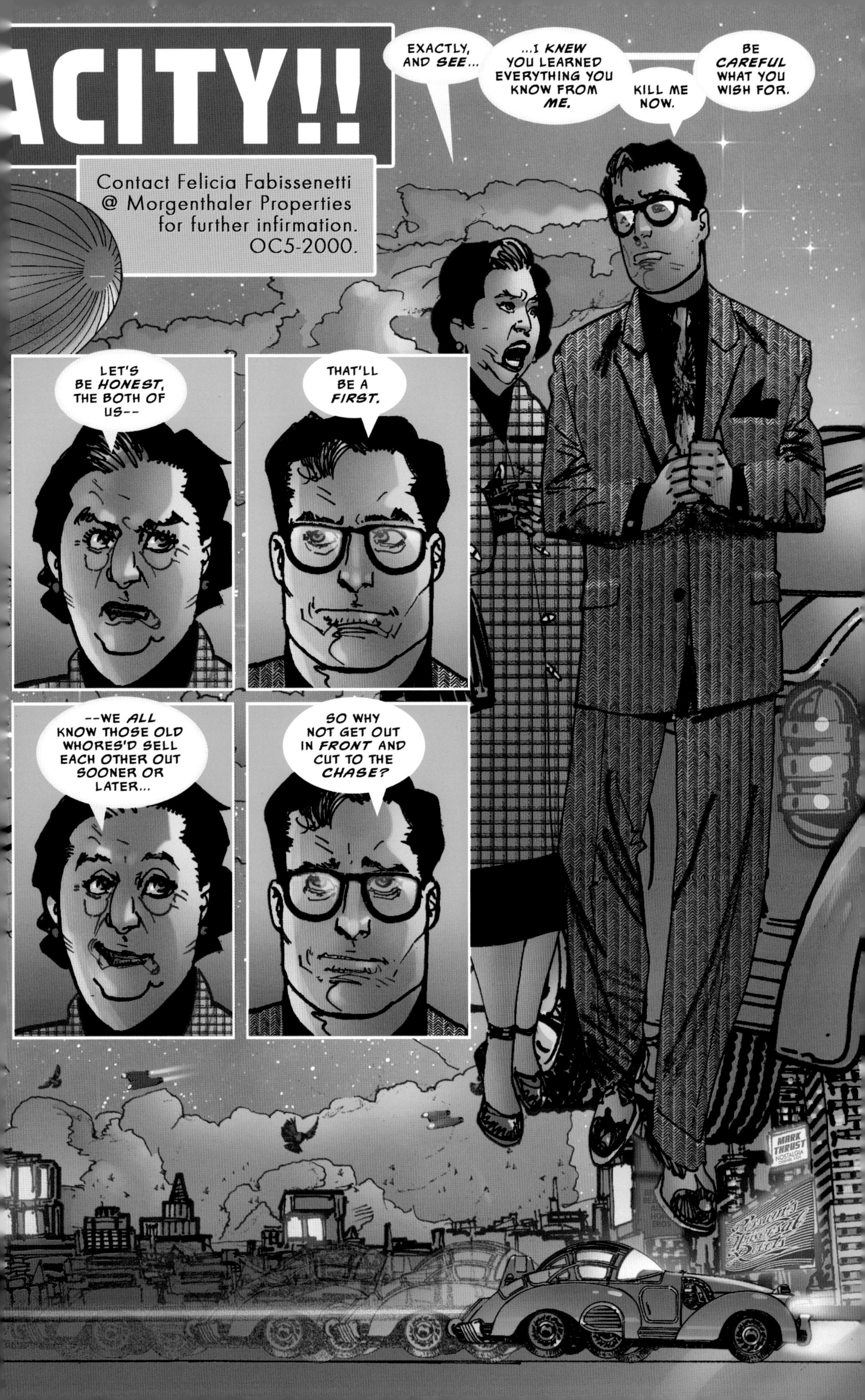

ACITY!!
Contact Felicia Fabissenetti @ Morgenthaler Properties for further infirmation. OC5-2000.
EXACTLY, AND SEE...
...I KNEW YOU LEARNED EVERYTHING YOU KNOW FROM ME.
KILL ME NOW.
BE CAREFUL WHAT YOU WISH FOR.
LET'S BE HONEST, THE BOTH OF US--
THAT'LL BE A FIRST.
--WE ALL KNOW THOSE OLD WHORES'D SELL EACH OTHER OUT SOONER OR LATER...
SO WHY NOT GET OUT IN FRONT AND CUT TO THE CHASE?
MARK THRUST
NOSTALGIA

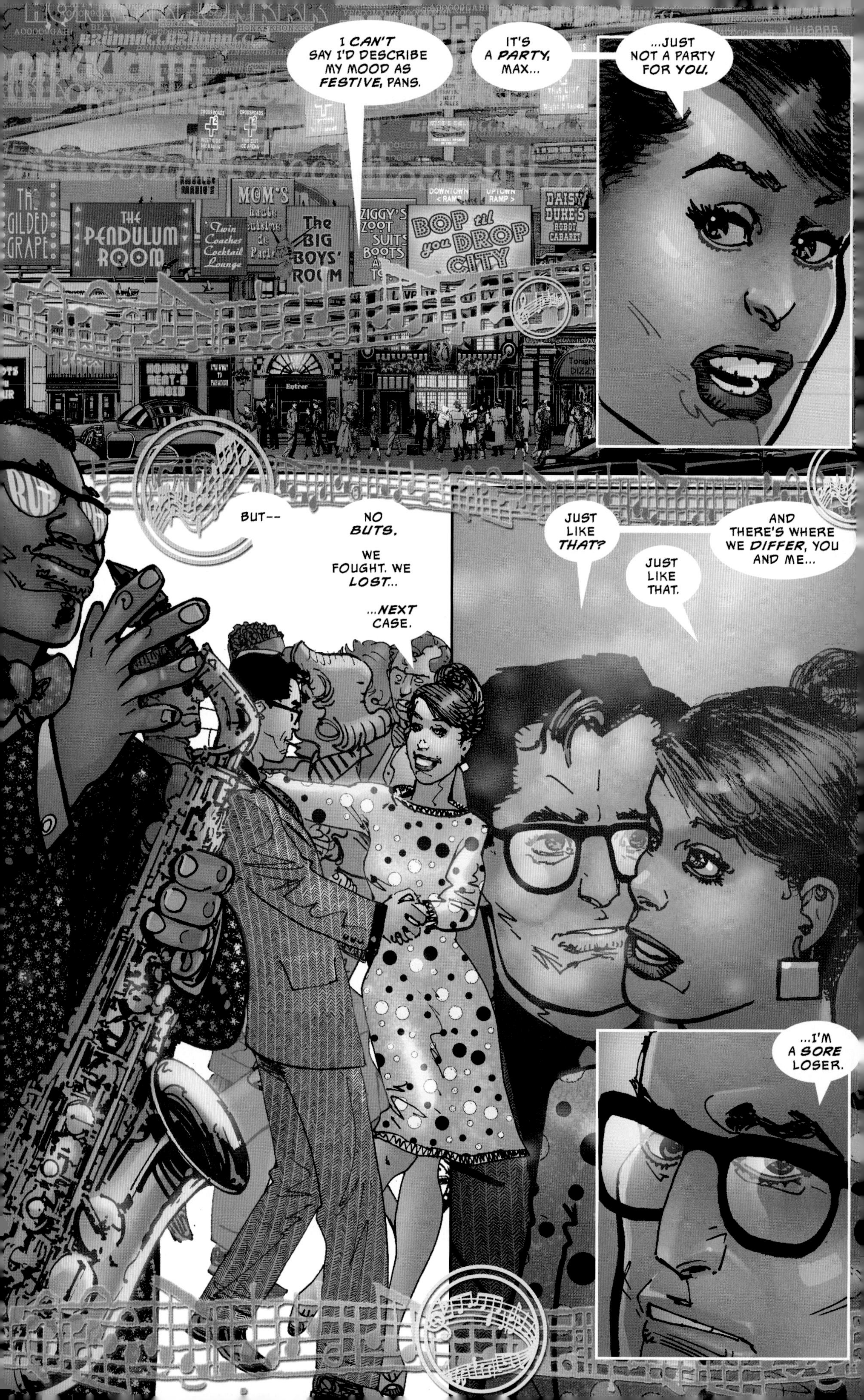
THE GILDED GRAPE
THE PENDULUM ROOM
MOM'S haute cuisine de Paris
Twin Coaches Cocktail Lounge
The BIG BOYS' ROOM
ZIGGY'S ZOOT SUITS
BOP til you DROP CITY
DOWNTOWN < RAMP
UPTOWN RAMP >
DAISY DUKE'S ROBOT CABARET
HOURLY RENT-A DROID
I CAN'T SAY I'D DESCRIBE MY MOOD AS FESTIVE, PANS.
IT'S A PARTY, MAX...
...JUST NOT A PARTY FOR YOU.
BUT--
NO BUTS.
WE FOUGHT. WE LOST...
...NEXT CASE.
JUST LIKE THAT?
JUST LIKE THAT.
AND THERE'S WHERE WE DIFFER, YOU AND ME...
...I'M A SORE LOSER.

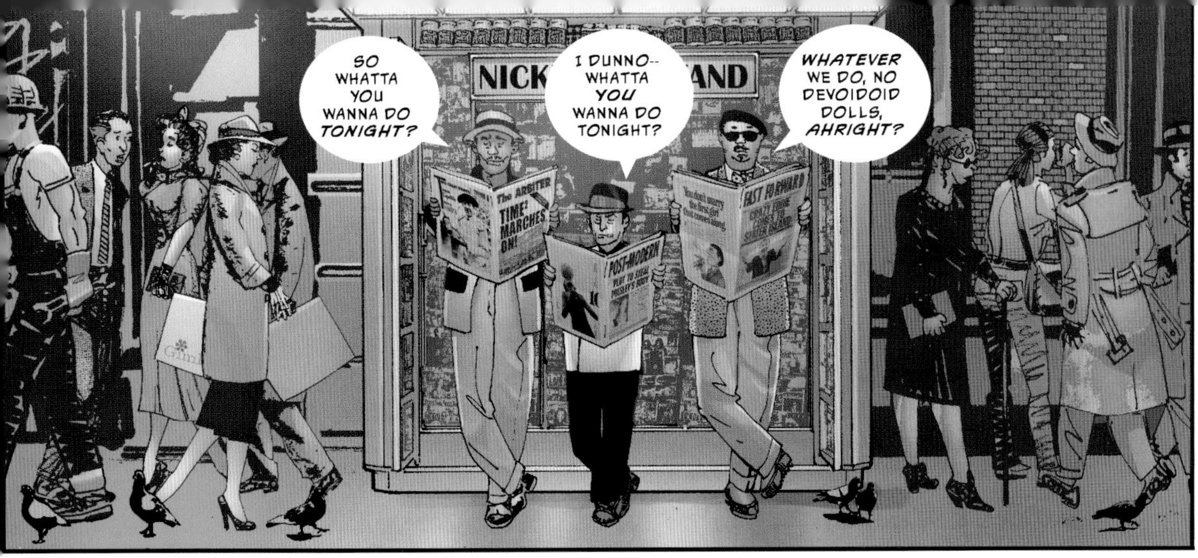
SO WHATTA YOU WANNA DO TONIGHT?
I DUNNO-- WHATTA YOU WANNA DO TONIGHT?
WHATEVER WE DO, NO DEVOIDOID DOLLS, AHRIGHT?
NICK ... AND
The ARBITER TIME MARCHES ON!
POST-MODERN
FAST FORWARD

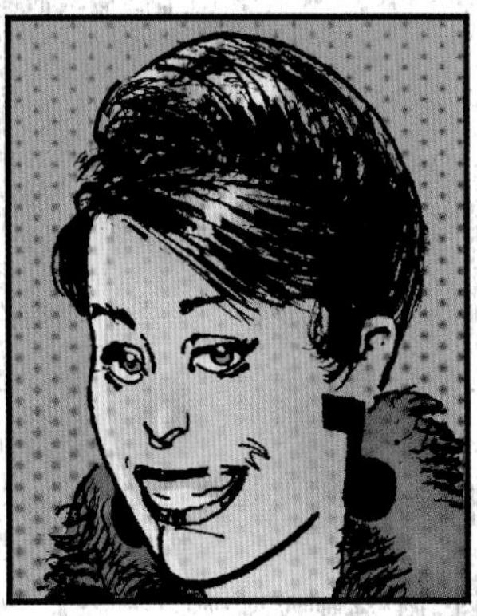

PANSY'S PASSIONS

by PANSY MATTHIAS

No surprise to anyone there's a distinct stink of disappointment on the Main Stem these days and nights, *mon petit choux*-...but as I told the main squeeze only last night, we'll get by as long as I have you.

The Square has always been a magnet for slummers and high hats from the OverCity...it's high--or is it low?--time they had a chance to see us in our natural habitat, engaging in our unnatural habits...

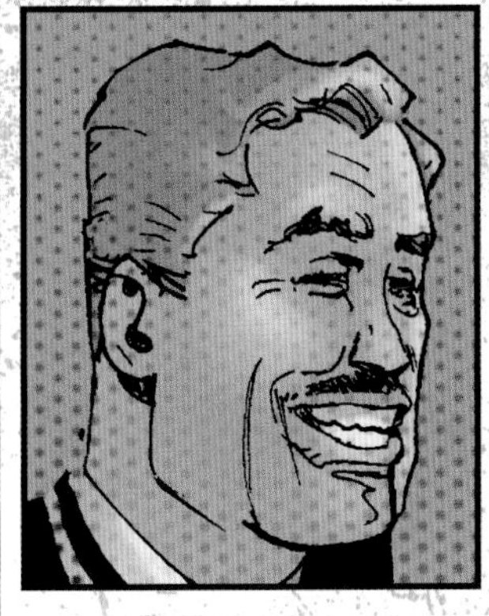

THE LAMP IS LIT

by **DIOGENES PILGRIM**

Looking for an honest man...had a wonderful dinner with Square newcomer Yeshua Morgenthaler and returning gal-pal Felicia Fabissinetti at Standup Katz's new imbibery last night...

...And believe you me, Lamplighters, you could eat the delight at the table with a spoon. Well-wishers couldn't gush enough about the clean-as-the-proverbial whistle, brand-spanking-new look that's a gift to the Square and everyone on the Main Stem.

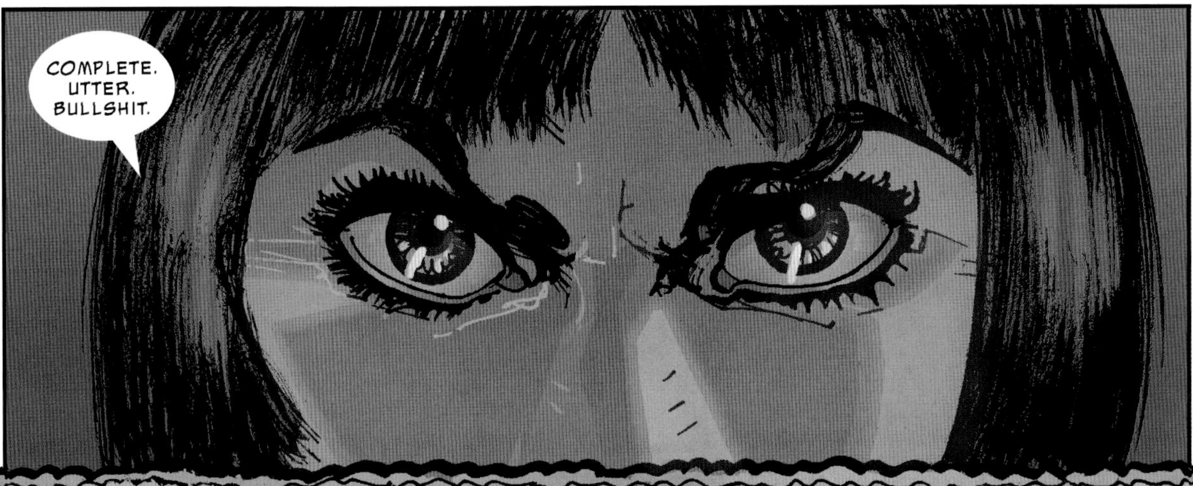
COMPLETE. UTTER. BULLSHIT.

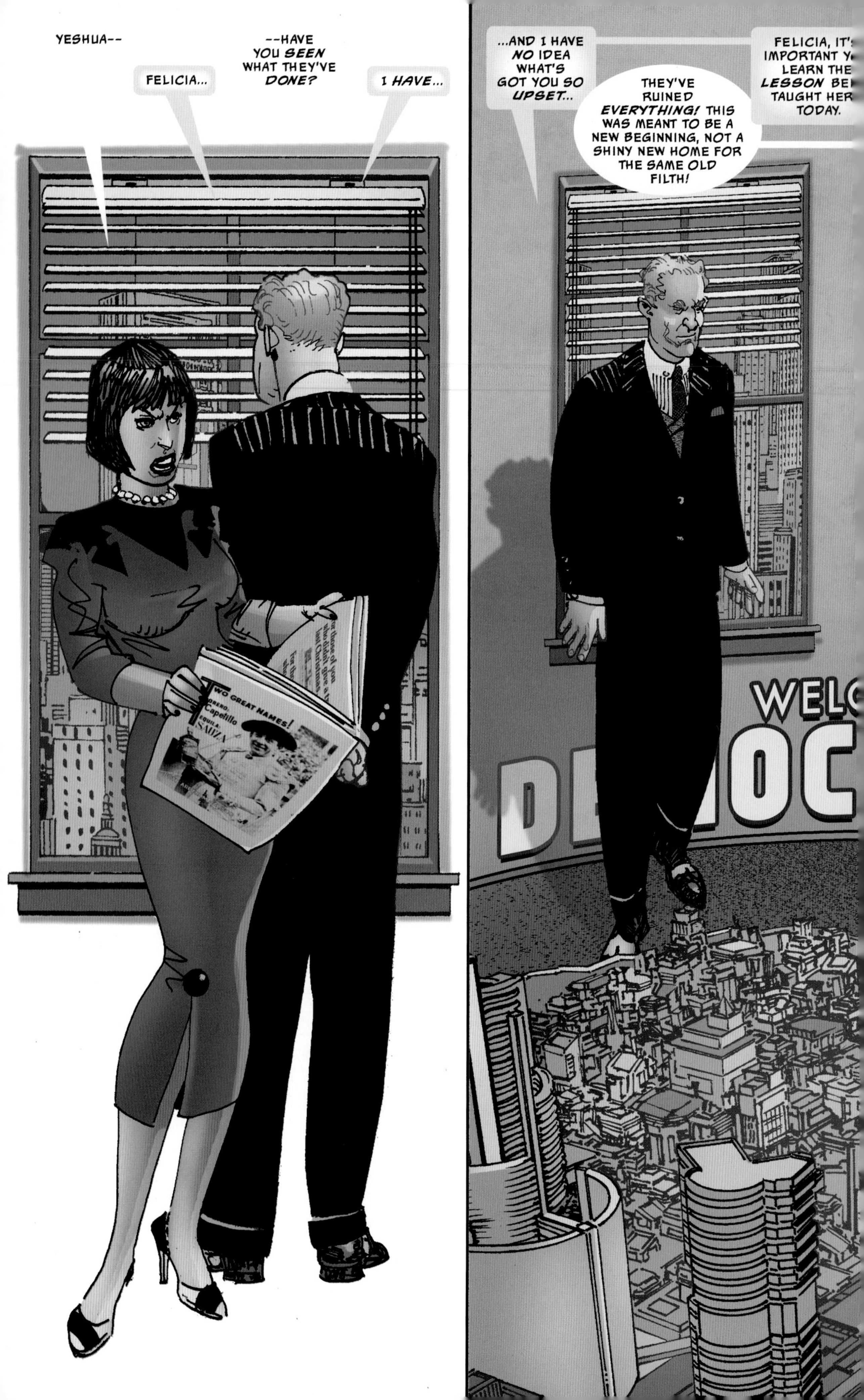
YESHUA--
FELICIA...
--HAVE YOU SEEN WHAT THEY'VE DONE?
I HAVE...
TWO GREAT NAMES!
...AND I HAVE NO IDEA WHAT'S GOT YOU SO UPSET...
THEY'VE RUINED EVERYTHING! THIS WAS MEANT TO BE A NEW BEGINNING, NOT A SHINY NEW HOME FOR THE SAME OLD FILTH!
TODAY.

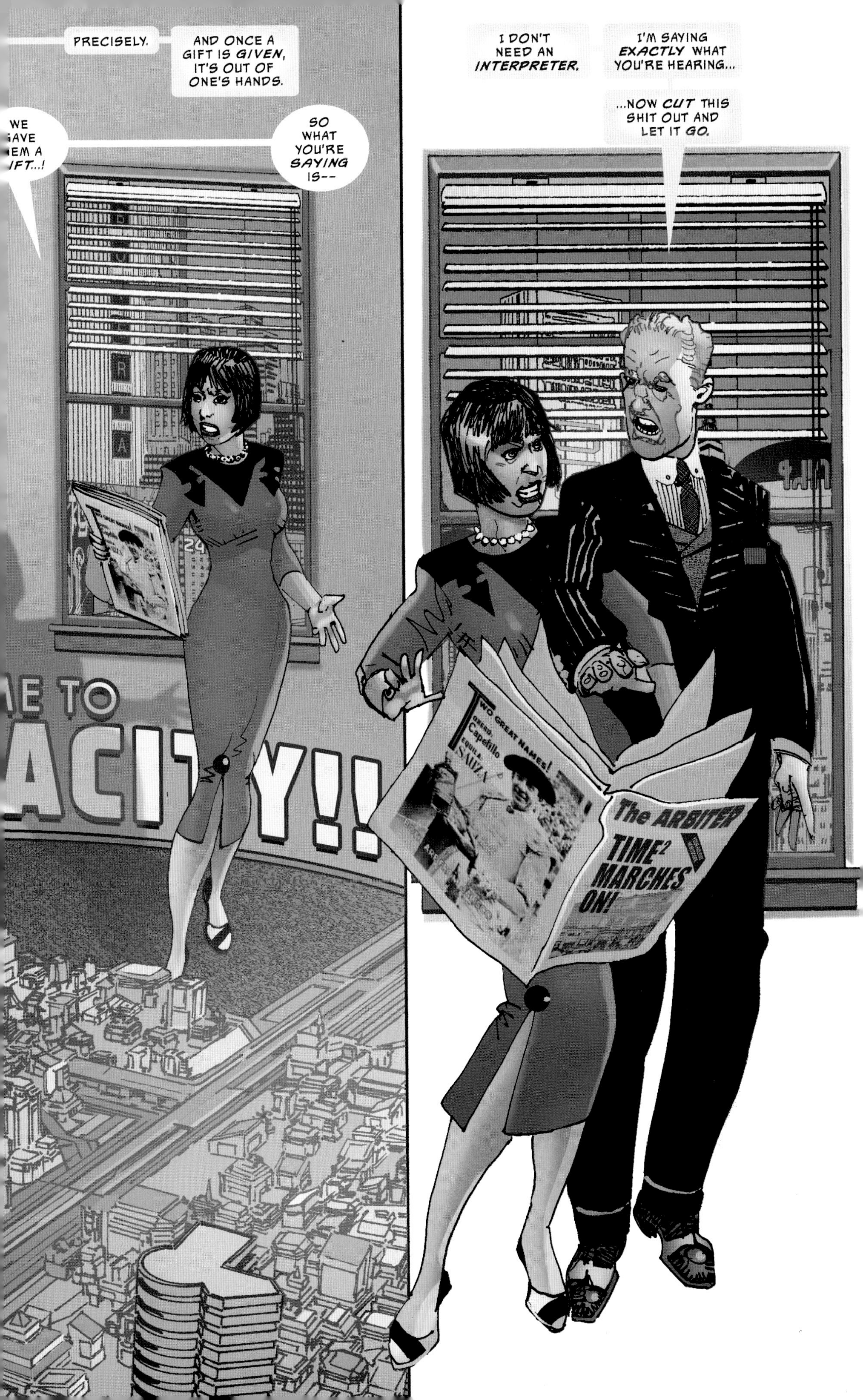
PRECISELY.
AND ONCE A GIFT IS *GIVEN*, IT'S OUT OF ONE'S HANDS.
WE GAVE EM A IFT...!
SO WHAT YOU'RE *SAYING* IS--
AE TO
ACITY!!
I DON'T NEED AN *INTERPRETER*.
I'M SAYING *EXACTLY* WHAT YOU'RE HEARING...
...NOW *CUT* THIS SHIT OUT AND LET IT *GO*.
TWO GREAT NAMES!
Capefillo
SAUZA
The ARBITER
TIME² MARCHES ON!

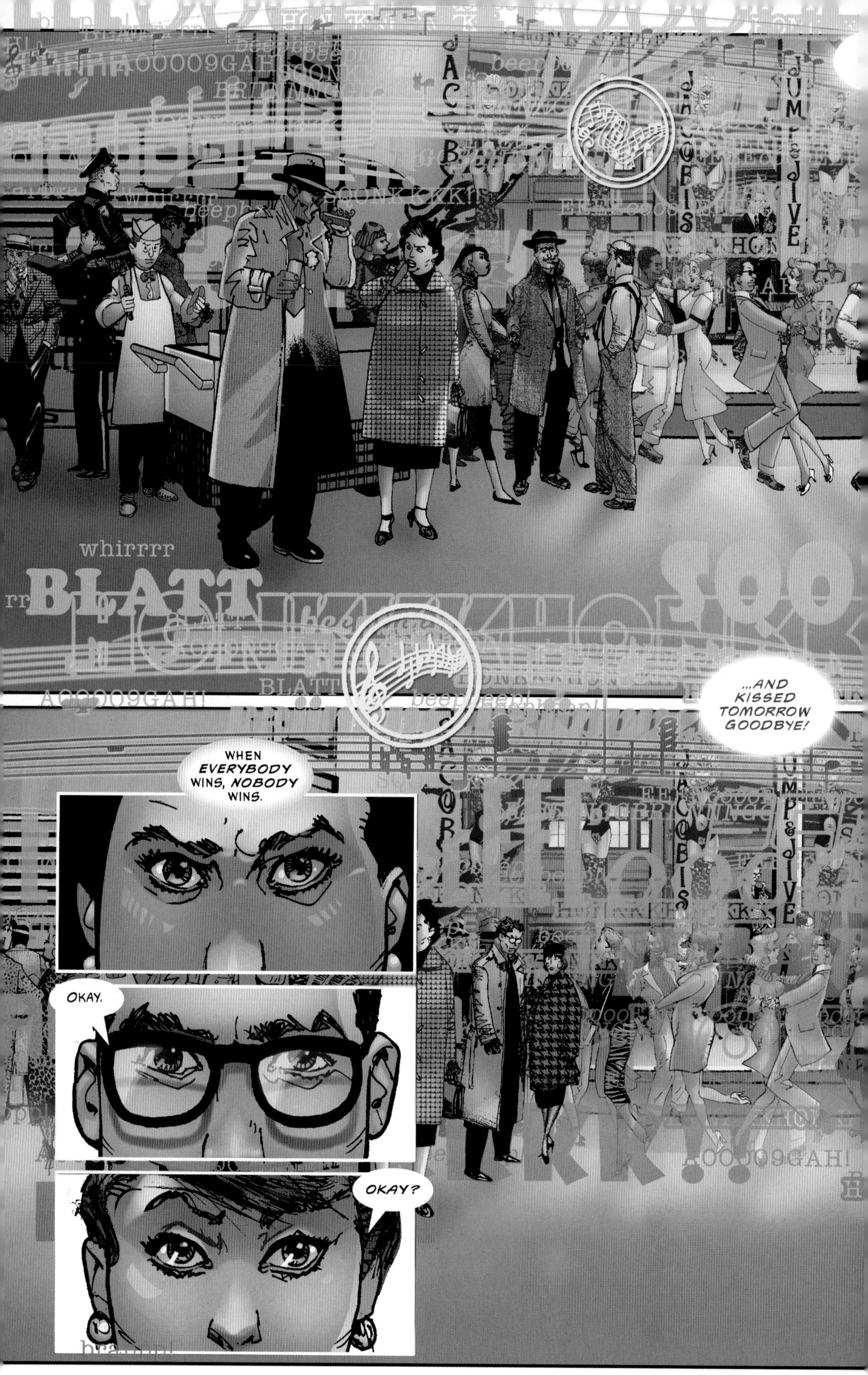
whirrrr
BLATT
WHEN EVERYBODY WINS, NOBODY WINS.
...AND KISSED TOMORROW GOODBYE!
OKAY.
OKAY?

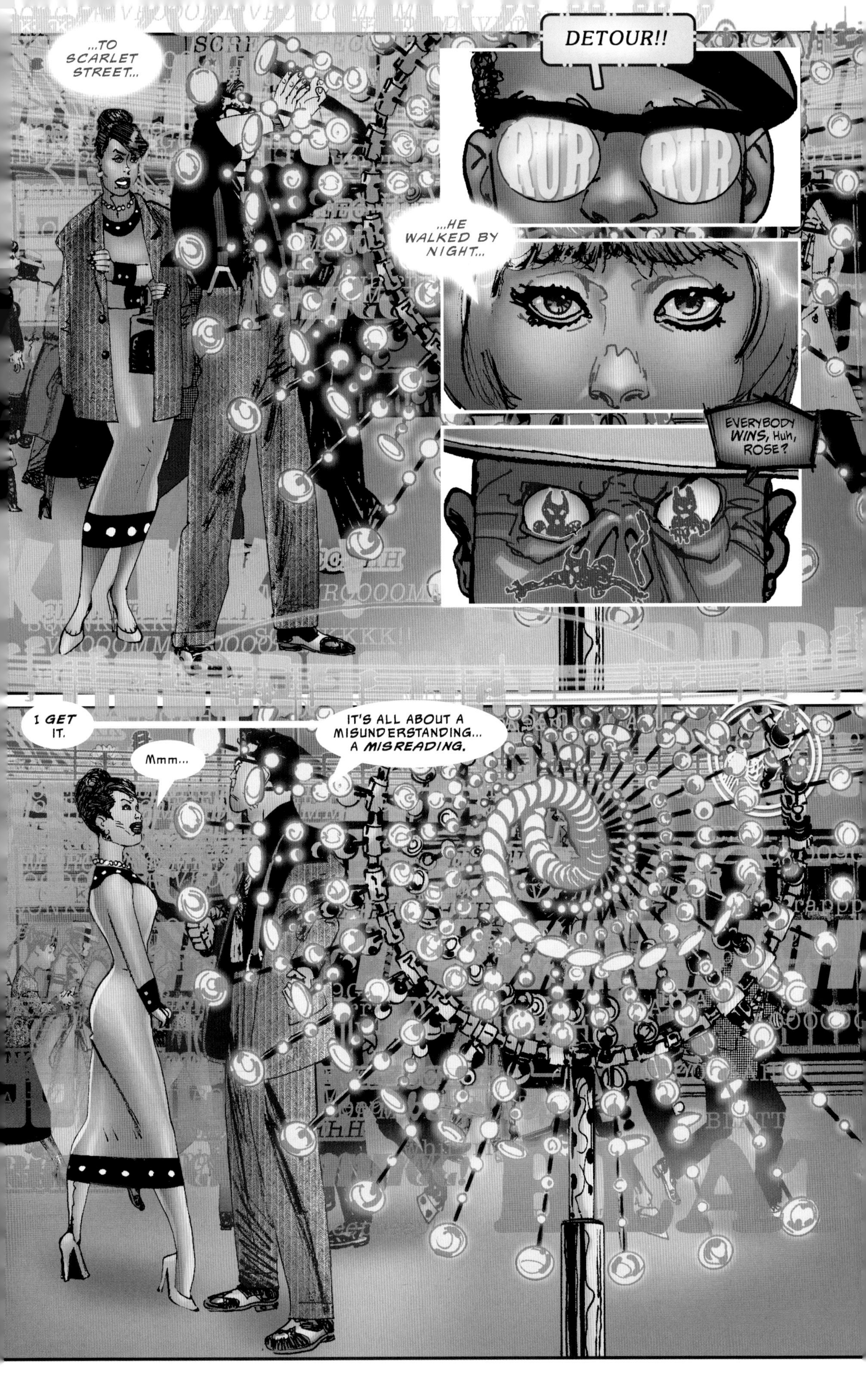
...TO SCARLET STREET...
DETOUR!!
...HE WALKED BY NIGHT...
EVERYBODY WINS, Huh, ROSE?
I GET IT.
Mmm...
IT'S ALL ABOUT A MISUNDERSTANDING... A MISREADING.

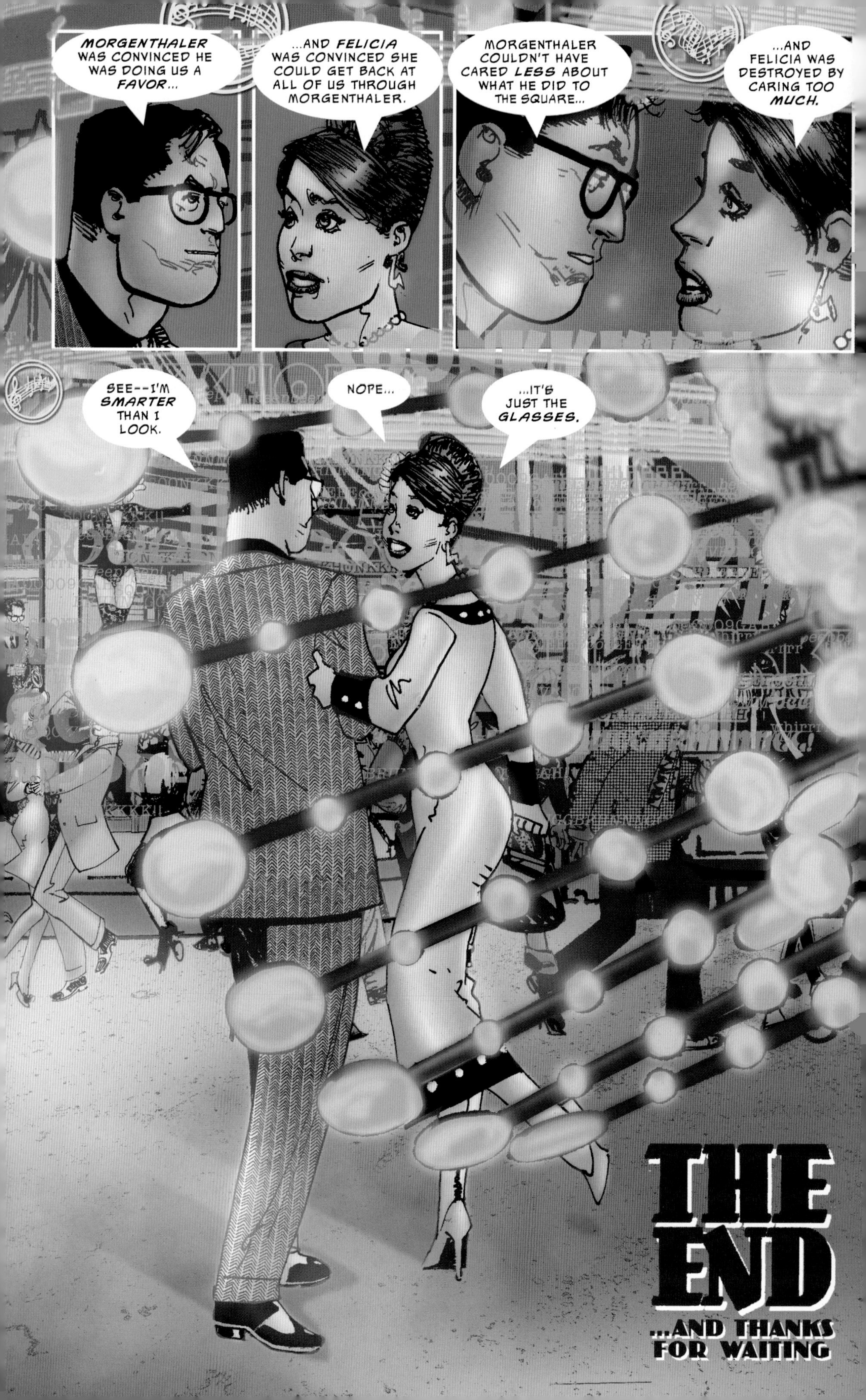
MORGENTHALER WAS CONVINCED HE WAS DOING US A FAVOR...
...AND FELICIA WAS CONVINCED SHE COULD GET BACK AT ALL OF US THROUGH MORGENTHALER.
MORGENTHALER COULDN'T HAVE CARED LESS ABOUT WHAT HE DID TO THE SQUARE...
...AND FELICIA WAS DESTROYED BY CARING TOO MUCH.
SEE--I'M SMARTER THAN I LOOK.
NOPE...
...IT'S JUST THE GLASSES.
THE END
...AND THANKS FOR WAITING

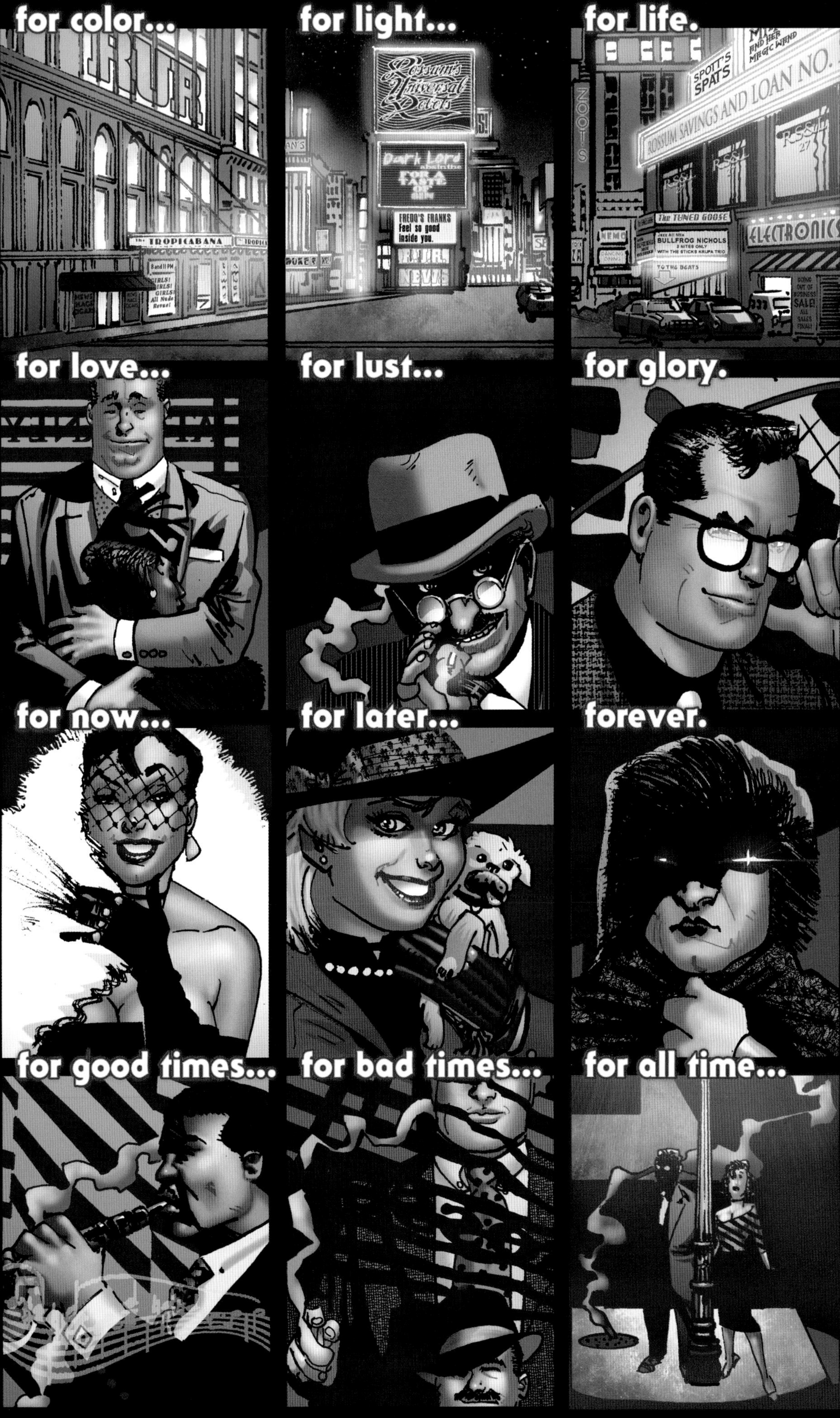
for color...
RUR
TROPICABANA
GIRLS! GIRLS! GIRLS! All Nude Revue!
for light...
Rossum's Universal Robots
Dark Lord absinthe
FREDO'S FRANKS Feel so good inside you.
for life.
SPOTT'S SPATS
ROSSUM SAVINGS AND LOAN NO.
The TUNED GOOSE
BULLFROG NICHOLS
3 NITES ONLY
WITH THE STICKS KRUPA TRIO
ELECTRONICS
for love...
for lust...
for glory.
for now...
for later...
forever.
for good times...
for bad times...
for all time...

...for the thrill of it all...

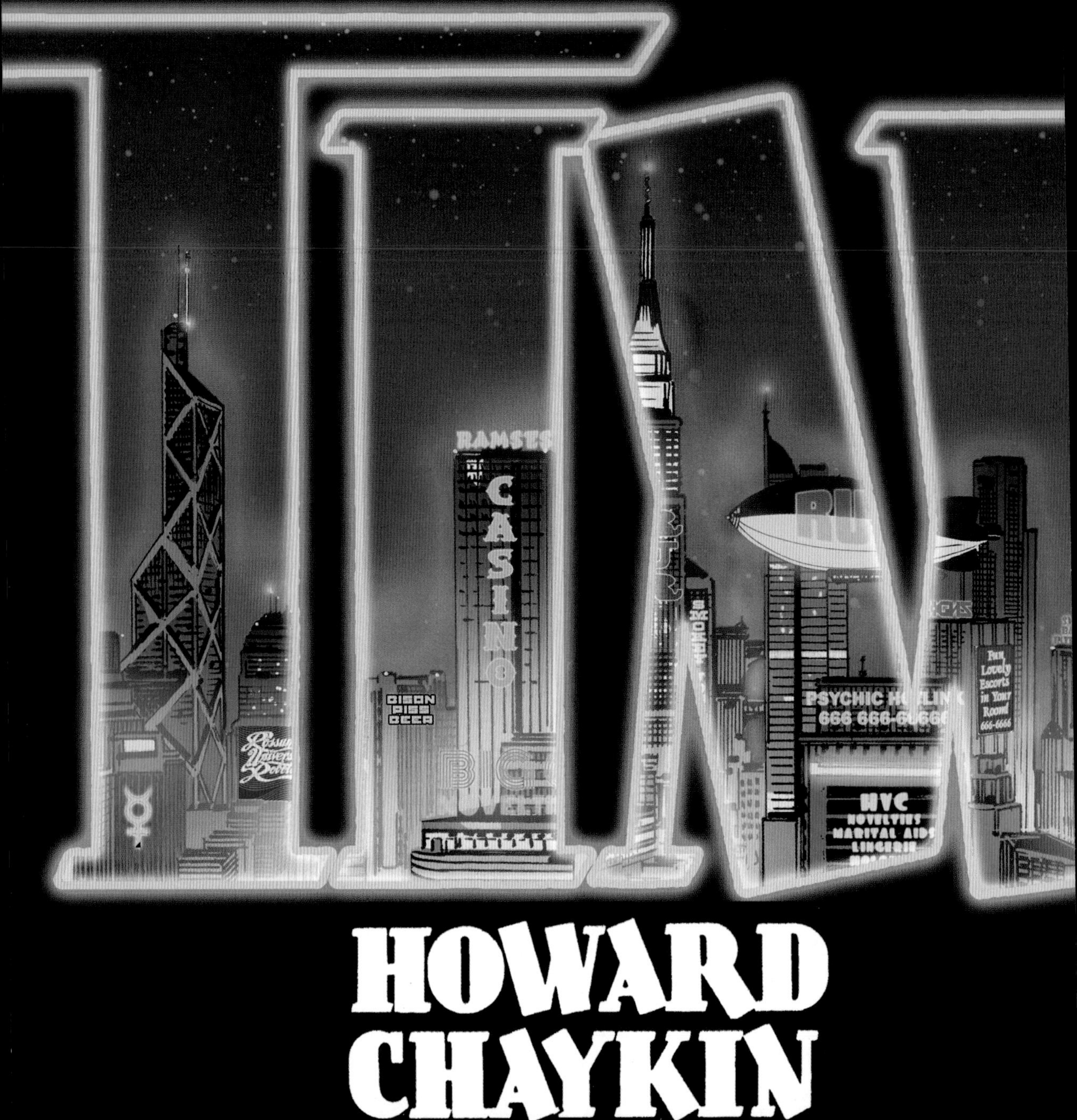
RAMSES
CASINO
NVC
MARITAL AIDS
Lovely
Escorts
in Your
Room!

HOWARD CHAYKIN

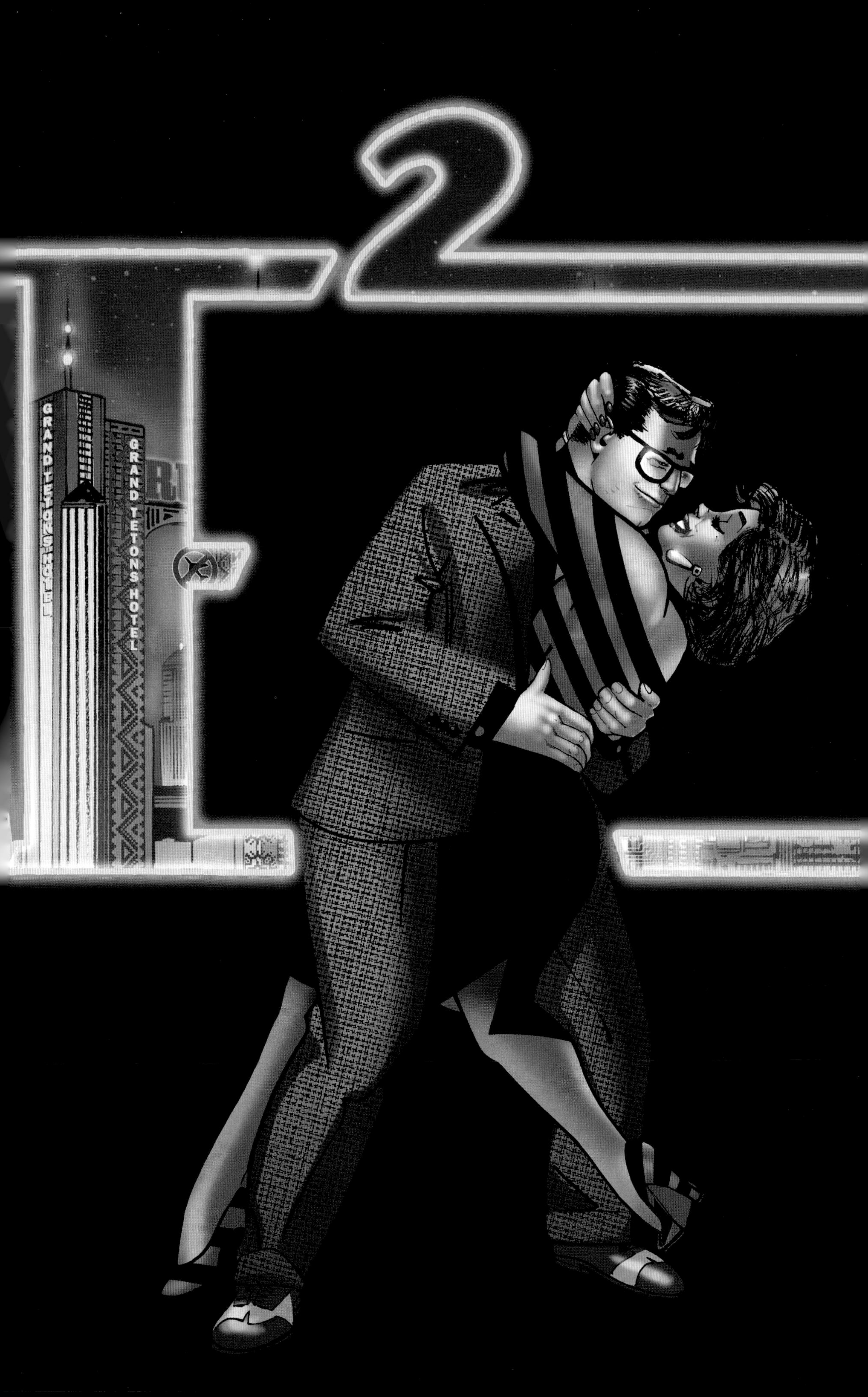
GRAND TETONS HOTEL
GRAND TETONS HOTEL

TIME²

EXTRAS

OH, *NOW* YOU GET IT?

TIME²
FIRST GRAPHIC NOVEL
The Epiphany
HOWARD CHAYKIN

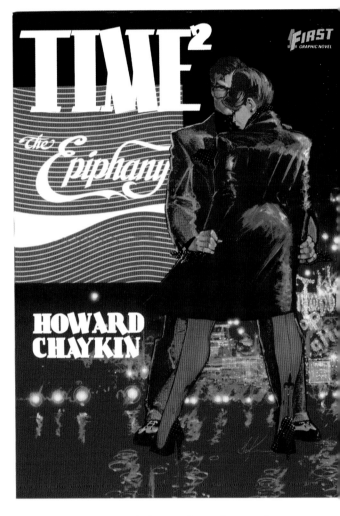

For many of us who were there, the 1960s were personified by exuberant and unjustified overconfidence, the 1970s were the 1960s with better drugs, nihilism, and more active commodification of nonconformism, and the 1980s were ten years of cynicism and hubris.

And just in case you hear an accusatory tone of scold here, let's all just calm down. I was there, and was guilty of most if not all of these cultural misdemeanors...

...and the cultural malfeasance we're here to talk about is hubris, and its bastard offspring, ***Time²***.

I had made critical gold with ***American Flagg!***, and took this as a sign that I could write my own ticket.

Naturally, that's where my trouble began.

When the pair of ***Time²*** graphic novels came out in 1986 and 1987, readers regarded them as, to be kind, enigmatic.

Also confounding, what the fuck is this?, confusing, fucking awful, and how could you do this to me?

Not to mention a lot of, "Huh?"

Needless to say, the book didn't find an audience, since ***American Flagg!*** was far more a *succès d'estime* than the commercial blockbusters flanking it. Add to this the reasonable expectation, based on how comics had been since their birth, that ***Time²*** would be ***American Flagg!*** in a different suit, and even those who'd been fans of ***American Flagg!*** hired buses to avoid it in droves.

That said, within a decade, and in all the years since, I cannot tell you how many people have come up to me and declared, "NOW I get it."

I look forward to two things in 2050: a cake with 100 candles, and hearing from all of you about ***Hallowed Ground⁰*** finally clicking for you after years, maybe even decades, of head-scratching consternation.

That said, and while we wait for my

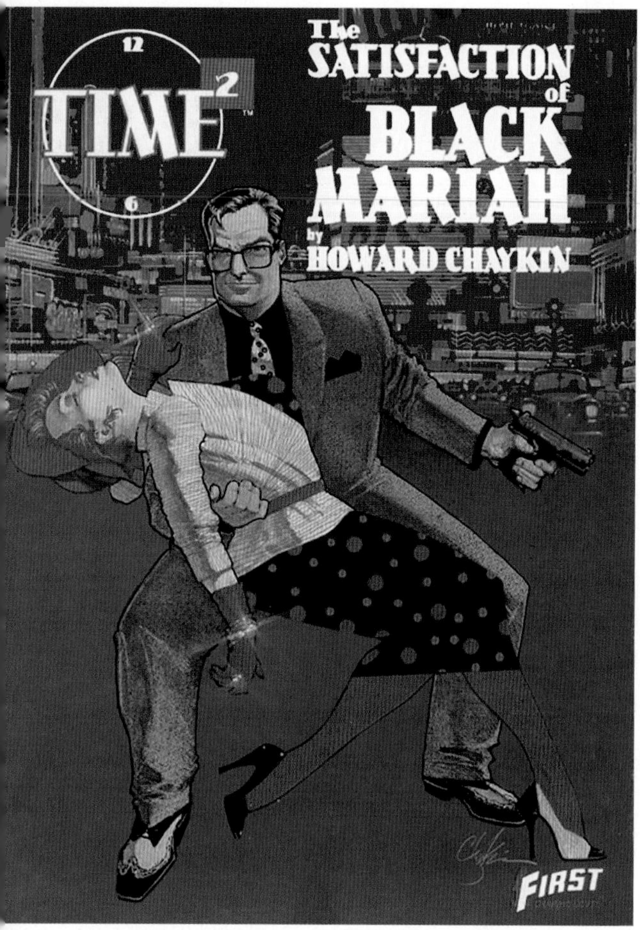
TIME²
The SATISFACTION of BLACK MARIAH
by HOWARD CHAYKIN
FIRST

centenary, just to set at rest the hearts of those who were confounded, and to be sure those who remain confused, by any or all three volumes, rest assured: I take full responsibility.

To make it explicitly clear...none of this was your fault.

As noted above, when those first two volumes hit the stores, I had recently extricated myself from the grind of ***American Flagg!***, and its themes, style and delivery were how I was now and, to be sure, newly perceived by fandom.

At the insistence of the justifiably paranoid editors and publishers of First Comics, for whom I'd done ***Flagg!***, I created a one-off one-shot to exploit the familiarity of ***Flagg!*** as a gateway to ***Time²***, a special reprinted in this volume for the very first time.

Comics is, to a profound degree, a business of one-trick ponies. Don't kid yourself. Try as they may to convince you otherwise, it's still really the House of Idea.

Time² wasn't anything like ***Flagg!***, and the graphic novels were not the work that was expected of me by my audience at the time. There was a theme running through what little critical reaction it received, that often boiled to down to textual somersaults in an attempt to wonder why I had repeated myself.

Talk about your cognitive dissonance.

The stories and themes of ***Time²*** are often challenging and frequently nonlinear. Some narrative elements are clearly delineated, others merely insinuated. And yes, there's quite a lot of what might be regarded as obligatory connective tissue that isn't there at all.

And that's very much the point, and was, to be sure, my intention and goal.

It's work that addresses techniques, concepts, ideas and situations that I find interesting, of course. But, and just as important, ***Time²*** is about *how* I find those things interesting.

The adjustment of the zig-zag, ladder-based narrative organization to accommodate double-page spreads as a means of reconsidering design as an integral part of the story itself, as opposed to simply a delivery system for narrative.

An occasionally successful attempt to translate my love of jazz, its culture, its mathematics in the telling of a story as if in a visual and narrative equivalent of Be Bop.

Of course, it's about characters and stories, but clearly not in the ways in which they are typically experienced in mainstream, narrative-based comics.

Maxim Glory, the nominal hero, certainly has an arc in each of the three graphic novels, but this arc is often implied, as opposed to explicated, and then explicated again for the upper balcony.

In a marketplace wherein the dominant paradigm boils down, none too roughly I might add, to Joseph Campbell's Hero with a Thousand Faces filtered through the scrim of Chuck Jones' Road Runner/Coyote cartoons, is it any wonder this material confounded its intended audience?

Unlike the traditional hero-with-a-wound archetype that all too often identifies the depth of character of most comic book heroes, Maxim Glory's arc as protagonist is one of bits and pieces, some related to that narrative through line, some off-story and frankly random--much like the life I've lived, and would presume, perhaps at my peril, that some of you have, too.

I am frequently asked all the time when I'm going to do more ***American Flagg!*** I regret, for those with that question, to tell you the answer is I'm not. But I am genuinely delighted to have finally circled around to finish what I'd begun on *Time*².

Yes. I know. How curious and counterintuitive a choice this must seem, both to the experienced enthusiast as well as the casual onlooker.

American Flagg! is the signature accomplishment in this medium under my name, while ***Time***² is an obscure, not to say obscurantist, experimental comic book whose audience was and remains a small group of enthusiasts.

To me, though, returning to this world was the only sensible choice, because

HOWARD CHAYKIN
12
TIME²
6
HALLOWED GROUND⁰
JESTER'S CIGARETTES
BOP TOWN
ICE CREAM
FLEA
FANTASIA
VANITI
image

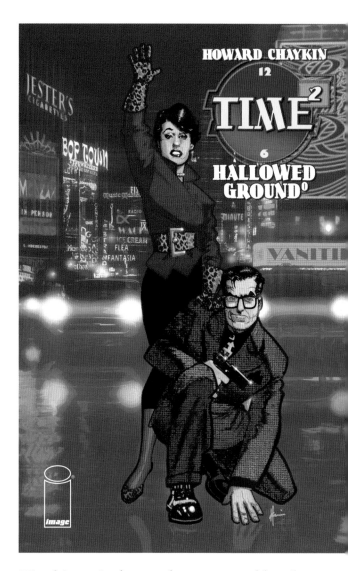

Time² is, at its heart, about my world and everything in it that interests me, and that's a place that's always worth visiting.

For me, certainly.

Others might disagree.

All that said, I do hope you've enjoyed taking this sentimental journey home with me as much as I enjoyed making it.

Howard Victor Chaykin...
A prince—
and most definitely of the City.

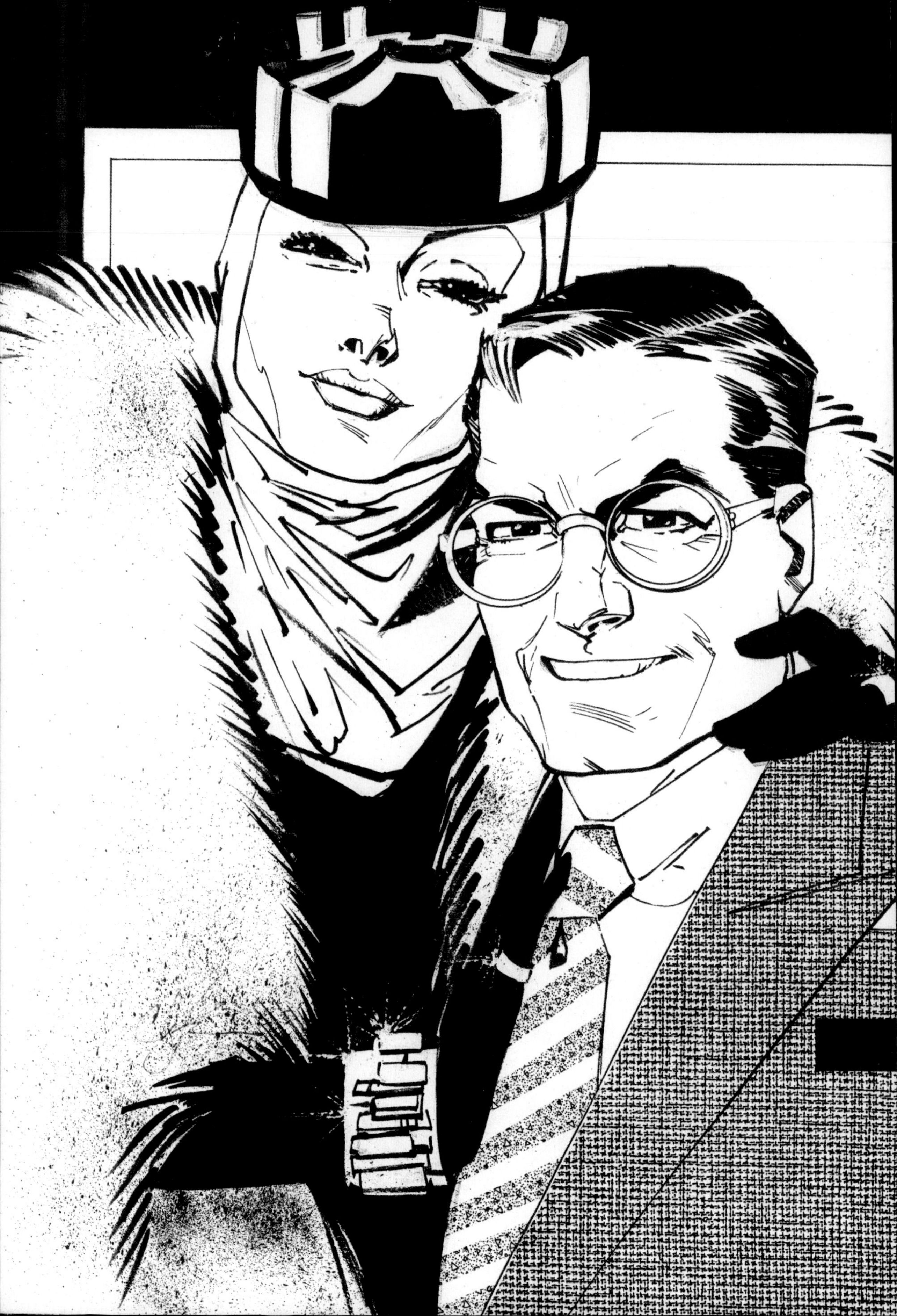

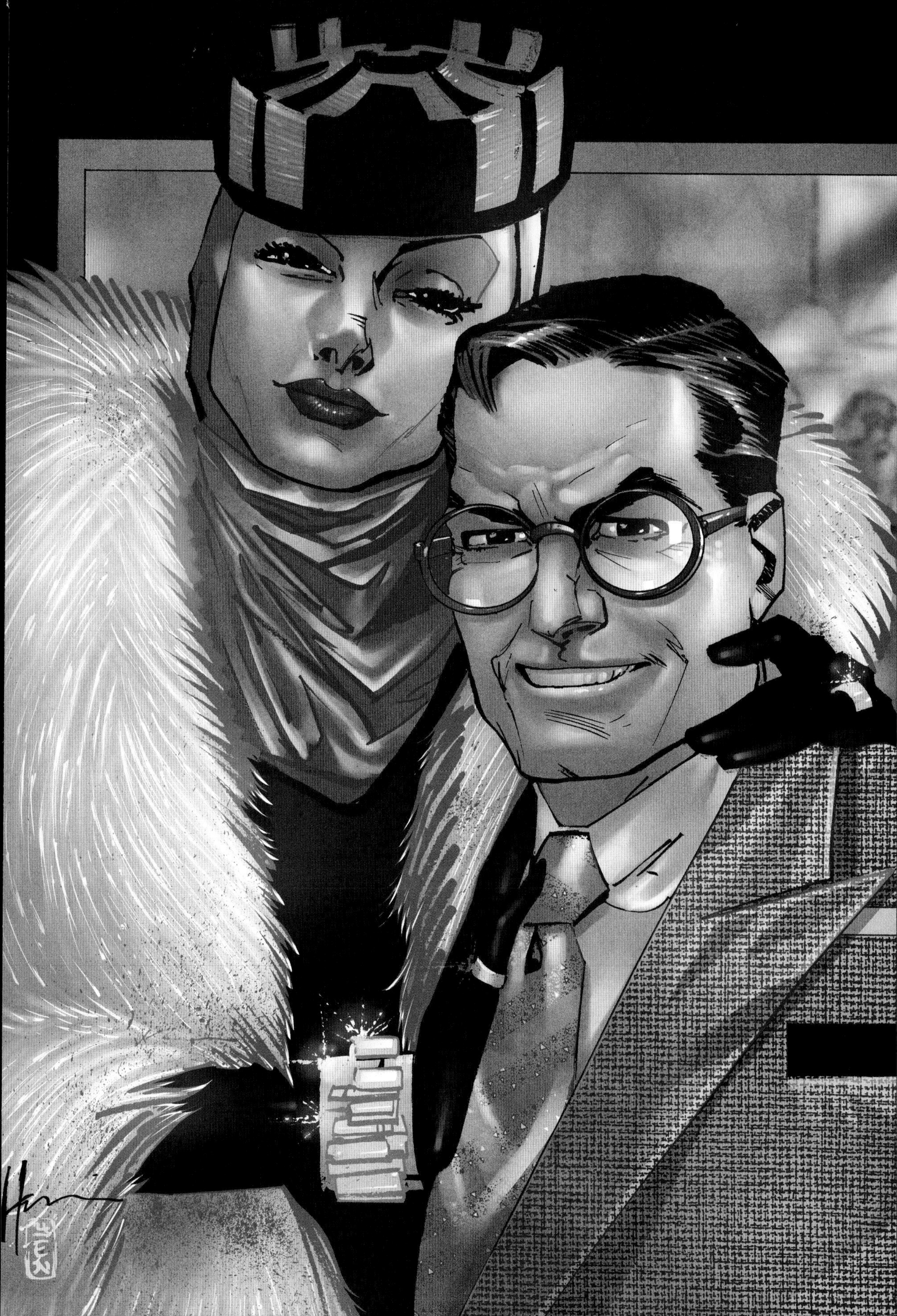

The SIGNS of the TIME^2

TIME2
HOWARD CHAYKIN'S
FRAMING DEVICE? ADAPTABLE TO ALL
6.

Designing the logo for *Time*^{2} began, as always, with a phone call from Howard Chaykin. Amid a verbal flood of still-evolving ideas were touchstone phrases such as "New York City, Damon Runyon, a horny sentient automobile," and "1950s jazz."

The ***American Flagg! presents Time*^{2} *Special*** had been part of the Flagg! universe, but this new project was to be a fully developed concept constructed around music, magic, and sexually hyperactive characters doing things witty and violent. Totally confused, I started sketching.

American Flagg! had been designed on a bedrock of Art Deco fonts, but ***Time***^{2} was set in the post-WW2 era, requiring a more jazzy, less industrial approach. The brief was to be evocative of a specific time and place, imaginative and polished in craftsmanship rather than organically hand-lettered. Street signs were an appealing gimmick, automatically conjuring an urban environment. Several fonts were developed in the late 1950s, but were *too* modern for the Be Bop *milieu*. Fluid script lettering was period accurate, but lacked the edgy *frisson* of improvisational jazz. One logo went too far into a psychedelic future approach. Who knew there were so many considerations for a simple comic book logo?

Working with a notebook of graph paper facilitated speed, accurate geometry and spacing as I attempted to find the match for what was in Howard's head in terms of tone and style. The goal at this stage was to search for a connective spark using a wide

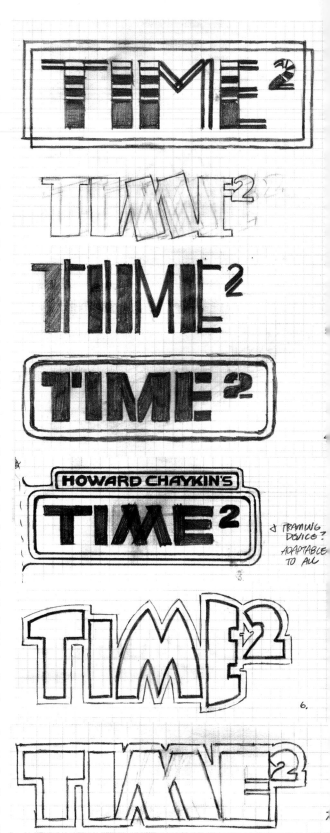

8.

9

10.

11

12

variety of font styles to trigger an immediate yes or no response. All the logos were valid, just not the most appropriate for a project which was still only a script and a few preliminary drawings.

Ultimately, Howard saw something that sent him to his own extensive files, where he found an old advertisement that was somewhat similar to sketch 2, consisting of five letters. It was by some anonymous artist from the 1920s, which I proceeded to extrapolate and hand-draw into a full alphabet and numbers for the logo, book titles and credits.

After *The Epiphany* was published, another development impacted the logo. A fan, whose name has been lost, sent Howard a note and a sketch in which he shortened the letterforms and installed them into a clock face configuration, complete with the 2 of *Time*[2] in the correct position. I was impressed enough to send him a check, and refined the new logo by boxing in the 2 for use on *Black Mariah*. Decades later, the logo has been further polished with digital effects and color enhancements.

From 1985 to 2022, *Time*[2] has marched on to the beat of a different drum, and I have done my best to keep in step.

--Ken Bruzenak...on cowbell.

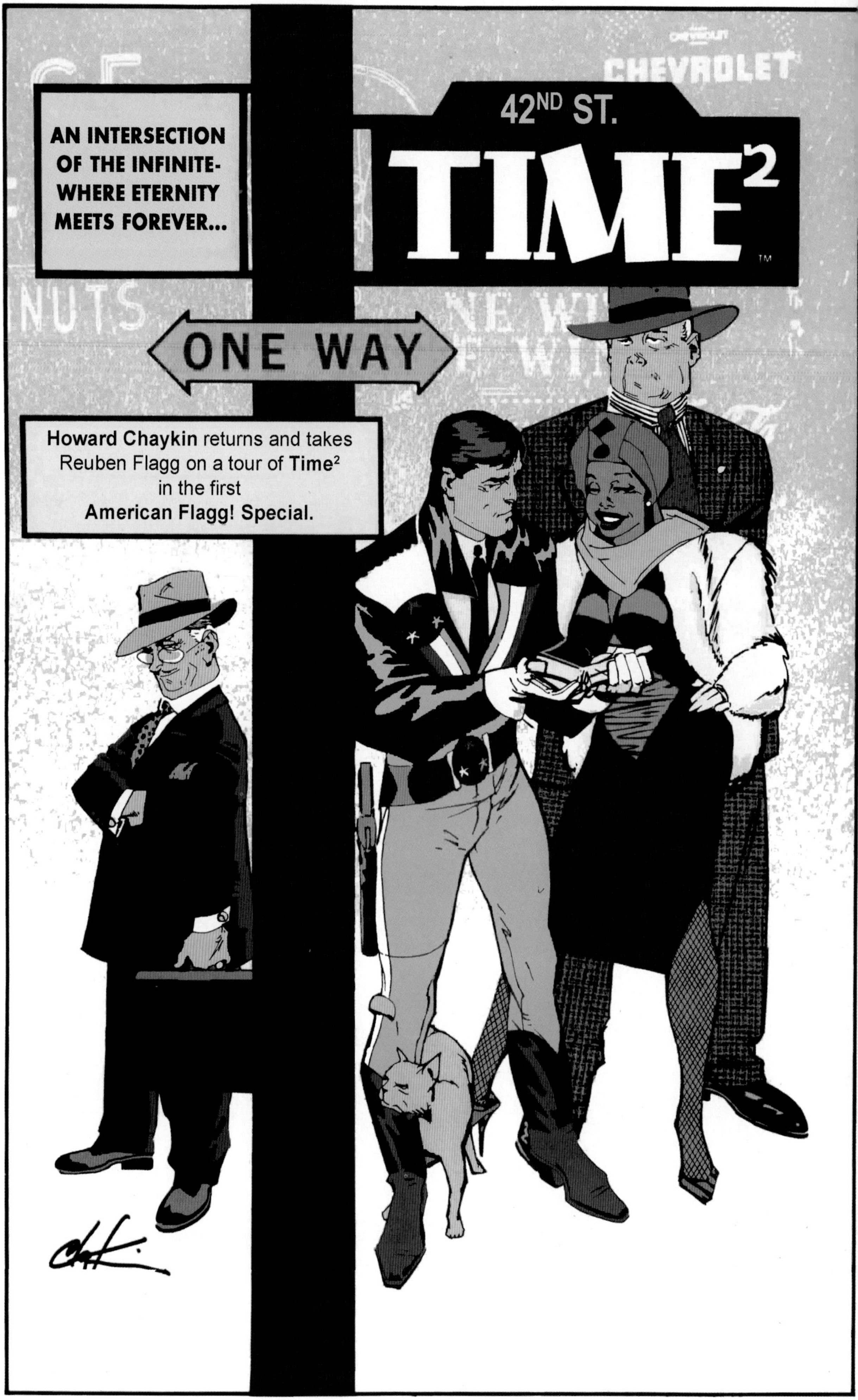
CHEVROLET
42ND ST.
TIME²
TM
AN INTERSECTION OF THE INFINITE- WHERE ETERNITY MEETS FOREVER...
ONE WAY
Howard Chaykin returns and takes Reuben Flagg on a tour of Time² in the first American Flagg! Special.

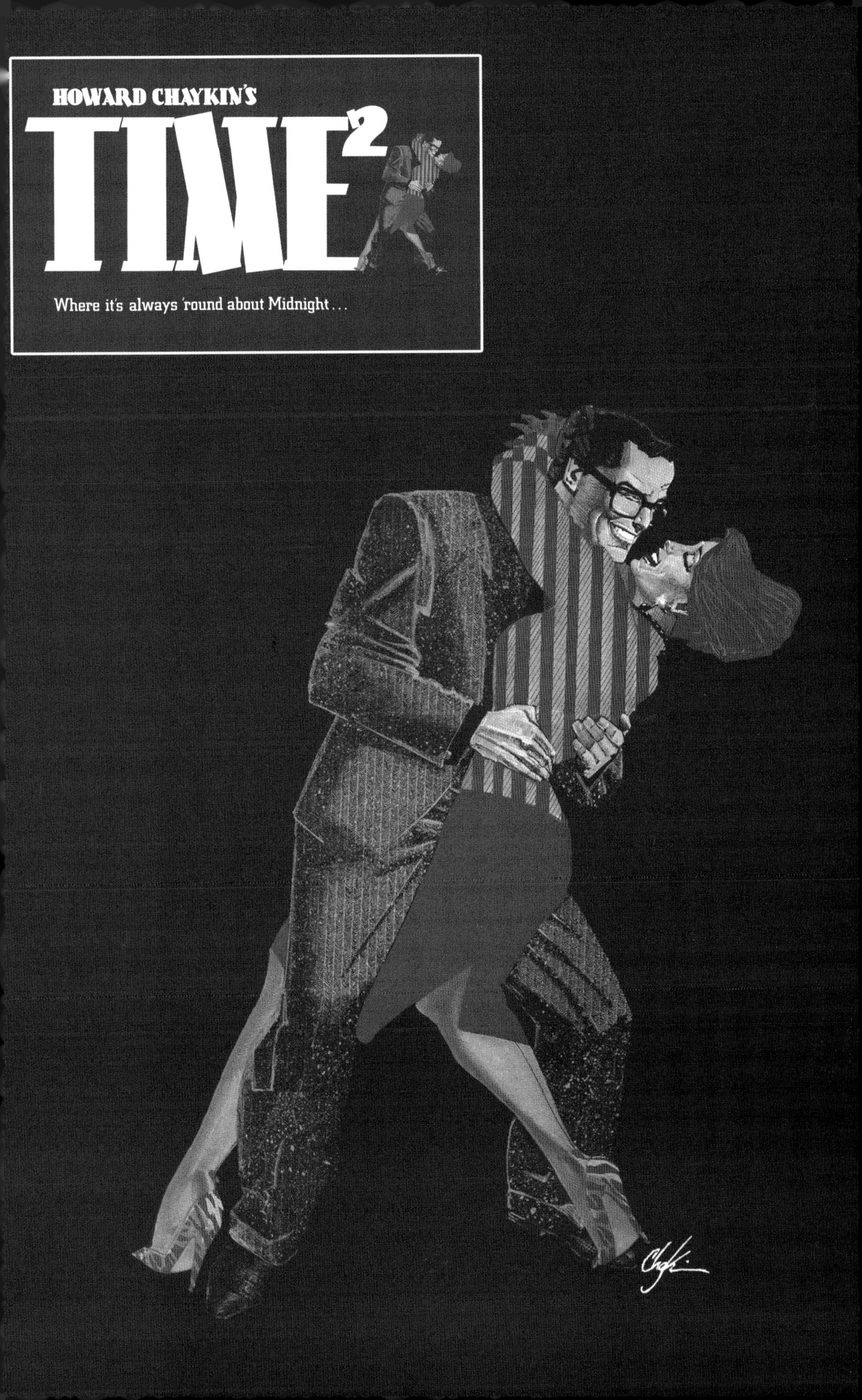
HOWARD CHAYKIN'S
TIME²
Where it's always 'round about Midnight...

The COLOR of TIME^2

On a historical backstory note, among the first reactions my generation had upon seeing what was being done with color in European comics were dismay, envy and curiosity.

The process, once it became comprehensible to us, who'd become first accustomed to the utter shittiness of comics, then resentful of that shittiness, grabbed many of us by the creative throat. Through fiat and force of will we convinced the powers that be that comics printed on better stock, with crystal-clear reproduction and color that wasn't a Ben-Day dot pattern smear, might have commercial value.

That said, in an effort to achieve the richest visuals available at the time, *The Epiphany* and *The Satisfaction of Black Mariah* utilized this European-derived painted blueline color, a full-color method that represented the state of the art before the introduction of computer coloring, which can and should, although all too often doesn't, recreate much of the effects of this now-somewhat-forgotten technique.

Colorist Steve Oliff in volume one, and Richard Ory with him in volume two, utilized gouache, acrylics, Pantone film and colored pencil coloring directly onto three-ply Bristol board midway in size between the originals and the comic book page—upon which a page's line work was printed in non-reproducible blue.

That same image was created in black on an acetate transparency, register marked to be placed and read over the blue-lined Bristol board, which the colorist could place over the painted work as reference for how the finished work would look when composited.

Once painted, the boards were photographed and directly used for the book's color, with black line work laid over them in production, plus additional overlays, an example of which is the big green KLOOGYAMOP effect on page 13 of *Black Mariah* that isn't present in the color reproduced at bottom left on the page facing this one.

Seen here for the first time in their original states are examples of the blueline colors for *Black Mariah*, highlighting the nuance and texture they brought to everything from scene atmosphere to individual character balloons.

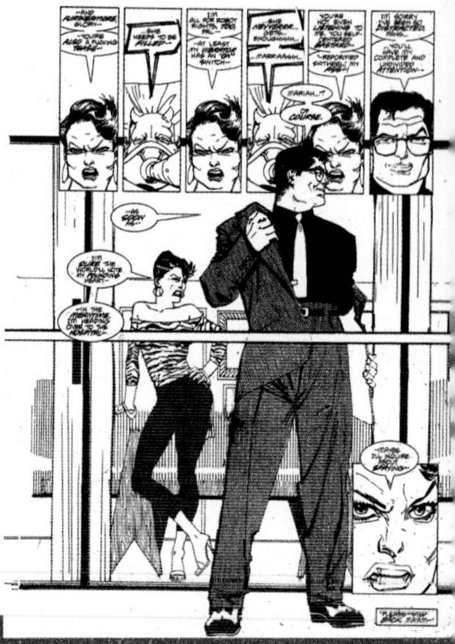

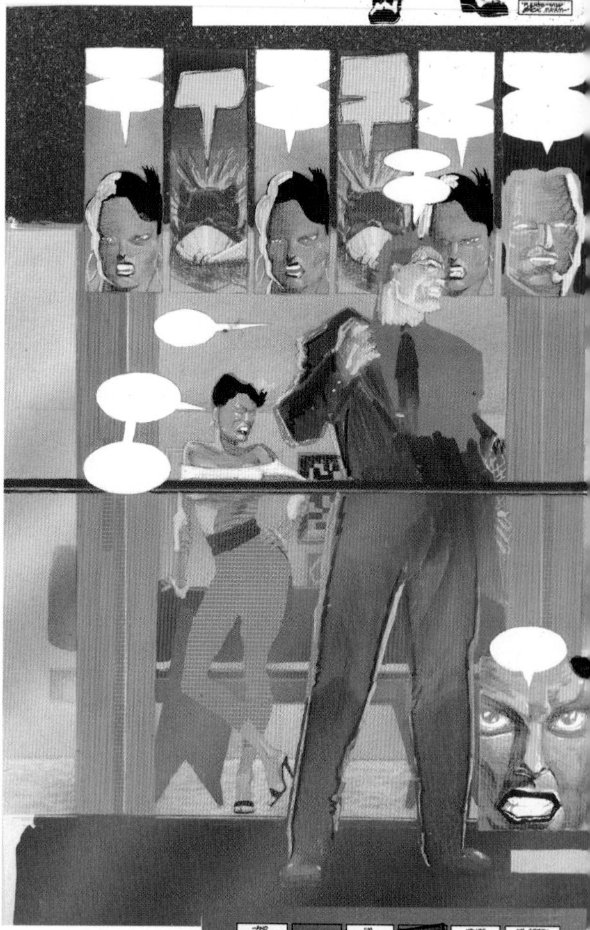

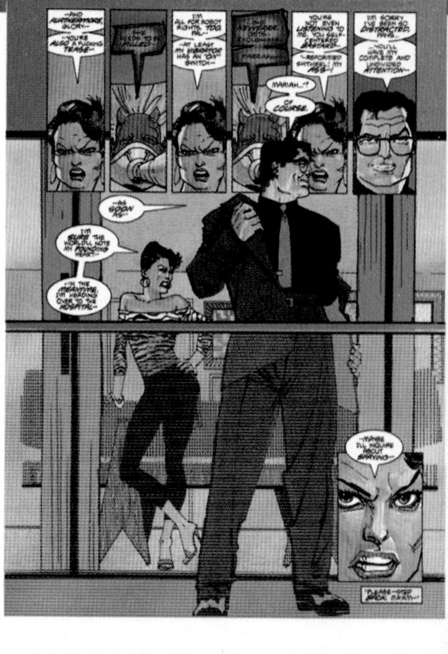

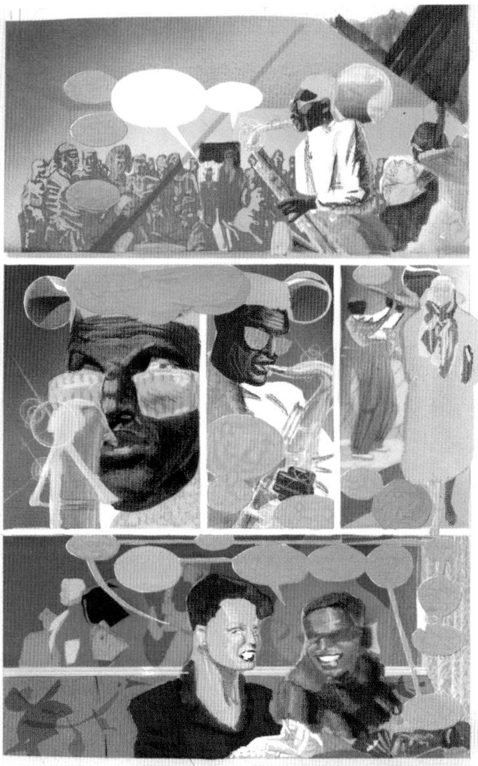

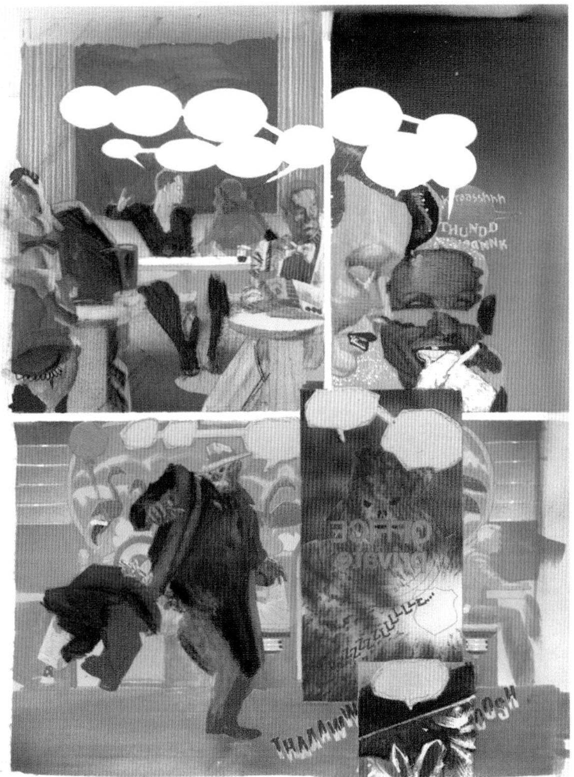

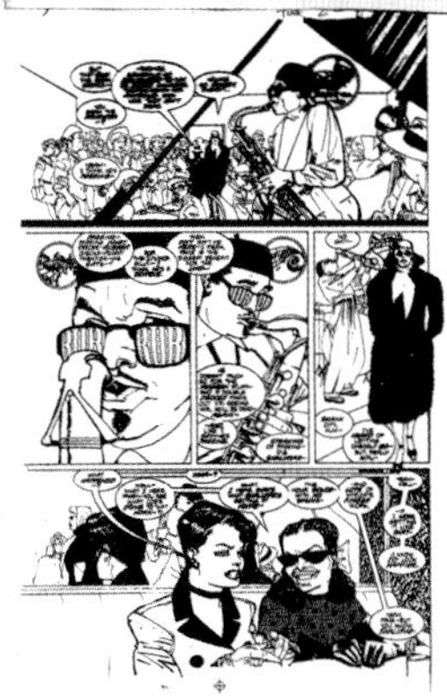

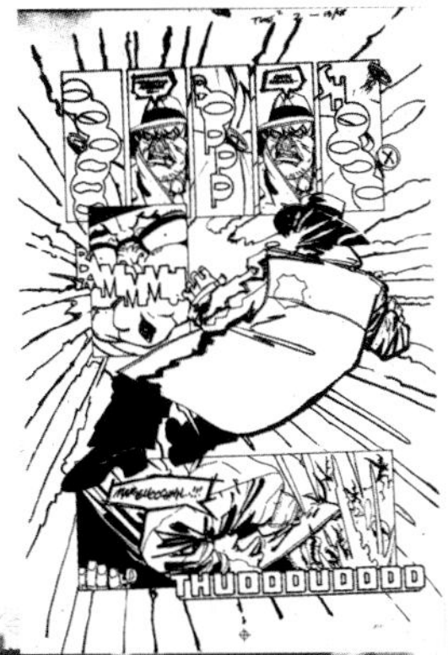
THUDDDUDDDD

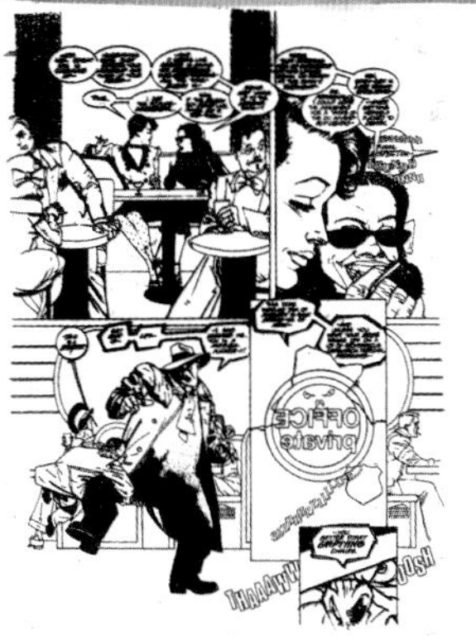

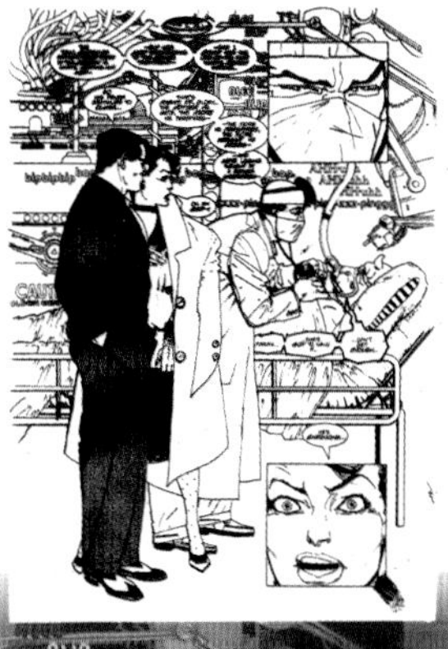

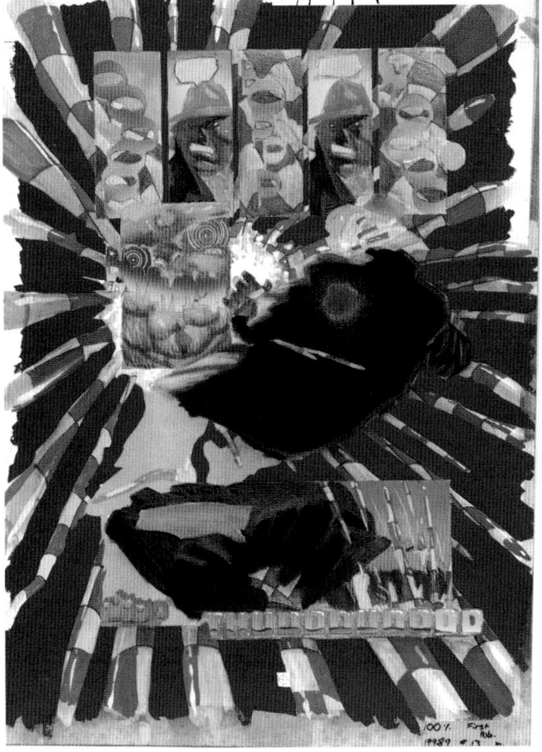

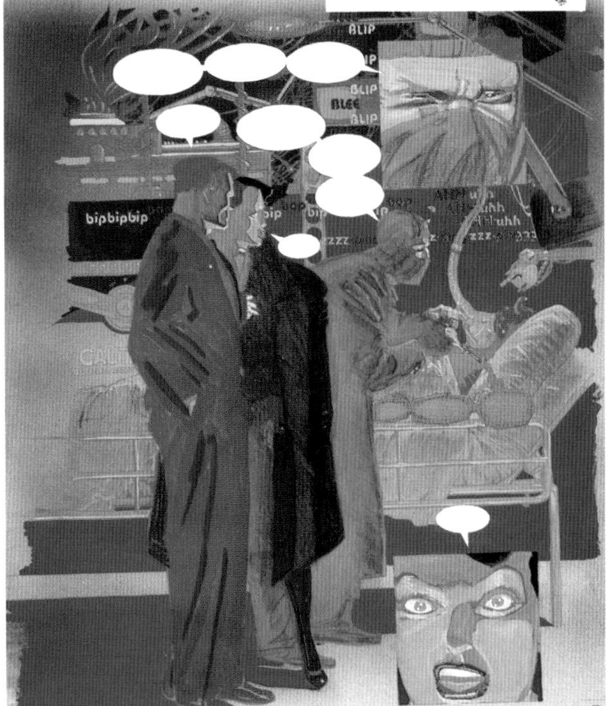
BLIP
BLIP
BLEE
bipbipbip

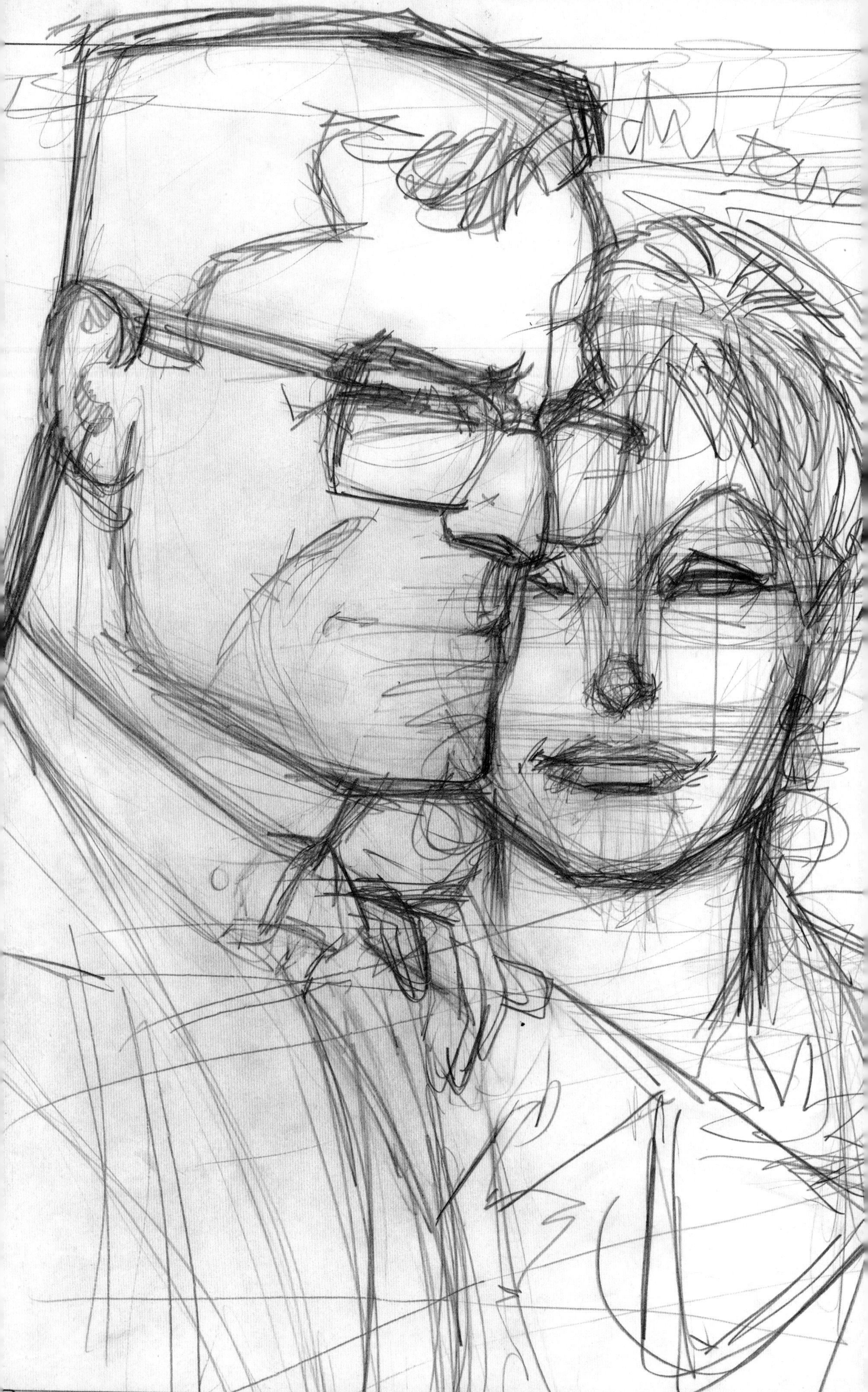

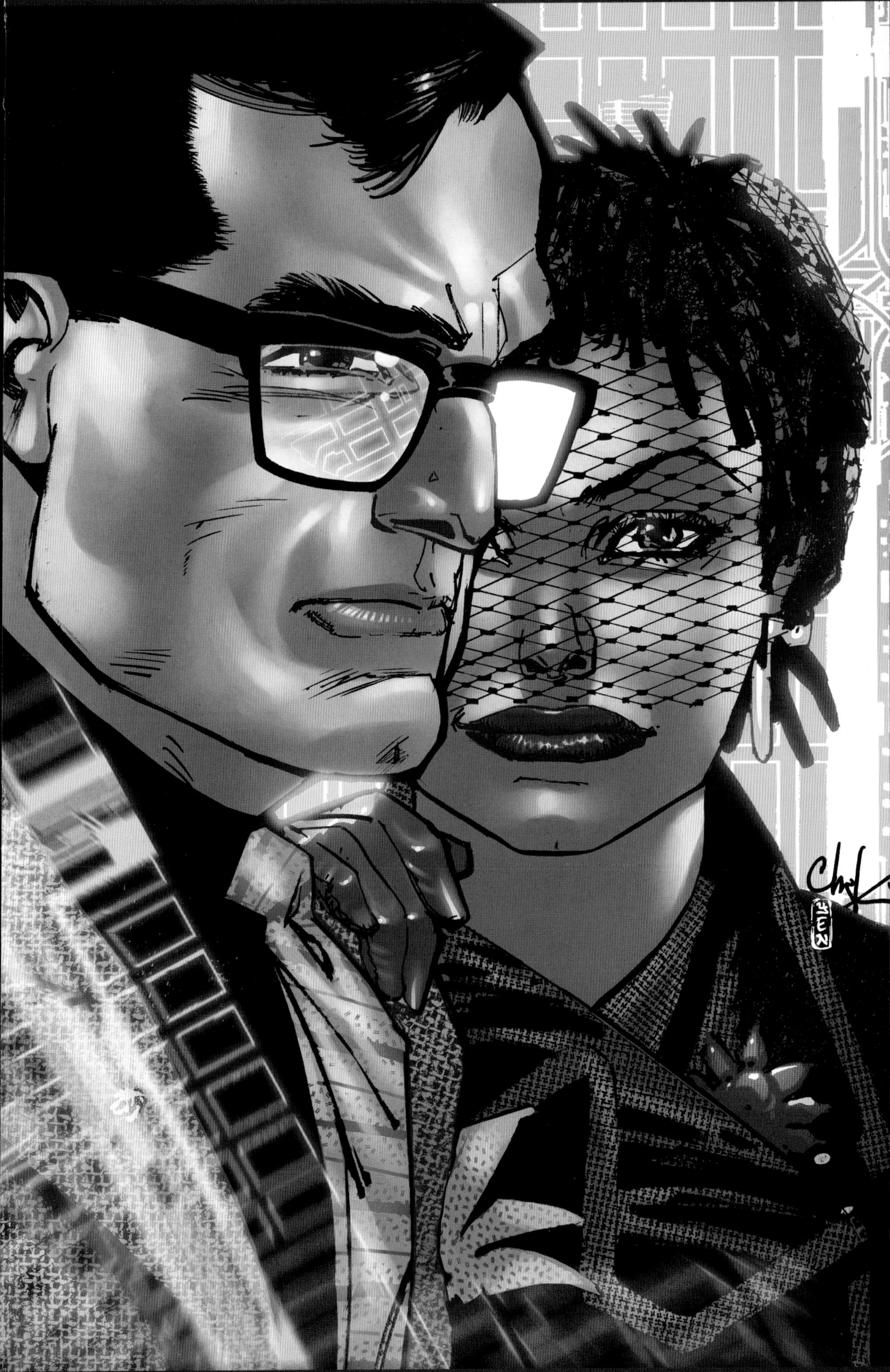

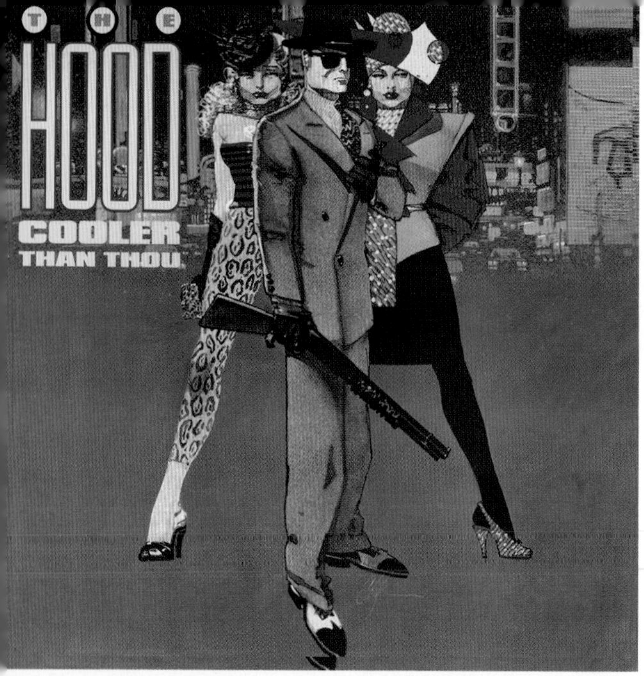
THE
HOOD
COOLER
THAN THOU

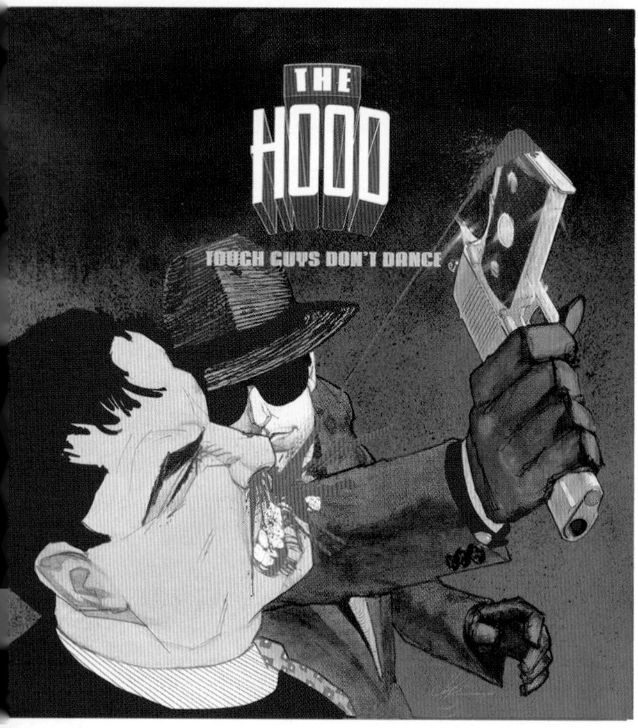
THE
HOOD
TOUGH GUYS DON'T DANCE

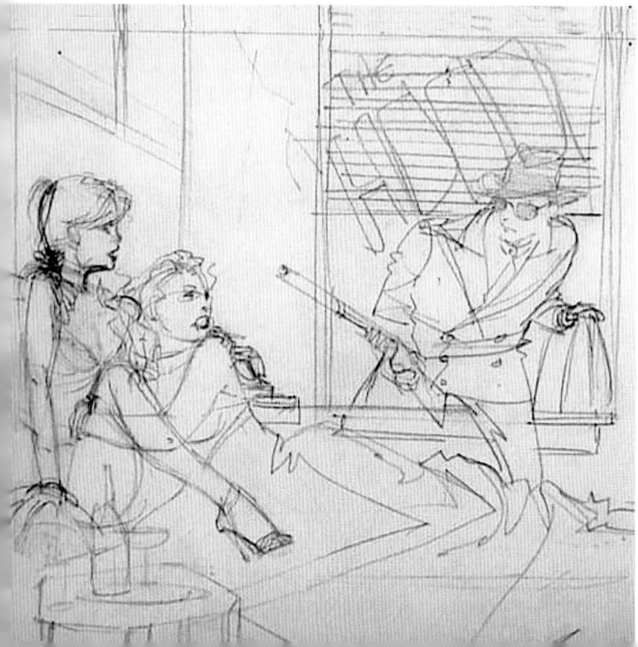

MEET ME on the MAIN STEM

An important factor in establishing an identity for the first two ***Time***² volumes was their covers; to make an initial impression that this project had grander aspirations than the average comic, they were developed in a vein similar to the painted covers I'd produced for a number of clients at the time, and, to be sure, comparable to the cover art on the then-nascent stream of so-called graphic novels.

I produced that first cover with my usual blur of mixed media—ink, acrylic paint, colored markers, colored pencils and even that tried-and-true aspect of my stuff, the late, lamented Zip-a-Tone. The cover displayed the three leads—Max Glory, Pansy Matthias, and the Main Stem itself—in an approach inspired by those great photographers who chronicled Manhattan nightlife in its heyday, in order to evoke elegance, style, sophistication and just a *frisson* of fantasy.

The result was successful enough to carry from volume one to volume two (see the unused pencil rough for *Black Mariah,* above right), and, curiously enough, beyond. In 1987, I was asked to provide artwork for Crépuscule Records' release of material by New York club mainstay John Hood.

I delivered artwork for three covers for The Hood releases - to accompany the 12-inch singles "Tough Guys Don't Dance" and "It Takes a Thief" (the latter never completed, left), as well as the LP *Cooler Than Thou*. Produced around roughly the same time as the cover art for *The Satisfaction of Black Mariah*, the Hood covers strongly echoed that aesthetic, creating unofficial companion pieces to

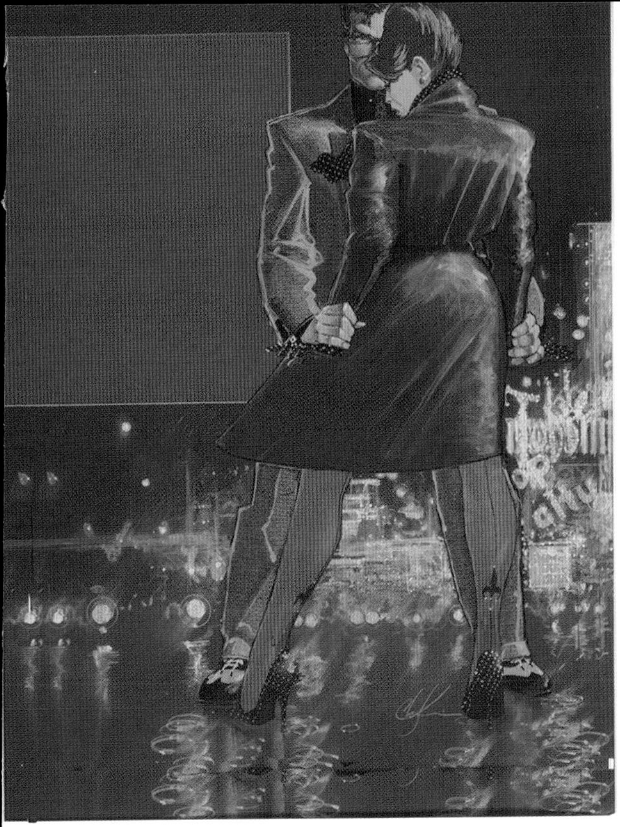

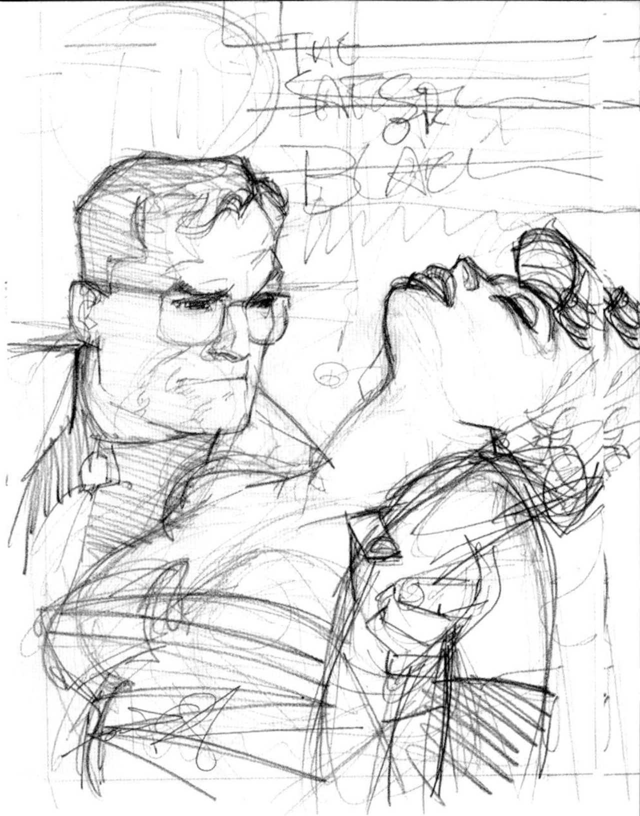

its established urban-fairy-tale vibe and look. Three decades plus have passed since then, and times had definitely changed by the time a third and final volume of what had always been intended to be a trilogy became reality.

I no longer paint at all, but in conceiving the cover for *Hallowed Ground*[0], returning to the timeless look and motifs that had worked so well in the past seemed the only way to go. Enter Don Cameron, a colleague who has built a serious career in the digital world of computer-generated graphics.

Working from a finished line drawing, Don stepped in and ran with it, developing a digital finish for the new cover that evoked the series' established look without slavishly imitating it.

The resultant cover has its own character—taking advantage of the most modern technology available even as it returns us to our favorite part of town.

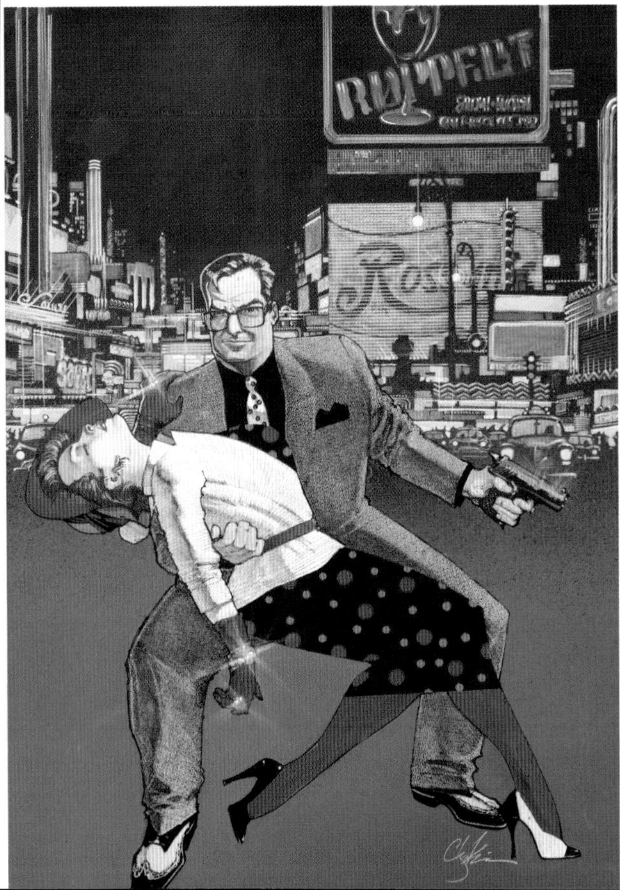

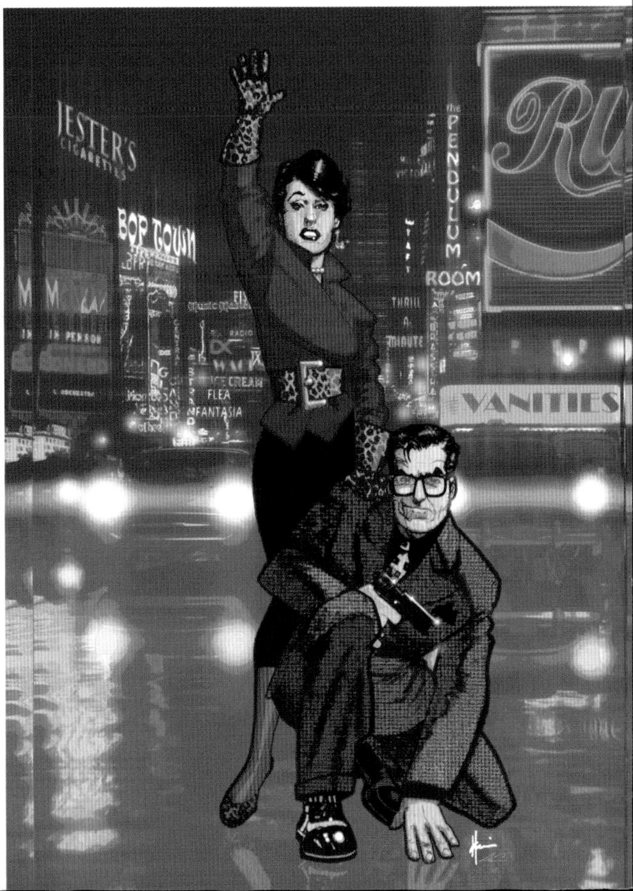
JESTER'S
CIGARETTES
BOP TOWN
the PENDULUM ROOM
VANITIES

LOST by the WAYSIDE

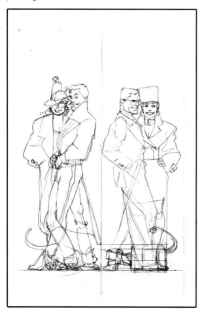

Over the fifty years of my career — and allow me to briefly choke on the acknowledgment of that number — I've had a number of assignments and jobs that never came to be. An apocalyptic western, based on the designs of Jo Mora, my version of *Forever Maelstrom and the Tomorrow Breed*, a *Legends of the Dark Knight* arc as writer with an artist who shall remain nameless, not to mention twice hired and twice fired in the span of 18 hours each – in the same calendar year, no less - on two dreadful television series, one of which never even got to the pilot stage.

I'm certain there are more, but hey, half a century, right?

Which brings us to these two pieces of artwork, begun but never finished in my time as a freelancer for First Comics, a company to which I will remain forever grateful for the faith it showed in me and my work, when such faith seemed utterly unwarranted. The company that bears the name today has nothing else whatsoever to do with that original iteration — don't fall for nonsense.

Which in turn brings me to these two unfinished pieces, both *Time*[2] related. Back in the 1980s, comics publishers would occasionally commission posters from talent, to serve as advertising in comics shops as well as sales product for retailers.

I have no recollection whatsoever of doing

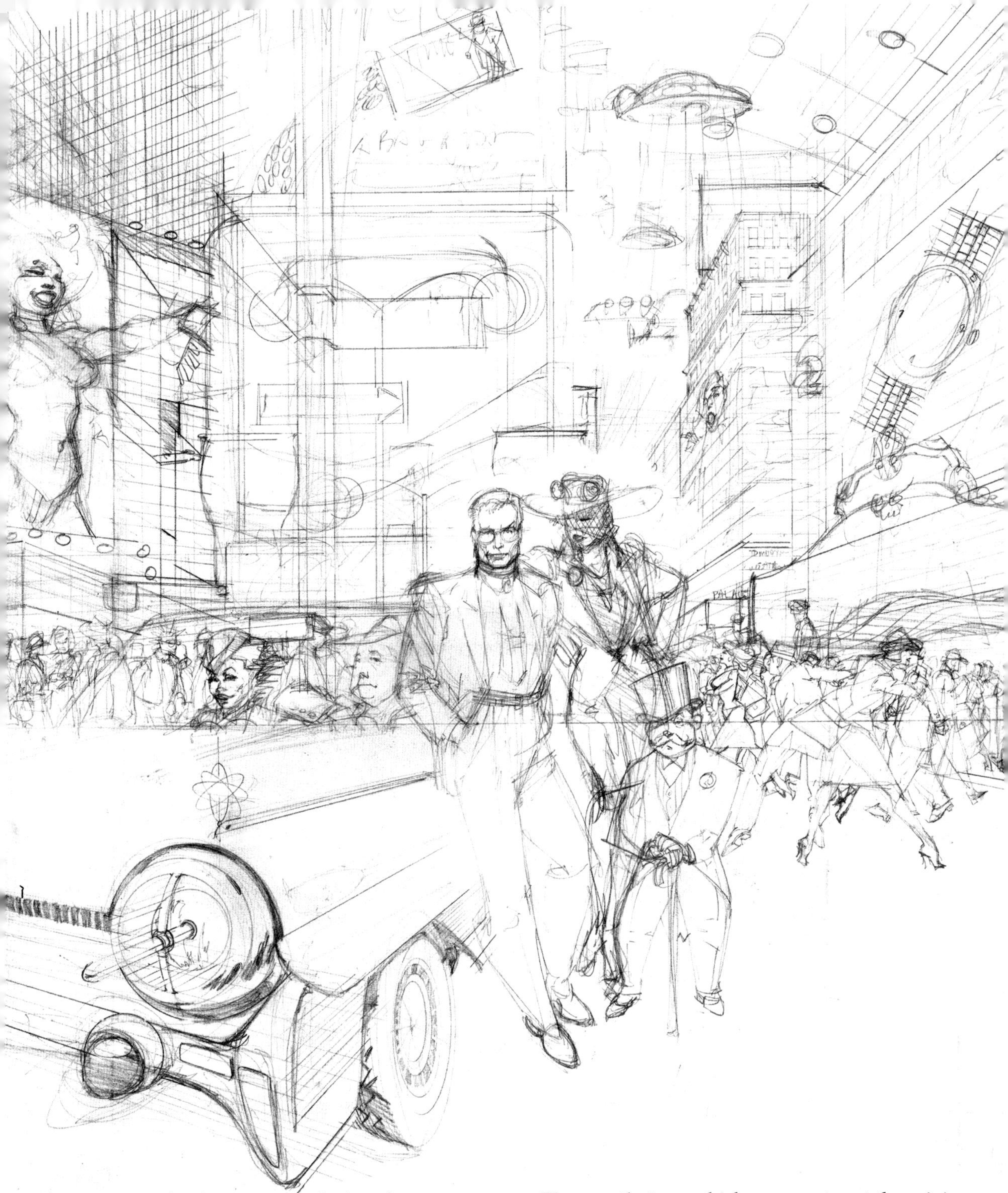

either piece; or, for that matter, whether they were requested as assignments or begun on my own initiative with the presumptuous assumption that they would be paid for, printed and published.

I was cocky even then, with considerably less of a justification for that sort of thing.

That said, these two pieces couldn't be more different. The foursome, which got as far as transference to the 20 x 30 illustration board seen at top left, with basic color blocked in, is all about charm, romance and insouciance. When we were looking for a lead-in to the ***Flagg! Special*** in this book, I recalled this piece and produced a new version with the spirit of the unfinished original.

The pencil piece, which never got past the original size, is all about crazed ambition. I mean, will you look at that work, for heaven's sake? It's insane. And I would forgive the assumption of the presence of mind-altering substances in its conception and making, but it's worth noting that no amphetamines of any kind figured into this drawing.

There's also a great deal of love and affection lavished on the concept, the world and the characters of ***Time***^{2}, a book which has been identified more than once as the perfect example of my overestimation of the audience, its tastes, and its sophistication.

Needless to say, that's for you to decide.

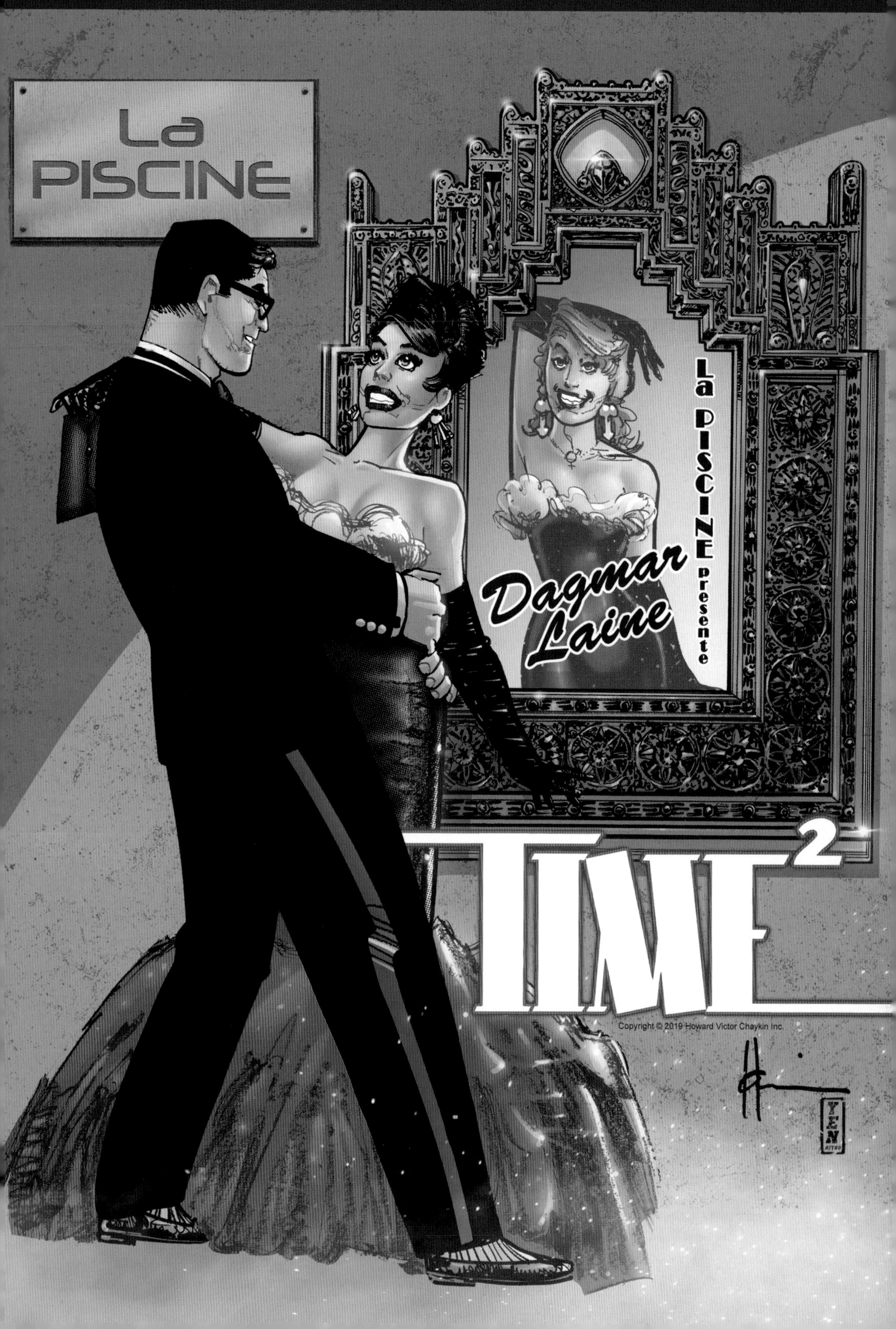
La PISCINE
La PISCINE presente
Dagmar Laine
TIME²
Copyright © 2019 Howard Victor Chaykin Inc.
YEN

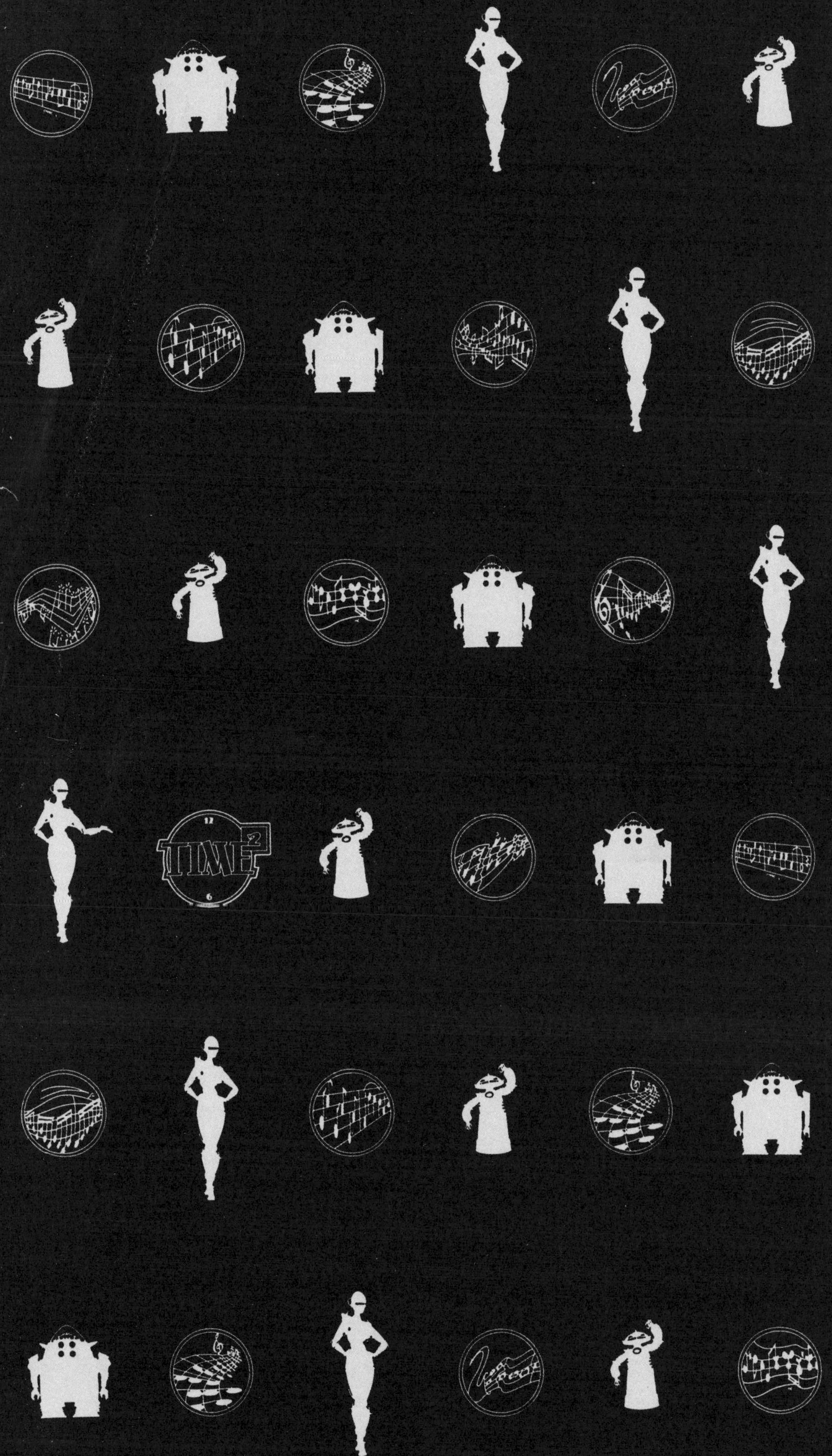
12
TIME 2
6

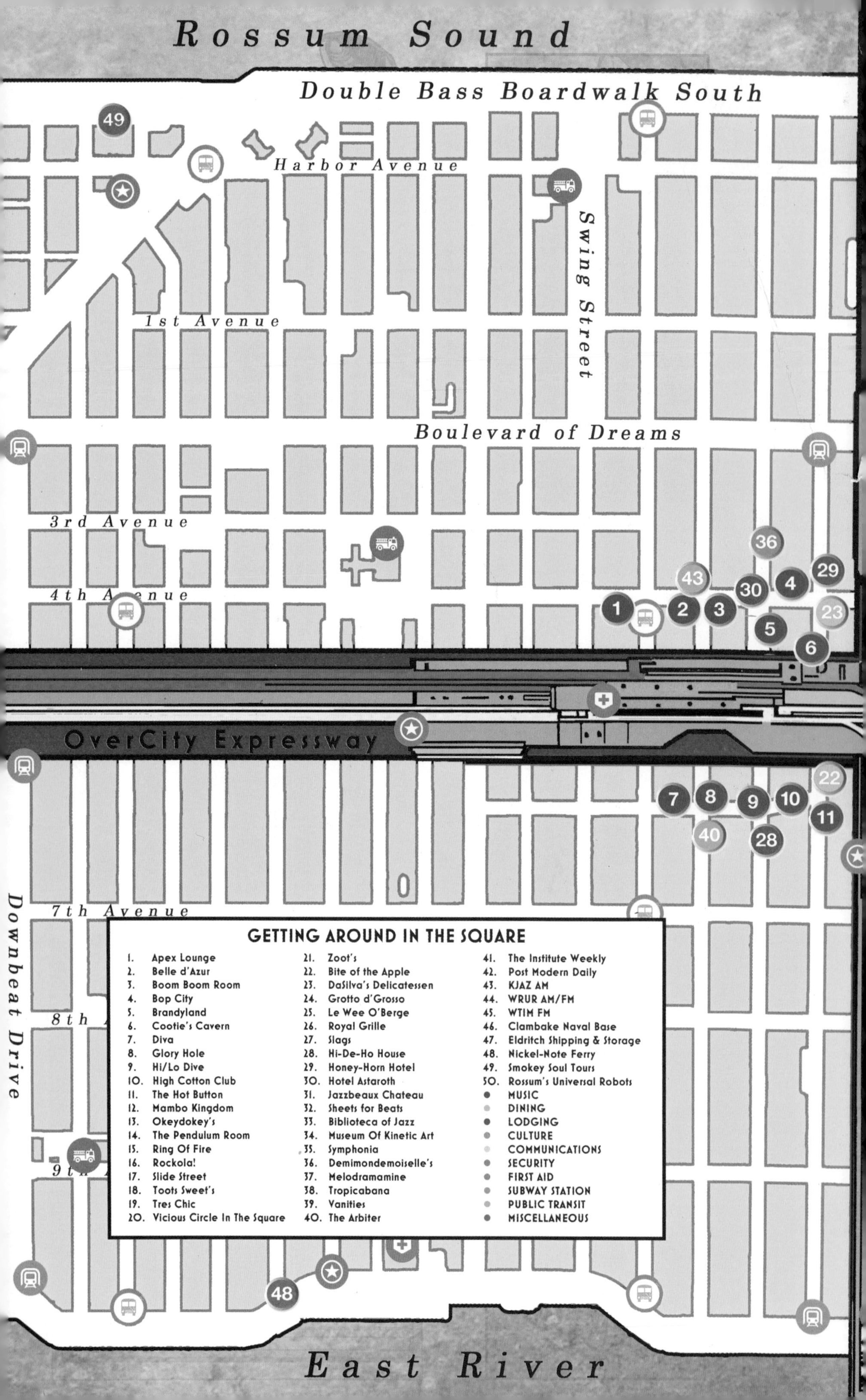

Rossum Sound
Double Bass Boardwalk South
Harbor Avenue
Swing Street
1st Avenue
Boulevard of Dreams
3rd Avenue
4th Avenue
OverCity Expressway
7th Avenue
8th
Downbeat Drive
East River
GETTING AROUND IN THE SQUARE
1. Apex Lounge
2. Belle d'Azur
3. Boom Boom Room
4. Bop City
5. Brandyland
6. Cootie's Cavern
7. Diva
8. Glory Hole
9. Hi/Lo Dive
10. High Cotton Club
11. The Hot Button
12. Mambo Kingdom
13. Okeydokey's
14. The Pendulum Room
15. Ring Of Fire
16. Rockola!
17. Slide Street
18. Toots Sweet's
19. Tres Chic
20. Vicious Circle In The Square
21. Zoot's
22. Bite of the Apple
23. DaSilva's Delicatessen
24. Grotto d'Grosso
25. Le Wee O'Berge
26. Royal Grille
27. Slags
28. Hi-De-Ho House
29. Honey-Horn Hotel
30. Hotel Astaroth
31. Jazzbeaux Chateau
32. Sheets for Beats
33. Biblioteca of Jazz
34. Museum Of Kinetic Art
35. Symphonia
36. Demimondemoiselle's
37. Melodramamine
38. Tropicabana
39. Vanities
40. The Arbiter
41. The Institute Weekly
42. Post Modern Daily
43. KJAZ AM
44. WRUR AM/FM
45. WTIM FM
46. Clambake Naval Base
47. Eldritch Shipping & Storage
48. Nickel-Note Ferry
49. Smokey Soul Tours
50. Rossum's Universal Robots
MUSIC
DINING
LODGING
CULTURE
COMMUNICATIONS
SECURITY
FIRST AID
SUBWAY STATION
PUBLIC TRANSIT
MISCELLANEOUS